A Survey of Modern English

TITLES OF RELATED INTEREST

A History of the English Language[*]
Albert C. Baugh and Thomas Cable

International English Usage
Loreto Todd and Ian Hancock

A History of English
Barbara M. H. Strang

Variety in Contemporary English
W. R. O'Donnell and Loreto Todd

An Uncommon Tongue: the Uses and Resources of English
Walter Nash

[*] Not available in the US as a Routledge title.

A Survey of Modern English

Stephan Gramley
Kurt-Michael Pätzold

London and New York

First published 1992
by Routledge
11 New Fetter Lane, London EC4P 4EE

Simultaneously published in the USA and Canada
by Routledge
a division of Routledge, Chapman and Hall, Inc.
29 West 35th Street, New York, NY 10001

© 1992 Stephan E. Gramley and Kurt-Michael Pätzold

Set in 10/12 pt Times, Compugraphic by MCS, Salisbury, Wiltshire
Printed in England by Clays Ltd, St Ives plc.

British Library Cataloguing-in-Publication Data
A catalogue record for this book is available from the British Library

Library of Congress Cataloging-in-Publication Data
Gramley, Stephan, 1943–
    A Survey of Modern English/Stephan Gramley, Kurt-Michael Pätzold
        p.   cm.
    Includes bibliographical references and index.
    ISBN 0–415–04956–3. ISBN 0–415–04957–1 (pbk.)
    1. English language—20th century.   2. English language—Grammar 1950
    3. English language—Variation.   I. Pätzold, Kurt-Michael, 1941–
    II. Title.
    PE1087.G7 1992
    420'.9'04—dc20   92-5427
                                                                      CIP

ISBN 0–415–04956–3
ISBN 0–415–04957–1 pbk

To Kurt Konrad Leo Pätzold
Hannah Pätzold, geb. Zielge
The first, if not the only, begetters

For Hedda

Contents

Preface

A Survey of Modern English has grown, over more than a dozen years, from a vague idea in the late 1970s, by way of our German-language book *Das moderne Englisch*, to what it is here, a sometimes expanded, sometimes abridged, and, in any case, very differently structured volume.

This book is to a large extent the product of teaching the subjects treated here to several generations of students in Bielefeld. We need, therefore, to thank them for reminding us again and again to keep our feet on the ground and to remember what they need and want: a view of the language related to what they know, explanations for phenomena that are new for them, insights into structures difficult to analyse immediately, and descriptions of varieties of English never before (or at least not extensively) encountered. It is because of our students, whom we have constantly had in mind in writing, that we have tried to be so relatively comprehensive and have made continual efforts to give straightforward explanations and to avoid too much unnecessary terminology. Where we have used the terms of the field we have tried to be clear about what they designate either by using short glosses or by providing more extensive discussion.

We have also had our students in mind as we have made the often hard choices about what to include and what to leave out. Needless to say, the choices could have been different and not everyone who uses this book will agree one hundred per cent. Nor, we know, will everyone agree with us in all of our interpretations. We know this from our own experience with each other. For although we divided up the work more or less according to themes and chapters (KMP: 1, 2, 5, 6; SG: 3, 4, 7–10, 12–16; both: 11) and have read and discussed each other's work critically, there has not always been complete agreement between the two of us.

Finally, we would like to single out a few of the people who have not always agreed and to thank them for their time and constructive criticism. Käthe Henke-Brown of Bielefeld University deserves special mention for the care she has taken in reading and discussing material from this book. Elizabeth Archibald of the University of Victoria, British Columbia, has also given most generously of her time. Furthermore, Karin Achterholt, Ramsey Rutherford and Konrad Sprengel, all of Bielefeld, have been especially helpful as well. Our thanks also go to Richard Bailey of the University of Michigan for his extensive comments on the pre-final version of this book.

SG, KMP

Abbreviations

AdjP	Adjectival phrase
AdvP	Adverbial phrase
AmE	American English
AusE	Australian English
BlE	Black English
BrE	British English
CanE	Canadian English
CaribE	Caribbean English
EAE	East African English
EFL	English as a Foreign Language
ESP	English for Special/Specific Purposes
EST	English for Science and Technology
FN	First name
GenAm	General American
H	Hearer
IndE	Indian English
IrE	Irish English
LN	Last name
KT	Kinship term
ModE	Modern English
NP	Noun phrase
NZE	New Zealand English
OE	Old English
PE	Pidgin English
PP	Prepositional phrase
RP	Received Pronunciation
S	Speaker
SAE	South African English
SingE	Singaporean English
s.o.	someone
s.th.	something
SSE	Scottish Standard English

StE   Standard English
T   Title
VP   Verb phrase
WAE   West African English
WAPE   West African pidgin English

LIST OF MAPS AND FIGURES

Maps

Figures

Introduction

This is a book about the English language as it exists today. But just what is English? It is most certainly several things at once. To begin with, it is an assortment of national and regional varieties, as discussed in chapters 10 to 15. Note that this includes not only Britain and Ireland (chapter 10), North America and the Caribbean (chapter 12) and Australia, New Zealand and South Africa (chapter 13), where there are millions of native speakers of the language, but also East and West Africa (chapter 14) and South and Southeast Asia (chapter 15), where there are relatively few native speakers but millions of users of English as a second language. We have drawn the line only at looking at English as a foreign language, not because this does not belong, but because it is too mammoth a task to include in this book. Within all the areas outlined above there are also regional, social and ethnic varieties of the language, and we have endeavoured to provide a glimpse at some of this diversity as well. This even includes language forms which are only marginally English, as in chapter 16, 'Pidgin and Creole English'.

Furthermore, English is also a language used by all sorts of people in all sorts of situations. It is used by the young and the old, by women and by men, by the rich and the poor, by people whose skin colour is white, black, brown, yellow or red, by illiterates and by the highly educated, and so on. While it has not proved feasible − in this framework − to look at all these types of users specifically, we have chosen to touch on most of these (and some other categories) in an illustrative way in chapter 9 ('Using English: modes of address') and to deal extensively with one of them in chapter 8 ('Language and gender').

How people use the language − whoever or whatever they are − depends on what purposes they are pursuing and with whom they are communicating. This includes questions of medium, style, purpose, addressee, subject matter, and more. One general chapter (chapter 6, 'Spoken discourse') and one which looks at a particular area of use (chapter 7, 'Special Englishes') deal with many of the questions of use.

English, finally, is a network of relations of a grammatical, lexical, phonological, orthographic and textual nature. Chapters 1 to 5 deal with these areas. Yet here the question arises once again as to what English is. This time, however, it lies within a different dimension. Whose English or which English should serve as the basis for a description of the linguistic levels just mentioned? For this book, this basis will be what is known as Standard English (StE).

Standard English

There is little explicit agreement about just how StE should be regarded. Almost everyone who works with English assumes at least implicitly that it exists, but the descriptions made of it – for example, in dictionaries and grammar books, to say nothing of manuals of style – indicate how much diversity there is in people's ideas about StE. Yet, there *are* dictionaries, grammars and style books, and what they document – some would say encode – is what is most often understood by StE.

Any standard language is, in an important sense, 'a codified form of a language, accepted by, and serving as a model to, a larger speech community' (Garvin 1964: 521). How necessary this is is highly evident in the cases of so many indigenous languages in Third-World countries which for lack of broad acceptance of a native language as the national standard have adopted a standardized European language such as English, hoping in this way to ease the path to 'economic prosperity, science and technology, development and modernization, and the attractions of popular culture' and paying the price of loss of self-expression and diminishment in feelings of cultural worth (Bailey 1990: 87). The result is that 'the old political empire with its metropolis and colonial outposts has nearly disappeared, replaced by a cultural empire of "English-speaking peoples"' (ibid.: 83).

Many people object to the idea of codification, and they are justified in doing so when codification means defining what may occur in a standard right down to the point at which no more variety is admissible. Certainly, that is neither desirable, nor is it possible.

To look at it from another angle, StE is 'the kind of English which draws least attention to itself over the widest area and through the widest range of usage' (Quirk and Stein 1990: 123). It is most clearly associated with the written language, perhaps because what is written and especially what is published is more permanent, is largely free of inadvertent slips and is transmitted in spelling, which is far more standardized than is pronunciation. Compare the relatively few AmE–BrE differences in orthography (cf. chapter 11), but the numerous national and regional accent standards (chapters 3, 10–15). Two criteria may be set to establish what 'draws least attention to itself' over the widest geographic spread and stylistic range. For one, there is the criterion of educated usage, sometimes broadened to include common usage and probably to be most reasonably located some-where between the two (whatever they may be). The other criterion is appro-priateness to the audience, topic and social setting (Stalker 1986: 50). However these criteria are finally interpreted, there is a well-established bias towards the speech of those with the most power and prestige in a society. This has been the well-educated and the higher socio-economic classes. The speech – however varied it may be in itself – of the middle class, especially the upper middle class, carries the most prestige. It is the basis for the overt linguistic norms of English-speaking society. This is not to say that working-class speech or, for example, what is called Black English (see chapters 10 and 12) is without prestige, but these varieties represent covert norms in the groups in which they are current. Not to conform to them means to distance oneself from the group and its dominant values and eventually to become an outsider. Language, then, is a sign of group iden-tity. Public language and the overt public norm is StE. (See also 8.2.3 for more on overt and covert norms.)

Although a great deal of emphasis has been put on *what* StE is, including lists of words and structures often felt to be used improperly (see below), it is perhaps more helpful to see *how* language use is standard. One attract-ive view is that accommodation is what makes language usage standard, as speakers communicate in a manner that is (1) socially appropriate (whether middle class or working class), (2) suitable to the use to which the language is being put (register; cf. chapter 1), and (3) clear (cf. Stalker 1986: 52–6). Comments on points (1) and (2) have been made above, and these are important criteria underlying the description of StE in the first part of this book. This means that we recognize the effects of the varying characteristics of users as well as the diverse uses to which the language is put. Yet, lest there be any doubt, it should also be made clear that we have oriented our-selves along the lines of educated usage, especially as codified in diction-aries, grammars, phonetic-phonological treatments, and a wide assortment of other sources. In doing this we are more Anglo-American than Antipo-dean, more middle than working class, more Eurocentric than not, and look more to written than spoken language (except, of course, in the treatment of pronunciation).

The third criterion listed above, clarity, is often evoked. Its loss, and the resultant demise of English, is often lamented by popular grammarians and their reading public. This is best treated in connection with the question of language attitudes.

Language attitudes

Language can be evaluated either positively or negatively, and the language which is judged may be one's own or that of one's own group, or it may be that of others. It may be spoken or written, standard or non-standard, and it may be a native-, a second-, or a foreign-language variety. Whatever it is, an evaluation is usually reached on the basis of only a few features, very often stereotypes which have been stigmatized as 'bad' or stylized as 'good'. And because language is such an intimate part of everyone's identity, the way people regard their own and others' language will lead to feelings either of superiority or of denigration and uncertainty.

These individual feelings are strengthened by the attitudes prevalent in any given group. Sometimes a whole group can be infected by feelings of inferiority. It is reported, for example, that 'there is still linguistic insecurity on the part of many Australians: a desire for a uniquely Australian identity in language mixed with lingering doubts about the suitability and "goodness" of [AusE]' (Guy 1991: 224). They seem to feel that a middle-class British or Cultivated Australian accent is somehow better, and they rate speakers with a Broad AusE accent less favourably in terms of status and prestige though highly as regards solidarity and friendliness (Ball *et al.* 1989: 94). In England the attitudes people have towards Received Pronunciation (RP) (see pp. 305–15) vary from complete identification, through all sorts of attempts at emulation, to rejection of it as a 'cut-glass accent' or as talking 'lah-di-dah' (Philp 1968: 26).

Few people would hold up RP as a world-wide model and most seem to accept the multiplicity of English pronunciations used, hoping to understand them, joking about unexpected or odd differences, yet inadvertently judging people's character by the attitudes engendered by these accents. Matched-guise tests, for example, have revealed many such attitudes. In these tests people are asked to judge the features of people on the basis of their recorded accents. In reality the same person has recorded a standardized text with various accents. The intention is to eliminate the effect of individual voice quality by using the same voice in each guise. Although there is the danger that such speakers will involuntarily incorporate mannerisms not attributable to accent in some cases and thus prevent a fair comparison, the results have revealed such things as the tendency of English people to associate speakers of RP with intelligence, speakers of rural accents with warmth and trustworthiness, and speakers of non-RP urban accents with low prestige (with Birmingham at the bottom). GenAm speakers enjoy relatively high prestige in England, but are rated low on comprehensibility (Giles and Powesland 1975: chapter 5). In the United States, *network English* (GenAm) – the variety most widely used in national newscasting – has high prestige (see pp. 374f.); Southern accents, in contrast, have little standing outside the South; Black English often has negative associations for whites (Fraser 1973; Williams 1973). On American television British accents have increasingly replaced German ones for evil and/or highly intelligent characters in science fiction programmes. The list could easily be continued. See Bailey (1992: 1f) for an enumeration of notions about English.

With the enormous variety of feelings and the strength they often have, it is natural to ask where all this comes from. Fundamentally, attitudes are anchored in feelings of group solidarity or distance. It is normal to identify with one's own group; therefore, the real curiosity is why some people deprecate the speechways of the group to which they belong. To a large extent this is the result of the explicit and implicit messages which are constantly being sent out in the name of a single set standard. When this standard came into being in the centuries after 1600, it was the upper-class, educated usage of southern England that was adopted. The force of the court, the Church, the schools, and the new economically dominant commercial elite of London stood behind it, and it was supported by the authority of a huge and growing body of highly admired prose (starting with the King James (Authorized) Version of the Bible in 1611). To belong to this privileged elite, it was felt that a command of proper language was necessary. This led to increasing codification and to the growth of a new class of grammarians who prescribed the standard. In this atmosphere, keeping the standard has become something of a moral obligation for the middle class and those who aspire to it. The bible of this cult is the dictionary; its present-day prophets ('pop grammarians' such as Edwin Newman and Richard Mitchell, but also the authors of popular manuals of style such as the Fowler brothers in Great Britain or Wilson Follett in the United States) anathematize the three 'deadly sins': barbarisms, solecisms and improprieties.

Barbarisms include many things. They may be foreign expressions deemed unnecessary. Such expressions are fully acceptable if there is not a shorter and clearer English way to the meaning or if the foreign terms are not somehow especially appropriate to the field of discourse (*glasnost*, *Ostpolitik*). *Quand même* for *anyhow* or *bien entendu* for *of course* do indeed seem to be 'pretension and nothing else' (cf. Fowler and Fowler 1973: 36). But who is to draw the line in matters of taste and appropriateness? Other examples of 'barbarisms' are archaisms, regional dialect words, slang, cant, and technical or scientific jargon. In all of these cases the same questions ultimately arise. A skilled writer can use any of these 'barbarisms' to good effect, just as avoiding them does not make a bad writer any better.

Solecisms comprise such things as the violation of number concord, the choice of the 'wrong' case for pronouns, and multiple negation. These are all phenomena which are somehow considered to have to do with logic. A singular pronoun such as *everyone* is said logically to demand continued reference in the singular (*Everyone forgot his/her lines*). But there is just as much logic in recognizing the 'logical' plurality of *everyone* 'all people'; hence, why not, *Everyone forgot their lines*? (see 8.1 for more discussion). The point is that an appeal to logic is not enough. Most people accept and use *That's me* (say, when looking at an old photograph of themselves) rather than 'logical' *That's I*, but educated people would be hesitant to use multiple negatives (*Nobody didn't do nothing*) except in jest, although they have no trouble understanding them. Multiple negation is, to put it directly, socially marked; it is non-standard. Here the prescriptive purists' idea of good English is also in line with what this book considers to be StE.

Improprieties chiefly concern similar words which historically had distinct meanings, but which are commonly used as if identical. Most people, for example, use *disinterested* as if it were a synonym of *uninterested*. *Imply* and *infer*, *flaunt* and *flout*, *lie* and *lay*, and many other pairs are often no longer distinguished in the way they once were. In a similar vein, *hopefully* as a sentence adverb (*Hopefully, you can follow this argument*) is widely attacked (see 11.4.1). Some of the many improprieties often named are malapropisms due to ignorance or carelessness, but others are fully in the current of a changing language which dictates that when enough (of the 'right') people are 'wrong', they are right (Safire quoted in McArthur 1986: 34). Once again, in other words, no general verdict is to be expected. (For a readable discussion of these questions and of barbarisms, solecisms and improprieties, see Nunberg 1983.)

Descriptive linguists, in contrast to the prescriptive grammarians just treated, try to do precisely what the term indicates: describe. The aim is to discover how the language is employed by its users whatever their sex, age, regional origins, ethnicity, social class, education, religion, vocation, etc. Explicit evaluations are avoided, but implicit ones, centred on educated middle-class usage, are almost always present, since this provides the usual framework for reference and comparison. It is in this tradition that this book has been written.

REFERENCES

Bailey, R. W. (1990) 'English at its twilight', in L. Michaels and C. Ricks (eds) *The State of the Language*, Berkeley: University of California Press, pp. 83–94.
—— (1992) *Images of English, A Cultural History of the Language*, Cambridge: Cambridge University Press.
Ball, P., Gallois, C. and Callan, V. (1989) 'Language attitudes: a perspective from social psychology', in P. Collins and D. Blair (eds) *Australian English: The Language of a New Society*, St Lucia: University of Queensland Press, pp. 89–102.
Fowler, H. W. and Fowler, F. G. (1973) *The King's English*, 3rd edn, London: Oxford University Press.
Fraser, B. (1973) 'Some "unexpected" reactions to various American English dialects', in R. Shuy and R. W. Fasold (eds), *Language Attitudes: Current Trends and Prospects*, Washington: Georgetown Roundtable in Linguistics, pp. 28–35.
Garvin, P. L. (1964) 'The standard language problem: concepts and methods', in D. Hymes (ed.) *Language in Culture and Society*, New York: Harper & Row, pp. 521–6.
Giles, H. and Powesland, P. F. (1975) *Speech Style and Social Evaluation*, London: Academic Press.

Guy, G. R. (1991) 'Australia', in J. Cheshire (ed.) *English around the World: Sociolinguistic Perspectives*, Cambridge: Cambridge University Press, pp. 213–26.

McArthur, T. (1986) 'The problem of purism', *English Today* 6 (April), pp. 34f.

Nunberg, G. (1983) 'The decline of grammar', *Atlantic Monthly* (December), pp. 31–46.

Philp, A. M. (1968) *Attitudes to Correctness in English*. Programme in Linguistics and English Teaching, Paper No. 6, London: Longman.

Quirk, R. and Stein, G. (1990) *English in Use*, Harlow: Longman.

Stalker, J. C. (1986) 'A reconsideration of the definition of Standard English', in G. Nickel and J. C. Stalker (eds) *Problems of Standardization and Linguistic Variation in Present-Day English*, Heidelberg: Julius Groos, pp. 50–8.

Williams, F. (1973) 'Some research notes on dialect attitudes and stereotypes', in R. Shuy and R. W. Fasold (eds) *Language Attitudes: Current Trends and Prospects*, Washington: Georgetown Roundtable in Linguistics, pp. 113–28.

Part 1

English as a linguistic system

Chapter 1

Vocabulary

In this and the next chapter the words of the modern English language will be at the centre of our discussion. The second chapter will deal above all with combinations of words (so-called *multi-word units* such as idioms and proverbs).

In this chapter the English vocabulary will be looked at from various points of view. First, the concept of *word* and the relationship between words and meaning will be discussed (1.1). Then there will be a section on the origins of the English vocabulary (1.2). The discussion of words borrowed from other languages (*loan words*) will be followed by brief sketches of new words (1.3) and *euphemisms* (1.4.1). Then will follow a more extensive treatment of the major word formation processes in present-day English (1.4.3 to 1.4.7). The last two sections will concentrate on how words change their meanings (1.5) and on some of the models which have been used in the analysis of the English vocabulary (1.6).

1.1 Words and meaning

The vocabulary of the English language is conveniently recorded in dictionaries, of which the second edition of the *Oxford English Dictionary* (1989; abbreviated as OED in the following) is the most recent and comprehensive. Although many people think it the greatest dictionary in the world, reviewers have no difficulty in pointing to words and phrases that are missing. Linguists draw a distinction between a dictionary, which is only the latest incomplete recording of the English vocabulary, and its total word stock, which they refer to as its **lexis** or **lexicon**.

It is not only because new words are coined all the time that it is impossible to say precisely how many words there are in English. It is also perhaps because of the vagueness of the everyday term *word*. For example, how often is the word *dictionary* used in the preceding paragraph? *Dictionary* and *dictionaries* are each found once, while there are two examples of *dictionary*. If we say that there are three different words (*Dictionary*, *dictionary*, *dictionaries*) we are simply referring to the physical shape of words, in this instance the black marks that appear on the paper of this book. Linguists have coined the term **word form** for this use of *word*. From a different point of view we might say that there are two examples of *dictionary*, one in the singular and the other in the plural. Linguists use **word** to refer to this second, the grammatical use. If we say, finally, that there are four occurrences of the single word *dictionary* we are basing our answer on the fact that, though different words and word forms are involved, they all show the same meaning. Word forms seen from the meaning point of view are called **lexemes**. As lexemes can have many meanings, the need has been felt for a term which refers to the combination of one meaning with one word form. This is called a **lexical unit**. The lexeme *old*, for instance, represents at least two different lexical units. This becomes clear when one thinks of the opposite of *old*: one antonym is *young*, but *old* in *my old friend* contrasts with *new* rather than *young*. What we find as main entries in dictionaries are lexemes, while the various meanings listed in these entries should be thought of as lexical units. Having said all this, we will use the everyday term *word* in this book where there is no danger of confusion.

Words (in whatever sense) are, however, not the smallest meaningful units recognized in linguistics. Word formation goes beyond words such as *star* (called **free morphemes** because they can stand alone) and also recognizes forms such as *-dom* as meaningful. Such **bound morphemes** occur only in combination with free morphemes. On the other hand, it is no less important to recognize that there are combinations of more than one word, so-called **multi-word units**, such as the **idiom** *pull someone's leg* or the **proverb** *he who pays the piper calls the tune*, which linguists regard as lexical items in their own right (see chapter 2). Dictionaries might well differ in whether or not they include both free and bound morphemes, idioms and proverbs in the total number of items counted in their word lists.

In the case of *dictionary* there is likely to be universal agreement that it is a word (in all senses), not least because it is easy to state its meaning. It is quite different for words such as *the*, *mine* or *upon*. These **grammatical** or **closed-system items** (articles, pronouns, prepositions, etc.; see chapter 4) have grammatical functions rather than lexical meanings (the *to* in *he likes to play chess*). Indeed, they are also called **function words** because their function is often more important than their meaning. Lexical items, on the other hand, are members of **open classes**: classes which have no determinate number of members and which are constantly added to. Lexical items are therefore often called **open-class items**.

The combination of word forms with meaning is also unproblematic in the case of *dictionary* because there are only one or two meanings (*lexical units*) involved. There are, however, many words which have a great number of meanings. Different linguists and lexicographers can have very different views on how many lexical units, and indeed lexemes, to set up in these cases. Table 1.1 shows how some dictionaries deal with such a more complicated example, viz. *romance*.

The table mirrors the difficulties involved in deciding whether to view a given word form with several meanings as a case of **polysemy** (the existence of one lexeme with many related meanings) or of **homonymy** (the existence of different lexemes that sound the same (**homophones**) or are spelt the same (**homographs**) but have different meanings; see Zöfgen 1989 for a summary; cf. also Lyons 1977). RHED and WNC seem to think the meaning 'piece of music' sufficiently different to warrant a separate entry. CED, WNC and LDOCE do the same for the Romance language meaning of the word form. While lexicographers thus have different views on differences in meaning, linguists find it no less difficult to reach agreement on the more fundamental question of the nature of meaning, how it is produced, processed and analysed, and how it can best be described (cf. 1.5 below on new meanings; for general discussions of meaning, see Lyons 1977; Allan 1986; Jackson 1988; Chierchia and McConnell-Ginet 1990; LePore 1987 is a state-of-the-art survey; Gordon 1987 offers a bibliographical guide).

In addition to meaning, four other factors can influence the decision to set up separate entries in dictionaries, namely spelling, word class, inflection and etymology. If two word forms differ in spelling, for example lower-case as against capital letters, lexicographers often decide on separate entries. This seems to be a contributing factor for the arrangements in CED,

Table 1.1 Some dictionary entries for the word *romance*

	COD	RHED	CED	LDOCE	WNC
noun					
atmosphere	+	+	+	+	+
love (affair)	+	+	+	+	+
literary genre/work	+	+	+	+	+
medieval tale	+	+	+	0	+
exaggeration, falsehood	+	+	+	0	+
language family	+	+	R	0	+
piece of music	+	r2	+	0	r3
adjective					
relating to the Romance language family	+	+	R	R	R
verb					
exaggerate	+	+	+	r2	r2
court, woo	+	+	+	r2	r2

Legend: COD = *The Concise Oxford Dictionary*; RHED = *The Random House Dictionary of the English Language*; CED = *Collins English Dictionary*; LDOCE = *Longman Dictionary of Contemporary English;* WNC = *Webster's Ninth New Collegiate Dictionary*.
+ = first/only entry; r2, r3 = second, third entry; R = separate entry, capital letters; 0 = not recorded.

LDOCE and WNC. Separate lexemes or dictionary entries can also be set up for the different word classes of a word form. This principle is clearly behind the arrangement in LDOCE and WNC, both of which have a sub-entry for the verbal meanings. Meanings that are tied to a particular inflected form (no example in the table) can also appear as entries in their own right, for example, *fell* as past tense (of *fall*) or as present tense (of *fell*). Finally, though the meanings of a given word form may be (widely) different, they can be put into one entry if they go back to the same word form (etymon). All the meanings listed in the table derive from a non-attested form *Romanice* 'in the vernacular' (as opposed to 'in Latin'); for this reason COD and other dictionaries with a historical orientation use one main entry only.

1.2 The origin and frequency of words

English has changed dramatically in the course of the centuries, from a language which was highly inflected in Old English times to one which has extremely few inflections today, and from one whose lexis was almost completely Germanic to one which has taken in lexical material from the most diverse sources (for histories of the English vocabulary, see Sheard 1970; Strang 1970; Baugh and Cable 1978; Jespersen 1982; Bolton 1982). Foreign influence also shows in **loan translations**, for example, *loan word* and *loan translation*, which are themselves both translations of German words, and *loan shifts*, where only the meaning has been borrowed, (cf. OE *cneoht* 'farm hand' > ModE *knight* under the influence of Old French *chevaler*). In the following we will concentrate on loan words only.

1.2.1 Celtic loan words

Very few words have been taken over and kept from the language of the Celts, the people whom the Anglo-Saxons conquered: for example, *bin*, *crag*, *luh* (Scots *loch*, Irish *lough*; 'lake'). These were supplemented by a few more in later centuries: *blarney*, *cairn*, *plaid*, *slogan*, *Tory* and *whiskey*. Others survive in place names: 'By Tre-, Pol- and Pen- | Ye may know the Cornishman' (Cameron 1969: 42). Examples are *Tregair*, *Tremaine*, *Trerose* (*tre*[v] 'homestead, hamlet'); *Polperro*, *Polruan*, *Polscol* (*pol* < *porth* 'port'); *Penare*, *Penryn*, *Penzance* (*pen* 'head, end, hill'; note Scots Gaelic and Irish *beann* 'peak', as in *Ben Nevis*). The Celtic name for the invaders, *Sassenachs* (ultimately derived from Latin *Saxones*, 'Saxons'), is still in use in Ireland and Scotland as a pejorative term for the English.

1.2.2 Scandinavian loan words

These are more numerous and less recognizable because of the close relationship between Old Norse and Old English. *Get*, *give*, *hit*, *skirt* and *take* are just a very few examples. Sometimes these loans ousted a native word (*take* supplanted OE *niman*); sometimes the immigrant and the native lexeme continued side by side with different meanings, for example, Scandinavian *skirt* and OE *shirt*, or Scandinavian *cast* and OE *werpan* 'throw' > ModE *warp*. Perhaps most remarkable is the fact that English borrowed not only lexical but also grammatical words from Scandinavian, for example, the pronouns *they*, *their* and *them*. Later borrowings include *rune*, *saga* and *ombudsman*.

1.2.3 German and Dutch loans

Other than in specialist fields such as geology and mineralogy, High German has had little influence on English (see Pfeffer 1987). Generally known items are all recent, and include food terms such as *lager*, *sauerkraut* (which has become in its shortened version, *Kraut*, a pejorative term for a German) and, more recently, *quark* (a type of cheese). Other loans have been taken from war and politics, for example, *ostpolitik*, *blitzkrieg* (where *blitz* is used in a transferred meaning, 'energetic intensive attack', as in *we're going to have a blitz on the house*) and *flak*, which is frequently used outside the military context to mean 'criticism, objection' (*they came in for a lot of flak*). More German loans have entered American English (AmE), particularly in the midwest and, often via Yiddish, in the northeast for example, *gesundheit* (in response to a sneeze), *kvetch* ('complain'), *schlep(p)* ('drag, lug') and *schlock* ('trash, inferior goods').

Low German and Dutch have contributed such items as *gin*, *kit*, *landscape*, *luck*, *snap* and a number of nautical lexemes such as *buoy*, *cruise*, *deck*, *skipper* and *yacht*.

1.2.4 Latin and Greek loans

Much more profound has been the impact of Latin and Greek. Though there are a number of Latin borrowings in Old English, both popular (*camp*, *cheese*, *chest*, *cook*, *pipe*, *silk*, *table*) and learned (*circle*, *consul*, *giant*, *legion*, *talent*), the two classical languages really became influential in the early Modern English period, from around 1500 onwards. Sometimes the same lexeme has been borrowed more than once, for example, the ancient Greek *diskos*, which appears as *dish* (< OE *disc*; from Latin *discus*), *dais* (from Old French via Latin), *desk* (<medieval Latin *desca*), *disc* or *disk* (< French *disque* or Latin *discus*; note *diskette*) and *discus*. More importantly, however, the two classical languages have provided English as well as most other (European) languages with countless technical terms in all branches of human knowledge, a need that was perhaps first strongly felt by English humanists who wanted English to become a medium capable of expressing the most refined thought, on a par with Latin and Greek. *Lexis, lexeme, lexical, lexicographer, diction(ary)* and *vocabulary* are all derived from Greek and Latin elements, while only the rarer *word book* and *word stock* are Germanic. The same goes for *poet, rhythm, metre* and *romance*, as opposed to *writer* and *wordsmith*. Before this period, Greek items had entered English via Latin and/or French, but now that Greek studies were getting a boost such lexemes as *anonymous, catastrophe, lexicon, polemic, thermometer* and *tonic* were borrowed directly into the language. The only recent field that seems to have more native coinages and native items used in special meanings than neo-classical loans is the jargon of computers and computing (*fanfold paper, formfeed, spreadsheet*; McCarthy 1990: 65). Sometimes it is impossible to see whether a loan is from Latin or French (*diverse, importation, information, solid*).

1.2.5 Romance loans

Lexemes from Anglo-Norman and, from about 1200, Central (Parisian) French have poured into the language in great numbers, profoundly changing its lexical character. Earlier loans during Middle English times tend to come from the areas of law, war and government (*assault, judge, jury, lance, parliament, siege, sue, tower, war*), while later borrowings reflect perhaps French domination more in the spheres of fashion, life style, the arts and sciences (*dress, fashion, garment, gown, habit, petticoat; court, courtesy, curtsy, joust, luxury, tournament; chapter, comedy, copy, page, romance, story, title, tragedy; engineer, college, lecture, library, medicine, physician, surgery, university*). Later loans include numerous gastronomic items (*bonbon, casserole, champagne, crème brûlée, crêpe, fondant, hors d'oeuvre, menu, praline* and *restaurant*). Many loans have been adapted over the centuries to conform to English sound patterns (*baron, button, chief, madam, mutton*), but later loans, especially after the English Restoration (1660), often keep some of the phonetic or intonational features of the donor language (*balloon, bassoon, chef, mademoiselle, platoon*). Thus one can hear *garage* completely /ˈgærɪdʒ/ or partially assimilated: /ˈgærɑɪdʒ/, /ˈgærɑːʒ/ (esp. BrE) and, with even more French-sounding pronunciations, /gɑˈrɑɪdʒ/ or /gɑˈrɑːʒ/ (esp. AmE).

Other Romance languages are less important. Italian has, above all, provided words from music, the arts and literature (*sonnet, stanza, canto, opera, sonata, solo, piano, prima donna*, etc.). Spanish has contributed *breeze, embargo, Negro, tango, vanilla*, and various items from its colonies, often ultimately from Amerindian languages (*barbecue, cannibal, canoe, maize, potato* and *tobacco*).

1.2.6 Other languages

Russian is the only other European language that has supplied a considerable number of loans to English, for example, *bolshevik*, *glasnost*, *perestroika*, *pogrom*, *sable*, *soviet*, *steppe*, *troika*, *ukas*, and *vodka*.

Arabic loans in English include, for example, *admiral*, *alcohol*, *cotton*, *mattress*, *saffron*, *tariff*, *zenith*. Of African origin are, for example, *chimpanzee*, *gnu*, *safari*, *voodoo* and *zebra*. Among Amerindian loans we find *caucus*, *rac(c)oon*, *squash*, *tomahawk*, *totem*, *wigwam*. Indian loans include *bungalow*, *calico*, *cashmere*, *cheroot*, *loot*, *pariah*, *pukka* and *shampoo*.

1.2.7 Present-day loans

Some major changes seem to have happened in recent times. First, loans as a source of new words seem to have become much less important. An explanation might be that only a few of the many traditional reasons for borrowing are active nowadays. Loan words have been imported in the past because the terms arrived with new imports (Scandinavian *ski*, Russian *vodka*), or because of the tendency to complete word families (Scandinavian verb *die* complemented the Old English adjective *dead* and the noun *death*). Borrowing also occurred because of the etymological link of an item with one which was already in the language, and of course because of sheer laziness or love of a new term (which may have sounded better, more learned or more fashionable, etc.).

It would seem that most new loan words nowadays refer to new things for which the foreign term is taken over (so-called **cultural borrowings**), while the other factors are of minor importance. In addition, English has increased its range of donor languages (Cannon 1987: 89, mentions at least eighty-four), the main contributors being French, Japanese, Spanish, Italian, Latin, Greek, German, African, Yiddish, Russian and Chinese. The share of Indo-European loans has dropped in comparison with earlier times. The prominence of the Asian and African languages is something qualitatively new. Often loans are changed in form, and particularly in spelling. Third, only three open-word classes are represented, with nouns dominating massively over the few adjectives and even fewer verbs (for more detail, see Cannon 1987: 90–3).

1.2.8 Word frequencies

The English vocabulary is no doubt a prime example of a lexically mixed language, but that is true only with reference to the 616,500 word forms which we find in the OED. When we look at the items actually used in writing and speaking we find that the front runners are native English words. The most frequent two hundred words in English consist overwhelmingly of one syllable; there are a few two-syllable ones (forty in AmE, twenty-four in British English (BrE)), and a handful of trisyllabic forms (three in AmE, two in BrE), while only AmE has a single four-syllable item, the word *American* itself (see the two word counts and frequency listings in Francis and Kučera 1982 for AmE, and Hofland and Johansson 1982 for BrE). Although Francis and Kučera count grammatical words and Hofland and Johansson list word forms – an illustration of the importance of the distinctions made in 1.1 above – their results are independently confirmed by other counts. It has been computed that, of the 10,000 most frequent English words (presumably lexemes, though this is not made clear), 31.8 per cent go back to Old English, whereas for the 1,000 most frequent words it is as high as 83 per cent (quoted from Berndt 1982: 69). This shows the paramount importance of the inherited Germanic vocabulary in the central core of English. Loan words are, generally speaking, more peripheral, though relative frequencies vary by different text type (see chapter 7) and stylistic level: the more formal the style and the more specialized and remote from everyday experience the subject matter, the higher the number of foreign loans. In everyday language, the English word will often be preferred because it is vague and covers many shades of meaning, while loan words are more precise and restricted and therefore more difficult to handle. Thus, when faced with the choice between *acquire*, *obtain* and *purchase* on the one hand, and *buy* or *get* on the other, most people will go for the short (Anglo-Saxon) words.

In formal situations it may seem appropriate to *extend* or *grant a cordial reception*, while in less stiff situations one will *give a warm welcome*. The old-established items are usually warmer, more human, more emotional, while many (polysyllabic) loans from Greek, Latin or the Romance languages are cold and formal and put a distance between sender (speaker, writer) and addressee (listener, reader). This division of function is reversed in the following example, which explains why the narrator feels the need for an explicit comment:

> 'I see – how nice', said Julia, imparting to these words a degree of coldness which one might have supposed sustainable only by some more polysyllabic observation.
>
> (S. Caudwell, *The Sirens Sang of Murder*, pp. 15–16).

(*Nice* derives in fact from Latin *nescius*, 'ignorant', but has long since lost any foreign flair).

1.3 New words

Great numbers of new words have been taken into English from other languages; even more are formed by productive word formation processes from items that are already in the language. The four supplementary volumes to the first edition of the *Oxford English Dictionary*, published from 1972 to 1987, are the most complete inventory of new words in English, but there are also other collections, such as Barnhart *et al*. 1973, 1980; Barnhart *et al*. 1990; Lemay 1989; Mish 1983; Mort 1986; Ayto 1989 and 1990. Mention must also be made of the journal *American Speech*, which devotes a regular column ('Among the New Words') to neologisms and new meanings. Research into words and meanings will be made much easier through the CD-ROM version of the second edition of the OED. Meanwhile, the first full-length study has appeared (Cannon 1987), which presents the results of detailed investigations into the 13,683 items recorded in three American collections of neologisms, Barnhart *et al*. 1973 and 1980, as well as the 1981 Addenda Section to *Webster's Third New International Dictionary of the English Language*.

Of the many new lexical items only some words and expressions from the vocabulary of the environment will be presented here which are now in *general* use. Particularly frequent are the forms *bio-* (*bio-diversity*, *bio-gas*, *bio-sphere*) and *eco-* (*ecoclimate*, *eco-labelling*, *ecosphere*, *ecosystem*); perhaps the single most frequently used word is the lexeme *green* in the sense of 'concerned with or supporting the protection of the environment'. Less cumbersome than *environmental(ly friendly)*, which it can often replace in the spoken language, it is used in countless combinations (*green* + *consumer*, *equities*, *ideas*, *issues*, *lobbyists*, *management*, *policies*, *products*, *protection*, *regulation*, *reputation*, *revolution*, *shoppers*, *standards*, *technology*, *voters*, etc.) One can *turn green*, *buy greenly* or *use one's funds greenly*, and politicians can make *green speeches*. Compare these examples:

No force will more powerfully drive the greening of world industry than the growing hostility of people, as they grow richer, to those installations that they see as polluting.

('A Survey of Industry and the Environment', *The Economist*, 8 September 1990, p. 14)

... an EC scheme offers West German companies a better way to sell throughout Europe products developed for their own long-greened customers.

(ibid., p. 8)

Companies that want to be greener are developing new ways to build greenery [= 'green ideas and methods'] into management.

(ibid., p. 23)

And companies fear that the more information they have to provide on a product's greenness, the more a label will cost them.

(ibid., p. 8)

The prefix *re-* is frequently employed to refer to reusing valuable materials, as in *recirculate* (water), *reprocess* (spent fuel), and above all *recycle* (bottles, garbage, metal, paper, plastics, raw materials, tins, etc.). *Recycle* can be used metaphorically as well, as in 'revenues from a carbon tax might be recycled to improve economic growth' ('Survey on Energy and the Environment', *The Economist*, 31 August 1991, p. 36).

The paragraphs which follow demonstrate some of the many new coinages found in non-technical discussions of environmental issues.

One of the most urgent problems is the *greenhouse effect* or *global warming*, which refers to the recent rise in the earth's temperature. This is caused by various *(greenhouse) gases*, such as *carbon dioxide*, *methane*, *nitrous oxide*, *tropospheric ozone* and *chlorofluorocarbons* (abbreviated to *CFCs*). The CFCs (used, for example, in refrigerators and air-conditioning systems) are doubly dangerous because they also nibble a hole in the *ozone layer*, which screens out ultraviolet rays from the sun. It is therefore vital that they are replaced with *ozone-friendly* substances. Global warming will result in flooding and droughts and the world may soon have millions of *environmental refugees* on its hands. One thing is clear: the *NIMBY* (not in my backyard) attitude must give way to international cooperation. It is therefore the aim of governments and *environmentalists* to reduce the *emission* of these *pollutants*, for example, by only allowing new cars that run on *unleaded petrol/gasoline* and have a *(three-way) catalytic converter* (or *catalyst*), and by *retrofitting* old cars with one. This may help to reduce the *pollution* caused by *acid rain*, which lowers the *pH* of soils and waters in rivers and lakes.

Another problem area is that of energy. *Fossil fuels* have provided most of our energy, but with their depletion and because of the pollution they cause, other and cleaner ways of producing power are being looked for. One option is nuclear power, another is various forms of *alternative energy* or *renewable energy sources*. Wind can be harnessed through single turbines or in *wind farms*; the sun's energy can be converted and stored in *photovoltaic* or *solar cells* and *solar panels*; *hydro(electric plant)s* can take power from dams, tides and waves; and various *biofuels* (which are of an organic origin and are found in much *domestic* and *industrial waste*; *biomass* 'power from burning vegetation') offer the prospect of cheap energy. *Alternative power* from *renewables* is thus likely to play an increasingly important part in the future.

A fundamental rethink of transport policy should be a top priority for any *environmentally conscious* government. Better public transport, more *pedestrianized areas* (*pedestrian precincts*), *cycle* and *bus lanes* will be necessary to lower air and noise pollution. *Gas guzzlers* ('cars that use a lot of gasoline/petrol') should be replaced by *gas sippers* ('cars that use little fuel'), and charges for the use of roads (*road pricing*) might reduce the volume of traffic significantly.

Waste management is another problem. To avoid waste, fewer *disposables* and *throwaways* should be bought and produced. By separating waste at source, and reusing the materials which can be *reprocessed*, there will be less waste to dispose of. Governments could set up *collection sites* for *recyclable* materials, such as glass, paper and plastics. More waste glass should be *returnable* and collected in *bottle banks*, separated into *clear* and *coloured glass*. *Recycled paper* saves trees. Most plastics should be boycotted as they do not *(bio)degrade/*are not *biodegradable*. Producers should avoid *overpackaging* and the use of *chlorine bleached paper*, which causes *ground* and *water contamination* with dioxins. Waste should no longer be burned at sea, particularly as not all ships are fitted with *scrubbers* to filter toxic fumes. No less controversial is the *deep burial method* of (intermediate and high level) radioactive waste disposal.

Intensive farming uses all sorts of *pesticides*, *insecticides*, *fungicides* and *herbicides* to produce blemish-free products that appeal to consumers, but which are dangerous to human beings either directly or indirectly when they enter the *food chain* through animals. It has led to overproduction and to *battery* or *factory farming*, which uses inhumane rearing methods for pigs, poultry and dairy herds. More environmentally friendly farming methods are used by *organic farmers*, who do not believe in piling on fertilizers, but turn instead to compost, seaweed and manure, and from whom one can buy *free-range poultry* and *eggs*. *Organic farming* might also help to reduce the massive surpluses (*the butter-, grain-* and *beef mountains*; *the wine lake*) in the EC.

1.4 Euphemisms, non-sexist language and word formation

This section discusses recent words which have been formed by some of the productive word-formation processes in present-day English. Euphemisms and non-sexist language will be dealt with first because they are not restricted to any single type of word formation.

1.4.1 Euphemisms

Euphemisms are the result not of changes in, for example, science, technology or the environment, but of changes in the moral sense of a society in areas where it has a communal bad conscience or is afraid to talk about a taboo subject. These areas have traditionally been the human body, death, crime, sex, war, money and government (see Neaman and Silver 1990). Now they include racial and sexual minorities, for example, non-white people, some of whom want to be called *African-American*, a word which has replaced *Afro-American*, which replaced the term *black*, which replaced *Negroes*, which in turn replaced *coloured*, which replaced *black*. But other fields are also involved, for example, menial jobs, so that servants can be referred to as *domestic engineers*, and refuse/garbage collectors as *disposal operatives* (GB) or *sanitation engineers* (USA). It is as if society were embarrassed and trying to avoid unpleasant realities by putting a good label on them, as is seen in this comment on developments in the United States:

> Prisons have become 'rehabilitative correctional facilities', housewives are 'homemakers', deaf people are 'hearing-impaired', the Cerebral Palsy society tells journalists never to use the word 'suffer' about those with that 'disease' (forbidden), 'affliction' (forbidden), condition [sic] (allowed).
>
> (*The Economist*, 28 July 1990, p. 11)

Euphemisms cannot upgrade low jobs or change reality, nor can they cover things up for very long. Soon the new word becomes firmly associated with the unpleasant or embarrassing meaning, and the need for a new euphemistic lexeme arises. A Jules Pfeiffer cartoon from 1965 captures this mechanism perfectly: 'I used to think I was poor. Then they told me I wasn't poor, I was needy. They told me it was self-defeating to think of myself as needy, I was deprived. Then they told me underprivileged was overused. I was disadvantaged. I still don't have a dime. But I have a great vocabulary' (quoted from Redfern 1989: 98). This example shows clearly how euphemistic tendencies cause the same meaning to be expressed by different words (this is called **lexical swap**) and also how words take on new meanings (called **semantic change** or change of meaning; see below 1.5). Not only are euphemisms the cause of increased lexical turnover, but they can also cause the loss of a lexical unit. A recent case is that of *gay*, both noun and adjective, which is currently used almost exclusively in the sense of 'homosexual'.

1.4.2 Non-sexist language

While the creation of euphemisms seems to be a never-ending story, the finding of non-sexist equivalents for offensive sexist items is more recent and perhaps more finite. Dissatisfaction with sexist language leads to

1 the replacement of lexical items or parts of lexical items that have an exclusively male meaning with neutral forms when the reference is to human beings generally or to both sexes;
2 the creation of new terms when the reference is to women only;
3 the avoidance and/or creation of new terms where lexical items, often with a pejorative meaning or connotation, have come to be associated exclusively with women.

Notes on 1:
Many compound lexemes containing the form *-man* have been, or are in the process of being, replaced, often by compounds ending in *-person*: *chairperson*, *spokesperson*. *Humankind* is an alternative to *mankind*, as are *beat up*, *push/kick around* or *maltreat* for *manhandle*, as Maggio (1988: 87) points out. The verb *man* has many possible alternatives, for example, *operate*, *staff*, *run*, *supply a crew/personnel for*, *work*, *serve at/on* (all from Maggio 1988: 86).

Notes on 2:
Terms such as *chairman* now have parallel terms such as *chairwoman*, *spokeswoman*, etc. *Housewife* is often avoided in American English and replaced by (euphemistic?) *homemaker*.

Notes on 3:
This is perhaps the most difficult. Often there is no alternative to the offensive expression (cf. the entries for *femme fatale*, *hussy* and *Jezebel* in Maggio). In other cases, such as *bitch* or *groupie*, there are a number of non-sexist options available. For more detail, see the discussion in 8.1.

1.4.3 Word formation

Word-formation processes account for almost 80 per cent of the new lexical items in Cannon's material (see his table, Cannon 1987: 279), as compared with new meanings (14.4 per cent) and borrowings (7.5 per cent). In this section we will look at some of the productive word formation processes (see table 1.2), using the two operations of deletion and combination as the basis of the present treatment (see Algeo 1978).

Cannon has found that **composite forms**, which consist of derivations and compounds, take the lion's share, with 54.9 per cent, followed by **shifts** (19.6 per cent) and **shortenings** (18 per cent). Compounds (4,040, of which 3,591 are nouns) are the oldest category, and while they are still the largest class overall – as they have been throughout the history of the English language – Cannon thinks that 'shortenings provide the newest and perhaps potentially the most productive categories for the near future' (ibid.: 246).

Shifts and **blends**, as well as **acronyms** and **back-formations**, are processes of which few native speakers are aware. Not many people will know,

Table 1.2 Word formation processes

wf process	combination	deletion	example
shift	–	–	(it's a big) if
blend	+	+	faction < fact + fiction
shortening	–	+	tech(nical)
composite forms	+	–	toyboy, cordless

for instance, that the verb *beg* is derived from *beggar* by back-formation, or that the verb *beggar* (as in *they had been beggared by the war*) is a shift which comes later in time than the noun, or that *smog* combines *smoke* and *fog*. Speaking synchronically, we would analyse the *beg–beggar* relationship like any other pair such as *lie–liar* or *bake–baker* and assume that the noun is derived from the verb by adding a suffix. The word form *beggar*, we would say, shows multiple class membership (noun and verb), and *smog* is an unanalysable addition to the lexicon. On the other hand, *composition*, *derivation* and *shortening*, (where the long form is retained), are more obvious as processes even to the lay person who knows only the contemporary language.

The following discussion relies for many of the examples and all its figures and percentages on Cannon's findings, though it does not always adopt his categories. A general word of caution is also in order, namely that not all the examples in Cannon's corpus or, for that matter, in the following pages will become a permanent part of the English language. They illustrate, however, certain trends and structural possibilities which are important in the modern English language. The discussion below is largely non-technical and concentrates above all on processes which are of particular relevance today. For more in-depth treatments see the standard work by Marchand 1969. Briefer introductions can be found in Hansen *et al.* 1985; Bauer 1983; Quirk *et al.* 1985; Tournier 1985; Allerton and French 1988; and, with a comprehensive bibliography, Welte 1988.

1.4.4 Shifts

Shifts (also called **zero derivations**) are typical of English and have been made possible through the loss of inflectional endings early in the Middle English period. Shifts are lexemes that have been assigned a new word class without change in the form of the underlying lexeme, which is why one also finds the terms **functional shift** or **conversion**. Cannon notes that this process has probably never been as productive as it is at present, that quite a few word forms come into use in more than one word class (this is called **multiple class membership**), and that they participate in the full inflectional potential of the new word class (this is referred to as **complete conversion**), especially when they are converted to a noun or verb (Cannon 1987: 57). Conversion most often results in nouns (239), followed by verbs (201, all but 13 of which shifted from nouns) and adjectives (108; figures from Cannon's corpus, ibid. p. 55). Examples of nouns are:

commute ('way to work': *the commute is too long*)
eats ('food': *healthy eats*)
edit (as in computerese: *save all your edits*)

shop ('shopping': *the weekly shop at the supermarket*)
update (*let's have an update on the traffic situation*).

Examples of verbs are:

handbag ('treat ruthlessly')
impact ('have an impact on': *how will this impact our plans?*)
intake ('they do intake their breath when the women kiss'; *The Times*, London, 24 May 1991, p. 12)
rubbish, trash ('criticize heavily'; frequent objects are books, films, etc.)
condo, mall ('provide with malls and condo[minium]s': '[they] cover the planet like one big enclosed shopping mall. We're getting malled and condoed.' (E. Leonard, *LaBrava*, p. 39).

This is perhaps a convenient place to mention **secondary shifts**, in which word forms move from one sub-class to another within the same part of speech while showing related meanings. Thus, *press*, as in the *American press* or *meet the press*, is a mass (non-count) noun, but the word can also be used as a count noun ('journalists': *how many press were there?*). *Okay* has been in adjectival use for a long time, usually in predicative position (*don't worry, she's okay*), but it is now found in attributive position as well, i.e. before a noun: 'Don't worry, Mom. I'm having an OK time' (A. Lurie, *The Truth about Lorin Jones*, p. 70). We will illustrate two productive processes for verbs. First, transitive verbs can be formed from intransitive ones, as in *the house sleeps five*. In the examples below, the new transitive verbs stand in a causative relationship to the intransitive verbs:

disappear (*he kidnapped you, disappeared you*; 'he caused you to disappear')
hurry (up) (*hurry one's stride; I tried to hurry him up*)
shut up (*it surprised him and shut him up*)
sit (*she sat the baby on the sofa*)
stand (*stand the chair in the corner*).

Second, intransitive verbs are formed from transitive ones, with a passive meaning. The best-known example is perhaps the verb *sell*, as in *the book sells well*, which is also found in a more complex structure such as *the novel has sold a million copies* ('a million copies of the novel have been sold'). These are called **notional** or **adverbial passives** (cf. 4.4.4), the latter because they often take an adverb of manner (*I don't anger/bruise/frighten easily*). More recent examples include the following: the cream *beats* well; her hat *blew off*; this wine will *drink* well for the next few years ('can be enjoyed by drinking'); cold lamb *eats* beautifully, especially if cooked with herbs and mustard ('can be enjoyed by eating'); the car *handles* easily; do you *hurt*? ('are you in pain?'); she *interviews* well ('she is good at being interviewed'); this weed *pulls* easily ('is easy to pull'); the play *translates* well into French.

1.4.5 Blends

Blends (also called **telescope** or **portmanteau words**) are the fusion of the forms and meanings of two lexemes. The first item usually loses something at the end, and the second something at the beginning (cf. Redfern 1989: chapter 17). Traditionally, blends have had at least one shared element (*motel* < motor and hotel) but more recent formations show no common elements (*brunch* < breakfast and lunch). They are characteristic of English, though they represent only 1 per cent (131 items) of new formations in Cannon's corpus (this may have something to do with his definition of blend). Blends are very popular in journalism, advertising and technical fields (especially names) and tend to belong to a more informal stylistic level. The majority of portmanteau words are nouns, with only ten adjectives and three verbs in Cannon's corpus (cf. Bryant 1974, who counted 251 nouns, 54 adjectives and one verb).

Verbs: *gues(s)timate* < guess, estimate
  skyjack < sky, hijack
Adjectives: *glitzy* < glitter, ritzy
Nouns: *camcorder* < camera, recorder
  Chunnel < Channel, tunnel
  sexploitation < sex, exploitation
  squarial < square, aerial
  stagflation < stagnation, inflation

1.4.6 Shortenings

Of the many processes which come under the heading of **shortenings** we will give examples for **back-formations**, **initialisms** and **clippings**, or **stump words**. The smallest group is **back-formations** (Cannon counts 151 examples), which have lost what is mistakenly thought to be an affix or inflection, as in *edit* < *editor* and *buttle* < *butler*. Indeed, the major traditional class change found in Cannon's material is noun to verb (96); the remaining third is made up of new nouns (41) and adjectives (14). The major patterns in the corpus are loss of *-ion*, *-er* or *-ing* in nouns, and loss of *-ic* in adjectives to form new nouns. There are also a host of new formations. Most striking among these are perhaps the result of the loss of *-y* (*complicit*, *funk*, *glitz*, *laze*, *raunch*, *sleaze*), the loss of a presumed prefix as in *ept* (< *inept*) and *flappable* (< *unflappable*), various additions after shortening (especially *-e*: *back-mutate* < *back-mutation*, *mitose* < *mitosis*) and the rare loss of a root in *hyper* (< *hyperactive*). Not all back-formations can be found recorded in dictionaries, though the type has great productive potential: in the family of one of the authors of this book *shevelled* (*<dishevelled*) is a much used, indeed essential, new adjective.

Initialisms are historically the most recent group; two types are usually distinguished, **acronyms** and **abbreviations**. Though both consist of a number of first letters, acronyms are pronounced as words (they are also called **syllable words**) whereas abbreviations are pronounced as a series of letters (**letter words**). Well-established acronyms are *laser* (*<l*ightwave *a*mplification by *s*timulated *e*mission of *r*adar) and *scuba* (*<s*elf-contained *u*nderwater *b*reathing *a*pparatus); more recent are *Aids* (*a*cquired *i*mmune *d*eficiency syndrome), *dinky* (*<d*ual income, *n*o *k*ids + -*y*), *NIMBY* (*<* *n*ot *i*n *m*y *b*ack *y*ard + -*y*), *RAM* (*<* *r*andom *a*ccess *m*emory), *ROM* (*<* *r*ead *o*nly *m*emory), and *yuppy* (*<* *y*oung *u*rban *p*rofessional + -*y*). There are 153 acronyms (all but four of them nouns) in Cannon's corpus as opposed to 460 abbreviations. Of the latter, all but three are nouns. They consist for the most part of three letters (usually all capital) and belong to fields such as chemistry or health (84), transport (31), the military (30) and computers and education (28). Examples are *AI* (*A*mnesty *I*nternational; *a*rtificial *i*ntelligence); *ATV* (*a*ll-*t*errain *v*ehicle in AmE; *A*ssociated *Te*l*e*vision in BrE); *BP* (*b*eautiful *p*eople, AmE; *B*ritish *P*etroleum, BrE); *CAD* (*c*omputer-*a*ided *d*esign); *CAT* (*c*lear *a*ir *t*urbulence in AmE; *C*ollege of *A*dvanced *T*echnology in BrE); *CR* (*c*onsciousness *r*aising); *IUCD* or *IUD* (*i*ntra-*u*terine [contraceptive] *d*evice); *VIP* (*v*ery *i*mportant *p*erson); *HTGR* (*h*igh *t*emperature *g*as-cooled *r*eactor); *VSOP* (*v*ery *s*uperior *o*ld *p*ale (brandy)).

There are two major types of **clipping**, front- and back-clippings. The second is the more frequent (341 items in Cannon as opposed to 110), while medial (95) and mixed (82) shortenings, though not uncommon, are less frequent.

Mixed: *comp* < accompany; *van* < advantage
Medial: vegan < vegetarian; *veggies* < vegetables
Front: *fiche* < microfiche; *foil* < hydrofoil
Back: *autoland* < automatic landing; *detox* < detoxification; *flip* < flippant; *glam* < glamorous; *limo* < limousine; *lit*(erary)-*crit*(icism); *metro* < metropolitan; *rehab* < rehabilitation; *sitcom* < sit(uation) + comedy

1.4.7 Composite forms

These can be roughly divided into **compounds** and **derivations**. **Compounds** consist of two or more free morphemes, which can be either **simple** (as are the morphemes in *book token*) or **complex** (*childhood sweetheart*). **Derivations** are made up of one or more free morphemes and at least one bound morpheme (the -*y* in *handyman* < hand, -y and man, while *nation* is the only free form in *denationalization* < de-, nation, -al, -ize, -ation). Bound morphemes in word formation are called **affixes**, of which **prefixes** come before, and **suffixes** after the free form. A third type of bound form, called *combining form*, is introduced below. It is not always easy to decide whether a given lexeme is a compound or a derivation, witness *householder*: is this *household* + *-er* or *house* + *holder* (Allerton and French 1988: 131)? Composite forms of more than two elements often combine both processes, as in *baby boomer*, *gas-guzzler* or *ungentlemanly*.

There are also a small number (2 per cent in Cannon's corpus) of formations (often technical) which combine only bound forms, for example, *afrophile*, *allozyme*, *anglophone*, *audiophile*, *hologram*, *telegamy* ('marriage between people who live far apart') and *telethon*. These bound forms are called **combining forms**, and the combinations they enter into are like compounds except that they consist of bound rather than free forms. There are also lengthier bound-item forms: *desalinate* is an example of a combining form with both a prefix and a suffix (de- + salin- + -ate). For free forms plus combining forms see **derivations** below.

Compounds are usually classified in semantic terms, namely whether or not the compound as a whole is equivalent to (at least) one of its parts. Thus, *goldfish* is a kind of fish, and *house party* is a kind of party. These compounds are called **endocentric**, as opposed to **exocentric**, where the compound meaning is 'idiomatic', i.e. where it is not equivalent to any of the constituent free forms. This is the case, for example, in *hunchback*, which is neither a hunch nor a back, and *turnkey*, which is neither a turn nor a key. Cannon has counted 3,579 new endocentric compounds as against 461 exocentric ones. Noun compounds constitute overwhelmingly the most frequent group (3,591, of which only 207 are exocentric), followed by adjectives (290, of which only 83 are endocentric) and verbs (135, of which 109 are endocentric and 60 consist of verb + particle). Again, with the noun compounds, the structure noun + noun (1,921) is more than twice as common as that of adjective + noun (938). A structure found frequently is lexeme plus particle (*churn out*). Compounds are most commonly endocentric and consist of two free forms; however, there are 577 items with three or more free forms, of which 524 are endocentric. Cannon sees exocentric structures consisting of two-word compounds as a new development, while as far as endocentric structures are concerned he regards items of three or more elements as innovative (see table 1.3; Cannon, 1987: 224, 239–240).

There are almost as many **derivations** (3,313 = 24 per cent of Cannon's corpus) as compounds. Of these, derivations with prefixes (**initial affixations**) are more frequent than those with suffixes (**terminal affixations**). The main types of bound forms used in derivations are combining forms, which are especially common in scientific terms of a formal nature. Prefixes, suffixes and inflections, on the other hand, occur in less technical items.

Table 1.3 Compounds

A *Endocentric compounds*

Two elements	cash dispenser, electronic banking/library/mail/shopping, glass ceiling ('invisible barrier that hinders women in their careers'), me generation; to blow-dry, index-link, zero-rate
Three	lead-free petrol, non-fossil fuels, sell-by date
Four	combined-cycle gas turbine (CCGT), sudden infant death syndrome, three-way catalytic converter
Five	smaller European elm bark beetle, coal-fired *or* fossil-fuel burning power station, Washington-based public-policy group
Six	experimental coal-fired combined-cycle plant

B *Exocentric compounds*

Nouns	an around the world (sc. trip), dog and pony show ('elaborate sales or publicity campaign'), freeze-frame; shoot-'em-up ('a film without much shooting')
Adjectives	before-tax (income), hatch-back (car), no-win (situation), towaway (zone; 'no-parking zone from which parked cars may be towed away'), on-the-job (training), off off Broadway (production; 'experimental, avant-garde'), larger-than-life (leader; 'very impressive')
Verbs	car-top ('carry on top of a car'), blind side ('attack critically'), nickel-and-dime ('to ruin financially little by little')

C *Lexeme plus particle*

Verbs	fall out ('burst out laughing'), leaf in (of trees, 'put forth leaves'), mouth off ('talk back'), pig out (on something, 'eat a lot of something')
Nouns	cookout, fry-up ('fried food platter'; BrE, colloquial), matchup ('comparison; political contest between two rivals'), shoot-out, sick-out ('organized absence from work'), square out ('a pass pattern in American football')

In **initial affixations,** there are six times more new items containing combining forms than prefixes. There is a strong word-class link between combining forms and nouns on the one hand, and prefixes and the remaining three open-word classes on the other. Never before have so many combining forms in initial position been used in English (Cannon counts 239). The most frequent of them are *micro-* (68), *bio-* (65), *immuno-* (31), *multi-* and *photo-* (26), and *neuro-* (25).

micro-: chip, code, floppy, mesh, surgery, wave
bio-: degradable, degrade, engineering, mass
immuno-: assay, chemistry, deficiency, suppression

The few remaining native prefixes show low productivity (*un-* (18) and *mis-* (9)). Most have been ousted by affixes of Latin and French origin, of which the most frequent are *anti-* (117), *non-* (71), *de-* (67), *pre-* (50), *super-* (40) and *sub-* (26).

anti-: convulsant, depressant, hero, nuclear
non-: art, Black, degree, event, hero, sexist, starter
de-: regulate ('remove government controls from'), selection,
    toxification

Derivations with initial combining forms are more frequent than those formed with prefixes (973 to 675). On the other hand, as the figures mentioned above show, individual prefixes are easily more productive than any single combining form.

In **terminal affixations** the ratio between combining forms (407) and suffixes (906) is reversed. All but one of the 407 new formations belong to the sciences. The frequency list of final combining forms for Cannon's corpus is as follows: *-ology/-ologist* (39), *-in* (20; as in *sit-in*, etc.), *-genic* (11), *-meter* (10), *-emia* (9). However, some other combining forms are similarly productive:

-gate ('major political scandal', from *Watergate*):
    Inkathagate, Irangate, Koreagate
-scape (after *landscape*), as in *moonscape, seascape,*
    street-scape, mindscape or *dream-scape* and *sound-scape*
-speak ('language of', used in a slightly derogatory way, as in Orwell's
    newspeak): *artspeak, computerspeak, winespeak*
-(a)thon: this combining form is derived from *marathon*, as in *talkathon,*
    telethon; the 1991 Edinburgh Festival organized a *poethon* ('long
    poetry reading').

There are more than twice as many different suffixes (98) as prefixes (42), but they are less productive (only 31 occur at least seven times, whereas 25 prefixes occur at least eight times). Most productive is native *-er* (130), followed by *-ist* (100), *-ism* (89), *-ize* (51), *-ic* (49), *-in(e)* (37) and native *-y* (35). It has to be borne in mind, however, that native suffixes such as *-y* or *-ish* are likely to be more productive than suggested by Cannon's list, although not all are recorded because they often appear in nonce formations in the spoken language (see below in 1.6.7). Examples are:

-er: *backpacker, butterflyer* ('a swimmer who specializes in the
        butterfly'), *car pooler, flasher*
-ist: *dartist, kineticist*
-ism: *ableism* ('discrimination against handicapped people'), *chimeraism,*
        ghettoism, middle-of-the-roadism, weightism ('discrimination based
        on a person's weight').

New formations with native suffixes are few though *-ness* seems to be an exception, cf. *generousness* beside *generosity*, *normalness* (*-ality/-alcy*) and *soberness* (*-briety*). Productive suffixes come chiefly from Latin and French. There are a few examples of multiple affixation, with prefixes plus suffixes (*antifoulant, demister, unflappable*) or with pre- and post-combining forms (*bioautography, sopropollenin*). In other cases affixation takes place together with compounding: fuck*ed* up, wheel*er*-deal*er*. These combined cases show again that the term **composite form**, which is used in this book, serves a useful purpose.

1.5 New meanings

While euphemisms and isolated examples such as *gay* ('cheerful' > 'homo-sexual') are deliberate creations, most shifts in meaning seem to be uninten-tional. Also, most changes take place in small steps, and one can often trace the semantic relationship between new and old meanings. Meanings are usually related by way of association, either because of their *similarity* or their nearness (*contiguity*). These associations can involve either the form of lexemes or their meaning; consequently, there are four different *processes* of meaning change (see table 1.4).

1.5.1 Folk etymology

When speakers cannot (or can no longer) analyse a form, they may replace it with one that is morphologically transparent; this process is called **folk etymology**. This happened to MidE *bridegome* (bride 'bride'; *gome* 'man'), where the second element ceased to be understood and was altered to *groom*. A more complex example is the verb *depart* ('separate'), which was used in the wedding ceremony . . . *till death us depart*. It became obso-lete and was reanalysed as *do* and *part*, and sometimes the word order was regularized (*till death do us part*). Though of considerable historical interest, folk etymology has never been a productive process. Mention should be made, however, of another process that is also triggered by formal similarity: where there are two formally similar lexemes, speakers often settle for one of them, usually the weightier, which then takes on the

Table 1.4 Processes of meaning change

	similarity	contiguity
form	folk etymology	ellipsis
meaning	metaphor	metonymy

meaning of the other. Examples are *technological* instead of *technical*, *sociological* instead of *social, nationalistic* for *national*, and *realistic* for *real* (cf. Barber 1985). Finally, a meaning change occurs when the meanings of two similar sounding words (often of Latin and Greek origin) are confused, as in 'The Council is not a *paradigm* of virtue' (where *paragon* is intended; see Amis 1980: 27, who offers more examples). These **malapropisms** start life as idiosyncratic usages; few of them, if any, will find their way into dictionaries.

1.5.2 Ellipsis

In **ellipsis**, part of a compound is deleted and the remaining part takes on the meaning of the whole:

Adidas < Adidas trainers/running shoes
anchor < anchorman or -woman
Danish < Danish pastry
life < a – sentence, as in *he got life*
microwave < – oven
the pill < the contraceptive pill

1.5.3 Metaphor

Metaphor usually involves deletion and/or addition of meaning elements or **semantic features**. *Mafia* in *the literary, mental-health* or *office mafia* is no longer restricted to the meaning element [organized crime] and is now applied to any group that exerts an apparently sinister influence. When *dove* is applied to a politician, the meaning element 'peaceful' stays, but the feature [animal] is replaced by [human]. *Bank* in *blood bank* or *bottle bank* has kept the element [collection point], but has obviously lost the financial meaning. Compare also *farm* in *beauty, health,* or *wind farm,* and *park* in *national, theme, science, technology* and *business park. Literate* can be extended to mean 'knowledgeable', as in *America's most economically literate green campaigner.* The language of computers is full of metaphors, for example, *breadboard* 'board for making a model of an electric circuit', *mouse* 'small device which controls the cursor', and *window* 'any of the separate data displays on a single video screen'. Indeed, metaphors are as indispensable as our daily bread (cf. Lakoff and Johnson 1980).

Metaphorical extension of verbs is seen in *launder*, which can now have as object not only articles of clothing but also *image* or *money*; in the latter case it means 'transfer to foreign banks, etc., so as to disguise its illegal source'. *Nurse* can take as its object *pride* or alcoholic drinks instead of human beings, and *park* is found with computer hard drive heads, chewing gum and even babies: 'She couldn't take the twins to work with her, so she parked them with the woman she was renting her room from' (K. Amis, *My Enemy's Enemy*, p. 105).

1.5.4 Metonymy

A common type of metonymy is that of a proper name which becomes used as the generic term for a commodity produced by a firm, for example, *Xerox* or *Kleenex*. Other types of metonymy can be seen in *the leadership* 'the leaders' (abstract for concrete); *answer the door/phone* 'respond to somebody who is using the door/phone to communicate' (instrument for agent); *save somebody's pocket* 'save someone money' (receptacle for content). Compare also *fare* (from money to person), *gossip* (from person to product, activity) and *shot* (as in *he is a good/poor shot*; from act [ivity] to person).

1.5.5 Meaning change

Besides the four associative processes just discussed, there are four types of meaning change which describe the semantic results: **specialization** (or *narrowing*, *restriction*), **generalization** (or *widening*, *extension*), **deterioration** (or *pejoration*, *catachresis*) and **amelioration** (a change for the better). These types will be exemplified below. Specialization and generalization are changes in the denotative meaning of words, while deterioration and amelioration concern their affective meaning. Cannon has found that generalizations are more numerous than specializations and that ameliorations outnumber pejorations (Cannon 1987: 45). Also, most changes in his corpus are from concrete to abstract meanings. In this process nouns (mostly composite forms) provide almost two-thirds of the new meanings; the remainder are accounted for chiefly by verbs and adjectives (p. 65).

Specialization and generalization The adjectives *straight* and *bent* have, in informal BrE, taken on specialized sexual meanings, with *straight* moving from 'conventional, respectable' to 'heterosexual', and *bent* from 'curved' > 'morally crooked' > 'homosexual'. Similarly, *glove box* has developed from 'a box for gloves' to 'a chamber with sealed-in gloves for handling radioactive material' (metaphor). Finally, *wet* 'feeble, weak' (informal BrE) refers to Conservative politicians who are suspected of Liberal tendencies (metaphor). One and the same lexeme can undergo both these processes, witness *girl*, which in Middle English referred to young people in general. While its present meaning is restricted to the female sex, it is no longer always confined in its reference to young women, though this sense is frowned upon by many, as in this quotation about middle-aged female farm hands in Canada: 'They were called the Girls not only by my mother and her friends but by themselves as well, so it mustn't have been as derogatory as it sounds today' (I. Huggans, *The Elizabeth Stories*, p. 83). Because of its present derogatory meaning Maggio suggests using (*young*) *woman* instead of *girl*, though the women themselves may go on using the term 'either out of long habit, local custom, or because they still think of themselves that way' (Maggio 1988: 53).

A recent change has taken place in AmE in the phrase *you guys*, which is no longer restricted to men and can refer to mixed company, or even women only. Other examples of generalization: *scenario* originally applied only to the plot of an opera, film, etc., but is now used to mean 'a likely sequence of events' ('the death of democracy becomes quite a likely scenario'; *Collins COBUILD English Language Dictionary*; metaphor). *Bullish* has changed from the stock exchange sense of 'causing or associated with a rise in prices' (COD) to 'optimistic' (*we're very bullish about the future*). *Sell-by date* also shows an extended meaning (metaphor), as in *Kennedy kept Hoover on past his sell-by date*.

Amelioration and deterioration   The phrase *the state of the art* was originally a typical (sub-)title of a report on what had been achieved in a particular field. From being neutral and merely descriptive, the adjective *state-of-the-art* has moved to denote the latest, and therefore the best of its kind (*state-of-the-art technology*). *Exposure* ('revelation of an embarrassing truth') is no longer always something to be feared, for example, 'he had, in a few short days of intense exposure, become a folk hero' (COBUILD; 'publicity'). *Cowboy*, on the other hand, has taken on a negative meaning in informal BrE: 'an unscrupulous or reckless person in business, esp. an unqualified one' (COD). *Mental* has developed an additional meaning: as well as 'of or in the mind' it can now mean 'insane' (*he's gone completely mental*).

Meaning and society   Changes in the affective meaning of words often reflect changes in the evaluation that societies, or certain groups in society, put on them. Thus to get publicity in the media, even if unfavourable, may well be regarded by some as valuable, which could explain the revaluation of *exposure*. People who are keen to sell their latest products have a vested interest in the equation 'most recent' = 'best' (*state-of-the-art*). The old as well as the insane, who do not work and earn or spend a lot of money, are increasingly marginalized in our consumer society, which might account for the pejorative meaning of *mental*. English is rich in examples of lexemes referring to members of minorities that have undergone pejoration or powerless groups (e.g. blacks; homosexuals, cf. *bent* above; women, cf. Schulz 1975; also 8.1). Homosexuals have tried to fight this by consciously using *gay*, and blacks have mounted a campaign with the slogan 'Black is beautiful'. The attempt to reverse the semantic status imposed by the powerful groups in society can also be seen in the new meanings of *bad* ('He's a bad man on drums, and the fans love him'; RHED), *tough* 'excellent' and *mean* (*she plays a mean game of chess*) 'skilful, formidable', which seem to have originated in the black community in the United States, possibly on African language models. For earlier examples of the link between language and society, see Leith 1983 and Hughes 1988, who mention, among other things, the moralization of status words: inferior position > moral disapproval, as in *churl, knave, villain* (perhaps this is also the reason behind the recent change in the meaning of *cowboy*); high social status > moral approval, (*free, gentle, noble*); the secularization of religious terminology (*clerk, office, sanction*) and the moralization of learning (*lewd*, which has changed from 'lay, unlearned' to 'lascivious, obscene').

Meaning and the language system   It must be stressed that semantic change does not occur in isolation. Rather, semantic changes are conditioned by changes in society. However, certain causes also lie in the language system itself, which may at least set the scene for some meaning changes. When **semantic fields** adopt new members, or when established members develop new meanings, this often has consequences for other members of the field. It has been shown how the OE and early MidE term for 'animal', *deer*, changed to its present meaning 'ruminant animal, hooved, antlered, and with spotted young' under the pressure of the loans *beast, creature* and *animal* (McLaughlin 1970: 303–13). On the other hand, when one lexeme develops a meaning that makes it a member of a new field, then other members of the original field can develop similar meanings: 'semantically related words show parallel semantic changes' (Lehrer 1984: 284). *Mad* and *crazy* mean not only 'insane' but also 'wildly excited', which is now one of the meanings of *daft* as well as *mental* (e.g. *she is mental about punk rock*) in BrE. Cookery verbs are another case in point: when said of people, *boil* has the metaphorical sense 'be greatly agitated, esp. by anger' (COD), while *broil* can express 'burn with impatience, annoyance, etc.' (RHED), at least in American English. Similarly, with human beings as objects, the following three verbs have developed meanings in the field of inflicting pain, discomfort or punishment: *grill* can mean 'interrogate', *fry* 'electrocute' and *roast* 'ridicule or criticize severely or mercilessly' (RHED; for more examples, see Lehrer 1984).

1.6 Words in use: the register approach

This final section discusses two models that provide analyses of the structure of the English vocabulary. The earlier is found in the preface to the OED, quoted in a revised version from the *Shorter Oxford English Dictionary* (SOED; 1977). The second approach, while it also takes lexical matters into account, goes beyond lexis to all possible aspects involved in language use; it is called the **register approach**.

1.6.1 The OED model

Two ideas lie behind the diagram in the SOED (see figure 1.1). One is the opposition between the centre and the periphery; the other is that of the relatedness of the various layers. The central core of the English lexicon is occupied by lexical items that are common to all native speakers and are not specifically marked for any of the other categories. **Literary** English refers to written and formal vocabulary, the language of science and literature. **Colloquial** English comprises spoken and informal items. **Archaic, foreign** and **scientific** language belong in the formal part of lexis ('are the specially learned outposts of the literary language', SOED, p. x), while **dialectal**, **vulgar** and **slang** vocabulary 'form a group of lower or less dignified status' (ibid.) Moving in a clockwise direction, one can see how the terms on the periphery are related to one another. Archaic items, often met with in poetry, also survive in dialect, and both are 'outcrops of older strata of the language' (ibid.); dialect items, vulgarisms and slang share their informal character; vulgarisms and slang items are both sub-colloquial and can cause offence through their coarse nature; slang (as in *public school slang*, *RAF slang*) and **technical** both refer to specialized languages. The same applies to scientific; furthermore, the language of science is rich in foreign loans (see 1.2.4 above). The only exception is the pair foreign and archaic, where there is no link, *pace* the SOED, which is why we have put between the two a dividing line that is not found in the original diagram.

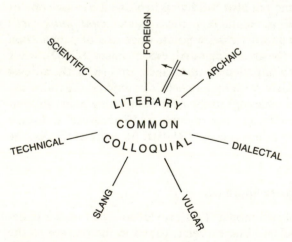

Figure 1.1 The English vocabulary
Source: The Shorter Oxford English Dictionary

While the diagram offers valuable insights into the structure of English vocabulary and the interrelationships of its parts, it also sometimes suggests classifications and similarities that are wrong or at least doubtful. First, it is not immediately obvious how scientific, foreign and archaic all derive from literary. *Literary* is perhaps not the best of labels because it seems to refer to formal as well as written language. Similarly, technical and scientific vocabulary items, for example, are clearly used both in speech and in writing and are not restricted to one medium. It seems that *literary* and *colloquial* refer to two aspects that are better kept apart; the one is medium (spoken or written language), the other is formality (formal or informal). Second, the status of *slang* is far from obvious: here the SOED lexicographers have conflated two rather different meanings of the term, one which refers to the language of particular social or professional groups, now usually called **jargon**, and the other the racy, informal type of language, often called **general slang**, which does not seem to be so restricted. It is only because slang refers to these two rather different layers that the SOED can suggest an affinity between technical and slang (in the sense of 'insider talk') on the one hand, and slang and vulgar (in the racy, forceful sense) on the other. It is tempting, therefore, to draw another dividing line for the two senses of *slang*. Finally, no provision is made for socially determined lexis, based on sociolinguistic categories such as gender, age, etc.

1.6.2 The register model

The **register** approach includes the terms of the SOED model, adds some new ones, and puts the whole on a more systematic footing. Its aim is to explain language variation in terms of the people who use the language and of the situations in which people find themselves. The more permanent characteristics, those of the language users, are called **dialects**, while the various situational factors that influence language use are collectively referred to as **diatypes** or **registers** (for general treatments, see Halliday *et al.* 1964; Crystal and Davy 1969; Gregory and Carroll 1978; O'Donnell and Todd 1990; Shopen and Williams 1980, 1981; Ure 1984; Coupland 1988; Quirk and Stein 1990; Benson and Greaves 1984 offer exercise materials).

1.6.3 Dialects

These come in various guises, **temporal**, **regional**, **social**, **standard** and **individual**. This book is not much concerned with Old or Middle English. But this is not to say that some knowledge of the **temporal dialects**, or earlier stages of English, is not relevant to a full and correct understanding of the present-day language. Reading Shakespeare or trying to understand items such as *let* (in tennis), *kith and kin* and *ye olde tea shoppe* involves historical information of one kind or another which can be found in histories of the language (see 1.2 for references) and etymological dictionaries. Again, not much needs to be said about **regional varieties** at this point, as the whole of part three of this book is devoted to questions of geographical variation.

Social dialects will also be treated extensively in part three, so that only a few lexical points need be mentioned in this chapter. While the link between pronunciation and the social class of speakers has frequently been studied, lexical differences have not been so often, or so rigorously, researched. Much has been made of the distinction in British English between **U** and **non-U**, i.e. between what the upper class use and what they do not use (see Ross 1954; Mitford 1959; Buckle 1978; Cooper 1980). Almost everything and anything can indicate class: what names you give your children, where you live, your family and friends, hobbies and occupation, wealth, education, etc. Meal names are well-known class indicators: 'Any Englishman who does call lunch dinner indicates at once and for sure to any other Englishman that he hails from somewhere below the middle of the middle class' (Smith 1985: 153). Other, perhaps more contentious generalizations, which nevertheless contain a certain amount of truth, are that *afternoon tea* is U, starts at four and typically consists of tea, thin sandwiches and cakes. Non-U *tea* (South) or *high tea* (North) are middle- and working-class events starting at about 5 to 6 p.m. They are much more serious meals and usually include one cooked course in the North. Other well-known non-U items are *lounge* (U: *drawing room*), *pardon?* (U: *what?*), *settee* (U: *sofa*) and *toilet* (U: *lavatory* or *loo*; cf. the short list in Buckle 1978: xviii—xix). Mention should also be made of the suffix *-er(s)*, which is typical of public schools (in the BrE sense) and is used to produce informal variants of nouns and adjectives. These class-marked derivations are unlikely to be used by non-U speakers. Examples are *champers* ('champagne'), *preggers* ('pregnant'), *rugger* ('rugby football'), *soccer* and *starkers* ('stark naked'; ellipsis, cf. 1.5.2; cf. Honey 1991: 49).

In his entertaining book on class differences in the United States, Fussell (1984) agrees with Cooper (1980) that the upper and lower classes generally use much blunter language than the middle class, who are insecure about their social status and therefore strive after elegance, becoming pompous and affected in their language. Thus, upper *boyfriend* and *driver* become middle *fiancé* and *chauffeur*, while *cross* can be replaced by the grand sounding *transit*, as in 'several ships transited the area'(Fussell: 155). Formulas such as *goodbye* and *how do you do?* are upper and upper middle class; all others use *have a nice day* and *pleased to meet you*. These details need to be treated with some caution because they may be somewhat subjective and fashions can change quite rapidly. Also, the link between language and class is not always direct, as some non-upper-class people affect certain U-usages while some (younger) upper-class people in Britain may imitate non-U accents. All in all, however, there is no doubt that class connotations often attach to the choice of at least some lexical items just as they do to pronunciation.

The term **standard dialect,** or **standard** for short, indicates that it is only the first among equals and that it is that dialect of a language which is universally acceptable in almost all public situations and for all non-local purposes. It is taught in schools, used in educational books and in the national mass media as well as in all types of official business: it is 'that kind of English which draws least attention to itself over the widest area and through the widest range of usage' (Quirk and Stein 1990: 123). Standard English is essentially a written, or even printed, form of English, and can be spoken with various accents (see ibid.: chapter 9, and the Introduction above for more on StE).

The standard dialect has been included in this section out of deference to most linguists who work with the register approach. But the features just discussed (written medium, formal situation, particular purpose) would seem to make the standard dialect as much a feature of language use, if not more so, as of the language users.

Idiolect or a person's **individual dialect,** finally, must be mentioned. This refers not so much to a different sort of dialect as to a selection from all of the above dialects, which together make up a large part of a person's linguistic individuality. Although idiolect can contain a few items that only this person or his or her family use, it usually consists of the established vocabulary common to most speakers of his or her speech community. It is no easy task to describe someone's idiolect, as it tends to change over time and according to the circumstances s/he finds herself/himself in: 'In a sense we possess several styles over the course of a lifetime, each one a typical reflection of our individuality' (Gregory and Carroll 1978: 25). Idiolect will, for example, reflect a person's sex in the choice of lexis (see 8.2.1 below) and it may well show dialect mixes of one kind or another. British and American mixtures are particularly common: the term *mid-Atlantic accent* has been coined to refer to the accent in which many pop singers sing or disc jockeys speak. In vocabulary matters, American writers may well use British items such as *tarted up* or *roof rack,* or use native *faucet* beside British *tap.* Idiolect is therefore nothing that is fixed once and for all, but something dynamic which can change depending on time, place, occasion, etc.

1.6.4 Registers

Variation in language clearly depends then on when and where one lives and on one's gender and social class, but it is also a function of 'what you are speaking about; who your addressees are; how well you know them; whether you are addressing them orally or in writing' (Quirk and Stein

1990: 41). This second set of factors relates not so much to the individual user as to language use in certain situations. Use varieties are called **diatypes** or **registers**.

1.6.5 Field

This is the first category of register, also called **province**. It reflects the fact that one needs different words to talk about different subjects. There are many terms that are typical of one particular subject, for example, *etymology*, *lexeme* and *loan word* are found only in linguistics. Others take on special meanings, for example *boot* (verb), *hardware*, *mouse*, *store* (verb) and *window* in computing. There are also combinations of lexical items that are typical of certain fields, for example, *desirable residence*, *tastefully modernized* or *compact patio-style garden*, which are found in the advertisements of property agents in England (McCarthy 1990: 64).

We are all perfectly capable of carrying on a general conversation about people, the weather, our holidays and the latest sports results. These everyday uses of language, though essential to life in society, are easy because they do not make great demands on our minds or linguistic abilities. But when we move from the general field of small talk and everyday conversation to that of computers, gene technology or heart surgery, the number of people who understand the language, or could themselves use it, is rather more limited. In the next example vocabulary items, as well as the larger context of the novel, make it clear that the field is heart surgery, but not many readers will understand all the technical terms without the help of a dictionary:

> . . . preliminary test . . . pulmonary congestion common after a myocardial infarction . . . backup of blood, leakage into the lung tissue . . . hydralazine . . . inflammation of the pericardium . . . Dilantin . . . skin rashes, diarrhea, loss of hair . . . hate to go to a pacemaker for a man his age . . .
>
> (J. Updike, *Rabbit at Rest*, p. 139).

General language is most obviously distinguished from technical language by its lexis, though other factors are also important (see chapter 7 for more detail). Clearly, education and/or experience of a great number of different specialist fields is crucial for an understanding of technical registers. The use of technical terms by a surgeon in a hospital, as in the example above, may be regarded as justified (the expert using the precise terms of his profession), or interpreted as an attempt to impress the patient's wife and, perhaps, therefore to suppress any opposition on her part to the treatment decided on by the surgeon. This must remain speculation, however, because the novel does not comment on his motivation.

The acceptability of technical language is given when experts talk among themselves. It also seems to be higher in the written than in the spoken language. Certainly, speakers in face-to-face situations usually express what they have to say in a more casual, non-technical way. Physical nearness, it seems, often translates into social and emotional nearness. This is apparently not well served by the many **hard words**, derived from Latin and Greek, which characterize technical registers, particularly those of science and medicine. For this reason everyday conversations consist of short everyday words, mostly native English items that engage the emotions and express feelings, or items that have been naturalized and are no longer felt to be foreign and distant. But, as the example shows, speakers are free to choose the level on the formality and distance scale at which they want to pitch their message, even in spoken language. So, while there is a link between spoken language and relaxed, informal speech, it is not one of cause and effect.

1.6.6 Personal tenor

Personal tenor, also simply **tenor** or **status** or **style**, refers to the formality of any given piece of language, for which dictionaries have such labels as *formal, familiar, informal, colloquial, slang.* Most lexical items are not labelled because they are stylistically neutral. There is often little agreement on whether an item is slang, or on how many stylistic levels ought to be set up. One quite well-known model is the five-term one proposed by Joos (1962), which Strevens (1964: 29) illustrates as shown in Table 1.5. Notice that a change in tenor involves much more than a simple change in the stylistic level of the lexemes (*visitors* vs. *chaps*). There is, for example, a change in the length and explicitness of the message: from *make their way* to *go*, and from *to the upper floor* to *up*.

Formality choices often go hand in hand with medium differences, but they are ultimately determined by the relationship between the people concerned. The closer the sender (speaker or writer) feels to his or her addressee(s), the more informal the language which the sender can use.

Table 1.5 Five-term model of personal tenor

Style	Example
Frozen	Visitors should make their way at once to the upper floor by way of the staircase
Formal	Visitors should go up the stairs at once
Consultative	Would you mind going upstairs, right away, please.
Casual	Time you all went upstairs, now.
Intimate	Up you go, chaps!

Conversely, the more distant the personal relationship, the more formal the personal tenor is likely to be. The frozen and formal versions above are likely to be announcements over a ship's PA system, where the speaker does not see his or her addressees, while the other three versions can only be uttered when speaker and hearer see each other. Personal tenor is thus often determined by physical closeness or distance. Again, it has to be stressed that speakers are free to stick to the generally accepted conventions or to flout them, for whatever reasons or purposes. Foreign learners should in any case be careful of using very informal or potentially offensive lexemes with people they do not know well.

1.6.7 Medium or mode

The five stylistic variants quoted above illustrate once again that there is no causal link between formality and **medium**, or **mode**, as all the examples belong to the spoken language. Although medial differences go far beyond lexical choices, the focus of the present discussion is on the lexis and syntax typical of the two media (for a recent study of speech and writing see Halliday 1989). First, however, a few more general notes are in order (see also chapters 5 and 6).

Speech is primary. This view is supported by the fact that speech, but not writing, is found in all societies. Speech is acquired in early childhood more or less informally, while writing is learned much later and by far fewer people, usually in a formal educational establishment. This is one reason (besides the obvious instrumental advantages of literacy) why writing confers greater prestige in society. Speech is typically used to create, maintain and enhance social bonds (which Brown and Yule call 'interactional' uses; see Brown and Yule 1983: 11), while writing is mostly concerned with the transfer of information ('transactional' uses; ibid.). Speech meets basic human needs, while writing satisfies less immediate ones. The following list of uses (from Leech *et al*. 1982: 140) starts with those typical of the spoken language and ends with those that are exclusive to writing: conversation in a pub, seminar, telephone conversation, personal letter, job interview, radio discussion, television advertisement, lecture, sermon, script of a play, television news, newspaper, business letter, this book. Writing is uni-modal while speech is multi-modal: the transmission of the writer's message usually relies exclusively on linguistic means, while speech can also employ paralinguistic means, both vocal and non-vocal.

> **Speech (conversation)**: intonation, pitch, stress, rhythm, speed of utterance, pausing, silences, variation in loudness; aspiration, laughter, voice quality; timing, including simultaneous speech; co-occurrence with proxemic and kinesic signals; availability of physical context.

Writing (printed material): spacing between words; punctuation, including parentheses; typography, including style of typeface, italicization, underlining, upper and lower case; capitalization to indicate sentence beginnings and proper nouns; inverted commas; graphics, including lines, shapes, borders, diagrams, tables; abbreviations; logograms and symbols; layout, including paragraphing, spacing, margination, pagination, footnotes, headings and sub-headings; permanence and therefore availability of the co-text.

(Stubbs 1980: 117)

This list should not be taken to imply that the written language has in no case a way of representing what spoken language achieves through intonation. A spoken sentence such as *Chris didn't say it*, with nuclear stress on the first word, can be rendered in the written medium in a slightly more elaborate way as *it was not in fact Chris who said it*. On the other hand, writing has features for which there is no clear counterpart in the spoken language, for example, paragraphs, italics, quotation marks (Quirk *et al.* 1985: 25).

There are also more narrowly linguistic differences. In pronunciation, spontaneous speech is notable for reductions, elisions, and assimilation processes of many different kinds, so that the foreign learner 'finds that many of the pronunciation rules he has learned for words in isolation have to be un-learned when the words are put together into sequences' (Crystal and Davy 1975: 108).

As regards syntax, the sentence is the syntactic base for the description of the English language in most standard grammars. In spoken English, however, there are many stretches of language where the concept of sentence makes no sense. Various alternative terms are in use for the units of spoken language, among them **information unit**, **utterance chunk** or **idea unit**. Spoken language units usually belong to one of a small set of syntactic structures which are typically characterized by a coherent intonation contour and are bounded by pauses. Each idea unit has a mean length of approximately two seconds, which is about six words (Chafe 1980).

While it is quite common in speech to find ellipsis of subject and predicate as well as referring words (deictics) such as *him* or *that one over there*, writing has to be more explicit because writers are isolated from readers and cannot rely on the situation or on paralinguistic means to help make their message clear. As there is more time for planning than in speaking, ideas can be ordered in such a way that they form a linguistic whole. Processing a written text takes place at the leisure of the reader, who can skip pages, go back and forth, or go over the same passage again as desired or needed. This is one of the factors that make literature and its appreciation possible. Spontaneous speech, however, leaves no time for thought or revision, and therefore it is characterized by syntactic blends or false starts, repetitions, digressions, loose ends, inconsistencies and changes of construction that are not permitted in formal written texts. The great speed of production can also explain why speakers use afterthoughts (e.g. clause-final, retrospective *though*), or, conversely, why anticipatory structures (such as *on the one hand*) are more typical of writing. Sentence connectors such as *because, since, therefore*, which indicate causal or temporal relationships, are more typical of writing than of speech. In unplanned discourse speakers rely more on structures learned early in life, while planned discourse uses those acquired at a later stage. Because of lack of time for planning and revision and for greater ease of understanding on the part of hearers, speakers will in general package their information less densely (i.e. use fewer lexical items than grammatical items), and will also choose less highly structured forms. Pieces of information are given one at a time, and the syntax is much simpler. Paratactic constructions are common with clause conjunctions such as *so, and, then, but*; noun phrases tend to be simple, but are often modified, in an afterthought, by a following phrase. Writing, on the other hand, shows a greater verbal density and a greater density of ideas, and is characterized by more complex syntactic structures, such as 'heavily premodified noun phrases with accompanying post-modification, heavy adverbial modification and complex subordinating syntax' (Brown and Yule 1983: 7). It has been said that the written mode is characterized by less predictable syntax, while in the spoken medium the predictability of syntactic structures is higher.

Among the features particular to writing we find the passive rather than the active, and relatively many declaratives but few imperatives, interrogatives and exclamations. In the written language there is a higher frequency of gerunds, participles in non-finite clauses, attributive adjectives, subjective and objective genitives, conjoined phrases, complement clauses, and modal and perfective auxiliaries. In contrast, noun clauses, infinitives and progressive auxiliaries are more common in speech than in comparable written samples (cf. chapter 4 for these terms). Speech shows the effects of interpersonal relations: there are more tag questions and items of personal reference, for example, first and second person pronouns and expressions such as *I think*, *in my opinion*, or *as far as I am concerned* (see also chapter 7).

Less research has been carried out on the lexical differences between the two modes. Spontaneous conversation is full of discourse markers such as *well* (*now*), *oh, uhuh, I mean, you know*, which serve a wide variety of purposes (see 6.5).

Written language is primarily message-oriented, often involving specific lexis. Spoken language is primarily listener-oriented and shows a lack of specificity. Thus writing is characterized by technical terms, hard words and polysyllabic lexical items, while speech prefers short or monosyllabic words, which tend to be general and are often vague and imprecise (see 1.2.8 above on Germanic vs. Latinate words). Indeed, spontaneous conversation is held to be characterized by three lexical features – imprecision, intensification and neologisms (Crystal and Davy 1975: 111–16). Imprecision, often as a result of emotional factors, loss of memory and lack of concentration, or the informality of the situation or the subject under discussion, is visible in items such as *things, thingy, whatsit(s)*, etc., where a more exact word is not available to the speaker. Other imprecise items include vague, summary phrases at the ends of lists such as *and things, that sort of thing, and so on and so forth*. Furthermore, mention must be made of vague generic terms and collective nouns such as *heaps of, bags of, oodles of* used in positive contexts, while *for anything, for the world* or *for worlds* are found in negative contexts (*I wouldn't go there for the world*). Finally, there are many ways of expressing the concept of approximation in English, particularly with numbers and quantities: *sixty-odd people, about* or *around sixty people, there were getting on for sixty people, sixty people as near as makes no difference*, etc. Especially frequent and useful, though little known to foreign speakers, is the suffix *-ish*: *tallish, shortish, fortyish, whitish*, etc.

The second category of lexical items typical of spoken English, but equally of an informal conversational atmosphere, are words and phrases that express a high or exaggerated degree. Examples are adverbs and adjectives such as *absolutely, definitely, horribly, perfectly, furious, horrible, terrible*, etc., and vogue words such as *ace, brill(iant), cool, great, super, smashing*, etc. The turnover among these words is rapid: they soon become overused and lose their force, so that speakers have to find new ones. Exaggeration in language is called **hyperbole** and has rather similar effects to euphemisms (see 1.4.1).

Most new meanings and new formations, the third category, are created on the spur of the moment and are unlikely to be recorded in dictionaries. Frequently used word-formation elements are *non-, mega-* and *semi-*, as well as the suffixes *-y, -like* and *-wise*, (*weatherwise, we can't complain*). Note that few of the above listed categories and items are the exclusive function of the spoken medium, but rather of medium and informality together.

Research into the spoken language has often suffered from unacceptable methodology. Many linguists who have taken informal spoken texts and compared them with formal written texts have mixed up the parameters of medium and formality. Other factors that have not always been given due weight are (1) the context and purpose of the speech event; (2) the nature of the communicative task appropriate to the speech event; (3) topic and associated register peculiarities; and (4) participants' background and level of linguistic knowledge. (Akinnaso 1982: 103). More recent studies therefore start from a specific task, such as describing, explaining, arguing, protesting, etc., and then analyse the linguistic means used in both media (see Akinnaso 1985). A comparison of spontaneous conversation with scripted dialogue has revealed differences in addressee interest, number and type of topics, and hearer–addressee agreement: 'whereas many scripted conversations are interesting, most naturally occurring conversations are extremely boring unless you happen to be an active engaged participant in one. Conversations. . .usually concern local, transitory, matters and deal with purely personal concerns' (Brown and Yule 1983: 33). The interactional language of small talk is, moreover, characterized by 'constantly shifting topics and a great deal of agreement on them' (ibid.: 11; see 6.3.1. for more detail on interactional language).

A recent study which casts new light on medial differences looks at a wide variety of genres from both speech and writing (e.g. face-to-face conversation, personal letters, spontaneous speeches, broadcasts, general fiction, professional letters, official documents), and characterizes them with respect to six dimensions, which consist of clusters of linguistic features:

1 interactive, involved discourse versus edited, informational discourse;
2 reported, narrative discourse versus non-narrative types of discourse;
3 explicit versus situation-dependent reference;
4 overt expression of persuasion;
5 formal, abstract information versus non-abstract types of information;
6 influence of real time on information production (Biber 1988: chapter 6).

No absolute differences between the two media were found ('there is no single dimension of orality versus literacy', ibid.: 162), which means that 'speakers and writers sometimes thwart the situational factors operating in each mode and produce discourse that is atypical for that mode' (ibid.: 161). On the other hand, oral and written genres are relatively well distinguished for dimensions 1, 3, and 5. The difference is one of the range of forms that can be produced in each mode, 'with the most informational and formal written genres using a greater frequency of literate features than any of the spoken genres' (ibid.: 163). Dimensions 2, 4, and 6 are not specific to conversation, nor do they distinguish it from, say, personal letters. In fact, these dimensions have little to do with whether a text is spoken or written.

1.6.8 Functional tenor

While it is intuitively obvious that we use different means to instruct, threaten or persuade others, it is less obvious how many functions language can have and how to classify them. One approach distinguishes six functions, which are derived from six essential features of human communication. The **emotive** (or **expressive**) function is related to the sender, who wants to express emotions. The **conative** (or **directive**) function is addressee-related: it refers to attempts to influence others in order to achieve some goal, typically realized by orders and requests. The **meta-communicative**, or **metalingual**, function is related to the code used. It is involved in a question such as 'What is the meaning of *let* in tennis?'. There is a particularly close link between the message and the **poetic** or **aesthetic** function. This function can be defined as the use of language for language's sake, i.e. for a special aesthetic effect. The **informational** or **referential** function derives from the context or subject matter of communication and is concerned with information transfer. The final use of language is the **phatic** function, in which language is used to keep the channel of communication open and to keep social relationships in good repair (cf. the interactional uses mentioned above in the section on medium). Small talk is one well-known form which the phatic function can take. Phatic language is diametrically opposed to aesthetic language: with phatic communion what is important is not the news value of what one says or the originality or creativity of the language used, but that something is said at all, that silence is avoided so that speaker and addressee may both feel that their company is enjoyed (Jakobson 1960; cf. Leech 1981: 40–2; Quirk and Stein 1990: 4–5; see also chapter 7, where a different set of rhetorical functions is used: description, report, exposition, instruction and argumentation).

Transitions between these functions can be fluid. The same stretch of language can serve different functions, for example, *I'm dying for a cup of coffee*, which can in the right circumstances be read as a piece of information, as an expression of the speaker's emotion, or as a veiled order to the addressee to get the speaker something to drink (cf. 6.2.1 on speech acts).

Advertising   The aesthetic function, though typically realized in poetry and fiction, is not restricted to poetry. Creative use of language is also often found in the language of English **advertising**, which serves a directive-persuasive purpose. In the famous slogan *Beanz Meanz Heinz*, spelling (*beans* and *means* are the normal forms) and assonance (the /iː/ sounds and the sibilant /z/) all contribute to establish a close association between the product and the producer's name (Heinz). Even more characteristic are puns: *Give your girlfriend a cheap ring*, a British Telecom advertisement, where *ring* equals both 'phone call' and 'piece of jewellery'; or *Flaming Tasty*, an advertisement on London cabs for a brand of hamburger, where *flaming* refers to the grill one can see on the poster and also has an intensifying force; *Heathrow Takes Off More*, where *take off* refers to what aeroplanes normally do ('get airborne'), but also to the price of duty-free goods ('reduce in price'). Other, less original features of advertising include the use of a few very common verbs (*buy*, *give*, *make*, *need*, *set*, *try*), typically in the imperative: this form is used less, however, in advertisements which sell their product more indirectly (the so-called *soft-sell approach*). Also typical of the lexis of advertising is the occurrence of highly evaluative adjectives such as *clean*, *fresh*, *soft* and, recently, *natural* and *organic*, which are often repeated to drive home the message. Short, one-syllable lexemes and short sentences are preferred. Verbs are usually in the present tense. Readers/viewers/listeners are often engaged in a pseudo-conversation, the tenor of which is intimate and informal (for more on advertising language, see Leech 1966; O'Donnell and Todd 1991: chapter 6; Vestergaard and Schroder 1985).

1.6.9 Recent research

Vocabulary choice, and language use in general, can clearly be described by the four dimensions of field, medium, personal tenor and functional tenor. Registers have been divided into those where linguistic choice is limited (**marked registers**), for example, greetings, forms of address and instructions, and those where there are more options available (**unmarked registers**), for example, the language of journalism. Much research has been concerned with looking at a very general register, such as the language of journalism or advertising, and setting up sub-types within it. One approach differentiates in advertising between radio, TV and newspaper adverts, and discusses, in addition to the genre of traditional commercial consumer advertising briefly described above, a new type which addresses more material needs in contrast to the social and symbolic needs met by luxury products. This type of advertisement is meant to sell goods and services presented as necessary, whether they are or not, for example, cars, suits, transatlantic flights, and the latest colour TV. These 'no-frills' advertisements are simple and factual; they mention the product's price and contain little hyperbolic language. Thus the difference in the perception of the product comes through in a no-nonsense style (Toolan 1988; for other refinements of registers, cf. Ghadessy 1988; Carter and Nash 1990).

Another aspect in register research is the question of whether the four categories are always equally important. It has been said that the language of science is dominated by considerations of field, the language of diplomatic protocol by personal tenor, and the language of advertising by functional tenor. More generally, it has been claimed that it is genre or the type of text which determines choices in field, mode and personal tenor. This has resulted in a rejection of functional tenor as a category on a par with the other three (see Gregory 1988; cf. also 7.3). A great deal of research is being conducted at present and it is too early to say anything final about either the number of categories or possible hierarchies.

Finally, one should also ask whether the register model captures enough of the situational factors to be able to give an adequate description of language in use. Among the more permanent (dialect) characteristics, gender is rarely mentioned, though there is an enormous body of research into this subject (see chapter 8). Similarly, people's ethnic affiliations might be of interest. Other neglected (diatypical) factors are the setting of a situation, i.e. the physical and temporal context (cf. Hymes 1972; see also Biber 1988: 28–33 for a detailed list of situation components). If the register model is seen not so much as a closed system but rather as an open approach which needs refining and extending, it will prove to be a very useful tool.

REFERENCES

Akinnaso, F. N. (1982) 'On the differences between spoken and written language', *Language and Speech* 25: 97–125.

—— (1985) 'On the similarities between spoken and written language', *Language and Speech* 28: 323–59.

Algeo, J. (1978) 'The taxonomy of word making', *Word* 29: 122–31.

—— (ed.) (1991) *Fifty Years among the New Words. A Dictionary of Neologisms 1941–1991*, Cambridge: Cambridge University Press.

Allan, K. (1986) *Linguistic Meaning*, 2 vols, London: Routledge & Kegan Paul.

Allerton, D. with French, M. (1988) 'Morphology: the forms of English', in W. F. Bolton and D. Crystal (eds) *The English Language*, London: Sphere, pp. 71–132.

Amis, K. (1965) *My Enemy's Enemy*, Harmondsworth: Penguin.

—— (1980) 'Getting it wrong', in L. Michaels and C. Ricks (eds) *The State of the Language*, Berkeley: University of California Press, pp. 24–33.

Ayto, J. (1989, 1990) *The Longman Register of New Words*, Harlow: Longman.

Barber, C. (1985) 'Linguistic change in present-day English', in S. Bäckman and G. Kjellmer (eds) *Papers on Language and Literature Presented to Alvar Ellegard and Erik Frykman*, Gothenburg: Gothenburg University Press, pp. 36–45.

Barnhart, C. L., Steinmetz, S. and Barnhart, R. K. (1973) *Dictionary of New English: 1963–1972*, Bronxville, NY: Barnhart.

—— (1980) *The Second Barnhart Dictionary of New English*, Bronxville, NY: Wilson.

Barnhart, R. K., Steinmetz, S. with Barnhart, C. L. (1990) *Third Dictionary of New English*, Bronxville, NY: Barnhart.

Bauer, L. (1983) *English Word-Formation*, Cambridge: Cambridge University Press.

Baugh, A. C. and Cable, T. (1978) *A History of the English Language*, 3rd edn, London: Routledge & Kegan Paul.

Benson, J. and Greaves, W. (1984) *You and Your Language*, Oxford: Pergamon.

Berndt, R. (1982) *A History of the English Language*, Leipzig: Enzyklopädie.

Biber, D. (1988) *Variation Across Speech and Writing*, Cambridge: Cambridge University Press.

Bolton, W. F. (1982) *A Living Language: the History and Structure of English*, New York: Random House.

Brown, G. and Yule, G. (1983) *Teaching the Spoken Language*, Cambridge: Cambridge University Press.

Bryant, M. (1974) 'Blends are increasing', *American Speech* 49: 163–84.

Buckle, R. (ed.) (1978) *U and Non-U Revisited*, New York: Viking.

Cameron, K. (1969) *English Place Names*, London: Methuen.

Cannon, G. (1987) *Historical Change and English Word-Formation*, New York: Lang.

Carter, R. and Nash, W. (1990) *Seeing Through Language*, Oxford: Blackwell.

Caudwell, S. (1990) *The Sirens Sang of Murder*, Glasgow: Collins.

Chafe, W. L. (1980) 'The deployment of consciousness in the production of a narrative', in W. L. Chafe (ed.) *The Pear Stories: Cognitive, Cultural, and Linguistic Aspects of Narrative Production*, Norwood, NJ: Ablex, pp. 9–50.

Chierchia, G. and McConnell-Ginet, S. (1990) *Meaning and Grammar*, Cambridge, Mass.: Massachusetts Institute of Technology.

Collins COBUILD English Language Dictionary (1987) editor-in-chief J. Sinclair, London: Collins.

Collins English Dictionary (1986) 2nd edn, ed. P. Hanks, London: Collins.

The Concise Oxford Dictionary of Current English (1990) 8th edn, ed. R. E. Allen, Oxford: Oxford University Press.

Cooper, J. (1980) *Class*, London: Corgi.

Coupland, N. (ed.) (1988) *Styles of Discourse*, London: Routledge.

Crystal, D. and Davy, D. (1969) *Investigating English Style*, London: Longman.

—— (1975) *Advanced Conversational English*, London: Longman.

Francis, W. N. and Kučera, H. (1982) *Frequency Analysis of English Usage: Lexicon and Grammar*, Boston: Houghton Mifflin.

Fussell, P. (1984) *Class*, London: Arrow.

Ghadessy, M. (ed.) (1988) *Registers of Written English*, London: Pinter.

Gordon, W. T. (1987) *Semantics: a Bibliography, 1979–1985*, Metuchen, NJ: Scarecrow Press.

Gregory, M. (1988) 'Generic situation and register: a functional view of communication', in J. D. Benson, M. J. Cummings and W. S. Greaves (eds) *Linguistics in a Systemic Perspective*, Amsterdam: Benjamins, pp. 301–30.

Gregory, M. and Carroll, S. (1978) *Language and Situation*, London: Routledge & Kegan Paul.

Halliday, M. A. K. (1989) *Spoken and Written Language*, 2nd edn, Oxford: Oxford University Press.

Halliday, M. A. K., McIntosh, A. and Strevens, P. D. (1964) *The Linguistic Sciences and Language Teaching*, London: Longman.

Hansen, B., Hansen, K., Neubert, A. and Schentke, M. (1985) *Englische Lexikologie*, Leipzig: Enzyklopädie.

Hofland, K. and Johansson, S. (1982) *Word Frequencies in British and American English*, Bergen: Norwegian Computing Centre for the Humanities.

Honey, J. (1991) *Does Accent Matter?* London: Faber & Faber.

Huggans, I. (1987) *The Elizabeth Stories*, New York: Viking.

Hughes, G. (1988) *Words in Time: a Social History of the English Vocabulary*, Oxford: Blackwell.

Hymes, D. (1972) 'Models of the interaction of language and social life', in J. Gumperz and D. Hymes (eds) *Directions in Sociolinguistics*, New York: Holt, Rinehart & Winston, pp. 35–71.

Jackson, H. (1988) *Words and their Meaning*, London: Longman.

Jakobson, R. (1960) 'Linguistics and poetics', in T. A. Sebeok (ed.) *Style in Language*, Cambridge, Mass.; Massachusetts Institute of Technology, pp. 350–77.

Jespersen, O. (1982) *Growth and Structure of the English Language*, 10th edn, Oxford: Blackwell.

Joos, M. (1962) 'The five clocks' *International Journal of American Linguistics* 28: 9–62.

Lakoff, G. and Johnson. M. (1980) *Metaphors We Live By*, Chicago: University of Chicago Press.

Leech, G. (1966) *English in Advertising*, London: Longman.

—— (1981) *Semantics*, Harmondsworth: Penguin.

Leech, G., Deuchar, M. and Hoogenraad, R. (1982) *English Grammar for Today*, London: Macmillan.
Lehrer, A. (1984) 'The influence of semantic fields on semantic change', in J. Fisiak (ed.) *Historical Semantics – Historical Word-formation*, Berlin: Mouton, pp. 283–96.
Leith, D. (1983) *A Social History of English*, London: Routledge & Kegan Paul.
Lemay, H. (1989) *The Facts on File Dictionary of New Words*, New York: Facts on File.
Leonard, E. (1985) *LaBrava*, Harmondsworth: Penguin.
LePore, E. (1987) *New Directions in Semantics*, London: Academic Press.
Longman Dictionary of Contemporary English (1987) 2nd edn, ed. D. Summers, Harlow: Longman.
Lurie, A. (1989) *The Truth About Lorin Jones*, London: Sphere.
Lyons, J. (1977) *Semantics*, 2 vols, Cambridge: Cambridge University Press.
McCarthy, M. (1990) *Vocabulary*, Oxford: Oxford University Press.
McLaughlin, J. C. (1970) *Aspects of the History of English*, New York: Holt, Rinehart & Winston.
Maggio, R. (1988) *The Nonsexist Word Finder: a Dictionary of Gender-Free Usage*, Boston: Beacon.
Marchand, H. (1969) *The Categories and Types of Present-Day English Word Formation*, 2nd edn, Munich: Beck.
Mish, F. C. (ed.) (1983) *9,000 Words: a Supplement to Webster's Third New International Dictionary*, Springfield, Mass.: Merriam-Webster.
Mitford, N. (ed.) (1959) *Noblesse Oblige*, Harmondsworth: Penguin.
Mort, S. (ed.) (1986) *Longman Guardian New Words*, Harlow: Longman.
Neaman, J. S. and Silver, C. G. (1990) *Kind Words* 2nd edn, New York: Facts on File.
O'Donnell, W. R. and Todd, L. (1980) *Variety in Contemporary English*, London: Allen & Unwin.
The Oxford English Dictionary (1989) 2nd edn, prepared by J. A. Simpson and E. S. C. Weiner, 20 vols, Oxford: Oxford University Press.
Pfeffer, J. A. (1987) *Deutsches Sprachgut im Worschatz der Amerikaner und Engländer*, Tübingen: Niemeyer.
Quirk, R. and Stein, G. (1990) *English in Use*, Harlow: Longman.
Quirk, R., Greenbaum, S., Leech, G. and Svartvik, J. (1985) *A Comprehensive Grammar of the English Language*, London: Longman.
The Random House Dictionary of the English Language (1987) 2nd edn, ed. S. B. Flexner, New York: Random House.
Redfern, W. (1989) *Clichés and Coinages*, Oxford: Blackwell.
Ross, A. S. C. (1954) 'Linguistic class-indicators in present-day English', *Neuphilologische Mitteilungen* 55: 20–56.
Schulz, M. R. (1975) 'The semantic derogation of woman', in B. Thorne and N. Henley (eds) *Language and Sex*, Rowley, Mass.: Newbury House, pp. 64–75.
Sheard, J. A. (1970) *The Words We Use*, London: Deutsch.
Shopen, T. and Williams, J. M. (eds) (1980) *Standards and Dialects in English*, Cambridge, Mass.: Winthrop.
—— (1981) *Style and Variables in English*, Cambridge, Mass.: Winthrop.
The Shorter Oxford English Dictionary (1977) ed. W. Little, 2 vols, Oxford: Oxford University Press.
Smith, G. (1985) *The English Companion*, Harmondsworth: Penguin.
Strang, B. M. H. (1970) *A History of English*, London: Methuen.
Strevens, P. (1964) 'Varieties of English', *English Studies* 45: 20–30.

Stubbs, M. (1980) *Language and Literacy: the Sociolinguistics of Reading and Writing*, London: Routledge & Kegan Paul.

Toolan, M. (1988) 'The language of press advertising', in M. Ghadessy (ed.) *Registers of Written English*, London: Pinter, pp. 52–64.

Tournier, J. (1985) *Introduction descriptive à la lexicogénétique de l'Anglais contemporain*, Paris: Champion-Slatkine.

Updike, J. (1990) *Rabbit at Rest*, New York: Ballantyne Books.

Ure, J. N. (1984) *An Introduction to Systemic Grammar and its Application to the Study of Register in Contemporary English*, London: Allen & Unwin.

Vestergaard, T. and Schroder, K. (1985) *The Language of Advertising*, Oxford: Blackwell.

Webster's Ninth New Collegiate Dictionary (1983) ed. F. C. Mish, Springfield, Mass.: Merriam-Webster.

Welte, W. (1988) *Englische Morphologie und Wortbildung*, Frankfurt am Main: Lang.

Zöfgen, E. (1989) 'Homonymie und Polysemie im allgemeinen einsprachigen Wörterbuch', in F. J. Hausmann, O. Reichmann, H. E. Wiegand and L. Zgusta (eds) *Dictionaries*, Berlin: de Gruyter, Vol. 1: 779–87.

Chapter 2

Words in combination

Language involves choice from among many possibilities that are restricted only by whether they are good grammar or not. This is the position taken by most people who write on grammar. But making a choice at one point often commits one to further choices. Words are not independent of each other, certainly much less so than the proponents of grammatical choice would have one believe. The *open choice principle* must be complemented by the *idiom principle*, which means that 'a language user has available to him or her a large number of semi-preconstructed phrases that constitute single choices, even though they might appear to be analyzable into segments' (Sinclair 1991: 110). The subject of this chapter is some of the types of such prefabricated language, called **multi-word units** or **lexical phrases**. They are well-established lexical combinations which consist of one or more *word forms* or *lexemes* (for these terms see 1.1) To indicate what is typical of the respective units, we will look at a variety of stylistic, situational, formal, semantic and syntactic aspects.

For our purposes, fixed expressions can be divided into two groups (see table 2.1), one of which expresses meanings (or *speech acts*; see 6.2.1) such as promises, warnings, requests, etc., while the other group does not. Another criterion is whether or not the expression is equivalent to a whole sentence or free utterance. On the next level down, the left branch is split into expressions which are used in set social situations and those which are not, a pragmatic criterion. The right branch, on the other hand, is subdivided by the semantic criterion of idiomaticity, i.e. a meaning which cannot be deduced from the meaning of the individual words. Some examples:

[1] Pragmatic idiom: *say when*; *how do you do*?
[2] Proverb: *don't count your chickens before they're hatched*; *like father, like son*; *birds of a feather flock together*.
[3] Idiom: *red herring*; *beat about the bush*; *put two and two together*.
[4] Collocation: *meet demand*; *confirmed bachelor*; *spring leak*.
[5] Commonplace: *orders are orders*; *you only live once*; *it's a small world*.

Table 2.1 Some fixed expressions in English

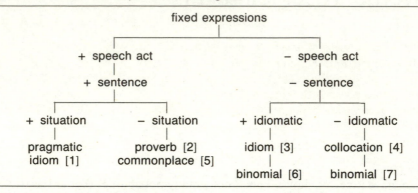

[6] Binomial: *kith and kin*; *high and dry*; *head over heels*.
[7] Binomial: *bed and breakfast*; *bacon and eggs*; *forgive and forget*.

The table shows the classification of the expressions dealt with in this chapter. A complete list would also include slogans, which have a definite purpose, and allusions and quotations, which have a known author, as opposed to the items listed, which do not. Also omitted are, for example, non-situational pragmatic idioms, among them discourse structuring devices such as *well*, *I see*, *you know* (some of which are treated in 6.5). (General treatments of the field include Alexander 1978–9; 1987; the standard handbook by Burger, Buhofer and Sialm 1982; Gläser 1986; Redfern 1989; Welte 1990 (with extensive bibliography); Welte 1992; and Zöfgen 1992.)

Multi-word units are so common in normal language that they 'may well be the basic organizing principle in language production' (McCarthy 1990: 11; cf. also Bolinger 1976). They are certainly known to the vast majority of native speakers. This distinguishes them from idiosyncratic turns of speech such as the following:

> Turning and turning in her bed, restless as a pride of stallions (why should that marvellous word be confined to lions and peacocks?), she wished with all her dark romantic heart: anywhere but here! anywhere but in the bonds of marriage!
>
>   (S. Scobie, 'A marriage of convenience', p. 202)

The narrator shows that he is aware of the restriction that operates on the frame *a pride of*, though he takes the liberty to extend the range of nouns conventionally possible. Note also these examples:

> Her clothes smell faintly of the Smeaths' house, a mixture of scouring powder and cooked turnips and slightly rancid laundry . . .
>
>   (M. Atwood, *Cat's Eye*, p. 52)

Alex was scared stiff and Joseph was scared sober for what would happen when Nora came to collect him.

(C. Nolan, *Under the Eye of the Clock*, p. 20)

The combinations *rancid butter* and *scared stiff* are what one would expect, while *rancid laundry* and *scared sober* are highly unusual. This chapter cannot go into the creative, unconventional use of language typical of poetry and prose fiction (but see below 2.1 on clichés), where authors often attach greater importance to expressive language than to the desire simply to make themselves understood in conventional language (for linguistic studies of literary language, cf. Sebeok 1960; Leech 1969; Burton 1980; Leech and Short 1981; Carter 1982; Sandig 1983; van Dijk 1985; Fowler 1986; Carter and Nash 1990). What is clear in any case is that, whatever the motivation for the variation, all these examples presuppose the conventional, institutionalized form of the expressions for their effect.

2.1   Clichés and fixed expressions

Clichés are routine or stereotypic forms that are found in many areas of life, for example, art, thought, behaviour, visual images or urban architecture. Some language clichés consist of single lexemes, for example, the journalistic items *bombshell, bonanza, brainchild, to harmonize, to orchestrate* and *scenario* (Howard 1984: 92), but most consist of more than two items.

Language clichés have often been the pet hate of writers on good English: 'Stereotyped, unoriginal, stale – these are the epithets that might be, and indeed often are, applied to them' (Vallins 1969: 136). The charge is that people do not think when they use expressions such as *acid test*, *psychological moment* or *leave no stone unturned*. Redfern calls them 'first thoughts, unexamined, in fact often non-thoughts or automatisms' (Redfern 1989: 7). This ties in with their psycholinguistic classification as part of **automatic speech** as distinct from more creatively produced language, which is referred to as **propositional speech** (Bolinger 1976).

What causes offence is the lack of style: 'There is a central aura of stylistic poverty about cliché: a suggestion of overuse' (Mackin 1978: 165). On the other hand, Howard points out that many clichés say what they say in a very economical way: 'they . . . express ideas that cannot be expressed otherwise without intolerable circumlocution and periphrasis' (Howard 1984: 98). But whether overused or not, clichés of one kind or another are used by everybody, not just the 'uneducated masses', even though Alexander thinks that proverbs are typically used by the working class, while the middle class is fond of literary quotations and allusions, for example to the Bible, Shakespeare and *Alice in Wonderland* (Alexander 1978–9: 190, 198). Indeed, there are large areas where consciously thought-out language is unusual, if not inappropriate. Redfern lists funerals, disasters, the writing of references and testimonials or letters of protest (Redfern 1989: 20ff). In much of everyday life, clichéd language is not only unavoidable but can actually be assigned a more positive function. On everyday small talk Redfern remarks:

> chatter . . . indicates the dread of silence: clichés stop us thinking of nothing, of nothingness. If not life enhancing, they are life-preservers. 'Phatic speech', speech used as social cement . . . is not necessarily empty speech . . . . It can be sorely missed, conspicuous by its absence.
>
> (ibid.: 22)

This provides a partial answer to the important question 'what is it about fixed turns of speech which make [*sic*] them in some instances preferable to novel utterances?' (Luelsdorff 1981: 1). Another aspect is that fixed expressions are known, and what is known does not intimidate: 'People like clichés . . . . They have a warm, familiar ring' (S. Raven, *Places where they Sing*, p. 55). By using clichés one signals that one has acquired part of the socio-cultural competence of a given speech community, that one is a member of the same group. Far from always breeding contempt, universally familiar language such as clichés can help to create an in-group feeling of sympathy, solidarity and good will ('familiarity breeds contentment', a memorable comment quoted in Redfern 1989: 131). Clichés therefore fulfil in many situations an important social function. Also, the stylistic case against clichés suffers when one notices how subjective published lists of clichés are: 'Whether we call a phrase an idiom or a cliché generally depends on whether we like it or not' (Brook 1981: 14).

Moreover, not every use of a cliché is to be condemned out of hand. Ricks, for instance, notes a playful use in everyday conversation that 'finds wit and humour and penetration in a conscious play with clichés' (Ricks 1980: 59; cf. also Redfern 1989: 166–7). The same playful impulse can be seen in the use of slightly altered clichés by politicians or journalists, as in 'France's ski industry: No business like snow business' (variation on the slogan *there's no business like show business*; *The Economist*, 3 March 1990, p. 65). A feature on an American socialist politician in Vermont is headed 'Painting Vermont Red' (*The Economist*, 22 September 1990, p. 53), where *red* is to be taken in its political sense of 'left wing' and the underlying fixed expression is *to paint the town red* 'enjoy oneself flamboyantly'. An article in the same magazine on exaggerated wage demands is entitled 'The Sin of Wages', a witty reversal of the biblical quotation *the wages of sin*. These examples illustrate the possibilities for word play inherent in these expressions: they consist of more than one word, they are characterized by a more or less fixed form, and they often have idiomatic meaning. Speakers can thus vary the conventionally established lexical constituents (*show business* > *snow business*). The trigger here seems to be the nearness in sound. One can also flout the conventionally fixed word order (*sin of wages*) and thus revive or revitalize a well-known expression. Finally, one can play with the meaning, as in *painting Vermont red,* where the constituents *Vermont* and *red* are given independent meaning, while the constituents in the idiom *paint the town red* do not have a meaning which can be isolated in this manner (see 2.5). In summary, clichés are employed universally, should not be avoided in those social situations where they meet important needs, and may be used creatively, so that each example of a cliché should be judged on its stylistic and other merits.

So far we have talked about questions of style, effect and function, which are central to an understanding of the cliché. We now turn to the linguistic description of clichés. Luelsdorff defines them as phrases, clauses and sentences which, owing to very frequent occurrence, have become hackneyed and trite (Luelsdorff 1981). Many clichés come from foreign languages and are often restricted to educated users, though native coinages are more frequent and are found in all walks of life (for examples arranged according to field, see Howard 1984).

Taking the 2,500 items collected in Partridge's *Dictionary of Clichés* (1954) as his corpus, Luelsdorff isolates prosodic, phonological, grammatical and semantic features. At the phonological level, clichés often show iambic or trochaic patterning (*the coast is clear, free and easy*), assonance (*cut and thrust*), rhyme (*fair and square*) and, more frequently, alliteration (*to have and to hold*). When one leaves aside clichés from foreign languages, the native items can be divided on the grammatical level into nominal, verbal and sentence structures. Nominal patterns include modifier-noun (*acid test, burning question*) and noun (phrase) plus preposition (*of* or *in*) plus noun (phrase) (*the apple of discord, an enemy in our midst*). Verbal structures show greater variety, for example, verb plus adverb (*plunge heavily*), verb plus noun (phrase) (*discard precedent*), verb plus noun plus adverb (*cry wolf too often*), verb plus prepositional phrase (*damn with faint praise*), and verb plus noun (phrase) plus prepositional phrase (*drown one's sorrows in drink*). Luelsdorff also lists sentence clichés (*Accidents will happen*; *Time marches on*). Howard distinguishes only between non-idiomatic and idiomatic clichés; Luelsdorff, in contrast, sets up a semantic hierarchy for his corpus material, saying that, on a scale from completely transparent expressions via clichés that contain some figurative constituents to completely idiomatic units, 'the overwhelming majority of clichés lies somewhere in the middle: the majority of clichés contains some figurative constituents' (Luelsdorff 1981: 6). We can use his findings as a background and an introduction to our treatment of fixed expressions, because he looks, among others, at collocations (*breathe freely*), binomials (*rough and ready*) and idioms (*cut off one's nose to spite one's face*).

2.2 Pragmatic idioms

In this section we will discuss lexical items and expressions whose occurrence is determined by a particular social situation. We will use the term **pragmatic idiom** to refer to them, though there are many other terms, such as **routines** or **social formulas** or **gambits**. Pragmatic idioms are not to be confused with pragmatic markers or expressions, often called **discourse markers**, such as *well*, *you know*, *I mean*, etc., which are discussed in 6.5.

Among the many situations in which stereotypic, or routinized, language is used are the beginnings (greetings, introductions) and endings (leave-takings) of social encounters and letters, eating and drinking, and all sorts of business transactions, as for example at a (railway) ticket counter (*Single or return?*), in a shop (*Can I help you?*), or in a café (*Black or white?*) or wine bar (*White or red?*).

Situations differ in the degree to which the language used in them is pre-determined. In many cases there is no choice, for instance in letters, where one has to use the salutation *Dear* even when one has no friendly feeling for the addressee – as in this example of a letter written by a wife who wants to divorce her husband:

'Dear Ricky, Please sign these papers and give me a divorce. I think you owe it to me . . . I'm sorry. Yours Chessie.'

Yours Chessie, thought Ricky dully, what a ridiculous way to end a letter when she's not mine anymore.

(J. Cooper, *Polo*, p. 125)

In this case, *Dear* and *Yours* are almost the only options, provided writers want to keep up appearances and go through the appropriately polite social motions (see Gülich and Henke 1980: 26–7).

In other situations participants have various options open to them. When one first meets people and introductions are made one can use *How do you do?*, *Hello, Hi, Nice|Pleased to meet you* and *I have been looking forward to meeting you (for some time)* (see Blundell *et al.* 1982; Lee 1983 for study materials). How do the expressions listed differ from one another? First, they belong to different levels of personal tenor (see 1.6.6), with *How do you do?* at the formal end, *Hi (there)* at the informal end, and *Hello* and the other two somewhere in the middle. *How do you do?* is becoming increasingly rare, not least because of the growing informality of English. When it is used, speakers often try to make it less distant and formal by combining it with *Hello* or *Pleased to meet you*. It is also felt to be typical of a certain social class (upper middle to upper), while *Pleased to meet you* is perhaps more often used by lower-middle and upper-working class people. Besides personal tenor and social dialect, there are also regional dialect associations: *Pleased to meet you* and *Hi* are still felt by some British speakers to be especially typical of Americans.

Formulas that are exclusive to Britain are, for example, *Straight or handle?* (referring in a pub to whether one wants a glass with or without a handle) or *Time, gentlemen please* (landlord's cry to get his customers to drink up and leave), while it is as yet only waiters in the United States who say *Enjoy!* (*your food* to be understood) to their customers when they have served them. In British papers and journals, letters to the editor are headed *Dear Sir* or *Sir*, while there is often no form of address in American printed letters. While Americans usually supply some information about the people introduced (job, titles, etc.), this is considered bad form by members of the British upper and upper-middle class (see Smith 1985: 126). The following quotation provides a final example, amusing and perhaps only slightly exaggerated.

> It takes four thank-yous for a ticket to be bought in an English bus. First the bus conductor heaves in sight and calls out thank-you (I have arrived). The passenger then hands over his 30p with an answering call of thank-you (I note that you have arrived and here is my fare). The conductor then hands over the ticket with another thank-you (I acknowledge receipt of your fare and here is your ticket in return) whereupon the passenger replies thank-you (thank-you).
>
> This elaborate and formal ritual amazes Americans, who can do the whole transaction with hardly a single thank-you being exchanged. It certainly slows life up, but oils the gears of everyday intercourse.
>
> (G. Smith, *The English Companion*, p. 233)

In contrast to the other types of fixed expression discussed in this chapter, pragmatic idioms often need the context of situation to be understood correctly. In the last quotation, Smith felt it necessary to provide glosses for the first three *thank-you's* because only the last use of that expression has its expected meaning. *Black or white?* in a different context (e.g. *Was the waiter black or white?*) has a completely different meaning. The semantic opaqueness of pragmatic idioms results in many cases from ellipsis: *Say when* is presumably shortened from *Say when I am to stop pouring* or *Say when you have enough*, and *Many happy returns* from *Many happy returns of the day*, which is, of course, still found. Moreover, many situational idioms show a weakened meaning. This is obvious in *How are you?*, which is usually no more than a ritual recognition of the other's presence, and does not express a deeply felt interest in his or her well-being. However, in certain circumstances it is not impossible for such a ritual question to be met by a genuine response (see Edmondson and House 1981: 190). In the (fictional) letter quoted above it is clear that neither the *Dear* nor the *Yours* have their usual full sense. They are just conventional tokens without any real meaning. It is not their meaning which is of primary importance; rather, it is the function they serve (beginning and ending a letter) that needs to be understood. *How do you do?* is semantically extreme in that it is difficult to state what meaning it has. *The Concise Oxford Dictionary of Current English* (COD) explains it as 'a formal greeting' (s.v. *how*), the *Collins COBUILD English Language Dictionary* (COBUILD) says it is 'a polite way of greeting someone when you meet them for the first time' (s.v. *how* 4). Neither dictionary defines its meaning, but instead both describe its function. Semantically, then, pragmatic idioms often need the context of situation to be fully and correctly understood, and they range from expressions which have full meaning to expressions which do not have any meaning, but only function.

However, to characterize pragmatic idioms from the point of view of regional and social class dialect and with regard to their syntax and semantics is still not to treat them adequately. It is also important to know the linguistic context (often called the **cotext**). If introductions are effected by a third party, and one speaker says *How do you do?*, how does the second participant react? This is what the *Longman Dictionary of Contemporary English* (LDOCE) has to say on the subject (s.v. *how* 6): 'a phrase used to someone you have just met for the first time; this person replies with the same phrase. They usually shake hands at the same time.' In other words, in order to behave in a socially appropriate way one needs to know that *How do you do?* is only the second and third step in a sequence which involves three parties (the person introducing and the two being introduced to each other). Moreover, LDOCE also points out that linguistic behaviour is accompanied by non-linguistic behaviour in this case (the hand-shake). However, LDOCE is not totally correct in implying that speakers have no choice. Consider the following example:

> 'Come here, Lisa. . . . I want you to meet your new governess. Miss Talbot, this is my daughter Lisa.' A firm hand propelled the child forward. 'Say 'how do you do', Lisa.'
> The child stumbled through the stiff formality of the greeting, bringing a lump to Helen's throat as she clasped the small hand extended towards her and felt the nervous twitching of the fingers against her palm.
> Her softly spoken 'Hello, Lisa. I've been looking forward to meeting you', was lost on the child.
>
> (Y. Whittal, *Scars of Yesterday*, p. 43)

The governess as the social superior with the higher status selects a less formal greeting in order to make the situation less fraught. This is often possible, while a selection up the formal scale is unusual because 'it may be said to imply "Keep your social distance, you upstart!"' (Edmondson and House 1981: 189). Secondly, people these days often do not shake hands when they are introduced.

Hi and *Hello*, besides being informal, also differ from *How do you do?* in that they can be used when meeting the same person or people on a later occasion (often with an added *again*, as in *Hi/Hello (there) again)*, while

How do you do? can be used only once. This also sets it apart from *How are you?*, which can be used more than once to the same person(s), though usually not on the same day.

To sum up, a full description of pragmatic idioms has to take into account their register characteristics (regional and social distribution, personal tenor, etc.), their syntactic and semantic peculiarities, at what point in a social situation or sequence they come, whether they occur alone or whether reciprocity is usual and indeed necessary, and if so whether the same idiom or a different idiom can or must be used, whether speakers must change, and, finally, whether the idiom can be used in an identical situation on a later occasion.

2.3 Collocations

In this section collocations will be defined and different types illustrated. This will be followed by a discussion of the claims made for an independent lexical level in language based on collocational organization. The section will be rounded off by a summary of some of the most important research in this area. For reasons explained in the final paragraph of 2.3.3, from now on collocations will usually be quoted in this form: *demand-meet*; *bachelor-confirmed*; *leak-spring*.

2.3.1 Definition

The term **collocation** is used by different linguists to refer to what are often very different combinations of word forms. As used in this chapter, it refers to combinations of two lexical items which make an isolable semantic contribution, belong to different word classes and show a restricted range.

Apart from the restriction to two word forms, a few explanations are in order. A first criterion (two lexical items, not grammatical ones) separates lexical combinations (**collocations** in a wider sense) from grammatical combinations. Note that the term collocation is sometimes used to refer to combinations of lexical items with grammatical items or grammatical constructions, like *do in*, *put up with*, *on approval*, *under consideration*, *proud of*, and *finish/stop* + *-ing*-construction (see Benson *et al.* 1986: ix–xxiii, who distinguish between *lexical* and *grammatical* collocations). The third criterion (independent meaning of constituents) marks non-idiomatic combinations off from idiomatic ones (see next paragraph). Finally, the criteria of different word class and restricted range allow us to distinguish collocations in the narrow sense used here from other lexical, non-idiomatic combinations (for more discussion see below).

Meaning The important point about collocational meaning is that each lexeme makes an independent contribution to the meaning of the whole collocation, or as Cruse (1986: 40) puts it, 'each lexical constituent is also a semantic constituent'. This means that the constituents of a collocation can have special meanings which are restricted to one particular collocation. Indeed, a collocation may sometimes appear illogical, as in this example, where Adrian Mole, the titular hero of Sue Townsend's novel *The Growing Pains of Adrian Mole*, p. 173, is struck by the apparent semantic incompatibility of something fluid (*rain*) with the adverb *solidly* ('continuously'): 'Sunday March 20th . . . 8 p.m. Rained solidly all day. 10.30 p.m. How can it rain "solidly"? What a strange mistress is the English language.' If we consider the meaning of *white* in *white paint* or *white snow* as the most frequent meaning, then *white* in *white coffee* ('with milk'), *white currant*, *white grape* or *white wine* are different, while the meanings of the adjective in *white lie* ('harmless'), *white night* ('sleepless') or *white sale* ('of household linen') are more opaque and are linked closely to the respective noun. In *white horses* ('white-topped waves') and *white coal* ('water as energy source'), it is not only the adjectives, but also the nouns that show special (metaphorical) meanings; one might be tempted to call them idioms if one were not aware of the metaphor (for a discussion of the meanings of *white* see Carter 1987: 21–2; for more collocations with *white* see Bennett 1988: 273–94).

Most research has concentrated on combinations of lexemes like *river-rise*, *agree-entirely*, or *fine-heavy*. These are indeed collocations from the semantic point of view because each constituent has independent meaning. Contrast with this idioms like *paint the town red* or *fly off the handle*, where it is hardly possible to say what the individual constituents contribute to the meaning of the combination as a whole. In between these two clear-cut cases are, however, many expressions which are at least partly idiomatic. Combinations like *It's raining cats and dogs*, often mentioned as a typical English idiom, do not qualify for full idiomatic status because at least one constituent is independently meaningful (*rain*) while the other is idiomatic (*cats and dogs* 'heavily'). These intermediate cases are sometimes called **partial** or **unilateral idioms**.

Word classes The fourth criterion is that lexemes belong to different word classes. Examples are *demand-meet* (noun-verb), *hopes-high* (noun-adjective), and *apologize-profusely* (verb-adverb). This sets them apart from a series of lexemes of the same word class which are often found together in texts (e.g. *poetry . . . literature . . . reader . . . writer . . . style*), and which contribute to the **textual cohesion** of the texts concerned (in as much as they all belong to the field of literature, its production and reception; example from Hasan and Halliday 1976: 286; for cohesion, see chapter 5). The different-word-class criterion together with the lexical-items-only criterion put combinations such as *a pride of lions*, *a cake of soap* as well as items such as *fraught with difficulties*, *bed and breakfast* and *bacon and eggs* in different classes of lexical combinations (for more on the last two see 2.4 on binomial expressions).

Range   The last criterion, restricted range, helps to set up different classes within the two-lexeme type of combination, namely **free combinations** as opposed to **collocations**. As used by Firth the term *collocation* refers to any combination of two lexical items. *Night*, for example, combines not only with *dark* (Firth 1957: 196), but also with *brooding, dull, frosty, hopeless, long, mantling, naked, perpetual, tedious, waxing* (to quote from only the first two of forty-nine lines of adjectives and verbs from Rodale 1947). This contrasts sharply with the four verbs (*spend*; *bid, wish somebody a good night*; AmE to *work nights*) and a mere fourteen adjectives in *The BBI Combinatory Dictionary of English* (Benson *et al.* 1986; BBI). The difference must be explained by different selection principles in the two dictionaries. *Dull, hopeless, tedious*, as well as *cheerless, difficult, eventful, fatal, fateful, ghastly, grim, lonely, memorable, peerless, precarious, previous, tolerable, unspeakable* in Rodale can no doubt be found together with *night*, but it could not be argued that they are particularly closely linked to *night*, let alone that they are typically found with it. Items that are not closely related to others enter into **free combinations** (other scholars use the term *unrestricted collocations*) while the closer associations between lexemes are called **collocations** (or *restricted collocations*). Rodale, therefore, includes both types while BBI restricts itself to collocations. Lexemes that belong to the core vocabulary of English are typically found in free combinations (*cheap, expensive, fast, great, interesting, new, nice, old, round, slow, small, square, young*; *buy, get, go, meet, put, run, talk*, etc.). The number of combinations formed with them is enormous. When one talks about the number of lexemes (or **collocates**) that occur together (or **collocate**) with the lexeme under discussion (the **node**), one is concerned with that lexeme's **range** (see Jones and Sinclair 1974 for these and other terms). It is common to express the difference between free combinations and collocations in terms of their ranges: the range of lexemes in collocations is smaller than that of lexemes in free combinations. Members of (a sub-set of) a range are often characterized by shared semantic features, as in the case of the verb *meet*, which collocates, for example, with *need, condition* and *requirement* on the one hand and *bus, plane* and *train* in the other. These similarities often provide the basis for recognizing different meanings (i.e. lexical units) in dictionaries, for example, 'satisfy' for the first meaning of *meet* and 'be there at the arrival of' for the second.

In **fixed (unique, frozen) collocations** lexemes have only one collocate. Well-known examples are furnished perhaps by the combinations of *ajar* with *door* (*the door was* or *stood ajar*), of *auburn* and *hair, kick* and *foot, nod* and *head, shrug* and *shoulders*, and *sorely* ('very much') and *miss* ('feel the loss of'). There are not many frozen collocations, and it would in general be rash to say that the range of a certain lexeme is limited to one collocate only as lexemes can extend their range and individual usage varies. Is it, for example, impossible to use *ajar* with *gate*? The combination of *cats and dogs* with *rain* is not unique, because *pour* and perhaps *hail* and *sleet* can also collocate with it. Note that frozen collocations are frozen only from the perspective of the lexeme that has been mentioned first in the examples above. *Door*, *foot*, *head*, as well as *miss*, enter into many other collocations than the ones cited. Also, it is essential to distinguish between the different lexical units of a word form. *Nod*, for instance, means 'move one's head up and down' and enters into the unique collocation mentioned; but it also means 'indicate by nodding', as in *to nod one's agreement*, *approval*, *greeting*, etc.

Problems   The distinction between collocations and free combinations is not unproblematic. There is no empirical research based on corpora large enough to allow the criterion of repeated co-occurrence to be tested conclusively and convincingly. Jones and Sinclair (1974) base their investigations on a corpus of 135,000 words of spoken text; Johansson and Hofland use the LOB (Lund–Oslo–Bergen) Corpus of about one million words of written text, but remark: 'we would like to have a distributional lexicon . . . summarizing the grammatical and collocational properties of words. This requires a far larger material [*sic*]' (Johansson and Hofland 1989: 14). In the entry for *night* Johansson and Hofland list only the three adjectives *good*, *previous* and *whole* (ibid.: 343), far fewer than the subjective, non-computer-assisted works by Rodale or Benson *et al*. It remains to be seen whether the dictionary of collocations announced from Collins-COBUILD, which is based on the computerized corpus of twenty million words at the University of Birmingham in England, will be able to resolve this problem. This seems unlikely, however, because there is a more fundamental difficulty to overcome: it has not been specified in absolute numbers what *limited range* means. Greenbaum (1970) and Roos (1975) consider collocations to be those lexical combinations which were named in 10 per cent or more of their informants' answers, while other linguists do not bother to give any figures at all. Roos's research is based on thirty informants, so that it needs only three informants to confer the status of collocation on a given combination.

Furthermore, there is a conflict between the criteria for collocations, namely close association, repeated co-occurrence and limited number of collocates (Benson *et al*. 1986: xxiv). For instance, in the entries for *man* and *woman*, BBI lists the adjectives *fat*, *old*, *short*, *tall*, *thin*, *ugly*, *wise* and *young*. But there must be some doubt whether combinations of *man* and *woman* with these adjectives can form collocations. Both the nouns and the adjectives are lexical items that belong to the core vocabulary of the English language, which, as remarked above, enter into countless lexical combinations, all of them free combinations. The adjectives listed above no doubt repeatedly combine with *man* and *woman*, but they are clearly not bound specifically to them. As long as the defining criteria are in conflict with each other there is no easy solution in sight to the problem of distinguishing between collocations and free combinations.

Fixedness   Collocations show various degrees of fixedness:

Morphology: in some collocations the adverbs are not formally marked by the *-ly* morpheme: swear-*blind*; drunk-*blind*; forget-*clean*; naked-*stark*; sober-*stone cold*.

Substitutability: lexemes can often be replaced by close synonyms, for example, *hardened criminal* is found side by side with *confirmed criminal*, though **hardened burglar* or **hardened murderer* are not found. *Conditions* can be *met*, *fulfilled* or *satisfied*, and *hopes* can be *pinned*, *placed* or *put on* something. *Conflict* collocates with *end* and *resolve*, though not with **finish* and **solve*.

Additions: additions, most often pre- or post-modifying nouns, are normal:

> He was critical of the ministry . . . of Henry Addington . . . for its failure . . . to put the country into an adequate state of defense to meet Napoleon's invasion threat
> (threat-meet; 'Fox, Charles James', in *Encyclopædia Britannica*, 15th edn, Vol. 7, p. 579)

> The oil-exporting nations . . . may soon restrict production below the level needed to meet still rising world demand
> (demand-meet; B. Ward, *Progress for a Small Planet*, p. 15)

Deletion: although deletions are not impossible they are much rarer than additions: *I have not got the faintest, foggiest* (sc. *idea*).

Displacement: personal pronouns may replace the actual collocational items (underlined in the following): 'Instead of banishing or shunning clichés, haven't we got to *meet* them imaginatively' (Ricks 1980: 55); 'Her heart wasn't very strong and her life assurance premiums weren't cheap. It can't have been easy to *meet* them' (P. D. James, *Death of an Expert Witness*, p. 325); 'QUALITY is our promise. Cancellation is Your Privilege if we fail to meet it' (advertising material, *The Economist*, May 1991).

Separability: some collocations cannot be separated, for example, *foot the bill* and *curry favour*, which are called **bound collocations** (Cruse 1986: 41).

Distribution: finally, the distribution or word order of the constituent lexemes in collocations is relatively free: *they met their demands*; *their demands, which were not met completely . . .*; *it was these last demands which the parents did not want to meet.*

Syntactic transformations are thus possible and do not change, or destroy, the meaning of collocations. On the whole collocations are less fixed than pragmatic idioms and the other types of expression to be discussed below. This low degree of formal fixedness in combination with the composite (isolable) semantic structure can also explain why collocations are rarely, if ever, the object of word play (see 2.1 above and 2.7 below for examples). Playful variation can, therefore, really focus only on the lexical constituents. The examples *rancid laundry*, *scared sober* and *a pride of stallions* (given earlier) seem to suggest that it is above all lexical combinations with a very restricted range ([frozen] collocations) that present a linguistic challenge.

2.3.2 Lexis as a linguistic level

As a result of their research into collocations, linguists have investigated the properties of lexical organization and tried to answer the question whether or not lexis is independent of grammar, meaning and phonology. At present the answer seems to be 'yes-but', i.e. there are features that speak both for and against the independence of lexis (for a summary, more detail and references, see Butler 1985: 128–37). It should be noted that in the following discussion collocation is often used in the wider sense of 'any lexical combination'.

Lexis and grammar   Consider some of the collocations of *strong* and *powerful*: *strong/powerful argument*; *strong tea*; *?powerful tea*; *powerful car*; *?strong car*. *Strong* and *powerful*, then, show different ranges (collocation potentials) though they are in identical grammatical structures (adjective plus noun). Conversely, different grammatical structures show identical collocational patterns: compare *the argument is strengthened/is made more powerful*; *the strength/power of his argument*; *he argued strongly/powerfully*; *the strength/?power of her tea*; *the ?strength/power of his car*. This demonstrates not only that collocational patterning is independent of grammatical structures, but also that collocations are also independent of such grammatically relevant considerations as word order (see above). Furthermore, while most grammatical units are described within the confines of the sentence, collocations hold across clause and sentence boundaries (cf. the examples above under 2.3.1 *displacement*). Finally, while a major focus in grammar is on the properties of simple words, lexis is also interested in the collocations of such complex items as *cats and dogs* (with *rain*) and *like a house on fire* (with *get on*). These are points which are said to argue in favour of an independent level of lexis.

On the other hand, grammar does play a part in the acceptability of at least some collocations. While the collocations *he drinks heavily*, *he is a heavy drinker* and *he put in some heavy drinking* are grammatically acceptable, the collocation *the drinker is heavy*, *heavy drink*, or *heavily drunk* are not, at least not in the relevant sense of *heavy*. Other examples are *confirmed bachelor*, *hardened criminal* and *hot pursuit*, where *the bachelor was confirmed*, *it was confirmed that the bachelor was*, *the criminal was hardened* and *?the pursuit was hot* are not acceptable in the relevant sense. The same restriction operates on *odd* in the collocation *odd socks*; in this case *his socks are odd* is grammatical, but has a completely different meaning.

Differences in subject or word order, for example, between British and American speakers, can also influence collocational preferences; see below 2.3.3.

Finally, one might well not accept the analysis of the *strong/powerful* example above, but set up two separate lexical units *strong*₁ ('sturdy') and *strong*₂ ('concentrated'). *Strong*₁ can be said of material or abstract objects, especially those that can stand up under attack, as *fort*, *argument*, *train* and *health*, while *strong*₂ refers to objects that can be perceived by the senses of smell, taste or sight, as *odours*, *tea* and *light*, but not *noise*.

Lexis and meaning   Arguments for lexis as an independent level can be seen in the fact that different meanings are realized through the same word form, as in *romance* (see 1.1) or the *nod*-examples above (2.3.1). Conversely, similar or identical meanings are realized by different lexical items. The meaning 'great amount' is expressed by *heavily* for the verbs *drink*, *smoke* and *rain*, but not *eat*, which takes *heartily*, *voraciously*, *inordinately*, etc. The meaning 'beginning' is expressed, for example, by *start/begin* (theatre performance, etc.), *kick off* (soccer match), *fall* (night) and *break* (day, or dawn in poetic language). Collocations are unpredictable not only in one and the same language but even more so between languages, as anybody knows who has learned a foreign language. Of the two verbs used with French *nuit* ('night') *tomber* is predictable, *descendre* is not. German uses verbs that are all unpredictable when one equates English *fall* with German *fallen* (*die Nacht kommt, bricht an, sinkt hernieder, zieht herauf*; the last three are poetic).

While there seems to be no reason why *night* should collocate with *fall* rather than *break* or some other verb, this does not mean that there are no semantic ties at all between the lexemes of a collocation. In the frozen collocations above, there are semantic features in *kick* which demand *foot*, and the same goes for *nod* and *head*, and *shrug* and *shoulders*. These are called **inherent** semantic **features**, and they have been distinguished from **selection restrictions**, which determine what may occur with given verbs. However, in this case the verb demands not a specific lexeme, but a whole semantic class of nouns, for instance, *spend*, which combines with numerous time nouns such as *day*, *evening*, *holiday*, *hour*, *life*, *spare time*, *time*, *war*, *weekend*, *one's youth*, etc. Other examples are provided by *eat*, whose object must have the meaning element [solid], and *drink* plus nouns with the meaning element [liquid]. Similarly, some adverbs show a certain semantic bias in their collocates, for example, *a bit* and *a little* tend to enter into collocations with adjectives that express something negative (*a bit*: *dull*, *frightened*; *a little*: *drunk*, *jealous*, *plump*, *tetchy*, *unkind*), while *highly* collocates more often with positive items (*important*, *intelligent*, *profitable*, *recommended*, *sensitive*; see Bäcklund 1973). These inherent and selectional features seem to militate against the setting up of lexis as an independent level (see Kastovsky 1980: 80–3 for a summary).

Phonology and **personal tenor** seem also to have some influence on the selection of components in collocations. Take, for instance, *highly*, which is an intensifier of high degree. Here the semantics seem to require its collocates to be made up of more than one syllable (see the examples in the last paragraph). On the other hand, *dead* is also a high-degree intensifier, but it tends to take words of one or two syllables, often informal, for which its short form and informal nature suggest themselves as explanations. Examples of *dead-* collocates are *beat*, *boring*, *certain*, *drunk*, *good*, *nervous*, *sad*, *scared*, *slow*, *stupid*, *sure*, *tired* and *worried*. Words of three and more syllables cannot be ruled out, but again tend to be stylistically neutral or informal, for example, *chaotic*, *disappointed*, *embarrassing*, *good-looking*, *horrible*, *pathetic*, *superior*, *symbolic*, *threatening* and *well-behaved* (all from S. Townsend's novels *The Secret Diary of Adrian Mole Aged 13¾* and *The Growing Pains of Adrian Mole*). These phonological and stylistic tendencies can perhaps explain why *dead* is not acceptable in collocation with **mature*, **positive*, **exhausted* and **intoxicated* (examples from Bolinger 1972: 54).

2.3.3 Research findings

Bäcklund (1973) deals with the collocations of adverbs of degree, basing his book on examples he has collected from various written sources. While he has found enough contexts for the more common adverbs, this is not the case, for example, for *heavily*, where his description rests on a mere seven examples. As a result, he concludes that *heavily* collocates with past participles in adjectival function that express something negative, and that verbal collocates are rare (other than *depend* and *rely*). Yet it is not too difficult to find further collocations including neutral *heavily built* as a reference to physique, or *heavily freckled* (as an intensifier). Furthermore, verbs are found quite often with *heavily*: besides *drink* and *smoke*, there are money-related lexemes (*be in debt* or *indebted*, *pay*, *subsidize*), verbs of (metaphorical) obligation such as *depend*, *lean on*, *rely*, *be indebted*, and weather verbs, a group not mentioned at all in Bäcklund: *pour down*, *rain*, *snow* (cf. also Bäcklund 1976; 1980).

As it is difficult to find a sufficiently large corpus, Greenbaum (1970) used questionnaires which he asked students to fill in. He concentrates on only a few degree adverbs (*certainly, really, badly, (very) much, greatly, utterly, completely, entirely*) and demonstrates convincingly that the choice of collocates is determined by semantic considerations in the majority of cases. *Utterly* and *completely* take pejorative verbs and adjectives (*detest, despise, indefensible, unsuccessful*), while *completely* collocates in addition with *forget* and *ignore. Greatly* and *(very) much* are found above all with attitudinal verbs: *greatly* and *much* prefer *admire* and *enjoy; very much* on the other hand is more frequent with *like* and *enjoy. Greatly* also enters into collocation with attitudinal adjectives, many of them past participles such as *appreciated, beloved* and *missed*. In adjective collocations, *entirely* is found with semantically positive or neutral lexemes, in contrast to *wholly*, which occurs more often with negative than positive lexemes. Frequent verbs with *entirely* are *disagree* and *agree. Certainly* is closely associated with *know*, as is *really* with *love. Badly* has a high-frequency collocation with *need* and a less frequent one with *want*.

Greenbaum's results also throw light on the interaction between syntax and collocations. Choice of subject is apparently the explanation for a difference in frequency: *I entirely agree* is more common than *my friend entirely agrees*. In a follow-up study in the United States, Greenbaum found that American students had lower scores than their British counterparts for such frames as *I badly* . . . or *I entirely* . . ., which he explains in the following way: 'It appears that American speakers prefer these intensifiers to be positioned finally . . . . Since the intensifiers were in pre-verb positions in the experiments, they did not evoke the verbs to the same extent as they might have done if positioned finally' (Greenbaum 1974: 85).

The three studies mentioned above are typical of much research in this field, where linguists take an adverb and then find out what its collocates are. This approach establishes links between lexemes, but it does not consider what actually happens in language production. Here, namely, one starts, say, with the noun *debate* and looks for an adjective to describe the kind of debate which one has just had. It is rarely the case that one has produced *bitter, heated, lively* and is now looking for a suitable noun (see Hausmann 1984). In the linguistic analysis of collocations, one can indeed make either the adjective or the noun the focus of attention, the **node**, but in language production one starts from the **base** and looks for acceptable partners, the **collocates** or **collocators**. The analytic approach, in other words, is divorced from natural language use and therefore sees no need to set up a hierarchy among the members of a collocation. In both Rodale and BBI, however, the search direction is from base to collocator, and this is the principle on which all entries are established: the noun entries list verbal and adjectival collocates, while adjective and verb entries record only adverbs as collocates. It is only when one is in the situation of looking for a suitable collocate that one appreciates what an immense improvement this arrangement really represents.

2.4 Binomials

Binomials, like collocations, consist of two constituents. These belong to the same word class and are linked by a grammatical item, frequently *and*. Their constituents can be independently meaningful (as in *bed and breakfast* or *hire and fire*), or they can be idiomatic (*bag and baggage, head over heels*). There are also three-member combinations (**trinomials**; *left, right and centre* or *hook, line and sinker*), but they are much less numerous. The two constituents can be identical, as in *face to face* and *so-and-so*. The basic structure can be expanded, as in *from rags to riches*, *by fair means or foul, few and far between, the quick and the dead, every Tom, Dick and Harry*. Binomials often preserve words which are rare (*hale* in *hale and hearty*) or which survive only in the binomial expression (*kith* in *kith and kin*). The collocative potential of binomials varies as with other lexical combinations. *Bed and breakfast, high and mighty* and *odds and ends* enter into free combinations, while *high and dry* forms a collocation with *leave*, and *hook, line and sinker* with *believe* or the synonymous verbs *accept, fall for, swallow* and *take*.

Syntactically, the two constituents belong to the same word class, as in these examples: *aid and abet, forgive and forget, part and parcel*. Exceptions include *by and large* and *up and coming*. With these examples in mind, Norrick (1988: 74) suggests as a defining criterion not syntactic parallelism but a parallelism on any level. This would also cover examples without *and*, such as *sooner or later* and *head over heels*. Binomials can have syntactic functions which neither constituent on their own could have; for example, the three nouns *hook, line and sinker* function as an adverbial phrase (as in *he accepted the story hook, line and sinker*), while the two adverbs *so-and-so* form a noun phrase (as in *what do you think of so-and-so?*).

The fixed expressions with which we are dealing in this section are called **irreversible binomials** because their word order is, in contrast to collocations, completely unchangeable. This is no doubt connected to the fact that the second (or third in trinomials) constituent is usually phonetically more weighty than the first – *bacon and eggs* being one of the few exceptions (see Gustafsson 1974). Also, none of the items can be exchanged for synonyms: there is no **help and abet* or **aid and help* or **kith and relatives*. Insertions are possible, though infrequent: *they really offered a marvellous bed and an even better breakfast* is a possible expansion of *bed and breakfast*, as is *they do you excellent bacon and not bad eggs*. On the other hand, **this is all an important part and even more important parcel of the whole initiation process* is not acceptable. This example would suggest that the nearer the binomials are to the idiomatic end of the semantic scale the more fixed they become. (For more discussion, see Gustafsson 1976.)

The fixed nature of many binomials is heightened by assonance or alliteration. Rhyme is also not uncommon, for example, *hire and fire*, *make or break*, *town and gown* and *wine and dine*.

Formally and syntactically, then, binomials are more fixed than collocations. Various semantic relationships between the two halves of binomials have been distinguished (cf. Malkiel 1959: 125–9). Repetition of the same lexeme, found more often in naturally occurring conversation than in written texts, can mirror real-life situations (*hand in hand*) or can be hyperbolic. Other binomials consist of two near-synonyms, which often complement or intensify each other, for example, *rules and regulations*, *fuss and bother* and *over and done with* (Norrick 1988: 77–80). They can also stand in semantic opposition to each other, as in *assets and liabilities*, *give or take* and *war and peace*. More generally, binomials range from completely transparent (*bed and breakfast*; *bacon and eggs*; *here, there and everywhere*) to semi-transparent (*kith and kin*; *left, right and centre*; *with all one's might and main*; *part and parcel*; *town and gown*) to opaque or completely idiomatic (*high and dry*; *hook, line and sinker*; *on the up and up*).

2.5 Idioms

While *collocation* and *binomial* are unambiguous technical terms, **idiom** has a non-technical meaning as well. This can be paraphrased as 'a form of expression peculiar to a language, person, or group of people' (COD). Thus, the fact that the first person singular pronoun is spelt with a capital letter is characteristic of English, as are also such grammatical phenomena as the expanded form (in the category of aspect) or some kinds of complementation with *-ing*. The fact that many verbs can be used both transitively and intransitively without any formal difference, and that intransitive verbs can have a passive meaning, are also features that are typical of English (cf. 1.4.4). As a lexical peculiarity one might mention the great number of sports terms, both in British and American English, which have gained general currency (see 11.4.4).

2.5.1 Definition of idiom

In linguistics, idiom is defined more narrowly as a complex lexical item which is longer than a word form but shorter than a sentence, and which has a meaning that cannot be derived from a knowledge of its component parts. Meaning is thus the decisive, if not the only, criterion for idioms. To contrast collocations and idioms once again, one can say that **collocations** consist of two word forms which are at the same time semantic constituents, or **lexical units**, while the word forms in an **idiom** do not constitute lexical units and do not make an isolable contribution to the meaning of the whole.

An idiom, it has been said, is a 'lexical complex which is semantically simplex' (Cruse 1986: 37), or, to put it slightly differently, idioms show **unitary meaning**. As a consequence of this, some linguists also use a special term for the constituents of idioms, namely **formatives**. A test for a semantic constituent is that of **recurrent semantic contrast** (see Cruse 1986: 26–9). In the sentence *you need not jump down my throat* (COD 'reprimand or contradict a person fiercely'), take *need* and substitute for it the semantically different but syntactically identical item *may*. This changes the meaning of the sentence, of course, but the point is that the same substitution of forms in a completely different sentence will produce a parallel change of meaning, as in *they need/may not sit the exam*. The same test shows that *you* is also a semantic constituent, but that *throat* is not, as in semantically unacceptable **you need not jump down my wind pipe*. In other sentence frames *throat* and *wind pipe* are in recurrent semantic contrast: *he hit me in the throat/wind pipe* and *they operated on my throat/wind pipe*. In fact, *jump*, *down* and the possessive *my* are all part of the idiom *to jump down -'s throat*. Similarly, if *hit* and *pail* are contrasted with *kick* and *bucket* in the expression *to kick the bucket* it becomes clear that *kick the bucket* is an idiom. The same goes for an adjectival idiom such as *red herring*: *red herring* is not to *green herring* as *red book* is to *green book*.

Recurrent semantic contrast does not mean that all idioms are equally difficult to decode. Idioms show different degrees of **semantic opacity** (see Cruse 1986: 39–40): *green light* in *give somebody the green light* is less opaque than *red herring*. Knowledge of the world will play a part in the degree to which speakers feel idioms to be opaque. Many idioms have originated in metaphors which some speakers recognize while others remain unaware of their origin. Thus, while *bury the hatchet*, *give somebody the green light* and *gnash one's teeth* are likely to be known and easily intelligible to many, only few will know that *white elephant* ('something expensive which is completely useless') apparently derives from a king of Siam who used to make a present of a white elephant to people he wished to ruin. Equally hazy are the origins of the archetypical idiom *kick the bucket*, for which one explanation is that it 'originates from the practice of a prisoner standing on the only article available in his cell, namely the bucket, in order to hang himself' (Fernando 1978: 321; cf. the OED s.v. *bucket* 2 for a different view). More relevant to an understanding of the idiom are present-day *kick* (*in*, *off*) or *kick it*, all meaning 'die', where *kick* seems to be a shortened form of the idiom *kick the bucket* (Ruhl 1989: 67). Dead metaphors often allow substitution of constituents by synonyms, near-synonyms or a semantic paraphrase. Some of the literal meaning is still relevant for the interpretation of *sweeten the pill* or *give somebody a piece of one's mind*, but another part remains obscure, for example, the pejorative, scolding meaning in *give somebody a piece of one's mind*. Cruse uses the adjective 'translucent' for this semantic state of affairs (Cruse 1986: 44).

Few readers will apply the recurrent semantic contrast test, so there arises the question of what other means there are to recognize that an expression is an idiom. Many idioms have two meanings, a literal and an idiomatic one (*kick the bucket*, *go to the country*, *pull one's leg*). In such cases only the context can give a clue as to which meaning is intended. In other cases, when a literal reading does not make sense in terms of the world as we know it, the likelihood is that we are dealing with an idiom. This applies to *jump down someone's throat*, *fly off the handle*, and *cats and dogs* (in *rain cats and dogs*). The same conclusion should suggest itself when an expression is formed in a way that is contrary to the syntactic rules of contemporary English, as in the definite articles in *kick the bucket* and *fly off the handle*, or *one* in *pull a fast one*. The definite article normally has the function of indicating that an item has already been mentioned or is considered unique in the context of the language community, while the pro-form *one* refers to a noun that must precede it. Neither of these conditions is fulfilled in the idioms cited. Finally, idioms can be phonologically irregular in that they have an unpredictable stress pattern. In free syntactic groups, the last lexical item usually carries the tonic stress, for example, *they ran into the ' house*. This is not so in *like a ' house on fire, you can say ' that again*, *learn the ' hard way*, and *have a ' bone to pick with somebody*. Also, in connected spoken discourse, idioms are often signalled by slight pauses or an audible intake of breath (Strässler 1982: 95). Finally, there is a certain amount of lexical repetition in the environment of idioms, which makes for greater lexical cohesion. Often a state of affairs is described, then the sender refers to it with an idiom, before it is picked up again by a non-idiomatic, literal lexical item (ibid.: 95–6).

2.5.2 Classifications of idioms

Idioms have been classified in applied linguistics according to the image or picture they evoke (e.g. *pull someone's leg* or *that is rather a mouthful* would appear under the heading of *body idioms*). This can of course scarcely be called semantic, for hardly any of the formatives that seem to refer to a body part have that meaning in the idiom. Another approach is to see what idioms there are to express a concept such as *fear* or *happiness* in English. A recent attempt to make idioms teachable and learnable is made by Latty (1986), who divides the 500 idioms she has examined into four categories. There are idioms with a focus on the individual (*keep a stiff upper lip, throw in the towel, die a thousand deaths*); those with a focus on the world (*go down the drain, be touch and go, that takes the cake* (BrE *the biscuit*)); those that refer to the interaction of individuals (*lend somebody a helping hand, somebody is not fit to hold a candle to somebody else*); and those which express the interaction between the individual and the world (*take up arms for something, know something inside out, it's all*

Greek to me). It remains to be seen whether these attempts will significantly improve the learning of idioms.

Idioms have also been categorized according to various syntactic criteria. It has been mentioned above that idioms fall into two groups, depending on whether they are formed in accordance with the rules of present-day English or not. Another classificatory scheme lists idioms according to their part of speech, i.e. nominal (*black market*, *red herring*), adjectival (*down-to-earth*, *happy-go-lucky*) or verbal (*go in for*, *put up with*, *cook the books*, *blow one's top*; see Gläser 1986). More revealing about the structural peculiarity of idioms at sentence level is the classification of idioms according to what transformations they allow (Fraser 1970). Fraser sets up a so-called **frozenness hierarchy** in which idioms have been arranged into six groups, ranging from those which are totally frozen, i.e. admit no transformation at all, to those at the other end of the scale which show almost no restrictions. The transformations Fraser takes into account are, for example, insertions, transpositions, gerund, passive and cleft-sentence transformations. The fixed nature of idioms is shown by the fact that there are no idioms which allow all six transformations, while there are some which do not allow any transformation at all, as in *bite off one's tongue* and *face the music*. As we saw with binomials, there seems to be a link between the degree of syntactic frozenness and the degree of semantic opacity.

Some of the reasons why certain idioms do or do not allow transformations seem to be idiosyncratic; for others, semantic reasons can be given. Idioms will resist the isolation of one formative for emphasis, for example, in cleft-sentence constructions (**it was her throat that he jumped down*) as well as adjectival and adverbial modification (**he jumped down her sore throat*) because both operations presuppose that formatives are semantic constituents, which they are not. *Throat* in *he jumped down her throat* has no isolable meaning in the idiom and can therefore not be modified (cf. Cruse 1986: 38). For the same reason, substitutions are not usually possible in idioms: **kick the pail*, **inter the hatchet*, **leap down someone's throat*, **in a russet study*. Insertions are, however, possible in some cases (they are printed in bold): *that rings a **faint** bell*; *he is going to come a **hell of a** cropper*; *the recipes are no great **culinary** shakes*.

2.5.3 Idioms and simple lexemes

As idioms, like single-word lexemes, show unitary meaning, linguists have wondered whether idioms behave more like simple lexemes or more like phrases or clauses. The answer is that they show characteristics of both. If *jump down -'s throat* behaved like a single-word lexeme the past tense would be **he jump-down-my-throated*, which it is not. Neither **redder herring* nor **red herringer* are attested, nor is **roll out the red carpets*, though *red herrings* and *John has bees in his bonnet about many things* (Cruse 1986: 38) are found. It would seem, then, that formatives (nouns, adjectives and verbs) are restricted in their freedom to share in the inflectional processes typical of their part of speech.

2.6 Proverbs and commonplaces

The last two types of fixed expression, **proverbs** and **commonplaces** (or **truisms**, **platitudes**), are free utterances or self-contained statements (Norrick 1985: 35). Both can be equivalent to a complete sentence:

> Yesterday, I had a narrow escape. A bullet came through the windshield and creased my helmet. But a miss is as good as a mile [proverb] and if I am for it, I am for it [commonplace].
>
> (J. Gray and E. Peterson, *Billy Bishop Goes to War*, p. 397)

In this section the most important criteria for defining and classifying proverbs and commonplaces will be reviewed (for a detailed treatment, see Norrick 1985: 31–79; Mieder 1989: 13–27 provides a concise overview).

2.6.1 Definition

Commonplaces are usually complete sentences, but this is not always the case with proverbs, where shortened versions are quite common. Shortening and other changes (additions, variations, transpositions) do not necessarily affect the intelligibility of proverbs, presumably because they are so well known that even fragments and mutations are easily associated with the full form, and indeed appreciated for their novelty, by senders and addressees alike:

> I will write a long letter to my old mucker in Melbourne, I thought, and kill two birds with one tome. I'll get it all off my chest . . . and at the same time relieve the dreariness of his Australian exile by providing an opportunity for jealousy, irritation, disapproval and condescension.
>
> (M. Frayn, *The Trick of It*, p. 17; *tome* instead of *stone*)

> He could be quite bad-tempered to his clients. You'd have thought as they were paying the money that they'd call the tune and do the bullying. That wasn't so. Santonix bullied them.
>
> (A. Christie, *Endless Night*, p. 23; the essence (*pay*, *call*, *tune*) is kept in this variation on *He who pays the piper calls the tune*.)

> It would have been a chance to have a quick word with Gabrielle before Wellieboots turned up . . . but her husband still looked as if he was being a bit soppy and I felt as if I'd sort of be barging in on a two's company situation.

(S. Caudwell, *The Sirens Sang of Murder*, p. 131; this shortened form of *Two's company, three's a crowd/* . . . three is none (AmE) is here used as part of a noun phrase, in the function of attributive modifier).

Proverbs as a class cannot be completely frozen, as is shown by the possibility of various additions and insertions (for more examples, see Gläser 1989: 46-50). There are expressions that mark proverbs as such, for example, *(as) they say*, *it is said*, or *as the proverb goes*, which can precede, interrupt or follow the respective proverb. Norrick calls these **proverbial affixes** and contrasts them with **proverbial infixes** such as *proverbial, ever-lovin'*, and *(good) ol'*, which 'can be inserted before any stressed noun phrase in a proverb' (Norrick 1985: 45). An example is *The proverbial pen is mightier than the sword* (ibid.). Proverb collections often list a number of variant forms, which shows that variability is a characteristic trait of proverbs. Transformations such as the cleft-sentence construction do not change proverbs out of all recognition (*It is while the iron is hot that it should be struck*), in contrast to most idioms which, treated the same way, would become meaningless or allow only a literal reading.

Proverbs often show irregular syntax (*Like father, like son* 'a son will resemble his father'; *Penny wise, pound foolish*; *Handsome is as handsome does* 'what counts is not appearance, etc., but one's actions'), while truisms conform to the syntactic rules of contemporary English. The vocabulary used in proverbs tends to be Anglo-Saxon or at least everyday-English lexis, and is more varied than that in truisms. Both proverbs and commonplaces are concerned with general rather than specific meanings, which is why the past tense is not normally found with them (Norrick 1985: 70). Proverbs make a claim to wide, but perhaps not universal, validity (see Redfern 1989: 119), while commonplace remarks are expected to apply everywhere and at all times. Proverbs are therefore sometimes semantically restricted, which comes through in modifications such as restrictive relative clauses (*People who live in glass houses should not throw stones, he who pays the piper calls the tune*). Truisms do not have this feature: *You/we (all) live and learn*; *You only live once*; *Business is business* or *Enough is enough*. Many proverbs are metaphorical and may pose problems for understanding, while commonplaces are usually literal and easy to process. Proverbs also show other features such as hyperbole, metonymy and paradox (see Norrick 1985: 101–43). Proverbs survive 'presumably because they derive from some deep-rooted need of the mind for formulaic expression, in catchy form' (Redfern 1989: 125), but the proverb pattern is no longer productive. Commonplaces seem to have taken over from proverbs in this respect, and three patterns are often distinguished: **tautologies** (*Enough is enough*, *Orders are orders*), **truisms** (*We only live once*) and **sayings based on everyday experience** (*Accidents happen*; *You never know*; *It's a small world*). Particularly productive is the pattern of tautologies, many of which are produced every day without making their way into the dictionaries (contrast the common *Enough is enough* with the nonce formation *A cupboard is a cupboard*). Proverbs on the other hand are well established and traditional, recorded in many collections and dictionaries (cf. Smith 1970; Simpson 1982). Proverbs contain 'a good dose of common sense, experience, wisdom and above all truth' (Mieder 1989: 15). One perhaps surprising aspect of folk wisdom is that it expresses the complexities of life in sayings which contradict each other: compare *Opposites attract* and *Birds of a feather flock together*, *Fine feathers make fine birds* and *Clothes do not make the man*, and finally *Out of sight, out of mind* and *Absence makes the heart grow fonder*. Proverbs show structural patterns as well as prosodic features not (typically) found with commonplaces, such as a two-part structure, alliteration, rhyme and lexical repetition: *Once bitten, twice shy*; *Easy come, easy go*; *A friend in need is a friend indeed*; *All that glitters is not gold*. Indeed, some writers think that 'it is the shape, the clinchingness, that matters even more than the content' (Redfern 1989: 121).

Proverbs, like collocations, binomials and idioms, are folklore items, have no known authors and cannot be traced to specific sources. It has been said that people who use proverbs belong to the lower classes (cf. Alexander 1978–9), but this seems doubtful. Perhaps a more useful distinction is between those who change them deliberately in order to achieve a special effect, and those who do not change them. It seems safe to say, however, that both proverbs and commonplaces tend to be used by older people rather than younger ones. This fact is exploited in S. Townsend's novel *The Secret Diary of Adrian Mole Aged 13¾*, where one finds comic entries such as this from the hero (almost 14 years old): 'My father was right. I didn't need two suitcases of clothes. Still it is better to be safe than sorry, I always say' (p. 70).

In sum, various aspects of the definition of proverbs and commonplaces have been mentioned. Commonplaces are complete sentences, fall into three classes, claim universal validity and are non-metaphorical, which explains both why they are easy to understand and why there is no need to list them in dictionaries. Proverbs are traditional, express general ideas and show non-literal meaning (metaphorical, metonymic); they can be added to, transformed and abbreviated. Proverbs are equivalent to a sentence and are also prototypically characterized by certain metrical, structural and prosodic features. Both types of expression tend to be used by older speakers.

2.7 Fixed expressions in texts

The discussion so far has concentrated largely on the description of fixed expressions from a structural, systematic point of view. This final section will take a brief look at how these expressions function in texts. The present treatment will necessarily be sketchy, but see Gläser (1986: 153–64), and the essays in Gréciano (1989) and Földes (1992).

The first point is that fixed expressions, like birds of a feather, tend to flock together: one often finds more than one such expression in the same place, as in the following example:

> RONALD: . . . I think the bank could probably see their way to helping you out.
> SIDNEY: Ah well, that's wonderful news . . . that means I can put in a definite bid for the adjoining site – which hasn't incidentally come on the market. I mean, as I said, this is all purely through personal contacts.
> R: Quite so, yes.
> S: I mean, the site value alone – just taking it as a site – you follow me?
> R: Oh, yes.
> S: But it is a matter of striking while the iron's hot – before it goes off the boil . . .
> R: Mmm . . .
> S: I mean, in this world it's dog eat dog, isn't it? No place for sentiment. Not in business. I mean, all right, so on occasions you can scratch mine. I'll scratch yours . . .
> R: Beg your pardon?
> S: Tit for tat. But when the chips are down it's every man for himself and blow you, Jack, I regret to say . . .
> R: Exactly.
>
> (A. Ayckbourn, *Absurd Person Singular*, p. 38)

Here both speakers use fixed expressions, which characterizes an informal atmosphere (the scene takes place at a New Year's Eve party): *see one's way to doing something, help someone out, put in a bid, come on the market, strike while the iron is hot, tit for tat*, etc. The massing of fixed expressions in Sidney's language is, however, unusual and reflects his desperate attempt to get Ronald's approval. What Sidney has in mind does not, however, seem to be entirely above board, and he uses all his rhetoric to convince Ronald that what he, Sidney, is planning to do is not only necessary but also common business practice, and therefore quite acceptable. He uses fixed expressions in the belief that Ronald will find it difficult not to agree with them because they express widely accepted maxims. Sidney speaks as one businessman to another, in the hope that this appeal to their common situation will win Ronald over to his side. Ronald's rather curt reactions suggest, however, that he does not see himself on the same level as Sidney (he is Sidney's bank manager), and perhaps resents Sidney's attempt at establishing common ground between them. As Ronald does not seem to be convinced by the first proverb (*strike while the iron* . . .) and idiom (*go off the boil*) Sidney pulls in one more proverb (*dog eat dog* 'no quarter is given') to make his point. He also emphasizes the need for cooperation (proverb: *you scratch my back and I'll scratch yours*). Sidney's final volley consists of another proverb (*tit for tat*) and a commonplace (*it's every man for himself*), a barrage which wears Ronald down so that he concedes the point. Proverbs and commonplaces are here used 'as silencers . . . the last word on the subject' (Redfern 1989: 120).

In this example, Ronald does not openly disagree with Sidney even though he does not seem to like him particularly. The social relationship of small business customer and bank manager puts certain restraints on possible behaviour, as does the party situation. In the next example we find serious disagreement between a wife, who wants a divorce, and her husband, who does not want to grant it:

ARNOLD: I can't bring myself to take you very seriously.
ELIZABETH: You see, I don't love you.
A: Well, I'm awfully sorry. But you weren't obliged to marry me. You've made your bed and I'm afraid you must lie on it.
E: That's one of the falsest proverbs in the English language. Why should you lie on the bed you've made if you don't want to? There's always the floor.
A: For goodness' sake don't be funny, Elizabeth.
E: I've quite made up my mind to leave you, Arnold.

(W. S. Maugham, *The Circle*, p. 56)

Why does Arnold use a form of the proverb *You've made your bed and you must lie on it*? A possible contextual paraphrase of the third sentence in his second speech would run *As you did* [*marry me*]*, you must accept the consequences*. As a synonymous expression for *marry*, the first part of the proverb conveys some meaning, in contrast to the pro-form *do* in the paraphrase, which has no meaning but only reference. In comparison with the literal *marry*, a simple lexeme, *You've made your bed* is figurative language and a multi-word expression. Figurative language can be regarded as unusual when compared with literal language; it stands out and attracts attention to itself. Speakers are especially likely to use figurative language in situations where they want to highlight what they have to say. The proverb is also more weighty than *marry* as it consists of at least four word forms. It makes Arnold's refusal more emphatic. The relative position of literal and figurative expressions is important. When the figurative expression comes first, the literal counterpart has a rational function, usually to comment or provide a gloss. When the literal expression precedes, the figurative item gives the message an emotional colouring, as here. The meaning of a figurative expression is always more than the sum of its parts, so that by using the proverb after the literal counterpart Arnold avails himself of the semantic surplus value of the proverb. There is of course another proverb with similar meaning (*In for a penny, in for a pound*), but the *bed* proverb seems much better suited to the marital context.

Proverbs are said to have a **didactic tendency**: they suggest a course of action (Norrick 1985: 70) or provide a gloss (ironic, pedantic, consolatory, etc.) after the event (Redfern 1989: 119–20). This is sometimes expressed directly (*When in Rome do as the Romans do*; *People in glass houses should not throw stones*), but more often indirectly (*The early bird catches the worm*; *Too many cooks spoil the broth*). This indirect quality of the proverb suits Arnold's nature well; he does not show his anger openly but in a veiled way (*I'm awfully sorry*), although on stage his intonation and gestures may give him away. The proverb relieves him of the burden of thinking up a good argument for his refusal; it is there ready-made, waiting to be used. It also allows him to remain nice to his wife, pretending to side with her against the moral demands of society (*I'm afraid . . .*), while at the same time making his point.

What has been said so far does not, however, explain Elizabeth's very emotional reaction. This is only understandable if she has been put under extreme pressure. Proverbs contain the practical wisdom of a culture as it has accumulated through the centuries. They are thus authoritative state-ments which carry considerable weight and are difficult to contradict. Arnold hides behind the proverb, which he can expect to do a more effective job than he could by flatly refusing his wife's request. But how can Elizabeth hold her own against the overwhelming weight of proverbial wisdom (cf. Hamm 1989: 181)? One possible move is to counter the proverb with another proverb that proves the opposite point (see 2.6.1 for examples of contradictory proverbs). Another possibility is to leave the level of direct interaction and talk about the (use of) the proverb and what it means. Eizabeth here takes this option and makes a meta-communicative statement about the validity of the proverb. But calling it false will not on its own do the job of debunking the proverb. That is why she adds two more sentences. The first is a rhetorical question, quite suited to the emotional atmosphere. The second sentence, on the other hand, is thought highly inappropriate by Arnold. To indulge in word play to contradict him strikes him as frivolous and unacceptable. But it is of a piece with her overall strategy of fighting against conventions: just as she does not accept the truth of conventional wisdom (as encapsulated in proverbs), so she does not accept the con-ventional idiomatic meaning of the proverb and feels free to put a literal interpretation on it. Arnold's use of the proverb, aimed at crushing his wife, has been foiled by the ridiculous effect achieved by Elizabeth, who reactivates the literal meaning of the proverb and thus robs it of any weight it might have.

The use of fixed expressions for word play can be seen as characteristic of certain situations and text types. Punning is common in newspapers (see 2.1 above for examples) and commercial advertisements (see 1.6.8). Puns are also found in the titles of plays (e.g. Oscar Wilde's *The Importance of Being Earnest*) or works of fiction (e.g. Alison Lurie's novel *Foreign*

Affairs, which deals with the love affair of two Americans in England). Fixed expressions, and word play based upon them, are more frequent in social science texts than in the natural sciences (Gläser 1986: 163), and more frequent in popular works on science than in technical scientific texts.

Fixed expressions can have several functions. They generally make people feel at ease and create a sense of belonging to the group (see 2.1). This nearness between the sender of a message and its addressee can make it difficult for the addressee to disagree with the sender – this is clearly the effect that Sidney and Arnold want to exploit. Fixed expressions (idioms, binomials and proverbs) provide stylistic variety and lend emphasis to statements (cf. also Gläser 1986: 153–64). It has also been suggested that speakers use idioms to organize their discourse and to make evaluations (Moon 1987). Proverbs and commonplaces deal with social situations, and their uses are manifold: 'to strengthen our arguments, express certain generalizations, influence or manipulate other people, rationalize our own shortcomings, question certain behavioral patterns, satirize social ills, poke fun of [*sic*] ridiculous situations' (Mieder 1989: 21).

REFERENCES

Alexander, R. (1978–9) 'Fixed expressions in English: a linguistic, psycholinguistic, sociolinguistic and didactic study', *anglistik und englischunterricht* 6: 171–88; 7: 181–202.

—— (1987) 'Problems in understanding and teaching idiomaticity in English', *anglistik und englischunterricht* 32: 105–22.

Atwood, M. (1989) *Cat's Eye*, London: Abacus.

Ayckbourn, A. (1979) *Absurd Person Singular* in *Three Plays*, Harmondsworth: Penguin.

Bäcklund, U. (1973) *The Collocation of Adverbs of Degree in English*, Uppsala: Uppsala University Press.

—— (1976) 'Frozen adjective–noun collocations in English', in P. A. Reich (ed.) *The Second Lacus Forum 1975*, Columbia, SC: Hornbeam Press, pp. 255–71.

—— (1980) 'Candid and frank', *Cahiers de lexicologie* 36: 57–79.

Bennett, T. J. A. (1988) *Aspects of English Colour Collocations and Idioms*, Heidelberg: Winter.

Benson, M., Benson, E. and Ilson, R. (1986) *The BBI Combinatory Dictionary of English*, Amsterdam: Benjamins.

Blundell, J., Higgens, J. and Middlemiss, N. (1982) *Function in English*, Oxford: Oxford University Press.

Bolinger, D. (1972) *Degree Words*, The Hague: Mouton.

—— (1976) 'Meaning and memory', *Forum Linguisticum* 1: 1–14.

Brook, G. L. (1981) *Words in Everyday Life*, London: Macmillan.

Burger, H., Buhofer, A. and Sialm, A. (1982) *Handbuch der Phraseologie*, Berlin: de Gruyter.

Burton, D. (1980) *Dialogue and Discourse*, London: Routledge & Kegan Paul.

Butler, C. S. (1985) *Systemic Linguistics*, London: Batsford.

Carter, R. (ed.) (1982) *Language and Literature: an Introductory Reader in Stylistics*, London: Allen & Unwin.

—— (1987) *Vocabulary*, London: Allen & Unwin.
Carter, R. and Nash, W. (1990) *Seeing through Language*, Oxford: Blackwell.
Caudwell, S. (1990) *The Sirens Sang of Murder*, Glasgow: Collins.
Christie, A. (1967) *Endless Night*, London and Glasgow: Collins.
Collins COBUILD English Language Dictionary (1987) ed. J. Sinclair, London: Collins.
The Concise Oxford Dictionary of Current English (1991) 8th edn, ed. R. E. Allen, Oxford: Oxford University Press.
The Oxford Dictionary of English Proverbs (1970) ed. W. G. Smith, rev. F. P. Wilson, 3rd edn, Oxford: Oxford University Press.
The Concise Oxford Dictionary of Proverbs (1982) ed. J. A. Simpson, Oxford University Press.
Cooper, J. (1991) *Polo*, London: Transworld.
Cruse, D. (1986) *Lexical Semantics*, Cambridge: Cambridge University Press.
Edmondson, W. and House, J. (1981) *Let's Talk and Talk About It*, Munich: Urban & Schwarzenberg.
Encylopædia Britannica (1974) 15th edn, Chicago.
Fernando, C. (1978) 'Towards a definition of idiom: its nature and function', *Studies in Language* 2: 313–43.
Firth, J. R. (1957) 'Modes of meaning', in *Papers in Linguistics 1934–1951*, London: Oxford University Press, pp. 190–215.
Földes, C. (ed.) (1992) *Deutsche Phraseologie im Sprachsystem und in der Sprachverwendung*, Vienna: Ernst.
Fowler, R. (1986) *Linguistic Criticism*, Oxford: Oxford University Press.
Fraser, B. (1970) 'Idioms within a transformational grammar', *Foundations of Language* 6: 22–42.
Frayn, M. (1989) *The Trick of It*, London: Viking.
Gläser, R. (1986) *Phraseologie der englischen Sprache*, Tübingen: Niemeyer.
—— (1989) 'A plea for phraseo-stylistics', in D. Kastovsky and A. Szwedek (eds) *Descriptive, Contrastive and Applied Linguistics*, Vol. 2 of *Linguistics Across Historical and Geographical Boundaries*, Berlin: Mouton de Gruyter, pp. 41–52.
Gray, J. and Peterson, E. (1986) *Billy Bishop Goes to War*, in J. Wasserman (ed.) *Modern Canadian Plays*, Vancouver: Talon Books.
Gréciano, G. (ed.) (1989) *Europhras 88 phraséologie contrastive*, Strasbourg: Université des Sciences Humaines, Département d'Études Allemandes.
Greenbaum, S. (1970) *Verb-intensifier Collocations in English*, The Hague: Mouton.
—— (1974) 'Some verb-intensifier collocations in American and British English,' *American Speech* 49: 79–89.
Gülich, E. and Henke, K. (1979/1980) 'Sprachliche Routine in der Alltagskommunikation', *Die neueren Sprachen* 78 (1979): 513–30; 79 (1980): 2–33.
Gustafsson, M. (1974) 'The phonetic length of the members in present-day English binomials', *Neuphilologische Mitteilungen* 75: 663–77.
—— (1976) 'The frequency and "frozenness" of some English binomials', *Neuphilologische Mitteilungen* 77: 623–37.
Hamm, A. (1989) 'Remarques sur le fonctionnement de la négation dans les proverbes: l'exemple de l'anglais', in G. Gréciano (ed.) *Europhras 88 Phraséologie Contrastive*, Strasbourg: Université des Sciences Humaines, Département d'Études Allemandes, pp. 177–194.
Hasan, R. and Halliday, M. A. K. (1976) *Cohesion in English*, Harlow: Longman.

Hausmann, F. J. (1984) 'Wortschatzlernen ist Kollokationslernen', *Praxis des neusprachlichen Unterrichts* 31: 395–406.

Howard, P. (1984) 'Cliché', in *The State of the Language*, London: Hamish Hamilton, pp. 87–99.

James. P. D. (1981) *Death of an Expert Witness*, London: Sphere.

Johansson, S. and Hofland, K. (1989) *Frequency Analysis of English Vocabulary and Grammar*, 2 vols, Oxford: Oxford University Press.

Jones, S. and Sinclair, J. M. (1974) 'English lexical collocations', *Cahiers de lexicologie*, 30: 15–61.

Kastovsky, D. (1980) 'Selectional restrictions and lexical solidarities', in D. Kastovsky (ed.) *Perspektiven der Lexikalischen Semantik*, Bonn: Bouvier, pp. 70–92.

Latty, E. (1986) 'Pragmatic classification of idioms as an aid for the language learner', *International Review of Applied Linguistics* 24: 217–33.

Lee, W. R. (1983) *A Study Dictionary of Social English*, Oxford: Pergamon.

Leech, G. N. (1969) *A Linguistic Guide to English Poetry*, London: Longman.

—— (1981) *Semantics*, 2nd edn, Harmondsworth: Penguin.

Leech, G. N. and Short, M. H. (1981) *Style in Fiction*, London: Longman.

Longman Dictionary of Contemporary English (1987) 2nd edn, ed. D. Summers, Harlow: Longman.

Luelsdorff, P. (1981) *What is a Cliché?*, Trier: LAUT Papers, Series A, no. 85.

McCarthy, M. J. (1990) *Vocabulary*, Oxford: Oxford University Press.

Mackin, R. (1978) 'On collocations: "words shall be known by the company they keep"', in P. Strevens (ed.) *In Honour of A. S. Hornby*, Oxford: Oxford University Press, pp. 149–65.

Malkiel, J. (1959) 'Studies in irreversible binomials', *Lingua*, 8: 113–60.

Maugham, W. S. (1931) *The Circle*, in *Collected Plays*, vol. 2, London: Heinemann.

Mieder, W. (1989) *American Proverbs*, Berne: Lang.

Moon, R. (1987) *Idioms in Text*, MS. Birmingham: English Language Research.

Nolan, C. (1988) *Under the Eye of the Clock*, London: Pan.

Norrick, N. (1985) *How Proverbs Mean*, Berlin: Mouton.

—— (1988) 'Binomial meaning in texts', *Journal of English Linguistics* 21: 72–87.

The Oxford English Dictionary (1989) 2nd edn, prepared by J. A. Simpson and E. S. C. Weiner, 20 vols, Oxford: Oxford University Press.

Partridge, E. (1954) *Dictionary of Clichés*, London: Routledge & Kegan Paul.

Raven, S. (1985) *Places where they Sing*, London: Granada.

Redfern, W. (1989) *Clichés and Coinages*, Oxford: Blackwell.

Ricks, C. (1980) 'Clichés', in L. Michaels and C. Ricks (eds) *The State of the Language*, Berkeley: University of California Press, pp. 54–63.

Rodale, J. I. (1947) *The Word Finder*, Emmaus, Pa.: Rodale.

Roos, E. (1975) *Kollokationsmöglichkeiten der Verben des Sehvermögens im Deutschen und Englischen*, Berne: Lang.

Ruhl, C. (1989) *On Monosemy*, Albany: State University of New York Press.

Sandig, B. (1983) *Stilistik*, 2 vols, Hildesheim: Olms.

Scobie, S. (1984) 'A marriage of convenience', in J. Metcalf and L. Rooke (eds) *Best Canadian Short Fiction*, Toronto: New Press.

Sebeok, T. (ed.) (1960) *Style in Language*, Cambridge, Mass.: Massachusetts Institute of Technology.

Sinclair, J. M. (1991) *Corpus, Concordance, Collocation*, Oxford: Oxford University Press.

Smith, G. (1985) *The English Companion*, Harmondsworth: Penguin.

Strässler, J. (1982) *Idioms in English*, Tübingen: Narr.

Townsend, S. (1983) *The Secret Diary of Adrian Mole Aged 13¾*, London: Methuen.
—— (1985) *The Growing Pains of Adrian Mole*, London: Methuen.
Vallins, G. H. (1969) *Good English*, London: Deutsch.
van Dijk, T. A. (ed.) (1985) *Discourse and Literature*, Amsterdam: Benjamins.
Ward, B. (1979) *Progress for a Small Planet*, Harmondsworth: Penguin.
Welte, W. (1990) *Englische Phraseologie und Idiomatik*, Frankfurt am Main: Lang.
—— (1992) 'On the properties of English phraseology', in A. Bammesberger and T. Kirschner (eds) *Language and Civilization*, Frankfurt am Main: Lang, pp. 597–624.
Whittal, Y. (1978) *Scars of Yesterday*, London: Mills and Boon.
Zöfgen, E. (ed.) (1992) 'Idiomatik und Phraseologie', *Fremdsprachen Lehren und Lernen* 21.

Chapter 3

The pronunciation and spelling of English

This chapter deals with the phonology of English together with a certain degree of phonetic detail and the essentials of English orthography. Naturally, a treatment of this length cannot take the place of a textbook in phonetics and phonology or a manual of spelling. Its aim is, rather, to present fundamental and systematic characteristics as well as tendencies in the development of English pronunciation and to give the principles of English spelling in outline. A readable introduction to phonetics and phonology is Roach 1991; for phonetics, Gimson 1989 and, less technically, Knowles 1987; for spelling, see Wijk 1966 or Venezky 1970.

3.1 The phonology of English

In order to talk about the sound structure of English it is necessary to make certain abstractions from actual sounds. This means that the varied phonetic realization of the many speakers and the many varieties of English (idiolects, dialects, network standards, registers, etc.) will be less at the centre of attention than what these various pronunciations share. This procedure stands in contrast to an **acoustic, auditory** or **articulatory** description of a particular variety, which is what the discipline of **phonetics** would provide. Instead we assume a system that ignores the exact phonetic details of actual speakers, but rather deals with the meaningful sound contrasts or oppositions of the spoken language of as many varieties as possible. This then, is a sketch of the **phonology** of English (see below 3.1).

Fortunately for such a description, the inventory of the phonemes of those forms of English which speakers of Standard English (StE) use all over the world reveals only relatively small differences (cf. Wells 1982: 122ff, 178). This observation relies on the recognition of 'standard' pronunciations, above all, of the widely accepted ones called **Received Pronunciation** or **RP** (in England) and **General American (GenAm)** in North America. These and other standard accents such as Cultivated Australian (see 13.1.1), Conservative South African English (13.3.1), or Standard Scottish English (10.2.3) are in many respects artificial; for example, they gloss over a great many differences based on the class, gender, age, or even region of the speakers. General American, for one, is ill defined in the extreme and covers a wide array of geographical areas (cf. Van Riper 1986). RP, for its part, is frequently divided into 'conservative', 'advanced' and 'affected', categories which correspond at least partly to age (see 10.1.2). In addition, studies all over the English-speaking world have revealed class and male–female distinctions in pronunciation. Nevertheless, speakers everywhere do seem to recognize the existence of pronunciation norms and even to agree to an astonishingly high degree on what they are. Furthermore, this is not the case with numerous non-standard dialects such as Lowland Scots (10.2.2), pidgin and creole English (chapter 16), or English as a second or foreign language (chapters 14 and 15). It is because of this that we feel justified in proceeding as we do and outlining here, based chiefly on RP and GenAm, what we call 'the pronunciation of English'.

This presentation of English pronunciation deals first with the consonants and the vowels, i.e. the segmental sounds, and after that with the suprasegmentals, viz. juncture, stress and intonation.

3.2 Segmental sounds

It is possible to divide up completely every linguistic utterance into segments which belong to a limited inventory of sounds. These sounds are called **phonemes**, and they are central to the approach used here. This concept is of great usefulness because it provides for an abstract level of description which embodies the systematic sound contrasts of the language without becoming lost in minute phonetic detail. Nevertheless, it is not so abstract that it does not reflect the actual sounds of the language.

The segmental sounds are divided into vowels and consonants. A **vowel** is defined, *phonetically*, as a sound which is produced without audible friction or blockage in the flow of air along the central line of breath from the lungs through the mouth. To this must be added the *phonemic* or structural observation that vowels always form the centre of a syllable. All other sounds are consonants. Note, however, that these two approaches do not lead to the same results. In this description, the phonemic view will generally be favoured (see 3.3).

For English it is possible to postulate twenty-four consonants as well as sixteen vowels (in GenAm) or twenty vowels (in RP). Each of these phonemes should be fully distinct from each of the others within its (RP or GenAm) system. The idea behind the concept of the phoneme is that it designates the smallest unit of sound which causes a potential difference in meaning. This principle can be demonstrated through the use of what are called **minimal pairs**: if two words which differ in regard to one sound only have different meanings, then the two differing sounds are not the same phoneme. By a process of extension to ever more such oppositions in sound and meaning, it is theoretically possible to establish just which sounds are the phonemes of a given language such as English or a particular accent of a language such as RP or GenAm. In figure 3.1 *mat* differs from *gnat, met* and *mad* in meaning. This demonstrates that /m/ is not the same as /n/, that /t/ is distinct from /d/, and that /æ/ and /e/ are not identical. Eventually all the possible combinations might be tried out until it is established that English has the number of phonemes mentioned above.

In reality, however, sounds occur that cannot always be clearly attributed to one single phoneme. For example, the second sound in the word *stop* is, despite the spelling, neither unambiguously a /t/ nor a /d/. This has to do with the fact that /p, t, k/, which are normally **aspirated**, i.e. pronounced with a brief puff of breath, are not aspirated after a preceding /s/ in the same syllable; as a result the **unaspirated** sounds /b, d, g/ cannot be distinguished from them. This is all the more the case since /b, d, g/, which are typically **voiced** (i.e. the vocal chords vibrate when they are pronounced), tend to lose their voicing (to become **devoiced**) following /s/ and so to resemble /p, t, k/, which are always **voiceless**. Here, in other words, the difference between /t/ and /d/ and between /g/ and /k/ is **neutralized** (*disdain* is pronounced identically with *distain*, and *disgust* is indistinguishable from *discussed*). A sound which realizes two or more neutralized phonemes is sometimes referred to as an **archiphoneme** and transcribed with a capital letter symbol, in this case as /T/ (see Davidsen-Nielsen 1974).

The example of neutralization shows that phonemes may have phonetic traits or characteristics in common; that is, indeed, why /t/ and /d/ are so similar. An explanation for this may be seen in the fact that each phoneme is defined by a number of features that are characteristic for it and for it alone. /t/, for example, can be (a) **alveolar** (articulated at the tooth ridge; see figure 3.2 on page 90), (b) aspirated, (c) voiceless, and (d) plosive. A **plosive** phoneme (also called a **stop**) is one which is articulated by momentarily stopping the flow of air and then releasing the built-up pressure with a

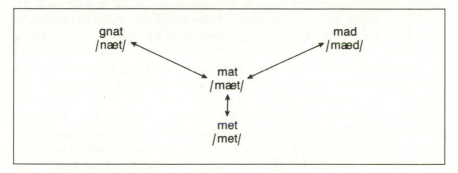

Figure 3.1 Examples of phoneme oppositions

kind of explosive force. /d/ is also alveolar and plosive; however, it is not aspirated and, while sometimes voiceless, is typically voiced. Common features characterize the similarities between phonemes while the particular combination of features distinguishes each from all others.

Within the system of English consonants, three features are sufficient to distinguish all the consonants from each other: **place of articulation**, **manner of articulation** and **force of articulation** (hard or **fortis** versus soft or **lenis**). Lenis is regularly associated with voicing (vibration of the vocal chords) and fortis with voicelessness. For the vowels three features are also sufficient to make all the necessary distinctions of English: **the height of the tongue**, **the horizontal position of the tongue** and the **complexity of the vowel** (short vs. long/diphthong). The features named, which distinguish every phoneme from every other one, are only a selection from among all the many possible features possessed in reality by any of these sounds; for this reason they are called **distinctive features**. These features have been chosen for the purposes of representing the systematic oppositions within the sound system of English; as such they belong to the area of phonology, which deals with the sounds of a particular language as a system, rather than to phonetics, which deals with all the sound features of speech.

In the sense of phonetics, or actual articulation, any particular phoneme may sound very different from occasion to occasion. In particular, the phonetic environment in which a phoneme is produced may cause extremely noticeable differences in actual pronunciation. However, as long as the exchange of one such variant for another does not cause a difference in meaning, each of the realizations may be regarded as one and the same phoneme. Varying pronunciations of each 'single sound' are known as the **allophones** of a phoneme. It is usual to enclose the symbol for an allophone in square brackets, [ ], while phonemes are put between slanted lines, / /.

A readily observable example of such allophones is /l/, which may be pronounced as a **clear** [l], as in *million* (it has some of the quality of the vowel /iː/ as in *fee* associated with it). This pronunciation typically occurs when /l/ precedes a vowel in RP. However, the /l/ may be **dark** [ɫ], as in *pull*, which means it has some of the sound quality of the vowel /ʊ/ as in *foot*. This is the way an /l/ is pronounced in RP when it is not followed by a vowel. The difference between the two is easy to hear; however, if they are exchanged one for the other, the words in which they occur do not become different words or unidentifiable sound sequences. (For more on /l/, see below 3.3.1 **The lateral**).

This is not always unproblematic, for in some accents of English (Cockney, various areas in the United States), /l/ is completely **vocalized**, that is, realized more or less like the vowel /ʊ/. In this case there is the possibility that new **homophones** (words which sound alike, but carry different meanings) may be created. The following words may, for example, be pronounced similarly in Cockney: *Paul* [pɔːʊ] or [pɔɪə], *paw*, *pore*, *poor* [pɔː] or [pɔːə] (cf. Wells 1982: 316). The question is whether the [ʊ] of [pɔːʊ] (*Paul*) is an allophone of /l/ or whether it has merged with the phoneme /ʊ/.

Besides such allophonic problems in the description of the consonants and the vowels there are two other areas which belong to the subject of the segmental sounds: phonological processes (3.3.5) such as the phonemic realization of particular morphemes (roots, prefixes, suffixes, inflectional endings) and phonotactics (3.3.6), which has to do with the possible and specifically English distribution and combination of phonemes.

3.3 Consonants

The inventory of English consonants has remained stable to a remarkable degree over several hundred years. As a result it is the consonants which contribute most to the phonological unity of the English language in its many and often quite different-sounding accents throughout the world. The form of any English word is most easily characterized by the position and type of combination of its consonants: 'Consonants are, in general, the more permanent elements in a language: they are, as it were, the skeleton' (Potter 1979: 64).

Since the first Germanic sound shift (also known as Grimm's Law) in the third or second century BC, there have been no major changes. However, in the Middle English period (roughly between 1050 and 1500) the three sounds [ð], [ʒ] and [ŋ], which up until then had been allophones of /θ/, /ʃ/ and /n/, became independent phonemes. In the same period the phoneme /x/ (the consonant sound of German *ach* or *ich*, which once regularly appeared in words still written with ⟨gh⟩ such as *right* or *thought*) disappeared in all but a few regions, most particularly the local dialects of Scotland. In addition, the phoneme /hw/ (as in *which*) is presently losing its status as an independent phoneme for more and more speakers as it converges with /w/ (as in *witch*) — something that has already happened in RP and for most GenAm speakers.

The consonants may be divided up into the following types as far as the degree of their consonant-like nature is concerned:

Semi-vowels are consonants which are usually produced without audible friction in, or stoppage of, the air coming from the lungs; phonetically, therefore, they are vowel-like. However, they do not form the centre of a syllable, but are peripheral; that is, they are found initially or finally. In this phonological sense, they are consonants. The semi-vowels of English include /w, r, j/, though each also has variants (allophones) which involve friction and/or stoppage. /r/ is also sometimes regarded as a **frictionless continuant** or **approximant** (cf. Gimson 1989: 206–12). /h/ may be said to belong here as well; for, although it is not **sonorous** (that is, it is not produced with vibration of the vocal chords), but voiceless, it has as many variants (or allophones), as there are vowels which may follow it. For this reason it will be designated a **voiceless vowel** (i.e. it is whispered). However, it is also often termed **glottal fricative** (e.g. Gimson 1989: 192–4), which would put it in the group of obstruents below.

The **sonorants** are sounds which are articulated with a partial closure of the respiratory passage and vibration of the vocal chords. They are usually found at an initial or a final position in the syllable; however, under certain circumstances they may also be **syllabic**, i.e. central to a syllable. This is, for example, true of the /l/ in *bottle* [bɒtl̩] (the small stroke under the *l* indicates that it is syllabic). In this sense sonorants sometimes resemble vowels phonologically. They include the nasals /m, n, ŋ/, which are articulated with closure of the mouth (the air stream is released through the nose) and the lateral /l/, which has partial closure of the mouth at the alveolar ridge, with a lateral release of air around the sides of the tongue where it touches the top of the mouth.

The **obstruents**, finally, are the 'true' consonants, which are produced with friction (the **fricatives**), for example /f, ð, ʃ/, complete closure and blockage of the air stream (**stops** or **occlusives** or **plosives**), for example /p, d, g/, or a combination of the two (the **affricates**), /tʃ, dʒ/. Furthermore, they are always peripheral to the syllable.

Phonologically, the system of English consonants is characterized by a high degree of symmetry. Twenty-four (with /hw/, twenty-five) consonants

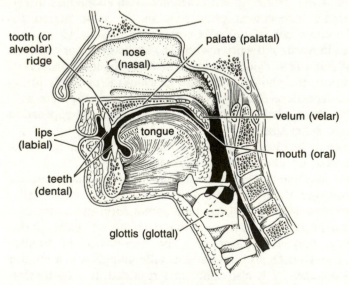

Organs of speech (and corresponding adjectives)

Figure 3.2 The places of articulation

can be distinguished according to three distinctive features, as mentioned above. These are

1 **place of articulation**, of which there are four main ones (lips, alveolar or tooth ridge, the post-alveolar or pre-palatal region between the alveolar ridge and the palate, and the palate itself) and one less frequently used one (the teeth);
2 **manner of articulation**, of which there are seven types (stop or plosive, affricate, fricative, nasal, lateral, semi-vocalic, and voiceless vocalic);
3 **force of articulation**, which distinguishes soft or **lenis** from hard or **fortis**. This distinction generally coincides with voicing, that is, the distinction between **voiced** and **voiceless**. This third opposition involves only the stops, affricates, and fricatives (i.e. the obstruents). For more detail see the following sections.

Despite the stability of the system mentioned above, many of the phonemes listed in table 3.1 are involved in a noticeable process of change in one or another variety of English somewhere in the world. These changes are, however, seldom of phonological significance. In the following the distinctive features will first be briefly explained (3.3.1 and 3.3.2). Following this there will be some comments on restriction in distribution (3.3.3) and a few of the changes in progress (3.3.4) before phonological processes (3.3.5) and phonotactics (3.3.6) are reviewed.

Table 3.1 The consonants of English

Manner	Labial	Dental	Place Alveolar	Post-alv.	Palatal
stop[1]	p b		t d		k g
affricate[1]				tʃ dʒ	
fricative[1]	f v	θ ð	s z	ʃ ʒ	
nasal	m		n		ŋ
lateral[2]			l		ɫ
semi-vowel[3]			j	r	w
voiceless vowel[4]			h		

[1] The left-hand symbol represents the fortis or voiceless phoneme; the one on the right, the lenis or voiced one.
[2] [l] and [ɫ] are allophones of /l/; see below.
[3] /hw/ is present in some accents.
[4] /h/ is realized in numerous positional variants, see below.

3.3.1 Manner and place of articulation

Obstruents The high degree of symmetry in the occurrence of the stops and the fricatives is very noticeable. (Note that labio-dental /f/ and /v/ are classified as labial.) There are four pairs of stops and four of fricatives if the affricates /tʃ/ and /dʒ/, which consist of a close connection of a stop and a **homorganic** fricative (one produced at the same place or organ of speech), are counted with the stops, as has been done in the table. There has long been discussion about whether /tʃ/ and /dʒ/ are each a single phoneme or a combination of two. It seems there is no unambiguous phonetic evidence which might help to settle this question. Phonologically, however, the freedom with which both may appear initially (*cheese, job*), medially (*bachelor, major*) or finally (*rich, ridge*) in words is a small indication of their unitary (one-phoneme) status (for a summary of evidence, see Roach 1991: chapter 13). Aside from this point, note that there is a lack of balance between the stops and the fricatives, a 'mismatch' which is caused by the lack of the palatal fricatives /x/ and /ɣ/ and the presence of the dental fricatives /θ/ and /ð/. Note also that the fricative /x/ (like the *ach*-sound of German) with its allophonic variant [ç] (the *ich*-sound) has, as already mentioned, been retained in various Lowland Scots dialects, for example in *night* /neçt/ or *loch* /lox/. Furthermore, many people use it in the pronunciation of foreign words or names such as *Bach* or the interjection *ugh* /ʌx/.

Nasals The nasals do not occur in lenis–fortis (voiced–voiceless) pairs, for they are sonorants and therefore, phonologically speaking, are always voiced. There are only three nasals, since the post-alveolar /ɲ/ of Spanish (*mañana*), Italian (*senior*), or French (*compagnon*) is not phonemic in English; instead, the analogous sound in English is seen as a sequence of two phonemes /nj/ as in *canyon* /kænjən/. Furthermore, the historically more recent addition to the nasals, the phoneme /ŋ/, is not fully equivalent to /m/ and /n/ since it cannot occur initially in a word, nor does it occur after all the vowels of English (in RP it follows /ɪ, æ, ʌ, ɒ/; in GenAm /ɪ, æ, ʌ, ɑː, ɔː/; cf. *sing, sang, sung, song*, the last with /ɑː/ or /ɔː/ in GenAm depending on the region).

The lateral The lateral /l/ differs from the preceding examples of manner of articulation inasmuch as clear [l] and dark [ɫ] are allophones which do not stand in phonemic opposition to each other. Indeed, there are accents such as those of southern Ireland in which clear [l] appears exclusively, and other areas, such as Scotland and some parts of the United States, in which only dark [ɫ] occurs. RP, as previously mentioned, is characterized by the **complementary distribution** of the two allophones. This means that in one set of circumstances only the one may occur and in another set only the other. Concretely, clear [l] is used before vowels (*look, teller*) while dark [ɬ] appears before consonants (*help*) or at the end of a word (*goal*); this includes syllabic [ɬ̩] as in *bottle*).

The semi-vowels   The semi-vowels are difficult to adapt to the scheme of classification used here because, phonetically speaking, they are not consonants at all, but vowels which occur in the typical position of consonants, peripheral to the syllable (see above 3.3). In many classifications /w/ and /hw/ are given as bilabial. The rounding of the lips which is typical of /w/ and /hw/ is, however, of secondary importance and need not be present. Note that prevocalic /r/ is often produced with lip-rounding as well. The criterion which has been used in positioning the semi-vowels in table 3.1 is the position of the tongue: /j/ corresponds to the high front vowel /iː/ because it has the same sound quality as /iː/. /j/ differs only inasmuch as it is extremely short (non-syllabic). Like /iː/ it requires a tongue position close to the alveolar ridge; hence it has been classified as alveolar. /r/ corresponds to the central vowel /ɜː/, which is more or less post-alveolar; and /w/ corresponds to /uː/, a high back vowel, which takes a tongue position close to the velum.

The Voiceless Vowel   /h/ occurs only before vowels and is often designated as a glottal fricative. Since, however, /h/ has a different resonance depending on what vowel follows it, the term voiceless vowel is also employed, a term which does justice to the fact that /h/ is seldom associated with much audible friction and that it has as many allophones as there are vowels which may follow it (namely the entire range).

The glottal stop   This sound, [bʔ],does not have the status of a phoneme, but is so obvious in some accents of English that it will be treated below under 3.3.4.

3.3.2 Force of articulation and voicing

All of the obstruents are members of pairs of phonemes that share the same features in regard to place and manner of articulation. However, the members of each pair differ from each other inasmuch as the one is pronounced with more force or energy ('hard', 'fortis') and is always voiceless, i.e. the vocal chords do not vibrate while it is being pronounced; the other member of each pair is pronounced with relatively less force or energy ('soft', 'lenis') and is often, though not always, voiced. The pair /ʃ /–/ʒ/ differs from the other obstruent pairs inasmuch as /ʒ/, which occurs relatively seldom, appears only at the beginning (*Zhivago*) or at the end (*rouge*) of words which have been borrowed from other languages and have been only imperfectly incorporated into English. In a medial position (*measure*) it is perfectly unexceptional.

The nasals, semi-vowels, and the lateral are always regarded phonologically as voiced, and, indeed, they are usually voiced phonetically as well. However, in a voiceless environment they may, as a matter of actual phonetic realization, become devoiced. /h/ is always voiceless. The voiced obstruents are fully voiced only in a voiced environment, such as between two vowels (the *v* in *giving* or the *d* in *sadder*). At the beginning of a word the sonority or voicing sets in during the course of articulation, which means that voicing may be very imperfect. In word final position the voicing may be completely missing. In both of these cases the lack of voicing is not generally noticed because the distinction between the obstruent pairs is maintained more by force of articulation than by voicing. The /v/ of /laɪv/ is, for example, seldom voiced. The contrast to the /f/ of /laɪf/ is maintained, rather, because /v/ is lenis while /f/ is fortis. In addition, the opposition between the 'voiced' and the 'voiceless' stops in initial position is supported by the aspiration which is associated with the fortis as opposed to the unaspirated lenis phoneme. In English no stops are aspirated after an /s/, as mentioned above in 3.2.

In AmE the distinction between voiceless /t/ and voiced /d/ is neutralized in intervocalic position (provided the following syllable is unstressed); both are pronounced with voicing. Pairs of words such *latter–ladder* cannot, for this reason, be distinguished on the grounds of sonority or force of articulation. (For some speakers, however, the vowel preceding the stop may be longer when a /d/ follows (cf. Sheldon 1973; Fox and Terbeek 1977; Kahn 1980; see also 11.1.3).

3.3.3 Restrictions in distribution

The system of twenty-four consonants which has been assumed here does not mean that the various consonants are fully equivalent. The infrequency of /ŋ/ in comparison with /m/ and /n/ and that of /ʒ/ in comparison with /ʃ/ has already been pointed out. In much the same way the occurrence of initial /ð/ is restricted to the so-called grammatical or function words only, which include pronouns (*they*, *thou*, etc.), the definite article (*the*), the demonstratives (*this*, *that*, *these*, *those*), and such basic adverbs as *there*, *then*, *thus*, etc. In addition, /ð/ never occurs directly before another consonant within the same syllable. The only exception is where inflectional endings are involved, but here the /ð/ is separated from the following consonant by a morpheme boundary, for example, the regular inflectional {D} (=/d/ of the past tense and past participle), as in *smoothed*, or {S} (=/z/ of plural nouns or the third person singular simple present of verbs), as in *paths* or *breathes*.

3.3.4 Consonant changes

All the points in this section have to do with differences which vary considerably from accent to accent. The following will be treated: /hw/, non-prevocalic /r/, non-prevocalic /l/, /h/, [ʔ], /ð/ and /θ/, /j/, palatalization and the simplification of final consonant clusters.

/hw/ is the only consonant that seems to be disappearing completely. Many speakers today use /w/ where once /hw/ was pronounced. In this way numerous ⟨w-⟩ and ⟨wh-⟩ words have become homophonous, for example, *wear* and *where*, *wheel* and *we'll*, *which* and *witch*, etc. Nonetheless, many speakers still use /hw/ as an emphatic variant of /w/, as in *Why?!* /hwaɪ/. As a result there are cases in which people have been known to produce an unhistorical /hwaʊ/ *wow!* (Metcalf 1972: 33). The /hw/−/w/ opposition is still maintained in various American and British accents (e.g. the Northern dialect area in the United States, and Scotland in Great Britain).

Especially noticeable is the disappearance of non-prevocalic ⟨r⟩ in many accents of English. While /r/ is pronounced wherever it is written in GenAm, Irish English, Scottish English, and various parts of the southwest of England, it is missing in such accents as RP, the English of New England and wide areas in the American South, Australia and New Zealand. In these latter accents an /r/ can occur only before a vowel. In talking about this split in the accents of English, it is convenient to speak of **rhotic** and **non-rhotic accents**, i.e. those which have and those which have not retained /r/ in all positions.

In those accents which have retained non-prevocalic /r/ the quality of this phoneme differs considerably. In America, Northern Ireland, parts of Scotland and the English southwest this /r/ is realized chiefly through the quality of the preceding vowel, which is *r*-**coloured**. In parts of southern Ireland and Scotland the /r/ may be rolled at the tip of the tongue [r]. In (old) County Durham and Northumberland it was traditionally realized as uvular /r/, i.e. the 'French' [R] (see Påhlsson 1972: 20, 113, passim).

Just as non-prevocalic *r* has become vocalic ('*r*-coloured vowels'), so, too, is non-prevocalic /l/ not only dark, as mentioned above, but completely vocalic in such widely separated accents as Cockney and Southern American: the tongue no longer touches the top of the mouth; instead, only the dark resonance of the back vowel /ʊ/, which is associated with it, remains (cf. the examples of homophonous *Paul* and *paw* given above for Cockney).

One of the stereotypes of BrE for an American is H-dropping, and, indeed, this is regularly the case not only for much of BrE, but for much of AmE too as far as the change from /hw/ to /w/ is concerned. Beyond this, although an ⟨h⟩ is written in such words as *her*, *him*, *he*, all native speakers drop the /h/ when these words are unstressed (in the so-called weak forms). The stereotype which the Americans mean is the loss of /h/ in such words as *hat, house, horse*, which are normally stressed. In a great many urban accents of England (but not of Ireland and Scotland) these words are pronounced *'at, 'ouse, 'orse* (cf. Hughes and Trudgill 1979: 7, 34, 39, and passim; Wells 1982: 322, 371, 374, 391).

The simultaneous pronunciation (co-articulation) of /t/ and the glottal stop [ʔ] is typical of many urban accents of Great Britain. For the same phenomenon in GenAm see Kahn 1980. In BrE, however, it very often happens that /t/ is completely replaced by [ʔ]. It is this phenomenon which explains the humour of the remark of a Glaswegian: 'My name's Pa'erson, with two ts' (McIntosh 1952: 53).

The two dental fricatives /θ/ and /ð/ are often replaced by other fricatives. When this happens voicing/force of articulation retains its original distribution. The Cockney accent realizes the pair as /f/ and /v/ (*muvver* for *mother*; *nuffink* for *nothing*). New Yorkers often use /t/ and /d/ (*tanks* for *thanks*; *dis* for *this*) or the affricates [tθ] and [dð]; many blacks in America have /t/ and /d/ at the beginning of a word, but /f/ and /v/ at the end (*dem* for *them*; *wiv* for *with*). In Ireland it is common to hear [t̪] or [t̪θ] and [d̪] or [d̪ð] for /θ/ and /ð/. In addition and independently of this, almost all speakers pronounce words such as *clothes* or *months* without /ð/ or /θ/, namely as /kləʊz/ or /kloʊz/ and /mʌns/ when they are speaking casually.

Almost all accents of English have the pronunciation /juː/ for the spellings ⟨u, ui, ew, iew/ieu, eu, ue⟩ unless the preceding consonant is dental or alveolar. (An exception is the traditional accent of East Anglia, in which the /j/ does not occur for these spellings, e.g. *pew* /puː/; cf. Hughes and Trudgill 1979: 35). When there is a preceding dental or alveolar consonant (/s, z, n, t, d, l, θ/), as in *suit, exuberant, new, tune, dew, revolution, thews*, the pronunciation varies between /uː/ and /juː/. Most accents of AmE have /uː/ everywhere. RP varies a bit, especially after /θ, s, z, l/ (Gimson 1989: 213–15); elsewhere /juː/ is usual in RP (see 11.1.3 **Dental and alveolar consonants + /j/**).

The sequence /h/ + /j/ as in *pew* [pʰjuː], *cue* [kʰjuː], *Hugh* /hjuː/, etc., is realized as [ç] (the sound of ⟨ch⟩ in German *ich*). (In *pew* and *cue* the [h] is the result of aspiration following /p/ and /k/ in word initial position.) [ç] is basically a voiceless fricative allophone of /j/; however, because of the meaningful opposition *who – Hugh – you* [huː] - [çuː] – [juː] the [ç] has marginal phonemic status.

3.3.5 Phonological processes

Palatalization Wherever historical /j/ has occurred before an unstressed syllable, but especially in the suffixes *-ion* and *-ure*, some degree of palatalization of preceding /s, z, t, d/ has taken place everywhere in the English-speaking world, though not always in a fully predictable way. Such palatalization means that /s, z, t, d/ are pronounced slightly farther back (at the palate rather than the alveolar ridge), as in the following examples:

	unpalatalized	palatalized
-ion:	/s/ (missile)	/ʃ/ (mission)
	/z/ (fuse)	/ʒ/ (fusion)
	/t/ (motive)	/ʃ/ (motion)
-ure:	/s/ (fissile)	/ʃ/ (fissure)
	/z/ (please)	/ʒ/ (pleasure)
	/t/ (Advent)	/tʃ/ (adventure)
	/d/ (verdant)	/dʒ/ (verdure) (GenAm only)

In many accents the process of palatalization has been uneven. Therefore, while *literature* is generally pronounced as palatalized /lɪt(ə)rətʃə(r)/, some (American) accents have /lɪtərətuːr/. Likewise, both RP and GenAm agree in using unpalatalized forms for *Tuesday*: RP /tjuːzdɪ/ and GenAm /tuːzdiː/ (GenAm with no /j/ cannot undergo palatalization). However, many non-RP speakers of BrE have the palatalized form /tʃuːzdɪ/ (*'Chewsday'*, as it were). RP has /edjuːkeɪt/ (unpalatalized) for *educate*, while GenAm has /edʒuːkeɪt/ (palatalized). RP has both /ɪmiːdiːɪt/ (unpalatalized) and /ɪmiːdʒɪt/ (palatalized) for *immediate* and /ɪsjuː/ (unpalatalized) and /ɪʃuː/ (palatalized) for *issue*, while GenAm has only the unpalatalized form in the former and the palatalized form in the latter case.

Simplication of final consonant clusters Whenever several consonants occur together at the end of a word, one of them is frequently left out. In the case of the few words which according to the spelling and the phonotactics of English can have a cluster of four consonants, such simplification is very common, for example, *exempts* or *twelfths* are simplified from /egzempts/ and /twelfθs/ to /egzemps/ and /twelfs/. In addition, it is relatively normal, especially in casual speech, to drop final consonants in shorter clusters when the following word also begins with a consonant, for example, *west side* becomes *wes' side* [wesɪaɪd] and *left leg* becomes *lef' leg* /lefleg/.

Assimilation A number of the cases of consonant loss or change so far described are really cases of assimilation. A large part of the allophonic variation in English is due to this. The loss of the aspiration of fortis stops in word final position or the voicing of intervocalic /t/ in AmE, for example, may be explained in this way. In the former case assimilation is in the direction of a pause or silence; in the latter, /t/ adapts to the sonority of the preceding and following vowels. Assimilation is also involved in palatalization. Indeed, whenever the pronunciation of one sound becomes in some way similar to that of a neighbouring sound, it is possible to speak of assimilation. Often only one single feature is changed. The following are well-known examples in modern English of assimilation which occurred long ago and have remained frozen or irreversible:

- a change in voicing and force of articulation: in *have to* 'must' /hæftə/, the /v/ of *have* has become a voiceless, fortis /f/ owing to the influence of the following /t/;
- a change in the manner of articulation: the original /d/ of *soldier* has become /dʒ/ under the influence of following /j/: (RP) /səuldʒə/ (GenAm) /souldʒər/. (This is a case of palatalization; the place of articulation has also changed.)

Other instances of assimilation are dependent on the style of speech. What in careful, formal style is

(RP) /ðɪs hɪə/ or /wɒt duː juː wɒnt/
and
(GenAm) /ðɪs hɪr/ or /wʌt duː juː wɑːnt/
become
(RP) /ðɪʃɪə/ or /wətʃə wɒnt/
and
(GenAm) /ðɪʃɪr/ or /wədəjə wɑːnt/

in the casual style of colloquial language.

Morphophonemic alternations   If assimilation were seen as a purely sound-conditioned phenomenon, many cases of alternation in form could not be explained because they are limited to certain grammatical and lexical classes of words. The form /beɪ/ *bay*, for example, is given the ending /z/ in order to form the plural *bays*. Since it is not possible to have a fortis /s/ here, this appears to be a case of assimilation to the preceding vowel. However, since there is also the word /beɪs/ *base*, in which there has not been a similar instance of assimilation, it becomes clear that the /z/ of *bays* is a case of assimilation restricted to particular circumstances. It involves only the inflectional ending and is therefore termed **morphophonemic**. It can be illustrated by the following examples.

First, the endings {S} (for the regular plural and the possessive of nouns and for the regular third person singular of the present simple form of the verb) and {D} (for the past tense and past participle forms of regular verbs) are realized in differing ways depending on the phonological environment in which they occur.

The morpheme {S} is realized as
/-ɪz/ when the word that is to be inflected ends in a homorganic fricative
(/s, z, ʃ, ʒ, tʃ, dʒ/), e.g. *mixes* /mɪksɪz/, *bushes* /buʃɪz/
/-z/ when the word to be inflected ends in any other phonologically lenis or

voiced phoneme, including a vowel, e.g. *boys* /bɔɪz/, *lugs* /lʌgz/, *child's* /tʃaɪldz/

/-s/ when it ends in any other phonologically fortis or voiceless phoneme, e.g. *bikes* /baɪks/, *raps* /ræps/, *life's* /laɪfs/

The morpheme {D} is realized as

/-ɪd/ when the word that is to be inflected ends in a homorganic (alveolar) stop (/t,d/), e.g. *headed* /hedɪd/, *heated* /hiːtɪd/

/-d/ when the word to be inflected ends in any other phonologically lenis or voiced phoneme, including a vowel, e.g. *allowed* /əlaʊd/, *rammed* /ræmd/, *saved* /seɪvd/

/-t/ when it ends in any other phonologically fortis or voiceless phoneme, e.g. *licked* /lɪkt/, *brushed* /brʌʃt/

Exceptions include such common, but irregular forms as *wife–wives* or *burn–burnt*.

The second example of morphophonemic alternation concerns the numerous lexical words of Latin origin which end in the syllable /-ɪk/. Such words as *public*, *historic*, etc., show a change from /k/ to /s/ when a suffix beginning with ⟨i⟩ or ⟨e⟩ is added. This alternation is due to assimilational processes in Latin and does not apply to words of non-Latin origin, cf. RP.

public /ˈpʌblɪk/   *publicity* /pʌbˈlɪsɪtɪ/
                       publisher /ˈpʌblɪʃə/ (here palatalized)
historic /hɪsˈtɒrɪk/ *historicity* /hɪstəˈrɪsɪtɪ/

but no such alternation in the following words:

stick /stɪk/   sticker /stɪkə/
picnic /ˈpɪknɪk/ *picknicker* /ˈpɪknɪkə/

English spelling emphasizes the semantic–historical relationship involved in the Latin material inasmuch as the letter ⟨c⟩ can represent both /k/ and /s/. For extensive presentations and a critical discussion of morphophonemic alternations, see Chomsky and Halle 1968, especially chapter 4; Shane 1973; Sommerstein 1977.

3.3.6 Phonotactics

Several facets of distribution (involving /ŋ, h, ʒ, ð/) have already been mentioned. Distribution is really a part of phonotactics. To round out the picture in this area a few examples of regular combinations of sounds will be presented.

It is not possible, for example, to begin an English word with a combination of nasal and stop (**mbit* /mbɪt/ or **dnime* /dnaɪm/). ⟨Pn-⟩,

Table 3.2 Final and medial nasal-stop clusters

labial	*camp* /-mp/	*bomb* /-m/
	camping /-mp-/	*bombard* /-mb-/ but *bombing* /-m-/
dental	*Lent* /-nt/	*land* /-nd/
	Lenten /-nt-/	*landing* /-nd-/
palatal	*think* /-ŋk/	*long* /-ŋ/
	thinker /-ŋk-/	*longer* /-ŋg-/ (but
		singer /-ŋ-/)

[1] In *bombard* /m/ and /b/ occur in two different syllables; note also *iambic*; /-mb-/ does not occur within a single syllable.

[2] Before the inflectional ending {ING} the letters ⟨mb⟩ and ⟨ng⟩ are pronounced without the stops /b/ and /g/. The ⟨g⟩ of ⟨ng⟩ is, however, pronounced when followed by the comparative and superlative endings {ER} and {EST}, as in *stronger*, *younger* or *longest*. The ⟨g⟩ is not pronounced when the agent ending {ER} is added to a verb, as in *singer*, *wringer*, *banger*, etc.

⟨gn-⟩, and ⟨kn-⟩ are, as is well known, only written: the stops are not pronounced. In the middle or at the end of a word combinations of nasal plus stop are completely unproblematic in the case of the fortis stops and of /d/, while nasal plus the lenis stops /b/ or /g/ can appear only in the middle of a word (see table 3.2).

The phonotactics of English permits consonant clusters in which the semi-vowels /j, r, w/ and the lateral /l/ can occur after almost all the stops and some of the fricatives at the beginning of a word, for example, /pr-, br-, fr-, tr-, dr-, θr-, ʃr-, gr-, kr-/. Only /s/ can occur before /p, t, k, m, n, f/ at the beginning of a word. At the end of a word considerably more combinations are possible. A large number of these consonant clusters are due to morphological endings such as {D} or {S} discussed above or the {TH} (= /θ/) of many derived nominals (*twelth*, *truth*, *depth*). For details, see Gimson 1989: 241–59; Ashby and Ashby 1990.

3.4 Vowels

The inventory of vowels can be determined by three features: the height of the tongue, the horizontal position of the tongue, and the complexity of the vowel. In this brief presentation of the vowels of English, twenty in RP and sixteen in GenAm, first the distinctive features (3.4.1 and 3.4.2) and then the status of non-prevocalic ⟨r⟩ (3.4.3) will be examined.

The nasality of a vowel (as in French, for example) is a further phenomenon; however, it is peripheral since its presence varies individually and regionally. Although it is typical of many varieties of AmE, it does not appear to be phonemic in any of them.

3.4.1 The position of the tongue

The sound quality of each vowel of English is determined by the horizontal position of the highest point of the tongue, which can be in the front, centre, or back of the mouth (or oral cavity). Three vertical levels are recognized: high, mid and low. Theoretically, a combination of these dimensions should provide for nine possibilities. However, among the short vowels of English only six of these are realized. A further short vowel is /ə/ (often called **schwa**), which, however, is essentially different since it is always unstressed (see below figure 3.3).

The system of the short vowels of English is of significance because it is the short vowels that have remained relatively stable over several centuries. With notable and clearly defined exceptions, the short vowels are phonotactically limited to occurrence in **checked syllables,** that is in syllables which end in a consonant. This means that words cannot end in short vowels without a following consonant. Unstressed schwa /ə/ is not restricted in this manner. As a result there are no words of the form /be/ or /sæ/ (cf. Wells 1982: 168).

The notable exception to this phonotactic regularity is the use in RP (and the accents of Northern England) of the vowel /ɪ/ as the realization of final ⟨-y⟩ or ⟨-ie⟩ in words such as *lazy* or *Suzie*. Most other accents (for example, in southern England, North America, Australia, etc.) have long /iː/ here.

The vowel /ə/ is the form which many vowels may be regarded as 'taking' when they occur in unstressed syllables in the natural flow of speech. Schwa is never stressed. Because of the high incidence of unstressed syllables in English it is easily the most frequent vowel in the language.

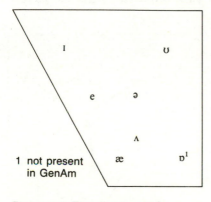

Figure 3.3 The short vowels

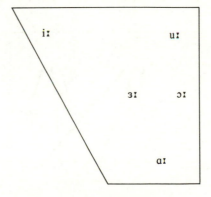

Figure 3.4 The long vowels

3.4.2 Complexity: length and diphthongization

Every deviation from the short nature of a vowel will be regarded here as a case of complexity. Length is one such deviation. Since, in addition, the long vowels have a distinct tendency in many varieties of English to be at least somewhat diphthongized, there is some justification for grouping length and diphthongization together. In addition, the short vowels are produced without special muscle tensing of the tongue (i.e. they are **lax**) while both the long vowels and the diphthongs are **tense**. (For extensive discussion, see Lass 1976: chapter 1; cf. also for the suggestion that RP maintains long–short distinctions while GenAm has tense–lax ones, see Lindsey 1990). The degree of diphthongization varies considerably, but it is usual to speak of three long **closing diphthongs** and two slightly diphthongized closing ones. Closing refers to the closing movement of the mouth during the articulation of these diphthongs. The arrows in figure 3.5 show the direction of the movement from the first to the second element of the diphthongs. Length in monophthongs is indicated by ɪ.

The two diphthongs /eɪ/ and /əʊ/ (RP) or /oʊ/ (GenAm) are realized in many varieties (e.g. Standard Scottish English) or in certain phonetic environments (especially before fortis stops) in GenAm as long monophthongs, for example, *gate* [geɪt] or *goat* [goɪt]. Three further diphthongs, /aɪ, aʊ, ɔɪ/, are pronounced as diphthongs in almost all accents.

The centring diphthongs (see figure 3.6) are a further set which is present is RP, but not in GenAm. For background on them, see below 3.4.3.

In addition to the phonological differences in length which are of central importance here, there are also non-phonological length differences. All vowels, whether short or complex, are relatively shorter when followed by a fortis consonant and relatively longer when followed by a lenis one or,

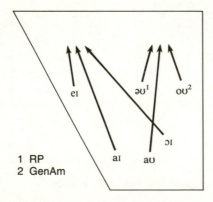

Figure 3.5 The closing diphthongs

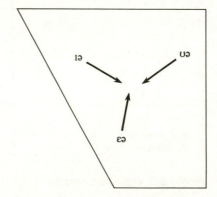

Figure 3.6 The centring diphthongs

for those where this is possible, when no consonant follows (in free or unchecked syllables). For this reason the /eɪ/ of *late* is shorter than the /eɪ/ of *laid* or the even longer /eɪ/ of *lay*; the /æ/ of *back* is shorter than that of *bag*. This length difference may sometimes be used to distinguish *writer* from *rider* in GenAm, where both words have a voiced and flapped [ḍ] in the middle. Since the [ḍ] of *writer* was historically a /t/, this means that for some (but not all) speakers the /aɪ/ of *rider* may be longer than the /aɪ/ of *writer*. Otherwise, the two words are indistinguishable. The same distinction may differentiate other pairs, such as *latter* and *ladder*. It is not, however, clear whether such differences in length are perceived in normal speech (cf. Sheldon 1973; Fox and Terbeek 1977).

3.4.3 Non-prevocalic /r/

Up to this point a system of seventeen (RP) or sixteen (GenAm) vowels has been assumed. This system and the comparability of these two standard accents becomes considerably more complicated when non-prevocalic *r* (traditionally termed 'post-vocalic' *r*) is included. Non-prevocalic *r* refers to an orthographic ⟨r⟩ which is not followed immediately by a vowel (either within the same word or linked to an initial vowel in the following word); instead, it is followed by a consonant (*hard*) or comes at word-end (*here*).

In the rhotic accents orthographic ⟨r⟩ is regularly pronounced in all environments. In many such accents the vowel system is noticeably simplified in the sequence vowel +/r/. (Note that this does not apply to all rhotic accents, for example, Scottish English.) In GenAm the oppositions are neutralized that otherwise exist between /iː/ and /ɪ/, between /eɪ/, /e/ and /æ/, between /ɔɪ/ and /ou/, and between /uː/ and /ʊ/ when /r/ follows. This leads to a system of just ten vowels (see table 3.3).

Furthermore, in GenAm /r/ usually has the features of a vowel (it is a semi-vowel). (An actual consonant, such as rolled [r], occurs in few accents of English.) Combinations of vowel +/r/ in GenAm are often really phonetic diphthongs whose final element is an *r*-coloured schwa. This means the schwa has the sound quality of a retroflex [ɻ] – produced with the tip of the tongue curled back towards the rear of the mouth – or a constricted [ɹ] – articulated with lateral tension of the tongue). It is sometimes written with the symbol [ɚ]. This is the case, for example, with *fear* /fɪr/ = [fɪɚ] or cure /kjʊr/ = [kjʊɚ]. The central vowel /ɜː/ is *r*-coloured without the need for a schwa [ɜː], for example, *purr* /pɜːr/ = [pɝː]. This can be the case with /aɪ/ +/r/ as well, which may show up as [aɪ] as in *car* /kaɪr/ = [kɑˈɪ].

Table 3.3 shows the full GenAm system of vowels on the left and the restricted system of vowels that occurs before non-prevocalic *r* on the right. Note that the neutralized vowels are transcribed with capital letters, to indicate their status as archiphonemes (cf. Moulton 1962: 77ff).

Table 3.3 The vowels of General American

Full system		Before /r/	
/iː/	bead	/ɪr/ (also /Ir/)	beard
/ɪ/	bid		
/eɪ/	bade		
/e/	bed	/ɛr/ (also /Er/)	bared
/æ/	bad		
/ɑː/	bod(y), father	/ɑːr/	barred, farther
/ɔː/	bawd		
/oʊ/	bode	/ɔr/ (also /Or/)	bored
/ʊ/	Budd(ha), book		
/uː/	booed	/ʊr/ (also /Ur/)	boor, toured
/ʌ/	bud	/ɜːr/	bird
/ə/	baba, NASA	/ər/	barbered, Nasser
/aɪ/	bide	/aɪr/ or /aɪjər/	buyer, tired
/aʊ/	bowed	/aʊr/ or /aʊwər/	bower, towered
/ɔɪ/	Boyd, coy	/ɔɪr/ or /ɔɪjər/	Boyer, coyer

Note: The triphthongs /aɪr, aʊr, ɔɪr/ (= [aɪɚ, aʊɚ, ɔɪɚ]) are not stable and are therefore often pronounced as two syllables. This may result in an epenthetic [j] or [w] (conditioned by movements necessary in articulation). Bronstein also counts [eɪɚ] as in *mayor* and [oʊɚ] as in *blower* as triphthongs (Bronstein 1960: 201).

In the left-hand column there are only fifteen phonemes because /ɜː/ appears exclusively before an /r/ in GenAm. For this reason an analysis is conceivable in which no /ɜː(r)/ appears at all, but only /ʌ(r)/. After all, /ɜːr/ and /ʌr/ do not stand in opposition in AmE since there are no minimal pairs contrasting them (Wells 1982: 480f). However, this analysis has not been adopted because it would only complicate the already difficult comparison of the vowel systems of GenAm and RP.

In the non-rhotic accents, in which non-prevocalic /r/ does not occur, there is also a reduced vowel system where non-prevocalic ⟨r⟩ is involved. For RP the situation is as shown in table 3.4.

Instead of the sequence 'vowel + /r/', RP has either 'vowel + schwa', schwa alone, or a long vowel alone. The six sequences of vowel or diphthong plus /ə/ are termed **centring diphthongs** or **triphthongs** because in each case their final element consists of the central vowel schwa. Historically /r/ was lost after the development of an epenthetic [ə] (Wells 1982: 214). This suggests that /r/ turned into /ə/ or, to put this somewhat differently, that GenAm /r/ and RP /ə/ are somehow equivalent in words with a post-vocalic ⟨r⟩.

Such an assumption is, however, questionable in a synchronic description of present-day RP (and other non-rhotic accents), as will be explained in the following. The reason for this is that both /ɪ/ and /ɪə/ (the stressed vowels

Table 3.4 The vowels of Received Pronunciation

Full system		Before ⟨r⟩ plus consonant	
/iː/	bead	/ɪə/	beard
/ɪ/	bid		
/eɪ/	bade		
/e/	bed	/ɛə/	bared
/æ/	bad		
/ɑː/	bah, father	/ɑː/	barred
/ɒ/	bod(y)		
/ɔː/	bawd	/ɔː/	bored
/əʊ/	bode		
/ʊ/	Budd(ha)	/ʊə/	boor, toured
/uː/	booed		
/ʌ/	bud	/ɜː/	bird
/ə/	baba	/ə/	barbered
/aɪ/	bide	/aɪə/, /aːə/, /aː/	buyer, tired
/aʊ/	bowed	/aʊə/, /aːə/, /aː/	bower, towered
/ɔɪ/	Boyd, coy	/ɔɪə/, /ɔːə/	Boyer, coyer

Note: There is a strong tendency towards simplification of the triphthongs in RP, called smoothing. Instead of the possible further triphthongs /eɪə/ or /əʊə/ one finds smoothed diphthongs as in the words *player* /eːə/ or *mower* /ɜːə/ or the monophthongs /ɛː/ or /ɜː/ respectively (Wells 1982: 238; Gimson 1989: 139–41).

of *mirror* and *nearer* respectively), as well as /e/, /eɪ/ and /æ/ (*merry*, *Mary* and *marry* respectively), appear in opposition before a following (inter-vocalic) /r/. Note that the schwa of the centring diphthongs is present together with /r/ in *nearer* and *Mary*. Consequently, it cannot be seen as a replacement for /r/. Furthermore, /aɪ/ as in *bar*, /ɔɪ/ as in *bore*, and /ɜː/ as in *purr* are all monophthongs without a second schwa-element which might be thought to 'replace' the /r/. When these forms occur pre-vocalically, as in *barring*, *boring* and *purring*, the so-called linking /r/ is realized (see below 3.5.1).

The oppositions /ɪ/–/ɪə/ and /e/–/eɪ/–/æ/, however, only occur before a prevocalic (hence intervocalic) /r/:

spirit /ˈspɪrɪt/ – spear it /ˈspɪərɪt/
Harry /ˈhærɪ/ – hairy /ˈheərɪ/
herring /ˈherɪŋ/ – hair ring /ˌheəˈrɪŋ/

In GenAm *spirit* and *spear it* are indistinguishable, but *marry* and *Harry* are often (regionally) distinguished from *Mary/merry* and *hairy* (Moulton 1962: 78; Bronstein 1960: 152f). In rural New England the opposition

/oː/–/ɔː/ is maintained both before pre- and non-prevocalic /r/, *hoarse, boring* /oɪr/, but *horse, warring* /ɔɪr/; however, this opposition is highly recessive (Kenyon 1969: 229f); Bronstein 1960: 167, 169; Moulton 1962: 78).

3.4.4 Transcriptional systems

Depending on the purpose being followed as well as the phonetic features which are considered important, the symbols used for a **broad** or **phonemic transcription** of the vowels of English vary considerably. Naturally, an analysis based on RP will differ from one based on GenAm, for the simple fact that the number of vowel phonemes recognized will be different. Many dictionaries use symbols that are close to the sounds suggested by the spelling of English, for example, ⟨o⟩ for /əʊ/ or /oʊ/ and ⟨a⟩ for /æ/, etc. For use by non-native speakers most learners dictionaries employ a system based on the International Phonetic Alphabet (IPA). Table 3.5 provides a synopsis of the symbols used for the vowels of English in a number of important works.

3.4.5 Phonetic variety in the area of the vowels

The intention so far has been to present the vowels as phonemes. However, it is important not to forget that the phoneme is an abstract concept and that there is a large variety of differing realizations of each phoneme. It is this variety in pronunciation which often makes it difficult to understand an unfamiliar accent of English. To illustrate this point, this section will take an exemplary look at one phoneme, /aɪ/, which will serve to show how varied actual pronunciation may be.

The phoneme /aɪ/ varies noticeably in the one or the other accent in one or more of the following four ways:

1 retraction of the first element;
2 raising of the first element;
3 weakening of the second element, resulting in some cases in a monophthong;
4 a split of the single phoneme into two distinct allophones in complementary distribution.

Retraction of the first element is noticeable especially in London Cockney and in the less prestigious accents of Australia, New Zealand and South Africa. Here the first element is frequently a back, open and, in some areas, slightly rounded vowel, resulting in [ɒɪ]. The settlement history of Australia, New Zealand and South Africa from the late eighteenth century on, with a large number of immigrants from the home counties (around London) where Cockney is centred, offers an explanation for this wide-

Table 3.5 Transcriptional systems

Key words		Gimson 1989	Jones 1950	MacCarthy 1965	Kenyon 1969	Trager and Smith 1951	RHWCD 1991
bead	keyed	iː	iː	ii	i	iy	ē
bid	kid	ɪ	i	i	ɪ	i	i
bed	kedge	e	e	e	ɛ	e	e
bad	cad	æ	æ	a	æ	æ	a
bard	card	ɑː	ɑː	aa	ɑ(r)	a(r)	ä(r)
bod(y)	cod	ɒ	ɔ	o	ɑ	a	o
bawd	cawed	ɔː	ɔː	oo	ɔ	ɔh	ô
Budd(ha)	could	ʊ	u	u	ʊ	u	o͡o
booed	cooed	uː	uː	uu	u	uw	o͞o
bird	curd	ɜː	əː	əə	ɜr	ə(r)	ûr
bud	cud	ʌ	ʌ	ʌ	ʌ	ə	u
be(deck)	c'ld(could)	ə	ə	ə	ə	ə	ə
bade	cade	eɪ	ei	ei	e	ey	ā
Boyd	cloyed	ɔɪ	ɔi	oi	ɔɪ	oy	oi
bide	Clyde	aɪ	ai	ai	aɪ	ay	ī
bode	code	əʊ	ou	ou	o	ow	ō
bowed	cowed	aʊ	au	au	aʊ	aw	ou
beard	cleared	ɪə	iə	iə	ɪ(r)	ir	ēr
bared	cared	ɛə	ɛə	eə	ɛ(r)	er	âr
board	cord	ɔə	ɔə	oo	ɔ(r)	or	ôr
boor	cured	ʊə	uə	uə	ʊ(r)	ur	o͞or
(bar)bared		ə	ə	ə	ɚ	ər	ər

Symbols from the International Phonetic Alphabet (IPA) are used in Gimson 1989, Jones 1950 and Kenyon 1969 (1924). The differing conventions reflect both phonetic differences (RP vs. GenAm) and changes in time (1950 vs. 1989). The conventions employed by MacCarthy 1965 as well as Trager and Smith 1951 share the use of only a limited number of special symbols, which makes typewriter use feasible. In addition, Trager and Smith base their transcription on systematic considerations concerning English phonology (single symbols for short simple vowels; double symbols for complex vowels, which are always a combination of a simple vowel and a high front element (/y/), a high back element (/w/) or an element of length (/h/), as well, of course, as (/r/). The final system given (*Random House Webster's College Dictionary*, ed. R. B. Costello, 1991) is typical of many dictionaries intended for native speakers (especially in North America): it uses the symbols suggested by common English spellings and modified by such traditional conventions as diacritical marks for short (⟨ ˘ ⟩) and long (⟨ ¯ ⟩) vowels.

ranging similarity. Some other independent reason must, however, be found to explain why [ɒɪ] is also the pronunciation traditionally found on the Outer Banks, the islands off the coast of North Carolina, which were settled considerably earlier. A degree of retraction, though less extreme, is, by the way, also sometimes to be found in RP: [ɑɪ] (Wells 1982: 292). This is perhaps indicative of the way in which RP may evolve, for various other developments were first (and more extremely) observed in Cockney before they became the accepted realization in RP.

Raising of the first element is to be found in Norwich, in the far north of England, in Wales, in Ireland, in New England, and in Barbados and the Bahamas. The quality of the phoneme may be symbolized as [ʌi] (Norwich, Barbados, the Bahamas), [ʌɪ] (Ireland), [ɛɪ] (the far north of England), or [əɨ] (Wales, New England) (Wells 1982: 340, 358, 381f, 426, 526, 585, 588). Raising is also typical of Canada ('Canadian raising'; see 12.2.1) and in parts of Maryland, Virginia, North and South Carolina, Georgia and Florida (the Tidewater South). Here, however, [əi] or [əɪ] occurs only before a voiceless-fortis consonant. In other phonetic environments the pronunciation of /aɪ/ is [aɪ] (Canada) or [aː(əɪ)] (for example, Virginia) or [ɑːɪ] (for example, South Carolina). This means that the vowels in *rice* and *rise* are clearly different:

rice [rəɪs]   *rise* [raɪz] (Canada)
              [raːəz] (Tidewater Virginia)
              [rɑːɪz] (Tidewater SC)
              (Wells 1982: 494, 538)

A split of /aɪ/ is also the case in Scotland and the Scots-speaking areas of Northern Ireland. In Scotland a pronunciation without raising, [ae], is used in final position, before a voiced-lenis fricative, or before /r/, as in *buy*, *prize* or *fire*. Otherwise [ʌi] or [əi], for example in *wipe*, *tribe*, occurs (ibid.: 405ff, 444). Morphological boundaries also play a role here, which is the reason why, for example, *tied* [taed] and *tide* [tʌid] constitute a minimal pair (ibid.: 406).

In a final group of accents /aɪ/ is realized as a monophthong. Many speakers in the American South, for example, have exclusively [a(ː)] or lightly diphthongized [aᵉ]. However, other more prestigious accents of the South have [ae] or [aɪ], before voiceless-fortis consonants. For speakers of the latter type there is thus a split of /aɪ/, as illustrated by the two vowels of *nighttime* ['naɪtːam] (ibid.: 437). A further example of monophthongization of /aɪ/ may occasionally be found in Cockney; this leads to pairs such as *laugh* = *life*, both as [lɑːf] (ibid.: 308).

Monophthongization is, by the way, to be found for further diphthongs of both RP and GenAm such as /aʊ/, which is realized as [æ] in Cockney (*about* is pronounced as if it were spelled *abaht*) (ibid.: 308, 318f). A further example is RP /ɛə/, which becomes [e] through the process of smoothing in Cockney, South African, or Australian English, so that *bed* and *bared* may be distinguished only by length (Cockney) or hardly at all (ibid.: 305f; Lanham and Traill 1962: 200f; Lanham 1978: 151; Bernard 1967: 52f).

3.5 Suprasegmentals

3.5.1 Juncture

Juncture is the suprasegmental area which, perhaps, has the most to do with the segmental phonemes. Basically juncture is concerned with the way in which neighbouring words and sounds are joined. A word sounds different depending on whether it is enunciated very carefully as a single word or uttered in the flow of speech. When a pause follows a word, there is what is called **open juncture**; otherwise, there is **closed juncture**. The distributional differences between clear [l] in prevocalic position and dark [ɫ] before consonants or open juncture as well as cases of assimilation have already been recounted and are part of the area of juncture. When one word ends with a consonant and the next begins with a vowel, the final consonant of the first word is normally bound to the second word in what is often called **liaison**. When this liaison does not occur the speaker of English often uses a glottal stop [ʔ] to separate the two sounds. Glottal stops are particularly common in emphatic styles of speech.

One particularly important kind of liaison in English is the use of what is termed the **linking /r/**, which occurs in several non-rhotic accents (especially RP, Eastern New England; the American South, however, while non-rhotic, does not have a linking /r/). This means that a word-final postvocalic ⟨r⟩ is pronounced if the following word begins with a vowel. By itself or before a word that begins with a consonant the word *Peter* takes the form /piːtə/; *Peter Andrews*, however, appears with a linking /r/ as /piːtərædruːz/. For some speakers the pattern of the linking /r/ leads to the articulation of /r/ where no ⟨r⟩ occurs in the spelling. This is especially the case following /ɔː/, /ɑː/, and /ə/ and is referred to as an **intrusive /r/**, as, for example, in *I saw Ann* /aɪ sɔːræn/. Not all speakers of non-rhotic accents share this pattern, and for many speakers it is stigmatized.

Juncture seldom has a phonemic function (cf. Hoard 1966: 166). Nevertheless, it is not difficult to provide examples of minimal pairs, such as *an oat – a note*, which are distinguished, it seems, on the basis of juncture and syllable boundaries (cf. Gimson 1973: 100f; Jones 1973: 154; Kahn 1980; Wells 1990).

3.5.2 Stress

The phenomenon of stress is difficult to define. Functionally, it serves to emphasize something against the background of its environment. This can take place in the form of a change in loudness, a change in pitch, or a change in duration (cf. Brazil *et al.* 1980: 3f). Usually two or three, sometimes four, distinct levels of stress are recognized, viz. primary ('), secondary (,), tertiary (not used in the following) and unstressed (unmarked). Stress has an immediate influence on how a phoneme is realized inasmuch as unstressed syllables tend to have vowels with a schwa. Note the initial vowel of *'atom*, which is (stressed) /æ/, while the unstressed first syllable of *a'tomic* is /ə/. The weak stress of some syllables can lead to an identical realization of otherwise differing words, for example, *drive* and *derive* may both be /draɪv/. Naturally, these words are hardly likely to occur in contexts in which they might be confused, and even if they did, speakers could easily remedy the possible confusion by using a more careful pronunciation of *derive*, /dəraɪv/.

Aside from its influence on the realization of phonemes, stress has two further important functions. For one thing it differentiates lexical pairs such as *'Main ₁ Street* and *₁main 'street* or *'pass on* ('to judge' as in *we didn't feel capable of passing on her qualifications*) and *₁pass 'on* ('hand to the next person'). For a detailed treatment of word stress, see Fudge 1984; Poldauf 1984.

Secondly, it marks (in connection with intonation) the word which carries the syntactic or sentence stress. In the careful style of spoken prose, for example, a speech read at a meeting or the news read on radio or television, this is usually the last lexical word (noun, full verb, adjective or adverb) in a clause. Most frequently the rheme (see 4.4.4), or that part of the sentence which contains new information, carries the stress. If a different word, for example, a function word such as an article, a pronoun, an auxiliary verb, a preposition or a lexical word besides the final one is to be stressed, this will be a case of contrastive stress. This means that the item which carries the stress is consciously emphasized in opposition to what might otherwise be the case, for example, *Jerry doesn't eat pickled herring (even though Diane does)*. Halliday calls this second function of stress, in which a particular word that contains new information is emphasized, **tonicity** (Halliday 1970: 40ff; 1973: 116f; for a recent differentiated view, see Maidment 1990).

The connection between rhythm and stress is an important feature of English. All lexical words carry a primary or secondary stress. The pattern which arises from this series of stresses provides the skeleton of English rhythm, for all the remaining syllables are (relatively) unstressed. English (like German) is, for this reason, referred to as a **stress-timed** language (as compared with a **syllable-timed language** such as Spanish). Note that West and East African English (14.3.1 and 14.6), Singaporean English (15.4.3), Philippine English (15.7) and, to some degree, Caribbean English (12.7) are syllable-timed. It is often suggested that English has largely even rhythm, or **isochrony**, with each of the stresses occurring at equal time intervals (however, this hypothesis has yet to be confirmed; cf. Halliday 1973: 106–8; Lehiste 1977; Brazil *et al.* 1980: 5f; and Scott *et al.* 1985 think that isochrony may be more perceptual than actual).

3.5.3 Intonation

The final major area of phonology is intonation, or the use of changes in the pitch of the voice. There are numerous variations in the details of its use from region to region (cf. for example, Macaulay 1977: 49f). Nevertheless, the basic function of intonation is probably very similar for most varieties. Intonation has an affective, a grammatical and a discourse function. Thus it is possible to use the same sequence of words to express a wide range of feelings, such as joy, indifference, sarcasm, etc., by employing what often amounts to only the finest of differences in intonation. Intonation can also be used grammatically to signal whether a particular sequence of words is to be understood as a statement or a question, as a list of single features or as a combination of common characteristics. Finally, it has also been pointed out that intonation is used pragmatically to add 'specific interactional [discourse] significance to lexico-grammatical items' (Coulthard 1987: 46; see below).

English employs five basic intonational contours, which are referred to as **tones**. They are:

1 fall ↘
2 rise ↗
3 level —
4 fall–rise ∨↗
5 rise–fall ∧↘

(cf. the following sources, not all of which use the preceding list: Brazil 1985: 104; Brazil *et al.* 1980: 6–9; Cruttenden 1986; Crystal 1975; Gimson 1989; Halliday 1967, 1970, 1973; Kingdon 1958; O'Connor and Arnold 1961; Pike 1945; Roach 1991).

There are numerous factors which might be taken into consideration, but which cannot be presented here. For example, the intensity, duration and range of the pitch change. The pitch change usually occurs within a single syllable, which is called the **nucleus** or **tonic syllable** or **segment**. It may, however, be spread over further syllables which follow the actual nucleus and are called the **tail** or the **enclitic segment**. This is especially the case for the complex tones, where the speed of the fall or rise or the abruptness of the change from fall to rise (as in 4) or from rise to fall (as in 5) is involved. Even more complicated are the variations that are possible preceding the nucleus. This stretch of speech may, in general, be called the **proclitic segment** (Coulthard 1987: 47) or, more specifically, the **pre-head** or **pretonic** if it contains no stressed syllables. If one or more are present, the whole stretch from the first stressed syllable (the **head**) to the nucleus is called the **body** (sometimes, however, simply the head), and what precedes this is the **pre-head**. For example, in answer to the question with rising intonation, *When did they leave?* (2), someone might say *They left at* *five* (1). Here *five* would be the nucleus with tone (1), a fall; *left* is the head; *at*, the body (alternatively *left at* is the head); and *They*, the pre-head. In a simplified reply consisting only of the words *At five* (1), *At* is the pre-head; *five*, the nucleus; and there is no head or body. The affective function of a low pre-tonic and relatively level nucleus in *At five* (3) might be to convey lack of interest. In *They left at five* (2) a jump from a high pre-head to a low head leading into a rise on the nucleus could signal mild astonishment, as if to say 'Didn't you know?' Almost needless to say, the number of variations that actually may occur are so great that there has been little agreement as to what the significant contours are, what meaning they convey, and why this is so.

There do, however, seem to be some things of significance which can be said. One has to do with the general meaning of rises and falls, and the other is concerned with how intonation serves to structure information in discourse, as when a fall to low signals 'that a particular mini-topic is ended' (Coulthard 1987: 60).

The general meaning of falling and rising intonation   Halliday's analysis and interpretation of the intonation of English comes to the following conclusion:

> Tone marks the kind of activity involved, by a complex pattern built out of a simple opposition between certain and uncertain. . . . If . . . certain, the pitch of the tonic falls; if uncertain, it rises.
>
> (Halliday 1973: 124)

In this way it is possible to understand both the affective and the grammatical functions of intonation as aspects of the same general criterion. A series of examples may serve to clarify this.

Statements are usually spoken with falling intonation (1) because they express certainty; if, however, the speaker is less certain or wants to appear less certain or dogmatic, this attitude can be conveyed by means of a final rise, as in *It's getting pretty late* (4) as opposed to the same with (1).

The yes—no question is in order if a speaker is not sure whether something is the case or not. The appropriate intonation will normally be rising (2). Even a sentence without the inversion of subject and auxiliary verb will probably be interpreted as a question or at least as contradiction, astonishment or the like if it is uttered with rising intonation, as with *It's getting pretty late* (2).

Wh-questions differ from *yes—no* questions in containing a premise which is in any case asserted. In the question *Where is your sister?* (1), the assumption is made that you do, indeed, have a sister. For this reason *Wh-*questions always contain an assertion, and it is understandable that they take falling intonation. However, a low rise at the end is not unusual: it permits a question to sound more open and friendly, less absolute. Thus a low rise together with the sequence of words *When are you going home?* (2) is less certain than the same with falling intonation (1); the result is that the speaker comes across as more polite and friendly, because a rise (2) leaves more room for the addressee to answer freely, even, for example, by perhaps remarking that he/she is not planning to go home at all right now (on politeness, see also 4.4.2, 6.1 and 8.3.3).

An interesting alternative to Halliday's general principle is that of Brazil, which Coulthard has expressed as follows:

> We can generalize . . . that a basic function of the fall-rise tone is to mark the experiential content of the tone unit, the *matter*, as part of the shared, already negotiated, common ground, occupied by the participants at a particular moment in an ongoing interaction. By contrast, falling tone marks the matter as new.
>
> (Coulthard 1985: 105; cf. also House 1990)

In these terms a statement with falling intonation, *It's getting pretty late* (1), is rather more peremptory because it *proclaims* something new to the hearer. The same statement with fall–rise (4) creates more social solidarity because it *refers* to common knowledge. When applied to questions, the same principle is valid. A referring tone, (2) or (4), 'projects the speaker's wish to have his assumptions confirmed with respect to a truth which he presents as having been negotiated'; proclaiming tones, (1) and (5), 'project a wish that the respondent should provide a selection from a so-far unnegotiated set' of choices (Brazil 1985: 171). In this sense, *wh*-questions usually have falls because the information requested has normally not yet been negotiated. Rising *yes–no* questions suggest: 'I think I know the answer: please tell me whether I am right' (ibid.: 172f). Perhaps the greatest disadvantage to this approach is that it applies better to RP than to other accents of English. The widespread use of (4) described here is, for example, relatively unfamiliar in American English as well as in areas in the British Isles outside southern England.

The approach espoused by Brazil includes the idea of **pitch concord**, which helps to predict what type of response will follow. A nucleus which falls from a high or mid-level pitch will suggest a response which starts on the corresponding level. A rise which ends high or mid will tend to have a similar effect. Ending a statement at a mid-level pitch has the effect of asking for agreement (4; a common ground is assumed); ending it at a high level would tend to call forth a definitive statement (1; *yes?* or *no?*). A fall to low or a rise from low does not have the same constraining effect on the response: the hearer is free to respond as he or she wishes or not at all. Note that in BrE a perfunctory *Thanks* which falls to low releases the other from any obligation to reply and may therefore terminate an encounter. In AmE in the same situation *Thanks* is more likely to end at mid or even high, which allows for the more usually American *You're welcome* or the like (Coulthard 1985: 115–17).

Tonality   The information expressed by a sentence may be affected not only by the choice of tones and by the distribution of stress in the sentence, i.e. tonicity, but also by the number of intonational contours which correspond to a clause (according to Halliday: tonality). Tonality affects the structure of information. When a simple sentence or a single clause corresponds to a single intonational contour, Halliday speaks of **neutral tonality**, which is the 'normal' or unmarked case. However, an intonational contour can be longer or shorter than a clause.

Non-restrictive (or non-defining) **relative clauses**, for example, can have their own separate contour, something which is not possible with **restrictive** (or defining) relative clauses, which must share a contour with the sentence in which they are embedded. If someone has only one brother, then the sentence given below is non-defining and may appear as either (a) or (b), i.e. either with or without a separate contour for the non-restrictive relative clause, and the (b) version will be with a comma. If the speaker has several brothers, the relative clause serves to identify which is meant and is defining; hence only one contour, as in (b), is possible (and there may be no comma):

(a) *That's my brother* (1), *who lives in Oregon.* (1)
(b) *That's my brother* (,) *who lives in Oregon.* (1)

Alternative questions have different interpretations depending on which contours they have and whether or not they have more than one contour. *Can you speak Spanish or French?* may have the following interpretations depending on the tones and the tonality:

(a) *Can you speak Spanish or French?* (2) neutral: 'Can you speak either one?'
(b) *Can you speak Spanish* (2) *or French?* (1) 'Which of the two?'
(c) *Can you speak Spanish* (2) *or French?* (2) 'Or maybe another one?'
(d) *Can you speak Spanish* (1) *or French?* (1) 'Do you know any foreign languages at all?'

In conclusion, it should be pointed out that the relationship between tone, tonicity and tonality is complex and that the global interpretations presented here are far from being universally accepted. Despite the fact that intonation and stress are of central importance, not enough is known about either. Both contribute to the expression of speaker attitude and speaker intention and to the information structure of the sentence; however, tempo and **voice quality** are two further factors which very evidently play a similarly significant role (cf. Addington 1968; Laver 1980; see 8.2.3).

3.6 The orthography of English

Orthography refers to the set of conventions which are employed when writing a language. Since written conventions are not sufficient to express all the information which the spoken word transmits and because the written language has a long tradition and a set of regularities of its own, the two systems, that of speech and that of writing, correspond only imperfectly (for more discussion, see 1.6.7). To begin with, almost everything that is written is a part of StE and presumes a certain minimum degree of education. In addition, the written language cannot match the many elements which in the spoken language identify the emotional state and the regional and social origins as well as the gender and age of the speaker. Of course, handwriting may offer some hints, and young children as well as less highly educated writers of the language may be fairly readily identified. Some writers (especially those of fiction) also use dialect spellings for the regional and/or educational classification of people. When such information about language-users is to be expressed in writing, it is best done explicitly, for example, by saying in so many words that someone is a male or a female, is tired, angry, happy, or old, young, poorly educated, etc. Clearly, everything which has to do with accent and voice quality is lost in the written language. Only the choice of vocabulary and use of syntax remain as elements of style which may contain hints as to region, class, gender or age.

3.6.1 Punctuation

As one part of orthography punctuation serves two main purposes:

(a) it separates units;
(b) it specifies grammatical function.

Punctuation is governed largely by conventions but individual preference is also important: 'I should define punctuation as being governed two-thirds by rule and one-third by personal taste' (Carey 1972: 13).

The **separating function** is probably clear without further explanation. Included here are indentation or free lines to mark paragraphs, spaces between words and the full stop (BrE) or period (AmE) [.], the semi-colon [;], the comma [,], the dash [–], brackets (BrE) or parentheses (AmE) [( )], etc. Commas, dashes, brackets/parentheses and inverted commas (BrE)/quotation marks (AmE) [" " or ' '] are generally used in pairs when they mark embedded material.

The **grammatical function** of punctuation includes the following: the use of the question mark [?], the exclamation point/mark [!], the apostrophe ['] as a marker of possessive case, underlining (in handwriting) or italics (in print) for emphasis or to mark the use of linguistic material or foreign words as well as other less central conventions.

Many modern monolingual dictionaries of English contain a presentation of the rules and conventions of English punctuation. In addition, special books such as Carey 1972 or Partridge 1963 may be consulted. See also Salmon 1988.

3.6.2 Spelling

English spelling has a bad reputation. This is partly because numerous words have more than one spelling, partly because many phonemes can be represented by a whole series of different **graphemes** (units of spelling consisting of a letter or sequence of letters), and partly because one and the same grapheme may represent various phonemes. Emery quotes the following sentence:

> In a *cozy* house *cater-cornered* from the palace a *finicky caliph* who maintained that a *jinni* had revealed to him the secrets of the *cabala*, spent much of his time smoking *panatelas* – sometimes *kef* – and training his pet *parakeet*.

and remarks that if all the permutations and combinations of different spellings for the nine words in italics as given in five different American dictionaries were added up, there would be 11,197,440 different *correct* versions of this sentence (Emery 1975: 1f).

This kind of variation is interesting to note, but is basically trivial. For the spelling of English is fundamentally based on phonemic principles. However, there is a very imperfect degree of correspondence between sound and sign owing to such factors as

1 historical spellings which have been retained (*cough, plough, though, through*);
2 etymological spellings (*subtle* and *doubt* with a ⟨b⟩ despite the lack of /b/ in the pronunciation; this on the model of Latin *subtilis* and *dubitare*, even though older English had *sutil/sotil* and *doute* without a ⟨b⟩);
3 a variety of foreign borrowings (*sauerkraut, entrepreneur* or *bhang*).

The spelling of consonants   The situation is less complicated in the area of consonants than with vowels. In most cases there is a fixed correspondence between one letter and one sound; ⟨k⟩ represents /k/ and ⟨b⟩, /b/. The exceptions are relatively few and easy to remember: the ⟨k⟩ of ⟨kn-⟩ (*know, knife*, etc.) and the ⟨b⟩ or ⟨-mb⟩ (*comb, lamb*, etc.), for example, are never pronounced.

When there is no letter available in the Latin alphabet to represent a particular phoneme, a combination of two letters is used, for example, the graphemes ⟨th⟩, ⟨ch⟩, ⟨sh⟩, or ⟨zh⟩ (⟨zh⟩ in foreign words for /ʒ/). The fact that ⟨th⟩ is used for both /ð/ and /θ/ and that ⟨ch⟩ is used for /tʃ/, /k/, and /ʃ/ is, of course, inconsistent, but the principles behind this are easy to grasp. Initial ⟨th⟩ represents

1 /ð/ in grammatical or function words, i.e. pronouns (*they*, *them*, *their*, *this*, *that*, etc.), the basic adverbs (*then*, *there*, *thus*), or the definite article *the*;
2 /θ/ in all the other (lexical) words, such as *thing*, *think*, *theatre*, *thunder*, *thin*;
3 /t/ in a few exceptional cases such as *Thomas*, *thyme*, *Thames*, *Thailand*.

In the middle of a word ⟨th⟩ is /ð/ if it is followed by ⟨(e)r⟩ as in *leather*, *weather*, *father*, *brother*, *either*, *other*, etc. Only a few words of Greek origin, such as *aesthetic*, *anthem*, *menthol* or *ether*, are exceptions to this. When no ⟨e⟩ follows, ⟨th⟩ is /θ/, as in *gothic*, *lethal*, *method*, *author*, *diphthong*, *lengthy*, *athlete*. Exceptions with /ð/ are the result of inflectional endings which have been added on, especially {ing}, for example, *breathing* (from *breathe*), but also exceptionally *worthy* (from *worth*).

At the end of a word /ð/ is sometimes marked by a following silent ⟨e⟩, for example, *seethe*, *bathe*, *breathe*, *teethe*, *clothe*, but individual words such as *mouth* (verb) are not differentiated in this way.

There is also an alternation between voiceless/fortis singulars and voiced/lenis plurals for some words, for example,

path /θ/	paths /ðz/
bath /θ/	baths /ðz/
mouth /θ/	mouths /ðz/, etc.

However, there are also numerous exceptions to this, for example, *math—maths*, both with /θ/ or *lath—laths*, both with either /ð/ or /θ/.

The use of ⟨ch⟩ for three different phonemes can be explained by reference to the history of the language: words which were present in Old English have ⟨ch⟩ at the beginning of a word to represent /tʃ/, for example, *cherry*, *cheese*, *church*, *cheap*, etc. Words which entered the language from French after the Middle English period are by and large pronounced with /ʃ/ though spelled with ⟨ch⟩, for example, *chalet*, *chandelier*, *champagne*, *Chicago*, *chic*, etc. In learned words, finally, which ultimately stem from Greek or Latin, initial ⟨ch⟩ is pronounced /k/, for example, *chaos*, *character*, *chemistry*, *chorus*, *chord*, etc. For a history of English spelling, see Scragg 1974.

Two letters are sometimes used for a single consonant phoneme when one would be sufficient. For example, final /k/ can be spelled ⟨k⟩, ⟨c⟩ or ⟨ck⟩ (*took*, *tic*, *tick*); ⟨g⟩ and ⟨gh⟩ both stand for /g/ (*ghost*, *goes*); ⟨j⟩, ⟨g⟩,

⟨dg⟩ all represent /dʒ/ (*jam*, *gem*, *bridge*); ⟨f⟩ and ⟨ph⟩ are both possibilities for /f/ (*fix*, *phone*); and ⟨s⟩ and ⟨ss⟩ may be used for /s/ (*bus*,
dress), just as ⟨z⟩ and ⟨zz⟩ may be for /z/ (*fez*, *fuzz*), etc. The reasons
for this are sometimes of an etymological nature (for example, ⟨ph⟩ for /f/
in words from the Greek). Often, however, the use of a single **graph** or letter
versus a **digraph** (a two-letter combination) is important because it provides
information about how the preceding vowel grapheme is pronounced, as
will be illustrated in the following.

The spelling of vowels　When one of the single-letter-vowels of the
alphabet, namely ⟨a, e, i/y, o, u⟩, occurs singly (i.e. neither doubled nor
together with another letter-vowel, as in ⟨ee, ie, ea⟩ etc.) and it represents
the vowel of a stressed syllable, its phonemic interpretation varies according
to the graphemic environment. When a single letter-vowel is followed by a
single letter-consonant plus another letter-vowel, it has the phonemic value
of the alphabet name of the letter, i.e. long ⟨a⟩ = /eɪ/, long ⟨e⟩ = /iː/,
long ⟨i⟩ = /aɪ/ (also for ⟨y⟩), long ⟨o⟩ = /əʊ/ (RP) or /oʊ/ (GenAm), and
long ⟨u⟩ = /(j)uː/, as in the words *made*, *supreme*, *time/thyme*, *tone*,
and *mute*.

　When, however, two letter-consonants or one letter-consonant and the
space at the end of a word follow, the letter-vowels are interpreted (in the
same order) as /æ/, /e/, /ɪ/, /ɒ/ (RP) or /ɑɪ/ (GenAm), and /ʌ/. Examples
are *mad(den)*, *pet(ting)*, *hit(ter)*, *hot(test)*, *run(ner)*. In a number of words
⟨u⟩ is not /ʌ/, but /ʊ/, for example, *bush*, *push*, *bull*, *pull*, *bullet*, *put*,
cushion, *butcher*, *puss*, *pudding* (Holmberg 1964: 50). It is interesting to
note that in all those words where /ʊ/ rather than /ʌ/ occurs there is a /p,
b, ʃ, tʃ/ immediately next to the vowel and each of these consonants is

Table 3.6 The 'long' vowels, spelling and pronunciation

Spelling		Examples	Exceptions
⟨a⟩ + C + V = /eɪ/		rate, rating	have, garage
⟨e⟩	/iː/	mete, scheming extreme	allege, metal, extremity
⟨i/y⟩	/aɪ/	ripe, rhyme divine	machine, river divinity
⟨o⟩	RP /əʊ/ GenAm /oʊ/	joke, joking verbose	come, lose, gone verbosity
⟨u⟩	/(j)uː/	cute, renewal	–

Note: Words ending in *-ity*, *-ic* and *-ion* (*divinity*, *mimic*, *collision*) have a short
vowel realization of ⟨a, e, i, o, u⟩ as a result of historical processes (cf. Venezky,
1970: 108f).

pronounced with lip-rounding, as is /ʊ/. (This seems to be a necessary though not a sufficient condition, since quite a few words have central, unrounded /ʌ/. Note, for example, *put* /ʊ/ vs. *putt* /ʌ/ or *Buddha* /ʊ/ vs. *buddy* /ʌ/.)

In one final set of circumstances an ⟨r⟩ follows the letter-vowel. In such cases a whole new system of correspondences applies. One type involves ⟨r⟩ followed by two letter-vowels (*various*) or a single letter-vowel at word end (*Mary*); a second type provides for ⟨r⟩ followed by a letter-vowel plus a letter-consonant (*arid*) or double ⟨rr⟩ (*marry*); and a third type has ⟨r⟩ followed by a letter-consonant or a space (*mar, part*).

There are, of course, numerous exceptions to these rules, as has been indicated. In addition, there are all those representations of vowels which make use of combinations of two letters (digraphs). Venezky (1970: 114–19) refers to these as '*secondary vowel patterns*' and distinguishes between major correspondences and minor correspondences.

Major correspondences include the use of ⟨ai/ay/ei/ey⟩ for /eɪ/ (*bait, day, veil, obey*) or of ⟨ea/ee⟩ for /iː/ (*each, bleed*) or of ⟨oo⟩ for /uː/ (*boot*).

Table 3.7 The 'short' vowels, spelling and pronunciation

Spelling		Examples	Exceptions
⟨a⟩ + C + C/∅ = /æ/		rat, rattle[1]	mamma
⟨e⟩	/e/	met, mettler	–
⟨i⟩	/ɪ/	rip, ripping	–
⟨y⟩	/ɪ/	system	–
⟨o⟩	RP /ɒ/	comma	gross
	GenAm /ɑː/		
⟨u⟩	/ʌ/	cut, cutter	butte
	/ʊ/	put, bush[2]	

[1] see table 3.8.
[2] see text for discussion.

Table 3.8 Words with /ɑː/ in RP, but /æ/ in GenAm

Spelling		Examples	Exceptions
⟨a⟩ + ⟨f⟩ = /ɑː/		after, daft	baffle, raffish
⟨s⟩		ask, pass	gas, as, basset
⟨th⟩		path, father	math, hath
⟨a⟩ + ⟨m⟩ + C = /ɑː/		example, sample	ample, ramble
⟨n⟩ + C		advance, trance	random, Atlantic
⟨a⟩ + ⟨l⟩ + ⟨f⟩ = /ɑː/		half, calf	Ralph, Alfred
⟨m⟩		palm, calm[1]	Talmud, almanac

[1] GenAm has /ɑː/ or /ɔː/

Table 3.9 The pronunciation of vowels before ⟨r⟩ (cf. Venezky 1970: chap. 7)

Spelling	RP	GenAm	Examples	Exceptions
⟨ar⟩ + V + (V/∅) =	/ɛə/	/ɛr/	wary, warier	are, aria, safari
⟨er⟩	/ɪə/	/ɪr/	here, cereal	very
⟨ir⟩	/aɪə/	/aɪr/	fire, inquiry	delirium
⟨yr⟩	/aɪə/	/aɪr/	tyre	–
⟨or⟩	/ɔː/	/ɔr/	lore, glorious	–
⟨ur⟩	/ʊə/	/ʊr/	bureau, spurious	bury, burial
⟨ar(r)⟩(+ VC) =	/æ/		arid, marriage	catarrh, harem
⟨er(r)⟩	/e/		peril, errand	err
⟨ir(r)⟩	/ɪ/		empiric, irrigate, iris	*GenAm* squirrel
⟨yr(r)⟩	/ɪ/		lyric	–
⟨or(r)⟩	/ɒ/	/aː/	foreign, oriole, borrow	worry, horrid
⟨ur(r)⟩	/ɜː/		burr, furry, purring	muriel, urine
				RP hurry, turret[1]
⟨ar⟩ + ∅/C =	/aː/		par, part	scarce
⟨er⟩	/ɜː/		her, herb	concerto, sergeant, *RP* clerk
⟨ir⟩	/ɜː/		fir, bird	–
⟨yr⟩	/ɜː/		Byrd	–
⟨or⟩	/ɔː/		for, fort	attorney
⟨ur⟩	/ɜː/		cur, curd	–

[1] see text for discussion.

Minor correspondences involve such 'exceptions' as ⟨ai⟩ for /e/ (*said*) or ⟨oo⟩ for /ʊ/ (*book, wool, foot,* etc.).

Spelling reform   English spelling seems to be regular and systematic enough to resist any serious attempts at reform. Nevertheless, two important tendencies may be noted. Popular spellings – especially in America and in the language of advertising (cf. Gläser 1972) – affect numerous words, in particular ones originally with ⟨-gh⟩ such as *donut* (*doughnut*), *nitelite* (*nightlight*), *thruway* (*throughway*), but also such expressions as *kwik* (*quick*) or *krispy kreme* (*crispy cream*). Besides these unofficial reforms, a certain regularizing tendency has been standardized in AmE spelling with the levelling of ⟨-our⟩ to ⟨-or⟩ (*honour > honor*), ⟨-re⟩ to ⟨-er⟩ (*centre > center*), etc. (for a discussion of AmE-BrE spelling differences, see 11.2.1).

Spelling pronunciations   Spelling also exerts a certain influence on speech habits, so that so-called spelling pronunciations come into existence. Traditional /fɒrɪd/ (RP) or /fɔːrɪd/ (GenAm), for example, becomes /fɔːhed/ (RP) or /fɔːrhed/ (GenAm) and the previously silent ⟨t⟩ in *often* is pronounced by many speakers. Of this Potter writes: 'Of all the influences affecting present-day English that of spelling upon sounds is probably the hardest to resist' (Potter 1979: 77).

There are, in other words, tendencies for people to write the way they speak, but also to speak the way they write. Nevertheless, the present system of English spelling has certain advantages:

> Paradoxically, one of the advantages of our illogical spelling is that . . . it provides a fixed standard for spelling throughout the English-speaking world and, once learnt, we encounter none of the difficulties in reading which we encounter in understanding strange accents.
>
> (Stringer 1973: 27)

A further advantage (*vis-à-vis* the spelling reform propagated by George Bernard Shaw) is 'that there can often be greater visual resemblance between cognates than would otherwise be the case, since many vowel quality changes and vowel omissions concomitant with a shift of stress are not recorded in the new spelling' (MacCarthy 1972: 60). As an example of this, remember the comment (above, 3.3.5) on ⟨c⟩ to represent both /s/ in *historicity* and /k/ in *historic*.

REFERENCES

Abercrombie, D. (1967) *Elements of General Phonetics*, Edinburgh: Edinburgh University Press.
Addington, D. W. (1968) 'The relationship of selected vocal characteristics to personality perception', *Speech Monographs* 35: 492–503.
Ashby, M. G. and Ashby, P. D. S. (1990) 'Generalisations on RP consonant clusters', in S. Ramsaran (ed.) *Studies in the Pronunciation of English*, London: Routledge, pp. 168–77.
Bernard, J. R. L. (1967) 'Length and the identification of Australian English vowels', *Australian Modern Language Association* 27: 37–58.
Brazil, D. (1985) *The Communicative Value of Intonation in English*, Birmingham: English Language Research.
Brazil, D., Coulthard, M. and Jones, C. (1980) *Discourse Intonation and Language Teaching*, London: Longman.
Bronstein, A. J. (1960) *The Pronunciation of American English: an Introduction to Phonetics*, New York: Appleton Century Crofts.
Carey, C. V. (1972) *Mind the Stop*, Harmondsworth: Penguin.
Chomsky, N. and Halle, M. (1968) *The Sound Pattern of English*, New York: Harper & Row.
Coulthard, M. (1985) *An Introduction to Discourse Analysis*, 2nd edn, London: Longman.
—— (1987) 'Intonation and the description of interaction', in *Discussing Discourse*, Birmingham: English Language Research, pp. 44–62.
Couper-Kuhlen, E. (1986) *An Introduction to English Prosody*, Tübingen: Niemeyer.
Cruttenden, A. (1986) *Intonation*, Cambridge: Cambridge University Press.
Crystal, D. (1975) *The English Tone of Voice*, London: Edward Arnold.

Davidsen-Nielsen, N. (1974) 'Syllabification in English words with medial *sp*, *st*, *sk*', *Journal of Phonetics* 2: 15–45.

Emery, D. W. (1975) *Variant Spellings in Modern American Dictionaries*, 2nd edn, Urbana, Ill.: National Council of Teachers of English.

Fox, R. A. and Terbeek, D. (1977) 'Dental flaps, vowel duration and rule ordering in American English', *Journal of Phonetics* 5: 27–34.

Fudge, E. (1984) *English Word-Stress*, London: Allen & Unwin.

Gimson, A. C. (1973) 'Implications of the phonemic/chronemic grouping of English vowels', in W. E. Jones and J. Laver (eds) *Phonetics in Linguistics*, London: Longman, pp. 88–93.

—— (1989) *An Introduction to the Pronunciation of English*, 4th edn, rev. S. Ramsaran, London: Edward Arnold.

Gläser, R. (1972) 'Graphemabweichungen in der amerikanischen Werbesprache', *Zeitschrift für Anglistik und Amerikanistik* 20: 184–96.

Halliday, M. A. K. (1967) *Intonation and Grammar in British English*, The Hague: Mouton.

—— (1970) *A Course in Spoken English: Intonation*, London: Oxford University Press.

—— (1973) 'The tones of English', in W. E. Jones and J. Laver (eds) *Phonetics in Linguistics*, London: Longman, pp. 103–26.

Hoard, J. E. (1966) 'Juncture and syllable structure in English', *Phonetica* 15: 96–109.

Holmberg, B. (1964) *On the Concept of Standard English and the History of Modern English Pronunciation*, Lund: Gleerup.

House, J. (1990) 'Intonation structures and pragmatic interpretation', in S. Ramsaran (ed.) *Studies in the Pronunciation of English*, London: Routledge, pp. 38–57.

Hughes, A. and Trudgill, P. (1979) *English Accents and Dialects*, London: Edward Arnold.

Jones, D. (1950) *The Pronunciation of English*, Cambridge: Cambridge University Press.

—— (1973) 'The "word" as a phonetic entity', in W. E. Jones and J. Laver (eds) *Phonetics in Linguistics*, London: Longman, pp. 154–8.

Kahn, D. (1980) 'Syllable-structure specifications in phonological rules', in M. Aronoff and M.-L. Kean (eds) *Juncture*, Saratoga, Calif.: Anma Libri, pp. 91–105.

Kenyon, J. S. (1969) *American Pronunciation*, Ann Arbor, Mich.: Wahr.

Kingdon, R. (1958) *The Groundwork of English Intonation*, London: Longman.

Knowles, G. (1987) *Patterns of Spoken English*, London: Longman.

Lanham, L. W. (1978) 'South African English', in L. W. Lanham and K. P. Prinsloo (eds) *Language and Communication Studies in South Africa*, Cape Town: Oxford University Press, pp. 138–65.

Lanham, L. W. and Traill, A. (1962) 'South African English pronunciation', *English Studies in Africa* 5: 171–208.

Lass, R. (1976) *English Phonology and Phonological Theory*, Cambridge: Cambridge University Press.

Laver, J. D. M. (1980) *The Phonetic Description of Voice Quality*, Cambridge: Cambridge University Press.

Lehiste, I. (1977) 'Isochrony reconsidered', *Journal of Phonetics* 5: 253–63.

Lindsey, G. (1990) 'Quantity and quality in British and American vowel systems', in S. Ramsaran (ed.) *Studies in the Pronunciation of English*, London: Routledge, pp. 106–18.

Macaulay, R. K. S. (1977) *Language, Social Class, and Education: a Glasgow Study*, Edinburgh: Edinburgh University Press.

MacCarthy, P. A. D. (1965) *A Practice Book of English Speech*, Oxford: Oxford University Press.

—— (1972) *Talking of Speaking: Papers in Applied Phonetics*, Oxford: Oxford University Press.

McIntosh, A. (1952) *An Introduction to a Survey of Scottish Dialects*, Edinburgh: Nelson.

Maidment, J. A. (1990) 'Focus and tone in English intonation', in S. Ramsaran (ed.) *Studies in the Pronunciation of English*, London: Routledge, pp. 19–26.

Metcalf, A. (1972) 'Directions of change in Southern California English', *Journal of English Linguistics* 6: 28–34.

Moulton, W. G. (1962) *The Sounds of English and German*, Chicago: University of Chicago Press.

O'Connor, J. D. and Arnold, G. F. (1961) *Intonation of Colloquial English*, London: Longman.

Påhlsson, C. (1972) *The Northumbrian Burr: a Sociolinguistic Study*, Lund: Gleerup.

Partridge, E. (1963) *You Have a Point There*, London: Hamish Hamilton.

Pike, K. L. (1945) *The Intonation of American English*, Ann Arbor: University of Michigan Press.

Poldauf, I. (1984) *English Word Stress*, Oxford: Pergamon.

Potter, S. (1979) *Our Language*, Harmondsworth: Penguin.

Random House Webster's College Dictionary, (1991) ed. R. B. Costello.

Roach, P. (1991) *English Phonetics and Phonology*, 2nd edn, Cambridge: Cambridge University Press.

Salmon, V. (1988) 'English punctuation theory', *Anglia* 106: 285–314.

Scott, D. R., Isard, S. D. and Boysson-Bardies, B. de (1985) 'Perceptual isochrony in English and in French', *Journal of Phonetics* 13: 155–62.

Scragg, D. G. (1974) *A History of English Spelling*, Manchester: Manchester University Press.

Shane, S. A. (1973) *Generative Phonology*, Englewood Cliffs, NJ: Prentice-Hall.

Sheldon, D. R. (1973) 'A short experimental investigation of the phonological view of the *writer–rider* contrast in U.S. English', *Journal of Phonetics* 1: 339–346.

Sommerstein, A. H. (1977) *Modern Phonology*, London: Edward Arnold.

Stringer, D. (1973) *Language Variation and English*, Bletchley: Open University Press.

Trager, G. L. and Smith, H. L. (1951) *An Outline of English Structure*, Washington: American Council of Learned Societies.

Van Riper, W. R. (1986) 'General American: an ambiguity', in H. B. Allen and M. D. Linn (eds) *Dialect and Language Variation*, Orlando: Academic, pp. 123–35.

Venezky, R. L. (1970) *The Structure of English Orthography*, The Hague: Mouton.

Wells, J. C. (1982) *Accents of English*, Cambridge: Cambridge University Press.

—— (1990) 'Syllabification and allophony', in S. Ramsaran (ed.) *Studies in the Pronunciation of English*, London: Routledge, pp. 76–86.

Wijk, A. (1966) *Rules of Pronunciation for the English Language: an Account of the Relationship Between English Spelling and Pronunciation*, London: Oxford University Press.

Chapter 4

Grammar

This chapter deals with the grammatical structure of StE. It is, however, impossible to do this without, on the one hand, commenting on other aspects of the structure of English (phonology, lexis, text types) and, on the other, making at least occasional reference to regional and social variation in syntax and morphology. Note that a more detailed treatment of American and British differences in grammar is to be found in 11.3.

The following pages will concentrate on a presentation of English grammar which begins on the level of individual words, moves on to make some observations about functional word groups or phrases, and then explores the fundamental syntactical relations of English at the clause or sentence level. The first level, that of the word, is concerned with an identification of word classes or parts of speech, and it briefly reviews the inflectional morphology of English. The second step introduces functional groupings of words, the noun, verb, adjective, adverb and prepositional phrases. The third stage goes more extensively into the way sentences in English are constructed; it identifies and comments on the various clause elements and on how clauses vary and how they are combined into more complex structures. The role of grammatical processes in texts is treated in chapter 5.

4.1 Word classes

Within English grammar nine word classes are traditionally recognized: nouns, pronouns, verbs, adjectives, adverbs, prepositions, conjunctions, interjections and articles. While this division is useful, it also has several drawbacks. Positive aspects include the fact that these classes are familiar and widely used – including their employment in the description of numerous other languages – and the fact that their number is manageably small. What is problematic is that many of these parts of speech include sub-classes that are often dramatically different from one another. As a result, it is sometimes difficult to find a clear common denominator and to be definite about class membership (see below).

Open and closed classes   One of the most noticeable disparities within the traditional classes is that between open classes and closed sets. This is the case, for example, with the verb. Most English verbs are lexical items; they may be regarded as having a relatively concrete content, often but not always easily visualized, for example, *run, read, stand, investigate, take out, consist of*. Additional verbs can be added to the language or the meanings of old ones extended as needed to name new concepts, such as *bio-degrade* or *recycle*. These examples are part of the open class of lexical verbs because their number can be extended. Other verbs, however, belong to groups which may not be added to in this way; they are parts of closed sets. Prominent examples are the auxiliary verbs, both non-modal (*be, have, do*) and modal (*must, can, shall, will, may*, etc.). The items in these sets may be listed in their entirety. Furthermore, none of them is easy to picture: for they are not content or lexical words; rather, their meaning is grammatical. They are commonly referred to as **function**, **grammatical** or **structure** words.

Nouns consist exclusively of lexical words, since the grammatical words with a noun or nominal function have traditionally been separated out into the class of pronouns. Adjectives are also a lexical class, but adverbs consist of both lexical and functional items (see below 4.1.5). Prepositions are usually regarded as grammatical, but there is, in fact, a wide range of types within this class, stretching from the highly grammatical (for example, *of*) to the highly lexical (say, *to the left of* or *at the foot of*). Conjunctions and articles are functional classes, though conjunctions have important lexical dimensions to them (time, cause, concession, condition, etc.). Interjections, finally, are a ragbag of linguistic and non-linguistic items; they include single nouns and verbs (*Hell!, Damn!*), phrases and clauses (*Good morning!, Break a leg!*), special interjectional items (*Wow!, Whew!*), and sounds such as whistles, coughs and sighs. They may mark surprise, disgust, fear, relief and the like; or they may function pragmatically as greetings, curses, well wishes and so forth. They will not be considered in the following since they are governed less by formal consideration of syntax and morphology than by expressive and situational demands.

Morphological and syntactic criteria   Word classes may be determined by observing their possible inflectional morphology and syntactic position. The former is the more restricted since several classes have no inflections at all (conjunctions, prepositions and articles). Not even all nouns, pronouns, verbs, adjectives and adverbs can be inflected. In the sections on the individual parts of speech below, the inflectional paradigms of the noun, of pronouns and of the verb will be presented in tables.

Syntactic position means that the part of speech of a word can typically be identified by word order. Concretely, a noun, for instance, can appear by itself immediately after an article (*the lamp, an expression, a book*).

Prepositions appear before nominal expressions (*after the show*, **because of the accident**, **in spite of them**). Adjectives may appear after articles and before nouns (*the red car*, *an **unusual** sight*, *a heavy load*). There are some problems involved in this way of defining word classes. Not all members of each class conform to the positional criteria. For example, some nouns are seldom if ever preceded by an article (proper nouns such as *Holland* or *Lucy*; some nominalized forms such as the gerunds *working* or *being happy*). Some prepositions follow their objects (*two years **ago***). Some adjectives are not used attributively (**the ajar door*). Furthermore, there is overlap since, for example, some nouns take the same position as adjectives (*the **dilapidated*** (adj.) *house* vs. *the* **brick** (noun) *house*). Similar objections apply to positional definitions of the other parts of speech. Furthermore, each of the definitions presumes an understanding of some of the other word classes. What this means is that we are dealing with partially intuitive classes grouped around prototypical members of the various word classes. For some further discussion of word classes see below 4.1.1–7 and, for example, Fries 1952: chapters 5–7; Gleason 1965: chapter 6; Ross 1972; Huddleston 1984: chapter 3; Quirk *et al*. 1985: 34–45.

4.1.1 Nouns

At the centre of the class of nouns are those items which fulfil the positional requirements elaborated above; added to this is the typical inflection of a noun (possessive {S}, plural {S}); finally, semantic criteria may be applied: a noun is the name of a person, place or thing. Obviously there are numerous nouns which do not inflect and fulfil the positional criteria, as mentioned in the previous paragraph; furthermore, there are also innumerable abstract nouns, i.e. ones which are not designations for concrete persons, places or things, for example, *truth*, *warmth*, *love*, *art*.

Words that do, however, conform to the characteristics enumerated are prototypical nouns. They may be simple, consisting of one word (*bird*, *book*, *bay*), or complex (*string bean*, *sister-in-law*, *sit-in*). Grouped around them are further items which conform only partially, yet are regarded as nominal because they can be part of the same kind of phrases, noun phrases or NPs (see below 4.2). It is this functional similarity that serves most broadly to define the limits of the class of nouns.

Inflection   Nouns are prototypically concrete ('persons, places, things') and, as such, refer to objects which can be counted. As a result they characteristically take the inflectional ending {S} for plural number. Inasmuch as they refer to something animate they take a further inflection for possession (also {S}). This results in the paradigm shown in table 4.1.

The spellings -'s, -s, -s' are not differentiated in pronunciation; hence these three forms are homophones. The way {S} is realized phonologically

Table 4.1 Noun inflections

	singular	*plural*
common case	student	students
possessive case	student's	students'

Note: **Common case** in the table covers all the non-possessive occurrences of a noun, such as what is traditionally called the nominative or objective/accusative.

(as /z/, /s/ or /ɪz/) depends on the preceding phoneme (see 3.3.5). In addition, there are a small number of inflectional exceptions in plural formation (*child/children, man/men, deer/deer, goose/geese*). Non-animate nouns are seldom found in the possessive (exceptions are time expressions: *a day's wait*). Numerous mass or non-count nouns (ones not normally used to designate discrete, countable units) have no plural (*snow, water, information, advice, furniture*), though the latter three are frequently pluralized in non-native second language varieties of English in Africa and Asia (see chapters 14 and 15).

For more detail on this and the other topics discussed in this chapter, see any one of the numerous grammars available. The following short list may be of help: Alexander 1988; Close 1975; Dixon 1991; van Ek and Robat 1984; Greenbaum 1991; Leech *et al*. 1982; Huddleston 1988; Leech and Svartvik 1975; Quirk *et al*. 1985; Quirk and Greenbaum 1990; Thomson and Martinet 1983.

4.1.2 Pronouns

Those words which can replace NPs are called pronouns. They are a closed class, and they are divided into several well-known sub-sets: the personal (including reflexive and intensive pronouns), impersonal and reciprocal, demonstrative, relative, interrogative, and indefinite pronouns.

Personal pronouns These are used to distinguish the speaker (first person), the addressee (second person), and a further or third party (third person). They have, for English, a fairly elaborate set of case, number and gender forms.

Case in English does not reflect grammatical function (subject, object) strictly. Predicative complements after copular verbs (*be, seem, appear, become*, etc.) are most frequently and naturally in the objective case (*That's me in the picture*). This may well be the case because the position after the predicator (the verb) is the object position. Objective case forms can be subjects as well, especially if conjoined, for example, *Me and him, we're going for a swim*. This may be attributed to the disjoined or **disjunctive**

Table 4.2 The English personal pronouns

| | 1st person | | 2nd person | |
	singular	*plural*	*singular*	*plural*
nominative	I	we	you	you
objective	me	us	you	you
possessive	mine	ours	yours	yours
reflexive/intensive	myself	ourselves	yourself	yourselves

| *singular:* | 3rd person | | | |
	masculine	*feminine*	*neuter*	*plural*
nominative	he	she	it	they
objective	him	her	it	them
possessive	his	hers	its	theirs
reflexive/intensive	himself	herself	itself	themselves

position of the two objective form pronouns in the example. Finally, the objective occurs as a disjunctive pronoun when the pronoun stands alone, for example, Q: *Who did that?* A: *Me.* (but *I did*, where the pronoun does not stand alone).

Two further pronouns are closely related to the personal pronouns. The first is the third person singular pronoun *one*. It is used for general, indefinite, human reference and frequently includes the speaker or listener, as in *One does what one can*. It is often regarded as stylistically affected. Like the other indefinite pronouns that end in *-one*, it has a possessive (*one's*, *everyone's*, *no one's*, but also *(n)either's*). It differs from the other indefinite pronouns, however, in also having a reflexive form: *oneself*.

The second type closely related to the personal pronouns are the **reciprocal** pronouns *each other* and *one another* (which are virtually interchangeable). They have possessive forms (*each other's*, *one another's*), but no reflexive, which is logical since they function much like reflexives, referring to a previous referent. In contrast to the reflexives they must have a plural subject (e.g. *we*, *you* or *they*); the verbs with which they occur express a mutual relationship (*we saw each other = I saw you + you saw me*).

Relative and interrogative pronouns   These pronouns, specifically *who* and *which*, are the only other pronouns that have case distinctions.

The interrogative *what* is used for persons when the desired answer is a class of people, for example, a vocation (*What is she? She's a chemist*), rather than a particular person (*Who is she? She's my sister/Susan*). The determiner (see 4.5.2) *what* may be used not only for things, but for persons as well. Asked about their sister someone who has none might say: *What*

Table 4.3 The pronouns *who* and *which*

	animate/personal	inanimate
nominative	who	which
objective	who(m)	which
possessive	whose	whose

sister? This stands in contrast to someone with several, who might say *Which sister?* There is one other relative pronoun in common use in modern English: *that*; it may refer to animate or inanimate antecedents; it is never inflected. For more on relative pronouns (and relative adverbs), see below 4.5.5.

Demonstrative and indefinite pronouns   The former are inflected for number (*this, that; these, those*). Some of the indefinite pronouns are inflected like adjectives for the comparative and superlative (*(a) few–fewer –fewest; little–less–least; many–more–most*); the remainder are not inflected (*some, any, both, all, each*, etc.) except for those mentioned above which take a possessive {S}.

One special case is that of the pro-form *one*. While the NP *the red house* is replaced by the pronoun *it*, the replacement for just the single noun *house* is the pro-form *one*: *the red one*. This pro-form is inflected for number and possession like a noun (*one's, ones, ones'*), as are the forms of *other*, which may also replace single nouns, but which, unlike *one*, may not be modified by an adjective (*the (*red) others*).

4.1.3 Verbs

Lexical verbs   Lexical verbs are an open class. They follow NPs in patterns such as *the government issued a statement; my left foot hurts*; or *that symphony is a masterpiece*. Prototypical verbs designate actions (*issued*), but other verbs also refer to states (*hurts*) or relations (*is*). They inflect for person (third person singular, present tense), for tense (past), and as participles (present and past). This provides the paradigm shown in table 4.4.

On the pronunciation of the regular morpheme endings {S} and {D}, see 3.3.5. As for the approximately two hundred irregular verbs in English, there are various inflectional patterns. Among other things, some verbs have no distinct past and past participle forms (*set, let, burst*). The verb *be*, on the other hand, has eight distinct forms (*be, am, are, is, was, were, being, been*). See also 11.3.1.

Table 4.4 Verb morphology

	irregular verbs	*regular verbs*
infinitive and present (except third person sing.)	write	fix
3rd person sing.	writes	fixes
past	wrote	fixed
present participle	writing	fixing
past principle	written	fixed

Verbs may be complex and consist of more than one word. At least the following types are distinguished:

(a) **Verb + adverbial particle** (phrasal verb): *put up, set out, hand over*, etc. For example, *put up* in *they put up my cousin* means 'to provide with a place to stay'. The particle is stressed in pronunciation, which indicates that it is lexical rather than grammatical (see (b) below). If the VP is transitive and the direct object is a noun, the word order is variable: *they put my cousin up*. This word order is normally the only kind possible with pronouns: *they put him up*, but not: **they put up him*.

(b) **Verb + preposition** (prepositional verb): *look at, count on, reckon with*, etc. For example, *count on* in *we are counting on you* means 'to trust in, depend on'. The preposition is not stressed, which indicates that it is more grammatical than lexical. Word order is invariable.

(c) **Verb + adverbial particle + preposition** (phrasal-prepositional verb): *put up with, stand up for, run out on*, etc. This is a combination of (a) and (b). Since the preposition is always the element before the object, word order is invariable, as in *they are standing up for their rights*. On types (a)–(c), see Bolinger 1971; Cowie and Mackin 1978; Courtney 1983; Palmer 1987: chapter 10.

(d) **Verb + noun**: *take a bath, give a talk, do (some) work*, etc. For example, *take a bath* is one of the meanings of 'to bathe'. The noun is syntactically restricted (possible are *take a bath, take two baths*, etc., but not normally *?*take the bath*). This is part of what is referred to as nominal style (see 7.2.2).

Sometimes such combinations are idiomatic, as in *bite the dust* 'to die' or *beat around the bush* 'not to get directly to the point' (see 2.5).

(e) **Verb + adjective**: *be satisfied, become angry, turn sour*, etc. A copular (linking) verb and a predicative adjective express a unitary meaning, which it is generally not possible to express with a single word in English (but *grow red* = 'to redden'). This type of construction is also dealt with as copula + adjective (see below 4.3.1 and 4.3.3).

The auxiliary verbs   As has already been pointed out, auxiliary verbs are a closed set of function words. The non-modal auxiliaries are *be, have* (four forms: *have, has, had, having*), and *do* (three forms as an auxiliary: *do, does, did*). The modal auxiliaries are defective. None of them has the {S} inflection of the third person singular present tense. In fact, some have only one form *must, ought (to)*. This applies to *dare, need, used (to), had better* inasmuch as they are modal verbs at all. There are four paired sets of modals: *shall, should; can, could; will, would; may, might*. These pairs are seldom related to each other like the present and past tenses of lexical verbs (see below 4.4.5).

A final unusual formal feature of some of the auxiliaries is the pronunciation many of them have in RP when combined with the contraction of *not*: *do* /duː/ becomes *don't* /dəʊnt/ (the vowel of *do* becomes /ʌ/ in *does*); *will* /wɪl/ becomes *won't* /wəʊnt/; *shall* /ʃæl/ becomes *shan't* /ʃɑːnt/; *can* /kæn/ becomes *can't* /kɑːnt/ (in RP); *am* /æm/ becomes *aren't* /ɑːnt/ (for some speakers). In GenAm the /əʊ/ of *don't* and *won't* is, of course, /oʊ/, and the /ɑː/ of *shan't, can't* is /æ/. Furthermore, there is no contracted form **mayn't* in either variety for most speakers.

Syntactically, the auxiliaries differ from the lexical verbs in four ways. First of all, they may be negated directly, (cf. auxiliary *I couldn't come* and lexical **I camen't*). Secondly, auxiliaries may invert with the subject (for example, in interrogatives): *Could you come?*, but not **Came you?* Thirdly, auxiliaries can freely and easily be stressed, as in *I could come*, something possible but less usual with lexical verbs alone. Finally, reduced, elliptical forms are possible with auxiliaries (A: *Could you come tomorrow?* B: *Yes, I could*), but uncommon with lexical verbs alone (A: *Did you come yesterday?* B: *?Yes, I came*).

These operations are carried out on lexical verbs that do not already occur with an auxiliary by introducing the dummy auxiliary *do*. This results in negative *I didn't come*, interrogative *Did you come?*, emphatic *I did come*, and elliptical *Yes, I did*.

The only lexical verbs which allow direct negation and question inversion are the lexical verbs *be* and, for some speakers, in some cases, *have* (*Aren't you afraid?* or *Haven't you an idea?*). In order to be able to refer easily to verbs with these syntactic features, whether an auxiliary or lexical *be* or *have*, the term **operator** is sometimes used.

Catenative verbs   The fact that some exceptional lexical verbs are operators leads to the question of whether some auxiliary verbs are not perhaps non-operators. Although no final position on this question will be taken here, it should be pointed out that non-operators are often semantically very much like auxiliaries. This includes pairs such as *must : have got to* (*Must we do that? : Do we have to do that?*) or *will : want* (*He won't go : He doesn't want to go*).

Lexical verbs which, like auxiliaries, are followed by non-finite verb forms (infinitives, gerunds and participles), but which are not operators, are catenative verbs. See below 4.7.

4.1.4 Adjectives

Adjectives are an open class with numerous semantic sub-groups (colour terms, terms of size, age, weight, value, etc.). They typically attribute qualities or properties which are gradable in terms of more or less. These properties and qualities may be **stative**, i.e. not subject to wilful control. An example of this is *tall*; either a person is or is not tall. It is not possible to direct someone (**Be tall!*), nor can a person be temporarily tall (**She's being tall today*). Other adjectives may be **dynamic** and hence subject to will (*Be careful!* or *We're being very careful with the good china*). It is chiefly dynamic adjectives which can be made into adverbs by adding *-ly* (see next section).

Attribution of quality or property may be to a noun; here adjectives generally appear before the noun (attributively), for example, *an old man*. Or it may be to a whole NP; in this case they appear most commonly after a copula (predicatively), for example, *the left-over milk turned sour*. Some adjectives can be used only attributively; others, only predicatively: in *the system of criminal justice* 'the court system for dealing with crime' the adjective has a different meaning and it should be regarded as a different lexical item (lexeme) from when the same word form is used predicatively, in *the system of justice is criminal* 'the court system is unjust/dishonest'. Some adjectives occur after nouns (post-positively), either in fixed expressions (*secretary general*, *court martial*) or as the head of a complex adjectival construction (*an author famous for her/his words*).

The inflection of adjectives is restricted to those which express some kind of relative degree (gradability), and it is realized either by the endings {ER}, {EST} or by the periphrastic elements *more*, *most*. Only monosyllabic and some bisyllabic adjectives take the endings (for exceptions see most grammar books: *cute–cuter–cutest*; *pretty–prettier–prettiest*; but *beautiful–more beautiful–most beautiful*). All negative forms use *less* and *least* regardless of the number of syllables (*less cute*, *least beautiful*). There are also some adjectives with irregular comparatives and superlatives, for example, *good–better–best*; *bad–worse–worst*; *much–more–most*. A few have no comparative, but superlatives only, for example, *inner–innermost*; *outer–outermost*. Where degree is not involved comparatives and superlatives do not exist, for example with adjectives of material (usually derived from nouns), such as *atomic, metal, wooden*, etc., where there is *an atomic power plant*, but no **a more atomic power plant*.

4.1.5 Adverbs

Adverbs are more difficult to define than nouns, verbs and adjectives because there are so many sub-classes and positional variations. Some of the basic semantic areas are those of time, place and manner, as represented by the adverbial pro-forms *then/now, there/here* and *thus/so*. However, intensifiers (such as *very, awfully, hopelessly*) and conjuncts (connective adverbs such as *however, nevertheless, furthermore*, etc.) also belong here.

Inflection is involved in two ways. First, numerous adverbs are derived from the corresponding dynamic adjectives by adding the ending {LY}. This is the case with **adverbs of manner** (*quick* → *quickly*), which tell how something is done (*He left quickly*). This also includes **sentence adverbs**, or **disjuncts** (*hopeful* → *hopefully*), which modify a whole sentence (*Hopefully, it won't snow*). Note that adverbs are not derived from other adjectives; hence there is no *oldly or *greenly.

The second way in which inflection is involved is in connection with the comparatives and superlatives of adverbs of manner (*quickly–more quickly–most quickly*). In addition, a few adverbs have comparatives and superlatives with the endings {ER} and {EST} ([*to work*] *harder/hardest*); however, this is not common since these endings can be used only with adverbs which do not end in {LY}.

Adverbial expressions derived from adjectives in *-ly* (*friendly*), *-like* (*ladylike*), *-style/-fashion* (*western-style*) must be constructed periphrastically, for example, *in a friendly way/manner/fashion, in the style of the west*.

Some adverbs are not derived from adjectives. Generally these are parts of various closed (sub-)sets, for example, time adverbs (*yesterday, today, tomorrow*), place adverbs (*here, there, yonder*), but also numerous adverbs identical in form to prepositions (*above, below, ahead, behind*, etc.) or derived originally from prepositional phrases (*abroad, outside, upstairs*).

4.1.6 Prepositions

Prepositions are often close to adverbs because, like adverbs, they express time, place and manner/modality. In addition, they are used for degree (*over two hours, under twenty pounds, about sixty years old*) and comparison (*like, as*), subject matter (*about*) and motivation/contingency (*because, despite, in case of*). As a group they are more a closed than an open class, but it is hard to draw the line between complex prepositions and similar constructions which are not prepositional. That is, the commonest simple prepositions, *about, at, by, from, for, in, of, on, over, through, to, with*, are clear cases, and so are highly fixed complex prepositions such as *in front of* or *in regard to*. More marginal are *at the front of* or *in sight of*. At the farther extreme are such clearly non-prepositional constructions as *in the considered opinion of* or *at the new shop of*, which consist of individual units joined by normal syntactic processes. For a discussion of criteria see Quirk and Mulholland 1964; Quirk *et al.* 1985: §9.12.

Prepositions can definitely not be defined by inflectional morphology; they have none. Perhaps the most satisfactory criterion is positional: they are followed by an NP, together with which they form a prepositional phrase (PP). This distinguishes them from (subordinating) conjunctions, which are followed by clauses (preposition: *after the party* vs. conjunction: *after we left the party*). It also tells them from adverbs, which are not followed by any particular types of word or phrase (preposition: *they dropped a letter in the box* vs. adverb: *they dropped in*). However, this also means that such items as *e.g.* or *viz.* must be included, which are regularly followed by NPs, but which are not traditionally considered to be prepositions.

4.1.7 Articles and conjunctions

These are the final parts of speech to be considered. Since there are only two words which are articles, the definite *the* and the indefinite *a/an*, the best definition of them is simply naming them. However, a large group of **determiners** might be included here. These are comprised of the demonstrative adjectives (*this*, *that*, *these*, *those*); the possessive adjectives (*my*, *your*, *our*, *her*, etc.); interrogatives and relatives (*what*, *which*, *whose*, etc.); and quantifiers such as *some*, *any*, *no*, *all*, *double*, *half*, *both*, *(n)either*, *each*, *every*, *many*, *more*, *most*, *enough*, etc., as well as both cardinal (*one*, *two*, *three*, etc.) and ordinal (*first*, *second*, *third*, etc.) numerals. They all share the feature of appearing before attributive adjectives as part of an NP (see below 4.5.2).

Conjunctions are basically of two types, coordinating (*and*, *or*, *nor*, *but*, *yet*, *for*) and subordinating (*after*, *because*, *although*). Both groups consist of relatively limited sets. They include not only single word items but also double (correlative) forms such as *both . . . and* or *either . . . or* as well as phrasal constructions such as *ever since*, *in case* or *as soon as*.

4.2 Functional phrases

In the preceding section the focus of attention was on individual words, even though they are sometimes actually complex (*string bean*, *one another*, *put up*, *ever since*, etc.). This section will point out that words do not so much occur individually as in groups of syntactically related items, called **phrases**. Nouns, for example, may appear in such phrasal structures as determiner + adjective + noun + prepositional phrase (*the large apples on the table* or *a weak spot in your argument*). Phrases of this sort are referred to as noun or nominal phrases (NPs) because the noun is the member (or constituent) which must be present. It may, however, appear with or without a determiner, an adjective or a prepositional phrase. Hence in the following even the single word *apples* is an NP:

NPs: *the large apples on the table*
    the large apples
    the   apples
            apples

An NP always consists of at least a noun (or nominal or pronoun) which is its **centre** or **head**. Determiners and modifiers are optional.

Three other types of phrases also consist of either single words as minimal obligatory elements or of these plus further accompanying words. They are the verb phrase (VP), the adjective phrase (AdjP) and the adverb phrase (AdvP), for example:

VP: *go, will go, would have gone*
AdjP: *green, amazingly green, amazingly light green*
AdvP: *gently, very gently, very gently indeed*

The final type of phrase, the prepositional phrase (PP), differs from the others inasmuch as it must consist of at least two elements, a preposition and an NP. Without the preposition this would be an NP. Hence it is the preposition which gives the phrase its name, for example:

PP: *in trouble, in big trouble, in very big trouble*

Phrases occur within other phrases. For instance, PPs may be part of a higher level NP and so, too, may AdjPs. In the following presentation, however, the chief concern will be with phrases as the realization of the functional elements which make up the parts of a sentence or clause. These elements are realized exclusively and completely by the phrase types just enumerated.

Before looking more closely at the two most important and complex phrasal types, the VP and the NP, the functional elements of English sentences as well as a typology of English sentence patterns will be introduced. (For more discussion, see Huddleston 1984: 3.3; cf. also Quirk *et al.* 1985: §§2.25–28)

4.3 Functional sentence elements

4.3.1 The predicator

Within the description of the structure of English in this chapter the clause or sentence is the highest level unit (for larger units, see chapter 5). It always contains, for our purposes, a **predicator**. There are, however, sentences without predicators, for example, *The sooner, the better*. These are called **minor sentence types** and will not be treated here. The predicator is the central syntactic element in a sentence. This is the case because it is the predicator which determines the number of complements that will occur and, indeed, whether a particular element is a complement or an adjunct (see below).

4.3.2 Complements

Connected with every predicator is at least one kind of element which serves to complete the predication. Such elements are called **complements**. If there is only one it will be the **subject** of the predicator and therefore of the sentence/clause (*She fell asleep*). If there are two the second will be either the **direct object** *(She lost her keys)* or the **predicative complement** (sometimes termed **subject complement**: (*She became a specialist*). If there are three such complements, there will be a subject, a direct object, and either an **indirect object** (*She gave us her report*) or a predicative complement (*She named him her assistant*). There are never more than three (see 4.3.3).

In addition to filling the grammatical functions of subject, object, indirect object and predicative complement, the complements also realize a variety of differing **semantic roles** or relations depending on the verb involved. The most common of these roles are

agentive: the deliberate instigator of an act or activity (*My brother has gone to Chicago*);

cause: the inanimate source of an event or process (*The storm ruined the harvest*);

experiencer (sometimes **dative**): the animate subject of thoughts, feelings, sensations (*We think you're right*);

instrumental: the inanimate tool used to do something (*I used a pen to make my notes*);

objective: the goal affected by a predication (*I read the book*);

factative: the object created by the activity of the predicator (*I baked a pie*).

These roles are not necessarily associated with any particular sentence function (such as subject or object); rather, any one verb will have a certain constellation of roles associated with it. For example, the verb *make* will have an agentive (*the carpenter*), a factative (*a table*) and an instrumental (*his tools*). The favoured realization has the agentive as the subject, the factative as the object, and the instrument as a prepositional phrase (*The carpenter made a table with his tools*). Other constellations are also possible, such as passive *The table was finished by the carpenter with his new tools* (see below 4.4.4; see also Fillmore 1972; Anderson 1971; Dirven and Radden 1987).

4.3.3 Sentence patterns

Just how many complements there are in a sentence depends on the type of verb in the predicator. The following are the major types of verbs.

A **Predicators with one complement only**:

I **Intransitive verbs**: *sleep* (*I was sleeping*); *walk* (*She walked to work*); *be worried* (*He's worried*).

II **Impersonal (weather) verbs**: *rain* (*It was raining*); *snow* (*It's going to snow*); *thunder* (*It's thundering*). These verbs are often regarded as having no complement at all on semantic grounds since the subject *it* has no reference and is only a 'dummy', which must appear because predicators in finite sentences must have (grammatical) subjects.

B **Predicators with two complements**:

III **Transitive verbs**: *read* (*Did you read the report?*); *carry* (*She was carrying the groceries*); *delight* (*The weather delighted me*).

IV **Copular verbs with predicative complements**:

(a) **With a predicative nominal or NP**: *be* (*I'm a student*); *become* (*The teacher became a bore*); *sound* (*That sounds a mess*). Verbs of physical appearance such as *sound*, *look*, *feel*, etc., cannot be followed by a predicate noun in AmE; a PP with *like* must be used in AmE (see 11.3.1).

(b) **With a predicative adjective (AdjP)**: *be* (*We were tired*); *get* (*They got drunk*); *look* (*You look happy*). It is also possible to regard the 'copula + adjective' construction as a single VP (see above 4.3.1).

(c) **With a predicative adverbial (of place)**: *be* (*Who's in there?*); *live* (*She lives in Wilmington*); *there + be* (*There was no one at home*). The immediately preceding example (the 'existential *there*' construction) consists regularly of a dummy subject *there*, some form of the verb *be*, an NP which is the 'logical' subject, and an expression of place. Although verbs other than *be* may occur and the place expression may occasionally be missing, the pattern given is the predominant one.

V **Intransitive verbs + adverbial complement**: *last* + duration (*The concert lasted (for) two hours*); *weigh* + amount (*My brother weighs 200 pounds*); *cost* + value (*The peaches cost $2.00 a pound*); *walk* + distance (*We walked twenty miles*).

C **Predicators with three complements**:

VI **Ditransitive verbs**: *give* (*We must give her a party*); *show* (*Who showed you the way?*); *tell* (*I told him a joke*). The indirect object often appears after the direct object and is introduced by the preposition *to* or *for* (*We must give a party for her*; *I told a joke to him*).

VII **Transitive verbs with predicative complements**:

  (a) **With a predicative nominal (NP)**: *call* (*She called me a weak-ling*); *elect* (*They elected her captain*); *declare* (*The newspaper declared you an enemy of the people*).

  (b) **With a predicative adjective (AdjP)**: *call* (*She called me stupid*); *make* (*That made me mad*); *find* (*The court found them guilty*).

  (c) **With a predicative adverbial**: *spend* + place (*He spent the day in bed*), *put* + place (*Who put the peanut butter in the fridge?*); *behave/treat* + manner (*The CD player is behaving (itself) capriciously/in an unpredictable way*; *maybe you should treat it better*).

If any of these predicators are used in the imperative form, the subject, of course, does not appear and the number of complements is lessened by one (*Give the money to her*). The same applies when a transitive predicator (III, VI, VII) is passive (*She was given the money*).

The complements are, as the examples have shown, usually NPs, but in a number of cases they have also been PPs and AdvPs, and, of course, the predicate adjectives have been AdjPs. In fact, as a rule subjects are NPs; direct objects usually are as well, although some appear as PPs. Indirect objects vary between NPs and PPs with *to* or *for*. Adverbial complements may be PPs, AdvPs or NPs. (For VPs as subjects or objects, see below 4.4.)

4.3.4 Adjuncts

The third type of functional sentence element is the **adjunct**. As its name suggests, it is adjoined or added to the sentence. This means that its status is one of optionality. In other words, an adjunct, however important it may be for the meaning communicated, is not grammatically necessary: if it is left out the sentence is still 'well formed'. A complement, on the other hand, may not be omitted without the sentence becoming ungrammatical or a grammatically different structure. The predicative adverbial, a comple-ment, in *The waiter set the plate on the table* cannot be left out, cf. **The waiter set the plate*; the adjunct of place in *I cut the meat on the table* may be, cf. *I cut the meat*.

Adjuncts and complements are thus theoretically distinguishable according to the criterion of omissibility. In reality this criterion is extremely hard to apply. Indirect objects as complements, for example, are part of the 'essential' structure of sentences with ditransitive verbs, yet they can often be left out without the sentence becoming ungrammatical (*I told (him) a joke*); the resulting sentence is, however, a different structure: type VI (ditransitive) has become type III (transitive).

Adjuncts may be realized as NPs, AdvPs, PPs, and even as subordinate clauses:

They drove the car two miles (NP);
They drove the car too fast (AdvP);
They drove the car to town (PP);
They drove the car till it got dark (subordinate adverbial/temporal clause).

Adjuncts may indicate time, place, manner, means, agent, instrument, cause, condition, purpose, concession, etc. What is a complement in one sentence may be an adjunct in another. Status as a complement or as an adjunct is a syntactical question, not one of semantic role: *The craftsman* (agent, complement) *used a special tool* (instrument, complement) *to cut the tiles*, as compared with *The tiles were cut by a craftsman* (agent, adjunct) *with a special tool* (instrument, adjunct).

For more on sentence elements and sentence patterns see van Ek and Robat 1984: chapter 1; Quirk *et al.* 1985: §§2.13–24.

4.3.5 Connectors

The final sentence element is the connector (or **connective**). It is used to connect sentence elements with each other, or to link clauses with each other. Connection can be realized by conjunctions, but also by PPs, AdvPs, relative pronoun NPs, and some special elements called complementizers, which will be introduced later (4.6). Here are some short examples of all but this last type:

Conj: *John and I played tennis* (coordinating conjunction);
        I left as it was late (subordinating conjunction);
PP: *We went skiing; in addition, we did some skating*;
AdvP: *It was cold; nevertheless, we went skiing*;
NP: *I just met someone who knows you.*

4.4 The verb phrase (VP)

The verb phrase may be sub-categorized into two major types, **finite** and **non-finite**. The difference between the two is that the finite ones always occur as clause predicators, always include tense, and always have a subject. For example, in *I was looking for a solution* the finite VP *was looking* is the clause predicator; it is in the past tense; and it has a subject (*I*).

Non-finite VPs, in contrast, need not be clause predicators and need not have a subject of their own. For instance, in *He seems to like me*, where *like* is the predicator of the infinitive clause *to like me*, it has to 'share' its subject (*he*) with *seems*. In other cases, non-finite forms may be **modifiers** instead of predicators and therefore adjectival in nature, for example, the past particle in *a broken window*; the present participle in *a raging fire*; or the infinitive in *the way to do that*. Furthermore, non-finite forms can also be nominal in nature, for example, the infinitive subject in *To err is human* ... or the gerund prepositional object in *She is in charge of renting additional office space*.

The following section deals exclusively with finite VPs. Non-finite forms will be taken up again in a later section on catenative verbs (4.7).

Three particularly useful, discursive treatments of the English verb which may be consulted throughout section 4.4 are Joos 1968; Leech 1987; Palmer 1987.

4.4.1 Finite VPs

There is at least one and as many as six elements in any given finite VP. The six can be illustrated by the following sentence, in which each of the elements represents one of the grammatical choices of English in the area of the verb.

[Henry] might have been being entertained [royally] .

might: expresses modality; this takes the form of a modal verb, which is followed by an infinitive; if a modal verb is present, it always occupies the initial position;

might: also expresses tense, here the past of *may*; the first element in every finite VP must be either past or present;

have: expresses perfect aspect; this is always introduced by *have* and followed by a past participle; it is in the second relative position;

been: expresses progressive aspect; this is always introduced by *be* and followed by an *-ing* form; it is in the third relative position;

being: expresses (passive) voice; this is frequently introduced by *be*, but sometimes by *get* or *have* followed by a past participle; it is in the fourth relative position;

entertained: expresses the predication; this may appear as any lexical verb and may consist of more than one word; it may also appear as one of the pro-forms, *do* or *so*, where appropriate; it comes in final position in the simple VP.

VPs in which all six categories are represented are highly infrequent. However, any combination of the categories may occur so long as the relative order is not changed. In the vast majority of cases the lexical verb, indicating the predication, will be present, but in cases of repetition it is often elided or replaced by a pro-form (*do* and with inversion *so*), as in *A: Have you turned in your paper? B: Yes, I have* (Or: *Yes, I have done*, a form more common in BrE than in AmE, see 11.3.1) *A: So have I*. Note that more than just the lexical verb is elided (or replaced by *done* and *so*):

the direct object is as well. (This is one circumstance that speaks for an alternative analysis of the constituent parts of the sentence, one in which everything which does not belong to the subject is considered to be part of the VP.)

Although modality was named first above, its treatment will be postponed until 4.4.5. Tense will be considered first.

4.4.2 Tense

This is the category of the verb which was described above as being obligatory in the finite VP. In terms of form alone, the first element in every finite VP will be one of two tenses, present or past. In this sense a sentence with *will* (often called the 'future tense'), such as *When will you get an answer?*, is really present, because *will* is the present tense form just as *would* is the past tense form of *will*. The same applies to all other initial forms. Hence the present also includes, for example, *it's raining*, *it has rained* and *it must have rained*; and the past includes *it would be nice*, *it had been nice* and *it was nice*. (Note that modals such as *must*, *dare* and *need* have only one form and therefore only one tense.)

Concord   All the verbs of the language except the modals have an inflectional {S} in the third person present singular. This is all that is left in English of a system of marking agreement between subject and predicator, a system which was at one time considerably fuller and which served to mark the subject and the predicator as belonging together through concord or agreement in person and number. Besides the single instance of third person singular present tense {S}, there are the further special forms of *be* (*I am*, *he/she/it is*, *we/you/they are* in the present; *I/he/she/it was*, *we/you/they were* in the past). The fact that it has grown so weak in modern English has been compensated for by relatively strict word order. The subject is usually the NP which comes directly before the VP.

The subject normally determines concord according to its own grammatical number. This is called **grammatical concord**. If the subject is singular, the verb is singular, and if it is plural, so, too, is the verb. However, not only the grammatical number of the subject, but also the concept of number which lies behind the form of the noun subject may determine concord. This is called **notional concord**. Since a team consists of various members, it is possible for singular *team* to be a plural subject, for example, *The team are playing in Bristol next week*. This type of concord is more prevalent in BrE (especially with subjects such as *government*, *committee*, *family*) than in AmE, although it is not unknown in the latter (see 11.3.1). Conjoined subjects are often notional units, such as *apple pie and cheese* or *bread and water*, and may therefore sometimes have singular verb concord, as in *Bread and water is good for you*. Plural amounts are

usually singular (and sums of money almost always are), as in *$2 is a lot*.
Furthermore, a subject such as *a number of people* is usually regarded as
plural according to *people* rather than singular according to *number*. The
nouns *people* and *police*, although unmarked, are always plural, just as
apparent plurals such as *the United States* or *news* are always singular.

A third principle is **concord by proximity**. This principle may be partly
responsible for concord of the type just mentioned. More clearly it applies
in the *there is/are* construction, in which the first noun after the verb
determines the concord, for example, *There is a plate and three forks on
the table*. A second instance is with conjoined *either . . . or* subjects, in
which the latter element conventionally decides the concord, for example,
Either you or I am mistaken.

Time and tense   There is little doubt that tense is related to time. However,
the relationship is definitely not one-to-one. In everyday thinking the continuum of time is commonly divided up into three: past–present–future.
Tense, as has been pointed out, is binary (divided into two): present and
past. Furthermore, the present tense may be used for non-present time (see
next section), and the past tense has a function which is wider than that of
marking time (see the section after next).

Present simple   This is the 'unmarked' tense. 'Unmarked' may be understood morphologically as the general lack of a special ending such as the
past {D} (except for the third person {S} discussed above). However, it also
refers to the fact that the present simple may be used to designate something
temporally unrestricted:

(1) *Characterization* [*general truth*]
The foundation of Congress's power as a political institution is its
control of the budget. Money to do any and all of the things the federal
government undertakes must be raised, authorized, and appropriated by
acts of Congress.
(W. J. Crotty and G. C. Jacobson, *American Parties in Decline*, p. 228)

Furthermore, the present may be used for past reference (though the
converse is not possible) as in the so-called historical present:

(2) *Narration* [*historical present*]
Of the screaming which people afterwards claim to have heard from the
granary, I hear nothing. At every moment that evening [*that* indicates
distance and hence past time] as I go about my business I am aware of
what might be happening, and my ear is even tuned to the pitch of
human pain.
(J. M. Coetzee, *Waiting for the Barbarians*, p. 4f)

Text (1) is an example of present tense used for general situations which
extend beyond the present into both the past and the future; they are

sometimes referred to as 'general truths'; more suitably, they may be called characterizing statements. Text (2) is an example of what is sometimes called the 'historical present', which is typical of an especially immediate or vivid style of story-telling. In addition, the present tense is used in the following ways: for reporting something just as it takes place, as in sports broadcasting or in stage directions (3):

(3) *Report* [*stage directions*]
Light rises on the kitchen. WILLY, talking, shuts the refrigerator door and comes downstage to the kitchen table. He pours milk into a glass.
(Arthur Miller, *Death of a Salesman*, Act I, p. 1068)

for reporting or explaining what one thinks or feels:

(4) *Mental or emotional state*
BIFF: I just wonder though. I wonder if Oliver still thinks I stole that carton of basketballs. . . . I think that's why I quit.
(ibid.: 1067)

for performing an act:

(5) *Performative act*
In the Name of God, the Father, the Son, and the Holy Ghost, I now join you together to live in holy wedlock as husband and wife.
(*Hymnal and Liturgies of the Moravian Church*. Bethlehem, Pa: Provincial Synod, 1948, p. 42)

for comments immediately accompanying a demonstration and explaining the individual acts involved:

(6) *Demonstration*
Now watch − I drop the tablet into this warm water, and you see it dissolves quite nicely.
(Joos 1968: 105)

and even for future time, especially in temporal clauses (see also below **Future**)

(7) To accompany me I have chosen three men. I call them together the afternoon before we leave [future reference].
(J. M. Coetzee, *Waiting for the Barbarians*, p. 58)

For further discussion, see Joos 1968: chapter 5; Palmer 1987: chapter 3.

Past simple   The past tense has three clearly delineated functions. The easiest to recognize is its use to mark a situation as having taken place in the past time:

(8) In July, Allen shipped the locomotive by river and canal to Honesdale, Pennsylvania, and there on August 8 a fire was kindled under the boiler, and the 'Stourbridge Lion' was readied for its first test.
(D. Brown, *Hear That Lonesome Whistle Blow*, p. 21)

The second function is to mark indirect speech after a reporting verb in the past tense (see 4.7.3 and 4.7.5):

(9) Joyce Johnson said she didn't know what had come over her last night, but she felt okay, though her husband was mad at her. He said she had barked like a dog.

(G. Keillor, *Lake Wobegon Days*, p. 412f.)

The final use is in unreal (10) and contrafactual (11) conditional constructions (see below 4.4.5):

(10) In theory, if the market paid workers exactly their 'worth', there would be enough work to go around, and no unemployment.

(11) By the early 1960s the Japanese steel industry would have had a competitive advantage over the U.S. industry even if the Japanese government had kept hands off.

What each of these three seemingly different uses of the past tense have in common is the idea of **remoteness**. The past has even been termed the 'remote' tense (cf. Joos 1968: 121). First of all it is remoteness in time (as in 8). Secondly, what is reported is put at a distance to the person reporting (as in 9). Interestingly enough, the time shift to the past need not be made when the speaker identifies with what he or she reports. Accepted facts, for example, do not normally undergo a backshift to the past (*He pointed out that blood is* [not: *was*] *thicker than water*). In the third case, the past tense indicates remoteness to reality (as in 10 and 11). Note that a likely condition (a 'real conditional') has the present tense and differs from an unreal conditional inasmuch as there is less likelihood that the latter will be realized: the likelihood is more remote. Compare *If I had time, I'd write* [unreal conditional, writing is unlikely] with *If I have time, I'll write* [real conditional, writing is less unlikely].

One further use of the past tense may well be related to this: the past tense for politeness as in *There's something I wanted to ask you*. With a first person subject, as in this example, the past expresses more tentativeness and unobtrusiveness. This is accomplished thanks to the remoteness of the past, which puts greater distance between the speaker and his/her request ('I wanted to ask you something, but I don't necessarily still want to'). This distance makes a refusal on the part of the addressee easier (B: *Sorry, I don't have any time at the moment*. A: *Oh well, it doesn't matter, I was just wondering*). When the subject is in the second person, the past serves to soften a request by making it less immediate (*Could you spare me a moment?*); see 6.2.2 on the politeness principle.

Future Tense consists of only two options, as mentioned above: past and present. For lack of a special future tense, the language must resort to a number of different constructions to express future time:

1 present progressive: *We're meeting tonight at eight.*
2 *be going to*: *I'm going to sell my car.*
3 simple present: *They leave tomorrow.*
4 *will* and *shall*: *She'll probably help you.*
5 *will* + progressive: *He'll be dozing off directly.*

In addition, what has not (yet) taken place is regularly referred to by other modal verbs (*We can meet tomorrow*), semi-modal verbs (*The fire is about to go out*), numerous lexical verbs (*Do you plan to stay long?*), and all imperatives (*Buy me a doughnut, please*).

The forms (1)–(5) are by no means freely interchangeable. They fall more or less roughly into two groups, those which stress intention and those which express prediction. Intention is strongest with (1) and (2); prediction is more prominent with (3), (4) and (5).

Notes on 1: The progressive form is used to indicate something which is going on (see below 4.4.3). If the actual act lies in the future (*meeting tonight*), then the current activity can only be seen in the fact that a decision (intention) to meet has at present already been made. This means of expressing the future is frequently supported by a future time adverbial.

Notes on 2: The form with *be going to* is used with wilful agents to indicate that a course of action has been decided on. Therefore when determination to do something is evident, only this form is appropriate (*It doesn't matter what you say; he says he's going to move out*). *Will*, in its contracted form *'ll* is inappropriate here; however, the full form spoken emphatically might be used by some speakers to indicate great wilfulness. With inanimate subjects, in contrast, *be going to* makes predictions, but ones of great certainty, for example, *Look at those heavy black clouds: it's going to pour*. Here again, *will*, contracted or not, cannot be used.

Notes on 3: The simple present (always used with an adverbial expression of future time) is another way of expressing the certainty of a future event. This is basically the report function of the present which was mentioned above; here, however, it is something in the future which is being reported. This works best with verbs which express dynamic, prescheduled acts (*meet*, *depart*, *decide*, etc., as in *We finish at eight o'clock*) rather than activities (*hike*, *discuss*, *read*, etc.).

In addition, the simple present is the usual form found in temporal clauses referring to the future ([*We will be home*] *before you are*). Although the verb *are* is clearly future in reference, none of the other four forms could replace it. The same holds for the *if*-clauses of real conditionals unless volition is explicitly to be expressed (*If it rains* [not *will rain*], *the picnic will be ruined*, for rain cannot have volition).

Notes on 4: *Will* and the less frequent *shall* (restricted to the first person; chiefly heard in southern England) also make predictions, but ones which are vaguer, less certain. If someone says *Well, we'll see*, that person may well forget about the whole thing soon. Often this form appears after an introductory expression which indicates this vagueness (*I think I'll go to bed*).

Notes on 5: *Will* + the progressive, in contrast, comes close to being a 'pure' future since this construction is used for future situations which are set and will take place as a matter of course. It indicates certainty without suggesting intention (*It will be getting light soon*). Notice how it can be used without necessarily indicating intention on the subject's part: *You'll be taking your exam in just two days and I know you'll be quivering in your boots*.

For more on the future see Binnick 1972; Wekker 1976; Close 1988.

4.4.3 Aspect: perfect and progressive

The tense system of English as presented in the previous section cannot really be understood without including the category of aspect. Both tense and aspect have to do with time, but in differing ways:

> . . . tense is a deictic category, i.e. locates situations in time, usually with reference to the present moment. . . . Aspect is not concerned with relating the time of the situation to any other time-point, but rather with the internal temporal constituency of the one situation; one could state the difference as one between situation-internal time (aspect) and situation-external time (tense).
>
> (Comrie 1976: 5)

In English there are two types of aspect, the perfect and the progressive (the latter is also referred to as the continuous or the expanded form).

The perfect   This form is more closely related to tense than is the progressive. Situations which are reported in the present perfect refer, for instance, to the past. If *someone has bought a sweater*, then the act of buying is over. What is of importance as far as aspect is concerned is that the implication is different when the same act is reported in the past (*someone bought a sweater*). The difference is frequently described as involving **current relevance** in the case of the perfect; this is a kind of expansion of the actual event (its situation-internal time) to include the present. The past, on the other hand, as the unmarked form, may, but need not, involve such relevance. This might be explained as follows: if someone says they have bought a sweater, they are making the purchase the theme of conversation and probably expect an interested comment or question from their interlocutor (*Oh, really, show me* or *Where did you find it?*). The use of the past might, of course, provoke a similar reaction, but what it is primarily doing is reporting something which happened in the past.

There are two different ways in which the perfect may be relevant to the present. If the verb in the predicator indicates a completed act or event (*buy something*, *arrive somewhere*, *read something*, *meet someone*, etc.) it may be referred to as the **resultative perfect**. Something has happened and the results are of current or present interest. The other possibility is that the verb designates an activity or process which does not presuppose completeness or a conclusion (*sleep*, *read*, *live somewhere*, *learn*, *grow wise*, etc.). When there is no result, furthermore, the activity or process will be reported in the perfect progressive and will indicate something which began in the past and is still going on: *I have been living in Birmingham since 1979* (I am still living there); *she's been sleeping all afternoon* (she's still sleeping). This is what is called the **continuative perfect**. While the continuative perfect may occur in both the simple and the progressive form, the resultative perfect can occur only in the simple form. If a verb which indicates an unfinished activity occurs in the simple perfect, it will either be non-sensical (*?I have slept*) or will be reinterpreted in a resultative sense (*He has grown wise* 'he is now wise'). (See table 4.5.)

Adverbial specification   The occurrence of the perfect is restricted not only by the type of verb in the predicator, but also by the adverbials used. A past time adverbial (*last year*, *an hour ago*, *formerly*) cannot occur together with the perfect; there is no **He has done it yesterday*. As a result, when there is an indicator of past time, current relevance cannot be expressed with the perfect. A speaker would have to indicate relevance non-grammatically, such as with an explicit statement (*He did something yesterday which I find very interesting for us*).

Just as there are adverbials which are incongruent with the perfect, there are a few which demand the perfect. These are ones whose scope includes not only the past, but also the present, for the present perfect includes both past and present. The most prominent of these is temporal (not causal) *since*. Examples are *The weather has been rainy since we arrived*, a continuative perfect; or, *I haven't seen them since last year*, a resultative perfect. Note that both sentences would be ungrammatical in the past tense. Occasionally *since* occurs with the present tense (*I like French cooking since our vacation in Burgundy*). It may even be used, exceptionally, with the past to avoid ambiguity, as in *I was in America since we met last* (implies one visit) vs. *I have been in America since we met last* (implies a continuous stay).

Several other adverbials have a strong, but not necessarily imperative tendency towards use with the perfect; they include *still*, *(not) yet*, *already*, *just*, *so far*, *up to now*, adverbials of indefinite time such as *ever* and *never*, and *recently*. BrE tends to employ the perfect more strictly with these than AmE does. A few adverbials, especially those containing a referentially ambiguous use of *this*, are sometimes past in reference and demand the past tense, and sometimes present in reference and allow the perfect. For example, if someone says *this morning*, and it still is the morning, the adverbial is present in scope; in the afternoon of the same day, however, it is a past adverbial.

The comments so far made on the perfect have been concerned with the present perfect (*have gone*). In the case of the past perfect (*had gone*) and the future perfect (*will have gone*), there are no adverbial restrictions of the types just outlined. Indeed, both sometimes express relevance in regard to a past or future time point just as the present perfect does to the present; but sometimes they are more tense-like and provide further levels of temporal differentiation, such as a 'deeper' past (*I had read his books before I met him*). Indeed, the perfect of non-finite forms seems to be one alternative way of indicating anterior time in non-finite VPs, which cannot otherwise be marked for tense (see below 4.7.3).

A final remark about the perfect is that it is often used within texts, especially narrative or reporting texts, to provide backgound information. Since relevant results of past situations as well of continuing activities are expressed via the perfect, this fits quite nicely:

(12) Australia has always mythologized the pioneers who settled the continent's interior, even though relatively few Australians have ever ventured far from the coast. Today the country is among the world's most urbanized: almost 90% of the people live in cities on the edge of the vast land

(Time, 11 June 1990, p. 53)

For more extensive treatments see McCoard 1978; Fenn 1987.

Progressive aspect   The progressive (or **continuous**) form in English is closely related to the idea of incompletion. It distinguishes **acts** and **events**, which are complete, from **activities** and **processes**, which are not. If someone is reading a book, reading is an activity that this person is not yet finished with. If, however, someone read a book, then this is an act which they are through with. From this distinction it is only a small step to the frequent characterization of the progressive as a form which marks limited duration. Aspect, in other words, is concerned with the internal constituency of an activity such as reading; it emphasizes the fact that an activity lasted for some time. When the non-progressive form is used, an act or event is simply reported as completed, regardless of how much time it may, in actual fact, have taken.

Often a speaker has a choice whether he or she wants to express one and the same happening as having temporary duration (and therefore in the progressive) or as permanent (and therefore in the simple form), for example, *I am living in Utah* vs. *I live in Utah*. The simple form is once again the unmarked form. Using it does not exclude the possibility of temporary duration, while the progressive marks this aspect of meaning explicitly.

Narration and background description The most impressive evidence for this distinction between the simple and the progressive forms can be observed in narrative texts. When someone tells what happens, one event after the other, each of these events is regarded as an individual step in a sequence and each is reported in the simple form (usually simple past, sometimes simple or historical present). What lies outside this narrative chain is background information which overlaps with the narrative events. From the perspective of these events, it is therefore incomplete. Consequently, this background information is presented in the progressive form:

> (13) Father's head lolled back and Shane caught it and eased it and the big shoulders forward till they rested on the table, the face down and cradled in the limp arms.
>
> Shane stood erect and looked across the table at mother. . . . She was watching Shane, her throat curving in a lovely proud line, her eyes wide with a sweet warmth shining in them.
>
> (J. Schaefer, *Shane*, p. 103.)

In this passage the mother was watching while all the other things mentioned took place (*lolled–caught–eased–rested–stood–looked*); this watching is outside the narrative chain. All the acts are in the simple past and might be linked in each case by the phrase 'and then'; they are treated as uniform points in a sequence regardless of whether one was longer or shorter than another. They are the focus of attention in the narrative foreground. In each case 'the whole of the situation is presented as a single unanalysable whole, with beginning, middle, and end rolled up into one' (Comrie 1976: 3). The activity of watching, in contrast, goes on all the while as a kind of backdrop; its duration is the central feature emphasized by the choice of the progressive.

Stative and dynamic verbs The use of the progressive is rendered more complicated by the fact that not every verb may occur freely in this form. Verbs which express states, for example, are restricted to the simple form. One of the main verbs of state is *be* (*The sky is cloudy*, not **The sky is being cloudy*). Yet almost any verb may be used in the progressive under the appropriate circumstances. With *be*, for example, we find *You're just being polite*, which indicates that the politeness of the addressee is temporary and perhaps not fully sincere. A convenient test to see whether a state verb is being used dynamically is to frame it as an imperative. If this is grammatical, the verb is dynamic (*Be polite*); if not, it is stative (**Be six feet tall*). This works because issuing a command presumes intention and control over action on the part of the addressee.

Most verbs are dynamic, which means that they can easily appear in the progressive if that is what is called for. Verbs of movement are clear examples (*run*, *jump*, *build*, *write*, etc.), but numerous others are also dynamic (*read*, *sleep*, *talk*).

It is convenient to divide the non-progressive or non-dynamic verbs into two sub-classes. The first of these is the **private verbs**, so called because they refer to what an individual alone can experience in his or her sensations, thoughts or feelings. When any of these are expressed, it is essentially a report and, like all other reports, appears in the simple form. Verbs of perception, cognition and evaluation (*see*, *hear*; *know*, *believe*; *want*, *love*, etc.) belong here. It is normal to hear a child say: *I love my mommy*; unacceptable is **I'm loving my mommy*. A verb of evaluation may be found in the progressive, but chiefly to indicate a growing intensification (*Are you smoking more and enjoying it less?*). Note, however, that some private verbs, such as *feel*, *itch* and *ache* may be used in both forms (*How are you feeling?* or *How do you feel?*).

The second sub-class is that of **verbs of state**, ones which designate relationships, which are not regarded as temporary even if they eventually turn out to be so: *equal*, *resemble*, *seem*, *cost*, *depend*, *adjoin*, and many others. Clearly *two plus two equals four*, and no one would venture to say **two plus two is equalling four*.

Perfect and progressive   The progressive and the present perfect can occur together, as was pointed out above (see above **The perfect**). However, not every type of verb may appear in this combination. Verbs which designate undifferentiated activities, that is, activities which do not logically include the idea of completion, must occur in the present perfect progressive and cannot appear in the present perfect simple. Compare *I have been thinking* vs. **I have thought*. These verbs may be used in the present perfect simple only as expressions of general experience (*?I have slept*), but people seldom say such self-evident things.

In contrast to verbs of undifferentiated activity there are verbs which are intrinsically perfective; that is, they designate an act which necessarily presupposes its conclusion, for example, *Goldilocks has eaten my porridge up*. Since *to eat something up* expresses completeness, it does not fit with the idea of incompleteness contained in the present perfect progressive. The sentence **She has been eating my porridge up* is unacceptable (unless it refers to repeated instances of this) because it is impossible to say that something is in the process of being completed when it is not yet clear whether it will, in fact, ever be successfully completed. Compare also **I have been discovering the answer to the world's energy problems*.

State verbs cannot, of course, occur in the present perfect progressive because they never occur in the progressive. In addition, state verbs cannot be in the present perfect simple either, for a state is something unchanging, while the present perfect simple is used for something which by implication has been completed in the past (though relevant in the present), for example, *I have been six feet tall or *Two plus two has equalled four or *I have known the answer.

Most verbs, however, allow either a perfective or non-perfective interpretation. In the former case they are examples of the resultative perfect (*I've done my homework*); in the latter they are instances of the continuative perfect (*I've been doing my homework*). Table 4.5 sums up the different verb types.

4.4.4 Voice

This category consists of the contrast between active and passive. The use of passive as opposed to the active causes a change in the perspective of a sentence, i.e. it affects the **sentence theme**. The passive is favoured in informative texts, especially academic and scientific ones (see 7.2.1).

Active and passive sentences are related to each other syntactically. What is the object of an active sentence is the subject of a passive one (*Schaefer wrote the story* ↔ *The story was written by Schaefer*). Conversely, the subject of the corresponding active sentence, which is usually the agent or is often referred to as the 'logical' subject, may be expressed in a passive sentence in a *by*-PP (*by Schaefer*). However, this is the case only approximately 20 per cent of the time. There are several reasons for this low frequency. For one thing, there is the strong tradition of apparent objectivity in scholarly texts, in which the first-person point of view is regarded as stylistically inappropriate (*In this section the passive is discussed*; less formal: *In this section we will discuss the passive*). In addition, the 'logical' subject may be non-existent (*Many factors are involved in the passive*) or

Table 4.5 Verb types and the present perfect

Verb types	pres. perf.	pres. perf. prog.
undifferentiated activity (*read, sleep, dream, talk*)	no	yes
perfective acts, events (*arrive, eat something up, discover the solution*)	yes	no
ambiguous for the above (*listen to the news, eat supper, read a book*)	yes [= resultative]	yes [= continuative]
state verbs (*know something, resemble someone, contain something*)	no	no

it may be unknown or indefinite (*Many texts are written with a high percentage of passives*).

Not every predicator can appear in the passive. Those without an object (intransitive, copular and weather verbs) can only be active. The verbs listed in table 4.5 above as verbs of state do not have a passive, for example, *He resembles you*, but not **You are resembled by him*; *The box contains two dozen pieces*, but not **Two dozen pieces are contained by the box*. On the other hand, ditransitive sentences (*We gave her the book*) have two passives, one less frequent one in which the direct object is the subject (*The book was given to her*) and a more common one in which the indirect object is the subject (*She was given the book*).

Statal and dynamic passives   While passives most frequently appear with the auxiliary verb *be*, two others are also common, *have* and *get*. The latter is particularly important because passive constructions with *be* are often ambiguous between the occurrence of an act and the result of such an occurrence. The first is called the **dynamic passive**; the second, the **statal** (or **stative**) **passive**. As an example, note that *John was hurt* can refer to a dynamic act in which someone inflicted damage or insult on John. It can also refer to the state or condition of being injured or insulted (because of something someone did or said). The sentence *John got hurt*, in contrast, has only the dynamic meaning.

Despite the advantage of its clearly dynamic meaning, *get* also has a disadvantage: it may be used only with some verbs (*get married, get involved, get done*; not **?get seen, *?get aided, *?get instructed*). *Get* is only suitable when a change of state is involved. Furthermore, style is also a factor: in more formal usage *get* is less acceptable than in casual conversation.

Other 'auxiliaries': the semi-passive   In some cases *get* is less a passive than a copula followed by a participial adjective. This can be confirmed by the fact that an intensifier such as *very, awfully* or *extremely* may precede the participle (*Towards midnight I got (terribly) tired*). Much the same thing is true of *become, grow, feel, seem* and a number of others. They resemble the stative passive, but are not usually regarded as true passives.

Passive-like structures   Both *get* and *have* are used in a structure in which the subject is experiencer (but not agent, see 4.3.2) of a passive act: *John got/had his arm broken in the fight*. Here John experienced something, but did not actually do it. In a different interpretation of this structure, the subject may be understood as the person who caused or instigated what was done (*John got/had his tonsils removed* 'asked the surgeon to do this').

Active constructions with passive meaning.   In conclusion it should be pointed out that there are a number of constructions in which the subject of an active sentence is the 'logical' object of the predicator. This gives these sentences a passive-like interpretation, and it is possible with such verbs as *blow*, *burn*, *ring*, *break*, *open*, etc. (*The leaves blew in the wind* 'were blown by the wind'; *The house burned down* 'was burned down').

A similar pattern applies to verbs which usually occur with an adverbial. Here the agent can be left out and the object can then be 'promoted' to subject; hence *We are selling that book awfully fast* becomes the passive-like *That book sells awfully fast* 'is being sold fast'. This is not truly a passive, for note that the same relationship holds with intransitive *You can write well with that pen*, which becomes *That pen writes well*. Here no passive paraphrase is possible, for the subject has the semantic role of instrumental. There do not seem to be any obvious restrictions on what predicators permit this so long as they (a) (usually) contain an adverbial of manner and quantity and (b) what is promoted to subject is an objective or instrumental semantic role; see 1.4.4 for more examples.

In addition to the constructions presented here, see 4.5.4 for non-finite constructions which are active in form but passive in effect. For further detail, see Stein 1979; Svartvik 1966.

The communicative structure of sentences   One final, extremely important question remains to be discussed: What function does the passive fulfil? In English what comes early in a sentence is its **theme** or **topic** and what follows is the **rheme** (from the Greek word meaning 'what is said') or **comment** on this topic. Since subjects usually come at the beginning of sentences, they also normally designate the theme. Sometimes, however, the object is the theme. By using the passive the object can become the subject and take the thematic position at the beginning of the sentence. For example, in *John's in the hospital. Someone hurt him in a fight*, the theme of the second sentence is John, as established by the first sentence. The two sentences would have more **cohesion** if the expected theme came first in the second sentence and the new material, the comment, towards the end. This can easily be accomplished with the passive: *John's in the hospital. He got hurt in a fight*.

Questions of the thematic meaning can, as this shows, be solved by the use of the passive; however, other devices are also available to change the placement of elements. One of these means of highlighting information is by **fronting** (*Roses, I like; violets, I don't*, or *He didn't go gracefully, but quickly he did go*). Notice that fronting is used especially for contrast.

Another way of contrasting elements is by means of **contrastive stress**, which can be indicated only imperfectly in writing by using italics or underlining for what, in speech, would be realized by loudness, pitch change or the like (see 3.5).

In formal writing especially, but not only there, use is made of **cleft** and of **pseudo-cleft sentences**. In the first type the rheme is introduced by *It* *is/was* and the theme follows in a relative clause (*It was my car keys which I lost*). This reversal of the usual theme-rheme order has, once again, a contrastive function. Any sentence element or part of a sentence element except the VP may be rhematized in this way:

> *It is the second question which concerns us.* [subject]
> *It is statements of this sort which the author prefers to deal with.* [object]
> *It was in a flash that they left.* [adjunct]

In the second type, the pseudo-cleft construction, even a VP may be highlighted. Here the element which is to be emphasized is preceded by the appropriate sort of relative clause and the verb *be*. The element highlighted may be

a verb: *What we did was (to) leave as fast as possible*;
a noun: *The person who got hurt was John*;
a manner adverbial: *The way (in which) he did it was by dishonesty*;
a place adverbial: *(The place) Where we met was (in) Ohio*;
a time adverbial: *The day (when) we left was Tuesday*.

A further means of changing the relative order of elements in a sentence is **extraposition** (see 4.8.7). For further discussion see Halliday 1967; Duškova 1971; Erdmann 1990.

4.4.5 Modality

Modality in English has to do with the world not so much the way it is as the way it might potentially be. This may revolve around people's beliefs about it or around their potential actions in it. There are various linguistic means of expressing this in English, for example, with AdvPs and PPs (***Probably** he's coming*; *It's **in their power** to decide the issue*), with AdjPs (*It's **likely** that he's coming*; *They're **able** to decide the issue*), with NPs (*the **probability** of his coming*; *their **capability** to decide the issue*), and with VPs (*He **might** come*; *They **can** decide the issue*). Here we will concentrate on the modal verbs.

Morphology and syntax   The modal verbs form a closed class whose central members are *will, would, may, might, can, could, shall, should, must* and *ought*. Somewhat less central are *need, dare, used to* and *had better*. All of the modals share the syntactic features of the auxiliaries/operators: direct negation, inversion with the subject, emphatic stress and elliptical or reduced forms (see 4.1.3). The central modals retain these features under all circumstances. The less central ones do not always exhibit them. *Dare, need* and *used to* may appear with *do*-periphasis. For example, *I needn't ask* is virtually the same as *I don't need to ask*. In addition, *had better* seems to have no widely acceptable interrogative form; certainly, *?Had I better buy a new one?* sounds awkward. In addition, none of the modals has the third person singular {S} (*she may*, never *she mays*), and all take the bare or unmarked infinitive except *ought (to)* and *used (to)*. For these reasons *needs/dares to* are often not regarded as modals; no further notice will be taken here of any of the more peripheral modals except for *needn't* as a negation of *must*.

The deficient nature of the modal verbs *vis-à-vis* lexical verbs can be seen in the fact that none of them (as modals) has either a present or a past participle. As a result they lack the perfect, progressive and passive. Furthermore, they have essentially no past tense. Four of the modals do, it is true, form present-past pairs *(will–would, shall–should, may–might, can–could)*, but the past tense forms function as past tenses only in the most restricted of circumstances (see below **Tense**).

Epistemic and deontic   There are two major types of modality in English. The one, epistemic, has to do with beliefs and knowledge about logically possible or logically necessary situations. The other, deontic, has to do with potential actions.

Epistemic modality indicates the degree of probability of a fact or proposition. Take a proposition such as *Sally is 170 cm tall*. This can be viewed as relatively unlikely or convincingly plausible or, of course, somewhere between the two. Expressed with modals, this produces *Sally might be 170 cm tall* at the unlikely end and *Sally must be 170 cm tall* at the certainty end. Each of these could be paraphrased as follows: *It is just possible that Sally is 170 cm tall* and *It is necessarily true that Sally is 170 cm tall*.

Likelihood and necessity, the two main poles of epistemic modality, can be expressed in terms of each other:

> *x may be* = 'it is possible that x'
>   'it is not necessary that not x'
> *x must be* = 'it is necessary that x'
>   'it is not possible that not x'

The epistemic modals can be arranged on a scale: *might–may–could–can–should–ought to–will–must*. This scale is a somewhat subjective estimate and is not always accurate. The modals are too vague to allow a more precise calibration. *Will*, for example, makes a prediction, sometimes on the basis of evidence (*The phone's ringing; that'll be my sister*) and sometimes 'out of the blue' (*It'll be nice at the party, I hope*). Note, too, that *would* and *shall* are not included.

Deontic modality has to do with ability, permission, volition and obligation with regard to an action. If you can or may do something, i.e. are allowed to do it, the possibility exists that you will carry out this action. If you must do it, there is an obligation or a necessity, rather than a possibility. The key terms are permission and obligation, both of which can be expressed in terms of each other.

you may do x = 'you are permitted to do x'
　　　　　　'you are not obliged not to do x'
you must do x = 'you are obliged to do x'
　　　　　　'you are not permitted not to do x'

Ability and volition are variants of permission (they are sometimes referred to as a third type of modality, **dynamic**, cf. Palmer 1987: 6.1.2; Huddleston 1984: 170). While permission comes from outside the agent, ability and volition are internal to the agent (see below **Subjective and objective**).

A scale like the one given above for epistemic modality must be less convincing for deontic modality because of the varying semantic elements; nevertheless, it might look something like this: *may/might–can/could–will/would–ought to–shall/should–must*. Note that the past forms are included here with their present tense forms; this is because they sometimes still function as past tenses when they are used to express deontic modality.

Tense   Deontic and epistemic modality have different structures for expressing the past. For epistemic modality there is only a two-way actual : past relationship; the latter is always realized by means of the perfect infinitive, for example:

it might be true : it might have been true
it may be true : it may have been true
it could be true : it could have been true
it must be true : it must have been true

Note that all of the epistemic modals, even the past tense forms, have a present or future meaning when used with the simple infinitive; furthermore, all of them may be used with the perfect infinitive to express conjecture about the past. The past form has a contrafactual or condition-contrary-to-fact effect about it at the more uncertain (*would have, could have, might have*) end of the possibility–necessity scale (see below **Conditional sentences**).

In reported speech there is no backshift of those modals which are already past in form or which have no past form, i.e. *might* remains *might* and *must* remains *must*; epistemic *will, can* and *may* can be shifted to *would, could* and *might*, though this need not be the case.

In their present tense forms the deontic modals have future or potential reference. For past tense there are substitute forms available; they include *be permitted/allowed to* for *may* and *can, be able to* for *can, be willing to* or *be going to* for *will, be supposed to* for *should*, and *have (got) to* for *must* (also possible for epistemic *must*).

The two past tense forms, *could* and *would*, are the only ones which fulfil all of the remoteness functions of the past tense: past time reference, distance in reported speech, unreality in conditional sentences, and politeness and tentativeness in statements (see 4.4.2). However, the past time reference of the two is not completely unrestricted. Note that both auxiliaries have past time reference chiefly when they are negated and only in non-permission meanings. The latter is logical since it is not possible to give permission for the past, but only for the future. For *can*, then, it is the ability meaning which is carried by the past negative *couldn't*. For *will*, it is the volition meaning (rather than prediction or future) which *wouldn't* conveys. The positive past of *can*-ability is usually not expressed by *could*, but by *be able to*, and the volition sense of *will* not by *would*, but by *want to* or *be willing to* (negative *He couldn't solve the problem* as compared to positive *He was able to . . .*; and negative *She wouldn't sell her stock* as opposed to positive *She wanted to . . .*). Note that there is a past ability use of *could* + perfect infinitive, which is contrafactual in interpretation (*You could have come earlier*).

The past permission meaning of *can* is never expressed by a modal, as in *He was permitted/allowed to stay up late*, while *He could stay up late* has an ability meaning. Likewise the future-in-the-past of *will* must be the non-modal *She was (not) going to sell* and not the volitional *She would(n't) sell*.

Both *could* and *would* as well as their substitute forms *be able to* and *want to* occur freely in the backshifted tense of reported speech, for example, *We said they were able to/could help out*. The fact that the two versions do not mean the same thing will be discussed below (see **Subjective and objective**). Both the modals and the substitute forms also occur in tentative statements and in unreal conditionals, for example, *I would help out if I had the time* (see below **Conditional sentences**).

Should, though past tense in form, never has past time reference. Past deontic time reference is possible either with the perfect infinitive, which has a contrafactual effect (*should have done* 'was/were supposed to, but did not'), or with the substitute forms *was/were supposed to do/have done*, which is not restricted to a contrafactual interpretation. The same applies to *ought to*. *Should* is not used as the tentative or unreal form of *shall*; however, it is employed as a backshifted form in reported speech, for example, A: *Shall I leave?* B: *She asked if she should (*shall) leave*. Much the same sort of thing applies to *might*, which is never found for past time reference and seldom as the unreal or tentative form of *may*. It can, however, be used for backshifted *may* in reported speech, as in A: *You may have some cake if you wish*. B: *She said we might* (more likely: *may*) *have some cake if we wished*.

Negation   Besides the effects of negation just mentioned for the past tense of *can* and *will*, there are some important complications that have to do with the question of whether *not* negates the modal or the following infinitive. Sometimes this is unimportant inasmuch as, for example, not having permission to smoke (*You can't smoke in here*) is what would usually be said. Having permission not to smoke (*You can not-smoke in here*), which sounds strange, would very likely be interpreted just like the former utterance. Much the same applies to the *should* and *ought* of obligation.

The most complicated case of negation is with deontic *must*. The negative of the modal is *needn't* (*You needn't go* 'it is not necessary that you go'). The negative of the lexical verb, in contrast, is *mustn't* (*You mustn't go* 'it is necessary that you not go'). Epistemic *must* cannot itself be negated directly; instead, *can't* and, of course, *needn't* are used, as in positive *That must be our bus* vs. negative *That can't/needn't* (**mustn't*) *be our bus*. However, the infinitive after *must* may be negated (*That must not be our bus* 'It must be that that is not our bus').

As a partial summary of the categories so far discussed in relation to the modals, see tables 4.6 and 4.7.

Subjective and objective As mentioned above, the sentence *We said they were able to help out* and *We said they could help out* do not mean the same thing. In the first case the ability to help out is introduced as an objective possibility. In the second case the subject of the main clause (*we*) attributes

Table 4.6 Can and be able to (ability and possibility senses)

		deontic	epistemic
pres.	*positive*	can, be able to	can
	negative	can't, not be able to	can't
past	*positive*	be able to (occasionally: could)	could (or can) have been
	negative	couldn't, not be able to	couldn't (can't) have been

Table 4.7 Must and have to (obligation and necessity senses)

		deontic	epistemic
pres.	*positive*	must, have to	must, have to
	negative	mustn't, needn't don't have to	can't, must not, needn't
past	*positive*	had to	must have been
	negative	didn't have to, needn't have	mustn't/needn't have been

this ability to the subject of the reported clause *they*; it is an assessment and as such subjective.

There are several such pairs, for example, subjective *must* and objective *have to*; subjective *needn't* and objective *not have to/not need to*; subjective *can* and objective *be allowed to*. The distinction is, however, not always clearly maintained, and this can lead to ambiguity, as when the Australian Prime Minister said of a politician who was accused of deceiving the Parliament: *Senator Withers may have misled Parliament*. As a case of subjective modality the PM would be committing himself to this possibility; as a case of objective modality [the actual intention] the PM would merely be admitting that others had made this accusation (example from Huddleston 1984: 167).

The deontic modal *must* is subjective, which means that it imposes an obligation stemming from the speaker; hence it is relatively forceful. Objective *have to* invokes an outside obligation, which takes the onus off the speaker. This may well be the reason why some dialects of English, for example, some varieties of Scottish English, do not have *must*, but only *have to*. Certainly, the difference between the impolite sounding *You must leave immediately* and the more neutral *You have to leave immediately* is evidence for this. If, however, something pleasant is expressed as an obligation, *must* is unproblematic (*You must try our new sauna*).

Conditional sentences   Four types of conditional sentences may be distinguished in English, and the modals play an important role in all of them. The types are

real: *If it rains, they'll get wet*;
unreal: *If it rained, they would get wet*;
contrafactual: *If it had rained, they would have got wet*;
implicational: *If it's raining, they must be getting wet*.

Modals do not usually appear in the *if*-clause (although *will* may when it expresses volition) and are restricted to main clauses. Real conditions refer to the future; since the modals are commonly used for future reference, they will appear frequently in such sentences. *Will* is the most common, but other central modals can occur in this type as well.

Unreal conditional sentences differ from real ones only inasmuch as they express less likelihood. The use of the past tense therefore fits very well as a marker of remoteness.

The third type of condition is used to say something about the past. Here a conclusion is drawn about a hypothetical state of affairs. The main clause always contains a modal (chiefly *would*, often *could*, sometimes *might*) plus a perfect infinitive. This combines the remoteness of the past with epistemic modality, which expresses the likelihood of something given the right

Table 4.8 Conditional clauses

Condition	Time	Main clause predicator
real	future	*will, can*, etc. + infinitive
unreal	future or present	*would, could, might* + infinitive *would* + infinitive
contrafactual	past	*would, could, might* + perf. inf.
implicational	present	*must* or present indicative
	past	*must have* or past indicative

conditions in the past. Since the past is not repeatable, this is 'contrary to fact' or contrafactual.

The final type of conditional, the implicational, states a relationship which the speaker logically supposes to be true. It is basically a variant of the real condition. The *if*-clause represents not a possibility but a circumstance whose truth is not definitively known. Hence *if it's raining* implies that the speaker does not know whether or not it is raining. However, if the condition is true, then by logical implication it is also true that *they must be getting wet*. Note that the predicator in the main clause will either be the epistemic *must* of logical necessity or it will be the straightforward indicative (i.e. *they are getting wet*).

Conjunctions   Conditional clauses have, for convenience and clarity, been referred to as *if*-clauses. While it is true that *if* is the most common conjunction employed, a variety of others are also to be found. Some of them, as well as non-conjunctional structures used in conditional sentences, are listed with style-usage labels.

supposing, suppose: formal; not used for implicational conditionals. Example: *Suppose demand falls, then unemployment will increase.*

in case, allowing that, in the event that, on (the) condition that: formal; not used for implicational conditions and unlikely for unreal and contrafactual ones. Example: *Payment will be made within twelve days on the condition that delivery is completed as specified.*

unless: negative ('if not'). Example: *This can't be true, unless I'm dreaming!*

lest: with a strong element of purpose 'in order that not'; formal, chiefly AmE; real conditions only. Example: *Plan in advance lest ill fortune bring you to a fall* ('if you do not want ill fortune to . . .').

subject–operator inversion: old-fashioned or formal; not used for real conditions. Example: *Were he to agree* (or: *Should he agree*), *I would be very astonished*; Had he agreed, I would have been astonished.

conjoined clauses: chiefly second person and frequently imperative; informal; real conditions only. Example [threat] : *(You) come here again and you'll get to know me.*

The semi-modals This label is used to refer to a number of non-defective verbs which have modal-like uses. They include, above all, the substitute forms mentioned above: *have (got) to, be willing to, want to, be allowed/ permitted to, be supposed to, be able to, be going to* and *be to*. Further evidence for their auxiliary nature may be seen in the irregularity caused by the assimilation of the infinitive marker *to* with the preceding element to form a single phonetic unit, i.e. *have to* is really *hafta* /hæftə/ (*has to* is *hasta* and *had to* is *hadda*), *have got to* is *gotta*, *supposed to* is *supposta*, *going to* is often *gonna, want to* may be *wanna*; even the less central modals with *to* have *usta* for *used to*, a possible *needa* for *need to*, and *oughta* for *ought to*. This kind of reduction does not apply to other verbs followed by an infinitive; there is no *beginna for *begin to* or *lofta for *love to*) (cf. Jaeggli 1980).

4.5 The noun phrase (NP)

The NP can consist of up to four parts: the obligatory noun head, pre-head determinative elements with several different positional possibilities, pre-modifiers and, finally, postmodifiers, also consisting of several possible elements.

4.5.1 The noun head

Nouns can be divided into common nouns, themselves subdivided into count and non-count, and proper nouns. This is of importance because of the implications each category has for the other elements.

Count and non-count nouns Count nouns are, as was pointed out above in 4.1.1, prototypical nouns because they have plurals and, in many cases, possessives. They also take all forms of the determiner (*the, a/ an* and zero). Non-count nouns, in contrast, have no plural and individualized singular. As a result they cannot appear with the indefinite article (there is no *a snow*). They may, instead, have either the definite article with specific reference or zero article with generic reference (see below). Non-count nouns may be concrete and include such mass nouns as *coffee, sand, wheat* or *mud*. More often, however, they will be abstract nouns such as *loudness, strength* or *entrepreneurship*. Furthermore, a large group of nouns includes both concrete and abstract nouns which are sometimes count and some-times non-count, for example, *cabbage, denial* or *sound*, as in *I bought a* *cabbage* (a head of cabbage), where *cabbage* is a count noun, and *I don't like cooked cabbage*, where it is non-count. In addition, mass nouns may be used as count nouns, when, for example, you order *two coffees* or a writer talks about the *snows* of yesteryear. Normally, however, this is accomplished by prefixing some measure or quality expression as in *two cups of coffee*, *a kind of snow* or a *grain of sand*. Article usage with count and non-count nouns can be summarized as shown in table 4.9.

Generic nouns refer to typical representatives of a class. With count nouns there are three common ways in which generic reference is realized, viz. the singular with the definite article (*The unicorn is a mythological beast*), the singular with the indefinite article (*A unicorn has a single horn*), and the plural with no article (*Unicorns do not exist*). The three differ from each other in that *the* + **singular** refers to the class represented; it has an informal alternative with *your* (*Your unicorn is a mythological beast*). *A* + **singular** is used much like *any*. It may occur only in subject position. **Zero article and the plural**, also restricted to subject position, is the same as saying *all* (or *no*, if negative). A variant of this is the definite article and plural nouns of nationality (*The Germans are orderly* = *Germans are orderly* = *All Germans are orderly*). Non-count nouns are generic when they occur without an article (*Snow is white*).

Proper nouns can be identified as those which are capitalized. Capitalization is a sign of the fact that each such noun refers to a unique entity (even if, in fact, there is more than one, say, Joe or Barbara in the world). Because the people, places or things referred to are unique, they cannot be further specified and therefore occur without an article. There are two important exceptions to this. The first and most general is that a name of a person can occur more than once. If we want to distinguish between two people with the same name we can specify further by saying, for instance, *the Joe I know* or *the Barbara with the red hair*. The second exception involves places. Many place names which are derived from common nouns retain their article, so *the United States*, *the Metropolitan (Opera)*, *the Mississippi (River)*, etc. Unfortunately, there is no easy rule to distinguish between, for example, *Buckingham Palace* (no article) and *the White House* (with the definite article).

Table 4.9 Articles with count and non-count nouns

definite	count	non-count
singular	the (song)	the (music)
plural	the (songs)	—
indefinite		
singular	a (song)	—
plural	(songs)	—

4.5.2 Pre-head

The elements of the pre-head are divided first into those which specify (tell which of a group) or quantify (tell how many or how much). These are the pre-determiners, determiners, and post-determiners. Second are adjectives and participles, which are all designations of quality. A small group of individual items also serve to refer to quality (viz. *such, what, quite* and *so* or *too* + adjective).

The most basic arrangement is the order article plus adjective, as in *the fresh eggs* or *a new car*. In place of the article, which is the most common determiner, various other sets of determiners may occur; they include:

demonstratives: *this, that, these, those*
possessives: *my, your, her; Ruth's, (the) boy's, whose*
indefinites: *some, any, no, every, each, (n)either*
interrogatives: *which(ever), what(ever)*

All the determiners except the indefinite ones follow the **quantifiers** *all, half, a/one third, both, double, twice,* etc. The small set of qualifying **pre-determiners** (*such, quite, what,* as well as the quantifier *many*) may precede the indefinite article (*such a day*); *quite* also comes before the definite article (*That was quite a party!*). With both *so* and *too,* adjectives are moved in front of the indefinite article (*so big a problem*).

The post-determiners are exclusively expressions of quantity: *many, much, few, little, several, a number of, a lot of,* etc., and the cardinal and ordinal numbers (including *first, next, last, further, additional, other*). No more than one representative of each class may appear in any one NP, for example, *all the many (books), many a last (drink),* or *half my few (dollars).*

4.5.3 The order of adjectives

This is not strictly fixed, but the following schema is indicative of the dominant principle, namely that the more accidental, subjective and temporary qualities are named before the more essential, objective and permanent ones. Hence evaluative adjectives (*beautiful, important, stupid*) tend to come first, and those which name the substance out of which something is made, or the subject matter something consists of, come last (*wooden, metal; economic, religious*). In between come first size (*tiny, tall, fat*), then shape (*round, flat, sharp*), then participles (*blazing, ruined*), followed first by age (*old, new, young*) and then colour (*red, green, blue*). After that comes nationality or provenance (*British, American, African*). Adjectives which are gradable may be preceded by adverbial intensifiers (*somewhat, astonishingly*, *pretty*, *really*). Here are some illustrative examples (more than three or four adjectives in one NP would be rare in actual use):

both my last very worthless old British pennies
all your shapeless old-fashioned felt carpet-slippers
the second dozen small somewhat wilted yellow roses
his confusing modern poetic works

4.5.4 Postmodifiers

The noun head can be followed by several types of modifying expression. A few adjectives can be post-positive, both fixed expressions (*secretary general*, *president elect*) and adjectives and participles with complements (*a woman true to her principles*, *a house made to order*). Those adverbs of time and place which can modify nouns also follow (*the valley beyond*, *that car there*, *years before*). Many of these adverbs are variants of PPs, which are the most frequent postmodifiers (*the valley beyond ours*, *a story about love and war*, *a person of distinction*). PPs themselves are sometimes, but by no means always, variations of clauses, both non-finite (*the valley situated beyond ours*, *the woman sitting beside you*, *the valley to visit*) and finite (*the valley which is situated beyond ours*, *a student who comes from Ghana*).

Most of these constructions present no difficulties. However, the postmodifying infinitive requires a brief comment. In the example above, *the valley to visit*, there are two interpretations, 'the valley which you ought to visit', and 'the valley which ought to be visited'. Underlying the first is a structure in which the infinitive has a subject and remains active (*the valley for you to visit*); for the second it is one in which *the valley* is the subject and the infinitive has passive force (*the valley to be visited*).

The relative order of postmodifiers is generally from short to long. The main exception to this is that PPs which provide information about the nature or provenance of the head noun (*a woman of virtue*, *the currency of Japan*) come before participles and adverbs (*a friend of the family waiting outside in the yard*).

Postmodifiers can be restrictive (defining) or non-restrictive (non-defining), whereas premodifiers are more likely to be restrictive only (on restrictive and non-restrictive, see below 4.5.5). As restrictive elements they often introduce new and distinguishing or identifying features. On further mention these restrictive, defining elements, now known or given, may be shifted to a premodifier position in much the fashion of the theme-rheme, given-new distinction (see 4.4.4). For example, a program may be introduced as *a program using a computer*; further mention can then be of *the computer program*. More detailed definition may add the information that this is *a computer program for the checking of spelling*, which can then lead to *the computer spelling-check program* and so on (cf. Dubois 1982). This is parallel to the way information is introduced via a predicative complement: *her car is black* which then becomes *her black car*. The preceding example also illustrates the restrictive nature of premodifiers as opposed to postmodifiers and predicative complements: predicative *black* adds (introduces) information; attributive *black* identifies which car is the subject of discourse.

4.5.5 Relative clauses

The restrictive vs. non-restrictive distinction just mentioned is also made for relative clauses. Restrictive relative clauses are used if the identity of the referent is not clear. If someone says, 'my mother', it is not possible to ask 'Which of your mothers?'; the identity is clear, so a postmodifying relative will be non-defining (*My mother, who loves flowers, is president of the garden club*). However, if someone says 'my brother' or 'my sister' and has more than one, the relative may be necessary to identify which one of them is meant (*My sister who is at university just turned twenty, but my other sister is only sixteen*). However, the distinction between referents which are already identified and ones which need further definition is often far from clear. One result is that many writers occasionally fail to make the distinction, namely that non-restrictive clauses are conventionally separated off by commas while restrictive ones are not.

Note that non-restrictive pronominal relatives consist of only the items *who(m)*, *which* and *whose*. *That* and zero relative are possibilities only in restrictive clauses. Non-restrictive relative clauses are always finite. Restrictive pronominal clauses, in contrast, may be finite (*We don't like people who complain all the time*) or non-finite (*a hotel at which to stay*). The non-finite relative clauses invariably involve a preposition plus a relative pronoun combination.

Among the non-defining pronominal relative clauses is the sentential relative, whose antecedent is a whole clause (*Grammar is interesting, which is why I study it*). Only *which* occurs in this type of construction. This is, of course, not a postmodifier in an NP, but a kind of sentence adverbial. See Quirk *et al.* 1985: §15.57 and Greene 1977.

A further important distinction among relatives is that there are both pronominal relative clauses, that is, ones introduced by a relative pronoun (*who(m)*, *whose*, *which*, *that*), and adverbial ones, introduced by a relative adverb (*when*, *where*, *how*, *why*).

Pronominal relative clauses distinguish between what they postmodify (their antecedents) according to whether this is personal or non-personal. *Who(m)* is used for the former (*the friend whom I met*) and *which* for the latter (*the computer which I use*). This distinction is neutralized in the possessive since *whose* refers to both (*the friend whose computer I use*; *the* *computer whose printer is so noisy*). The same is true of the relative pronoun *that* (*the friend that*. . .; *the computer that*. . .). The relative pronoun does not need to appear when it is not the subject of its own (restrictive) relative clause (*the friend I met*; *the computer I use*).

The relative adverbials are similar to pronominal relatives inasmuch as temporal *when* is equivalent to *the time in/at which* and local *where* to *the place in/at which*. Both can be defining or non-defining, as in non-restrictive *London, where Parliament sits, is the capital of the UK* as opposed to restrictive *The city where the meeting was held is somewhere in Illinois*. Those of manner (*how* 'the way in which') and reason (*why* 'the reason for which') are always defining. If the antecedent is general (*the place*, *the time*, *the way*, *the reason*) the relative word *that* is also employed (*the last time that I saw you*). Manner relatives never occur with both antecedent and relative (**the way how*), but only either the one (*He saw the way I did it*) or the other (*He saw how I did it*). When there is no antecedent, which can also be the case with time, place and reason clauses, the adverbial relative can be considered to be fused (see following paragraph). In such cases *how*, *when*, *where* and *why* are hardly distinguishable from indirect questions.

Fused relatives are the final type. They are called this because the antecedent and the relative are, as it were, fused into a single whole (*You must return what you borrow*, '. . . return that which you . . .'). Because there is no separate antecedent, this type is, like the sentential relative, not a nominal postmodifier. See Huddleston 1984: §12.4 for more on fused (or nominal) relatives; for further details on usage of the relatives, see Quirk *et al*. 1985: §§17.10–25.

4.5.6 Cohesion within the NP

In summary, it should be mentioned once again that the NP derives its cohesion chiefly by means of word order. However, this is supplemented first of all by explicit connectors such as prepositions and relative pronouns, but also by number concord, which can be seen in the fact that various, but not all, determiners are either singular (*a/an*, *much*, *less* (increasingly plural as well), *every*, *each*, *this*, *that*), dual (*both*, *either*, *neither*) or plural (*all*, *many*, *fewer*, *these*, *those*). Finally, gender agreement also provides a small amount of cohesion; here *who(m)* relates to persons and *which* to non-persons only. For more on cohesion see chapter 5.

4.6 Nominalization

While nouns are 'typically' concrete and countable, not all of them are. Many are abstract designations such as *liberty*, *relationship* or *art*. In addition, acts, events, activities, processes and states, which are usually expressed by verbs, can be nominalized – that is, put into a noun form. Such forms are called **nominals** (in contrast to nouns). Five types of nominals will be recognized here:

1 derived nominals: *his refusal to come, the warmth of July*;
2 action nominals: *the understanding of problems*;
3 gerunds: *your singing popular songs*;
4 infinitives: *for them to complain*;
5 nominal and interrogative clauses: *that they agreed*; *whether the police know*.

Nominals are somewhere between the classes of noun and of verb. Semantically they all refer more to time (occurrences) than to space (objects).

Derived nominals and action nominals are the most noun-like. The former may be pluralized in concrete reference, for example, *the governments of the EC countries*. Note that the abstract act of *government* 'governing' cannot be plural. Both (1) and (2) may be preceded by the article (*a/the refusal*). Furthermore, both (1) and (2) may be followed by postmodifying PPs (*the interviewing of people, the hatred of evil*). Most important, however, both nouns and nominals form the centre (or head) of NPs. For example, they may be the subject of a sentence as in *His writing poems keeps him busy*.

The gerund, the infinitive, and the nominal and interrogative clauses are more verb-like. Gerunds and infinitives take the verbal categories of aspect and voice (*writing, having written, having been writing*; *being written, having been written* and *to write, to be writing, to have written, to have been writing*; *to be written to, to have been written to*, etc.). Nominal and interrogative clauses, of course, have tense and modality in addition, since they contain full finite VPs. The gerund is perhaps more noun-like than the infinitive and the clauses because it is the only one which may appear after prepositions (*by doing that*; but not: **by to do that*); furthermore, progressive aspect is infrequent with gerunds since there is no **being writing*.

The gerund, infinitive, and nominal and interrogative clauses are associated with what are called **complementizers**. These are markers which signal the presence of a nominal. For the gerund it consists of the (optional) possessive pronominal adjective and the ending *-ing*, (*our cooking supper*); for the infinitive it consists of an initial *for*, which precedes the subject of the infinitive in at least some cases, and the marker *to* directly before the infinitive itself in most cases (*for you to type so quickly*). For the nominal clause it is the optional element *that* (*(that) I came*); and for the interrogative clause it is the mandatory presence of a *wh*-word (*when, where, why, whether, who, how*, etc.; *what he said*).

Nominals form NPs, but they cannot freely occur everywhere noun-headed NPs can. Few will ever appear as indirect objects. However, all of them occur frequently as the subjects of predicators with lexically appropriate verbs, though the passive form may be unlikely with some (*?To go jogging is liked (by my wife))*. And long, 'heavy' subjects may be moved to the end (this is called **extraposition**), leaving the dummy subject *it* behind, for example, *It was great that you remembered Mother's birthday* rather than *That you remembered Mother's birthday was great*.

What is most intriguing and complex about the nominals is the use of gerunds, infinitives, and nominal and interrogative clauses with a set of verbs referred to as catenatives. The following section is devoted to them.

4.7 Catenation

Catenatives are those predicators which can have gerunds, infinitives, and nominal or interrogative clauses as complements. Examples are *I remember seeing them* (gerund), *They told you to return the book* (infinitive), *My uncle said that we should go now* (nominal clause), *I doubt whether he's right* (interrogative clause). In describing how these verbs and their nominal complements are used together it is necessary (1) to distinguish verbs by their semantic classes, (2) to differentiate the internal forms of each of the nominal types, and (3) to recognize the time relationships between the predicators and their complements.

4.7.1 Verb classes

There are perhaps some thirty different classes of catenatives, each of them containing members which share important elements of meaning. All in all some 500 to 600 verbs (not including adjectives) are involved. Note, however, that some are counted more than once since multiple class membership is common.

It does not seem reasonable to attempt an even moderately complete review of the classes; however, a look at some of the more important ones can serve to clarify the way in which catenation functions. The following classes (with examples) will be observed:

perception: *see, hear, feel*
cognition: *think, remember, suppose, see*
speech: *say, declare, suggest*
imperative: *ask, demand, remember, suggest*
volition: *agree, love, wish*
evaluation: *like, love, hate*

What all of these verbs and verb classes have in common is that they say something about either a state or an action/happening. They may say something about the possibility that it existed/happened, when it began or stopped, or who caused it, observed it, wanted it, demanded it, etc.

4.7.2 Internal formal differentiation

An infinitive is not just an infinitive. As the following examples reveal, there are important formal differences (aside from possible progressive, perfect, and passive forms):

I can come	subjectless bare infinitive
I hope to come	subjectless marked infinitive
I saw you come	bare infinitive with subject
I asked you to come	marked infinitive with subject
I planned for you to come	complementizer *for* plus marked infinitive with subject

Just as there are five different kinds of infinitives there are three kinds of *-ing* forms (again without considering aspect and voice). (The term *-ing* form is being used because it covers both gerunds and present participles):

I began working	without a complement subject
I saw him working	with object case subject
I minded his working	with possessive case subject

Nominal clauses may also be differentiated:

I like it that he came	*it + that*
I established that he came	*that*
I thought (that) he came	no complementizer necessary
I reminded him that he should come	modal predicator
I recommend that he come	subjunctive predicator

The interrogative clauses, finally, are differentiated by the variety of different *wh*-words which can occur as introductory complementizers (see 4.6). In the following, interrogative clauses (indirect questions) will not be pursued any further.

4.7.3 Time relations

There is a basic temporal distinction between the infinitive and the *-ing* form. Non-finite complements which refer to a time before that of the main or catenative predicator are exclusively expressed by *-ing* forms (*remember doing something, admit doing something, deny doing something, mention doing something, justify doing something*). An infinitive complement can indicate past relative to the main verb only by appearing in the perfect form. This is really a report of a present state which has resulted from a past occurrence (*seem to have done something, happen to have done something, be rumoured to have done something*).

Non-finite complements which are future in regard to the catenative are infinitives (*command someone to do something, wish to do something, like to do something, promise to do something*). Only a relatively small group of verbs does not follow this pattern (*recommend doing something, urge doing something,* etc.).

Those complements, finally, which designate a state or action which is simultaneous with the main verb may be followed by either. One difference between the two involves progressive aspect (*see someone leave* vs. *see someone leaving*; *begin to understand* vs. **?begin understanding*, where stative *understand* resists use in the progressive). A second distinction is that of factuality (past/present) vs. potentiality (future), as in *I tried smoking, but didn't like it* 'actually smoked' vs. *I tried to smoke, but didn't manage to* 'did not actually smoke'.

Finite *that*-clause complements are, of course, freer in their temporal relations to the catenative which embeds them because they contain a finite verb. The tense of the predicator is, however, not fully free. Recall the rules of sequence of tense which applies to indirect speech (see 4.4.2). In general, a past tense form in the main clause will normally require a past tense in the *that*-clause of the reported speech; for example, *will go* becomes *would go*; *goes* becomes *went*; *have gone* becomes *had gone*. Furthermore, the imperative verbs which take *that*-clause complements are restricted to the mandative subjunctive or to the deontic modal of obligation *should* (see 4.7.5, **Suggest**).

4.7.4 Status of the nominals

The nature of the varying relationships between catenative and complement is indicative of the fact that each of the nominals is fairly closely associated with a particular status. In the case of the interrogative clauses this status would doubtlessly be that of a question. For nominal clauses it is something like an imperative where the subjunctive or modal must appear and a proposition (or the assertion of a fact) with the indicative. When *it + that* is used the status is that of a presupposition (see examples in 4.7.5).

The infinitive is stative and carries the status either of a complete act or event or of a state. It therefore stands in contrast to the *-ing* form, which designates an ongoing activity or process, i.e. something not completed. This distinction is, of course, much the same as that expressed by progressive aspect (see 4.4.3).

4.7.5 Examples

To illustrate how this works four verbs have been selected (*see, remember, love, suggest*), all of which take a variety of different complement types. As the complement observed changes it is also possible to see that the verb itself has changed classes according to the new status of the complement.

See   Note the contrast between *I saw them crossing the bridge* and *I saw them cross the bridge*: in the first case it is the *activity* of crossing which is attested to by the first-person subject. No conclusion can be made about whether the people crossing ever finished crossing, that is, got to the other side. The second case focuses on the *act*, viz. something completed. It is clear, on the authority of the perceiving subject, that the crossing was finished. In both cases something actually happening in time is witnessed.

The use of the marked infinite with a subject is possible though not terribly common with *see*. This would provide for *I saw them to have crossed the bridge*. Here the crossing is also complete, but it is not an occurrence in time which is reported, but a state, the state of having crossed. In fact, this need not be something physically witnessed; rather, it can be a conclusion drawn on the basis of other evidence, such as the fact that none of 'them' remains on the original side. Here the verb *see* has changed classes from being a verb of physical perception to being one of cognition. Other verbs of this class (*believe, find, know*; *I believed him to be friendly*, *she found the bread to be stale*) frequently take complements of this sort, which is sometimes called the **accusative with infinitive** or **a.c.i.** (from the Latin *accusativus cum infinitivo*). When the main clause predicator is put into the passive, the subject of the infinitive becomes the subject of the whole sentence (*They were seen to have crossed the bridge*). This is sometimes called the **n.c.i.** (*nominativus cum infinitivo*). Most verbs of speech enter only the n.c.i. and not the a.c.i. construction (*She was said to be clever*, but not **Someone said her to be clever*). As a cognitive verb *see* may also take a *that*-clause complement (*I saw that they have found a cure for the common cold*). The difference here is that the subject did not necessarily see any evidence which might have led to the conclusion; instead, he or she may have simply read this in the newspaper and accepted it as a fact because someone told him or her that this was the case. What is expressed is not a state which has been established, but a proposition which has been accepted.

In summary, the verb *see* may take a complement which is an activity, an act, a state or a fact.

Remember   When someone says *I remember doing my homework* (or with a subject: *I remember him doing his homework*), they are referring to an activity which they (or someone else) carried out at an earlier time. They can also refer to an earlier state resulting from an activity by using the perfect form, viz. *I remember having done my homework* (or *I remember his having done his homework*). This stands in contrast to a present or continuing state, as in *I remember him to have red hair*. In both cases *remember* is a verb of cognition.

In *I remembered to do my homework*, finally, the doing of the homework is future in regard to the remembering. In this latter example *remember* is like an imperative verb, as can be seen more clearly when a subject and the *for . . . to* construction occurs (in those varieties of English which have such a construction): *I remembered for him to do his homework* = 'I reminded him to do it'.

In summary, *remember* has complements which represent an activity, a state and a command.

Love   Potentially there is a contrast between *I love him sitting there* ('I love him when he is sitting there') and *I love his sitting there* ('I love the fact that he sits there'). In the first instance *sitting* is a participle which designates a simultaneous activity, and it modifies the object of the verb *him*. In the latter case *sitting* is a gerund and names an actual act or activity. In the first case the subject loves the person named in the object; in the second the subject approves of the activity. Both refer to factual situations, and both are instances of *love* as an evaluation verb. When there is no second NP, as in *I love sitting there*, the gerund interpretation is appropriate.

When the infinitive is used, as in *I love him to sit there*, or, in those varieties where this is possible, *I love for him to sit there*, the verb is volitional and directed towards what is desired in the future. The same is the case without the second NP, as in *I love to sit there*.

The final variation is *I love it that he sits there*. Here *love* is a verb of evaluation, and the complement is a proposition, viz. that he does in fact sit 'there'. The proposition is presupposed to be factual and then positively evaluated ('I love it').

In summary, *love* may have complements which are current activities, actual acts or activities, potential acts, or presupposed facts.

Suggest   This verb may be followed by a gerund or an infinitive complement. In the former case (*I suggest our taking a long walk*) it is a proposal about a future activity and is unusual inasmuch as gerunds are used for future reference with only the verbs of this class (*propose*, *intend*, *recommend*, *advocate*, *urge* and *oppose*). The sentence *I suggest taking a long walk* may, but need not, include the subject (*I*) in the suggestion.

In some varieties of English the *for . . . to* construction is possible after *suggest* (*I suggested for us to take a long walk*). The same is true of the construction with no subject and the simple infinitive (*I suggested to take a long walk*). These sentences are used to report a potential act. In such cases *suggest* may be regarded as a manner-of-speech verb such as *whisper*, *yell*, *moan*, etc. as well as *say*, where this type of complement is common (*He screamed (for us/to us) to pay attention*).

The mandative subjunctive is a further form which is possible after *suggest* (*I suggested that he take a long walk*). An alternative complement is with the modal *should* (. . . *that he should take* . . .). Both are the reported form of an imperative. The mandative subjunctive is used after predicates which introduce a demand or proposal (the adjectives *important*, *mandatory*, *imperative*, *advisable*, etc.; the verbs *demand*, *insist*, *order*, *request*, etc.; and even the nouns *decision*, *requirement*, etc.).

Syntactically, this subjunctive is marked by having the base or infinitive form after the subject in all persons (*It is desirable that he/they be informed*). Furthermore, negation is realized without *do*-periphrasis, but rather with simple pre-posed *not* (*I prefer that he/they not learn what happened*). In BrE the subjunctive is restricted more to formal contexts. In this variety the form with *should* is very common, but the present or past indicative is found as well (*I suggested that he takes/took a walk*). The latter form is likely to be misunderstood in AmE as a verb of speech (*suggest* 'insinuate') which is followed not by an imperative, but by a proposition ('In my opinion this is what he did').

In summary, *suggest* may be followed by a proposed act or activity, a potential act, an imperative, and a proposition.

The examples of these four verbs have demonstrated some of the main principles behind the way the catenatives and their nominal complements interact. Needless to say, an enormous amount of detail has been left out, including a considerable number of instances which often seem on the surface to be contradictory. For further detail, see Borkin 1973; Declerck 1981; 1983; Freed 1979; Gee 1975; Gramley 1987; 1988; Karttunen 1971; Ney 1979; Palmer 1987.

4.8 The clause

Among the phenomena which are relevant at the level of the clause are sentence patterns, mood, illocutionary force and complexity. Furthermore, some phenomena such as clause pro-forms, negation, thematic focus and word order are best observed at this level. The major syntactic or sentence patterns have already been introduced (4.3.3). We will continue here with illocutionary force.

4.8.1 Illocutionary force

It is well known that many a statement really pursues a different purpose than just, say, giving information. *I've just mopped the floor* may be intended as a prohibition ('Don't walk on it yet') or a request ('Say thanks'). In the appropriate setting the statement *It's warm and sunny* may be taken as a question ('Shall we go for a stroll?'), itself perhaps more a directive (see 6.2.1).

4.8.2 Clause types

As far as this chapter is concerned, each of the traditional moods is associated with a particular sentence type. The **indicative** is rooted in the declarative sentence, and this is the type used in 4.3.3 to illustrate sentence patterns: the subject comes first, followed by the predicator, and then by whatever further complements may be called for (direct object, indirect object, predicative complement).

The **interrogative** provides a variation on this inasmuch as most questions involve a *wh*-question word (*who, what, where, when, why, how*, etc.) and operator–subject inversion. For example, the declarative *She left us at noon* becomes the question *When did she leave us?*, in which the operator *do* is introduced since the declarative in the example has no operator. Of course, inversion does not always occur (*Who left us at noon?*, where the *wh*-word is subject); nor is there always a *wh*-word (*yes–no* questions such as *Did she leave at noon?*). If such a *yes–no* question is reported, however, the *wh*-word *whether* or *if* is used (*They asked whether/if she left at noon*). In reported questions there is usually also no inversion (*They asked when she left*). However, there is a tendency to retain inversion in informal usage (*They asked when did she leave*). Sometimes there is neither inversion nor a *wh*-word, as in *She left us at noon?* spoken with rising intonation. In writing, direct questions always have a question mark at the end.

The **imperative** typically appears as the base form of the verb without a subject (*Speak up, please*). Imperatives are, despite the lack of a subject, clearly second person, addressed to a hearer-reader. This is evident both in reflexive forms and anaphoric pronoun reference (*Help yourself to more potatoes if you're still hungry; Give me a hand, will you?*). Imperatives never contain modals, and there is never perfect aspect in imperatives. The lack of the perfect clearly has to do with the fact that imperatives refer to the future. The progressive is possible though infrequent (*Be working when the boss comes in*). Passives are found, but most often in the negative (*Don't be fooled by her*) or with the auxiliary *get* (*Come on! Get organized*). Note that *be* is negated with the auxiliary *do* in imperatives.

Although typical imperatives are second-person forms, the imperative construction with *let* is sometimes thought of as a first-person variant as in *Let's give a party* or as in the reflexive *Let me treat myself to a cup of coffee* or *Let's leave early, shall we?* with a pronoun tag. Sometimes third-person forms are also found (*If they have no bread, let them eat cake*). The negative is *Let's not go, Don't let's go* (BrE) or *Let's don't go* (AmE). (On the imperative, see Davies 1986; Hamblin 1987.)

Exclamatory mood may be imposed on practically any syntactic form if emphatic stress and strongly rising or rising-falling intonation is used. However, there is also one exclamatory sentence type, namely independent utterances introduced by *what* or *how* with or without a predicator, for example, *What a day (it was)!* or *How nice (they are)!* An exclamation point is often but not invariably used in writing.

4.8.3 Complexity

Clauses can also be linked by **coordination** and **subordination**. When two main clauses are connected, this is referred to as a **compound sentence**. Subordination may, as 4.7 has shown, involve finite and non-finite clauses embedded within main clauses, including reported speech. Relative clauses can expand NPs as postmodifiers (4.5.5). Furthermore, a subordinate (adverbial) clause may be joined to a main clause. These instances are all called **complex sentences**. A combination of the compound and complex sentences are referred to as **compound-complex**. Complexity is one means of establishing cohesion within texts (see chapter 5).

Two main clauses can be coordinated by means of the coordinating conjunctions *and, or, nor, but* and *for* (*It's warm, and the sun is shining*). There is also the possibility of using correlative coordinating conjunctions, *both . . . and, (n)either . . . (n)or, not only . . . but (also)*, in which one member comes at the beginning of the first and the other at the beginning of the second clause (*Not only is it warm, but the sun is also shining*). Coordination can also be achieved with **conjuncts**, i.e. adverbials which have a connecting function. They tend to be relatively formal in style. Some of the most common are *however, nevertheless, moreover, in addition, therefore, furthermore, in other words, on the other hand, rather, instead*; but there are many more. In writing, if the two clauses do not appear as separate sentences, the convention is to use a semi-colon before and a comma after them when they come between the two (*Conjuncts are connectors; nevertheless, they are not conjunctions*). If a conjunct occurs within the second clause the punctuation is as follows: *Conjuncts are connectors; they are, nevertheless, not conjunctions*. In addition, both coordinating conjunctions and conjuncts may link subordinate clauses, phrases or individual words with each other.

A final means of coordinating two clauses in writing is by simply putting them next to each other and connecting them with a semi-colon or colon (*The word 'but' is a conjunction; the word 'however' is a conjunct*).

Subordinate adverbial clauses fulfil much the same function as adjunct AdvPs and PPs. They are usually introduced by a subordinating conjunction which may express time (*when, before, after, as soon as*), cause (*because, as, since*), concession (*although*), condition (*if, in case, supposing, unless*, but conditional clauses are also introduced by means of subject-auxiliary inversion; *were you to go . . .*), purpose (*so that, in order that*), comparison (*as, like*), and a few other relations (see 4.3.4).

A subordinate adjunct clause may precede or follow the main clause; that is, the subordinating conjunction may occur initially in the sentence or between the two clauses (*We went swimming as it was hot* or *As it was hot, we went swimming*). A coordinating conjunction, in contrast, may only come between the clauses it joins (*We went swimming, for it was hot*; **For it was hot, we went swimming*).

The content of an introductory subordinate clause tends to be themat- ically given and therefore less prominent *vis-à-vis* the new information of the main clause. In the sentence *Although it was late, I read for a while before I turned off the light* the lateness of hour is treated as if already known, and the focus is on the continued reading. The final temporal adjunct clause carries more weight than the initial concessive one without having quite the same character of givenness; yet, it definitely is not high- lighted. If the two subordinate clauses are exchanged (*Before I turned off the light, I read for a while although it was late*), it is the temporal clause which is the given and the concessive one has more weight.

4.8.4 Pro-forms

Do is used as a pro-form when the predicate itself and all the complements which follow it are elided (*Jack hurt himself fetching water, and Jill did, too*). If another auxiliary is present, the pro-form *do* is less common (*Has Jack hurt himself? Yes, he has*; also: *Yes, he has done*; see also 11.3.1). Note that the pro-form *do* is not the same lexeme as the auxilliary *do*; the latter has only the forms *do*, *does*, *did*, while the pro-form has these as well as *done* and *doing*.

The pro-form *so* is used for the complements which follow the pre- dicator, as in *Jack broke his crown, and Jill did so, too*. Its negation would be . . . *but Jill did not*. Alternative negative forms are with *neither*, *nor* and *not* . . . *either* (*Jack didn't hurt himself and neither/nor did Jill* or *Jack isn't a child and Jill isn't either*). *So* is especially common as a pro-form for *that*-clauses after verbs of speech and cognition, for example, A: *Do you believe they're here?* B: *I'm not sure, but I believe so*; negative: . . . *but I believe not*, or . . . *but I don't believe so*.

4.8.5 Negation

Elements of all sorts can be negated at all levels and in a variety of different ways, viz. words (*partisan* : *non-partisan*; *skilled* : *unskilled*), phrases (*with malice* : *without malice*; *very carefully* : *not very carefully*) and clauses (*Someone yelled* : *No one yelled*; *I went* : *I didn't go*). At the clause level, it is normally the predicator which is negated. And this is normally done with the word *not*.

The use of *not* to negate a finite VP is always realized by putting this word after the operator (*I am working* : *I am not working*). If there is no operator in the unnegated version, an appropriate form of *do* is inserted

(*I left* : *I didn't leave*). Two exceptional usages are worth mentioning. The first is the negation of an imperative, in which even the verb *be* (although an operator) takes a pre-posed *don't* or *do not* (*Don't be upset*). The second is the negative of the subjunctive and of infinitives and *-ing* forms, all of which have *not* without *do* (*I suggest that you not be late again*; *To be or not to be*; *Not eating sweets is my New Year's resolution*).

4.8.6 Non-assertive contexts

A number of items are restricted to contexts in which there is negation or some other form indicating uncertainty about the truth or reality of a situation (this includes questions, conditionals, and some instances of modality). Many of the words which occur in such contexts correspond to others which appear in positive or assertive contexts. Such assertive : non-assertive pairs include *some* : *any, too* : *either, already* : *yet* and *sometimes* : *ever*. Hence there is assertive *He's already bought some*, *They sometimes go*, or *She did it, too* and non-assertive *He hasn't bought any yet*, *They don't ever go* or *She didn't do it, either*. This alternation is most stringent under negation. In questions, conditionals and modals, the non-assertive member of each pair is not always necessary (*Has he bought any yet/already?* or *Do they ever/sometimes go?*). *Either* may not, in fact, occur except with negation (*Did she do it, too/*either?*). Furthermore, the whole series of words formed around *some* and *any* involve numerous complications which depend on such things as the scope of negation and the meaning of *some* (definite or indefinite). (For more detail, see Huddleston 1984: §13.2; Quirk *et al*. 1985: §10.60f.)

A special effect of non-assertive elements is the occurrence of negative elements (*never, not once, at no time*, etc.) and semi-negative ones (*barely, hardly, infrequently, rarely, seldom, scarcely*) at the beginning of a sentence. When this happens there must be inversion of subject and operator (*Rarely did the sun appear that afternoon*).

4.8.7 Word order

The arrangement of words in sentences is one of the most important means of establishing grammatical cohesion in English (see chapter 5). Often word order is grammatically fixed. This has been mentioned at various points, such as 4.3.3 on sentence patterns. In 4.8.2 on mood it was pointed out that there is subject–operator order in declaratives and inversion in interrogatives. The effect of initial negatives and semi-negatives appeared in the preceding paragraph (4.8.6). The relative order of determiners and of adjectives has also been sketched out (4.5.2). Furthermore, word order is obviously an important factor in the way in which theme-rheme works, both in the communicative structure of sentences (see 4.4.4) and also in that of NPs

(4.5.3). The two guiding principles of cohesion are, in brief, those just mentioned: grammatical restrictions on word order and thematic focus.

The relative position of adjuncts   The order of adjuncts is perhaps the most difficult to present concisely. The overriding principle is that of focus. An adjunct which is to carry more weight will come at the beginning (thematic) or at the end of the sentence (rhematic). Very few restrictions can prevent this from happening. This does, of course, take for granted that the element which is fronted or which occurs finally would not normally be found there. In other words, it presupposes some kind of unmarked or normal word order from which it departs.

The usual position of adjuncts is after the predicator and its complements, with place before manner and manner before time *(We drove the car home* [place] *in a hurry* [manner] *before the storm broke out* [time]). There are several reasons why this pattern is seldom found. First of all, all three types of adjunct are not often likely to appear together in a single sentence. Secondly, manner adjuncts, especially in the form of single adverbs, such as *quickly* instead of *in a hurry*, will occur before the lexical verb *(We quickly drove...*). Secondly, time adjuncts freely appear in initial position, especially if this prevents the occurrence of a series of sentence final adjuncts *(Before the storm broke out we drove the car home quickly)*. Thirdly, the greater length or weight of an element will lead to its appearance closer to the end *(Yesterday we drove the car quickly to the place where we last remembered seeing the picnickers)*.

Displacement of a long element to the end of a sentence is almost a grammatical requirement in some instances. *That*-nominal clauses and infinitives which are the subjects of sentences are often felt to be too weighty and moved to the end. When this happens they leave the pronoun *it* behind to supply the necessary grammatical subject *(It was nice that you called* or *It was great to hear from you)*. With several common verbs this movement to the end of a nominal clause, which is called **extraposition**, is grammatically obligatory *(appear, seem, happen, occur, turn out*, as in *It happens that she likes you)*.

Extraposition can apply to sentence objects as well as subjects. Where a nominal clause is displaced, *it* may be, but usually is not, introduced immediately after the predicator *(We consider it important that you report to headquarters immediately*, but more usual *We hope very much that you have a safe journey home)*.

REFERENCES

Alexander, L. G. (1988) *Longman English Grammar*, London: Longman.
Anderson, J. M. (1971) *The Grammar of Case*, Cambridge: Cambridge University Press.

Binnick, R. I. (1972) 'Will and be going to', Publications of the Chicago Linguistic Society 8: 3–9.

Bolinger, D. (1971) The Phrasal Verb in English, Cambridge, Mass.: Harvard University Press.

Borkin, A. (1973) 'To be and not to be', Publications of the Chicago Linguistic Society 9: 44–56.

Brown, D. (1977) Hear That Lonesome Whistle Blow, New York: Bantam.

Close, R. A. (1975) A Reference Grammar for Students of English, London: Longman.

—— (1988) 'The Future in English', in W.-D. Bald (ed.) Kernprobleme der englischen Grammatik, Munich: Langenscheidt-Longman, pp. 51–66.

Coetzee, J. M. (1982) Waiting for the Barbarians, Harmondsworth: Penguin.

Comrie, B. (1976) Aspect, Cambridge: Cambridge University Press.

Courtney, R. (1983) Longman Dictionary of Phrasal Verbs, Harlow: Longman.

Cowie, A. P. and Mackin, R. (1978) Oxford Dictionary of Current Idiomatic English, Vol. 1, Verbs with Prepositions and Particles, Berlin: Cornelsen & Oxford University Press.

Crotty, W. J. and Jacobson, G. C. (1980) American Parties in Decline, Boston: Little, Brown & Co.

Davies, E. (1986) The English Imperative, London: Croom Helm.

Declerck, R. (1981) 'On the role of progressive aspect in nonfinite perception verb complements', Glossa 15: 83–114.

—— (1983) 'On the passive of infinitival perception verb complementation', Journal of English Linguistics 16: 27–46.

Dirven, R. and Radden, G. (eds) (1987) Concepts of Case, Tübingen: Narr.

Dixon, R. M. W. (1991) A New Approach to English Grammar, on Semantic Principles, Oxford: Clarendon.

Dubois, B. L. (1982) 'The construction of noun phrases in biomedical journal articles', in J. Høedt, L. Lundquist, H. Picht and J. Qvistgaard (eds) Proceedings of the 3rd European Symposium on LSP 'Pragmatics and LSP', Copenhagen: LSP Centre, pp. 49–67.

Dušková, L. (1971) 'On some functional and stylistic aspects of the passive voice in Present-Day English', Philologia Pragensia 14: 117–43.

van Ek, J. A. and Robat, N. J. (1984) The Student's Grammar of English, Oxford: Blackwell.

Erdmann, P. (1990) Discourse and Grammar. Focussing and Defocussing in English, Tübingen: Niemeyer.

Fenn, P. (1987) A Semantic and Pragmatic Examination of the English Perfect, Tübingen: Narr.

Fillmore, C. J. (1972) 'The case for case' in E. Bach and R. T. Harms (eds) Universals in Linguistic Theory, New York: Holt, Rinehart & Winston, pp. 1–88.

Freed, A. F. (1979) The Semantics of English Aspectual Complementation, Dordrecht: Reidel.

Fries, C. C. (1952) The Structure of English, New York: Harcourt Brace.

Gee, J. (1975) Perception, Intentionality, and Naked Infinitive: a Study in Linguistics and Philosophy, Dissertation, Stanford University.

Gleason, H. A. (1965) Linguistics and English Grammar, New York: Holt, Rinehart & Winston.

Gramley, S. E. (1987) 'The infinitive forms of English as verb complements', Belfast Working Papers in Language and Linguistics 9: 10–76.

—— (1988) 'Infinitive and -*ing* constructions as verb complements', in W.-D. Bald (ed.) *Kernprobleme der englischen Grammatik*, Munich: Langenscheidt-Longman, pp. 67–90.

Greenbaum, S. (1991) *An Introduction to English Grammar*, Harlow: Longman.

Greene, J. (1977) *The Use of 'Which' as a Non-Restrictive Relative Marker in Standard English*, Dissertation, Georgetown University.

Halliday, M. A. K. (1967) 'Notes on transitivity and theme in English', *Journal of Linguistics* 2: 37–81.

Hamblin, C. L. (1987) *Imperatives*, Oxford: Blackwell.

Huddleston, R. (1984) *Introduction to the Grammar of English*, Cambridge: Cambridge University Press.

—— (1988) *English Grammar: an Outline*, Cambridge: Cambridge University Press.

Jaeggli, O. (1980) 'Remarks on *to* contraction', *Linguistic Inquiry* 11: 239–45.

Jespersen, O. (1940-2) *A Modern English Grammar on Historical Principles*, Copenhagen: Munksgaard.

Joos, M. (1968) *The English Verb: Form and Meanings*, 2nd edn, Madison: University of Wisconsin Press.

Karttunen, L. (1971) *The Logic of English Predicate Complement Constructions*, Bloomington: Indiana University Linguistics Club.

Keillor, G. (1986) *Lake Wobegon Days*, New York: Penguin.

Leech, G. N. (1987) *Meaning and the English Verb*, 2nd edn, London: Longman.

Leech, G. N. and Svartvik, J. (1975) *A Communicative Grammar of English*, London: Longman.

Leech, G. N., Deuchar, M. and Hoogenraad, R. (1982) *English Grammar for Today*, London: Macmillan.

Lyons, J. (1977) *Semantics*, Cambridge: Cambridge University Press.

—— (1968) *Introduction to Theoretical Linguistics*, Cambridge: Cambridge University Press.

McCoard, R. W. (1978) *The English Perfect: Tense-Choice and Pragmatic Inferences*, Amsterdam: North Holland.

Matthews, P. H. (1981) *Syntax*, Cambridge: Cambridge University Press.

Mihailovic, L. (1962–3) 'Some observations on the use of the passive voice', *English Language Teaching* 17: 77–81.

Miller, A. (1960) *Death of a Salesman* in J. Gassner (ed.) *A Treasury of the Theatre*, New York: Simon & Schuster.

Ney, J. (1979) 'Semantic features and verbs with verbal complements in English', *Journal of English Linguistics* 13: 48–64.

Palmer, F. R. (1987) *The English Verb*, 2nd edn, London: Longman.

—— (1986) *Mood and Modality*, Cambridge: Cambridge University Press.

Poutsma, H. (1926–9) *A Grammar of Late Modern English*, Groningen: Noordhoff.

Quirk, R. and Greenbaum, S. (1990) *A Student's Grammar of the English Language*, London: Longman.

Quirk, R. and Mulholland, J. (1964) 'Complex prepositions and related sequences', *English Studies* 45: 64–73.

Quirk, R., Greenbaum, S., Leech, G. and Svartvik, J. (1985) *A Comprehensive Grammar of the English Language*, London: Longman.

Ross, J. R. (1972) 'The category squish: endstation Hauptwort', *Publications of the Chicago Linguistic Society* 8: 316–28.

Schaefer, J. (1980) *Shane*, New York: Bantam.

Stein, G. (1979) *Studies in the Function of the Passive*, Tübingen: Narr.

Svartvik, J. (1966) *On Voice in the English Verb*, The Hague: Mouton.
Thomson, A. J. and Martinet, A. V. (1983) *A Practical English Grammar*, School edn, Oxford: Oxford University Press.
Wekker, H. C. (1976) *The Expression of Future Time in Contemporary British English*, Amsterdam: North Holland.

Chapter 5

Written texts

The importance of texts is self-evident when we remember that all language occurs in communicative units usually larger than single words or sentences. All the same, texts have proved to be the hardest units to describe, perhaps because of the seemingly endless variations with which texts present us. Nevertheless, this chapter shows that quite a number of meaningful things can be said about texts. The phenomenon *text* will be treated under two points of view. The first (dealt with in 5.1 and 5.2) defines what qualities linguists have in mind when they speak of *texts*. Particular attention is paid to the means used to establish uniform discourse. The second attempts a classification of text types (5.3), which is then applied to the discussion of a concrete example (5.4).

This chapter and chapter 6, 'Spoken discourse', complement each other: the discussion of cohesion and coherence in this chapter is also relevant for spoken language, while the discussion of speech act theory (6.2.1) and global knowledge patterns (6.4.2) has a direct bearing on the production and reception of written language. While this chapter attempts a definition and classification of texts, chapter 7, 'Special Englishes', discusses one particular genre of written texts, that of English for science and technology.

The chapter headings 'Written texts' and 'Spoken discourse' have been chosen for practical reasons rather than terminological precision – many linguists use the two terms *text* and *discourse* interchangeably, as is done on occasion in this book. However, a distinction is often made between *text*, as a unified stretch of language without regard to situational context, and *discourse*, in which situational factors are taken into account (cf. Enkvist 1989: 371–2). General treatments of text linguistic matters include de Beaugrande and Dressler 1981; van Dijk and Kintsch 1983; Werlich 1983; van Dijk 1985; Brinker 1988; Petöfi 1988 and 1990; Heinemann and Viehweger 1991; McCarthy 1991.

5.1 Textuality

What distinguishes written (or spoken) texts from a random collection of sentences (or utterances) is the quality of **textuality**. Text units are connected with one another, and this unity is called **connectivity, connexity** or **continuity**. Textuality is the result of the interplay of the seven factors discussed in the following.

Cohesion and coherence   Textual unity manifests itself at different levels. Text sentences are linked above all by grammatical and lexical means (sometimes termed the **cotext**, Werlich 1983: 80) which prompt readers to interpret them as belonging together. This is called **grammatical** and **lexical cohesion**. A deeper semantic level is involved in discussions of **coherence**, which refers to the continuity of concepts and the relations between them. These two notions focus on the structure of texts; they will be discussed further in 5.2.

Intentionality and acceptability   The next two aspects relate to the attitudes of the participants. It is clearly necessary that senders (speakers, writers) intend to produce cohesive and coherent texts, and that addressees (hearers, readers) accept them as such, showing a certain tolerance towards texts where senders' intentions may be less than perfectly realized (this often applies to spoken language texts, cf. 1.6.7 on medium). Sender intentions and addressee acceptance are not based solely on knowledge of the language system but also on the participants' ability to bring their knowledge of the world to bear on text production and reception (see 6.4.2 on schemas). Of particular interest is the way receivers fill in gaps or breaks in the surface continuity of texts in order to make them cohesive and coherent (see 6.2.2 on inferencing processes based on conversational principles).

Informativity   Informativity is a receiver-centred notion of textuality and refers to the degree to which the text produced is expected or unexpected and whether it repeats what is known already or provides new information. No text provides only old or only new information, but the ratio of the two can vary considerably and depends on the sender's intentions and assessment of the addressee. Texts about well-known things are easy to produce and understand, but can also easily bore the reader. Texts that give a lot of new information, on the other hand, are more difficult to understand, though they are likely to be of greater interest to readers. There is, then, an inverse correlation between minimum effort (efficiency) by the participants and maximum impact of the message (effectiveness). In general, senders focus on the problematic or variable aspects of a topic because only they provide new information (de Beaugrande and Dressler 1981: 189). For instance, the midday meal is a well-established institution in many countries: when writing about lunch in England, therefore, one will concentrate on what is different from other countries, namely the class connotations that are attached to it (see the text in 5.2).

Situationality   Situationality concerns factors which make texts appropriate and relevant to a particular situation. This includes such aspects as using informal vocabulary and short sentences in informal situations. It also has to do with discourse **strategies**, for example the selection and sequencing of text units in such a way that they achieve the sender's goal.

Intertextuality   This stresses the fact that the production and reception of texts and text units often depend upon the participants' knowledge of other texts or text forms and their patterns or ways of expression.

Two comments need to be made on these aspects of textuality (summarized from de Beaugrande and Dressler 1981). The first is that their presence or absence depends on the individual reader or hearer. Different people will see different things in the same text and will obviously see different things in different situations (time, place, etc.): textuality is not an inherent property of a collection of sentences or utterances, but is attributed to it 'in a special context by an interpreter' (Petöfi 1983: 266). The other observation concerns the degree to which it is necessary to realize all seven standards. Again, this seems to be a subjective matter, not only with respect to the acceptability of a text but also, for example, in the degree to which sender and addressee are aware of the connections of any particular text or part of a text with other texts. For example, in the cases of *Vanity Fair* (Thackeray; allusion to an episode in John Bunyan's work *The Pilgrim's Progress*), *Ulysses* (Joyce; the Latin name of the hero in Homer's *Odyssey*) or *Paradise Postponed* (John Mortimer; allusion to Milton's epics *Paradise Lost* and *Paradise Regained*), the significance of the titles for the interpretation of the novels depends on the literary education of the reader. A text which does not seem to be dependent in very many or obvious ways on other texts would not, of course, be without textual status. This goes also for some of the other standards, for instance informativity. It has been shown that receivers will try to make texts relevant and informative even if it is far from clear what their communicative impact is (cf. 6.2.2 on conversational principles). It is obvious again that people vary in the extent to which they can decode a text's information successfully. It would seem therefore that a text fails to achieve textuality only if it fails to fulfil the standards mentioned to such an extent that no cohesion, coherence, relevance to a situation, etc. can be discovered by the interpreter (de Beaugrande and Dressler 1981: 34).

5.2 Cohesion and coherence

The continuity of forms and meanings necessary for textuality is achieved in various ways (see Halliday and Hasan 1976 for a comprehensive treatment of cohesion; also de Beaugrande and Dressler 1981: chapters 4 and 5; Brown and Yule 1983: chapter 6; Quirk *et al*. 1985: chapter 19 concentrates on grammatical means). We will illustrate these **cohesive devices** from the following text:

[1] **Lunch** [2] The word — and the thing itself — cause endless trouble still in England at that join in the class pyramid where it is still called dinner. [3] Any Englishman who does call lunch dinner indicates at once and for sure to any other Englishman that he hails from somewhere below the middle of the middle class. [4] The difficulty is relatively new in the long vista of English history, since the word till quite recently meant a snack between proper meals. [5] There was a time when everyone in England who could afford to do so dined in the afternoon and supped in the evening. [6] Then, with ease and affluence, lunch began its metamorphosis to a meal in its own right: an agreeable pause in the rhythm of the working day for deals and dalliance. [7] It is now a social divider of infinite power. [8] It distances husbands from their wives (he had roast beef in the cafeteria, she had cottage cheese salad in the kitchen). [9] It distances bosses from their workers (grouse and claret in the boardroom, sandwiches and tea on the building site). [10] It separates the employed from the unemployed (steak and kidney in the pub, baked beans by the telly). [11] The proliferation of the expense account has allowed a whole clutch of restaurants to spring up serving meals customers would never dream of eating at home. [12] Whether much business is achieved at these festivals of cholesterol is a moot point: in certain flash callings like showbiz and publishing the point is not so much what you eat but with whom you eat it. [13] It has become a handy way for royalty to entertain foreign potentates who are not worth putting up and for government to entertain middling visiting politicians; a convenient means for business to coddle new clients and a continuing solace to underdogs for their meagre rewards. [14] There may be no bonus at Christmas again but at least there's lunch to look forward to with old Ronnie at L'Escargot (see *Soho*). [15] Though a socialist government did its best to discourage lunch by making meals no longer tax-deductible it has had little effect. [16] In any event, the left seems as keen to go out to lunch as anyone else. [17] Lunch will cease to be a problem in England when it means the same to every Englishman as *déjeuner* does to every Frenchman.

(G. Smith, 'Lunch', *The English Companion*, p. 153)

5.2.1 Lexical links

For many text types, lexical-semantic ways of creating cohesion and coherence are more important than syntactic means: 'in non-narrative texts it is the lexical links that dominate the cohesive organization' (Hoey 1991: 74). Lexical links will therefore be discussed first.

Vocabulary items contribute to cohesion and coherence in many ways (see Phillips 1989). Most importantly, they constitute lexical fields; they establish semantic relationships; and they can activate larger text patterns, thus imposing structure on a whole text.

Lexical fields   The text under consideration deals with lunch in England. This is reflected in lexical sets which refer to the food consumed at lunch, to meal names and to typical places of eating:

food and drink: *roast beef, cottage cheese salad, grouse, claret, sandwich, tea, steak and kidney* (sc. *pie*), *baked beans*;
meal names and verbs: *lunch, dinner, snack, meal; sup, dine; have, serve* (*a meal*); *go out to lunch*;
places: *cafeteria, kitchen, boardroom, pub, restaurants*.

These sets of lexical items activate in readers stored knowledge (of things, places, people and their roles; cf. 6.4.2), with which they flesh out what is said in the text, and thus make the text coherent in their minds (cf. van Dijk 1977: 98–9 for another example).

Semantic relationships   The most obvious means of ensuring continuity is perhaps the exact **repetition** of a word. *Still* is thus repeated in [2], as is *Englishman* [3, 17] and *meal* [4, 6]. *Simple repetition* (the term is from Hoey 1991: 53) is found in *called* [2] and *call* [2], as well as *meals* [4] and *meal* [6]. This all seems very straightforward to the point of triviality. But it is far from clear what can count as repetition and what kinds of repetition should be distinguished (for a detailed discussion, see Hoey 1991: chapter 3). In our text, it is necessary to differentiate at least between the examples just mentioned, in which both word form and meaning seem to be identical, and the various occurrences of *lunch* [3, 6, 14–17], where this is not the case: *lunch* has the modern meaning of 'meal' in [3, 14–17] but refers to a snack in [6]. The basic requirement for Hoey is that there be 'repetition in context of the sense of one item by another, whether the wording has been the same or not' (ibid.: 69). *Lunch* in [6] cannot count as a repetition of *lunch* in [3] because the information contained in the two identical word forms is different.

Close in meaning, if not identical, are *difficulty* [4] and *problem* [17], both of which link with *trouble* in [2]. While *difficulty* and *problem* are loose **synonyms** independent of context, *distance* [8, 9] and *separate* [10] are made synonymous only for this passage. The same contextual synonymy is found in *handy* and *convenient*, and *way* and *means* in [13]. Also to be noted is the contextual synonymy of *meals* in [11] with the unmentioned compound *business lunch*, which is implied by the mention of *expense account* in [11] and *business* in [12].

Repetition in Hoey's sense (identical information content) is also present in words which stand in the semantic relationship of **hyponymy**, provided that the more general (**superordinate**) term follows the more specific. Thus, *meal* in [4] follows *lunch* and *dinner* in [3], as well as *snack* in [4]; furthermore, it does not add any information that was not contained in the three earlier words. The same goes for *the left* [16] and its hyponymous expression *socialist* (*government*) [15]. *Word* and *thing* [2] can also be seen to repeat *lunch* [1], with the difference, however, that they are much more general than *meal* is with respect to *lunch* or *dinner*.

A further instance is the example of words which, though they do not contain the same information, are related in meaning (for a detailed discussion of meaning relationships in lexical semantics, see Lyons 1977 and Cruse 1986). Here there is hyponymy with an increase of information, as in *calling* (superordinate) and *showbiz* and *publishing* [all 12]; cf. also *rewards* [13] and *bonus* [14].

The final group of examples all illustrate the relation of **opposition**; compare with the **complementaries** 'continue' and 'cease' contained in the words *still* and *cease* (*cause endless trouble still* [2] and *will cease to be a problem* [17]), or 'male' and 'female' encapsulated in *husbands* and *wives* in [8] (for a detailed, technical discussion of opposites, see Cruse 1986: 197–264). Examples of less exclusive forms of opposition are *lunch–dinner* [3], *lunch* [3, 14–17] and *lunch* [6], *dine–sup* [5], *bosses–workers* [9], *the employed–the unemployed* [10]. Of the pairs of places which are contrasted in [8-10], perhaps only *boardroom* and *building site* could be seen as opposite in meaning (in terms of social class) outside of a specific context, while the others (*cafeteria–kitchen*, *in the pub–by the telly*, *restaurants–home*) do not really exhibit either striking similarity or opposition in meaning in isolation. Finally, a contrast seems also to be involved in *discourage lunch* 'stop people from wanting to go out to lunch' and *seem keen to go out to lunch* [15–16].

Larger text patterns   Certain vocabulary items have the function of linking larger segments of text. Examples are *problem, issue, approach, solution, difficulty, drawback* and *question*. The function of these **procedural lexical items** is to organize and structure a text, to indicate the 'larger text-patterns the author has chosen, and build up expectations concerning the shape of the whole discourse' (McCarthy 1991: 76). The word *trouble* in [2] has great cohesive power because it activates in the reader what has been called the **problem–solution pattern**. The full pattern consists of the steps *situation–problem–response–result–evaluation* (see Hoey 1983 for discussion and exemplification). The word *trouble* makes the reader expect to be told at least what the problem is and, possibly, how to resolve it. Sentence [2] is a brief statement of the situation, and [3] and [7] through [12] give detailed descriptions of the problem. An actual response to the situation, and its result, is mentioned in [15]. The final text sentence [17] can be seen as a sort of evaluation. The problem–solution pattern, signalled by *trouble* [2], *difficulty* [4] and *problem* [17], thus acts as a device which helps to establish the unity of the whole text.

5.2.2 Syntactic links

The examples so far given have been of lexical words which establish connections with other words or organize the structure of the whole text. This section will be devoted to other means of creating links between text items: co-reference through pronouns, pro-forms and articles, ellipsis, connectives, and tense and time adverbials.

Co-reference   Pronouns, articles and other pro-forms cannot be interpreted in their own right, but rather direct the reader to look elsewhere (either in the text or outside it) for their interpretation. When receivers have to look back, or forward, to something, 'this has the effect of linking the two passages into a coherent unity' (Halliday 1985: 291). The relation between pro-forms and articles and the text entities referred to is called **co-reference**, to distinguish it from **reference**, which is the function of lexical items through which writers and speakers indicate what they are writing or talking about (Brown and Yule 1983: 205). Pro-forms and articles have two different uses, **anaphoric** and **cataphoric**: when they follow the items which explain them, they have anaphoric force, when they precede them, cataphoric force. In this book we can give only a brief, text-based introduction to anaphora. For more detail, see Brown and Yule 1983: chapter 6; Fox 1987; and Hofmann 1989.

Pronouns and pro-forms   *It* has only anaphoric uses, but its scope varies considerably. The first instance of *its* in [6] refers to *lunch*, and the second instance to *meal*. In other cases the pronoun does not follow immediately on its referent (see *it* in [2] where one has to go back to *the word – and the thing itself*). Close contiguity is no help either in deciding on the referent for the *it* in [7]: in making the connection with *lunch* in [6] one has to cross the sentence boundary. Slightly problematic syntactically is the use of *it* in [13]: the semantically nearest likely nouns are *festivals of cholesterol* [12] and *meals* in [11], but both are plural. *It* refers of course to *lunch*, the central topic, and picks up the pattern of initial *it* which is used in [7] through [10], but we need our knowledge of the text topic and the text as a whole to be sure of this (for problems with pronominal substitution see Brown and Yule 1983: 6.3.4). The almost exclusive co-referential function of *it* with *lunch* (exceptions are [12] and [15]) provide the text with strong cohesive force. In all the sentences except [5] *lunch* is present either in the form of lexical reference or co-reference with *it*.

All the other pronouns used in the text co-refer with something in the same sentence. Most of them are also anaphoric (*he* [3], *their* [8]). Note that *he* and *she* in [8] pick up *husbands* and *wives* respectively: both the nouns and the pronouns have generic meaning. A similar indefinite meaning ('one, people in general') attaches to *you* in [12].

There are only two cataphoric uses of pro-forms in the text. One is *that* [2], which points forward to *where it is still called dinner*. In the other example, *do so* [5] refers to *dined in the afternoon and supped in the evening*, the new information in the sentence. A change in word order would have destroyed the thematic structure by putting the semantically empty pro-forms in the informationally most prominent position at the sentence end.

No final answers can be given to the question why one form of reiteration is chosen rather than another, why, for example, a pronoun is preferred to a lexical item. One criterion is distance: there is a limit, though this may vary from case to case, to the distance across which a pronoun can still successfully co-refer to its antecedent. The use of lexical items does not seem to be restricted in this respect. Furthermore, there are stylistic grounds which may prevent the repetition of (lexical) items and require pronouns to be used. For both these reasons one might have expected *lunch* rather than *it* in [13]: the nearest instance of *lunch* in [6] is quite a distance away, and sentence [12] ends with an *it*, which does not link with *lunch*. The explanation lies perhaps in a different syntactic direction: when *it* co-refers with *lunch* in this text, it is identified with sentence-initial position and the subject function. This makes it easier to understand *it* in [13] and also accounts for the fact that the objects in [11], [12], [14] and [15] are realized not by *it*, but by lexical items. In cases where an item is stressed, only a lexical item, not a pronoun, is normally possible. This seems to be the more general reason behind the use of *lunch* in [14]. The same thing applies particularly to [17], which closes the topic in this text: it has been suggested that pronouns keep a text sequence open, while lexical items indicate the end of a text sequence (this is the central thesis of Fox 1987). For other explanations, see McCarthy 1991: 66.

The definite article   In [2], the definite articles in *the word* and *the thing* also have anaphoric force, making it clear that the *word* and *thing* meant is *lunch* in [1]. In [4], *the difficulty* co-refers presumably to the whole of [3], and *the word* points back to *lunch*, either in [3] or in [1].

In other examples co-reference is to things that are not mentioned in the text itself. Here the article signals 'you know which one I mean', implying that there is only one – 'or at least only one that makes sense in the context' (Halliday 1985: 293). The author relies on the reader's knowledge to make the text cohesive. Types of knowledge can range from worldwide (*the afternoon, the evening* [5]) to very local. Smith does not expect his readers to know the restaurant L'Escargot in London's Soho district, so he makes a cross-reference to his entry for *Soho*. This creates a minimal link (of repetition) between two articles in *The English Companion*. While the author feels that some explanation is necessary in this case, he does not make a cross-reference to *class* for *the class pyramid* [2] or to *pubs* for *the pub* [10], for a full understanding of which readers need to activate their knowledge of English society and institutions. Other concepts, such as *the cafeteria, the kitchen* [both 8], *the boardroom, the building site* [9], *the telly* [10] and *the left* [16], are not restricted to England in the same way and therefore can be expected to convey some meaning to a wider readership. (On the role of knowledge patterns in discourse, see 6.4.2.)

Ellipsis   The reader is also called upon to become active in several places and provide missing sentence parts. Subject and predicator are deleted in the brackets in [9] and [10], but can be easily supplied in analogy with [8]. In [13], *it has become a handy way* is to be supplied before *for government*, and subject and verb (*it has become*) are to be understood to complete the subject complements in the second half of [13]. It is less easy to say what has been deleted after the colon in [6] − presumably *lunch began its metamorphosis to.*

Conjunctions and connectives   What is striking in the *Lunch*-text is the lack of explicit markers of relationships between sentences and parts of sentences. There is only one connective (*in any event* [16]) and two conjunctions (*since* [4] and *though* [15]). Smith uses formal markers sparingly and relies instead largely on the readers' ability to provide the missing links themselves.

Tense and time adverbials   Smith is, however, careful to mark the temporal relationships clearly. He starts out in the present, but *still* [twice in 2] establishes a link between present and past, which is taken up again in *relatively new* and *till quite recently* [4]. A kind of natural order is then established from past back to present, and the passage ends with a reference to the future (see van Dijk 1977: 223; Altenberg 1987: 56). The past tense indicates the past in [4] to [6], and this is underlined by the time adverbials *there was a time* [5] and *then* [6]. The return to the present is signalled by the present tense and by *now* in [7]. The text stays with the present tense from then on, although the past is again included, in the form of the perfect, in [11], [13] and [15]. The only exception is the past tense form in [15], which is devoted to an action in the past but made relevant to the present by the resultative perfect *has had little effect* [15]. The text ends with the only reference to future time. (This text will be further discussed in 5.4 using the criteria established in 5.3.)

5.3 A typology of texts

Most of the recent models developed in text linguistics use a multi-level approach for the classification of texts. None of the ones offered so far, however, is sufficiently elaborated or has won general approval. There are also many differences in detail between the various models. The ideas which are presented in the following (see Heinemann and Viehweger 1991: 129–75; Brinker 1988: 93–138; Werlich 1983) should therefore be regarded only as a practical means of producing, predicting and processing texts and not as theories which lay down hard and fast rules for the distinction of text types: 'The conditions of communicating are simply too diverse to allow such a rigorous categorization' (de Beaugrande and Dressler 1981: 186).

The approach rests on the view that linguistic communication is an inter-active process. The first, or highest, level of observation consists, therefore, of the various functions that language serves in human communication. On the lower levels, types of texts are successively distinguished according to types of situation, of strategy, of structure and, at the lowest level, of patterns of expression.

5.3.1 Functions

Among the many functions that have been distinguished (cf. 1.6.8 and 7.1) four will be regarded as basic in this chapter. These are the **expressive function**, the **phatic** or **social-interactive function**, the **informative function** and the **directive function**. These four basic functions have to do with speech events in the real world. Another primary function is the **aesthetic function**, which relates, however, to literature. It may include elements typical of any of the other functions since it is usually subject to little restriction. Note, however, that certain poetic genres such as the sonnet or the limerick follow conventional prescriptions of uncommon rigour. The functions mentioned are not exclusively linguistic: traffic lights have informational and directive value, a blow or box on the ears clearly has directive force and gestures may have any of the functions. However, language is the primary means used by human beings to perform these functions.

All expressions of emotion (joy, anger, frustration) are subsumed under the expressive function. It is the most basic or general because all the other functions (interacting, informing, directing) always include some expression of self. Note that concrete texts (both spoken and written) often realize more than one function. Conversations or personal letters, for example, consist mainly of interactive language, in which the social bonds between sender and addressee are reinforced (this is called *phatic communion*; see 6.1), but they can also contain a part in which some business is transacted, as when news is exchanged (informative) or plans or instructions are discussed (directive).

Only a few examples of textual sub-classes will be given here, and none for the first function as it is realized implicitly in all the others. Phatic texts relate to social or seasonal occasions (births, deaths, birthdays, anniversaries, examinations, Christmas). The majority of texts are informative or directive.

Text types   When the informative and the directive functions are grouped together five major text types are often recognized: **descriptive**, **narrative**, **directive**, **expository** and **argumentative**. These are characterized by typical thematic types, surface features, semantic conceptual relations and global knowledge patterns (see de Beaugrande and Dressler 1981: 184; and 5.4). Werlich (1983: 28–30, 39–41), who is followed in much of the subsequent presentation, employs the term **instructive** where directive is used here.

The text types under discussion are general semantic-functional concepts and are not to be confused with such realizations as advertisements, editorials, sermons, shopping lists, poems, telephone books or novels, which are here referred to as **text forms**. The five types are examples of different realizations of the register category of **functional tenor** (see 1.6.8) or purpose, and, although further types may exist, these five are general enough for the classification of most texts. In addition, the five may be sorted into four basic categories according to the two criteria of concrete vs. cognitive and real vs. potential. This is represented graphically in table 5.1.

Narrative texts have to do with real-world events (time). It is immaterial whether a narrative is fictional (as in a fairy tale or novel) or non-fictional (as in a newspaper report). What is characteristic is the sequencing of events in which dynamic verbs (see 4.4.3) occur in the simple form and in which sequencing adverbials such as *and then* or *first, second, third*, etc., provide the basic narrative structure, for example, *First we packed our bags and then we called a taxi. After that we . . .*, etc.

Descriptive texts, in contrast, are concerned with the location of persons and things in space. For this reason they will tell what lies to the right or left, in the background or foreground, or they will provide background information which, perhaps, sets the stage for narration. Once again it is immaterial whether a description is more technical-objective or more impressionistic-subjective. State or positional verbs plus adverbial expressions are

Table 5.1 The catagories of text types

	concrete	cognitive
real	narrative (time)	expository
	descriptive (space)	
potential	directive	argumentative

employed in descriptions (*The operation panel is located on the right-hand side at the rear*; *New Orleans lies on the Mississippi*). Perfect and progressive forms typically give background information (*He was peacefully dreaming when the fire broke out*; *As the cabinet has agreed on the principles, an interministerial committee will work out the details*).

Directive texts are concerned with concrete future activity. Central to such texts are imperatives (*Hand me the paper*) or forms which substitute for them, such as polite questions (*Would you hand me the paper?*) or suggestive remarks (*I wonder what the paper says about the weather*). Stage directions use the simple present (*The maid enters, opens the door, and admits a visitor*). Assembly and operation instructions use sequences of imperatives (*Disconnect the 15-pin D-shell connector . . . and secure the signal cable firmly . . .*; *Shake well before using. Do not ingest with alcohol*).

Each of the three types just discussed has, as pointed out, grammatical forms associated with it which may be expanded to form sequences of a textual nature. Furthermore, all three are centred around real-world events and things. In contrast, expository and argumentative texts are cognitively oriented. This is the case because they are concerned with explanation and persuasion, both mental processes (though the former may include a considerable amount of description and the latter may have consequences in future action).

Expository texts identify and characterize phenomena. As such they include text forms such as definitions, explications, summaries, and many types of essay. Once again they may be subjective (essay) or objective (summary, explication, definition). Furthermore, they may be analytical, starting from a concept and then characterizing its parts; this is what is done by definitions and the *Lunch*-text which is discussed in 5.2 and 5.4. On the other hand, expository texts may proceed in the opposite, synthetic direction as well, recounting characteristics and ending with an appropriate concept or conclusion; this is the case with summaries, which exist as the sum of their constituent parts. Typical syntactic constructions which may be appropriately expanded in forming expository texts are identifying statements with state verbs or epistemic modals (*Pop music has a strong rhythmic beat*; *Texts may consist of one or more sentences*) or with verbs indicating characteristic activities or qualities (*Fruitflies feed on yeast*; *Most geraniums are red*).

Argumentative texts depart from the assumption that the receiver's beliefs must be changed. A frequent pattern would therefore be to start with the negation of a statement which attributes a quality or characteristic activity to something or someone. Even when a scholarly text provides positive support for a particular hypothesis there is almost always at least an implicit negation of previous assumptions. Advertising texts, often at the extreme opposite pole in terms of style, also try to persuade their readers that a particular product is somehow better, at least implicitly, than others.

Few texts are pure realizations of a single type. Advertisements, for instance, are frequently both argumentative-persuasive (*This is good because . . .*) and directive (*So buy now!*). The *Lunch*-text discussed in this chapter is expository (text form: definition), but also argumentative inasmuch as it implicitly pursues the thesis '*Lunch* is not what you think it is; it's really a socially problematic phenomenon' (see 5.4).

Expository texts can be neutral or contain evaluative elements (reviews, references, letters to the editor, rules and regulations, etc.). Whether or not they have directive force depends: in a review or newscast the information given is primary; an advertisement or set of instructions contains information, but the directive function predominates. Laws, decrees and treaties belong to a sub-group in which some aspect of life in society is regulated. Such texts fulfil the double function of informing the members of the society in question as well as directing their behaviour. They are thus partially expository and partially directive texts.

5.3.2 Situations

Any given text is not only a realization of a particular text type (including combined forms), but is also the product of the further register categories **field**, **medium** and **personal tenor** (see 1.6.5 to 1.6.7). Additional parameters are whether texts are part of non-verbal activities or not and whether they are used to accompany or accomplish practical or theoretical activities. A letter asking for a social security number, for instance, is characterized by these features: directive function; field of public (social) administration; medium of writing; personal tenor of dyadic communication in an asymmetric social relationship including, conventionally, the use of relatively formal language; practical-administrative activity.

5.3.3 Strategies and structure

On the level of strategy, senders have to make decisions on how to present their message in a way that is most likely to achieve their goal. A text strategy is, therefore, 'a goal-determined weighting of decision-affecting factors' (Enkvist 1987: 205; cf. de Beaugrande and Dressler 1981: chapter 8, who draw up a list of twelve strategies). Senders must therefore not only be clear about their intentions (cf. functional tenor, text types) and take into account other situational factors (field, medium, personal tenor), but must also ensure that the addressee can process the message easily. The relative easiness or difficulty of a text depends, among other things, on the number of participants mentioned in a text (i.e. the fewer people involved, the easier the text); on whether the features that distinguish between characters, in, say, a story, are memorable; on the simplicity and symmetry of spatial structures; on the simplicity and sequencing of temporal structures;

and on whether senders give explicit cognitive hints for the interpretation of the links (other than temporal and local), for example, those of purpose and reason in argumentation (see Brown 1989; for sentence length and other aspects, cf. Péry-Woodley 1991).

On a local level, in making a request, for example, senders have to decide on such matters as the degree of directness and politeness, and on whether to support their arguments or not (by giving reasons, explanations, or further details; cf. 6.3.3 on supporting moves).

A high-level strategic decision relates to what means senders employ in the pursuit of their intentions. Argumentative texts consist of 'events and states leading up to an intended GOAL' (de Beaugrande and Dressler 1981: 90–1). The step-by-step exposition is, for example, found in many expository texts (for more detail, see Quirk *et al.* 1985: §19.18; 5.4 and 7.4 below). Similar strategies have long been established in classical rhetoric. Enkvist (1987) has isolated the temporal, local and personal principles. In narration, events are presented in 'ordered sequences linked by time proximity and causality' (de Beaugrande and Dressler 1981: 90). This is basic to the overall structure of text types such as chronicles, histories and much narrative fiction. Descriptive texts centre on objects and situations and how they relate to one other. A general aspect of the matters to be described or a particular point of view or vantage point provides the organizing principle for the writer's presentation. Guidebooks are spatially oriented, but can also have passages that are temporally dominated. Note that biographies are agent-dominated texts, but that they are also temporally structured. Texts, in other words, can contain one, two or more strategies simultaneously.

It also follows that the mix of strategies can vary considerably. Long texts are more likely to be multi-strategic than short passages. As pointed out in 7.4.3, texts may even be organized cyclically, moving from one strategy to others in repeated waves. On the level of structure, in other words, senders have to make decisions about the number and sequence of text parts: where to place the central statement, for example, and whether or not to have introductory and closing parts. Similar decisions have to be taken for the individual text sentences that make up the various text parts. An important aspect of structure is also the choice of connections between text parts and text sentences (see 5.2.2).

Text types vary considerably in the number of their possible parts. For illustrative purposes we include a list of eleven text parts found in scholarly writing, though not necessarily in one and the same text: background information; statement of result; (un)expected outcome; reference to previous research; explanation of unsatisfactory result; exemplification; deduction; hypothesis; reference to previous research; recommendation; and justification (Jordan 1989: 159; see also Swales 1990). See 7.4.3 for five widely accepted parts in the scholarly writing of science and technology.

5.3.4 Language patterns

The choice of appropriate language for a particular type of text is partly a matter of individual preference, but partly also a matter of convention, which writers can of course flout if they think it will help them to achieve their goal. General maxims valid for an application for a social security number, for instance, are (a) factual approach, (b) concise style, and (c) polite tone. More specific patterns relate to typical lexical items and combinations of lexical items. In a description of elections in Great Britain there will be such expressions as *proportional representation*; *redraw the boundary*; *go to the country, go to the polls*; *declare the result*; *return an MP to Parliament*.

Of great importance for the reader are so called **text structuring devices**. These can give a preview of what is to come (*Let us now turn to X* [new topic], or *This chapter consists of five parts. The first . . . . The second . . .*), or refer to what has already been dealt with (*So much for X*). Here too belongs the class of **procedural lexical items** such as *problem, issue*, etc. (see 5.2.1).

5.4 Application: an example

In this final section, the criteria outlined in 5.3 will be used to interpret the example text 'Lunch' by G. Smith reproduced in 5.2.

5.4.1 Functions, text types and strategies

The text shows some features of the aesthetic function (see 5.4.4), of the directive and of the informative. However, the overall function of the text is to inform readers, not to get them to do something. Of the five types, Smith's text is nearest to the argumentative. Although the title would seem to hint at an exposition (definition) of lunch, there are many surface features (see 5.4.4) which show that it is rather more in the nature of an argumentative text.

In fact, the text shows features of other types as well. With narrative texts it has in common the chronological progression: from past [4−6] to present [7−16] to future [17]. However, the majority of text units are not located in the past, as is the norm in narrative texts, but in the present (cf. 5.2.2 **Tense and time adverbials**). The present tense system is characteristic of expository texts (see Hüllen 1987: 16−17). What it also shares with expository texts is a clearly stated theme or point of view, which is expressed in the first sentence of the main body of the text [2]. As is often the case in factual reports, the first sentence is particularly important because it summarizes the whole text (Hoey 1991: 47). Another feature is the enumeration of the various forms that lunch can take (see the brackets in [8−10]). But it is closest to argumentative texts because the writer wants his readers to share his belief that lunch poses a problem in English society. Note in this respect the order in which Smith arranges his text. He could have started with the history of the meaning of the word and then gone on to an explication of what lunch means in present-day England. This would have fitted in with an expository text. Instead, he tells his readers straightaway that lunch is a problem [2] and supports this assessment in [3] before he fills in the historical background. This is an indication that he is more interested in the argumentative evaluation of lunch than its explication. The same preference for evaluation over exposition is to be seen again in the overall structure of [7] to [10]: [7] contains his thesis, which is supported by three arguments in [8] to [10]. This order is also reflected in the structure of the three support sentences: first come the predicators, which paraphrase *social divider* in [7], then follow details. Smith uses the statement of what people have for lunch to illustrate social divisions in England. It is a means to his overall end of making the reader see things his way – a purpose typical of argumentative texts.

This is mirrored in Smith's discourse strategy. He uses the *stack strategy*, which is marked by a predetermined unity, clearly visible in the thematically central sentences [2], [7] and [17]. However, in this text the stack method of exposition contains elements of a *step-by-step* procedure in the brief historical sketch in [4–6] as well as of the *balance strategy*: the case against lunch [7–11] is contrasted with the various uses it has [13–16] (see Quirk *et al.* 1985: 1435-7 for these discourse strategies). [12] provides the transition between the pros and cons.

5.4.2 Conceptual and semantic relations

Among the conceptual, and more broadly semantic, relations that are often found in argumentative texts, three will be discussed: **opposition**, **value** and **reason** (cf. de Beaugrande and Dressler 1981: 184).

The most important semantic relationship is that of **contrast** or **opposition**. We have shown in 5.2.1 how individual words are opposed in meaning, but sentences also stand in that relationship to one other. The most comprehensive contrast in the example text is between the harmful effects of lunch [7–11] and the useful functions it fulfils [13–16]. The pros and cons also differ in degree. The lexemes indicating a positive evaluation (and thus realizing the conceptual relation of **value**), *handy*, *convenient* and *continuing solace* [13], express a low or middling degree, while the negative evaluations are located near the middle or the top of the scale: *endless trouble* [2], *difficulty* [4], *social divider of infinite power* [7], *a whole clutch of restaurants . . . meals customers would never dream of eating* [11], *festival of cholesterol* [12], *problem* [17].

Englishmen in general are set in opposition to one another in [3], and more specific groups are contrasted in [8] to [10]. In [17] the English are compared with the French. A further series of contrasts clusters around the concept of *lunch*. Elaborating on the disparity between *word* and *thing* in [2], Smith first mentions the changes in the meaning of the word in [4] and [6] before he proceeds to detail the differences in the thing itself, using places and foods to point up the contrast in [8] to [10]. The final contrast is between the *action* (*discourage* [15]) and the *state* (*be keen* [16]).

It would seem that the frequency of semantic contrasts on the levels of concepts, lexical items and text sentences reflects Smith's view of lunch as something which creates divisions and sets people against one another. Oppositions are therefore particularly apposite for the theme chosen.

Only slightly less important is the relationship of **reason** or **causality**. Thus, [3] provides the justification for the statement in [2], just as the second half of [4] and [5–6] give the grounds for the statement in the main clause of [4]. The same goes for the examples in [8–10] in relation to [7] and for the clause after the colon in [12] with respect to the statement before the colon. The frequency of the reason relation demonstrates once again that Smith wants to win over his readers to his view of lunch in England.

Two aspects of the surface realization of semantic relations in the text between sentences deserve brief comments. First, explicit markers of the relations are rare (see 5.2.2). This is in keeping with the finding that causal connectors in written English are only half as frequent as in spoken English (Altenberg 1987: 51). Second, in all cases the reason follows, rather than precedes, the statement for which it provides the justification. All four statements mentioned above, which are followed by statements of reason or cause, express central aspects of the topic 'lunch'. By putting them in first place Smith underlines their importance. This can perhaps be seen as part of his strategy of *persuading* the reader of his beliefs. If he had reversed the order, a more academic, formal text would have resulted with the intention to *convince* the reader (on linear ordering, see van Dijk 1977: 223–5; Altenberg 1987). Finally, putting the reasons in second place makes them seem afterthoughts, which are more typical of spontaneous conversation than carefully planned writing (see 1.6.7). This is in keeping with Smith's intention to take his readers on 'an informal ramble through things English' (G. Smith, *English Companion*, p. 6).

5.4.3 Situational aspects

The **informality** of the text is also signalled by other means, both grammatical and lexical. Among the grammatical means are the lack of explicit markers of the semantic relationship between sentences and the various ellipses (see 5.2.2). The lexical means used include ellipsis (*steak and* *kidney*, sc. *pie* [10]) and **hyperbolic expressions** such as *endless* [2], *at once and for sure* [3] and *infinite* [7]. Also important are mixtures in terms of the register categories: formal or neutral words are found beside informal items, just as in some cases archaic or neutral forms are contrasted with coinages of more recent origin. 'Serious' academic texts would perhaps more consistently maintain the same level of personal tenor or temporal dialect.

Informal items are: *telly* [10]; *clutch* [11]; *festivals of cholesterol* [12]; *showbiz* [12]; *old Ronnie* [14]; *though* [15]; also a number of idioms and phrasal verbs of a more or less informal nature: *spring up* [11], *put up* [13], *look forward to* [14], *do one's best* [15]. **Formal words** are *vista* [4]; *solace* [13]. The two levels clash in the combination *flash* (informal) *callings* (formal) [12].

Sup [5] is an **archaic item**, and a clash is seen again in *deals and dalliance* [6]. Smith very appropriately chooses the only retrospective passage in the text for these obsolete terms. Other contrasts, though of a less marked nature, can be seen in *ease and affluence* [6], *potentates* and *put up* [13], or in the **hard words** *metamorphosis* [6], *proliferation* [11] and *tax-deductible* [15] when compared with such (Anglo-Saxon) **monosyllabic words** as *word, thing, eat*. These register clashes contribute to the informal nature of the text, but they also add another dimension of contrasts to that of semantic opposition.

5.4.4 Surface features

Finally, there are a number of features which help to define the *Lunch*-text as an example of an **argumentative** text. These features are used mainly for emphasis and insistence (see de Beaugrande and Dressler 1981: 184). They include

repetitions: *still* [2], *Englishman* [3, 17], *England* [2, 5, 17] and *distances* [8, 9];

assonances and alliteration: *deals–dalliance* [6], *divider–distances* [7–8]; *cafeteria–kitchen* [8]; *boardroom–building* [10]; *potentates–putting up– politicians* [13]; *convenient–coddle–clients–continuing* [13]; *did–discourage –tax-deductible* [15];

parallel units: *The word – and the thing itself – cause endless trouble still in England* [2]; *when it means the same to every Englishman as déjeuner does to every Frenchman* [17]; *dined in the afternoon and supped in the evening* [5]; *with ease and affluence . . . for deals and dalliance* [6]; *It distances/ separates husbands/bosses/employed from wives/workers/ unemployed* [8] – [10]; *he had/she had roast beef/cottage cheese salad in the cafeteria/kitchen* [8]; *steak and kidney in the pub/baked beans by the telly* [9 and 10]; *what you eat but with whom you eat it* [12]; *for royalty to . . ., for government to . . ., for business to* [13].

These examples are certainly evidence of delight in language for its own sake as well, which is no doubt part of the author's intention to entertain. Such features of the **aesthetic** function can also be seen in the well-turned phrase *festivals of cholesterol* [12] and in speech rhythms (*with ease and affluence . . . for deals and dalliance* [6]).

REFERENCES

Altenberg, B. (1987) 'Causal ordering strategies in English conversation', in J. Monaghan (ed.) *Grammar in the Construction of Texts*, London: Pinter, pp. 50–64.

Brinker, K. (1988) *Linguistische Textanalyse*, 2nd edn, Berlin: Schmidt.

Brown, G. (1989) 'Making sense: the interaction of linguistic expression and contextual information', *Applied Linguistics* 10: 97–108.

Brown, G. and Yule, G. (1983) *Discourse Analysis*, Cambridge: Cambridge University Press.

Cruse, D. A. (1986) *Lexical Semantics*, Cambridge: Cambridge University Press.

de Beaugrande, R. and Dressler, W. (1981) *Introduction to Text Linguistics*, London: Longman.

van Dijk, T. A. (1977) *Text and Context*, London: Longman.

—— (ed.) (1985) *Handbook of Discourse Analysis*, 4 vols. New York: Academic Press.

van Dijk, T. A. and Kintsch, W. (1983) *Strategies of Discourse Comprehension*, New York: Academic Press.

Enkvist, N. (1987) 'Text strategies: single, dual, multiple', in R. Steele and T. Threadgold (eds) *Language Topics*, Vol. 2. Amsterdam: Benjamins, pp. 203–11.

—— (1989) 'From text to interpretability: a contribution to the discussion of basic terms in text linguistics', in W. Heydrich, F. Neubauer, J. S. Petöfi and E. Sözer (eds) *Connexity and Coherence*, Berlin: de Gruyter, pp. 370–82.

Fox, B. A. (1987) *Discourse Structure and Anaphora*, Cambridge: Cambridge University Press.

Halliday, M. A. K. (1985) *An Introduction to Functional Grammar*, London: Arnold.

Halliday, M. A. K. and Hasan, R. (1976) *Cohesion in English*, London: Longman.

Heinemann, W. and Viehweger, D. (1991) *Textlinguistik*, Tübingen: Niemeyer.

Hoey, M. (1983) *On the Surface of Discourse*, London: Allen & Unwin.

—— (1991) *Patterns of Lexis in Text*, Oxford: Oxford University Press.

Hofmann, T. R. (1989) 'Pragmatics and anaphora', *Journal of Pragmatics* 13: 239–50.

Hüllen, W. (1987) 'On denoting time in discourse', in J. Monaghan (ed.) *Grammar in the Construction of Texts*, London: Pinter, pp. 15–23.

Jordan, R. R. (1989) 'English for academic purposes', *Language Teaching* 22: 150–64.

Lyons, J. (1977) *Semantics*, Cambridge: Cambridge University Press.

McCarthy, M. (1991) *Discourse Analysis for Teachers*, Cambridge: Cambridge University Press.

Péry-Woodley, M.-P. (1991) 'Writing in L1 and L2: analysing and evaluating learners' texts', *Language Teaching* 24: 69–83.

Petöfi, J. S. (1983) 'Text, signification, models, and correlates', in G. Rickheit and M. Bock (eds) *Psycholinguistic Studies in Language Processing*, Berlin: de Gruyter, pp. 266–98.

—— (ed.) (1988) *Text and Discourse Constitution*, Berlin: de Gruyter.

—— (1990) 'Language as a written medium: text', in N. E. Collinge (ed.) *An Encyclopaedia of Language*, London: Routledge, pp. 207–43.

Phillips, M. (1989) *Lexical Structure of Text*, Birmingham: English Language Research.

Quirk, R., Greenbaum, S., Leech, G. and Svartvik, J. (1985) *A Comprehensive Grammar of the English Language*, London: Longman.

Smith, G. (1985) *The English Companion*, Harmondsworth: Penguin.

Swales, J. M. (1990) *Genre Analysis*, Cambridge: Cambridge University Press.

Werlich, E. (1983) *A Text Grammar of English*, 2nd edn, Heidelberg: Quelle & Meyer.

Part 2

Uses and users of English

Chapter 6

Spoken discourse

In chapter 1 we discussed some of the differences between spoken and written English in general (cf. 1.6.7). In this chapter we will look at one variety of spoken language, spontaneous conversation, for which collections of texts have been published in Carterette and Jones 1974; Crystal and Davy 1975; Svartvik and Quirk 1980; and Cheepen and Monaghan 1990. Naturally occurring conversation has received a great deal of attention over the last twenty years from scholars in such varied fields as ethnomethodology, philosophy, sociology and linguistics (for overviews, see Edmondson 1981; Stubbs 1983; McLaughlin 1984; Coulthard 1985; van Dijk 1985; Taylor and Cameron 1987; Owen 1990; Leech and Thomas 1990; Cook 1989 and McCarthy 1991 include teaching materials and exercises). We will try to indicate the underlying shared assumptions that make conversations possible, how meaning is built up by speakers and perceived by hearers, how conversations are structured in interactional terms, how speakers negotiate whose turn it is to talk, and how they select what they want to say. In conclusion, the many functions of words such as *well* and *you know* in spoken discourse will be discussed. To save space, S will be used for *speaker* and H for *hearer*.

6.1 General considerations

Conversation is a social activity in which language plays a decisive, if not exclusive, role. Non-verbal ways of communication such as gestures, body language and eye contact can underscore or contradict what is said and show whether someone likes people and is attentive to what they say or, indeed, it can signal whether someone is willing to talk to them in the first place. While non-verbal aspects of speech are of great importance, the focus of this chapter will be largely on the verbal aspects of conversation (for discussions of non-verbal behaviour, see 8.5; cf. also Hinde 1972; Morris 1977; Kendon 1981).

Many of the rules that make for smooth social intercourse in general also apply to talk between two or more people. Among these are, above all, consideration for others. In most cases, people are assumed to be honest, reasonable, truthful and trustworthy individuals. If life in society is to be tolerable, not to say profitable, then people must try to accept others the way they are or at least the way they choose to present themselves, avoid offending them, and help them to preserve face. For conversations this means, for example, that each S should accept the other's topics, let them have their say and give their opinions a fair hearing without challenging or interrupting them too often. Hs should make Ss feel at their ease, show them that they are prepared to give them their full attention, are interested in what they think, agree with them as far and as often as possible, and generally avoid saying unpleasant things to them. These are aspects of what has been called the **hearer-support maxim** (Edmondson 1981: 25). If Ss do not receive feedback, support and encouragement, they cannot be expected to do the same the other way round. Conversely, supporting the H implies not forcing one's own wishes and desires on others (too often and too blatantly), on the assumption that Hs will support Ss in their turn. Some writers have noticed a decrease in social reciprocity, i.e. in the ability to give and take, and put this down to economic and social insecurity in modern individualistic societies, which causes many middle-class people to promote themselves constantly and thus come to be 'preoccupied with themselves and unattentive to their companions' (Pin and Turndorf 1985: 162).

A further aspect of polite behaviour is that one should repay compliments or other verbal behaviour by which people show that they are interested in us. This is particularly easy to observe in what is called **phatic communion** (see Malinowski 1923; cf. 6.3.2 on phases). Awareness of the H also shows in the choice of when to talk and when to be silent. Silence causes embarrassment because it usually indicates a conversational breakdown. People who can only talk and not listen (conversational bullies or 'steamrollers'), or who can only listen and not talk, make others feel uncomfortable and are in danger of being shunned. How to begin a conversation, what topics to introduce and what particular aspects to mention − all these are matters of convention, which may differ from society to society. In many English-speaking countries, for instance, it is usual to keep away in everyday conversation from areas of potential conflict and to avoid introducing too many new ideas or going too deeply beneath the surface. Native speakers learn these conventions as they grow up in their societies as a matter of course, but foreigners do not necessarily share these tacit assumptions. Over and above a grammatical (i.e. syntactic, phonetic, phonological, lexical and semantic) knowledge of the language in question, non-native speakers have therefore to acquire what has been called a **communicative competence** in the foreign culture, memorably summed up by Hymes: 'competence as to when to speak, when not, and as to what to talk about with whom, when, where, in what manner' (Hymes 1972: 277).

An amusing example of an unproductive conversation comes in the children's classic animal fable *Charlotte's Web*. The young lamb has just said that it does not want to play with Wilbur, the pig, because 'Pigs mean less than nothing to me.' This is a very blunt refusal, to which Wilbur makes this angry reply:

> 'What do you mean, *less* than nothing? . . . I don't think there is any such thing as *less* than nothing. Nothing is absolutely the limit of nothingness. It's the lowest you can go. It's the end of the line. How can something be less than nothing? If there were something that was less than nothing, then nothing would not be nothing, it would be something – even though it's just a very little bit of something. But if nothing is *nothing*, then nothing has nothing that is less than *it* is.'
> 'Oh, be quiet!' said the lamb. 'Go play by yourself!'
>
> (E. B. White, *Charlotte's Web*, p. 28)

This exchange between the lamb and the pig flouts many of the norms we have mentioned. It is confrontational instead of cooperative, blunt and direct instead of tentative and indirect, and contains what amounts to a short philosophical treatise on the precise meaning of *nothing* instead of accepting the lamb's loose, everyday use of the word. It is no wonder that the conversational goal (i.e. the conversational outcome desired by one of the speakers) is not achieved. Conventionally, people do not ask searching questions that might embarrass others but stay with what is generally known and accepted, which is arguably the best method of establishing common ground with interlocutors. Banal and stereotypic thoughts are unacceptable in intellectual discussions but have their legitimate place in everyday talk: 'social harmony is only possible if there are things we can agree on' (Wardhaugh 1985: 17). In the discussion of clichés and fixed expressions the value of routinized language has already been pointed out (see 2.1). Note here that the 'routines, patterns, rituals, stereotypes of everyday existence provide us with many of the means for coping with that existence, for reducing uncertainty and anxiety, and for providing us with the appearance of stability and continuity in the outside world' (Wardhaugh 1985: 21f.).

6.2 Meaning

Every communicative act can be seen both from the point of view of inter-action between the partners in a conversation and with regard to the meanings that Ss want to express and Hs have to understand. Interaction will be dealt with in the next section; this section is concerned with how meaning is built up and perceived in conversation.

6.2.1 Speech acts

Often it is not difficult to understand what is meant if one knows the meaning of a word or phrase and the rules of how words are put together to form sentences. In particular, there are a number of verbs which are used to perform certain public acts and which leave no doubt about the intended meaning. Examples are *I hereby pronounce you husband and wife*; *I name this ship 'Cutty Sark'*; *I sentence you to five years in jail*. These verbs show that language can be used not just to talk about but to do things. Such acts performed by language have been called **speech acts**, and the verbs used are known as **speech act verbs** or **performative verbs** (for detailed treatments of speech act theory, see Austin 1962; Searle 1969; Leech 1983; Levinson 1983; de Souza Filho 1985; Flowerdew 1988, who also considers language teaching aspects). What can be questioned is not the truth of these performative utterances (**performatives** for short), but whether they are carried out appropriately or not. To be judged appropriate, performatives must be part of some ritual or well-established procedure, such as marrying, naming ships or passing sentences in court, as in the examples above. Other restrictions concern the people and the place: only certain people are allowed to make these utterances (in the first person, simple present tense), and they can usually make them only in certain officially established places (churches and/or registry offices for weddings). The procedure must also be executed fully and correctly: if a priest leaves out the crucial words the wedding ceremony is not valid, and the resulting offspring illegitimate (for a discussion of these **felicity conditions**, see Austin 1962; Searle 1969; Cohen and Perrault 1979).

Other verbs, such as *warn*, *promise* and *apologize*, fulfil the same function of doing something by saying something; in fact, by saying anything at all one is performing some kind of speech act (for classifications of speech acts, see Searle 1979: 1-29; Bach and Harnish 1979; Edmondson and House 1981; Leech 1983). The speech acts used in conversations can be divided into three basic categories, **meta-interactive**, **turn-taking** and **interactive**. The first concerns the organization of the conversation itself, i.e. the marking of beginnings and endings (examples: *now*, *right*; cf. also 6.3.3 on *meta-moves*); the opening of conversations (greetings such as *hello*, *hi*) or the structuring of the conversation in some way (*Sorry, I'm afraid I must go now*). Turn-taking speech acts are used to pass, hold or obtain the floor in public speaking (*what do you think?*; *if I may just finish this*; *could I come in on this?*). Interactive acts consist of

eliciting acts, which require some linguistic response, such as asking for information, a decision, agreement, or the clarification or repetition of an utterance;

informing acts, which offer information or respond in other ways to eliciting acts, such as agreeing, confirming, qualifying or rejecting;
acknowledging acts, which provide positive or negative follow-up or feedback; and
directing acts, which ask for an immediate or future action.
(For more detail, examples and a sample analysis, see Francis and Hunston 1987; cf. also Edmondson and House 1981: chapter 4, especially p. 98, and Coulthard 1985: 126–7).

Speech acts have been divided into those in which a performative verb actually appears (they are called **explicit**), and those which do not have one in their surface structure. The latter are called **primary**, because they are far more frequent than the other type. There are two tests to find out whether an utterance is to be considered a speech act. When the first person pronoun is used and the word *hereby* can be inserted, the utterance is a speech act (*I hereby agree, declare, refuse*, etc.). However, the presence of the first person simple present active is clearly not a necessary condition, as can be seen from *Patrons are kindly asked to refrain from smoking*, or *guilty*, as pronounced by the jury foreman in a court of law. The second test says, therefore, that utterances count as speech acts if they are reducible, expandable or analysable into the form 'I + present simple active verb', as in *I state that the jury finds the accused guilty*.

If all utterances do something, the question arises what it is that they do. Three aspects have been distinguished by Austin (1962). First, utterances perform a **locutionary act**, whose interpretation is concerned with *meaning*, for which both knowledge of the language system as well as extra-textual knowledge of the world is necessary. Second, by making an utterance one performs an **illocutionary act**. This is a linguistic act whose interpretation is concerned with the *force* of the utterance, for example, advising, ordering, urging or warning somebody. Third, utterances can have an effect on people, for instance, persuading or dissuading them. This non-linguistic act is called the **perlocutionary act**, and its effect is referred to as **perlocutionary force**. Illocutions are (potentially) under the control of Ss but perlocutions are not: 'I may warn you hoping to deter you but in fact succeed only in encouraging or even inciting you' (Coulthard 1985: 19). Two effects have therefore been distinguished according to whether they are intended by Ss (**perlocutionary object**) or not (**perlocutionary sequel**).

There are various difficulties about these distinctions, the most important of which relates to the illocutionary force of utterances. It is by no means always obvious what is meant, as shown by such expressions as *I didn't know what she was getting at, I couldn't make head or tail of what she said,* or *I had no idea what she was going on about* (for a review of difficulties with speech acts, see Stubbs 1983: 176ff). Indirect ways of getting things done by language, called **indirect speech acts**, are particularly difficult to process, though they are more normal in everyday talk than direct and unambiguous statements. Indirect speech acts are expressed through the performance of another speech act. They often show a discrepancy between grammatical form and communicative function inasmuch as the declarative, interrogative and imperative moods do not (exclusively) realize statements, questions and orders. In particular, in situations where the role relationships between participants are not clear, Ss may well choose indeterminate expressions such as *Is that the phone?*, which Hs can interpret as a genuine question or as a veiled order. Ss can thus get around imposing their will on others too openly and directly, and an unpleasant confrontation is avoided (Leech and Thomas 1990: 195). Some utterances in the form of statements are particularly difficult to interpret: when a wife writes to her husband 'I'll be back next Thursday', this may be no more than a piece of information, but she may well be asking him to meet her at the station, cook a nice dinner, etc. and be disappointed when none of these things happen. Exclamations can also be problematic, as in the case of Henry II's apocryphal utterance 'Will nobody rid me of this turbulent priest?' This may have been just an angry exclamation, but some of his knights took it to be an order to kill Thomas Becket and did so. Henry may, of course, have deliberately exploited the ambiguity of his exclamation, its 'illocutionary indeterminacy' (Leech 1983: 30), so as to claim later that he had never given an order. This ambivalence is the reason why it is sometimes necessary to point out explicitly how an H is meant to understand an utterance, for example, with an added *I was only joking* or *that is an order*. These phrases prove the general point that Hs may have different interpretations from Ss' intentions and that 'we cannot ultimately be certain of what a speaker means by an utterance' (ibid.). Meaning is an interactive category; it is the H who at any given time determines the meaning of utterances, not the S, though the S may self-correct in a later contribution to the conversation. This has been called the **hearer-knows-best principle** (Edmondson 1981: 50), and applies to the interpretation of spoken discourse just as much as to that of written texts, including literary works.

Notwithstanding this basic problem, much effort has been directed at specifying the conditions under which S intention and H interpretation will coincide. Thus it has been shown that the direct imperative *Pass the salt!* can take six different types of indirect form:

1 Sentences concerning hearer's ability   Can you pass the salt?

2 Sentences concerning hearer's future action   Are you going to pass the salt?

3 Sentences concerning speaker's wish or want   I would like (you) to pass the salt.

4 Sentences concerning hearer's desire or willingness	Would you mind passing the salt? It might help if you passed the salt.
5 Sentences concerning reasons for action	I don't think you salted the potatoes.
6 Sentences embedding either one of the above [sic] or an explicit performative	Can I ask you to pass the salt?

(Coulthard 1985: 27, summarizing Searle 1979: 36–9)

Five of these possibilities take the form of questions, so it would seem useful to find rules for when questions are questions and when they are something else. Three rules have been set up to predict when a question is to be read as a command (the social situation is that of classroom discourse).

Rule 1: A question is to be read as a command to do something if it refers to an action or activity which both teachers and pupil(s) know ought to have been performed or completed but has not. Thus, *Did you shut the door?* is not a command only when the teacher really does not know whether the action has been performed.

Rule 2: A question is a command to do something if it meets the following three conditions:

1 it contains one of the modals *can, could, will, would* (and sometimes *be going to*);
2 the subject of the clause is also the addressee;
3 the predicate describes an action which is physically possible at the time of the utterance.

Thus, *Can you play the piano, John*? will be understood as a command provided there is a piano in the classroom, while *Can John play the piano?* (subject not present in class) and *Can you swim a length, John?* (action not possible in classroom) will be understood as questions.

Rule 3: A question is a command to stop if it refers to an action or activity which is proscribed at the moment of utterance. If laughing is forbidden then both *Is someone laughing?* and *What are you laughing at?* will be heard as commands by pupils. If it is not forbidden, then *What are you laughing at?* is interpreted as a question (after Coulthard 1985: 130–1).

It should be added that the distinction between a question and a command or request is made easier when there is the adverb *please*, which is a sign of a polite order or request. It is clear that in their explanations both Searle and Coulthard take into account important grammatical as well as situational factors.

6.2.2 Conversational principles

Searle has said that, to derive the meaning of indirect speech acts such as *Can you pass the salt?*, Ss need 'a theory of speech acts, a theory of conversation, factual background information, and general powers of rationality and inference' (Searle 1979: 176). In his seminal article of 1975, Grice sets out to explain the inference process through which Hs derive meaning from S utterances. He starts from the basic assumption that people work together to achieve some goal in a conversation. This **co-operative principle** manifests itself in certain consequences, which he summarizes in four 'maxims' (Grice 1975: 46):

1 Quantity:
    (a) Make your contribution as informative as is required (for the current purposes of the exchange).
    (b) Do not make your contribution more informative than is required.
2 Quality:
    (a) Do not say what you believe to be false.
    (b) Do not say that for which you lack adequate evidence.
3 Relation: Be relevant.
4 Manner:
    (a) Avoid obscurity of expression.
    (b) Avoid ambiguity.
    (c) Be brief (avoid unnecessary prolixity).
    (d) Be orderly.

There are, of course, activities in which the maxims hardly apply at all, for example, talk between enemies, political speeches, press conferences or police interrogations. Parliaments which allow filibustering clearly suspend maxims 3 ('Be relevant') and 4 ('Be brief'). Grice recognizes that Ss can choose not to stick to the maxims, and therefore his point is rather that 'people will interpret what we say as conforming to the maxims on at least some level' (Levinson 1983: 103). Take this example, which seems to be in breach of the maxim of quantity 'be informative', since it is obvious from the answer that B is also aware of the low temperature:

A: Cold in here, isn't it?
B: Okay, I'll shut the window.

A's utterance is not informative, apparently, because it contains no new information for B. According to Grice, B will interpret A's utterance as implying that A wants B to do something about the low temperature, in fact, that A is uttering some sort of request. This is the obvious interpretation when B assumes A to be informative despite surface appearances (see Leech 1983: 38–43, for a detailed discussion of this example; for more examples, see Wardhaugh 1985: 65ff.) Another example involves the maxim of relation:

A: Can you tell me the time?
B: Well, the milkman has come.

The chain of inference is described by Levinson like this:

> Assume B's utterance is relevant; if it's relevant then given that A asked a question, B should be providing an answer; the only way one can reconcile the assumption that B is co-operatively answering A's question with the content of B's utterance is to assume that B is not in a position to provide the full information, but thinks that the milkman's coming might provide A with the means of deriving a partial answer. Hence A may infer that B intends to convey that the time is at least after whenever the milkman normally calls.
>
> (Levinson 1983: 107)

According to Grice's inference scheme, therefore, Hs make the assumption that, though Ss seem to be breaking the cooperative principle, at a deeper level they are not doing so. Grice's maxims are to be understood as a device to move from what people say to what they really mean. It can be doubted whether inference sequences such as the one above always take place. An analysis of the *Cold in here, isn't it?* example in interactional terms might draw attention to the conventional nature of this exchange (see 6.3 below). A scheme such as Grice's becomes unnecessary when the conversational inference becomes a conventional one (see Levinson 1983: 118–47 for tests and types of inferences, which Grice calls *conversational implicatures*).

Although the Gricean principle with its associated maxims can be useful in selecting and rejecting possible readings of utterances, the question of *why* speakers are so often indirect in expressing what they have in mind is not addressed by Grice. To go back to the last but one example above (*Cold in here, isn't it?*), why does A not say *Could you close the window*? or even *Close the window*. The answer seems to be that A wants to get B to do something and to be polite at the same time, and so chooses a form of expression which does not impose on B too much, thus giving B a certain freedom to react to this veiled order. A could have been more informative, but only at the cost of being rude to B. In this case, as in many others, the **politeness principle** overrules the cooperative principle with its four maxims, including the quality maxim. Other examples include white lies (*I'm terribly sorry but we've got something on already tonight*) which one tells so as to avoid having to do something one does not want to without giving offence (see Leech 1983: 79–84; on politeness in general, see Brown and Levinson 1987). There are various degrees of politeness in English, and, the more polite one's utterance, the more likely it is that one will achieve one's (perlocutionary) object. As Leech points out, the more indirect a speech act is the more polite it tends to be, because indirect speech acts 'increase the degree of optionality, and . . . because the more indirect an illocution is, the more diminished and tentative its force tends to be' (Leech 1983: 108). He lists these examples (in increasing order of indirectness and politeness): *Answer the phone*; *I want you to answer the phone*; *Will you answer the phone?*; *Can you answer the (tele)phone?*; *Would you mind answering the phone?*; *Could you possibly answer the phone?* (ibid.).

Irony is also sometimes linked to the politeness principle: in cases where one cannot avoid giving offence one should at least do it in a way that does not obviously clash with the politeness principle. Fixed expressions such as *That's all I need* ('Why did this have to happen to me?') or *that's a fine/pretty kettle of fish* ('a messy, confusing situation') clearly mean the opposite of what they seem to be saying, and thus go against the quality maxim. As there is often no reason why speakers should not be cooperative, the obvious explanation is that they say untrue things to save the politeness principle. This comes out even more clearly where the ironic expression is a comment on people and their actions, for example, *You're a real genius* ('You're an idiot') or *How brilliant!* ('How stupid'). It has to be admitted, however, that avoiding the offending terms does not mitigate the strong impression on the part of the H that the S thinks her- or himself to be wiser and superior to the H − an implication no doubt resented by the H (see Wardhaugh 1985: 96).

The politeness principle can account for some of the selections that Grice's maxims do not explain, as can other principles that cannot be discussed here (see, for example, the *charity principle* 'Construe the speaker's remarks so as to violate as few maxims as possible' and the *morality maxim* 'Ss should not do things, or make Hs do things, that they ought not to' mentioned in Bach and Harnish 1979: 68). But neither speech act theory nor the various inference schemes seem to be able to explain how utterances that can have many meanings in isolation come to have only one in a particular context. It has been said of the example *Cold in here, isn't it?* that it can be an indirect request to close the door, but as Sadock points out, it is infinitely flexible: 'But it can also convey a request to open a door or to bring a blanket or to pay a gas bill. In fact it's difficult to think of a request that the utterance could NOT convey in the right context'(Sadock 1978: 286). It should be added, however, that the speech context (or **cotext**) often constrains the interpretations that can be put on an utterance; see 6.4.1 on the concept of the *adjacency pair*.

To end this section on meaning, two areas should be mentioned that offer promising developments. One is the modelling of discourse for computers, which involves writing explicit rules for the relation between utterances and their meaning (see Cohen and Perrault 1979 and Grosz *et al.* 1986). The other is a book by Sperber and Wilson (1986) on the concept of relevance and work based on it, which has opened up new perspectives for discourse analysis and communication in general. Of particular interest is the claim that every utterance has only one meaning consistent with the principle of relevance (for a brief summary and some discussion of Sperber and Wilson's book, see *Behavioral and Brain Sciences* 10 (1987), 697–754; cf. also Blakemore 1988, 1992). However, it is too early to say whether this new theory offers the key to the fundamental unsolved problems of speech act theory and the various inference schemes mentioned in this section.

6.3 Conversational interaction

Each utterance in a conversation has a double status. Seen from the point of view of S meaning, it expresses what the S has in mind; seen from the point of view of the interaction between conversational partners, it is a move in the conversational game that S and H jointly play (cf. Klammer 1973). How Ss express what they mean and how Hs understand it has been examined in 6.2. Here we will discuss some aspects of the interactional structure of conversations, basing the treatment on Edmondson (1981) and Edmondson and House (1981), who present perhaps the most elaborate description (see also Francis and Hunston 1987; for a model of classroom interaction, cf. Sinclair and Coulthard 1975; Sinclair and Brazil 1982). In the discussion we will consider the definition and/or function of the element involved, state whether it is necessary or optional, and indicate how many occurrences of the same element are possible at the level to which it belongs, how it is linked to other elements of the same level, and how it affects the turn-taking structure.

Conversations are made up of **encounters**, which consist of one or more **phases**, which in turn consist of at least two **exchanges**. Exchanges are made up of two or more **moves**, which themselves consist of one or more **acts**. Note that an exchange is the only unit to have at least two lower units as its constituents. This reflects the fact that conversations are dialogic activities. In classroom interaction, which is among participants of unequal social status, exchanges usually show an additional third move in which the teacher provides some kind of feedback for the pupil(s) (Coulthard 1985: 135).

6.3.1 Encounters

Encounters are the highest unit of conversational structure. It is usual to distinguish three phases: an opening phase, a central phase in which the main business of the respective encounter is transacted, and a closing phase, in which the encounter is brought to an end. *Chaining* and *reciprocity* are particularly frequent at the beginning and end of conversations (see below 6.3.2). While people are fairly free to negotiate the topics for the substantial part of the encounter, opening and closing phases are marked by a great degree of conventionalization of the things that participants feel have to be said.

Openings   The opening phase consists of exchanges in which the partners in a potential conversation acknowledge one another's presence, decide whether they want to enter into a longer conversation and explore whether the other person is available for conversation. The first few moves also serve to establish the social roles that participants are going to play during the encounter. Often the first contact is made visually before a single word is said. A negative signal is given if the potential conversational partner is, say, reading a newspaper. This makes it unlikely that he or she will want to respond to an opening move. There are other, positive pre-opening signals of a non-verbal nature, however, that can be used to trigger a conversation: 'A gesture that indicates how cold it is can lead to a remark about the weather at a bus stop' (Wardhaugh 1985: 124). It has been observed that there are three types of expressions that can be used as **openers**: expressions directed to the other (*sleep well?*; *have a good journey?*), self-oriented expressions (*before I forget*; *thirsty work this*) and neutral remarks (on the weather, etc.) In non-solidary encounters where the social status of speakers differs, social superiors will use other-oriented expressions while social inferiors produce self-oriented ones (Laver 1975). This is so because social inferiors 'are not allowed to invade the psychological world of the superior, as this would infringe the status rules which hold between them' (Cheepen and Monaghan 1990: 33). But many conversations are also started with expressions that are both self- and other-oriented (*Excuse me*; *Sorry to bother you*; *I've been longing to meet you*), and which have been called *shared-world tokens* (ibid.: 37).

Encounters can be divided into **transactional encounters**, which have some business other than a simple social meeting (a job interview, a loan application, a purchase of some kind), and **interactional encounters**, whose sole purpose is the establishment and confirmation of social bonds (ibid.: chapter 1). In both types the exchange of greetings belongs to the pre-opening phase. On the other hand, while **small talk** (about the weather, a new dress or car, the behaviour of the cat/dog, or the height of a child) provides the topics in interactional encounters, it must be regarded as a pre-topic in transactional encounters, which move on to the real purpose of the encounter in the central phase. In interactional encounters with strangers, the opening phase involves a gradual, step-by-step disclosing of, and asking for, more or less personal details about the other person, for example, where they live, come from, went to school, etc., after which the conversation can move on to 'a common theme of discussion: movies, politics, restaurants, ballet, a foreign country, a book, flying experiences, hobbies, children's education, auctions, exhibitions, modern art, theatre and the like' (Pin and Turndorf 1985: 180). Topic changes are frequent and usual.

People not only direct their efforts in the opening stage towards establishing common ground by choosing safe topics, but also refrain from introducing controversial ideas or from disagreeing with the interlocutor, who might feel threatened. This is again in keeping with the general maxim that one should support the H. Dissent or contradictions, if they come up at all, tend to be introduced by appropriate softening devices, and will be kept back until a later stage in the encounter when enough common ground and mutual goodwill have been established (on *small talk*, see Schneider 1988).

Endings As a conversation is nearing its end, participants often make a comment about the quality of the current encounter (*it's been nice talking to you* or *it was nice meeting you*) and refer to possible future meetings (for detailed treatments, see Schegloff and Sacks 1973; Clark and French 1981; Cheepen and Monaghan 1990). Phrases such as *I mustn't keep you*; *I'd better let you go*; *I'm afraid I must get back to work* are used in order not to appear too ready to close the encounter. Again, non-verbal means are usually employed to hint at one's wish to bring the conversation to a close. Diminished eye-contact is one of them, as is a glance at a watch or clock, possibly accompanied by the exclamation *(Heavens,) is that the time!* or *is it already so late?* It can be difficult to get out of boring or unproductive conversations, so that one might have to use stronger signals such as standing up or tidying up the scene of action, which will bring the conversation to its end even if one's partner should not want to finish it just yet. As the ending of conversations is also a cooperative undertaking, both must agree to stop, usually by using such tokens as *right*, *okay*, or hesitations and references to some other topic or activity. It is only in extreme cases that one leaves using a direct excuse, such as *Sorry, I've got to run* or *Sorry, I must rush*. In this situation there is rarely the time, or the desire, to reassure the other that one likes his/her company and looks forward to renewing the contact (*I hope we'll meet again; hope to see you again*; *you must come and see me soon*; *I'll be in touch* or *I'll write soon*). It is also quite common to find pre-final **side sequences**, in which an earlier topic is briefly mentioned again. Final goodbyes come in various forms according to the situation ((*good*) *bye, so long, cheerio, see you, be seeing you*, etc.).

It should be stressed that many of the speech acts mentioned, though they may appear banal and trivial at one level, are an important part of the social competence of all native speakers. This becomes immediately apparent when one comes across someone who does not make the appropriate social noises. Some people do not feel like engaging in small talk, either because they think it silly or because they are not aware that it is expected of them. Such people are likely to be perceived as strange and difficult, if not unfriendly or threatening.

Central phase   While some research has been carried out into the **boundary sequences** (openings and closings), not much has been done on the central section of conversations. Cheepen and Monaghan (1990), however, have found that the central phase in interactional encounters (which they call **conversation**) consists of two main elements, **speech-in-action** and **stories**. **Speech-in-action** occurs at, or near, the beginning of an encounter and consists of comments by the participants on various aspects of their immediate environment. Comments on the nature of the social encounter (*how nice to see you*) are less common than those which relate to objects and conditions that are observable by the participants (such as the weather, the scenery, pet animals, the speakers themselves; for more details, see the discussion on openings above). Speech-in-action functions 'as a base for the telling of story, to which the speakers refer between instances of story, and from which the bulk of new conversational topics arise' (Cheepen and Monaghan 1990: 45).

Stories are contributions that consist of more than one turn, and special care must be taken by Ss in telling them as other participants are likely to break in at possible finishing points. Story-tellers therefore often get permission to tell a story by using a **story-preface** (*You know what happened to me this morning?* or *Have you heard the one about x?*). Ss must ensure that stories fit well into the conversation, and are clearly marked off from other talk. They can achieve this by a *disjunct marker* (*oh*) to indicate that what follows is not directly related to the preceding utterance and/or by *embedded repetition*, which links the following story to the prior talk by repeating a word, phrase, etc. (Jefferson 1978). The stories themselves tend to have clearly marked beginnings and endings, and some general point, 'some message about the world in which the speaker and hearer actually live' (Polanyi 1985: 189). Speech-in-action is used to bring the listeners back to the present time, and other Ss can then tell their stories, which often show similarities (in content, specification, moral) to the preceding story – another instance of speaker support in operation. This telling of parallel narratives enhances the point of the first story and thus achieves a shared world view, perhaps the most important function of conversations.

Stories in general are defined by the structure *state–event–state*, i.e. stories narrate an event, which arises out of a particular state and which brings about a change in the world, a new state. This is the most fundamental structure that shows up in everyday life and reflects the way we perceive and interpret the world. Stories in naturally occurring conversation are specifically about clearly defined human beings, are told in dialogue form, and allow participants to agree on evaluations (for other features, see Gülich and Quasthoff 1985, 1986). As participants can take control of the conversation at different times, they feel they are equals, which is an important prerequisite for good social relationships, the development of which is the ultimate goal of interactional encounters. Social bonding between co-conversationalists is also enhanced through the creation of a shared world view by agreeing on evaluations of the stories told.

The main body of the conversation can also contain passages in which conversational trouble arises. Sometimes this is overt and has to do with the wrong choice, or the misunderstanding, of lexical items, which temporarily interrupt the smooth flow of conversations and bring about side sequences (see Jefferson 1972). The more serious trouble, however, is covert and arises either because one or more of the participants feel threatened in their conversational status or because of a failure to agree on an evaluation (for examples, see Cheepen and Monaghan 1990: chapter 3). One type of repair of interactional trouble occurs in the form of a negative evaluation sequence of a highly exaggerated nature, in which all speakers make comments on an absent person. This *scapegoat repair* (ibid.: 81–4) helps speakers to create some sense of unity and harmony after a dangerous situation has been negotiated in the conversation. After a scapegoat repair speakers often move back to an earlier topic (*topic loop*; ibid.: 84–6). Presumably even more effective in re-establishing good relationships are *delayed repairs* (ibid.: 80), in which conversational trouble is put aside until a later stage in the conversation, when it can be fitted to some earlier topic and dealt with in such a way that offended parties are reconciled and interactional harmony restored. Both side sequences and the sequence trouble–repair–topic rerun/topic loop show that naturally occurring conversation is not an unstructured activity, as has often been asserted, but that conversations have a goal and that conversationalists monitor closely the way conversations develop and try to find the right moment for what they want to say.

6.3.2 Phases

A **phase** consists of one or more **head exchanges**, in which the main business is transacted. Related but less important matters are dealt with in minor exchanges, which occur before or after the head exchange. These **pre-** and **post-exchanges** are optional, though it is not uncommon to find more than one such subordinate exchange, especially in the case of post-exchanges.

Pre-exchanges have various functions, for example, to introduce a topic (*I've got a bit of a problem . . .*) or to gain advance commitment (*Could you do me a favour?* or *Could you spare a moment?*). They are also commonly employed by Ss to check on objections by Hs before they make their main move:

pre-exchange	A: Have you got anything on tonight?
	B: No, not really.
head exchange	A: Well, would you like to go to the cinema?
	B: I'd love to.

A can be sure that, whatever else B may come up with, B will at least not be able to say that he or she has other plans. If B had answered in the positive, A might well not have invited B in order to avoid the danger of being turned down. The benefits of pre-exchanges are, however, not all one-sided: B is also spared the potentially embarrassing situation of having to turn down an invitation. This example also shows that pre-exchanges lead directly to head (or other) exchanges, and that the S who initiates a pre-exchange also produces the first move in the directly following (head) exchange. The use of pre-exchanges is so well established that Hs frequently see through them and react to them as if they were the first move in the anticipated head exchange:

> pre-exchange   A: Have you got anything on tonight?
> head exchange   B: No, let's go to the cinema.

Both B's response (*No, not really*) in reply to A's pre-exchange move and A's invitation have been deleted in this example. B's turn must nevertheless be characterized as a response to A's anticipated but implicit *Well, would you like to go to the cinema?*

While Ss use pre-exchanges in order not to be turned down, Hs use them before they respond to a request (etc.) made by Ss (this is called a **pre-responding exchange**):

> A: Would you rather I wrote a cheque?
> B: Yeah – you got a card I suppose – a banker's card?
> A: Yes I have – yes –
> B: Yes I think so – in this case.

> (adapted from Owen 1983: 34)

The subordinate nature of the exchange is even more obvious in this example:

> A: Have you got anything on tonight?
> B: Why do you want to know?

Pre-responding exchanges can also have the function of confirming the content or significance of the preceding move:

(A wants to borrow records from B)
> A: I don't know how to put this, but could we take some of yours along?
> B: (deep breath)
> A: We'll be very careful.
> B: Which ones?
> A: Well, I mean, that's partly up to you . . .
> B: Mm . . . yeah okay . . .

> (adapted from Edmondson 1981: 107)

Despite A's assurance *We'll be very careful*, B hesitates to say yes and stalls by initiating a pre-responding exchange, thus acknowledging the significance of A's move. One can easily see that more than one pre-responding exchange might be employed by cautious Hs.

Post-exchanges, on the other hand, confirm, or make more precise, the outcome of a preceding exchange:

> A: We eating at home?
> B: Could I suppose.
> A: No. Let's go out. I've got to look for a book.
> B: OK. Give me a few minutes to get changed . . . Chinese food?
> A: Yeah. If you want. I'll take the dog out for a walk while you get ready . . .
>
> (adapted from Wardhaugh 1985: 193f)

The couple agree to eat out in the head exchange and solve the problem of what kind of food to have in the post-exchange. Examples with more than one post-exchange are quite frequent:

> (A and B have just reached a solution to Y's baby-sitting problem)
> A: I'll bring my friend round tonight.
> B: Yeah, okay.
> A: What time would you like?
> B: Oh any time . . . about eight thirty'll be fine.
> A: Oh, yes all right, fine. Well, I'll bring her round tonight.
> B: Yeah.
>
> (adapted from Edmondson 1981: 102)

This example shows that post-exchanges are often employed to bridge the business and closing phases of an encounter. Here the first post-exchange confirms the outcome reached in the preceding conversation, while the second settles a detail of the outcome and the third closes the conversational encounter. We can therefore say that post-exchanges can be either *substantial* (the second exchange in the last example) or *ritual* (exchanges one and three), where the outcome of the exchange is the same as that of the previous exchange. Typical ritual post-exchanges are the last two moves in a thank-you sequence, as in

> A: Thank you very much.
> B: That's okay/Don't mention it/etc.

So far we have dealt with one way of linking head exchanges to pre- or post-exchanges, that of subordination. Edmondson also proposes a second type, that of coordination, which takes either the form of **chaining** or of

reciprocation. The following question–answer sequence illustrates the chaining process:

A: Well, can you prescribe anything for the allergy?
B: Does it itch at all?
A: Yes, it itches quite a lot.
B: Do you get scabs forming on it?
A: No.
B: Hm hum. It's just on your face and hands, is it?
A: And my arms.
B: And your arms. Is it on any other place of the body?
A: Well, it's spreading, yeah.
B: Well, I think I can prescribe some ointment for you . . .

(adapted from Edmondson 1981: 110)

This question–answer sequence shows all the pre-conditions for chaining: the exchanges all have a common topic, the skin problem; the information asked for by the doctor could have been got in one block question which would have contained all the other questions; the pre-responding exchanges are of the same type (question–answer), and A's intentions are the same in all the exchanges (eliciting information).

Reciprocation is commonly found in small talk, where the partners to a conversation are nice to each other, asking about one another's health (*How are you? . . . And how are you?*), volunteering information about themselves, etc. Reciprocal exchanges can be started by either partner and can appear in chained sequences.

6.3.3 Moves and exchanges

Exchanges consist of two or more **head moves**. At least one partner to a conversation engages in talk in order to achieve some result. Once this goal is obtained, the participants can either embark on a new exchange or end their conversation. It is the conversational goals through which exchanges are defined, while the individual moves are characterized by the role they play in reaching these conversational goals. We will distinguish the head moves **initiate, satisfy, counter** and **contra**, and three **meta-moves: reject, re-run** and **prime**.

Head moves   In the simplest case, an exchange consists of two moves only: an S initiates a conversation and an H reacts positively to this move. The move that gets the conversation going is an **initiate**, and the H's positive reaction to it is a **satisfy**:

A: Excuse me, could you tell me the time?
B: It's half past three.

Moves need not always be realized, as is the case with B's satisfy in the next example:

A: Have you got coffee to go?
B: Milk and sugar?
A: Just milk.

(Owen 1983: 34)

This example can be made explicit in the following way:

A: Initiate
B: [Satisfy;] Initiate
A: Satisfy

The positive answer, the satisfy to A's initiate, must here be understood, or else B's question, a second initiate, would not make sense. On the other hand, just as a satisfy can be omitted, whole sequences may be added in an exchange before the outcome is achieved, as shown in the examples on pre-exchanges above (6.3.2).

Another way of keeping exchanges going is through negative reactions, of which Edmondson (1981) distinguishes two. The first, called **contra**, realizes an ultimate reaction in the negative, as in

Initiate   A: Like to come and see *The Canterbury Tales* tonight?
Contra   B: Sorry, I've got something else on.
Satisfy   A: Ah well, never mind.

Here B has been immediately successful in making A withdraw the initiate, though it is quite possible to find exchanges with more than one contra:

Initiate   A: Coming to Alan's party tonight?
Contra   B: 'Fraid I can't, I have to finish this essay.
Initiate   A: But the whole gang are coming.
Contra   B: Sorry, I really must hand it in first thing tomorrow morning.
Initiate   A: What a shame, we specially asked Susan to come along for you.
Contra   B: Yeah, well, I'd love to come but I really can't.
Satisfy   A: Oh well, some other time then.

In this example, B maintains his/her contra until the exchange is eventually closed by A, who takes back the initiate by offering a satisfy to B's third contra.

The second negative move, the **counter**, is only provisional and is taken back in the course of the exchange:

Initiate   A: I think we should invite the whole family.
Counter   B: Oh God, their kids are so loutish.
Satisfy   A: Yeah, I agree they're pretty horrible – but

Initiate   you know they did put up with our lot last time.
Satisfy   B: Oh God, all right, invite them then – and the bloody dog.

B's first reaction is a counter, not a contra, because it is taken back in B's second contribution. Note also that though A agrees with B's counter (= satisfy) A does not give up the initiate. Contrast the following exchange, in which again B's first reaction must be classified as a counter:

Initiate   A: I think we should invite the whole family.
Counter   B: Oh God, the kids are so loutish.
Contra   A: Oh come on – they're not that bad.
Satisfy   B: Yeah, perhaps you're right – but even so,
Contra   I don't want to have to cook for the whole family – I'll be exhausted.
Satisfy   A: Oh well – if you feel like that about it, let's forget the whole business.
    (both exchanges adapted from Edmondson and House 1981: 40–1)

Here A gives up the initiate in the last move, thus offering a satisfy to B's contra of the preceding move. A counter is, then, only a provisional negative reaction, and it also differs from a contra in its potential consequences. First, (as in the first *counter*-example above) the acceptance of a counter does not necessarily mean that the S who offers a satisfy to a counter takes back the initiate. Second, as in the second *counter*-example above, if a counter is met with a contra and the S who has produced the counter goes on to take back this counter, i.e. produces a satisfy to the other's contra, this nevertheless does not mean that he or she accepts the original initiate. It should also be noted that a satisfy always refers to the immediately preceding move, and that, while no exchange can be closed by a move other than a satisfy, producing one does not always bring the total exchange to an end. Thus there are, in the last two examples quoted above, two non-closing satisfys, one responding to a counter and the other to a contra.

Meta-moves   Apart from these four moves, Edmondson recognizes three other moves, which have the conversation itself as their topic, and which are called **meta-moves**. The first of these, the **reject**, objects to the fact that an initiate is being made, or to the manner in which it is made. The second is called **re-run**; it arises when an initiate is misunderstood and the S has to repeat it in a form that is easier to understand, as in

A: Could you give me the trousers, please?
B: Here you are.
A: Not these, sorry, the cords.

Reject and re-run do not occur very often because they are H-unfriendly. In the example, the re-run indicates that B has made a mistake and that

A does not accept the satisfy. The third meta-move, the **prime**, is a non-specific request for a verbal initiate (*What on earth am I to tell him when he asks me?*), such as are also made by chairpersons in formal debates or discussions (*Right, can we have the next question?*).

There seem to be very few restrictions on the order in which moves can follow one another. In theory, any move can be combined with any other move, with the exception of the satisfy as well as the prime, both of which must be followed by one of the other moves.

There are, however, restrictions on the number of moves Ss can make in any one contribution. The normal turn (for a definition, see 6.4.1 below) consists of one of the moves mentioned so far. Ss can make more than one move in any given turn only if their first move is the satisfy of a counter or contra. After the satisfy of an initiate, however, there is again competition between both participants, i.e. either speaker can make a move. Change of speaker within the exchange is thus determined by interactional structure, but conversationalists are free to negotiate whose turn it is outside the exchange structure.

Supporting moves The basic move inventory plus the three meta-moves are to be distinguished from supporting moves, which are relevant but subsidiary to head moves (see Edmondson 1981: 122 for a technical definition of these moves). Their function is defined in terms of their semantic relationship to head moves. **Grounders** give reasons for (conversational) behaviour, **disarmers** are used to apologize for a possible offence before it is committed, and **expanders** provide more than the absolute bare minimum of information asked for. Whether speakers make use of these moves depends on how they view the situation, and in particular on how appropriate, or necessary, they think them for their conversational goals. Though the use of supporting moves is thus partly a matter of speaker strategy (Edmondson 1981: 114–16), there are strong social pressures which make it almost obligatory, for example, to produce reasons for requests, or to apologize for potential offences. The following example of a grounder brings out the interactional structure:

A: John, can you lend me ten pounds?
B: Why?
A: I've forgotten my wallet and just remembered that it's Cleopatra's birthday today.

Speakers may well feel they have to use more than one grounder:

The woman stopped at her husband's shoulder. 'If the king of kings is ready it's high time we were going. Cathy's had quite enough sun for one day and the tide's coming in fast. And we're late for tea already.'

A nice voice, less refined than the expression, with affection taking all the sting out of the marching order.

(A. Price, *Our Man in Camelot*, p. 23)

Apart from showing the importance of non-verbal means (affection) in interaction, the last example also illustrates that Ss employ supporting moves strategically to anticipate possible wishes, doubts, questions or hesitations by the H with respect to a head move. Put in interactional terms, a supporting move is a satisfy to an anticipated initiate of pre-responding exchanges, which Hs might otherwise be expected to produce before they react to the S's initiate. The place of supporting moves is either after (as in the last two examples) or before the head move:

John, look, I've gone and left my wallet at home, and I've just remembered it's Cleopatra's birthday today. I was wondering, can you lend me ten pounds?

(after Edmondson 1981: 125)

Grounders can be so conventionalized that they are interpreted to convey that which they would normally serve to ground:

A: Can you come and see me tomorrow morning?
B: The buses are on strike.

Here the negative answer *I'm sorry, I can't* is missing and only the grounder remains.

Disarmers are used to make it difficult for others to take offence. Without appearing unfriendly and uncooperative the S tries through self-criticism to prevent the H from claiming that a real offence has taken place. Commonly used tokens are *Sorry to interrupt but*; *I don't want to sound bossy but*; and *I hope I'm not disturbing you*.

Expanders typically occur at the beginning of an encounter in what is called **small talk**. Here participants show that they are well disposed towards each other and are prepared to enter into a real conversation. In the following example (adapted from Edmondson 1981: 125), B's turns will be interpreted as unfriendly and uncooperative because they do not provide enough information:

A: Hello, nice party, isn't it?
B: Yes.
A: Do you know John and Mary well?
B: Yes I do.
A: Oh erm, you've been here before then, have you?
B: No.

The use of these supporting moves is a matter of knowing, and wanting to conform to, the social rules of English-speaking countries. The maxim behind the use of disarmers might be said to be, 'When your action is likely to give offence make sure you apologize for it.' Another such rule, governing the employment of expanders, is to give information freely when asked for it. B in the above example does not conform to this norm of social behaviour, suggesting that he or she does not want to talk to A.

6.3.4 Acts

The smallest units in Edmondson's model are called **acts**. One or more **head acts** or **heads**, optionally accompanied again, as in the case of moves, by elements before or after (**pre-** and **post-head acts**), combine to form a move. Interaction in the full sense of the word cannot be said to take place in individual acts or moves, but only at the level of the conversational exchange, for which at least two moves are necessary. Still, there is structure discernible at the level of the act and a list of interactional units would be incomplete without a description of it.

Three elements can be distinguished at this lowest level, a **head act** or **head**, which can be preceded by a pre-head act or **uptaker** and followed by a post-head act or **appealer**. Head acts are the same as head moves inasmuch as they realize illocutionary acts such as request, permission, invitation, apology etc. By contrast, uptakers and appealers do not constitute speech acts (or, to put it differently, do not have illocutionary force). They do, however, serve important communicative functions: uptakers link the preceding move with the ongoing move, and appealers connect the current move with the following one.

Appealers are used by Ss to get agreement, most often to a move that conveys some kind of information. They include tokens such as *okay*, *(all)right*, *don't you think?* as well as question tags and non-linguistic *eh*, *uh* and *mhm*.

Uptakers are signals of active listening on the part of Hs. Typical tokens include *hmm*, *uhum*, *aha*, *ah*, *uh*. The most frequent uptakers in English are *yes* or *yeah*, not to be confused in this function with their use to signal agreement. Besides these neutral tokens there are a number of more emotional items (*really*, *you don't say*, *good heavens*, *terrific*, *not again*, *bloody hell*, etc.). A most important interactional use of uptakers occurs when they do not precede a move but are used 'alone during a narrative or other extended turn at talk by one's conversational partner, without in any way constituting an interruption' (Edmondson and House 1981: 73), as in this example (uptakers in parentheses):

she's a very unique type, very very upper middle class English (yes yes) you see (yeah) – er sort of the general's daughter sort of type (yes yeah) and he was erm from Essex somewhere (yeah) . . .

(after Crystal and Davy 1975: 62)

This class of uptaker (called *go-on gambit* by Edmondson and House 1981: 73) clearly supports the S as they indicate to the S that he or she can go on with her/his turn. In fact, when Hs do not produce them, Ss are likely to stop talking altogether and ask whether something is wrong or, on the phone, whether the H is still there. By using an uptaker a person shows that they accept the other's contribution, but also indicates that they are ready to take a turn themselves (cf. 6.5 on discourse markers below).

While at least one head act is necessary for the communicative act to constitute a move, more than one head act is possible. A typical case is that of questions in an academic debate which are collected by a chairperson and then dealt with one by one by the speaker. Another example of the *collective head* is the shopping list, where again re-ordering has taken place so that we have one head move instead of many. Multiple head acts are particularly common in the opening and closing stages of encounters:

A: Fine, okay, see you next week.
B: Yes, okay then, bye bye.

(after Edmondson 1981: 162)

Two heads (more specifically each an initiate: *okay*; *see you next week*) are made by A, and both are acknowledged by two heads (more specifically each a satisfy) in B's turn.

Appealers and uptakers (when they initiate a turn) are optional elements because many moves contain them implicitly or presuppose them. If, for example, one refuses a request or agrees to one, this clearly presupposes that one has heard the request, and therefore it may seem unnecessary to make this fact explicit. However, when uptakers function to support the S and to show him/her that the H is still prepared to listen, they play an indispensable interactional role.

6.4 Turns, schemas and topics

This section is concerned with how Ss choose what to tell and to whom, i.e. how they select 'tellables' from the mass of potentially interesting things, and how they decide to whom to communicate them. First, though, a brief outline will be given of how participants in a conversation take turns as Ss and Hs.

6.4.1 Turns

Naturally occurring, spontaneous conversations differ from other types of spoken language in two important respects. First, the roles of speaker and hearer frequently change, and second, neither the change nor the size or order of turns is predetermined but are a matter for negotiation. This section deals with the turn-taking mechanism, i.e. how speakers get a turn, how they keep it and how they hand it over to the next speaker (Schenkein

1978 contains important articles; Levinson 1983: 294–370 provides an excellent summary; see also Coulthard 1985: chapter 4). Most research has focused on what happens in conversations with two people, but see Edelsky (1981) for remarks on conversations with more than two participants.

A common definition of **turn** states that a turn consists of all the S's utterances up to the point when another person takes over the role of S. This definition raises the question of what an **utterance** is (see McLaughlin 1984: 95–6). Utterances can be defined in terms of syntax: a stretch of talk that is an independent clause (including elliptical sentences such as *Super!* or *How?* and expressions such as *No, Really!*), a term of address or a tag (*You know?*, *Doesn't he?*). Utterance boundaries also tend to be marked by intonation contours and terminal junctures: low pitch on the final tone unit of an utterance 'is in fact a speaker's signal that he has reached a point of semantic completeness' (Coulthard 1985: 124). Finally, utterances are defined semantically in that they express propositions, i.e. they assert (or predicate) that there is some relation of the subject (an entity or entities) to an attribute or other entity. There is some disagreement over the status of items typical of conversation, such as *well*, *hmm*, *erm*, which have no propositional content, though they fulfil important communicative functions as discourse lubricants for 'the speaker (to cover his confusion, uncertainty and so on) and for the hearer (reassuring him, seeking to persuade him and so on)' (Edmondson and House 1981: 66). We will say that turns consist of one or more utterances that have a semantic content (called **illocutionary acts** in speech act theory; see 6.2.1). In actual fact, because there is great competition for turns, they consist mostly of only a single sentence, unless an S has been granted permission to tell a joke or a story (see 6.3.1, **Central phase**).

How do participants in conversations get their turn at talk? Sacks *et al.* (1974) found that there are two ways. Either the current S passes his/her turn to, and names, the next S, or the current S simply stops and allows the next speaker to self-select. The next S may, of course, be identical with the current S when nobody takes up the offered turn. These possibilities apply again at the next point in the conversation where speaker change can take place (Sacks *et al.* use the term *transition-relevance place*).

One of the questions not tackled by Sacks and his fellow workers is how Ss and Hs recognize change-over places in conversations. Later research has found both verbal and non-verbal signals used in getting and passing turns, though the linguistic ones are primary (witness telephone conversations where no gestures and the like can be perceived). Among the non-linguistic signs that people use are an increase in volume (S) and, for Hs, bodily tension, certain movements to draw the attention of the speaker, a deep intake of breath, or the clearing of the throat. *If I may come in here* or *Excuse me but* . . . are among the phrases commonly used to get a turn. Ss may complete the sentence begun by the previous S, but though this is less hostile than interrupting, it too must be used sparingly. Possible linguistic devices to signal that one is coming to the end of what one wants to say are pauses, a rising or falling intonation at the end of an utterance, expressions such as *you know*, *but*, *so*, an increase in volume and/or a drop in pitch together with these expressions, the completion of a clause, and, of course, expressions that make the end of a turn explicit. These last, however, are rare because they are considered too formal in spontaneous conversation. Non-linguistic means include relaxing one's body and stopping the movements of one's hands and starting another activity, for example, eating, drinking or smoking. When Ss want to keep a turn they will fill their own pauses (e.g. with a *well*) and leave the clauses incomplete. Ss can also use structural pointers such as *first of all*, *then*, *next*, *finally* or *to sum up*, which will allow them to say everything they have to say. An effective non-verbal means of continuing with a turn is averting the eyes, which makes interruptions or attempts to take the turn away from the speaker difficult.

Sometimes it is necessary to break somebody's flow of speech and be uncooperative. A permissible interruption is one in which the H asks the S to explain something that the H has not understood, using such tokens as *Excuse me, what did you say?*; *Would you say that again?*; *Sorry, you've lost me*; or *Sorry, I missed that*. On the other hand, interrupting to correct Ss or to question the truth of what they are saying is a much more delicate matter as it endangers the conversational standing of the Ss. Such hostile interruptions can be warded off by using structuring remarks that show how long you intend to speak (*I would like to comment on two points*; *I just have a few comments*); by using complex sentences; by saying *Let me finish*; *if I may just finish this*; or by raising one's voice to drown out the other. A frequent non-verbal means is to raise one's hand towards a (potential) interrupter as if to fend him/her off.

All this may explain why conversations go on with remarkably little overlap and few awkward silences. When overlap occurs this is likely to be unintentional because Hs usually recognize when an utterance is complete, and the reason for two participants speaking at the same time often is that the current S has not selected the next S. But this situation is quickly remedied: typically the participant who was the first to speak continues with his/her turn. Silences between turns are filled by questions (*Didn't you hear me*) or by repetitions on the part of the current S. The new S will use starting noises (*erm*, *um*, *mm*).

The rules outlined above do not take into account, however, that meaning can be important for the placing of utterances: 'turns initiated with *but* are more likely to occur at non-transition relevance places than turns initiated with either *so* or *and*' (Schiffrin 1988: 268). Also ignored by this approach is the fact that overlap, and its evaluation, is culturally determined: 'members of some ethnic groups interpret overlap as evidence of cooperative involvement and enthusiasm' (ibid.). It seems therefore that the rule-based account of turn-taking needs to be supplemented by a description of the roles that are played by linguistic as well as social meaning.

Most turns consist of single sentences, and conversations consist minimally of two turns. The ties between turns vary a good deal. They can be very close for what are called **adjacency pairs**, which consist of two utterances successively produced by different speakers in a fixed order. Examples of first parts of pairs are complaints, greetings, invitations, offers and questions. The first part of the adjacency pair usually selects the next S, and always the next speech act. This means that what follows after a complaint, invitation, etc., will be interpreted as a response to that first part. Thus, a move which comes after a complaint will be understood as an apology, justification, etc. Likewise, Hs will go to great lengths to interpret the move following on an invitation as expressing acceptance or refusal. Second parts can be reciprocal (greetings are answered by greetings); for some there is only one appropriate second part (a question can be reacted to appropriately only by an answer), while others are not so restricted (complaints can be followed by apologies, denials or justifications). Adjacency pairs show how the speech context or, more precisely, the linear ordering of utterances determines their meaning or illocutionary force.

Several qualifications must be made about this characterization (see Levinson 1983: 304–8). Often the two parts do not follow on immediately because other conversational matter is inserted, while in other cases there is no second part at all. However, Ss expect a second part and when no answers are forthcoming to questions or when greetings are not returned, they will comment on this behaviour as rude or impolite. Another problem is that the predictive power of first parts is diminished and with it the importance of adjacency pairs for the organization of conversation if there are very many alternatives for second parts. The number of second parts can be limited, however, because certain realizations are preferred: requests have grants as **preferred seconds**, and offers and invitations prefer acceptances and disprefer refusals. In other words, preferred seconds are unmarked, the most frequent alternative chosen, while **dispreferred seconds** are marked, unusual and structurally more complex. They are distinguished by various features such as delay (a pause before delivery as well as displacement over a number of turns), the use of markers or announcers (*uh*, *well*), the production of appreciations (for offers, invitations, etc.), the use of apologies (in the case of invitations or requests), or the giving of reasons for why the dispreferred alternative is chosen (ibid.: 334–5):

A: Uh, if you'd care to come and visit a little while this morning I'll give you a cup of coffee. [invitation]

B: Hehh [delay], well [marker], that's awfully sweet of you [appreciation]. I don't think I can make it this morning [refusal–

dispreferred second] − hh uhm, I'm running an ad in the paper and uh I have to stay near the phone [reason].

(adapted from Coulthard 1985: 71)

This principle of **preference organization** can also be invoked in the case of other behaviour, for example, when questions or invitations are met with silence, which will be interpreted as a negative answer or a refusal. Finally, when Ss make mistakes, they prefer to correct these themselves rather than have them corrected by someone else. Clearly, this is a way of avoiding loss of face, which is also the reason behind various sequences carried out before the actual requests, invitations, etc. are made (see 6.3.2 on pre-exchanges).

6.4.2 Schemas

This section addresses the question of how Ss select what they want to tell Hs (and how Hs process both what they are told and what they are not told). As a general rule, Ss will avoid speaking about events and situations which they can expect Hs to know. But how can they know what Hs know?

I woke up at seven forty. I was in bed. I was wearing pyjamas. After lying still for a few minutes, I threw back the duvet, got out of bed, walked to the door of the bedroom, opened the door, switched on the landing light, walked across the landing, opened the bathroom door, went into the bathroom, put the basin plug into the plughole, turned on the hot tap, ran some hot water into the wash basin, looked into the mirror . . .

(Cook 1989: 69)

This example illustrates the fact that, even if asked to tell the truth, the whole truth and nothing but the truth, witnesses in court will not produce texts like this when they have to account for their movements on a particular morning. They can assume that the information contained in the example is known to every person in court, so that its recital is superfluous, irrelevant and very likely boring. People have stored in their brains knowledge about what getting up in the morning involves, so-called **frames**, **schemas**, **scripts** or **plans** (for general discussions, see Schank and Abelson 1977; Johnson-Laird 1983; van Dijk and Kintsch 1983; Brown and Yule 1983: chapter 7; Bower and Cirilo 1985, especially 93−101). Only those features which are not in the getting-up schema need be listed, for example, what one had for breakfast and when one left for work. Details not mentioned by speakers will be assumed to be present unless this assumption is explicitly cancelled. Other examples are the motor car, the restaurant and the waiting-room schema.

Evidence for such **global knowledge patterns** comes from the close study of text production and processing (see de Beaugrande and Dressler 1981:

196–9 for an example). What all patterns have in common is that they are knowledge structures which tie together information in memory about things, sequences of events and actions, about goals and motivations, plans and interests (van Dijk and Kintsch 1983: 307–8). Different patterns have been distinguished.

Frames consist of commonsense knowledge about some central concept, for example, a restaurant. They store all the things that belong together, but do not specify in what order they will be done or mentioned.
Schemas, on the other hand, provide order for states and events and are arranged in a progression.
Plans are defined by the goal that events and states lead up to and must be made under consideration of all the relevant elements according to the criterion of whether they help to achieve the goal.
Scripts are well-established plans which specify the roles of participants and their actions (cf. de Beaugrande and Dressler 1981: 90–1).

Global knowledge patterns thus incorporate **background knowledge** (classes of relevant objects and participants; principles of possible actions; values attached to objects, actions, etc.) and **action knowledge** (description of circumstances or conditions; sequence of actions or events; possible choices; see Mohan 1987 for exemplification from gardening, bridge, statistics and parliamentary procedure).

The great advantage of having knowledge patterns such as these stored in memory is that it 'reduces complexity . . . and allows retaining much more material in active storage at one given time' (de Beaugrande and Dressler 1981: 91). Applied to written and spoken texts this means that speakers have stored patterns of jokes, stories, fairy tales or crime novels, as well as other text types which predict, for example, certain characters and their roles, and plot development. They also have patterns for turn-taking, length of turn and the general goal and development of conversations.

These global knowledge patterns are activated in Ss and Hs alike and thus help them to select what is relevant, both as Ss and Hs of discourse. Cook (1989: 74) points out that global knowledge patterns go a long way towards explaining Grice's maxims. Communication can be economical because Ss will give us new information after taking into account what Hs know already in their schemas. If too much information is provided, as in the getting-up example, or too little because too much knowledge is assumed in Hs, Ss violate the maxim of quantity. The clarity maxim is also broken 'when people make false assumptions about shared schemata. . . . Lastly, our perception of the truth of discourse is also a comparison of the schemata it evokes – its assumptions – and our own' (ibid.).

6.4.3 Topics

When Ss have made their selection of what to tell Hs with the help of the various knowledge patterns discussed in 6.4.2, they must decide whether what they have chosen to communicate is of potential interest to Hs. The concept of **newsworthiness** is not easy to apply to any given situation, and Ss can make wrong assessments, but it is obvious that Ss constantly assess Hs with regard to the what and when, not to mention the how, of communication:

> For instance, if one's sister becomes engaged, some relatives must be told immediately, others on a first meeting after the event, whereas some of one's friends might not know the sister or even that one has a sister, and for them the event has no importance or even interest.
>
> (Coulthard 1985: 79)

The topic that is the first to be mentioned in a conversation is of special importance as it is the only one which Ss are free to choose; all others are determined to a greater or lesser extent by what has gone before. The initial topic of conversation usually has to do with the reason for the encounter. There is a great expectancy that Ss say why they are seeking an encounter, as is borne out by cases where people are just paying social calls without any ulterior motive. In these cases they will say something like *I was just passing* or *I wanted to see how you are*. Some Ss will, of course, hold back the real reason until they can fittingly mention it.

A conversation, if it is to be satisfactory to participants, proceeds from topic to topic in such a way that Hs take up what Ss have said (**linked transition**, Levinson 1983: 313). We can all think of unrewarding conversations where there was no close fitting of topics but rather abrupt topic changes. To make participants enjoy conversations, Ss and Hs must be willing to talk not only about similar topics (e.g. where they went on holiday) but about the same topic (how prices have gone up in the respective country). Another unsatisfactory, though not infrequent, type of conversation is when Ss are unwilling to take up the previous utterance but stick to their own topic and refer back to their own contribution (this has been called *skip-connecting*). For longer speaker turns such as stories, see 6.3.1.

Topics can, but need not be, marked off from one another in various ways. One common way is to use *OK, well, right, now* or *good*, uttered with strong stress and high falling intonation, and followed by a pause (this has been called a **frame** or **framer**; see Coulthard 1985: 123). Another means of indicating a topic boundary is for one S to produce a brief summary (often in the form of a proverb) with which the H can and, indeed, is expected to agree. For endings, see above 6.3.1.

6.5 Discourse markers

This section provides a brief summary of the major aspects of discourse by discussing items that perform a number of different discourse functions. We will first introduce a discourse model in which five different components have been distinguished. Then there will be a brief description of the main characteristics of discourse markers. The section is rounded off by a discussion of three such markers, *now*, *you know* and *well*. Our presentation relies throughout on the treatment by Schiffrin (1987), who offers a detailed and sophisticated analysis, of which we can summarize only the most important aspects. Schiffrin's data are taken from AmE and can be complemented by various BrE corpora, for example, Svartvik and Quirk 1980; Cheepen and Monaghan 1990; and Crystal and Davy 1975, who also offer one of the first analyses of what they call *softeners* – now variously referred to as *gambits*, *pragmatic expressions* or, perhaps most often, *discourse markers*.

6.5.1 Discourse components

Schiffrin sees discourse as made up of five components: exchange structure, action structure, ideational structure, participation framework and information state (Schiffrin 1987: 24–9). The first two components are pragmatic because S and H are centrally important in determining its organization. The units of the **exchange structure** are variously referred to as *turns* and *adjacency pairs* (cf. 6.4.1), or *moves* and *exchanges* (cf. 6.3.3 and 6.3.4). As we have seen, Ss and Hs negotiate whose turn it is and use signals to indicate the beginning and end of their contributions as well as their willingness to listen. **Action structure** is also non-linguistic because it emerges through (perlocutionary) acts, i.e. units which are realized through language but which are not themselves linguistic. Questions here relate, for example, to the sequence of acts, to what actions are intended, and to what actions actually follow (cf. the distinction in 6.2.1 between *perlocutionary object* and *perlocutionary sequel*).

The third dimension, **ideational structure**, consists of linguistic units, ideas, topics or propositions; it concerns the organization of discourse into these units and how they relate to each other.

The **participation framework**, the fourth component, refers to two different aspects. First, it concerns the ways in which S and H can relate to each other; hearers can, for example, be differentiated into those who are intended to receive a message (**addressees**) and those who are not (**overhearers**). It also encompasses the various social role relationships, for example, teacher–pupil, doctor–patient, shop assistant–customer, which influence what roles Ss and Hs can assume. Second, it refers to **mode** or **orientation**, that is, the relations between Ss and utterances. This includes such aspects as whether Ss use direct or indirect speech acts to realize their meanings. Another aspect of S stance is the transition from the narration, or neutral presentation, of a story to its evaluation (see 6.3.1) or interpretation.

Information state, the fifth component, concerns what Ss and Hs know (knowledge), and what they know about their respective knowledge (meta-knowledge). S and H information determines to a large extent how Ss shape their message and how Hs receive it. Knowledge and meta-knowledge are differentiated by degrees of certainty and of saliency, or relevance (see 6.4.2).

The function of discourse markers is to make the various levels explicit and, by integrating them, to create coherent discourse, i.e. talk that is unified because it shows connections on the various discourse planes.

6.5.2 Discourse markers

Discourse markers, such as *now, right, well, you know, you see, I mean*, etc., share various features. First, they relate utterances to the two 'textual coordinates', **participants** (speaker, hearer) on the one hand, and **text** on the other. Markers refer either to preceding discourse (**anaphoric reference**) or to following discourse units (**cataphoric**), or both. This reference function is called **indexical function** (Schiffrin 1987: 322). The units of discourse are not further specified other than to say that they are not to be equated with units in syntax, semantics, phonology or speech act theory.

Second, markers appear at the boundaries of discourse units, but 'are not dependent on the smaller units of talk of which discourse is composed' (ibid.: 37). Schiffrin calls this the **sequential dependence** of markers and illustrates this aspect of the definition, for example, by pointing to combinations which are acceptable only at the discourse level. In 'Now these boys were Irish. They lived different [*sic*]' (ibid.: 38), *now* cannot be a temporal adverbial, because that meaning of *now* cannot co-occur with the past tense. Discourse markers are thus independent of syntactic organization (i.e. they are not attached to sentences). Other features are that they are commonly used at the beginning of utterances; that they show certain prosodic characteristics (e.g. tonic stress followed by a pause or phonological reduction); and that they have no, or only vague, meaning, which allows them to function on different planes of discourse (ibid.: 328).

6.5.3 Now

As table 6.1 shows, discourse markers have functions on several levels. The main function of *now* is mainly in the idea structure of discourse. Its specific function is to mark 'a speaker's progression through a discourse which contains an ordered sequence of subordinate parts' (ibid.: 240).

Table 6.1 Some discourse markers and their functions

	now	you know	well
Exchange structure		+	+
Action structure			* +
Ideational structure	* +	+	+
Participational framework	+	+	* +
Information state		* +	+

Note: the asterisk indicates the primary function.
(adapted from Schiffrin 1987: 316)

Comparisons, either explicit or implicit, completed or unfinished, and the expression of opinions are some of the larger structures in which *now* focuses on one of the subordinate parts:

Explicit comparison: 'They used t'keep them trimmed. Now, for us to do that oh it's gotta be a hundred dollar bill!' (adapted from Schiffrin 1987: 232).

Implicit comparison: 'They have an open classroom at Lansdon. Now there's lots of the mothers in that room are very upset about it. I'm not' (ibid.: 234). Here the topic statement is absent (*parents feel quite differently about this new type of classroom*) in relation to which the *now*-utterance contains an implied comparison.

Opinion: 'He was giving a spelling test. Now to me, if you're inviting parents t'come observe, y'don't give a spelling test!' (ibid.: 236) Here the S sets up a contrast between what she feels and what other people may feel, and this implicit comparison is introduced by *now*.

The other function of *now* relates to shifts in orientation, such as a change from statements to questions, or from narration to evaluation. *Now*, because of its cataphoric reference, is also used 'when the speaker needs to negotiate the right to control what will happen next in talk' (ibid.: 241). Tokens such as *Now listen to me and do what I tell you* show how Ss try to get back their turn at talk. *Now* also prefaces the most important move by the S in an argument, often indicating prior resistance to a command:

And my mother says, 'Now Jerry, and this is the God's honest truth, I'm not gonna hold no punches . . . I don't want you to marry that [girl] — and I want you to break it off right now'.

(adapted from Schiffrin 1987: 243)

The last two examples show that *now* focuses on the S's next contribution to the discourse rather than on the H's reaction to it. This reflects the deictic use of *now* as temporal adverb, which also expresses speaker nearness. In some cases *now* can display as much as three different shifts, in the ideational structure, in speaker orientation and in the hearer/speaker footing, as in this example:

> HENRY: Value. Your sense of value is lost. Now you take your father's a dentist.

(ibid.: 244)

The ideational shift is here from general (*your sense of value is lost*) to specific (*you take your father*), with *now* focusing on the new item, the example; second, S stance, and thereby the S–H relationship, changes from making a statement to involving the H in the assessment of this statement. Third, the S moves from the declarative mood to the imperative, which implies a change in his attitude towards the H.

6.5.4 You know

The basic function of *you know* derives from the meaning of the phrase. *Know* is a stative verb meaning 'have something in one's mind or memory'. *You* can either refer to the addressee or hearer, or it can have indefinite reference 'one, anyone, a person'. *You know* therefore marks meta-knowledge about either what S and H share or what is generally known (cf. also Erman 1987).

Ss use *you know* to 'create a situation in which the speaker knows about . . . knowledge which is shared with the hearer' (Schiffrin 1987: 268). This is why the main function of *you know* lies in the information state. However, as *you know* often causes Hs to react, it can also be regarded as an interactional marker. Schiffrin thinks that *you know* derives from *do you know*: it can therefore be regarded as the first part (question) of an adjacency pair, which sets up the strong expectancy of a second part. This is why it is marked in table 6.1 as having a function in the participant framework and the exchange structure. Take this example:

> JACK: And when you're a cripple . . . they're cripples because they're so religious is what − is the point I'm trying to make. In other words they're *sick*. Religiously. Like the: . . . you know what Hasidic is?
> DEBBY: Umhmm.
> JACK: The Hasidic Jew is a cripple in my eyes, a mental cripple.

(adapted from Schiffrin 1987: 269)

This example illustrates clearly that it depends on the H whether S has to provide information so that S and H share the same knowledge. As Debby has the information in question, Jack can go on and make his point.

In many other examples *you know* is used as a marker of general truths (*You know when you get older, you just don't keep socializing anymore*; ibid.: 277), which can take the form of fixed expressions such as proverbs, commonplaces, etc. The appeal to shared knowledge is used to win con-firmation of one's own point of view or to win over an opponent in an argu-ment (cf. also 2.7). All of Schiffrin's examples of the marker prefacing general truths, except one, show falling intonation, while all cases where the marker refers to what S and H share, again with one exception, have rising intonation. Schiffrin concludes that rising intonation indicates that Ss are less certain about shared knowledge than when falling intonation is used (cf. 3.5.3). This seems plausible because the more general a truth is, the greater is the likelihood that it is universally known.

The marker also has a function for the idea structure of discourse. *You know* causes Hs to focus on a particular piece of information (*Y'know what I like the best? I like the seashore area*; ibid.: 289). In story-telling *you know* helps Hs to focus either on what is important for the understanding of the point (see ibid.: 283 for an example and discussion) or on evaluations (*Like out of the clear blue sky! Y'know they just have such an arrogant air about them!*; ibid.: 289). *You know* thus often 'focuses on the centrality of a single proposition for the overall idea structure of a text' (ibid.: 317).

6.5.5 Well

In contrast to *now* and *you know*, where the semantic content influences the function the marker has, *well* has no meaning which could restrict its use to any one plane of discourse. Its primary function is in the partici-pation framework: the main participant role it defines is that of the respon-dent in an exchange. It is particularly frequent in question–answer as well as request–compliance pairs.

Schiffrin has found that the syntactic form of questions influences the use of *well*. It is, for example, rare after yes-no questions and tag questions but more frequent after *wh*-questions. In other words, '*well* is more frequent when a larger set of answer options is encoded through the form of the question' (ibid.: 105). Another important use is in cases where Ss do not limit themselves to the options offered in questions, or where they delay the core of their answer. An example of a complex deferral is found where Ss use a story to give an answer:

DEBBY: What happened?
ZELDA: Well . . . at one time he was a very fine doctor. And he had two terrible tragedies. [story follows]   (ibid.: 110)

In general, *well* is used by Ss when they have difficulty finding an answer because what they want to say does not fit the semantic options implied or mentioned in the question. This is also the reason for the marker's use in request sequences, where it is more likely to be employed to mark non-compliance than compliance. Put differently, *well* prefaces a dispreferred second, such as an insufficient answer, denial or disagreement (cf. 6.4.1).

Let us look at the five tokens of the discourse marker in the following extract:

> B: So we'll have to try and do something about the allergy and get your rash cleared up first, won't we?
> A: Well [1], can you prescribe . . . anything for the allergy . . .?
> B: Does it itch at all?
> A: Yes, it itches quite a lot.
> B: Do you get scabs forming on it or anything?
> A: No.
> B: Hm hum . . .. It's just on your face, is it?
> A: And my arms.
> B: And your arms. Is it on any other place of the body?
> A: Well [2], it's spreading, yeah.
> B: Hm hm (begins writing)
> A: All over.
> B: And is it painful at all?
> A: Well [3], only – well [4] if I scratch it, yes, it becomes very painful.
> B: Well [5], I think I can prescribe some ointment for you . . .
>
> (adapted from Edmondson 1981: 182–3)

A's first *well* prefaces an answer which does not consist of a simple yes or no and also demonstrates a lack of appreciation of B's contribution, perhaps even resentment of the particular form chosen: it is not *we*, but *you* whom A expects to do something about his rash. The context for the second use is again a contrast between B's question (*any other place*) and A's answer, which informs B that the rash has in fact spread all over his or her body. *Well* can be viewed, both here and in the first use, as a means of softening disagreement or deferring an embarrassing answer. This seems to apply also to the third and fourth tokens. But, more importantly, the fourth illustrates the use of the discourse marker in contexts where it introduces responses not to another participant's utterance but to one's own. Self-repairs are thus signals of a shift in speaker orientation.

The tokens discussed so far are all placed in contributions immediately next to the utterance that solicited them. This is different for the fifth token, which looks back to the beginning and answers A's first question/request for a prescription. Put in interactional terms, *well* functions in head exchanges which are preceded by a number of pre-responding exchanges. Another non-local use of *well* has already been mentioned (see 6.3.2): it can bridge the business and closing phases of an encounter. *Well* has therefore functions at both the local level of the exchange or adjacency pair and the global level of discourse phases.

REFERENCES

Austin, J. L. (1962) *How to Do Things With Words*, Oxford: Oxford University Press.

Bach, K. and Harnish, R. M. (1979) *Linguistic Communication and Speech Acts*, Cambridge, Mass.: Massachusetts Institute of Technology.

de Beaugrande, R. and Dressler, W. (1981) *Introduction to Text Linguistics*, Harlow: Longman.

Blakemore, D. (1988) 'The organization of discourse', in F. J. Newmeyer (ed.) *Language: the Socio-Cultural Context*, Vol. 4 of *Linguistics: the Cambridge Survey*, Cambridge: Cambridge University Press, pp. 229–50.

—— (1992) *Understanding Utterances: An Introduction to Pragmatics*, Oxford: Blackwell.

Bower, G. H. and Cirilo, R. K. (1985) 'Cognitive psychology and text processing', in T. A. van Dijk (ed.) *Disciplines of Discourse,* Vol. 1 of *Handbook of Discourse Analysis*, London: Academic Press, pp. 71–105.

Brown, G. and Yule, G. (1983) *Discourse Analysis*, Cambridge: Cambridge University Press.

Brown, P. and Levinson, S. C. (1987) *Politeness: Some Universals in Language Usage*, Cambridge: Cambridge University Press.

Carterette, E. C. and Jones, N. H. (1974) *Informal Speech: Alphabetic and Phonemic Texts with Statistical Analyses and Tables*, Berkeley: University of California Press.

Cheepen, C. and Monaghan, J. (1990) *Spoken English: a Practical Guide*, London: Pinter.

Clark, H. H. and French, J. H. (1981) 'Telephone *goodbyes*', *Language in Society* 10: 1–19.

Cohen, P. R. and Perrault, C. R. (1979) 'A plan-based theory of speech acts', *Cognitive Science* 3: 213–30.

Cook, G. (1989) *Discourse*, Oxford: Oxford University Press.

Coulthard, M. (1985) *An Introduction to Discourse Analysis*, 2nd edn, Harlow: Longman.

Crystal, D. and Davy, D. (1975) *Advanced Conversational English*, London: Longman.

van Dijk, T. A. (ed.) (1985) *Handbook of Discourse Analysis*, London: Academic Press.

van Dijk, T. A. and Kintsch, W. (1983) *Strategies of Discourse Comprehension*, New York: Academic Press.

Edelsky, C. (1981) 'Who's got the floor?' *Language in Society* 10: 383–421.

Edmondson, W. (1981) *Spoken Discourse*, London: Longman.

Edmondson, W. and House, J. (1981) *Let's Talk and Talk about It*, Munich: Urban & Schwarzenberg.

Erman, B. (1987) *Pragmatic Expressions in English*, Stockholm: Almqvist & Wiksell.

Flowerdew, J. (1988) 'Speech acts and language teaching', *Language Teaching* 21: 69–82.

Francis, G. and Hunston, S. (1987) 'Analysing everyday conversation', in M. Coulthard (ed.) *Discussing Discourse*, Birmingham: English Language Research, pp. 107–48.

Grice, H. P. (1975) 'Logic and conversation', in P. Cole and J. Morgan (eds) *Speech Acts*, Vol. 3 of *Syntax and Semantics*, New York: Academic Press, pp. 41–58.

Grosz, B. J., Sparck Jones, K. and Webster, B. L. (eds) (1986) *Readings in Natural Language Processing*, Los Altos, Calif.: Kaufmann.

Gülich, E. and Quasthoff, U. (1985) 'Narrative analysis', in T. A. van Dijk (ed.) *Dimensions of Discourse*, Vol. 2 of *Handbook of Discourse Analysis*, London: Academic Press, pp. 169–197.

—— (1986) 'Story-telling in conversation: cognitive and interactive aspects', *Poetics* 15: 217–41.

Hinde, R. A. (ed.) (1972) *Non-Verbal Communication*, Cambridge: Cambridge University Press.

Hymes, D. (1972) 'On communicative competence', in J. B. Pride and J. Holmes (eds) *Sociolinguistics*, Harmondsworth: Penguin, pp. 269–93.

Jefferson, G. (1972) 'Side sequences', in D. Sudnow (ed.) *Studies in Social Interaction*, New York: Free Press, pp. 294–338.

—— (1978) 'Sequential aspects of storytelling in conversation', in J. Schenkein (ed.) *Studies in the Organisation of Conversational Interaction*, New York: Academic Press, pp. 219–48.

Johnson-Laird, P. N. (1983) *Mental Models: Towards a Cognitive Science of Language, Inference and Consciousness*, Cambridge: Cambridge University Press.

Kendon, A. (ed.) (1981) *Nonverbal Communication, Interaction, and Gesture*, The Hague: Mouton.

Klammer, T. P. (1973) 'Foundations for a theory of dialogue structure', *Poetics* 9: 27–64.

Laver, J. (1975) 'Communicative functions of phatic communion', in A. Kendon, R. Harris and M. Key (eds) *The Organisation of Behavior in Face-to-Face Interaction*, The Hague: Mouton, pp. 215–238.

Leech, G. N. (1983) *Principles of Pragmatics*, London: Longman.

Leech, G. N. and Thomas, J. (1990) 'Language, meaning and context: pragmatics', in N. E. Collinge (ed.) *An Encyclopaedia of Language*, London: Routledge, pp. 173–206.

Levinson, S. C. (1983) *Pragmatics*, Cambridge: Cambridge University Press.

McCarthy, M. (1991) *Discourse Analysis for Language Teachers*, Cambridge: Cambridge University Press.

McLaughlin, M. L. (1984) *Conversation: How Talk is Organised*, Beverly Hills, Calif.: Sage.

Malinowski, B. (1923: repr. 1969) 'The problem of meaning in primitive languages', Supplement 1, in C. K. Ogden and I. A. Richards, *The Meaning of Meaning*, London: Routledge & Kegan Paul.

Mohan, B. A. (1987) 'The structure of situations and the analysis of text', in R. Steele and T. Threadgold (eds) *Language Topics*, Vol. 2. Amsterdam: Benjamins, pp. 507–22.

Morris, D. (1977) *Manwatching: a Field Guide to Human Behaviour*, London: Cape.

Owen, M. (1983) *Apologies and Remedial Interchanges*, Berlin: Mouton.

—— (1990) 'Language as a spoken medium: conversation and interaction', in N. E. Collinge (ed.) *An Encyclopaedia of Language*, London: Routledge, pp. 244–80.

Pin, E. J. and Turndorf, J. (1985) *The Pleasure of Your Company*, New York: Praeger.

Polanyi, L. (1985) 'Conversational storytelling', in T. A. van Dijk (ed.) *Discourse and Dialogue*, Vol. 3 of *Handbook of Discourse Analysis*, London: Academic Press, pp. 183–201.

Price, A. (1977) *Our Man in Camelot*, Sevenoaks.

Sacks, H., Schegloff, E. A. and Jefferson, G. (1974) 'A simplest systematics for the organisation of turn-taking for conversations', *Language* 50: 696–735.

Sadock, J. (1978) 'On testing for conversational implicature', in P. Cole (ed.) *Pragmatics*, Vol. 9 of *Syntax and Semantics*, New York: Academic Press, pp. 281–97.

Schank, R. and Abelson, R. (1977) *Scripts, Plans, Goals, and Understanding*, Hillsdale, NJ: Erlbaum.

Schegloff, E. and Sacks, H. (1973) 'Opening up closings', *Semiotics* 8: 289–327.

Schenkein, J. (ed.) (1978) *Studies in the Organisation of Conversational Interaction*, New York: Academic Press.

Schiffrin, D. (1987) *Discourse Markers*, Cambridge: Cambridge University Press.

—— (1988) 'Conversation analysis', in F. J. Newmeyer (ed.) *Language: the Socio-Cultural Context*, Vol. 4 of *Linguistics: the Cambridge Survey*, Cambridge: Cambridge University Press pp. 251–76.

Schneider, K. P. (1988) *Small Talk: Analysing Phatic Discourse*, Marburg: Hitzeroth.

Searle, J. R. (1969) *Speech Acts: an Essay in the Philosophy of Language*, Cambridge: Cambridge University Press.

—— (1979) *Expression and Meaning*, Cambridge: Cambridge University Press.

Sinclair, J. M. and Brazil, D. (1982) *Teacher Talk*, Oxford: Oxford University Press.

Sinclair, J. M. and Coulthard, M. (1975) *Towards an Analysis of Discourse: the English Used by Teachers and Pupils*, Oxford: Oxford University Press.

de Souza Filho, D. M. (1985) *Language and Action: a Reassessment of Speech Act Theory*, Philadelphia: Benjamins.

Sperber, D. and Wilson, D. (1986) *Relevance*, Oxford: Blackwell.

Stubbs, M. (1983) *Discourse Analysis*, Oxford: Blackwell.

Svartvik, J. and Quirk, R. (1980) *A Corpus of English Conversation*, Lund: Gleerup.

Taylor, T. J. and Cameron, D. (1987) *Analysing Conversation*, Oxford: Pergamon.

Wardhaugh, R. (1985) *How Conversation Works*, Oxford: Blackwell.

White, E. B. (1980) *Charlotte's Web*, New York: HarperCollins.

Chapter 7

Special Englishes

The ways in which English is used in particular situations vary according to these situations. In itself this is a trivial statement; yet the principle it incorporates lies at the centre of a major field of endeavour, viz. English for Special/Specific Purposes (ESP). As English has expanded to become the preferred language of international communication in more and more fields (cf. Large 1989: 171–3), the needs of ever more non-native users of English have become evident. The important assumption has been made that these users, as well as their native-speaker colleagues, employ English in a restricted range of social and thematic areas. Why, after all, should an Egyptian or Brazilian technician bother with the language of English poetry if what he/she is interested in is, say, a set of technical specifications or instructions? What is important for this technician is the communication of information, which necessitates the use of unambiguous terminology and clear grammar. This unambiguity and clarity is desirable from the perspective of both the writer (or speaker) and the reader (or listener).

7.1 Special Englishes and the register model of language

Special Englishes are, in the sense of the preceding paragraph, instances of **registers** (see 1.6 and 5.3). Two criteria within this model which are frequently used to classify Special Englishes are *field* and *purpose*. In addition to field of discourse and purpose, which is sometimes referred to as *functional tenor*, the further criteria of *personal tenor* (style, relationship of the speaker/writer to addressee) and *medium* (spoken/ written) are also significant. However, the latter seldom show up as the major criteria for the classification of special Englishes.

Field The various sorts of English as defined by their situation of use have frequently been divided up according to field. This has the advantage of following the relatively easily observable criterion of shared vocabulary. However, there is no agreement on the appropriate size of the fields. Major areas such as science, technology, law, medicine, the social sciences, business and economics are commonly named. However, finer (for example, biology, chemistry and physics) and ever finer divisions (such as biophysics, zoology, biochemistry, gene technology, etc.) can also be made (one author speaks of up to 300 fields, see Beier 1980: 25); yet it is not clear where the point is beyond which further distinctions cannot be expected to be helpful.

Purpose   A different approach is one oriented along the lines of purpose. Here the general divisions run across the boundaries of the individual disciplines, providing for such types as English for Occupational Purposes (EOP) or English for Academic Purposes (EAP). Within the latter the English of Science and Technology (EST) is recognized as an important subdivision. Nevertheless, even within and across these areas there are more specific communicative purposes which can be distinguished. These consist of the **rhetorical functions** of description, report, exposition, instruction and argumentation (cf. 5.3, discussed there as text types).

Style   Personal tenor is meaningful in connection with the neutral, unemotional and objective tone which scientific and academic prose characteristically has. The sender–receiver relationship will be different in such scholarly prose as appears in learned journals *vis-à-vis* popular science publications (such as The *Scientific American*) or science reports in general newspapers or magazines (such as *The New York Times* or *The Atlantic*). A related term is **functional style** (as developed by the Prague and Soviet schools of linguistics). It recognizes four to five larger functional styles: the scientific-technical style, the language of *belles-lettres*, everyday language, the language of business and administration and, perhaps, the journalistic style (Beier 1980: 20). This approach, of course, raises style to a criterion of classification.

Medium or mode   So far it has been exclusively the written language which has been referred to; yet a wide range of spoken usage belongs here as well, stretching from scholarly colloquia to technical training classes to salesroom explanations. EST will probably be more strongly oriented towards written forms, the English of business and economics, perhaps, somewhat more towards speech.

Special vs. General English   One of the major difficulties in describing Special Englishes, regardless of how they are subdivided, is deciding what the nature of the difference between them and everyday or General English is. Since, for instance, the latter includes *all* the regularities of the grammar of English, grammar offers no absolute criteria for making a distinction. Nevertheless, there is 'the intuitive notion of an everyday language and we would wish to uphold its existence' (Sager *et al*. 1980: 3), and there are meaningful distinctions which can be made (see below).

Part of this general–special/specific distinction is the question of whether to understand the S of ESP as meaning 'Special' or 'Specific'. The earlier designation was 'English for *Special* Purposes'. More recently, especially since the late 1970s, the term 'English for *Specific* Purposes' has largely displaced it. The rationale behind this is that 'special' implies restricted languages, while English for *Specific* Purposes focuses attention on the purposes of the learner, which are specific, viz. 'to perform a task in English' (Robinson 1989: 396). These determine the selection of skills needed (reading, listening, writing, talking) and the communicative or rhetorical functions involved (description, report, exposition, argumentation and instruction), as well as the vocabulary and grammar necessary for this. Practically speaking, this means that

1 the complete grammar of English belongs to ESP;
2 the same processes of morphology and word formation apply to it as are found in General English.

Yet this also recognizes that

1 there may be distinctly different frequencies in the use of individual syntactic and morphological constructions as well as of word formation processes;
2 the selection of vocabulary will be skewed by field;
3 terminology will be at least partially standardized to eliminate ambiguity;
4 certain conventions will be observed in regard to the individual elements of written texts and the way they are structured;
5 special visual phenomena (symbols, graphs, tables, etc.) may be employed in written texts that are not a part of everyday English or the way it is used.

In other words the Englishes involved here are, indeed, restricted, selective and special, though not in such an exclusive way as to offer absolutely definitive criteria: they are 'differences of degree rather than kind' (cf. Todd *et al*. in Robinson 1989: 418). Yet they should not be dismissed as non-essential. One author describes scientific texts in the following manner: 'Any divergence from the stylistic norm may induce shock or even anger; almost certainly it will reduce the credibility of the author' (Large 1989: 179).

It is because the present orientation of English for Specific Purposes is in the field of teaching English as a foreign language, while the subject of this book is the English language, that we have chosen the title 'Special Englishes' for this chapter. The remainder of the chapter will deal with some of the typical characteristics of those Special Englishes which have been most commonly studied, viz. academically oriented English of Science and Technology, or EST. The procedure will be to look first at grammar, then at vocabulary and, finally, at textual and other conventions.

7.2 Syntactic features of EST

A number of studies of the syntax of EST have been published which, among other things, point out such features as

1 nominal style (see 7.2.2);
2 the selection of pronouns employed (more frequent than in General English: *we, this/these*; less so: *I, he*; even less so *she, you*, cf. Johansson 1975: 6ff, 17; Brekke 1989: 259f);
3 the occurrence of new plurals (*fats, oils, greases*, etc., cf. Gerbert 1970: 40) and Latin and Greek plurals (*mitochondrion/-ia*; *bacterium/ -ia*);
4 the use of telegram style (see 7.2.2);
5 the greater frequency of the passive (see 7.2.1);
6 the greater relative frequency of non-defining relative clauses compared with defining ones, *viz.* 20 to 30 per cent (Gerbert 1970: 40), 26 per cent (Kok Lee Cheon 1978: 132) or 31 per cent (Huddleston 1971: 259);
7 specific, frequently employed rhetorical devices such as anaphora, parallelism, parenthetical elements, emphatic inversion, rhetorical questions and ellipsis (Gläser 1979: 45–9).

7.2.1 The verb

Voice What is typical of the form of the verb in EST is, more than anything else, the frequency with which the passive voice occurs. Gerbert cites studies showing frequencies of passives among the total finite verb forms of 32.6 per cent (Kaufman), 28 per cent (Barber) and 26 per cent (Rumszewica) (Gerbert 1970: 88). Kok Lee Cheon (1978: 41) quotes 26.2 per cent (Huddleston), 23.8 passives per thousand words (Svartvik) and (for himself) 26 per cent. Hanania and Akhtar (1985: 53) report 40 per cent (in Wingard) and 46 per cent for themselves. The comparative figures for literary texts are 2.2 per cent (Kaufman), 3 per cent (Rumszewica, cf. Gerbert 1970: 88), and 8.2 per thousand words (Svartvik, cf. Kok Lee Cheon 1978: 41).

This might seem to be all there is to say; however, two important additions must be made. For one, these figures, especially those with a decimal point, suggest an accuracy and objectivity which is illusory. The representativity of the corpora used is unlikely to be more than approximate and, in addition, the values given will vary depending on whether a percentage is taken of all the finite verbs in a corpus or only those which could potentially appear in the passive, such as transitive and prepositional-transitive verbs (cf. Tarone *et al.* 1981: 127).

The second point has to do with when and why the passive is used. One common explanation is that the passive allows the author to step back and the work reported on to stand at the centre of attention. According to one study, 'author's passives' make up a third of the total. These are passives which involve the action of the author(s), for example, *Several interviews were conducted to substantiate this hypothesis* ('We conducted several interviews . . .'). Passives which replace other agents account for approximately a tenth of the cases. A few passives can be explained by difficulties in expression with an active construction or similar problems. Half, however, are used for generally unspecified non-human causes (Beier 1980: 79). The motivation here is likely to have to do with the thematic focus of a sentence. In English, the topic of a sentence is usually named at the beginning, and what is said (predicated) about it at the end (cf. 4.4.4). The passive allows a direct or an indirect object which is the topic to occupy the initial thematic position and thus helps to realize the desired thematic focus of the sentence. A study of the use of the passive in two journal papers on astrophysics confirms the validity of this principle. In addition, however, the same study offers three further explanations of the use or non-use of the passive.

1 Standard procedural choices in astrophysics research are reported in the passive while unique procedures chosen by the authors of the articles are reported in the active (with the subject *we*).
2 Previous work in the same field is reported in the active *we*-form if it is the author's own and in the passive if it is by others and stands in contrast to the author's own work; if other work agrees with or supports the author's research the active is used.
3 Work which the author proposes to do in the future is referred to in the passive (Tarone *et al.* 1981: 128ff).

These three explanations from the astrophysics papers cannot be generalized to other fields or other text forms besides journal papers without further studies. However, there seems to be a deeper principle involved here which might usefully be pointed out. This is the use of voice for deictic purposes. In the astrophysics papers the active serves to highlight (bring closer) the author's procedures and decisions. The passive is used to express the writer's greater distance.

Tense and aspects   The same deictic functions can also be expressed through the appropriate use of tense. For example, the present tense is normally used to describe scientific apparatus. However, if the apparatus is historical and no longer in use, the past will be used. Furthermore, if writers use the past tense in reporting research done previously by themselves or others then that research is of secondary importance to the current work being reported on. If, on the other hand, the writer uses the present perfect or the present tense, then the research is of more direct and primary importance to the writer's work.

(Trimble 1985: 126; cf. also Heslot 1982; Malcolm 1987)

Above and beyond these points, it has also been established that the simple past far outnumbers other verb forms (Barber 1962: 27; Beier 1980: 72f) and that the progressive is especially infrequent (Swales 1971).

Modal verbs   A final point to be mentioned in this section is that modal verbs may occur in meanings which are relatively rare in the general language, such as what has been termed the 'non-standard uses of *should* and *may*'. This refers to the uses of these two auxiliaries to mean *must*. Here they indicate that there is no choice, rather than the standard meaning 'desirable but not necessary' in sentences such as:

Steel weld backing *should be* [= must be] sufficiently thick so that the molten metal will not burn through the backing. . . . For steel thicknesses other than gage material, a relief groove *may be necessary* [= must be used] .

(Trimble 1985: 119f)

7.2.2 The nominal

The nominal differs in several ways which have frequently been commented on. One of these is that EST has a higher proportion of nouns (but also prepositions and adjectives); in one count this is 44 per cent of all words in EST vs. 28 per cent in general texts. 'As a result of strong nominalization, verbs have less communicative value and are only half or a third as frequent as in general language' (Sager *et al.* 1980: 234; cf. also Gerbert 1970: 39; Beier 1980: 61).

Nominalization   This refers to the replacement of clauses, which contain finite verbs, with complex structures consisting of nouns and noun adjuncts, for example, *because the surface of the retina is spherical →* *because of the sphericity of the retinal surface*; or: [*something*] *is near the nucleus →* [*something*] *occupies a juxtanuclear position* (examples quoted from Gerbert 1970: 36). In a similar fashion, prepositional phrases 'disappear': *experiments of transfer of momentum* becomes *momentum transfer experiments*; and *a vessel for storage of liquids* takes the compact form *liquid storage vessel* (examples quoted from Trimble 1985: 132f). For a further characterization of nominal compounds, see Williams 1984.

Nominalization and thematic structure   The formation of complex noun phrases is itself a part of the theme-rheme structure of English. What appears in prenominal position may represent information shared by sender and receiver; it is, in other words, presupposed information. In contrast, what is new and is being introduced occurs in postnominal position. In a neurological text in which the branchlets of nerves are discussed, mention may, for example, be made of a *posterior branchlet of the saccular nerve*. At a later stage the now given and no longer new information that it is the saccular nerve that is being referred to can be adopted into a prenominal position as the *posterior saccular branchlet* (Dubois 1982: 53–63).

Nominal style   The tendency to use combinations of function verb + noun instead of simple verbs is part of what is known as nominal style. In these structures function verbs are 'general purpose verbs' of low communicative value, such as *do, make, take, have* or *give*:

to work	→ to do some work
to investigate	→ to make an investigation
to photograph	→ to take a photograph
to hypothesize	→ to have (or make) a hypothesis
to report	→ to give (or make) a report

The article   A further feature involving the nominal is the use or non-use of the article. On the one hand, the definite article is often dispensed with in instructions written in telegram style, for example, *Insert red tab into red slot and blue tab into blue slot*.

The opposite tendency can also be observed, namely the 'overuse' of the definite article, as in the following description of a process:

> *The* gas turbine engine fires continuously. The engine draws air through *the* diffuser and into *the* compressor, raising its temperature.

The first use of *the* is generic and might, but need not, be replaced with the indefinite article *a*; the third and fourth instances could appear as indefinite articles in general English. For, after all, the indefinite article is usual when something is mentioned for the first time in a text (cf. 4.5.1). Native-language text-users regularly interpret the third and fourth instances of the article differently, however. Here, for example, engineers reading the description of the gas turbine engine 'took the use of the definite article . . . to indicate that the machinery being described contained *only one* of whatever part was being marked by the article' (Trimble 1985: 122; cf. also Master 1987).

7.2.3 The sentence

The sentence as a whole differs between general languages and special languages. Sentences in the latter are, on the average, longer (cf. Brekke 1989: 255–9) and more complex. Yet the repertoire of clause types is more restricted; relative clauses, for example, are particularly frequent (Hoffmann 1987: 101). Declarative sentences clearly predominate. Interrogatives are limited to use as rhetorical questions and to study questions at chapter ends in textbooks. Imperatives, however, are regularly found for giving instructions (Sager *et al*. 1980: 201f).

7.3 The lexicon of EST and word formation

'. . . the lexicon of special languages is their most obvious distinguishing characteristic' (Sager *et al*. 1980: 230). This has always been and will surely always remain true of special languages. While their syntax is distinguished from that of General English only in the relative frequencies of constructions, the vocabulary of Special Englishes will often contain words that can be found nowhere outside the given field. No one can say how many such special words there are, but there are several million for chemical compounds alone. The numerous dictionaries, terminological clearing houses, databases, etc., clearly indicate that the number is large. There follows one example of each. A general dictionary of science is *The Longman Dictionary of Scientific Usage*; it contains 1,300 terms basic to all branches of science and 8,500 technical terms from biology, chemistry and physics. The terminological clearing house, Intoterm, was established within UNESCO in 1971 for the coordination of work on terminology on an international basis; it cooperates with the International Standardization Organization (ISO). EURODICAUTON is an on-line databank service for up-to-date terminology available for the use of translators using EC languages.

Important characteristics of the vocabulary of EST are the following:

1 it is international, often based on Greek or Latin elements;
2 it is standardized and as unambiguous as possible;
3 it is non-emotive in tone;
4 it favours certain processes of word formation;
5 it incorporates symbols.

In looking more closely at the vocabulary of EST, we will begin with terminology, including non-lexical items (i.e. symbols), move then to word formation, and finish with the results of frequency counts.

7.3.1 Terminology

Terms are special items of vocabulary whose meanings are fixed by convention. They are necessary in order to avoid the ambiguity to which a variety of regional, non-standardized meanings could lead. Needless to say, ambiguity poses a threat not only to the success of experiments and manufacturing processes, but also to health and safety. Among the qualities associated with systems of terminology are that they are

1 exact, i.e. they designate a particular meaning;
2 unambiguous, i.e. they cannot be confused with the meanings of any other terms;
3 unique, i.e. one and only one term is available;
4 systematic, i.e. they are part of a larger, ordered system of terms, preferably in a clearly structured terminological hierarchy;
5 neutral, i.e. they are oriented towards cognition and objective processes without including aesthetic or emotive elements;
6 self-explanatory or transparent, i.e. they include elements which reflect the important features of the concept designated (cf. Beier 1980: 31f).

These features are, of course, ideals that cannot always be realized. The demand for economy may, for example, be sacrificed to the greater need for exactness, lack of ambiguity and uniqueness. Furthermore, scientists and technicians may often use vocabulary which is more informal, at least in oral communication. This might include clippings and metaphors from everyday language. Hence, *streps* for *streptococci*, *mag sulf* for *magnesium sulphate*, or *juice* for *electrical current* (examples from Beier 1980: 35f).

A special sub-area of terminology is that of the signs and symbols employed in the various fields. The fact that they do not always have a widely accepted pronunciation indicates once again that EST is, to a large extent, a written language. Examples of signs and symbols drawn from EST are Σ, $\sqrt{\ }$, $+$, $>$, $=$, μ, $^{\circ}$, π.

7.3.2 Word formation

Considering both the absolute quantity of terms needed and the qualities expected of them, processes of word formation are of central importance. Terms are, in some cases, borrowed from General English, for example, metaphorical *memory* for *computer storage capacity*. More often, however, they are derived from other languages, especially Latin and Greek. In addition to direct borrowings, such as *apparatus*, *matrix* or *phenomenon*, this involves morphological elements including, for instance, prefixes (*aero-*, *astro-*, *baro-*, *cryo-*, *ferro-*, *gyro-*, *hydro-*, etc.) and suffixes (*-gram*, *-graph*, *-ology*, *-scope*, *-tomy*, etc.). In chemistry, for example, the order and status of roots and affixes are strictly provided for:

> Thus eth + an + ol signifies, in that order, a structure with two carbons, simply linked together and with one of these linked to a hydroxyl (−O−H) group, and no other combinations of these morphemes describes that structure.
>
> (Dermer *et al.*, quoted in Beier 1980: 32)

In addition to the ubiquitous elements of Latin and Greek, EST, of course, also uses the normal processes of word formation of General English (cf. 1.4) with or without Latin-Greek elements, be they

1 prefixing (*anti-, in-, mis-, non-, semi-, un-*);
2 suffixing (*-ar, -al, -ed, -er, -less, -ment, -ness*);
3 conversion/zero derivation (*to dimension < dimension*);
4 back formations (*to lase < laser*);
5 clippings (*lab < laboratory*);
6 abbreviations (*FBR < fast breeder reactor*);
7 acronyms (*laser* 'light amplification by stimulated emission of radiation');
8 blends (*pulsar* 'pulsating radio star');
9 composite forms (*aeroplane*).

Perhaps most distinctive in the field of word formation is the extremely high frequency of compound nominal phrases (or noun compounds), which were already exemplified in the section on syntax (7.2.2). These constructions were found to occur as follows in corpora of ten 2,000-word texts in each of three areas:

General English (GE)	0.87 per cent
Medical English (ME)	9.76 per cent
Technical English (TE)	15.37 per cent

(Salager 1984: 138f)

This degree of frequency in Medical English and Technical English is to be understood as a consequence of the exactness, non-ambiguity and uniqueness of technical terms:

> compounds are mainly used to refer to something which is conceived of as a single entity, as an item in a class of its own. This underlines the difference between the compound and the relative clause. . . . There is a semantic difference between the CNP [compound nominal phrase] *banana curve* and the related but not synonymous phrase *a curve shaped like a banana*.
>
> (ibid.: 141f)

7.3.3 Frequency

The proportion of technical words in EST texts has been estimated at approximately 25 per cent (Beier 1980: 40). In a count of the one thousand most common words, one comparison revealed 339 words in EST which were not among the first thousand words of General English. In addition to technical terms there is also a difference in distribution, which is also due to the higher frequency of what are called semi-technical or sub-technical words. For in contrast to words from the closed classes (auxiliaries, pronouns, articles, demonstratives, prepositions), which have approximately the same frequency in General English and in EST, there is a noticeable weighting in EST towards words associated with

1 exposition (*discussion, argument, result, conclusion*);
2 procedure (*analysis, experiment, measurement, observation, test*);
3 statistics (*sample, probability, distribution, significance*);
4 classification (*class, type, group, species, item, unit*);
5 relational words (*similar, distinct, average, relative, normal*) (cf. Johannson 1975: 22).

Furthermore, relatively less use is made of shorter, everyday words as compared with longer, more formal words.

EST	also	rather than General English	too
	certain		sure
	determine		decide
	large		big
	obtained		got
	thus		so

(ibid: 25f)

The fact that we are looking at more formal, written texts also accounts for such differences in style as the lack of contractions, the greater use of cohesive devices such as *this/these, above, below, preceding* or *following* for reference within a text, and the greater occurrence of such relatively formal adverbs as *moreover, overall, primarily, therefore* and *however* (ibid: 11, 17ff, 24).

7.4 The EST text

The type of text is, as the preceding remarks have revealed, an important factor in the linguistic character of EST. As was pointed out in the discussion of register, this involves the topic (*field*), the participants (*personal tenor*), the time and place (*medium*) and the purpose (*functional tenor*). The closer these are to the thematically non-specific, to the personally informal, to the temporally and spatially immediate (the 'here and now') and to the subjective-conversational, the more likely the text is to be General English. EST, in contrast, is oriented towards the formal, towards the written, towards independence of the immediate moment and place, and towards objectivity. While there are exceptions and mixed forms (talking shop, lecturing, note-taking, popular science writing, etc.), this observation is basically accurate.

7.4.1 Message types

One approach to texts which takes these factors into account suggests five basic message types: dialogue, memo, report, schedule and essay. The **dialogue**, as an exclusively spoken form, will not be considered here.

The **memo**, characterized as demanding a response of some sort, encompasses a wide range of genres. A large number of its realizations are administrative (minutes, business letters, invoices, contracts) or journalistic (advertisements). However, textbooks, manuals and handbooks of the appropriate field may be regarded as part of it.

Reports, which are records of acts or processes produced at someone's request, include, for example, the laboratory report.

Schedules order and classify material. They include such important instances of written EST as bibliographies, indexes, tables of contents, glossaries, the valency table of elements, or the Linnean system of biological nomenclature.

Essays, finally, as exclusively written texts, are central to EST in the form of dissertations, journal articles and university theses (cf. Sager *et al.* 1980: 104–23).

Typical EST texts will therefore be located within the range of published writing. More popular science texts will be relatively more accessible to the general public and hence less specifically cases of Special English.

7.4.2 Text forms

Well over 100 traditional text forms can be enumerated, ones such as *address, agenda, aide-memoire, announcement, article, bibliography, blurb, book review, brochure, bulletin*, etc. (ibid: 148-81). Gläser (1990) examines thirty-five text forms arranged primarily according to whether they are meant for academic peers, for students and the lay public, or for (potential) users. Just how many text forms may usefully be distinguished is not known; indeed, not even the criteria for a typology have been agreed upon. What is available is, rather, a number of individual studies of what have intuitively been viewed as distinct text forms. These include ones such as

1 articles in learned journals
2 dissertations

3 laboratory reports
4 MS theses
5 textbooks (university level)

all from a variety of fields. It is these texts which have been drawn upon most freely for the syntactical features of EST described in section 7.2.

7.4.3 Text models

EST texts are also relatively strongly formalized: it is possible to reckon with a number of rather highly conventionalized text models. Journal articles normally have the following five divisions:

1 an introduction, in which the purpose pursued/hypothesis investigated is presented;
2 a review section, in which previous work is summarized or evaluated;
3 a methods part, in which procedural sequences, criteria, etc., are evaluated;
4 a results section, in which the findings are presented;
5 a discussion part, in which the findings are evaluated in the framework of the initial hypothesis.

Longer texts such as textbooks and dissertations will be cyclically organized repetitions or partial repetitions of such sequences (cf. Hopkins and Dudley-Evans 1988; Dudley-Evans 1989). Note that not all texts will necessarily contain all five steps. Furthermore, it is possible to identify and analyse distinct sub-cyclical components such as the definition (cf. Darian 1982).

Studies of individual divisions have also proved fruitful. Swales (1981) investigates article introductions, which, regardless of the discipline involved, fall into a structure containing a series of four moves: establishing the field, summarizing previous research, preparing for the present research (motivation) and introducing present research. A study of discussion sections has revealed the presence of corresponding moves, but in the reverse order: statement of the results of the present study, redescription of the motivation, review of the literature, implication for further research (Huckin, quoted in Dudley-Evans 1989: 75). Another empirical investigation of scientific texts distinguishes three fundamental subtypes, viz.:

1 the controlled experiment type, which contains methods, results and discussion;
2 the hypothesis verification type, which has hypothesis, methods, results and discussion;
3 the technique-descriptive type, which is centred around methods and results (Gopnik 1972: 71–96).

Since these three types are based on short, 250-word articles, it is no wonder that none of them contain a review section.

The five textual divisions mentioned above can each be given partial linguistic profiles. For example, introductions-cum-reviews as well as conclusions make great use of *that*-clauses (a third and a quarter respectively). This is logical, since both report findings and findings are typically presented in reported speech, which uses *that*-clauses. Results sections have fewer *that*-clauses (about a sixth) and methods sections have virtually none (1.33 per cent) (West 1980). This is the result of the varying rhetorical purpose of each of the sections, for example, reporting vs. describing. A high proportion of the simple present tense correlates with the expository function of introductions (and of textbooks). Passives, for example, are by far more common in methods sections (two-thirds vs. one-third elsewhere), at least in chemistry and biology papers, in which procedures and experiments are prominent. The danger of overgeneralizing from field to field is demonstrated by the fact that in physics, which often remains highly theoretical and argumentative, the methods sections are hardly different from the other sections (Hanania and Akhtar 1985: 54).

Just as symbols are a special aspect of the lexis of EST, its texts very often contain visual material such as diagrams, graphs, outlines, formulas, charts and tables.

These visual elements as well as the various sections of EST texts are coordinated into a cohesive textual unit by means of the conventionalized occurrence of the individual sections, which is often reinforced by the editorial requirements of journals/publishers. Other cohesive devices include

1 the use of referential vocabulary (adverbs, demonstratives);
2 the deictic use of tense and voice;
3 the employment of enumeration, advance labelling, reporting, recapitulation, hypothesizing and rhetorical questions (Tadros 1989: 18);
4 adopting recognizable patterns of logical development, such as problem and solution, statement and justification, generalization and exemplification (ibid).

In conclusion, then, specialized EST texts have a distinct bias towards certain grammatical forms, lexical items and non-linguistic phenomena – all motivated by the nature of the communication. While the field may cause some of the variation in components, there is an astonishingly high degree of similarity over a wide spread of fields. This is probably due to shared rhetorical functions. Furthermore, these rhetorical functions (reporting, describing, directing, explaining and arguing) will be placed within the structure of scientific texts in a conventional sequence.

REFERENCES

Barber, C. L. (1962) 'Some measurable characteristics of modern English scientific prose', *Gothenburg Studies in English* 14: 21–43.

Beier, R. (1980) *Englische Fachsprache*, Stuttgart: Kohlhammer.

Brekke, M. (1989) 'The Bergen English for Science and Technology (BEST) corpus: a pilot study', in C. Laurén and M. Nordman (eds) *Special Language*, Clevedon: Multilingual Matters, pp. 253–64.

Darian, S. (1982) 'The role of definition in scientific and technical writing: forms, functions, and properties', in J. Høedt *et al.* (eds) *Proceedings of the Third European Symposium on LSP*, Copenhagen: LSP Centre, pp. 27–47.

Dubois, B. L. (1982) 'The construction of noun phrases in biomedical journal articles', in J. Høedt *et al.* (eds) *Proceedings of the Third European Symposium on LSP*, Copenhagen: LSP Centre, pp. 49–67.

Dudley-Evans, T. (1989) 'An outline of the value of genre analysis in LSP work', in C. Laurén and M. Nordman (eds) *Special Language*, Clevedon: Multilingual Matters, pp. 72–9.

Gerbert, M. (1970) *Besonderheiten der Syntax in der technischen Fachsprache des Englischen*, Halle: Niemeyer.

Gläser, R. (1979) *Fachstile des Englischen*, Leipzig: Enzyklopädie.

—— (1990) *Fachtextsorten im Englischen*, Tübingen: Gunter Narr.

Gopnik, M. (1972) *Linguistic Structures in Scientific Texts*, The Hague: Mouton.

Hanania, E. A. S. and Akhtar, K. (1985) 'Verb form and rhetorical function in science writing: a study of MS theses in biology, chemistry, and physics', *ESP Journal* 4: 49–58.

Heslot, J. (1982) 'Tense and other indexical markers in the typology of scientific texts' J. Høedt, L. Lundquist, H. Picht and J. Quistgaard (eds) *Proceedings of the Third European Symposium on LSP*, Copenhagen: LSP Centre, pp. 83–104.

Hoffmann, L. (1987) 'Syntactic aspects of LSP', *Fachsprache* 9: 98–105.

Hopkins, A. and Dudley-Evans, T. (1988) 'A genre-based investigation of the discussions sections in articles and dissertations', *ESP Journal* 7: 113–21.

Huddleston, R. D. (1971) *The Sentence in Written English: a Syntactic Study Based on an Analysis of Scientific Texts*, Cambridge: Cambridge University Press.

Johansson, S. (1975) *Some Aspects of the Vocabulary of Learned and Scientific English*, Gothenburg: Gothenburg Studies in English.

Kok Lee Cheon (1978) *Syntax of Scientific English*, Singapore: Singapore University Press.

Lackstrom, J., Selinker, L. and Trimble, L. (1973) 'Technical rhetorical principles and grammatical choice', *TESOL Quarterly* 7: 127–36.

Large, J. A. (1989) 'Science and the foreign-language barrier', in H. Coleman (ed.) *Working with Language: a Multidisciplinary Consideration of Language Use in Work Contexts*, Berlin: Mouton de Gruyter, pp. 169–92.

Malcolm, L. (1987) 'What rules govern tense usage in scientific articles?', *ESP Journal* 6: 31–43.

Master, P. (1987) 'Generic *the* in *Scientific American*', *ESP Journal* 6: 165–86.

Robinson, P. C. (1980) *ESP (English for Specific Purposes): the Present Position*, Oxford: Pergamon.

—— (1989) 'An overview of English for specific purposes', in H. Coleman (ed.) *Working with Language: a Multidisciplinary Consideration of Language Use in Work Contexts*, Berlin: Mouton de Gruyter, pp. 395–427.

Sager, J. C., Dungworth, D. and McDonald, P. F. (1980) *English Special Languages*, Wiesbaden: Brandstetter.

Salager, F. (1984) 'Compound nominal phrases in scientific-technical literature: proportion and rationale', in A. K. Pugh and J. M. Ulijn (eds) *Reading for Professional Purposes: Studies and Practices in Native and Foreign Languages*, London: Heinemann, pp. 136–45.

Svartvik, J. (1966) *On Voice in the English Verb*, The Hague: Mouton.

Swales, J. (1971) *Writing Scientific English*, Walton-on-Thames: Nelson.

—— (1981) 'Aspects of article introductions', *ESP Research Reports* 1 (Aston University).

Tadros, A. A. (1989) 'Predictive categories in university textbooks', *ESP Journal* 8: 17–31.

Tarone, E., Dwyer, S., Gillette, S. and Icke, V. (1981) 'On the use of the passive in two astrophysics journal papers', *ESP Journal* 1: 123–40.

Trimble, L. (1985) *English for Science and Technology: a Discourse Approach*, Cambridge: Cambridge University Press.

West, G. K. (1980) 'That-nominal constructions in traditional rhetorical divisions of scientific research papers', *TESOL Quarterly* 14: 483–88.

Williams, R. (1984) 'A cognitive approach to English nominal compounds', in A. K. Pugh and J. M. Ulijn (eds) *Reading for Professional Purposes: Studies and Practices in Native and Foreign Languages*, London: Heinemann, pp. 146–53.

Chapter 8

Language and gender

English varies in many different ways, as has been pointed out in the preceding chapters. The sex of the speaker is one of the features in which there is currently a vast amount of interest and one which makes itself felt in many ways. Not the least of these is the widespread concern of many people, but especially of feminists, that English not be used in a sexist way, where sexism is defined 'as words or actions that arbitrarily assign roles or characteristics to people on the basis of sex' (NCTE 1977: 182) rather than assessing people individually.

A person's sex is, of course, biologically given and therefore, for all intents and purposes, permanent. The ways in which the sociolinguistic category of sex or gender shows up as a social variable which affects language use is by no means equally fixed. It can, however, influence a wide variety of behaviour, verbal and non-verbal, such as topics of conversation, styles of talk, pronunciation, grammar, vocabulary choice, and much else as well. Yet despite wide areas of differentiation along the lines of the sex of the user, in English all these differences are relative. That is, there are quantitative tendencies for males/females to give particular forms their preference. For this reason it is common to speak of 'sex-preferential' differences rather than absolute (or 'sex-differential') ones.

In this chapter we will be looking at language both as it is used to make reference to males and females and how it is differently employed by males as opposed to females. Under the former aspect the focus of attention will be chiefly on vocabulary and on what is called 'generic reference'. The latter aspect deals with the differing ways in which English is pronounced by members of the two sexes as well as evidence of differences in grammar and vocabulary use. In a step which goes beyond the narrower framework of the system of the language, the often dissimilar behaviour of men and women in conversational interaction as well as male–female differences in non-verbal behaviour will be explored.

8.1 Language used to refer to males and females

Vocabulary differs significantly from pronunciation and grammar inasmuch as people are not only aware of their choice of words but consciously exercise much more control over them. In addition, words also clearly carry elements of referential content that grammar and pronunciation do not. It is for these reasons that interest in avoiding sexist language has been concentrated largely in this area. (See 1.4.2, Maggio 1988.)

Investigations have revealed that prejudicial use of language is or has been commonplace for a wide of variety of words. To begin with there has been considerable interest in unpaired words ending in -*man*, for which there are no traditional equivalents with a feminine suffix. One of the demands of reform-minded language users has been to replace such exclusive terms with more inclusive ones. So it is that for many people *firemen* have become *firefighters*, American *mailmen* have become *letter carriers* and *chairmen* have become *chairpersons*.

There are other terms which do not end in -*man*, but which are also unpaired. Some of them pose problems as far as avoiding exclusive use is concerned and solutions have not always found widespread acceptance: *bachelor's degree* (but BA), *master's degree* (but MA), *university fellowship, liberty, equality and fraternity*, etc.

In English a large number of designations for persons are paired. This includes areas such as religion (*nun/monk, prioress/prior*; but note that *priestess* is not equivalent to *priest*!), aristocratic titles (*duke/duchess, king/queen, prince/princess, count/countess*, etc.) and kinship (*sister/brother, mother/father, aunt/uncle*, etc.). In these examples feminine and masculine terms are roughly equivalent. However, a great number of further pairings are sexistically one-sided, with the masculine term being positive and the feminine 'counterpart' negative: *major* (an officer) vs. *majorette* (a women dressed in a short skirt and marching ahead of a band), *courtier* (an officer of the court) vs. *courtesan* (a prostitute with wealthy or aristocratic clients), *master* (boss, expert, etc.) vs. *mistress* (lover), *governor* (high political office-holder) vs. *governess* (private teacher). Even *poet* (writer of poems) is said to be different from *poetess* (female writer of poems of poorer quality).

It is, of course, debatable whether such asymmetrical pairs are the results of structural features of English or the way in which the language is used. It seems, in any case, to be possible to 'repair' many of these imbalances. The counterpart of a governor who is male, for example, may be called a *woman governor* if it appears necessary to indicate the sex of the governor at all. This seems to indicate that the alleged sexism of the language is, to a large extent, if not totally, the result of sexist usage, and this usage is rooted, it would appear, in the stereotypes entertained by the users of the language. Numerous sources point out these stereotypes. For example, women are friendly, gentle, enthusiastic, smooth, and they talk gibberish on trivial topics, while men are forceful, loud, dominating and get straight to the point (Scott 1980: 200; cf. also Thorne and Henley 1975: 15; Williams *et al.* 1977). Studies such as those reported by Condry and Condry (1976) also indicate that we attribute specifically male and female traits to very young children. In this particular study people observing the same video tape of an infant of nine months interpreted one and the same reaction (the child's startled reaction to a jack-in-the-box) as anger if they thought they were watching a boy and as fear if they were told it was a girl.

Just how pervasive stereotyping in language can be has been pointed out by studies of dictionaries. Nilsen (1977) reports on 385 dictionary entries which are clearly masculine (e.g. *son*) and 132 which are similarly feminine (e.g. *daughter*). Despite the larger number of masculine terms there were more negative feminine words than negative masculine ones by a ratio of 25 to 20. Masculine terms were six times as likely as feminine ones to include an element of positive prestige. Gershuny (1977) reports on an investigation of the *Random House Dictionary of the English Language* (1966), in which the example sentences quote women in domestic contexts, as mothers, wives, hostesses, launderers, cooks, shoppers, gardeners, servants ('She gave us *overdone* steak'); in the world of glamour and fashion ('She always wore a *crazy* hat'); in emotional situations ('*Tears* rushed to her eyes'); but only occasionally in professional positions. Men were often associated with delinquency ('He was *hauled* before the judge') or with business and investments ('He *got* ahead by sheer determination'). Male–female rivalry/ conflict is stressed ('She was *boiling* when he arrived late'), and female assertiveness is regarded as negative ('She's *death* on his friends from the office') (examples from Gershuny 1977: 146–9).

Graham found that males are overrepresented in children's textbooks compared with their actual numbers in society. At the same time girls are confronted with sets of values involving inactivity and good looks while boys are provided with models which emphasize activity and strength (Graham 1975: 58f; cf. also Nilsen 1977). This tendency to underrepresent females and/or to portray them as weak, passive and supportive is pervasive, be it in literature (Gershuny 1977; Martin 1972), in American textbooks (U'Ren 1972), or in foreign language textbooks (Stern 1976; Hellinger 1980).

Perhaps the most perfidious tendency in the language is what has been called **semantic derogation** or **pejoration**. Stanley (1977) collected as many words as she could for both females and males as 'sexually available', for example, *honey pot* or *hustler*. She found, first, that there are far more for women (220) than for men (she collected only 22) and, second, that all but four of the female terms (*lady of the night*, *entertainer*, *concubine*, *mistress*) are derogatory, i.e. demeaning and shameful (*leasepiece*, *loose woman*); they often involve allusion to cost (*put out*, *giftbox*) and frequently rely on metonymy, in which a part of the body stands for the whole (*ass*, *tail*), or on metaphor, especially animal metaphor (*bitch*, *bird*).

> Again and again in the history of the language, one finds that a perfectly innocent term designating a girl or woman may begin with totally neutral or even positive connotations, but that gradually it acquires negative implications, at first perhaps only slightly disparaging, but after a period of time becoming abusive and ending as a sexual slur.
>
> (Schulz 1975: 65)

This seems to be the case, on the one hand, because the association with sex seems to contaminate the terms and because, on the other, there is a constant need to look for new euphemisms as one established term after the other undergoes semantic pejoration (ibid: 72), i.e. the process of taking on a more negative meaning.

Along with terms which designate people, there is the related field of vocatives, or terms used to address people (see 9.2.6). Once again there is a certain asymmetry to the language system inasmuch as the title for a man is simply *Mr* while a woman is *Mrs* if married and *Miss* if unmarried. For many language users (but by no means all) this disequilibrium has been remedied by the introduction of the new title *Ms*, the abbreviation of /mɪz/, the Southern American pronunciation of both *Mrs* and *Miss*, for all women. In addition it is impressionistically reported that men are more likely to call a woman by her first name than vice versa (Lakoff 1976: 80). In a similar vein, male sales-clerks were found to address female students as *(young) lady*, *kiddo*, *ma'am*, *senorita*, *sweetie*, *miss*, *dear*, *lovey*, *baby*, etc., but male students as *sir* (Eakins and Eakins 1978a: 116).

Generic reference   A final look at the use of language to refer to males and females concentrates on what is known as 'generic reference'. This has to do with the use of a particular term for people without regard to their sex. It is said that the word *man* is such a term when it means any human being. The problem is that *man*, in fact, suggests men rather than both men and women (Schneider and Hacker 1973). Hence the (unintended) humour of a biology textbook which speaks of 'pregnancy in man' (Silveira 1980: 168).

At the centre of the discussion of generic reference is the use of *he*. According to the grammatical category of gender, the pronoun *she* is used to mark referents who are female while *he* is employed for males, for both, or for indeterminant referents. However, many people argue that the so-called generic *he* excludes females; and, indeed, studies have shown that this is the case: Graham counted 940 uses of *he* in a sample of 100,000 words. Of these, 744 referred to male humans, 128 to male animals and 36 to persons presumed to be male, such as sailors or farmers. This left only 32 as indeterminant and hence generic (Graham 1975: 58). One interpretation of this is that people, but especially males, will consequently tend to interprete generic *he* as masculine. Furthermore, the choice of the pronoun has an effect on attitudes: for example, women are reported to get better results on maths problems which are female-oriented (Martyna 1980: 71ff). An investigation by Stericker (1981) indicates that women may be less likely to apply for a job if its description is worded with generic *he*.

That *he* is not neutral may be further illustrated by noting how it is used in personification in children's literature. MacKay and Konishi counted 35,000 occurrences of *he*, *she* or *it* in an anthology. Animals were *he* 76 per cent of the time and *she* 24 per cent. The masculine pronoun was typically used for large mammals such as lions, gorillas and wolves, the feminine for small ones such as birds or insects (bees, ladybirds). The authors point out, among other things, that a switch to *it* would have the disadvantage of lessening the emotional and personal involvement of the reader (MacKay and Konishi 1980: 152ff).

Bodine (1975) has made the interesting point that none of the grammatical categories of the English personal pronouns, namely person, number and gender, is strictly observed in actual usage. It is, for example, well known that *we* may be used singularly in the so-called royal *we* (Queen Victoria's *We are not amused*) or editorial *we* (*We shall be looking at language and gender in this chapter*). Impersonal *you* is regularly used as a third-person form (*How do you* [=anyone] *get from here to the airport?*), but sometimes also as a first-person form (*When you're as tired as I am, you* [=I] *can't stand any extra noise*). On the basis of this rather loose and pragmatic application of categories Bodine argues for the use of singular *they* as a non-sexist generic. This not only works (*Ask anyone; they'll agree*), but is also natural to most speakers when they refer to indefinite antecedents such as *anyone*, *someone*, *no one*. This also makes logical sense since such pronouns, while grammatically singular, are notionally plural; *anyone*, for example, means 'all people'.

For other antecedents, such as the concrete nouns *doctor*, *writer* or *nurse*, speakers seem to know to what extent the typical representative in society is male, female, or fairly well distributed between the two sexes (MacKay 1983: 43). Since doctors in countries such as the United States are typically male, the use of generic *he* is not extraordinarily misleading. For nurses, speakers seem to use generic *she* since most nurses are, in fact, female. It is only with antecedents such as *writer* that there may be misunderstandings. Since writers are equally likely to be men or women, it is misleading to use generic *he* (generic *she* does not seem to be a viable choice here).

It is for cases like these that a number of people have suggested adopting a new sex-neutral third-person singular personal pronoun, a neologism, and these suggestions have included such candidates as the following: *thon*, *co*, *hir*, *e* or *E*, *tey*, *hesh*, *po*, *re*, *xe*, *jhe*, *per*. The difficulty with any of these suggestions is that none of them is natural or easily available to the speaker, even though they have the advantage of being sex-neutral. Since pronouns belong to those words which are integrally part of the structure or grammar of the language, change is not likely to come easily. Over the last one thousand years the system of English personal pronouns has, of course, changed, but not often or quickly (for example, *they* was added and *thou* was lost), and there is no reason to think change might be less difficult and/or slow today.

What seems to have more chances of success is the adoption of the double pronoun, *he or she*, or the use of a plural antecedent, such as *writers*, which then allows the use of sex-neutral but plural *they*. It is this that many of the now numerous guidelines for the avoidance of stereotyping or for the improvement of the image of women (cf. titles in Thorne *et al*. 1983: 203f) suggest.

8.2 Language as used by males and females

In the following comments on the differing use of English by males and females it is important to remember that there are, in reality, far more similarities than there are differences. It is, however, the differences that have caught people's attention. Furthermore, the variable 'gender' is only one of several factors and is seldom the sole element influencing usage.

> Sexual distinctions in language use overlap with various combinations of other distinctions such as age, geographic region, socio-economic class, ethnic identification, occupation, and specific social situation.
>
> (Eble 1977: 296)

8.2.1 Vocabulary use

There have been relatively few studies in the field of vocabulary choice, wide as it is. Nevertheless, a few areas have been subject to investigation. They include topics of discussion; emotive, supportive and polite language; colour terms; spatial concepts; taboo words and exclamations.

Topic The findings available concerning topics of conversation and, therefore, the related fields of vocabulary indicate that women seem to avoid certain subjects such as money, business and politics while concentrating more on people (men, other women, themselves), clothing and decoration. Men favour topics such as money, business and sports (see Komarovsky 1967; Landis 1926–7). To some extent this is understandable, for traditionally there has been greater engagement of men in paid employment, politics and sports and of women in person-oriented domestic (family) situations. This, of course, is a product of economic and educational opportunity (or its lack) as well as socialization and expectations.

Somewhat indirectly related to the alleged greater preference among females for talk about people is the often expressed feeling that women use more emotive language than do men (see Gleser *et al*. 1959). Indeed, a great deal is made, especially by feminists, of the supposedly less assertive, more supportive language and behaviour of women as opposed to the more competitive and dominating behaviour of men (cf. Bate 1988: 44f). The very fact that several attempts have been made to rehabilitate the tradition-ally negative term *gossip* as a positive feminine phenomenon, in which concern is more about social interaction than the exchange of concrete information, (see Jones 1980) is indicative of this as well.

Colour words, spatial terms and taboo language   One of the main theses pursued in regard to gender-specific vocabulary is that there are features which are said to be typical of female use, such as more exact colour terms, for example, *chartreuse* rather than (male) *greenish yellow* or *beige* instead of *light brown* (cf. Lakoff 1976: 8f). Furthermore, women are credited with using such intensifiers as *so*, *such*, *quite* and *vastly* (Key 1972: 19, based on Jespersen 1922: 249f) and adjectives such as *adorable*, *charming*, *sweet*, *lovely* or *divine* (cf. Lakoff 1976: 8ff). 'Masculine' counterparts of such feminine adjectives are definitely rarer, though ones such as *helluva* or *damn good* might come close (*We had such a lovely time* vs. *We had a hel-luva good time*). Despite these assertions there is, in reality, a great dearth of empirical research in this area.

Some studies have also indicated that males seem to have a stronger tendency to use spatial terms (see Gleser *et al*. 1959) and that they are more oriented towards conveying facts, while women are more expressive (Eakins and Eakins 1978a: 48ff; Kramer 1975; Thorne and Henley 1975: 21).

The single area which seems to have attracted the most attention is that of taboo language. In the extensive annotated bibliography in Thorne *et al*. (1983), thirteen or well over a quarter of the forty-three references listed in the section on word choice and syntactic usage have to do with profane/ obscene items or tabooed words referring to sex-related acts or the genitals. By and large, these, as well as further studies, show that men are more likely than women to use obscene expressions and that women are more likely to employ impersonal or clinical terms. It is perhaps fruitful in this context to recall the remark above about possible 'masculine' adjectives such as *hel-luva* or *damn good*: both are mildly profane, mild enough to be used in mixed company and profane enough to be regarded as masculine. Much the same thing can be said of exclamations, where the typically male form is more forceful and unrefined than the typical female expression: Lakoff suggests that *Oh dear!* is feminine and *Shit!* masculine (1976: 10).

In general, the use of abusive terms is associated with males rather than females; with blue-collar workers on the job rather than with professionals on the job; with parties and night clubs rather than with formal or quasi-formal public or religious gatherings.

(Eble 1977: 296)

Although much of what has been reported is taken from the realm of speculation, it may be noted that overly positive (euphemistic and superlative) and therefore semantically empty terms are viewed as feminine while abusive and obscene language is often regarded as masculine. Just why this is the case is harder to say. Later on in the chapter several of the explanations which have been proposed will be reviewed.

8.2.2 Grammar

In the area of grammar it is once again the case that there are no major divergences between males and females speaking English. Despite the fact that the well-known grammarian Jespersen advanced the thesis that 'men are fond of hypotaxis and women of parataxis', by which he meant that women prefer to string clauses together ('like a set of pearls') while men employ complex sentences ('like a set of Chinese boxes, one within another') (Jespersen 1922: 251f), there has been no substantiation for this. There is, however, some evidence of other differences in syntax.

Imperatives   Males may, for example, use more straightforward imperatives and other directive forms than females do. This is, of course, not only a question of grammar, but also one of speech style and power. In an investigation of the language used by two- to five-year-old children (average age four) in play situations in which two children of the same sex played doctor, it turned out that the girls had a clear tendency to soften their directives: 'many more of the girls' utterances were mitigated (65 percent as compared with 34 percent for boys' (Sachs 1987: 184). For example, 25 per cent of the boys' commands/requests were straightforward imperatives (*Bring her to the hospital*) and 11 per cent were prohibitions (*Don't touch it*), while for girls the results were 10 and 2 per cent respectively. On the other hand, girls used more joint directives (*Now we'll cover him up*), namely 15 per cent as compared with the boys' 3 per cent (ibid: 182). In another study of young children, Gleason found that mothers were more likely to use directives in the question form while fathers employed a higher proportion of direct imperatives and implied indirect forms (a statement to which a response in the form of an action is appropriate; for example, *Your car is blocking mine* suggests that the other move his/her car). By the age of four children were following the speech patterns of their same-sex parents (Gleason 1987: 197f).

The patterns reported by Sachs and Gleason for largely white, middle-class American children are substantially confirmed by Goodwin for

working-class black children in Philadelphia. She found that in a cooperative play situation girls' imperatives are suggestive rather than demanding,
that the right to give directions rotates in a group of girls, and that when
imperatives are used by girls they are modified in some way (emphasizing
group benefits or accompanied by laughter), as opposed to the boys'
unmitigated forms (Goodwin 1988: 88).

Tag questions   A further syntactical phenomenon which has generated a
great deal of attention is Lakoff's impression that women use many more
tag questions of the sort that seek confirmation of a personal opinion (*The
way prices are rising is horrendous, isn't it?*; Lakoff 1976: 16). In an
attempt to check this Dubois and Crouch counted the number of tag
questions used in an academic conference and found that all of them were
used by men. They then proceeded to interpret this by writing that these
tags, 'far from signalling lack of confidence, [were] intended to forestall
opposition' (Dubois and Crouch 1975: 292).

There seem to be two issues involved. The first is about whether men or
women use more tag questions. Dubois and Crouch, for example, found
men using more in formal talk, while the study by Sachs quoted above
revealed girls to use twice as many as boys (Sachs 1987: 184). Numerous
other studies have not clarified this question, since the conditions of the
setting vary considerably.

The second issue has to do with the purpose tag questions serve. Some
say they are used to sustain communicative interaction, for example, by
women to elicit a response from an uncommunicative male conversational
partner. In the opinion of one writer:

1 Women do not use more tag questions than men.
2 Even if they did, it would not necessarily mean they were seeking
   approval, since tag questions have a wide range of uses.
3 In any case women's use of tag questions will always be explained differently from men's, since it is cultural sex stereotypes which determine the
   explanation of linguistic phenomena, rather than the nature of the
   phenomena themselves. (Cameron 1985: 56)

This display of evidence and interpretation reveals that numerous factors
must be taken into account, such as the gender, age, relative status, etc., of
the conversational participants, the nature of the setting (formal/academic,
informal/chatty), the topic, and the purpose pursued by the person who
uses a tag question, and possibly much more.

Non-standard grammar   Perhaps the single most widely discussed question
in regard to sex-differential use of English has to do with how standard or
non-standard a person's utterances are. There seems to be a connection
in the minds of speakers of English between non-standard English and

masculinity. In the area of grammar, Cheshire reports the findings of a study in Reading, showing a much greater tendency for boys who are firmly embedded in local vernacular culture to use local non-standard forms than for girls to do so. The non-standard forms of the verbs investigated seem to reflect 'toughness' for the boys (Cheshire 1978: 64f). Much the same result has been established for speakers of American Black English in Detroit, where, for example, men have been found to use multiple negation (*Ain't nobody going nowhere noways*) 30 per cent more often than women (Shuy *et al.* 1967). Few grammatical structures, however, show such strong distinctions in use according to the gender of the speaker as negation does for these speakers in Detroit.

The association between 'non-standard' and 'masculine' has been advanced by a number of researchers, especially in regard to non-standard accents (see 8.2.3); however, this is not the only feasible association. The non-standard is also often identical with the vernacular, and in such cases it may have strong associations with local culture. This would fit in with the connection Stewart has found between broadest Black English Vernacular (the basilect) in Washington, typically used in the family, and 'little boy' language, which 'big boys' (from the age of seven or eight on) reject (Stewart 1964: 17), possibly because it is associated with the culture of the home. Here a masculine identity may work against (one variety of) the non-standard. In another American Black English community in South Carolina, it is the young men who turn out to maintain the broad vernacular because their work and social lives are shared with other men from the local community (Nichols 1984: 34ff).

8.2.3 Pronunciation

The final systematic level of language use is pronunciation. Here, once again, many of the same tendencies already mentioned can be found. This seems to be especially true of the findings of a number of important sociolinguistic studies of pronunciation variables in regard to the standard–non-standard distinction just discussed. However, before going into this point, some general observations on speech stereotypes are in order.

Voice quality and pitch Even the idea that male voices can be distinguished from female voices because of the lower pitch of the former is not all there is to the picture. Experiments show that children who have not yet entered puberty and whose vocal tracts do not yet differ in size can nevertheless be distinguished by sex. It seems to be the case that young boys typically speak as if they were larger than they really are and that young girls speak as if they were smaller (cf. Sachs *et al.* 1973: 75; Sachs 1975: 154). This may be due to distinctive configurations in the relative distance between the bands of sound frequency produced when articulating vowels:

the upper bands of vibrations, the formants, are closer to the lowest band, the fundamental, in boys than in girls. This may produce a configuration similar to that of adult males. Other factors may, of course, also be involved in the successful identification of the sex of pre-adolescent speakers, ones such as speed, intonation or fluency. Note that some confirmation of the finely developed human faculty for imitation is offered by Lieberman (1967), who found that two infants, a boy of ten months and a girl of thirteen months, when vocalizing (i.e. babbling), responded to their father with a lower fundamental and to their mother with a higher one.

Voice quality is, in other words, a finely tuned thing. Just what we are reacting to when we make judgements on the basis of vocal characteristics is not readily identifiable. Addington's report on the assessment given to each of seven different voice qualities (breathiness, thinness, flatness, nasality, tenseness, throatiness, orotundity plus speed and pitch) shows that people can perceive a great variety of differences, but it is not easy to verbalize just what lies behind each of these labels. His investigation reveals, for example, that breathiness is a feminine feature (suggesting prettier, more petite, more effervescent, more highly strung) and that breathy males are regarded as younger and more artistic. Flatness is masculine and comes over negatively (sluggish, cold, withdrawn) for both sexes. Throatiness is also masculine, but more positive in a male (older, more mature, realistic, sophisticated, well-adjusted) while negative for a woman (less intelligent, more masculine, lazier, boorish, etc.). An increased range of pitch is feminine (dynamic, extroverted) (Addington 1968: 499ff). Although Addington's findings are controversial (cf. Smith 1985: 76), there can be little doubt that people do evaluate male and female speakers differently on the basis of features of pronunciation other than individual, segmental sounds.

The high pitch of a woman's voice is supposedly not taken seriously in the English-speaking world, and this is accepted as reason enough not to employ more than the nominal woman news reader for broadcasting (Kramarae 1988). Furthermore, it has been found that, while women appear frequently on television commercials, they seldom tell a man what to do; it is the man who bears authority and gives commands, and in commercials it is the voice of an unseen man (a so-called voice-over) which confers approval on what is shown (Hennessee and Nicholson 1972).

Women do, of course, have higher overall pitch; in addition, the range of their pitch is wider, as a study of American speakers reveals:

> Men consistently avoid certain intonation levels or patterns: they very rarely, if ever, use the highest level of pitch that women use. That is, it appears probable that most men have only three contrastive levels of intonation, while many women, at least, have four.
>
> (Brend 1975: 86f)

Men who have or adopt a similarly wide range of intonation are perceived as effeminate (Eakins and Eakins 1978a: 101).

Women in Tyneside are reported to use a higher percentage of final rises than do men (Pellowe and Jones 1978: 110), and Brend reports similar findings for American English (1975: 87). Over and beyond this, speakers of English identify final falling intonations as masculine significantly more often and rising ones as feminine (Edelsky 1979: 22). The interpretation often given to rising intonation is that it shows a greater degree of uncertainty and/or a greater degree of reserve and politeness (see 3.5.3). This certainly fits in well with the general view of women in the English-speaking societies as less assertive and more polite and sensitive. It should be pointed out, however, that how people perceive and interpret intonation may have little to do with the actual nature of what they are listening to. (For more on the perception of pronunciation, see below.)

The pronunciation of individual sounds   The relatively large number of sociolinguistic studies of pronunciation variation in a large variety of urban areas has revealed that gender is an important social variant along with such other factors as class, ethnicity, age and education. For the most part the results of such studies reveal that women adopt pronunciations that are relatively closer to the accepted public norms of the given region while men of the same social class tend to be closer to the non-standard or vernacular norms. By no means all the sounds of the language are affected. While men and women in one speech community may have a tendency towards differing pronunciations of one particular phoneme, in other regions they may well have indistinguishable pronunciations of the same segmental sound. Occasionally in the English-speaking world a sex-preferential difference is nearly universal. The verbal ending {-ING} illustrates this. The velar nasal /ŋ/ is considered to be standard or 'correct' pronunciation, while the alveolar nasal /n/ is not regarded as appropriate in more formal situations requiring Standard English. Fischer, looking at children three to ten years old in New England, reported that a 'typical' boy (i.e. 'physically strong, dominating, full of mischief, but disarmingly frank about his transgressions') used /n/ more than half the time, but especially with informal verbs, for example, *punchin'*, *flubbin'*, *swimmin'*, *hittin'* (formal verbs had /ŋ/; *criticizing*, *reading*, *visiting*) (Fischer 1958: 49ff). Girls typically used more /ŋ/ endings, a result that was substantiated for adult speakers in Norwich (Trudgill 1972: 187).

It was not only the sex of the speaker which correlated with an orientation towards the standard or the non-standard form of pronunciation. The socio-economic class of the speaker was also important. In Norwich, women classified as, for example, upper working class share the pronunciation norms of men classified as lower middle class. This pattern repeats itself throughout all the classes, with women typically using pronunciations credited to the men in the class immediately above them. Trudgill speaks of a greater status consciousness of women in English society than men. As a result they tend to adapt 'upwards' towards the norm which possesses **overt prestige**. Trudgill finds confirmation for this in the fact that women, when asked to tell what pronunciation they themselves use, report more use of the overt norm than is actually the case; this is called **over-reporting**. Men behave in a converse fashion: they use more standard forms while purporting to use fewer; this is referred to as **under-reporting**. On the basis of this, the non-standard, non-prestige accent used by men, but especially working-class men, is said to have **covert prestige**. For these under-reporting men it may be assumed that working-class speech has positive connotations of roughness and toughness (Trudgill 1972).

Conclusions of this sort, especially that females conform more to the prestige pronunciation norm of a given area, have been made about English speakers in many other parts of the world as well, for example, Lanham and McDonald for white English-speaking South Africans (1979), Macaulay for Glasgow (1978: 135), Levine and Crockett for Piedmont, North Carolina (1966) and Labov for New York City (1966). Needless to say, these studies examined numerous different pronunciation variables, both vowels and consonants.

Although most of the results of pronunciation studies have revealed the tendency of females to be closer to the overt norm than males of the same class, age and location, not all variables have conformed to this pattern. One of the best-known divergences is that of young women in a section of West Belfast known as the Clonard. They were more likely than men of the same area, age and class to realize the variable (a) = /æ/ as in *hat* or *man* as non-standard [ɒ], i.e. with a higher degree of backing (Milroy and Margrain 1980: 66). The explanation given for this is that the particular group of women here studied are part of a highly integrated social network, that is, one in which the members share mutual acquaintanceship in a variety of ways, at work, in place of residence, in leisure time activities, as kin. This has the consequence of causing a mutual reinforcement of all sorts of values and behaviour, including language. What is unusual here is that this sort of mutual reinforcement of the local vernacular in traditional rural and working-class industrial environments is normally more typical of men than of women. In the Clonard widespread male unemployment had caused a thinning out of male social networks: there was no working place to share; as a result local speech norms would be reinforced less strongly with men than with women and their intact social networks. Nichols has applied this type of explanation to speakers in two communities in South Carolina, one black and one white, to make the dynamics of speech change clearer (Nichols 1984: 40f). Cheshire's findings on grammar in connection with vernacular culture in Reading (see 8.2.2) can be seen in this light as well.

Coates sums up the importance of networks as follows:

> In working class communities, then, it is more accurate to say that men's speech differs from women's because men's tight-knit networks exercise control over their members and maintain vernacular norms.
>
> (Coates 1986: 92)

The idea that speakers are attracted to vernacular speech because of its connotations of masculinity is clearly an inappropriate explanation of the young Clonard women's speech behaviour. Vernacular speech may have connotations of masculinity because of its traditional association with working-class *male* speakers. However it is important not to confuse effect for cause.

(ibid. 94)

The perception of pronunciation   There is one final point which needs to be re-emphasized about pronunciation differences, and that is the way in which speakers with various accents are perceived. This tells less about how males and females actually talk, of course, than about the stereotypes of male and female speech which people hold. Elyan *et al*. used what is called the matched guise technique 'to determine evaluative reactions to RP versus Lancashire (Northern) accented female speech' (Elyan *et al*. 1978: 125). In a matched guise test, one and the same speaker produces samples of speech with differing accents. These are then played from tape to judges who evaluate the supposedly differing speakers according to scales of personality traits. While this technique is used to eliminate idiosyncratic voice features which might influence the listeners' judgements, thus leaving accent alone as the variable to be evaluated, it can never be fully guaranteed that the speakers may not be unconsciously switching implicit stereotypes in voice quality as well as accent. Bearing this in mind, the results of Elyan *et al*. may be considered:

> RP-accented females in Britain are upgraded in terms of competence and communicative skills but downgraded in terms of social attractiveness and personal integrity relative to regional accented females. . . . Perhaps more interestingly, however, RP women are expected to bear fewer children, to create a more egalitarian relationship with their husbands and are seen to be more masculine in their sex traits (positive and negative) while at the same time being rated higher on the femininity trait than Northern accented females. Thus, we have a stereotyped picture of RP-accented women as highly competent, articulate, lacking in warmth, masculine in certain ways and yet feminine and espousing egalitarian ideals between the sexes.
>
> (ibid.: 129)

People who have both strongly masculine and strongly feminine features have been referred to as psychologically **androgynous**. Hence speakers perceived in the way summarized in the quotation above are described as having 'the voice of perceived androgyny' (ibid.: 130). Women with such voices may be seen as being in a position to enjoy both 'their femininity by use of expensive fineries while at the same time succeeding in male-dominated pursuits' (ibid.). There is, of course, a difference between being perceived as androgynous and actually being androgynous. Furthermore, the features attributed to such women are, in part at least, more closely associated with factors of social class than of sex (cf. Smith 1985: 87).

8.3 Communicative strategies

The focus of concern so far has been chiefly on differences in the use of the language system, i.e. the choice of vocabulary, differences in predilection for certain grammatical structures, and a sometimes differing orientation in regard to norms of pronunciation. In this section the central question involves the way speakers use the language to communicate. This comprises topic selection (already dealt with above in 8.2.1) and text types or genres, the amount of speech produced (i.e. the stereotype of the talkative woman) and length of utterances, interruptions and other means used to determine what will be talked about, and the question of politeness.

8.3.1 Topics and text types

Differences in topics of conversation and related questions of type of voca-bulary used, which emphasize a more expressive, person- and appearance-oriented style among women as versus a more fact- and space-oriented one among men, have already been mentioned (8.2.1). Beyond this, distinctions in type or genre of texts produced also seem to be relevant. For example, there is far more evidence of males engaging in verbal duelling and ritual insults (see especially Abrahams 1970; Kochman 1972) than of women doing so (but see Folb 1980).

Such texts, as well as the so-called toast (a long, obscene oral narrative poem), are closely related to the use of taboo language since they rely to a large extent on obscene expressions and language otherwise objectionable in 'polite company' – and this is generally considered to be inappropriate for females. Investigations of toilet graffiti have substantiated that male graffiti are preoccupied with sex acts and sex organs and far more deroga-tory (54 per cent) than women's toilet graffiti (15 per cent) (Bruner and Kelso 1980).

In a similar vein, joke-telling seems to be more a male than a female domain, especially in the case of dirty jokes (cf. Legman 1968). Mitchell (1976) credits men with jokes which are more competitive and aggressive (and dirty jokes, which frequently have women as their butt, are certainly aggressive). On women's use of bawdy jokes, see Green 1977; Folb 1980; Risch 1987.

There is a related phenomenon in men's greater use of witty remarks. At staff meetings in a mental hospital 'men made by far the more frequent witticisms – 99 out of 103 – but women often laughed harder' (Coser 1960: 85). Humour and wit, which 'always contain some aggression' (ibid.: 83), originated more often from senior staff than from junior staff or paramedical workers and was never directed upwards in the hierarchy (ibid.: 85f). Here it was not only the smaller number of women who were present (eight women versus nine or more men) that determined this outcome. It was also both the higher status of the men (all but two of the psychiatric staff while the paramedics were all women) and the fact that

> women are not expected to be witty. Their humor may be acceptable in some situations, but it is disapproved in those social situations in which there is danger of subverting implicit or explicit male authority.
>
> (ibid.: 86)

8.3.2 Dominance behaviour

The example just quoted involving laughter touches on the important question of who controls conversational interaction. Although the evidence is not unambiguous, there are indications that males dominate both in the amount of speaking they do and in the ways in which they seek to control topics.

Amount of speaking   There is a stereotype of the talkative and gossipy female:

Q: What are the three fastest means of communication?
A: Telegraph, telephone, and tell a woman.

However, it seems to be males who speak most, both as regards the number of turns they take and the average length of turns. While a few studies find no differences or even a greater amount of speaking by women, far more studies show men to produce more speech than women (Brooks 1982; Edelsky 1981; Swacker 1975; Swacker 1978). The variation in results may have something to do with the type of situation involved. In more formalized settings in which hierarchy and power are more obviously relevant, such as staff meetings, male dominance is almost paradigmatic. Eakins and Eakins report about an American college departmental faculty meeting as follows:

> in average number of verbal turns per meeting, the men, with the exception of one male, outweigh the women in number of verbal turns taken.

The women with the fewest averaged 5.5 turns a meeting, whereas the man with the fewest turns had over twice as many and exceeded all the women but one.

(Eakins and Eakins 1978b: 57)

The number of turns was, it must be added, also positively related to the hierarchy of status and power, rank, importance and length of time in the department. The length of turns for the males ranged from 17.07 to 10.66 seconds. For the females it was 10.00 to 3.0 seconds (ibid.: 58). Swacker (1978) found similar results in regard to questions asked in discussion periods at a scholarly conference: men out-asked females proportionally speaking, and on average they took longer by more than twice for each of their contributions.

Topic control: interruption   Perhaps the most direct way of determining who will speak and what the subject of discourse will be is through interruption, which is 'a device for exercising power and control in conversation' (West and Zimmerman 1983: 103). Once again, while the evidence is mixed, more studies show men interrupting women than vice versa.

The social setting is obviously an important element in this variable. In a widely reported investigation of conversations involving male–female couples in public places in California (e.g. a coffee-shop) 'virtually all the interruptions and overlaps are by male speakers (98 per cent and 100 per cent respectively)' (Zimmerman and West 1975: 115). The conclusion drawn that females' 'rights to speak appear to be casually infringed upon by males' (ibid.: 117) may be too hasty. It does not appear to be justified without further qualification. Beattie found no such male dominance in conversational behaviour during university tutorials in England (Beattie 1981: 22ff). He suggests that other factors which might deter interruption by a female in an informal social encounter like those investigated by Zimmerman and West may be of importance, such as the need for social approval, i.e. to make a 'good impression'. Or interruption may be a sign less of dominance than of enthusiasm and involvement (ibid.: 17, 31). Kennedy (1980) goes into the question of interruption further and establishes, for a group of undergraduate students, that the following grounds account for interruption:

agreement   38 per cent
subject change   23 per cent
disagreement   19 per cent
clarification   11 per cent
tangentialization   8 per cent

Kennedy also noted that while women may be interrupted more than men, it may, in fact, be other women who are doing the interrupting.

There have also been reports of differing overall behaviour of women, who seem to engage in more overlapping or simultaneous speech than men. Zimmerman and West (1975) also noted overlap by women, but only with other women and never with men.

Topic control: questions Indeed, differing overall strategies may apply to the problem of topic control inasmuch as women seem, as a tendency, to approach this problem from a completely different angle. They have been found to use up to three times as many questions as men do. This suggests a strategy in which these questions function as 'sequencing devices' in conversation: because they demand a response, they may well serve to keep a conversation going:

> A question does work in conversation by opening a two-part (Q–A) sequence. It is a way to insure a minimal interaction – at least one utterance by each of the two participants. By asking questions, women strengthen the possibility of a response to what they have to say.
>
> (Fishman 1983: 94)

However, as was pointed out above in 8.2.2, neither is it clear that women really do use more (tag) questions, nor is the function of questions necessarily identical from situation to situation.

Minimal responses Nevertheless, Fishman's explanation gets a certain amount of reinforcement by way of the observation that women are more likely than men to produce minimal responses, that is, those *mm*'s, *uhuh*'s, and *yeah*'s which indicate active listening and encourage the speaker to go on. Apparently, women are more willing to play a supportive conversational role; see, for example, go-on gambits in 6.3.4.

8.3.3 Politeness

The word 'supportive' reintroduces an idea expressed in 8.2.1 on vocabulary. Various people ascribe supportiveness to women, while seeing assertiveness as typically masculine. Put more positively, it is possible to speak of different types of politeness: women practise positive politeness by intensifying their interest in the hearer via the use of tag questions, words signalling group identity and disagreement avoidance. Men display patterns of negative politeness, which means they seek to minimize imposition (Brown and Levinson 1978). They are also task-oriented, giving opinions, providing information, disagreeing (Piliavin and Martin 1978); they are interested in maintaining reputation (Abrahams 1976). Women, on the other hand, want to maintain respectability (ibid.), and they display socio-emotional behaviour, dramatizing, agreeing, showing tension (Piliavin and Martin 1978). Needless to say, if the behavioural norms of males and females are, on the whole, so different, this will have an effect on politeness; to pick up two key words just mentioned, are they interested in preserving face in the sense of reputation or of respectability?

8.4 Language acquisition and development

A look at language acquisition among children as well as at their use of English represents an attempt to understand better the many differences that exist between female and male use of the language. The central question is whether the differences are genetic or social, due, in other words, to nature or to nurture. While there is, indeed, evidence of girl–boy language differences, especially as concerns the age of acquisition (a result of girls' earlier maturation), there is an even greater amount of evidence which demonstrates the immense influence of socialization in the development of language patterns.

Certainly the influence of adults, especially parents, is unquestionably great. By the age of two or three, children are learning politeness patterns, with girls showing more cooperation (Ervin-Tripp *et al*. 1984: 134f). At four, boys are imitating male forms; girls are imitating female patterns, a process which may begin as early as the age of eighteen months (Gleason 1987: 198). Note also the greater number of unmitigated imperatives and other types of directives used by boys (discussed in 8.2.2), just as fathers use particularly many of them with their children, especially their sons (see below). Boys also talk more about sports and transmit more information, while girls talk more about school and sitting games, use fewer direct requests, laugh more and are more compliant (Haas 1979). At nursery-school age and beyond (three to seven), for example, children portray fathers' speech as straightforward, unqualified and forceful, mothers' speech as talkative, polite, qualified and higher pitched (Anderson 1977). This shows not only how unerringly children imitate models, but also how susceptible they are to gender stereotypes.

The models available have traditionally been considered to vary so much between men and women that the adult input language is often termed 'motherese', for it is mothers, above all, who simplify their language according to the child's age (Gleason and Greif 1983). Such language involves slowness, redundancy, simplicity and grammaticality. Utterances are shortened: mothers stay about 1.5 words in length ahead of the child. There is a great deal of repetition. There is present-orientation, and there is control (Engle 1980). Fathers have fewer exchanges with their children but tend to introduce more new words, to use more imperatives, to ask fewer questions and to make fewer repetitions (ibid.; cf. Gleason and Greif 1983; Gleason 1987). Nevertheless, 'motherese', in the sense of simplified language, is used by both parents. Interestingly enough, males who are daycare teachers conform to female speech patterns more than do fathers, who are generally secondary care-givers (Gleason and Greif 1983; cf. also Field 1978).

8.5 Non-verbal behaviour

Communication takes place not only by means of language, but also through other channels. This includes such non-verbal behaviour as gestures, mimicry, posture, eye contact, smiling, touch, and so on. Non-verbal communication is, in the words of Mehrabian, implicit communication as compared with explicit communication with words (Mehrabian 1972: 2). Indeed, so important is non-verbal behaviour for communication that the signals it provides may override the actual words a person uses. For example, we are all aware of the false smiles we sometimes encounter and are wary of their bearers. Body movements, which 'are normally outside our awareness (and hence less subject to censorship)' (Harper *et al.* 1978: 133), may provide us with numerous clear, though subliminal signals: 'In general, it was found that, when there was inconsistency among components, the implicit cues dominated the verbal cues in determining the total impact' (Mehrabian 1972: 103).

As far as gender-specific differences are concerned, it seems that women are generally more sensitive to non-verbal signals than men are (see especially Hall 1979: 35–42). This may have to do with the fact that women have less power and status in society and are therefore in greater need of interpreting implicit messages (Eakins and Eakins 1978a: 149; Rosenthal *et al.* 1974: 66), or it may be due to the requirements of motherhood, i.e. the need to respond to non-verbal signals from children (ibid.: 66) or both.

Smiling   Women have also been found to smile more than men, even when the smile has nothing to do with whether the person smiling is happy (Bugental *et al.* 1971). Just why this is the case is not clear, but explanations tend to emphasize either the greater politeness of women or the relatively weaker social position most women have.

> The traditional female role demands warm, compliant behavior in public situations; the smiling facial expression may provide the mask to convey this impression. . . . For her, the smile may be situationally or role defined, rather than being relevant to the immediate verbal interchange.
>
> (ibid.: 315)

Touch   Closely related to smiling is the area of touch. In general it seems to reflect socio-economic status: the higher the status, the more liberty one can take in touching others. It likewise reflects age, with the older person generally having the greater freedom to touch. Since women are generally touched more and do less touching, this fits in with what was just said:

women have less status and are often classed with children. This is reminiscent of the use of modes of address (see chapter 9), where the socially more powerful or the older has the right to initiate the use of first names. Touching behaviour is, however, further complicated by the factor of sex: if a women touches a man, her touch is very likely to be interpreted as a sexual gambit (Henley 1973).

Proximity and body posture   In a like manner, 'Women were approached more closely than men' (Willis 1966: 221), thus underlining the fact that women are allowed less personal space. Women are expected to move out of the way of men in passing on the streets. Body posture emphasizes this, too: men hold their arms and legs at a wider angle than women do (Birdwhistell 1970: 44). In other words, male territoriality is greater than that of females.

Eye contact   People look at higher status speakers more than lower status ones, and women maintain more eye contact than men do (see Harper *et al*. 1978: 216–18 for a review of the literature). One study of visual behaviour closes among other things with this remark:

> An understanding of how power, dominance, and status are communicated has practical value as well as theoretical importance. If, because of traditional socialization processes, men typically assume a dominant visual display and women adopt a submissive posture during mixed-sex interaction, then nonverbal cues can contribute to the perpetuation of perceived status differences between the sexes.
>
> (Dovidio and Ellyson 1985: 146)

This is fully in line with what was said above about smiling, touch and territoriality.

8.6 Explanations

Throughout the preceding section as well as in 8.3 a connection has been made between people's behaviour in regard to status and age on the one hand and their gender on the other. No doubt being female most often means having less social power and prestige and being male means having and asserting more power – two partially complementary sets of behavioural habits. Section 8.4 on language development in children illustrated the remarkable ease and strength with which patterns of deportment are passed on via socialization.

Section 8.2, which deals with differences in vocabulary, grammar and pronunciation use in English, emphasizes the importance of the social group for determining how the language is used. Here a person's gender is only one factor, along with others such as class, region and age.

The differing orientation of men and women, with men tending to use more local and/or non-standard forms and women tending to favour the overt norm of StE, has been explained in two somewhat varying ways. One of these is the supposed need on the part of women, who are said to be more status conscious than men, to seek prestige through language. This is reported to be the case most strongly among lower-middle-class women, who may try especially hard to compensate for their lack of a (prestigious) vocation by imitating the language styles of the classes above them (Trudgill 1972: 182f). Men, on the other hand, are said to prefer the rough and tough, 'masculine' language of the working class (including taboo language), which takes on the quality of a norm for them, too, albeit a covert norm (ibid: 183; Labov 1966: 108; Lanham and Macdonald 1979: 27, 56).

The other explanation relies on the concept of group identity and solidarity. It works with the idea of the social network, which may be a thick (**multiplex**) meshing of shared relationships, such as shared neighbourhood, shared work, shared kin and shared leisure time activities, or which may be a simpler perhaps singular (**uniplex**) relationship. The more firmly people are enmeshed in a network, the more likely they are to share values, including language use (Milroy and Margrain 1980). With such an approach the ideas of prestige-consciousness, as in the first explanation above, appear somewhat one-sided. Obviously they can still be meaningful, but prestige now is clearly a group norm and may dictate language forms which conform to the overt standard *or* the local covert norms depending on the nature of the social network involved.

There are numerous questions involving the sociolinguistic variable of gender (as well as the many other sociolinguistic variables) that are in need of further investigation. Above all, further data is needed to be able to say more about such questions as whether women really are more polite than men, whether men are linguistically more aggressive, how strong the factor of gender is in relation to other factors such as age, race, region, class or religion, what influence factors of the situation of communication (such as the relationship between the participants) have, and especially what can be done to change the sexist use of English.

REFERENCES

Abrahams, R. (1970) *Deep Down in the Jungle*, Chicago: Aldine.
—— (1976) 'Negotiating respect: patterns of presentation among black women', *Journal of American Folklore* 88: 58–80.
Addington, D. W. (1968) 'The relationship of selected vocal characteristics to personality perception', *Speech Monographs* 35: 492–503.
Anderson, E. (1977) 'Young children's knowledge of role-related speech differences: a mommy is not a daddy is not a baby', *Papers and Reports on Child Language Development* 13: 83–90.
Baron, D. (1986) *Grammar and Gender*, New Haven, Conn.: Yale University Press.

Bate, B. (1988) *Communication and the Sexes*, New York: Harper & Row.

Beattie, G. W. (1981) 'Interruption in conversational interaction, and its relation to the sex and status of the interactants', *Linguistics* 19: 15–35.

Birdwhistell, R. L. (1970) *Kinesics and Context: Essays on Body Motion and Communication*, Philadelphia: University of Pennsylvania Press.

Bodine, A. (1975) 'Androcentrism in prescriptive grammar: singular "they", sex-indefinite "he" and "he or she"', *Language in Society* 4: 129–46.

Brend, R. M. (1975) 'Male–female intonation patterns in American English', in B. Thorne and N. Henley (eds) *Language and Sex*, Rowley, Mass.: Newbury House, pp. 84–7.

Brooks, V. R. (1982) 'Sex differences in student dominance behavior in female and male professors' classrooms', *Sex Roles* 8: 683–90.

Brown, P. and Levinson, S. (1978) 'Universals in language usage: politeness phenomena', in E. N. Goody (ed.) *Questions and Politeness*, Cambridge: Cambridge University Press, pp. 56–289.

Bruner E. M. and Kelso, J. P. (1980) 'Gender differences in graffiti: a semiotic perspective', in C. Kramarae (ed.) *The Voices and Words of Women and Men*, Oxford: Pergamon, pp. 239–52.

Bugental, D. E., Love, L. R. and Gianetto, R. M. (1971) 'Perfidious feminine faces', *Journal of Personal and Social Psychology* 17: 314–18.

Cameron, D. (1985) *Feminism and Linguistic Theory*, London: Macmillan.

Cheshire, J. (1978) 'Present tense verbs in Reading English', in P. Trudgill (ed.) *Sociolinguistic Patterns in British English*, London: Edward Arnold, pp. 52–68.

Coates, J. (1986) *Women, Men and Language*, London: Longman.

Condry, J. and Condry, S. (1976) 'Sex differences: a study of the eye of the beholder', *Child Development* 47: 812–19.

Coser, R. L. (1960) 'Laughter among colleagues' *Psychiatry* 23: 81–95.

Dovidio, J. F. and Ellyson, S. L. (1985) 'Patterns of visual dominance behavior in humans', in S. L. Ellyson and J. F. Dovidio (eds) *Power, Dominance and Nonverbal Behavior*, New York: Springer, pp. 129–49.

Dubois B. and Crouch, I. (1975) 'The question of tag-questions in women's speech: they don't really use more of them, do they?', *Language in Society* 4: 289–94.

Eakins, B. W. and Eakins, R. G. (1978a) *Sex Differences in Human Communication*, Boston: Houghton Mifflin.

—— (1978b) 'Verbal turn-taking and exchanges in faculty dialogue', in B. Dubois and I. Crouch (eds) *The Sociology of the Languages of American Women*, San Antonio: Trinity University Press, pp. 53–62.

Eble, C. C. (1977) 'If ladies weren't present, I'd tell you what I really think', in D. L. Shores and C. P. Hines (eds) *Papers in Language Variation*, Birmingham: University of Alabama Press, pp. 295–301.

Edelsky, C. (1979) 'Question intonation and sex roles', *Language in Society* 9: 15–32.

Edelsky, C. (1981) 'Who's got the floor?', *Language in Society* 10: 383–421.

Elyan, O., Smith, P., Giles, H. and Bourhis, R. (1978) 'RP-accented female speech: the voice of perceived androgyny?', in P. Trudgill (ed.) *Sociolinguistic Patterns in British English*, London: Edward Arnold, pp. 122–31.

Engle, M. (1980) 'Family influence on the language development of young children', in C. Kramarae (ed.) *The Voices and Words of Women and Men*, Oxford: Pergamon, pp. 259–66.

Ervin-Tripp, S., O'Connor, M. C. and Rosenberg, J. (1984) 'Language and power in the family', in C. Kramarae, M. Schulz and W. M. O'Barr (eds) *Language and Power*, Beverly Hills: Sage, pp. 116–35.

Exline, R., Gray, D. and Schuette, D. (1965) 'Visual behavior in a dyad as affected by interview content and sex of respondent', *Journal of Personal and Social Psychology* 1: 201–9.

Field, T. (1978) 'Interaction behaviors of primary versus secondary caretaker fathers', *Developmental Psychology* 14: 183–4.

Fischer, J. L. (1958) 'Social influences on the choice of a linguistic variant', *Word* 14: 47–56.

Fishman, P. M. (1983) 'Interaction: the work women do', in B. Thorne, C. Kramarae and N. Henley (eds) *Language, Gender and Society*, Cambridge, Mass.: Newbury House, pp. 89–101.

Folb, E. (1980) *Runnin' Down Some Lines: the Language of Black Teenagers*, Cambridge, Mass.: Harvard University Press.

Gershuny, H. L. (1977) 'Sexism and dictionaries and texts: omissions and commissions', in A. P. Nilsen, H. Bosmajian, L. Gershuny and J. P. Stanley (eds) *Sexism and Language*, Urbana: National Council of Teachers of English, pp. 143–59.

Gleason, J. B. (1987) 'Sex differences in parent–child interaction', in S. U. Philips and A. Reynolds (eds) *Language, Gender and Sex in Comparative Perspective*. Cambridge: Cambridge University Press, pp. 189–99.

Gleason J. B. and Greif, E. B. (1983) 'Men's speech to young children', in B. Thorne, C. Kramarae and N. Henley (eds) *Language, Gender and Society*, Cambridge, Mass.: Newbury House, pp. 140–50.

Gleser, G. C., Gottschalk, L. A. and Watkins, J. (1959) 'The relationship of sex and intelligence to choice of words: a normative study of verbal behavior', *Journal of Clinical Psychology* 15: 182–91.

Goodwin, M. H. (1988) 'Cooperation and competition across girls' play activities', in A. D. Todd and S. Fisher (eds) *Gender and Discourse: the Power of Talk*, Norwood, NJ: Ablex, pp. 55–94.

Graham, A. (1975) 'The making of a nonsexist dictionary', in B. Thorne and N. Henley (eds) *Language and Sex*, Rowley, Mass.: Newbury House, pp. 57–63.

Green, R. (1977) 'Magnolias grow in dirt: the bawdy lore of Southern women', *Southern Exposure* 4: 29–33.

Haas, A. (1979) 'The acquisition of genderlect', in J. Orsanu, M. Slater and L. L. Adler (eds) *Language, Sex and Gender*, New York: New York Academy of Sciences, pp. 101–13.

Hall, J. A. (1979) 'Gender, gender-roles and nonverbal communication skills', in R. Rosenthal (ed.) *Skill in Nonverbal Communication: Individual Differences*, Cambridge, Mass.: Oelgeschlager, Gunn & Hain.

Harper, R. G., Wiens, A. N. and Matarazzo, J. D. (1978) *Nonverbal Communication: the State of the Art*, New York: John Wiley.

Hellinger, M. (1980) '"For men must work and women must weep": sexism in English language textbooks used in German schools', in C. Kramarae (ed.) *The Voices and Words of Women and Men*, Oxford: Pergamon, pp. 267–75.

Henley, N. (1973) 'The politics of touch', in P. Brown (ed.) *Radical Psychology*, New York: Harper & Row, pp. 421–33.

Hennessee, J. and Nicholson, J. (1972) 'NOW says: TV commercials insult women', *New York Times Magazine*, 28 May, p. 12f.

Jespersen, O. (1922) 'The woman', in *Language: its Nature, Development and Origin*, London: Allen & Unwin, pp. 237–54.

Jones, D. (1980) 'Gossip: notes on women's oral culture', in C. Kramarae (ed.) *The Voices and Words of Women and Men*, Oxford: Pergamon, pp. 193–8.

Kennedy, C. W. (1980) 'Patterns of verbal interruption among women and men in groups', quoted in B. Thorne, C. Kramarae and N. Henley (eds) (1983) *Language, Gender and Society*, Cambridge, Mass.: Newbury House, p. 282.

Key, M. R. (1972) 'Linguistic behavior of male and female', *Linguistics* 88: 15–31.

Kochman, T. (ed.) (1972) *Rappin' and Stylin' Out: Communication in Urban Black America*, Urbana: University of Illinois Press.

Komarovsky, M. (1967) *Blue-Collar Marriage*, New York: Vintage.

Kramarae, C. (1988) 'Censorship of women's voices on radio', in A. D. Todd and S. Fisher (eds) *Gender and Discourse: the Power of Talk*, Norwood, NJ: Ablex, pp. 243–54.

Kramer, C. (1975) 'Women's speech: separate but unequal', in B. Thorne and N. Henley (eds) *Language and Sex*, Rowley, Mass.; Newbury House, pp. 43–56.

Labov, W. (1966) 'Hypercorrection by the lower middle class as a factor in linguistic change', in W. Bright (ed.) *Sociolinguistics*, The Hague: Mouton, pp. 84–113.

Lakoff, R. (1976) *Language and Woman's Place*, New York: Harper & Row.

Landis, C. (1926–7) 'National differences in conversations', *Journal of Abnormal and Social Psychology* 21: 354–7.

Lanham, L. W. and McDonald, C. A. (1979) *The Standard in South African English and its Social History*, Heidelberg: Groos.

Legman, G. (1968) *Rationale of the Dirty Joke: an Analysis of Sexual Humor*, London: Jonathan Cape.

Levine L. and Crockett, H. J., Jr (1966) 'Speech variation in a Piedmont community: postvocalic *r*', in S. Lieberson (ed.) *Explorations in Sociolinguistics*, The Hague: Mouton, pp. 76–98.

Lieberman, P. (1967) *Intonation, Perception, and Language*, Cambridge, Mass.: Massachusetts Institute of Technology Press.

Macaulay, R. K. (1978) 'Variation and consistency in Glaswegian English', in P. Trudgill (ed.) *Sociolinguistic Patterns in British English*, London: Edward Arnold, pp. 132–43.

MacKay, D. G. (1983) 'Prescriptive grammar and the pronoun problem', in B. Thorne, C. Kramarae and N. Henley (eds) *Language, Gender and Society*, Cambridge, Mass.: Newbury House, pp. 38–53.

MacKay, D. G. and Konishi, T. (1980) 'Personification and the pronoun problem', in C. Kramarae (ed.) *The Voices and Words of Women and Men*, Oxford: Pergamon, pp. 149–163.

Maggio, R. (1988) *The Nonsexist Word Finder. A Dictionary of Gender-Free Usage*, Boston: Beacon.

Martin, W. (1972) 'Seduced and abandoned in the new world: the image of women in American fiction', in V. Gornick and B. K. Moran (eds) *Women in Sexist Society*, New York: Basic Books, pp. 26–39.

Martyna, W. (1980) 'The psychology of the generic masculine', in S. McConnell-Ginet, R. Borker and N. Furman (eds) *Women and Language in Literature and Society*, New York: Praeger, pp. 69–78.

Mehrabian, A. (1972) *Nonverbal Communication*, Chicago: Aldine, Atherton.

Milroy, L. and Margrain, S. (1980) 'Vernacular language loyality and social networks', *Language in Society* 9: 43–70.

Mitchell, C. A. (1976) 'The differences between male and female joke telling as exemplified in a college community', *Dissertation Abstracts* 37: 5270A.

NCTE (National Council of Teachers of English) (1977) 'Guidelines for nonsexist use of language in NCTE publications', in A. P. Nilsen *et al.* (eds) *Sexism and Language*, Urbana: NCTE, pp. 181–91.

Nichols, J. C. (1984) 'Networks and hierarchies: language and social stratification', in C. Kramarae, M. Schulz and W. M. O'Barr (eds) *Language and Power*, Beverly Hills: Sage, pp. 23–42.

Nilsen, A. P. (1977) 'Sexism as shown through the English vocabulary', in A. P. Nilsen *et al.* (eds) *Sexism and Language*, Urbana: NCTE, pp. 27–41.

Pellowe, J. and Jones, V. (1978) 'On intonational variability in Tyneside speech', in P. Trudgill (ed.) *Sociolinguistic Patterns in British English*, London: Edward Arnold, pp. 101–21.

Piliavin, J. A. and Martin, R. R. (1978) 'The effects of the sex composition of groups on style of social interaction', *Sex Roles* 4: 281–96.

Risch, B. (1987) 'Women's derogatory terms for men: that's right, "dirty" words', *Language in Society* 16: 353–8.

Rosenthal, R., Archer, D., DiMatteo, M. R., Hoivumaki, J. H. and Rogers, P. L. (1974) 'Body talk and tone of voice: the language without words', *Psychology Today* (Sept.): 64–8.

Sachs, J. (1975) 'Cues to the identification of sex in children's speech', in B. Thorne and N. Henley (eds) *Language and Sex*, Rowley: Newbury House, pp. 152–71.

—— (1987) 'Preschool boys' and girls' language use in pretend play', in S. U. Philips, S. Steele and C. Tanz (eds) *Language, Gender and Sex in Comparative Perspective*, Cambridge: Cambridge University Press, pp. 178–88.

Sachs, J., Lieberman, P. and Erickson, D. (1973) 'Anatomical and cultural determinants of male and female speech', in R. Shuy and R. W. Fasold (eds) *Language Attitudes*, Washington: Georgetown University Press, pp. 74–84.

Schneider, J. W. and Hacker, S. (1973) 'Sex role imagery and the use of the generic "man" in introductory texts', *American Sociologist* 8(8): 12–18.

Schulz, M. R. (1975) 'The semantic derogation of woman', in B. Thorne and N. Henley (eds) *Language and Sex*, Rowley, Mass.: Newbury House, pp. 64–75.

Scott, K. P. (1980) 'Perceptions of communicative competence: what's good for the goose is not good for the gander', in C. Kramarae (ed.) *The Voices and Words of Women and Men*, Oxford: Pergamon, pp. 199–208.

Shuy, R., Wolfram, W. A. and Riley, W. K. (1967) *Linguistic Correlates of Social Stratification in Detroit Speech*, East Lansing: Michigan State University Press.

Silveira, J. (1980) 'Generic masculine words and thinking', in C. Kramarae (ed.) *The Voices and Words of Women and Men*, Oxford: Pergamon, pp. 165–78.

Smith, P. M. (1985) *Languages, the Sexes and Society*, Oxford: Basil Blackwell.

Stanley, J. P. (1977) 'Paradigmatic woman: the prostitute', in D. L. Shore and C. P. Hines. (eds) *Papers on Language Variation*, Birmingham: University of Alabama Press, pp. 303–21.

Stericker, A. (1981) 'Does this "he or she" business really make a difference? The effect of masculine pronouns as generics on job attitudes', *Sex Roles*, pp. 637–41.

Stern, R. H. (1976) 'Review article: sexism in foreign language textbooks', *Foreign Language Annals* 9(4): 294–9.

Stewart, W. A. (1964) 'Urban Negro speech: sociolinguistic factors affecting English teaching', in R. W. Shuy (ed.) *Social Dialects and Language Learning*, Champaign, Ill.: National Council of Teachers of English, pp. 10–18.

Swacker, M. (1975) 'The sex of the speaker as a sociolinguistic variable', in B. Thorne and N. Henley (eds) *Language and Sex*, Rowley, Mass.: Newbury House, pp. 76–83.

—— (1978) 'Women's verbal behavior at learned and professional conferences', in B. Dubois and I. Crouch (eds) *The Sociology of the Languages of American Women*, San Antonio: Trinity University Press, pp. 155–60.

Thorne, B. and Henley, N. (1975) *Language and Sex: Difference and Dominance*, Rowley, Mass.: Newbury House.

Thorne, B., Kramarae, C. and Henley, N. (eds) (1983) *Language, Gender and Society*, Cambridge, Mass.: Newbury House.

Trudgill, P. (1972) 'Sex, covert prestige, and linguistic change in the urban British English of Norwich', *Language in Society* 1: 179–95.

U'Ren, M. B. (1972) 'The image of woman in textbooks', In V. Gornick and B. K. Moran (eds) *Women in Sexist Society*, New York: Basic Books, pp. 218–25.

West, C. and Zimmerman, D. H. (1983) 'Small insults: a study of interruptions in cross-sex conversations between unacquainted persons', in B. Thorne, C. Kramarae and N. Henley (eds) *Language, Gender and Society*, Cambridge, Mass.: Newbury House, pp. 102–17.

Williams, J. C., Giles, H., Edwards, J. R., Best, D. L. and Dawes, J. T. (1977) 'Sex-trait stereotypes in England, Ireland and the United States', *British Journal of Social and Clinical Psychology*, 16: 303–9.

Willis, F. N., Jr (1966) 'Initial speaking distance as a function of the speakers' relationship', *Psychonomic Science* 5: 221–2.

Zimmerman, D. H. and West, C. (1975) 'Sex roles, interruptions and silences in conversation', in B. Thorne and N. Henley (eds) *Language and Sex*, Rowley, Mass.: Newbury House, pp. 105–29.

Chapter 9

Using English: modes of address

Language use can reflect the social and linguistic background of its speakers and addressees, be it the gender of the participants (see the preceding chapter), their age, status, education, regional background, race, religion or whatever. Also relevant is the social situation, where the emotional content, number of participants or nature and purpose of the occasion may influence the type of language employed. One of the most illuminating ways to show the multiplicity of factors involved is to observe how people address each other. Put in other words: 'Personal address is a sociolinguistic subject par excellence' (Philipsen and Huspek 1985: 94).

There are two very prominent aspects to address. 'The social component consists of speaker–addressee relationship, speaker's evaluation of addressee (and situation), and of speaker's social background as expressed in the use of a given form of address' (Braun 1988: 258). However, a systematic level is involved as well, namely what forms of address the language has, for example, what second person pronouns are available. The procedure here will be to look first at the types of elements involved in the system of address and then to exemplify the ways in which the major social categories listed in the first paragraph may be perceived in the manner in which people address each other.

The pragmatics of address, or why people use vocatives in the first place, is touched on only in passing, usually in the sense that the choice of a particular form indicates solidarity or power (see below). It might be mentioned here, however, that in addition to the obvious deictic element, i.e. singling out one or more addressees within a larger group, the decision to use any vocative at all has to do with interpersonal dynamics. Emihovich (1981: 198) points out that relatively constant naming among children at play is used to guide play; adults may use it to control behaviour. Kramer (1975: 200f, 207) notes that in literary works address may be aggressive and is often coupled with an exclamation point or a question mark. Furthermore, she notes in this connection that men address women more than women do men. Finally, Fasold (1990: 15) mentions that speakers often avoid address altogether because they are confused about what the appropriate or expected form is or because they do not know the name of their addressee.

9.1 The linguistic elements of address in English

The forms of address of English include the pronouns used in the second person and vocative forms. The former offer very little variation in comparison with other languages, being largely restricted to *you*; the latter carry the burden of social differentiation. They are divided, on the one hand, into syntactically **bound** pronouns (those which carry a syntactic function such as subject or object) and, on the other, **unbound** pronouns (those which are used as vocatives).

Vocatives are not integrated into the structure of the clause, which explains their variable word order; they may precede, follow or interrupt a clause. They have separate intonation as well. Furthermore, there are some grammatical restrictions on them, for example, they may not contain a definite article (**Come here, the friend*), nor can they include any (unbound) personal pronouns other than the second person (**Hey them, come here*). Indefinite pronouns, however, do occur in vocatives, as in *Hey everyone, come here* (cf. Downing 1969).

There are a number of word forms that are exclusively vocative in the sense that they cannot also be used as bound forms (i.e. subjects and objects). This is especially true of common nouns without an article, such as *captain*, *professor*, *son*, etc., as well as specifically vocative forms such as *sir* and *ma'am/madam* and the M-forms, *mister*, *missus* and *miss* (which are not to be confused with the titles *Mr*, *Mrs*, *Miss*, *Ms*; see below). Some (especially) BrE speakers, however, treat *captain*, *miss*, and a few others as proper names; in such cases the word form without an article may also occur as a non-vocative (*Captain says you are to come immediately*).

9.1.1 Bound forms: pronouns

To all intents and purposes English has only one second person pronoun, *you*. Only in the reflexive (*yourself*, *yourselves*) is the singular and plural differentiated, but reflexives are not very frequent forms. The regional plural *you all* (American South) is a convenient but not consistently used form and dialectal constructions such as *youse* or colloquial ones such as *you guys*, *you fellows*, *you people*, etc., are not regarded as fully standard. In any case StE does not distinguish between a polite and a familiar singular form on the model of French *vous* and *tu*, Italian *Lei* and *tu*, German *Sie* and *du*, or Russian *vy* and *ty*. The historical second person singular form *thou* is no longer in use in current StE (but see below under 9.2.8 and 9.2.9; for this distinction in Shetland English, see 10.2.2).

The linguistic system, in other words, provides for no socially meaningful pronoun choices. Braun concludes, however: 'The non-differentiating pronomial address in English, *you*, does not necessarily make English speakers perceive each other as equals' (Braun 1988: 65); indeed, a lack of pronominal distinctions does not mean a lack of differences in politeness, respect, intimacy, etc. (ibid.: 62).

A minor possibility of bound address in English is by means of the third person. This does not involve pronouns, but is restricted to honorifics such as *your honour*, *your excellency*, *your highness*, etc., as in *Does Your Honour wish me to continue?* Kachru gives the following IndE example with the term *huzoor*, which is reserved for superiors: *'Would huzoor like to sleep on the veranda?'* (Kachru 1966: 273). In the military, third person address is also common in formal situations when addressing a superior officer, for example, *'May I have the General's indulgence for a few minutes?'* (Jonz 1975: 73; cf. also facetious use described in Ross 1967: 21).

9.1.2 Vocatives

These forms may be divided up into five distinct classes: unbound pronouns, names, kinship terms, titles and descriptors.

The pronoun   Pronouns are, as might be expected, of minor importance. Really the main contrast here is between *you* and no pronoun at all, as in *Hey you, watch out!* vs. *Hey, watch out!* The use of *you* without the introductory *hey* in the example above to soften its effect would be considerably more direct and therefore less polite (cf. the same sentence with rude *You there*). The use of vocative *you* is, consequently, infrequent. It is the noun vocative (titles, kinship terms, names and descriptors) which bear the burden of making social distinctions.

Names   As forms of address there are the following common types of names: first names in their full forms (FN), *Stephen*, *Elizabeth*; familiar forms, *Steve*, *Liz*; diminutive forms, *Stevie*, *Lizzie*; nicknames, *Tiger*, *Bunny*; and last names (LN), *Smith*, *Windsor*. LN alone is not a particularly common form of address. It seems to be used chiefly among men, particularly in the military (Jonz 1975: 74) and in British private schools. The diminutives include phonetic-morphological variations on names, *Stevio*, *Lizzikins*.

This final point is impressively illustrated for AusE, for which a sizable list of suffixes is given, including *-y*, *-o*, *-a*, *-s*, *-ers*, *-kin*, *-le*, *-poo*, *-pops* as well as multiple suffixing *Bobbles* (*le* + *s*), *Katiekins* (*y* + *kin* + *s*), *Albertipoo* (*y* + *poo*), *Mikeypoodles* (*y* + *poo* + *le* + *s*). However, it is not possible to combine just anything: *-kin(s)* cannot follow on a /k/ (*Mikekins) and *-y* cannot be appended to a vowel (*Di-y). The *-o* suffix is only masculine; furthermore, most suffixes to male names are mono-syllabic. The suffix *-y* is usually restricted to children's names (exceptions: *Terry*, *Tony*); forms such as *Jimmy* will, as a rule, be used for adult males only by their mothers and girlfriends or for teasing. In addition, there is 'a phenomenon regarded by many as peculiarly Australian, but not in fact limited to Australia, . . . the truncated forms of certain names whose initial syllable is open and whose second syllable commonly begins with *r*'. Here the shortened form closes with ⟨z⟩, producing forms such as *Baz* from *Barry*, *Shaz* from *Sharon* and *Tez* from *Terence* or *Teresa* (Poynton 1989: 61–4).

Multiple naming designates a practice in which people move freely from one form to another, whether first names, full or familiar names, nick-names or last names. This seems to indicate a great deal of intimacy (Brown and Ford 1964: 238).

Generic names (those relevant to any male regardless of his actual name), for example, *bud/buddy*, *mack* or *jack*, are applied to a few limited vocations, such as taxi drivers (ibid.: 236), or to express belligerent feelings, but also as markers of masculine solidarity – as what might be called **camaraderie forms** (see below 9.2.6).

Kinship terms   A kinship term (KT) may function as a name or as a title. *Grandmother*, *Father*, and diminutives of them, *Granny*, *Dad*, are used as names (notice that they are always capitalized in this use). Some KTs may combine with a name in the manner of a title, for example, *Aunt Liz*, *Uncle Steve*, *Gramma Brown*. They are generally used upwardly only, from a younger towards an older relative; however, older and rural usage may sometimes include *Cousin* + FN.

Titles   This type of vocative is probably most often used with a last name (T + LN, or TLN). Titles may be classed as vocational (*Dr*, *Prof.*, *Senator*, etc.), as ranks in the military or police (*Lt*, *Capt.*, *Gen.*, *Constable*, *Officer*, *Sheriff*, etc.) or as religious (*Father*, *Brother*, *Sister*, *Mother Superior*). Most common, however, are the M-forms (*Mr*, *Mrs*, *Miss*, *Ms*, *Master*), which are generic 'titles' applicable to anyone within the bounds of conven-tions regarding age, sex and marital status.

Although these titles, as vocatives, are usually combined with LN (some-times with FN alone; see below 9.2.3 and 9.2.5), most of them can be used alone. Exceptions include **Pope* (instead of *Your Holiness*), **King* (for *Your Majesty*) and **Representative* (for *Congressman*, *?Congresswoman*). Quite a number of these titles have alternative vocative forms, for example, the more informal *Judge* as opposed to the distinctly formal courtroom *Your Honour* or, similarly, *Prince* rather than *Your Highness*. The M-forms *Mr* and *Mrs* are used without LN only in relatively restricted circumstances (and then they are spelled out in writing): *Mister* sounds rude by itself; *Missus*, uncultivated. Instead, it is usual to hear the polite forms *sir* and *ma'am* (or the very formal madam).

Descriptors   This is the final category of vocatives. There are numerous general terms for males only (*buddy*, *chum*, *fellow*, *mate*, *old bean*, *pal*, etc.), some for females only (*babe*, *sister, toots*, etc.), and some for both (plural *folks*, *guys* and *people*). Besides these there are thing-designations for people, such as *taxi* or *room service*, as well as vocations and functions (*waiter*, *operator*, *nurse*, etc.) (cf. Whitcut 1980), sometimes even prefixed by an M-form, as in a note with the salutation *Dear Mr Milkman* or the traditional parliamentary address *Mr Chairman* or *Madam Chairman* (cf. also *Mr President* or *Mr Secretary*). Furthermore, there are numerous vocative terms of insult such as *stupid*, *jackass*, *dolt*, etc., on the one hand, and terms of endearment such as *dear*, *honey*, *darling*, etc., on the other. These latter two categories allow further lexical sub-classification. Most prominent are animal terms of endearment, some masculine, some feminine, some either (*bear*, *tiger*, *kitten*, *puppy*, *ladybird*, etc.) and of insult (*dog*, *swine*, *bitch*, *minx*, *vixen*, etc.). National and ethnic names used as vocatives are almost always insults (*nigger*, *Paddy*, *wog*, *wop*, *Yank*, *Yid*, etc.). Numerous insulting vocatives are taboo − not only the ones just listed, but also obscene and scatological terms of address, (*ass(hole)*, *bastard*, *cunt*, *dyke*, etc.).

9.2 Criteria of use

The use of the wealth of vocatives available in English depends on a wide variety of features of the speaker, the addressee and the situation. Before these are characterized more closely, a summary will be made of some of the general principles which lie behind the use of forms of address.

Vocatives indicate the nature of relationships between people. Of primary importance is whether the terms are used reciprocally or non-reciprocally. **Reciprocal** forms indicate some kind of equality while **non-reciprocal** ones indicate an imbalance in power or prestige. Examples of non-reciprocal relationships are parent−child, in which a parent is given KT (*Mum, Dad*), but gives FN or the like (*Steve, Liz*). Another example is teacher−student, which typically has TLN ↔ FN. This dimension is called the **power semantic** (Brown and Gilman 1972: 255).

Reciprocal dyads (a **dyad** is a pair of participants interacting with each other) are common within a status group. Children, students and fellow workers are all likely to exchange mutual first names (FN ↔ FN). However, there is also the possibility of mutual TLN ↔ TLN when people who are not well acquainted with each other interact, say, employees from different departments in a large firm (Slobin *et al.* 1968: 291) or military officers

(Jonz 1975). Reciprocal relations are examples of what is called the **solidarity semantic** (Brown and Gilman 1972: 258—60).

Just how the power and the solidarity semantics are applied varies by region/nation, according to the status, education, vocation, age, sex, race, religion, ideology and kinship of speaker and addressee. Furthermore, they reflect the situation of use.

9.2.1   Nation: BrE and AmE

If we abstract from the great variety of user characteristics (status, age, sex, race, etc.), we find that the AmE address system is basically a two-term system: either FN or TLN. The latter includes KT as a form of title. Non-reciprocality is the rule across generations within the family with the older generation receiving KT (*Gramma*) or KT + FN (*Uncle Steve*) from the younger generation and giving FN in return. Likewise, teacher—student is TLN ↔ FN; often boss—employee is TLN ↔ FN as well.

Adults are frequently introduced with mutual TLN, but the switch to mutual FN is rapid, especially among the young and where the dyads are of the same sex (Brown and Ford 1964: 236). In many familiar or informal situations introductions are in the form of mutual FN + LN and are followed by immediate use of FN ↔ FN. In cases of doubt, no-naming is a common strategy. The following precepts offer general guidelines:

> One may readily use FN with everyone except: with an adult (if one is an unrelated child); with an older adult (if one is markedly younger); with a teacher (if one is a student); with a clergyman or religious (particularly Roman Catholic and Orthodox); with a physician.
>
> (Hook 1984: 186)

Despite the impression that outsiders might have, FN does not necessarily indicate intimacy; it is simply a feature of American society. In fact, to refuse FN could be interpreted as unfriendly or snobby. 'First names are required among people who work closely together, even though they may not like each other at all' (Wardhaugh 1986: 260). For intimacy, either nicknames or multiple naming is employed in AmE.

In BrE the pattern is generally similar, although the move from mutual TLN to mutual FN may proceed at a slower pace; that is, the *bonhomie* connected with mutual first-naming is often regarded in England as very American (Whitcut 1980: 90).

University use   There are some BrE and AmE contexts in which there are differences. Ervin-Tripp mentions a three-option system in connection with British universities in which T (*Dr, Prof.*) + LN is used for most deference, the M-forms (MLN) as an intermediate stage, and only then FN. In addition, males may engage in mutual last-naming (without a title or M-form); such male LN ↔ LN is also practised at some private schools (Ervin-Tripp 1974: 274f).

In North American universities one study shows that there is little use of overt address between professors (teaching staff) and students at all; when there is any, TLN is used to the professors and FN address is rare: 'More than one informant spoke of the need to avoid expressing intimacy which does not exist, or indicated that such expression would be inappropriate so long as the student–teacher relationship pertains' (McIntire 1972: 290). Where there is movement to addressing a professor by his or her FN, the initiation does not come, as expected, only from the more powerful or superior, but in most cases from the inferior. The most important factor is age. Older male graduate students are the ones most likely to initiate FN with their professors, and then more easily with professors under than over 40 (ibid.: 289). A later study reveals that students, especially female ones, addressed young female professors (aged 26–33) by FN more often than they did their male teachers (Rubin 1981: 966). There were also some differences in the use of TLN. Male students preferred M-forms and *Dr* + LN, while women students preferred *Prof.* + LN for male professors. For female professors women students used M-forms and *Dr* + LN most often, while men students used M-forms + LN or FN. 'Thus, female students seem to be affording more status to their male professors' (ibid.: 970; cf. also McConnell-Ginet 1978; Baron 1978).

9.2.2 Nation: Australia, India, Singapore and Nigeria

The AusE use of address follows the same general lines as in AmE or BrE. As in AmE, FN has been widely adopted without necessarily implying equality or solidarity (Poynton 1989: 56).

> Sellers of cars and real estate assume the social utility of addressing potential buyers by personal name [i.e. FN], while the would-be Don Juan who uses diminutive forms to newly-met potential bedfellows can be seen as preparing the ground for physical intimacy by decreasing social distance linguistically.
>
> (ibid.: 57)

Countries such as India, where English is used as a second language, provide a real contrast. IndE, for example, uses forms of address which come from the non-native use of English in the context of Indian culture (Kachru 1966: 268). Special terms are used to express social relations such as master–servant and age–youth. While these relations exist in native-speaker English-language societies (however attenuated they may appear), the vocatives below, given according to several important social categories, are specific to IndE (ibid.: 272):

caste: *pandit, thakur, jamadar*
profession: *havaldar, inspector (sahib)*
> Note: *babu* or *baboo*: 'A term of respect used frequently in the north of India. In the south of India it is used for *sir, your honour*'. (ibid.: 286)

religion: *khwaja, pandit, sardar*
kinship: *brother-in-law, mother, sister, grandmother, father*
> Note: 'A term restricted to the kinship system of a [particular] language may be used with extended meaning in another culture and transferred to an L2' (ibid.: 272). Hence IndE has '*mother* as a term of respect, *sister* of regard, and *father-in-law* in the sense of abuse. *Bhai* ('brother') is used for any male of equal age, *father* for all elder persons, and an uncle may be referred to as *father*'. (ibid.: 273f)

superiority: *cherisher of the poor, king of pearls, huzoor, ma-bap* ('mother-father'), *friend of the poor*
neutral: *babu-sahib, bhai, master, dada* (male), *didi* (female), *sab*
> Note: *sab*: 'In colloquial language *sab* is used as the weak form of *sahib*. It is equivalent to *master* and may be used without religious or status restrictions when one wants to show respect. Originally it was used for Europeans in India'. (ibid.: 286)

Differences in forms of address transferred to English may also be illustrated by the usage of polite forms in Singapore English. Polite reference (not address) is via T + FN + LN (*Mr Arthur Orton*), but if well known T + FN (*Mr Arthur*). A woman who is unmarried is, for example, *Miss Tan Mei Ling* [*Tan* = LN]. If she marries *Mr Lim Keng Choon* [*Lim* = LN], she has three options: she may be called *Mrs Lim Keng Choon* (rarely), *Mrs Lim Mei Ling* or *Madam Tan Mei Ling*. Quite obviously, 'the conventions governing naming and forms of address in Malay, Chinese and Indian languages are quite different from those in English' (Tongue 1974: 104).

In Nigeria, finally, KT's may be used as they are in the West, but they may also be applied to the polygynous family, so that children of one father may address his several wives all as *mother*. Furthermore, *Father/Daddy* and *Mother/Mummy* are also used for distant relations or even unrelated people who are treated with deference and are of the appropriate age. 'Immediate bosses in their places of work get addressed as either *Daddy* or *Mummy* by subordinate young officers' (Akere 1982: 96). A further difference in modes of address in NigE is that TLN is often reduced to simple T; the M-forms, including the Muslim title *Malam*, can be used for direct address without the LN. Furthermore, multiple titles are also used, for example, *Chief Doctor Mrs* + LN (ibid.).

9.2.3 Region

Only a few examples of differences in usage due to regional factors will be mentioned. One relatively significant difference is in the southern United States, where the use of *ma'am* and *sir* is particularly common. In the South the usage balance between *ma'am* and endearments such as *honey* or *dear* in what are called service encounters (at petrol stations, stores, etc.) is 83.1 per cent to 16.9 per cent, while in the Northeast for equivalent types of speakers it is 24.5 per cent to 75.5 per cent (Wolfson and Manes 1980: 82f). *Ma'am* may even be used seriously (and not jokingly or ironically) among intimates. Indeed, it is so general in the South as to be considered formulaic and, therefore, not necessary to convey respect. It may even indicate people's momentary attitudes, as it may be omitted if the speaker feels annoyance. 'In general, however, the use of *ma'am* does indicate that the addressee is either of higher status or older than the speaker' (ibid.: 85).

Note that *ma'am* and *sir* are not always used as forms of address in the South. For one thing 'the single term *ma'am* [and *sir*], with rising intonation, can indicate that the speaker has not heard or understood what was said'; it is equivalent to saying *Pardon?*. In addition a use of '*ma'am* [and *sir*] which is specific to the south is the phrase "yes, ma'am" which functions as a variant of "you're welcome"' (ibid.: 84). Finally, note the colloquial AmE use of emphatic *yessir* or *yessiree* to signal agreement.

A further aspect of address in the American South is the use of T + FN. This is regarded as quaint or old-fashioned outside the South, but it offers a compromise between intimacy and respect for its users. Inasmuch as it is a relic of the older, racially tainted master/mistress–servant dyad with TFN ↔ FN (as used, for example, in the movie *Driving Miss Daisy*), it is certainly not acceptable to most people today. Where it exists independent of race it may be viable (President Carter's mother was widely known and addressed as *Miz Lillian*).

Other regional differences that are frequently encountered are ones involving the use of regionally marked descriptors. For example, *lass* is found most frequently in northern England and Scotland; *guv'nor* is Cockney; *stranger* or *partner* are stereotypical for the American West.

9.2.4 Status, education and vocation

There is frequently a general, though not absolute, correlation between level of education, prestige of vocation and power of status. Where these factors do not correlate, vocational status (achieved status) tends to override attributed status, including age. Hence in the business world the higher someone's position, the more likely they are to receive TLN and the more likely they are to give FN (Slobin *et al*. 1968: 289). However, since age is usually a powerful predictor of non-reciprocal relationships, it is not without its significance here: 'one may detect a residual feeling that age cannot be completely obliterated as a determinant of address' (ibid.: 293). Even so, in cases of mutual FN it is the more highly placed person who will probably allow a switch either from non-reciprocity or from mutual TLN to FN ↔ FN (cf. however, McIntire 1972: 290: in an academic setting 'it is by no means true that the dyad member with superior status will always initiate a move which signals greater intimacy'). For purposes of 'team spirit' superordinates may permit wide liberties otherwise not tolerated from their subordinates (Goffman 1967: 65).

It is worth mentioning that there is more to deference than the choice of a respectful form of address. The type of salutation (*Hi!* to intimates and subordinates, but *Good morning* to superiors), or the use of touch (superior to subordinate, not vice versa) are two further examples (cf. Brown and Ford 1964: 240, 243). Furthermore, a business person can ask an elevator operator about his/her children, but not vice versa (Goffman 1967: 64).

Some titles allow a compromise position between deference and intimacy, so the use of *Skipper* to a marine captain (Jonz 1975: 73) or *Doc* by an attendant to a physician (Goffman 1967: 61)

For some remarks on how to address upper-class people in England, especially in writing, see Ross 1967: 12–21.

9.2.5 Age

After status, age is the most potent factor in determining address relationships. Not only may it mitigate the effect of status, as just pointed out; it is also crucial to the use of KT's, where the older generation receives KT or KT + FN (*Gramma, Aunt Lizzie*) but gives FN. Age differences seem to be meaningful if they are approximately fifteen years or more (Brown and Ford 1964: 236). If they are less, FN ↔ FN seems to be no problem (unless there are major status distinctions). Even a KT will probably be dispensed with where, for example, aunts and uncles are of much the same age as their nieces and nephews. A compromise form (England, the American South) for an old servant to the son or daughter of an employer is M + FN (cf. Whitcut 1980: 91).

While there is only the single deference form *sir* for men, there are two for women, *miss* and *ma'am* (not counting the formal and infrequent variant *madam*). Young women receive *ma'am* if well dressed (status!); otherwise, *miss*. Women over thirty are more likely to get *ma'am* than *miss* from men (Kramer 1975: 204). A special M-form, *Master*, used in postal addresses when writing to young boys, still exists.

9.2.6 Sex

Address directed to men and women is far from equivalent. In service encounters (stores, public services, hospitals) women direct **endearments** (*sweetheart*, *honey*, *dear*, *love*, etc.) to women who are total strangers more frequently than to men; men also address women in this way, but they may never do so to other men. With the exception of females in service encounters the use of endearments towards a man on the part of a woman is likely to be perceived as a sexual advance. Endearments by men to women in service encounters, on the other hand, are, for some men, their standard form of address; for others it seems to be a way of putting women down, of showing 'the customer to be somewhat less than totally competent' (Wolfson and Manes 1980: 89; cf. also Kramer 1975: 203). A further indication that women are treated as incompetent or immature is that 'women are addressed as *girls* very much more frequently than men are addressed as *boys* and when men are so addressed it is usually in contexts where they are relaxing, not playing serious adult roles' (Poynton 1989: 59; cf. also Kramer 1975: 208).

What men can receive from total strangers are **camaraderie forms** such as *buddy*, *buster*, *mac*, etc. All of these, as designations of manliness, show male solidarity when supplied by other males; women are hardly likely to use such forms towards men since they are 'rough' terms (and not 'sweet' ones) and are therefore reserved for men (cf. Kramer 1975: 199).

When endearments and camaraderie forms as well as the **deference forms** *ma'am* and *sir* are used in service encounters, they are seldom reciprocal. However, it is not solely the sex of the members of the dyads that is decisive, for role relationships also play an important part. It is almost exclusively the service-giver who uses a vocative. Cases in which the person being served is the one who uses a vocative are restricted to *sir* and *ma'am* from persons *seeking help* from public agencies (the police, health services, welfare bureaux). Furthermore, endearments and camaraderie forms, on the one hand, and the deference forms *ma'am* and *sir*, on the other, stand in complementary distribution to each other inasmuch as both are not used together by the same speaker in a single situation. What determines which will be employed depends on both social and individual aspects of the service-giver. The status of the institution in which the encounter transpires reflects the former: in 'classy' establishments the deference forms are used towards the customers, patients, or clients unless the addressee is sufficiently young or obviously lacking in status. The latter, individual factor may be related to the relative egalitarianism of the service-provider: many people (outside regions such as the American South) find the deference forms hard to use. Hence if they use any vocatives at all to strangers, these will be endearments or camaraderie forms. For more on the factor of sex in the use of deference forms, see above **University use**.

The area of sex also supplies the vocatives of strongest abuse; what is said of AusE in the following quotation is true of AmE and BrE as well:

> Among the potentially most seriously insulting terms of address in Australian English are those impugning the heterosexual identity of males (such as *poofter*, *fag*), those attributing promiscuous sexual behavior to women (*moll*, *tart*), and identifying males or females (but particularly insulting when directed at males) in terms of female genitalia (*cunt*).
>
> (Poynton 1989: 60)

Males have a richer inventory of terms, including the -*o* suffix to names, the camaraderie terms and the possibility of **semantic inversion**, i.e. using insulting terms to each other as a sign of solidarity. For example, they may greet one another with an insult, such as the jovial *Well, you old son of a bitch, I haven't seen you for at least a year!* See also Kuiper on the use of sexually insulting terms among members of a New Zealand rugby team (Kuiper 1991: 205–7). There are, in contrast, no exclusively female morphological forms, no generic camaraderie names for women and hardly any ritual inversion, but far more endearments (cf. Poynton 1989: 65f).

Fun naming, which has nothing to do with a person's real name, also expresses solidarity and is practised by both males and females. It takes the form of appellations which rhyme with the last syllables of routine formulae or particular key words. Examples include the venerable *See you later, alligator*, to which the standard response is *In a while, crocodile*, but also *I'll be back, Jack*; *Alright, Dwight*; *No way, José*; *That's the truth, Ruth*; or *Here's the money, honey*.

9.2.7 Race and ethnicity

Differences in address based on racial or ethnic identity are highly ostracized today, yet there is little doubt that insulting epithets (*Chink*, *Jap*, *nigger*, *spick*, etc.) are often used. Similarly, some older non-reciprocal usage can still be heard in the American South, where blacks once regularly received FN and where black men were addressed as *boy* (a practice once common in many parts of the English-speaking world for non-whites), but where blacks had to give TLN or, perhaps, the more intimate form TFN. Even today continuing status differences often ensure that blacks give, but do not receive, *sir* and *ma'am* vis-à-vis whites.

9.2.8 Religion and ideology

The field of religious language is the only one in which the obsolete second person singular pronoun *thou* is still used by non-dialect speakers of StE. Note that some dialect speakers in the British Isles (cf. 10.2.2) and some

Quaker fellowships still use parts of the old second person singular forms in addressing some people. People invoke God with it, above all in liturgical language and in the still popular King James (Authorized) Version of the Bible, as in *Our Father, which art in heaven, Hallowed be thy Name.*

Vocatives specific to religious groups include, in particular, the KT's *Father* for God and for priests, *Brother* and *Sister* for members of religious orders, and *Mother (Superior)* for heads of female orders. In the Roman Catholic Church these KT's may be followed by FN in the case of *Brother* and *Sister* and by LN in the case of *Father*. In many Protestant bodies fellow members are addressed with their LN preceded by *Brother* or *Sister*. Blessings may be addressed to a *son, daughter* or *child*, as the faithful are regarded as the children of God. For religious terms used in IndE, see 9.2.2 above.

Ideological fellowships of a non-religious sort may also use special terms of address, be they any one of numerous lodges with a variety of titles or members of trade unions and socialist or communist groups, who use the term *comrade*, either by itself or before a LN.

9.2.9 Literature

Special features of the literary use of address is the old-fashioned, no longer productive, use of *thou*, for example, *Shall I compare thee to a summer's day* (Shakespeare, Sonnet 18), and the vocative *o* or *oh* in poetry which is still read, for example, *O Love, if death be sweeter, let me die* (Tennyson 'Elaine's Song' from *The Princess*).

Compare also the remarks on the pragmatics of address in literary works (Kramer 1975: 200f, 207, quoted in the introduction to this chapter).

9.2.10 Kinship

The basic system of giving FN name to the same or a younger generation and giving KT or KT + FN to an older one influences practice in non-kinship areas (cf. 9.2.8 above), perhaps because family is so basic to interpersonal relations. It is worth remarking, however, that this customary practice is not immutable, for many parents who consider themselves progressive encourage and accept FN from their children. This may be part of the general trend towards the suppression of asymmetric (non-reciprocal) relations which can be observed throughout the Western world. On the other hand, many mothers express a no-compromising attitude by reverting from FN (*Stephen*), diminutive (*Stevie*), or the like to FN + LN (*Stephen Smith*) or even, first, second, and last name (FN + SN + LN: *Stephen Arnold Smith*) (Brown and Ford 1964: 241).

In addition, many children learn to address unrelated friends of their parents as *Aunt/Uncle* + FN. Furthermore, older people, especially men, patronizingly address boys and young men as *son* or *sonnie*; *son* is also used by rank superiors in the military towards the lower enlisted ranks (Jonz 1975: 74). Finally, *sissy* (from *sister*) has become an insult directed to boys who do not show the degree of masculine behaviour which their peers expect of them.

9.3 Situation of use

In conclusion it is necessary to point out explicitly that no sure predictions about usage can be made. For one thing, the interplay between the various factors discussed is fluid; secondly, the participants in a dyad may well share more than one type of relationship.

In addition, factors in the communicative situation may be decisive. Titles and deference forms may serve to flatter an addressee or to insinuate the user into the addressee's good graces. How a student and a professor address each other may be very different in and outside the class. Officers of differing rank may stick strictly to TLN or at least to T alone while on duty, especially in the presence of either senior officers or enlisted men, but use mutual FN in their private quarters; when under fire all, or almost all, distinctions fall (Jonz 1975: 70, 75).

REFERENCES

Akere, F. (1982) 'Sociocultural constraints and the emergence of a standard Nigerian English', in J. Pride (ed.) *New Englishes*, Rowley, Mass.: Newbury House, pp. 85–99.

Baron, N. S. (1978) 'Professor Smith, Miss Jones: terms of address in academe', paper given at the annual meeting of the Modern Language Association, New York.

Braun, F. (1988) *Terms of Address: Problems of Patterns and Usage in Various Languages and Cultures*, Berlin: Mouton de Gruyter.

Brown, R. and Ford, M. (1964) 'Address in American English', in D. Hymes (ed.) *Language in Culture and Society*, New York: Harper & Row, pp. 234–44.

Brown, R. and Gilman, A. (1972) 'The pronouns of power and solidarity', in P. P. Giglioli (ed.) *Language and Social Context*, Harmondsworth: Penguin, pp. 252–82.

Downing, B. T. (1969) 'Vocatives and third-person imperatives in English', *Papers in Linguistics* 1: 570–92.

Emihovich, C. A. (1981) 'The intimacy of address: friendship markers in children's social play', *Language in Society* 10: 189–99.

Ervin-Tripp, S. (1974) 'Sociolinguistics', in B. G. Blount (ed.) *Language, Culture and Society*, Cambridge, Mass.: Winthrop, pp. 268–334.

Fasold, R. (1990) *The Sociolinguistics of Language*, Oxford: Blackwell.

Goffman, E. (1967) *Interaction Ritual: Essays in Face-to-Face Behavior*, Chicago: Aldine.

Hook, D. D. (1984) 'First names and titles as solidarity and power semantics in English', *International Review of Applied Linguistics* 22: 183–9.

Jonz, J. G. (1975) 'Situated address in the United States Marine Corps', *Anthropological Linguistics* 17: 68–77.

Kachru, B. B. (1966) 'Indian English: a study in contextualization', in C. E. Bazell (ed.) *In Memory of J. R. Firth*, London: Longman, pp. 255–87.

Kramer, C. (1975) 'Sex-related differences in address systems', *Anthropological Linguistics* 17: 198–200.

Kuiper, K. (1991) 'Sporting formulae in New Zealand English', in J. Cheshire (ed.) *English around the World: Sociolinguistic Perspectives*, Cambridge: Cambridge University Press, pp. 200–9.

McConnell-Ginet, S. (1978) 'Address forms in sexual politics', in D. Butturff and E. L. Epstein (eds) *Women's Language and Style*, Akron, Ohio: Lange and Springer pp. 23–35.

McIntire, M. L. (1972) 'Terms of address in an academic setting', *Anthropological Linguistics* 14: 286–92.

Philipsen, G. and Huspek, M. (1985) 'A bibliography of sociolinguistic studies and personal address', *Anthropological Linguistics* 27: 94–101.

Poynton, C. (1989) 'Terms of address in Australian English', in P. Collins and D. Blair (eds) *Australian English: the Language of a New Society*, St Lucia: University of Queensland Press, pp. 55–69.

Ross, A. S. C. (1967) 'U and non-U: an essay in sociological linguistics', in N. Mitford (ed.) *Noblesse Oblige*, Harmondsworth: Penguin, pp. 9–32.

Rubin, R. (1981) 'Ideal traits and terms of address for male and female college professors', *Journal of Personality and Social Psychology* 41: 966–74.

Slobin, D. I., Miller, S. H. and Porter, P. W. (1968) 'Forms of address and social relations in a business organization', *Journal of Personality and Social Psychology* 8: 289–93.

Tongue, R. (1974) *The English of Singapore and Malaysia*, Singapore: Eastern Universities Press.

Wardhaugh, R. (1986) *An Introduction to Sociolinguistics*, Oxford: Blackwell.

Whitcut, J. (1980) 'The language of address', in L. Michaels and C. Ricks (eds) *The State of the Language*, Berkeley: University of California Press, pp. 89–97.

Wolfson, N. and Manes, J. (1980) 'Don't "dear" me!', in S. McConnell-Ginet, R. Borker and N. Furman (eds) *Women and Language in Literature and Society*, New York: Praeger, pp. 79–92.

Part 3

National and regional varieties of English

Chapter 10

English in the British Isles

English is the primary language of both Great Britain (England, Scotland, Wales) and Ireland (the Republic of Ireland, Northern Ireland). There are, of course, numerous other languages spoken by the citizens of these various countries, some of which will be mentioned briefly below. Yet it is English that predominates. In fact, English is native to England and a major part of Scotland, from where it was transplanted to the other native-English-speaking areas in the British Isles and around the globe. It is perhaps because its origins are here that this variety, **British English (BrE)**, is often regarded by English-learners in many parts of the world as somehow the 'best' English. This is reason enough to examine English in the British Isles more closely and to try to find out more about its nature.

BrE comprises numerous, often greatly differing regional variants. Furthermore, in England, Scotland and Ireland there exist what are called **traditional dialects** (see especially 10.2.2). These grew up over centuries of relative geographic isolation and exhibit fairly obvious lexical, morphological, syntactic and phonological differences from each other and from StE.

Special attention will be paid to the status of one particular type of pronunciation, RP or Received Pronunciation, which enjoys special prestige in England.

10.1 England and Wales

The vast majority of the inhabitants of England (over 46 million) and Wales (approximately 2.8 million) speak English as their first language; yet there are considerable minorities who do not. This is perhaps most obvious in Wales, where around 20 per cent of the population speaks Welsh. In addition, there are large minorities in urban centres throughout Great Britain who immigrated from the Indian subcontinent or Cyprus and whose mother tongues are not English.

10.1.1 Wales

Wales is the only area in the British Isles where one of the original Celtic languages has been able to survive as the daily language of a large number of people (just under 19 per cent could speak Welsh in 1981; see data in Williams 1990). Although the future of Welsh is by no means assured, its use seems to have stabilized somewhat *vis-à-vis* English. There are Welsh-language schools in the predominantly Welsh-speaking areas in the north, and a fair amount of broadcasting is carried out in Welsh as well.

Welsh English shares many of the linguistic features of southern England (see below 10.1.2). What marks it off from the English of England is the effect of the Celtic substratum: 'there can be little doubt that the main influence on the pronunciation of English in Wales is the substratum presented by the phonological system of Welsh' (Wells 1982: 337; cf. also Parry 1972). One of the commonly noted characteristics of Welsh English is its sing-song intonation, presumably influenced by Welsh. In monolingual areas such as the southeast, the influence of Welsh is considerably weaker. Here, for example, monolingual English speakers generally have non-rhotic accents, while bilingual speakers further to the west are more likely to have rhotic ones (Thomas 1985: 213). Throughout Wales clear [l] is the rule, whether prevocalic or postvocalic. This, too, may be due to the substratum, but it is also typical of the English southwest. /h/ is not present. For more detail on pronunciation, see Russ 1984: 32f; Thomas 1984: 179–89; and several contributions in Coupland 1990. On attitudes towards Welsh English, see Giles 1990.

In grammar, Welsh English is for the most part no different from StE. However, Welsh-influenced English grammar (and vocabulary) is more likely to be heard in non-anglicized areas (Jones 1990). Moreover, non-standard Welsh English has additional forms for habitual aspect constructed with the uninflected auxiliary *do* (present) or *did* (past) plus the infinitive (*He do go to the cinema every week*) or with an inflected form of *be* plus an -*ing* form of the verb (*He's going to the cinema every week*). The latter construction correlates well with the equivalent Welsh form. The *do* form, which is predominant in the southeast, is an English construction apparently originally borrowed from the neighbouring English counties; as the speech form of the industrialized part of Wales it is relatively prestigious and is spreading into the *be* + V-*ing* area in the west (Thomas 1985: 214f).

Fronting for topicalization (*Singing they were*) is common in Welsh English and is a reflection of the substratum. The same is true of the practice of reporting indirect questions in the same word order as direct questions (*I'm not sure is it true or not*). Furthermore, possession can be expressed by using a prepositional construction (*There's no luck with the rich* 'they have no luck'). All of these examples have parallels in IrE (see

10.3.4). A further instance of influence from the substratum is the use of *there* in exclamations where StE would have *how* (*There's young she looks!* 'How young she looks!'). All examples are from Thomas (1985).

The use of an all-purpose tag question *isn't it?* (see Thomas 1984: 192) is reminiscent of the same construction in second-language Englishes in Africa and Asia (see chapters 14 and 15). Further non-standard grammatical features of Welsh English, as mentioned in Thomas (1985), are no different from many of the widespread non-standard forms of England; they are listed and illustrated as 2, 3, 6, 9 and 10 in the example below in the section on page 309.

10.1.2 England

This section reviews two subjects, the regional dialects of England and the RP accent. StE is dealt with in Part 1 of this book and special features of the StE of England are treated in a comparison with AmE in chapter 11. Remarks on the urban social dialects (sociolects) of Great Britain and Ireland are to be found in 10.4.

The regional dialects of England As one moves from area to area in England the variety of local forms in use can be impressively different. It may be difficult for Somerset and Yorkshire people to understand one another. Yet lack of mutual comprehension does not actually occur very frequently. The reasons for this lie in the fact that almost 90 per cent of the population of Great Britain live in cities and towns and the speech forms of urban populations are less noticeably different than those of traditional rural communities. Furthermore, speakers of the traditional dialects almost always have a command of the non-traditional dialect, be it StE or one of the non-standard urban vernaculars. For convenience of reference, Wells groups what is not traditional dialect together under the term **General English** (Wells 1982: 2; Trudgill 1990: 5 calls this 'Mainstream English').

The traditional dialects are fairly distinctively divergent from StE in grammar, morphology, vocabulary and pronunciation. Usually these divergencies are unpredictable because they do not stand in a regular correspondence with StE. In this chapter we will not be looking at them any further. A comprehensive investigation of English dialects was carried out in the Survey of English Dialects (SED), which was conducted in England and Wales in the 1950s and early 1960s (see Orton *et al.* 1962–71; Orton and Wright 1974; Orton *et al.* 1978; Kolb *et al.* 1979). For a detailed presentation of English dialects, see Wakelin 1977; for a shorter overview, Wakelin 1984 and the bibliography there; Trudgill 1990 is a readable introduction. Useful collections of articles are Wakelin 1972; Viereck 1985; Trudgill and Chambers 1991; these, however, are not limited to England nor always to traditional dialects.

Within the cities there has been a great deal of levelling (**koineization**) to a common denominator of forms, and here the more common, over-arching, public, media-orientated linguistic culture of General English has become dominant. This is not to say that there are no regional distinctions between the areas; for indeed there are. However, they are hardly as extreme as those between many of the traditional dialect areas. A very readable introduction to this diversity is Hughes and Trudgill 1979.

The major division within England is one between the north and the Midlands, on the one hand, and the south, on the other (see map 10.1). The chief differences are several features of pronunciation. In southern England, the vowel in such words as *luck*, *butter*, *cousin* or *love* is pronounced with a low central or fronted vowel /ʌ/ and is therefore distinctly different from that of *pull*, *push*, *could* or *look*, all of which have /ʊ/. In the north the two groups of words have an identical vowel, viz. /ʊ/, so that *look* and *luck* are homophones. A second distinction involves the distribution of /æ/ and /ɑː/. In such words as *bath*, *after*, *pass*, *dance* and *sample* the realization in the north is a phonemically short vowel, as in GenAm (see 3.6.2 and 11.1.4) though the quality of /æ/ is rather [a] in northern England. The south, in contrast, has a long vowel, either [aː] or [ɑː]. In a third group of words, viz. *quarry*, *swath*, *what*, which have a /w/ preceding the vowel, the northern vowel is fronted [a] while the south has back [ɔ]. A final distinction is the presence of a short low back vowel, /ɒ/ preceding a voiceless fricative in words such as *moss*, *off*, *broth* in the north. The south has a long vowel here, /ɔː/ (RP has, after a 'long' interlude, switched back to a short vowel).

Other important distinctions within the regional accents of England are the exclusive use of a clear [l] in the southwest and the presence of rhotic areas both in the southwest and in Lancashire in the north. For more detail, see Wakelin 1983; Glauser 1991.

Regional variation in vocabulary is infrequent outside the traditional dialects. Where it does exist, it is often restricted to the domestic, the local, the jocular or the juvenile. A wide display of different terms is provided, for example, by children's words for 'time out' or 'truce' in games: *fainties* (southwest and southeast), *cree* (Bristol), *scribs* (mid-southern coast), *barley* (western Midlands and northwards to eastern Scotland), *exes* (East Anglia), *crosses* (Lincolnshire), *kings* (Yorkshire and southwards), *skinch* (Durham–Newcastle) (Trudgill 1990: 119).

Grammatical variation within General English is probably less a regional dimension, though this can be the case, than an educational one. Those who value education are likely to use StE habitually, while those whose orientation lies elsewhere are more likely to use non-standard English, which shares a number of characteristics that transcend not only the regional boundaries of England but its national borders as well, and are to be found among native speakers of the language all over the English-speaking world.

These features include at least the following:

1 third person singular *don't* (*she don't know*);
2 non-standard past and past participial forms (*they come to see us yesterday*; *you done a good job*; *have you went to see them yet?*);
3 multiple negation (*she don't have none*);
4 widespread use of *ain't* for *be* and the auxiliary *have* (*I ain't interested*; *he ain't comin'*; *we ain't seen him*);
5 *never* for *not* (*Did you take them sweets? No, I never*);
6 various non-standard relative pronouns such as *what* or *as* (*he was the man what/ as did it*); or none at all as the subject of a restrictive relative clause (*he was the man did it*) (cf. 4.5.5);
7 the demonstrative adjective *them* (*where did you get them new glasses?*);
8 the reflexive pronouns *hisself* and *theirselves* (*he hurt hisself playing football*);
9 some unmarked plurals after numbers (*she's five foot tall and weighs eight stone*);
10 the ending {S} for all persons (in the west of England) (*I likes it*, *you likes it*, *she likes it*, . . .), and the lack of any {S} at all (in East Anglia) (*she like it*) (cf. Hughes and Trudgill 1979: chapter 2).

The RP accent   In England there is one accent which is not connected with a specific locality, though it is rather more southern than northern in its overall character. This is RP, which is short for Received Pronunciation. The term is derived from the meaning accepted (i.e. 'received') in the sense of being the accent current in the best social circles. This rather restricted reference is hardly appropriate in present-day English society, for RP is not limited in such a social way anymore. This is not to say that there are no social distinctions connected with it, for clearly there are. RP is closely associated with education and with the kind of higher social position and responsibility often associated with it (see below **The social argument**).

Despite the advantages of RP as a regionally neutral accent, it has not displaced the local accents of England. Estimates about the number of people who speak RP 'natively' (i.e. who learned it at home as children and not later in life) are usually set at 3 to 5 per cent of the population. As such RP is clearly a minority accent. However, its speakers occupy positions of authority and visibility in English society (government and politics, cultural and educational life, business and industrial management) far out of proportion to their actual numbers. Until World War II RP was also the exclusive accent of the BBC and it is still especially prominent there.

Perhaps because of its one-time dominance in broadcasting, RP is sometimes referred to as BBC English, even though a wide range of English and non-English (Scottish, Irish, North American, Australian, etc.) accents can be heard daily. Other designations for this accent include public school pronunciation, the King's/Queen's English and Oxford English. It is, of course, immaterial whether the one or the other name is chosen so long as there is reasonable agreement about what it refers to. In linguistic treatments of the accent, RP has become the accepted label.

The accent itself is neither changeless nor uniform, nor is there complete agreement about just what it is. With perhaps a few concessions to local pronunciation habits, it might be possible to extend the number of speakers to whom it applies. Within England this would include a total of 'not more than about 10 percent' (Wells 1982: 118), but it would also include many of the most prestigious accents in countries such as Australia, New Zealand and South Africa. Such an extended accent is called **near-RP** by Wells and is somewhat vaguely defined to refer 'to a group of accent types which are clearly "educated" and situated well away from the lower end of the socio-economic scale, while differing to some noticeable degree from what we recognize as RP' (ibid.: 301).

Within RP itself there are several streams to recognize. For one there is **U-RP**, that is, upper-class or upper-crust RP. Among the various characteristics Wells cites for it, the most likely diagnostic feature is a flapped [ɾ] in intervocalic position (ibid.: 282). This variety of RP has sub-varieties which are much like what Gimson called **Conservative** and **Advanced RP** (Gimson 1980: 91). The former counts as old-fashioned and will most likely be heard only among older speakers. It is characterized by a diphthongization of /æ/, something like [eæ]. Furthermore, /ɔɪ/ may still be realized as the centring diphthong [ɔə]. The centring diphthongs themselves end closer to [a] than to [ə]: [ɪa], [ɛa] and [ʊa]. /əʊ/ may be [oʊ], and, finally, the vowel in words of the type *moss*, *off* and *broth* can be old-fashioned /ɔː/ rather than /ɒ/. As for advanced RP, many people consider it affected. However that may be, it often shows the way that general RP will develop. Wells, who is otherwise very explicit, does not give any characteristics for this sub-variety.

A second major strand within RP is **adoptive RP**. This is the accent of someone who has learned RP as an adult, perhaps for vocational reasons. If well learned, it is no different from general RP. However, it may well be that such speakers retain their 'native accent' for more informal registers and that they have difficulty using RP in informal speech styles (ibid.: 284).

General RP has been characterized in chapter 3, and it is used as the basis for comparison with GenAm in chapter 11. Within the framework of the present chapter only a few of its present tendencies will be briefly outlined.

One of the most prominent on-going shifts within the RP vowel system is the increasing replacement of /ʊə/ by /ɔː/, especially in the words *sure* and *poor*. Where there is a preceding non-initial /j/, as in *pure*, /ʊə/ is more likely to be retained (but *your* with initial position is frequently /jɔː/). Instances of /ʊə/ which are the result of /uː/ in one syllable followed by /ə/ in the next (*fewer*, *brew a pot*) do not undergo this shift (Wells 1982:

287f). A second change is the backing of /æ/ which causes it to merge with fronted /ʌ/ and make *bank* and *bunk* homophones (ibid.: 292; Ramsaran 1990: 183).

One of the most widespread changes currently in progress in RP is what Wells calls **smoothing**. This is the simplification of a diphthong to a monophthong, or of a triphthong to a diphthong or a monophthong. This is most evident in pronunciations which reduce the vowels of *tower* and *tire* to the monophthong [ɑː] and [aː] respectively, sometimes even going so far as to produce homophonous *tower*, *tire* and *tar*, all as [tɑː] (ibid.: 292f). The centring diphthong /ɛə/ may also be smoothed to [ɛː] (ibid.: 293).

There has been quite a bit of discussion of the final unstressed vowel in words ending in ⟨-y⟩ or ⟨-ie⟩ (*happy*, *Susie*) (cf. Wells 1982: 294; Lewis 1990; Ramsaran 1990). The consensus seems to be that among the various realizations of this vowel, short /ɪ/ is giving way to [i], a somewhat shortened version of /iː/.

Among the consonants, Ramsaran mentions the variable realization of intervocalic /t/ before an unstressed syllable in words such as *butter* as tapped [ɾ] much like flapped [ɖ] in GenAm. Furthermore, she also sees the glottaling of /t/ before consonants (*hatrack = ha'rack* [hæʔræk]) as a change in progress in RP (Ramsaran 1990: 183). For further details, see Wells 1982: 285–300, and Ramsaran 1990.

About RP, Ramsaran remarks that it may be viewed

> as a kind of standard, not necessarily deliberately imposed or consciously adopted, not a norm from which other accents deviate, nor a target towards which foreign learners need necessarily aim, but a standard in the sense that it is regionally neutral and does undeniably influence the modified accents of many British regions.

(ibid.: 183)

Just what is the basis for the primacy of RP? In the vast literature in which this question has been batted around, four major positions have evolved.

The aesthetic argument An early stance maintained that RP 'is superior, from the character of its vowel sounds, to any other form of English, in beauty and clarity' (Wyld 1934: 606). This position can hardly be seriously defended, for it would find /paɪnt/ aesthetically pleasing when it is the pronunciation of RP *pint*, but unaesthetic as the pronunciation of Cockney *paint*. Furthermore, it is based completely on social prejudice that cannot be substantiated by native speakers of English who are unfamiliar with RP. North Americans, for instance, are not only incapable of distinguishing RP from near-RP, they cannot even be counted on to distinguish it from Irish, Scottish or Welsh English (since all are equally foreign and British-sounding). Hence the mirror image of Wyld is also invalid, namely that RP 'is a gross travesty of English speech . . . artificial, slovenly to a degree, absurdly difficult for foreigners to acquire, and . . . inharmonious' (Grieg 1928: 43). Few people today take such extreme positions as Wyld and Grieg, yet echoes can be heard in the ease/difficulty-of-learning argument, as when Trudgill and Hannah write: 'the RP accent is probably rather more difficult for many foreigners to acquire than, say, a Scottish accent, since RP has a large number of diphthongs' (Trudgill and Hannah 1982: 9f).

The intelligibility argument   When, early in the century, Jones chose RP as the basis for his description of English pronunciation, one of his arguments was that 'RP and approximations to it are easily *understood* almost everywhere in the English-speaking world' (Jones 1967: xviii). It is certainly true that RP is frequently heard in the media and is therefore easily accessible to many students of English as a foreign language (EFL). Furthermore, familiarity helps to guarantee comprehensibility. Yet the intelligibility argument should not be overvalued: in the words of Trudgill, 'Differences between accents in the British Isles are hardly ever large enough to cause serious comprehension difficulties' (Trudgill 1975: 53). In addition, it is conceivable that people in parts of the world where RP is not familiar (particularly in the sphere of influence of AmE) might find RP less intelligible than GenAm.

The scholarly treatment argument   RP has long been the basis of linguistic treatments of English pronunciation and has been used in EFL teaching materials (including tape recordings and pronunciation exercises) to a degree that far outdistances any other accent. Hence for purely practical purposes RP has a lot to recommend it. Material based on other accents, mainly GenAm, is also available. Most teachers see the advantage in using a single standard in the initial stages of EFL teaching, whichever it is, but few would dispute the necessity of exposing more advanced students to both RP and GenAm, at least, and preferably to other important accents as well.

The social argument   As the introductory remarks to this section indicate, RP does have social associations. While it is not exclusive to any particular class, it is, nonetheless, typical of the upper and the upper-middle classes. In sociolinguistic studies such as that of Trudgill in Norwich it has become clear that RP is the overt norm in pronunciation for most of the middle class (and especially for women). On the other hand, in Norwich local speech forms and London vernacular forms were said to be the covert norms in the working class (particularly strongly among men; see also 8.2.3). This fact should not be lost on the foreign learner, who needs to be aware of the connotations of accent within English society, not only to understand how the English see (hear) each other, but also to realize what the accent he or she has learned may suggest to his or her interlocutors.

In actual fact people seldom choose an accent. Rather, they have one. (EFL students, of course, get one – initially at least their teacher's.) What counts is the norms of the group they belong to or identify with. People simply have the accent they have because they are where they are in society. However, a few who move up in society 'modify their accent in the direction of RP, thereby helping to maintain the existing relationship between class and accent' (Hughes and Trudgill 1979: 7).

In other words, some people aspire to 'talk better' and are or are not successful; others disdain this as 'talking posh' or using a 'cut glass accent' (for more on attitudes, cf. Philp 1970). Just how strong the social meaning of accent is has been repeatedly confirmed by investigations designed to elicit people's evaluations of accents. In so-called matched guise tests subjects were asked to evaluate speakers who differed solely in accent (often the speaker was one and the same person using two or more accent 'guises'). The general results of such tests reveal that, *via-à-vis* other accents, RP has more prestige and is seen as more pleasant sounding, and its speakers are viewed as more ambitious and competent and as better suited for high status jobs. On the other hand, in early studies especially, RP speakers were rated as socially less attractive (less sincere, trustworthy, friendly, generous, kind) (see Giles *et al*. 1990 and the literature cited there).

What these studies demonstrate is 'the continuing significance of accent in British society in the closing decades of the twentieth century' (Honey 1989: 10). This significance lies in the social evaluations which people put on accents. A person who uses RP is perceived as more authoritative. Giles reports, for example, that the content of an argument on the death penalty, identically formulated but presented in four different accent guises, was more positively evaluated in the RP as opposed to three non-RP guises. Interestingly enough, the regional voices were, nevertheless, more persuasive (Giles and Powesland 1975: 93). Other experiments showed that people are more willing to comply with requests (e.g. filling out questionnaires, including the amount of written information provided) that are framed in an RP accent. Such results indicate the type of danger involved here. The expectation is that a distinctly non-RP accent may signal lack of competence and authority, and this is hardly justified in times such as these when education is no longer so clearly a class privilege. What is even less justified is the expectation many teachers have that children with the 'right' accent and who use StE are more intelligent or capable than those with a local accent who use non-standard English forms. Yet no investigations have indicated that the use of non-prestige forms correlates with people's intelligence or capability. What they do correlate with is class.

It is important for teachers to be aware of this and to avoid using the labels standard and non-standard as 'an easy way of concealing prejudice about socially stigmatized forms of speech under the guise of academic respectability'; instead, the teacher's job is to promote 'a process of

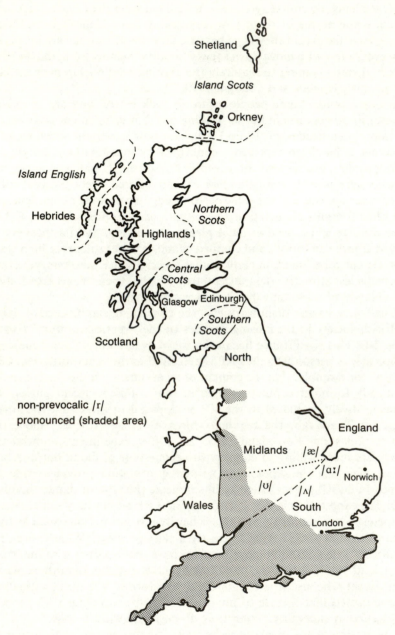

Map 10.1 Great Britain

intellectual development and the acquisition of knowledge' (Macaulay 1977: 72). Of course, imparting knowledge about the social evaluation of language is a legitimate part of this process. But this is different from wasting time trying to eliminate non-prestigious speech forms well anchored in regional peer groups. The latter is unlikely to meet with success. The need is really for more linguistic tolerance in society. Unfortunately, this is a distant goal. In the meantime, teachers and students should perhaps try to develop a moderate degree of bidialectalism, for a reasonable degree of competence in StE, especially in writing, is absolutely necessary for more and more jobs. This needs, however, to be coupled with open recognition of the legitimacy of the local non-standard norms in the appropriate spheres of activity.

10.2 Scotland

10.2.1 The languages of Scotland

The move from England to Scotland (population: just over five million) is one of the linguistically most distinct that can be made in the British Isles as far as English itself is concerned. Some people would even like to see Scotland as completely independent of StE (Aitken 1980: 61). This is certainly illusory since StE is well established throughout Scotland in government, schools, the media and business life in the specifically Scottish variety of the standard, which is usually referred to as **Scottish Standard English (SSE)**.

Yet in many areas of everyday life there is no denying that forms of English are used in Scotland which are often highly divergent. These forms are ultimately rooted in the rural dialects of the Scottish Lowlands, which differ distinctly from the dialects south of the border: there is 'a greater bundling of isoglosses at the border between England and Scotland . . . than for a considerable distance on either side of the border (Macaulay 1978: 142). An **isogloss** represents the boundary line between areas where two different phonetic, syntactic or lexical forms are in use. The traditional rural dialects as well as their urban variations are collectively known as **Scots**.

Besides SSE and Scots, one further non-immigrant language is spoken in Scotland. That is Scottish Gaelic, a Celtic language related to both Welsh and Irish. At present only a minuscule part of the population speaks Gaelic, and they are located in the more remote regions of the northwest and on some of the islands (the Hebrides). Those who speak Gaelic are, in any case, bilinguals who also speak English, though their English is often influenced by their Gaelic substratum (see below 10.2.3). The Highlands, also rural, are an English-speaking area where Gaelic was directly displaced by English rather than Scots. All the languages of Scotland are documented in Mather and Speitel 1975–7.

10.2.2 Scots

Scots is frequently 'associated with slang or slovenly language or socially unacceptable speech forms' (Low 1975: 18). The language is undoubtedly widely used,

> yet social pressures against it are so strong that many people are reluctant to use it or have actively rejected it. . . . The only use of it made regularly by the media is for comedy. . . . [it] is repeatedly associated with what is trivial, ridiculous, and often vulgar.
>
> (McClure 1980: 12)

While this statement is valid, it is also necessary to note that there are several different types of Scots, each with a different status and prestige. The variety so often and so subjectively regarded as vulgar is urban working-class Scots; considerably more positive are the often romanticized rural dialects; a third type is literary Scots (sometimes termed **Lallans** 'Lowlands'). This final variety is also sometimes pejoratively referred to as synthetic Scots because it represents an artifical effort to re-establish a form of Scots as the national language of Scotland and as a language for Scottish literature (much as was the case before the Union of the Crowns in 1603, when James VI of Scotland became James I of England, which eventually resulted in a linguistic reorientation in Scotland towards England).

Scots is commonly subdivided into four regional groupings: **Central Scots**, which runs from West Angus and northeast Perthshire to Galloway in the southwest and the River Tweed in the southeast. As such the region contains both Glasgow and Edinburgh and includes over two-thirds of the population of Scotland. Central Scots is itself sometimes further subdivided into South Central, West Central and East Central. Furthermore, it includes the Scots areas of Ulster (see 10.3.2). **Southern Scots** is found in Roxburgh, Selkirk and East Dumfriesshire. **Northern Scots** goes from East Angus and the Mearns to Caithness. **Island Scots** is the variety in use on the Orkney and Shetland Islands. The Shetlands are further distinguished by the continued presence of numerous words which originated in Norn, the Scandanavian language once spoken in the islands (see map 10.1).

The situation of Scots *vis-à-vis* SSE may be usefully summarized in regard to its historicity, its standardization, its vitality and its autonomy, all of which are criteria useful in assessing language independence (Stewart 1962: 20; see Macafee 1981: 33–37 for aspects of the following).

The historicity of Scots as the descendant of Old Northumbrian is clearly given, and Scots is consequently a cousin of the English of the East Midlands of England, which was the basis of StE. Of course, Scots has been highly influenced by StE, not least in the form of the Authorized or King James Version of the Bible (1611). Perhaps it is the success of the English Bible which has inspired the various more recent translations of the

Scriptures into Scots (cf. various samples in *English World-Wide*: 1983). Lallans as a language with literary ambitions has drawn heavily on the older Scots language for much of its vocabulary, but this is not a natural process and the words it has adopted have no real currency, for few will seriously use *scrieve* rather than *write* or *leid* rather than *language*.

Standardization is the goal of the creators of Lallans, but the tendencies of its champions are to reject as vulgar the Scots forms which have the most vitality or actual currency in everyday speech, namely those of the urban working class. A limited amount of success within the Lallans effort has been achieved in the area of standardization of spelling (cf. *The Scots Style Sheet* 1974, originally 1947).

> For *good*, a Glaswegian says 'guid,' a Black Isle speaker 'geed,' A North-Easterner 'gweed,' and a man from Angus or the Eastern borders 'geud,' with the vowel of French *deux*, but each could readily associate the spelling *guid* with his own local pronunciation.
>
> (McClure 1980: 30)

In a similar fashion ⟨aa⟩ is widely accepted as the spelling of either Central Scots /ɔ/ or Northern /a/ as in *ataa* 'at all'. But note that the common word /ne/ 'not' is spelled either as ⟨na⟩ or as ⟨nae⟩.

The autonomy of the Scots dialects is, in general, present. This is probably least so in point of vocabulary, for virtually all Scots speakers have long since orientated themselves along the lines of English, even though Scots has retained numerous dialect words such as *chaft* 'jaw', *lass* 'girl', *ken* 'know' or *ilka* 'each, every'. The lack of a standard in Scots is also reflected in the fact that there is sometimes a variety of local words for the same things, for example, *bairn*, *wean*, *littlin*, *geet* 'child' or *callant*, *loon*, *chiel* 'boy', or *yett*, *grind* 'garden gate' (cf. Catford 1957: 110), without there being any generally recognized Scots word.

More divergent, and hence more autonomous, are some of the grammatical forms. Among these note, for example, such non-standard morphology as the past and past participle forms of the verb *bake*, viz. *beuk* and *baken*, or *wrocht* and *wrocht* from *work*. A few words also retain older plural forms: *coo* 'cow' plural *kyn* 'cows' (cf. English *kine*), *soo* 'pig' (cf. English *sow*) plural *swine* 'pigs', or *ee* 'eye' plural *een* 'eyes' (ibid.).

The second person pronoun often retains the singular–plural distinction either using *thou/du* vs. *ye/you* or *yi/you* vs. *yiz/youse*. In the Shetlands the distinction between polite *you* and more intimate *du* is made, and seems 'to be rigidly observed' (Melchers 1985: 93; see also 9.1.1). Melchers, investigating language attitudes in the Shetlands, was moved to remark:

> I occasionally experience moments of glory, when, during interviews, talking about exciting subjects such as the Scandanavian heritage or the

history of knitting patterns, informants turn to me with 'du kens [you know]'.

(ibid.: 99)

Instead of StE relative *whose* one may find *that his* or *that her*. Furthermore, the demonstratives comprise a three-way system: *this/that/yon* and *here/there/yonder* (Catford 1957: 110; also Murison 1977: 38–47). Prepositions beginning with *be-* in StE often begin with *a-* in Scots, so *afore*, *ahind*, *aneath*, *aside*, *ayont* and *atween* (Murison 1977). The verb is negated by adding *na(e)* to the auxiliary, for example, *hasna(e)*, *dinna(e)*. Furthermore, the auxiliaries are used differently; for example, *shall* is not present in Scots at all.

The syntax of Scots includes the possibility of an {-S} ending on the present tense verb for all persons as a special narrative tense form, for example, *I comes*, *we says*, etc. (Catford 1957: 110; Macafee 1983: 49f; cf. 12.4.3 for a similar feature in American Black English).

The pronunciation of Scots, finally, is also tremendously important in defining its autonomous character. Quite in contrast to the other varieties of English around the world, 'Scots dialects . . . invariably have a lexical distribution of phonemes which cannot be predicted from RP or from a Scottish accent [i.e. SSE]' (Catford 1957: 109). By way of illustration, note that the following words, all of which have the vowel /u/ in SSE, are realized with six different phonemes in the dialect of Angus: *book* /ʊ/, *bull* /ʌ/, *foot* /ɪ/, *boot* /ø/, *lose* /o/, *loose* /ʌʊ/ (ibid.: 110).

The following list enumerates some of the more notable features of Scots pronunciation:

1 /x/ in *night*, *daughter*;
2 /kn-/ in *knock*, *knee* (especially Northern Scots);
3 /vr-/ in *write*, *wrought/wrocht* (especially Northern Scots); Island Scots: /xr-/;
4 the convergence of /θ/ and /t/ to /t/ and of /ð/ and /d/ to /d/ in Island Scots (the Shetlands);
5 /uː/ in *house*, *out*, *now*; Southern Scots: /ʌu/ in word-final position;
6 /ø/ or /y/ in *moon*, *good*, *stool*; Northern Scots: /iː/;
7 /eː/ in *home*, *go*, *bone*; Northern Scots: /iː/;
8 /hw-/ in *what*, *when*, etc.; Northern Scots: /f-/.

In urban Scots many of the features listed are recessive, for example, /x/, /kn-/ or /vr-/. However, /hw/ is generally retained; furthermore, Scots remains firmly rhotic. Yet some younger speakers do merge /w/ and /hw/, and some also delete non-prevocalic /r/ (see Macafee 1983: 32; Romaine 1978). Glasgow English is a continuum with a variety of forms ranging from broad (rural) Scots to SSE. This involves a fair amount of code-switching, as the following exchange overheard in an Edinburgh tea room illustrates:

A: Yaize yer ain spuin.
B: What did ye say?
A: Ah said, Yaize yer ain spoon.
B: Oh, use me own spoon.

(from Aitken 1985: 42)

Often only certain lexical items retain a more traditional Scots pronunciation, while other words have an SSE realization. For example, the vowel /ɪ/ is found in the items *bloody*, *does* and *used*; /i/ in *bread*, *dead* and *head*; /u/ in *about*, *around*, *brown*, *cow*, etc; and /e/ in *do*, *home*, *no*, etc. (cf. Macafee 1983: 37f for these and other pronunciation features involving limited sets of lexemes different from RP). Furthermore, Glasgow speakers have lost much of the traditional vocabulary of Scots; in its place, so to speak, they have available an extensive slang vocabulary of varying provenance, for example, Scots *plunk* 'to play truant'; local Glasgow *heidbanger* 'lunatic'; BrE *sky* 'to leave hurriedly'; AmE *fuzz* 'police' (ibid.: 43).

Grammatical features of Glasgow English which differ from StE are a mixture of Scots forms such as verb negation using enclitic *-nae* or *-ny* (*isnae* 'isn't') and general non-standard forms which can be found throughout the English-speaking world (e.g. multiple negation, as in *canny leave nuthin alane* 'cannot leave anything alone').

10.2.3 Scottish Standard English (SSE)

StE in Scotland is virtually identical to StE anywhere else in the world. As elsewhere, SSE has its special national items of vocabulary. These may be general, such as *outwith* 'outside', *pinkie* 'little finger' or *doubt* 'think, suspect'; they may be culturally specific, such as *caber* 'a long and heavy wooden pole thrown in competitive sports, as at the Highland Games' or *haggis* 'sheep entrails prepared as a dish'; or they may be institutional, as with *sheriff substitute* 'acting sheriff' or *landward* 'rural'.

Syntactically, SSE shows only minor distinctions *vis-à-vis* other types of StE. For instance, in the colloquial language, the modal verb system differs inasmuch as *shall* and *ought* are not present, *must* is marginal for obligation, and *may* is rare (Miller and Brown 1982: 7–11).

SSE has its own distinct pronunciation, as is the case with all national or regional varieties of StE. Some of its features are similar to those of Scots: it maintains /x/, spelled ⟨ch⟩, in some words such as *loch* or *technical*. /hw/ and /w/ are distinct. /l/ is dark [ɫ] in all environments for most speakers, though it is clear everywhere for some speakers in areas where Gaelic was formerly (the Highlands) or still is spoken (the Hebrides); it is also clear in

Dumfries and Galloway in the southwest (Wells 1982: 411f). This variation in the pronunciation of /l/ is rooted in the fact that SSE includes two very different traditions. One of these is the Lowland Scots background which was discussed above (10.2.2). The other tradition is that of Gaelic as a **substratum**. This means that the phonetic habits of Gaelic are carried over to English. Depending on how immediate the influence of Gaelic is, there will be more or fewer instances of English influenced phonetically by it (cf. ibid.: 412–14).

Outsiders are often struck by the fact that the glottal stop [ʔ] is widespread for medial and final /t/ in the central Lowlands, including Glasgow and Edinburgh (for more detail, see ibid.: 409f). In Glasgow its use has been shown to vary with age, sex and social class, being more frequent among the young, among males, and in the working class (Macaulay 1977: 48). This is, therefore, arguably not a feature of speakers of SSE.

SSE is a rhotic accent, pronouncing /r/ wherever it is written. The articulation of the /r/ is sometimes rolled or trilled [r], sometimes flapped [ɾ], sometimes constricted [ɹ]; however, some speakers even have non-rhotic realizations (see Romaine 1978; Macafee 1983). Whatever the case, SSE differs considerably from other rhotic accents because it preserves the /e/ – /ɪ/ – /ʌ/ distinction before /r/ in words such as *heard – bird – word*, where in RP and GenAm these vowels have all merged to central /ɜ:/. Note, however, that there are a number of local differences within Scotland. Moreover, Scottish English also distinguishes between /o/ and /ɔ/ before /r/ as in *hoarse* and *horse* (Wells 1982: 407f).

The vowel system of SSE does not, on the other hand, maintain all the vowel contrasts of RP. Where the latter has /u:/ in *fool* and /ʊ/ in *full*, SSE has undifferentiated /u/ in both and often central [ʉ] or even fronted [ʏ]. Not quite as widespread is the loss of the contrast between /ɒ/ and /ɔ:/ (*not* vs. *nought*), and the opposition between /æ/ and /a:/ is missing as well, though even less frequently. It has been suggested that these three stand in an **implicational relationship**, which here means that whoever neutralizes /æ/ to /a:/ also neutralizes the other two pairs. And whoever loses the opposition between /ɒ/ and /ɔ:/ also loses that between /u/ and /u:/, but not necessarily the /æ/ to /a:/ one (cf. Abercrombie 1979; Wells 1982: 400–4).

Scottish English does not rely on vowel length differences as both RP and GenAm do. Length does not seem to be phonemic anywhere. However, there are interesting phonetic differences in length which have been formulated as **Aitken's Law**. According to this all the vowels except /ɪ/ and /ʌ/ are long in morphemically final position (for example, at the end of a root such as *brew*, but also at the end of the first morpheme in bimorphemic *brew* + *ed*). Vowels are also longer when followed by voiced fricatives, /v, ð, z/ and /r/. Because of this, *brewed* contrasts phonetically with *brood*, which has a shortened vowel (Wells 1982: 400f). Closely related to this are the differing qualities of the vowels in *tied* and *tide*. The former is bimorphemic *tie + ed* with /ae/. The latter is a single morpheme in which the vowel is not followed by one of the consonants which causes lengthening; it has the vowel /ʌɪ/ (ibid.: 405f; see also Aitken 1984: 94–100).

10.3 Ireland

Ireland is divided both politically and linguistically, and, interestingly enough, the linguistic and the political borders lie close together. Northern Ireland (the six counties of Antrim, Armagh, Down, Fermanagh, Londonderry and Tyrone), with a population of approximately one and a half million, is politically a part of the United Kingdom, while the remaining twenty-six counties form the Republic of Ireland (population of about three and a half million). Although Irish English (IrE), which is sometimes called Hiberno-English, shows a number of standard features throughout the island, there are also a number of very noticeable differences (see 10.3.2 and 10.3.4). Most of these stem from fairly clear historical causes. The northern counties, for example, are characterized by the presence of Scots forms. These originated in the large-scale settlement of the north by people from the Scottish Lowlands and the simultaneous displacement of many of the native Irish following Cromwell's subjection of the island in the middle of the seventeenth century. In what is now the Republic a massive change from the Irish language (a Celtic language related to Welsh and Scottish Gaelic) began around the year 1800. The type of English which became established there stems from England and not Scotland, and shows some signs of earlier settlement in the southeast by people from the West Midlands of England. Most characteristic of southern IrE, however, are the numerous features in it which reflect the influence of Irish as the substratum language. In a few areas in the west called the Gaeltacht, Irish is still spoken; and Irish is the Republic's official language (English is the second official language). The percentage of population who actually speak Irish is, however, very low (around 2 per cent).

10.3.1 Northern Ireland

The split in Ireland as a whole is reflected once again within Ulster (the historical province), which is partly in the Republic (the three counties of Cavan, Donegal and Monaghan) and partly in Northern Ireland. The population of Northern Ireland itself is divided very much along confessional lines, approximately one-third Roman Catholic (the Republic is over 90 per cent Catholic) and two-thirds Protestant. This, too, reflects the historical movement of people to and within Ireland. The northern and eastern parts of the province are heavily Scots and Protestant; the variety of English spoken there is usually referred to as Ulster Scots or, sometimes, Scotch-

Irish. Further to the south and west the form is called Mid-Ulster English, and its features increasingly resemble those of English in the South as one moves in that direction, with South Ulster English as a transitional accent.

The same split, but also new, mixed or compromise forms, can be observed in Belfast, which with approximately half a million people is the largest city in the North and second only to Dublin in all of Ireland. Although there is a great and ever growing tendency towards sectarian residential patterns, speech forms in the city as a whole are merging (Barry 1984: 120). Harris, for example, states: 'The vowel phonology of Mid Ulster English can be viewed as an accommodation of both Ulster Scots and south Ulster English systems' (Harris 1984: 125). Phonetically, however, there are distinct Ulster Scots and South Ulster English allophones in Belfast. One of the most potent reasons advanced for the increasing levelling of speech forms is the weakening of complex (**'multiplex'**) social networks (with shared family, friends, workmates, leisure time activities). Especially in the middle class, where there is more geographical mobility, and in those parts of the working class where unemployment has attenuated some social contacts, there is a move away from complex local norms and distinctions, one of which is shared language norms (cf. Milroy 1991: 83f). The practical consequence in Belfast of the interplay of socio-economic patterns, regional origin and social networks of varying complexity is a zig-zag pattern of linguistic variants representing reality in which there is no unambiguous agreement on prestige models of speech (whether overt or covert; see 8.2.3). Furthermore, political affiliations (pro-British unionists vs. Republican nationalists), especially where residence patterns, schooling and place of work are so highly segregated, help to reinforce the fact that 'unionists and nationalists simply do not share the same set of prestige linguistic norms' (Harris 1991: 46; cf. Todd 1984).

10.3.2 Characteristics of English in Northern Ireland

Northern Ireland has a number of distinct speech areas (see map 10.2). These are reviewed in Gregg 1972; Harris 1984 and 1985; and Barry 1984. In the north and the east there is a band of Scots speech areas running from County Down through Antrim and Londonderry to Donegal. Its linguistic features are similar to those described above in 10.2.2, including Aitken's Law. Notably different is the lack of dark [ł] (see Harris 1985: 18–33 for more detail). Generally to the south of these areas comes Mid-Ulster English, which is also the variety spoken in Belfast. In the very south of Ulster there is what has been called South Ulster English; it is a 'transitional dialect' (Harris 1984: 118) between Ulster English and Ulster Scots and southern Hiberno-English (see below 10.3.4). The differences between these varieties are especially noticeable in their vowel phonologies, which are compared in Harris (1984: 118–29 and 1985: chapter 1). Harris (1985: 10)

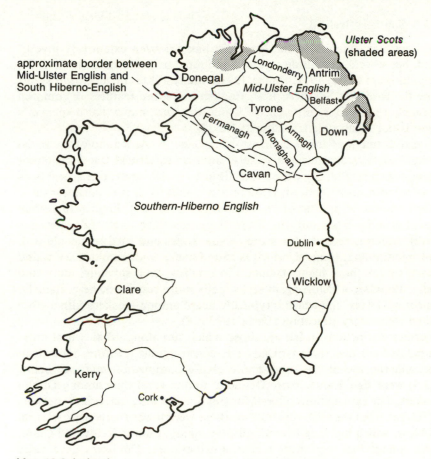

approximate border between
Mid-Ulster English and
South Hiberno-English

Ulster Scots
(shaded areas)

Londonderry
Donegal
Antrim
Mid-Ulster English
Belfast
Tyrone
Fermanagh
Monaghan
Armagh
Down
Cavan

Southern-Hiberno English

Dublin •

Wicklow

Clare

Kerry

Cork •

Map 10.2 Ireland

also emphasizes that the phonetic conditioning of vowel length in the Scots varieties as opposed to the phonemic length of the English varieties is mixed in Mid-Ulster English and Belfast Vernacular, 'the dialect upon which the regional standard pronunciation is based' (ibid.: 15). Belfast has also introduced some innovations, for example, more instances of dark [ɫ], the loss of the /w/ – /hw/ distinction, and some glottalization of voiceless stops before sonorants (*bottle* [bɑʔ(t)l̩]. Ulster Scots has considerably more glottaling. Belfast also has local forms for *mother*, *brother*, etc., without the medial /ð/ as in ['brɔ̃ər] (see especially Harris 1984: 130f).

Among the specifically northern grammatical forms the best known is probably the use of the second person plural pronoun *youse*. For other points, see Harris 1984: 131–3.

10.3.3 Southern Ireland

The linguistic situation in the Republic has not been extensively investigated, but several local studies have contributed useful insights (Bertz 1975; Filppula 1991; Henry 1957; Kallen 1991; Lunny 1981). In general, it seems to be the case that Southern Irish English has more features in common regionally than it does differences, which does not mean that a speaker's origin is not localizable (cf. Bliss 1977: 18f).

Social distinctions are, in contrast, much clearer. At the top of the social pyramid there is an educated variety, sometimes termed the **Ascendancy accent**, which is relatively close to RP (ibid.: 17). However, this accent does not serve as a norm. Indeed, if there is a standard of pronunciation, it is likely to be based on that of Dublin (Harris 1991: 39). English in Dublin is, of course, far from uniform. Bertz recognizes three levels: **Educated** (see above), which is reserved for more formal styles and used by people with academic training; **General**, which is found over a wide range of styles and is used by the more highly trained (journalists, civil servants, etc.); and finally, **Popular**, which is again stylistically more restricted, here, namely, to informal levels, and which is typically heard among speakers with a more limited elementary education (Bertz 1975: 78).

Further distinctions in IrE are those which run along urban—rural lines. Filppula found that three typically IrE constructions (clefting, topicalization, and the use of the subordinate clause conjunction *and*; see below 10.3.4) were significantly more frequent among rural than among Dublin speakers. The explanations offered for this are, for one, that urban speakers are farther from the Irish substratum: there were lower frequencies in rural Wicklow, which has long been English-speaking, than in Kerry and Clare, where change has been more recent. Furthermore, Dubliners have more contacts with the non-Irish English-speaking outside world (Filppula 1991: 58f).

10.3.4 Characteristics of English in the South

The most general characterization of IrE in the Republic is given by Bliss:

> In the pronunciation and vocabulary of southern Hiberno-English it is possible to trace the influence both of older strata of the English language and of the Irish language; in grammar, syntax and idiom the peculiarities of southern Hiberno-English depend exclusively on the Irish language.
>
> (Bliss 1984: 150)

Pronunciation In the area of the vowels there is phonemic identity with RP which is disturbed only by the fact that IrE, which is rhotic, does not have the centring diphthongs. Nor does it have /ɜː/, since words in RP with it, such as *purr*, are phonemically analysed in IrE as /ʌr/ (cf. Wells 1982: 420). The fact that there is such overall phonemic agreement between IrE and RP does not, of course, mean that the two actually sound alike. For one thing, the vowels of *gate* and *goat* are commonly the monophthongs /eː/ and /oː/. For another, the distribution of particular phonemes in various words may often differ. It is stereotypical of IrE, for example, to render a large number of words spelled with ⟨ea⟩ and pronounced in RP and GenAm as /iː/ with /eː/ in IrE: for example, *tea*, *meat*, *easy* and also *Jesus*. In addition, /ʌ/ and /ʊ/ are distributed in different and unpredictable ways so that /ʊ/ may occur in words such as *mother*, *sup* or *cut*. In addition, there is reportedly a great deal of variation between /ɒ/ and /ɔː/ in such words as *cross*, *loss*, *lost*, *often*, *cost*. Also /ɪ/ and /e/ regularly merge before a nasal so that *pin* = *pen*.

The actual quality of further vowels may differ markedly. /ɒ/ is usually unrounded [ɑ], more like the GenAm realization than the RP version. /æ/ is more open [a], and /ʌ/ is further back [ɔ̈]. The diphthongs /aɪ/ and /aʊ/ tend to have higher initial elements: [əɪ] and [əʊ], respectively; and /ɔɪ/ is not distinguished from /aɪ/ in all environments by all speakers. For more on the pronunciation of the vowels, see Bertz 1975; Bliss 1984; Wells 1982.

The twenty-four consonants of RP and GenAm are matched by twenty-two in some varieties and the full twenty-four in others. The difference of two lies in the fact that, for many speakers (in Cork and parts of Dublin), /θ/ and /ð/ have merged with /t/ and /d/ respectively. Most speakers, however, distinguish these phonemes, even though the distinction may not be recognizable to non-Irish ears: /t/ is articulated at the alveolar ridge while /θ/ is commonly dental [t̪], sometimes the affricate [tθ], and, in more sophisticated speech, [θ]; in the same fashion /d/ is alveolar, and /ð/ is [d̪] as well as [dð] and [ð]. The general lack of phonetic [θ] and [ð] as well as the split between dental and alveolar-palatal /t/ and /d/ can be attributed to the influence of the phonology of Irish. Furthermore, a final /t/ (sometimes even a prevocalic /t/) may be realized as a voiceless alveolar slit fricative [t̝] as in *hit* [hɪt̝]. This is regarded as particularly conspicuous of IrE. Note that intervocalic /t/ may be flapped and voiced [d̯] (as in GenAm) or even [ɾ], or it may be glottalized [ʔ] (as in much popular urban speech in England and Scotland) (Wells 1982: 428–31). Indeed, there seems to be increasing influence from urban British usage owing to the great amount of emigration to Britain (with the consequent return visits in Ireland) and also to a certain amount of permanent resettlement in Ireland after a period of work in Great Britain (Harris 1991: 45).

In IrE the two palatal stops /k/ and /g/ are differentiated into the velar allophones [k] and [g] and the more palatal ones [kj] and [gj], as in [kjar] *car* or [gjardən] *garden*, in some of the more conservative accents. The 'palatalized' realizations are conditioned by a following front vowel and hence correspond to the phonotactic regularities of Irish. Another instance of the influence of Irish phonology in IrE is the realization of /w/ as a voiced bilabial fricative [ß]. For much the same reason, IrE, both southern and northern, has a clear [l] everywhere. In words borrowed from Irish, /x/ may be retained (*Taoiseach* 'Prime Minister' [ţiːʃəx]) (Wells 1982: 433f; Bliss 1984: 138f).

A final interesting example of the influence of the substratum on pronunciation is the carry-over of what might be called consonant harmony within consonant clusters. In Irish the last consonant in a cluster determines whether the cluster as a whole will be made up of palatalized or unpalatalized consonants. In this sense the following consonants of IrE count as palatal: /t, d, ʃ, ʒ, n, l/, and the following as non-palatal: /ţ, ḑ, s, z, r/. Concretely this means that a cluster such as /str/ (*strong*) will be non-palatal because of cluster-final /r/. /s/ is already non-palatal and is unproblematic, but /t/ is palatal and will therefore be realized as [ţ], thus producing [sţraŋ]. Most non-Irish will not notice this, but more obvious is the following case: /l/ and /n/ and /t/ are palatal, hence a preceding /s/ in, say, *slow* or *snow* or *stop* must be palatal /ʃ/. The result is [ʃloː] and [ʃnoː] and [ʃtap]. For this explanation and these examples, see Bliss 1984: 138f. For more details on the consonants, see Wells 1982. There is little information available about the supra-segmental features of IrE.

Vocabulary The vast majority of words in IrE are identical to those in other varieties of StE. In non-standard usage, however, IrE does include a number of words which represent older or regional usage in Great Britain or which reflect the effects of the Irish substratum. Examples of older items are *cog* 'to cheat in an exam', *airy* 'gay, light-hearted', or *bowsey* 'a disreputable drunkard'; instances of dialect words are *kink* 'spasm of laughter or coughing' or *blather* 'to talk nonsense at length'; illustrations of words borrowed from Irish are found in *spalpeen* 'rascal' or *sleeveen* 'sly fellow'. The ending *-een* comes from Irish and is a diminutive frequently added to words for something small or young as in *girleen* 'a small or young girl' (for these and more examples, see Bliss 1984: 140–3).

Idioms and other expressions are frequently translations of Irish ways of saying things. The directions of the compass can therefore be *above* ('north') and *below* ('south'), *back* ('west') and *over* ('east') (Barry 1984: 109). The fact that Irish *fiadh* means both 'deer' and 'God', together with the fact that English has both the expressions *Oh dear* and *Oh God*, makes the IrE extension *The Dear knows* 'God knows' all the more easy to use (Bliss 1984: 142).

Grammar In this area the influence of the substratum is once again obvious: 'Southern Hiberno-English has precisely the same range of tenses as

Irish has, but the forms are built up out of English material' (ibid.: 143). This means that the present perfect for reference to the recent past is periphrastically realized as the preposition *after* + an *-ing* form of the verb, as in *All the week it's after being cold*. This construction is, of course, not employed to the exclusion of the StE form. In a study of Dublin usage, the *after* construction appeared to be used most frequently in friendly encounters among family and acquaintances (Kallen 1991).

Another important consequence of the fact that IrE is modelled so closely on Irish is that the progressive is more widely used than in standard BrE or AmE. The restriction of the progressive to dynamic predicators is, as a result, not so absolute, as in *Who is this book belonging to?* (Bliss 1984: 144).

The use of habitual tense-aspect forms (the **consuetudinal**) is an expansion of the StE system. This provides for *I do be* ('I usually am') next to simple *I am* ('I am right now'). This can be extended to all the verb forms, including *He bees writing* or *He does be writing* 'He usually writes' (ibid.: 143f).

Sentence structure also differs at various points. IrE does not, for example, dictate changed word order in indirect questions (*They asked when would you be back*), nor is *if* or *whether* necessary to report *yes–no* questions (*I wonder does she honestly mean it*) (examples from ibid.: 148).

Several structures which are particularly Irish include changes in theme-rheme structure (cf. 4.4.4). For one thing this involves the relatively frequent use of fronting of elements to topicalize them (*A pastime he used to have*). Even more well known is the use of clefting, very much parallel to usage in Irish, to bring an element into topic position, as in *It's looking for more land a lot of them are*. Filppula (1991) found both to be common in all the areas he investigated (Counties Kerry and Clare; County Wicklow; Dublin), but more common in the rural areas where, in comparison with Dublin, the influence of Irish is still strong.

The use of *and* with the effect of a subordinating conjunction is frequently found. How the conjunction is to be interpreted depends very much on the context, but usually it is temporal. In *He fell and him crossing the bridge* the effect is the same as that of *as* or *when*. Filppula, who investigated this construction as well as clefting and fronting, found that it is rarer than the other two (ibid.: 57).

IrE is further characterized by the extensive use that it makes of prepositions on the model of Irish. Possession is expressed by the verb *be* plus *on*, *at*, *near* or *by* (*There weren't any candles by this man* 'he didn't have any'; *It was a custom by them to go out on Christmas Eve* 'it was their custom . . .'; *It is not any common sickness that is on him* 'he doesn't have any . . .'). Existence is also expressed this way (*Sure there's no daylight in it at all now* 'there's none left'). A third typical use of prepositions is the dative of interest with *on* (*He was murdered on me one St Patrick's Day fair* 'this happened to me'). For these and other examples, see Bliss 1984: 149f; Barry 1984: 108).

10.4 Urban British English

Throughout this chapter the English of a number of cities has been referred to. These varieties have enjoyed increasing attention from linguists in the past couple of decades. Some of the better-known investigations have had to do with Norwich in East Anglia (Trudgill 1974), Glasgow (Macaulay 1977) and Belfast (Milroy 1981). Milroy (1984) and Cheshire (1991) provide very useful overviews of the work done. Urban language surveys have not only provided a great deal of systematic, empirical data, they have also helped to advance insights into how people identify linguistically and into some of the roles which language plays in modern urban society. Among the general conclusions which can be drawn from the work that has been done are the following.

1 Urban accents are related to the pronunciations of the regions in which they are situated, sometimes with a high degree of koineization.
2 There are relatively few local lexical items.
3 Non-standard grammatical features are often shared over a wide geographic range (nationally or even internationally).
4 Phonetic features are most suited as social indicators (class, gender, age).
5 Social indicators are most visible for pronunciations currently involved in change.
6 Phonetic realization is highly responsive to speech style (word list style, reading style, interview style, casual conversation).
7 Stigmatized pronunciations are most subject to variation according to style since they are most closely monitored.
8 Social indicators are based on relative differences in frequency rather than absolutely different variants.
9 Pronunciation change comes either from above (the overt norm) via the middle class or from below (the covert norm) via the working class.
10 Middle-class women are most often leaders in change towards the overt norm; working-class men are most often the initiators of changes towards the covert norm.

Discussion of some of these aspects is to be found in 8.2.3. In the remaining pages of the present chapter a short sketch of one urban variety, Cockney, will be attempted and a look at the role of ethnicity in language will also be undertaken in connection with British Black English.

10.4.1 Cockney

Of all the urban varieties of English in the British Isles, Cockney is doubtlessly the best known, not least because of its use in *My Fair Lady*. What it refers to may be more broadly or more narrowly defined. Traditionally, a Cockney is an inhabitant of London's East End. But, from the point of view of language, Cockney or near-Cockney can be heard throughout the city. In general, it is a working-class accent, and as such it has little or no overt prestige. Its covert prestige is, however, enormous. In the form of it which Wells describes under the label London English, it 'is today the most influential source of phonological innovation in England and perhaps in the whole English-speaking world' (Wells 1982: 301).

The grammar of Cockney is basically of the non-standard vernacular type sketched out in 10.1.2. Its vocabulary is equally unexceptional. However, it is well known for its **rhyming slang**. This is not an exclusively Cockney feature, nor is it typical of the everyday speech of most Cockneys. But it does help to contribute to the image of Cockney as colourful. In rhyming slang a word is replaced by a pair of words, the second of which rhymes with the one replaced. For example, *my wife* may disappear in favour of *my trouble and strife* or, more positively, *my fork and knife*. The new pair is often shortened so that someone may say *Use your loaf* instead of *Use your loaf of bread*; both mean the same: *Use your head*. The expression *Let's get down to brass tacks* ('Let's get down to business') is originally rhyming slang (*brass tacks = the facts*), though few people realize this. For more examples, see Barltrop and Wolveridge 1980; Franklyn 1960; Wright 1981. Sivertsen 1960 provides a detailed phonetic description of Cockney; Wells 1982: 301–34 is extremely useful; Hughes and Trudgill 1979: 39–43 offer a brief characterization with an accompanying recording.

What is most distinctive about Cockney is its pronunciation, and what is significant about this is the fact that Cockney pronunciations have often indicated the way in which RP would itself eventually develop. This does not mean, of course, that RP will indeed adopt all of the points which are sketched out below. Many of them are so highly stigmatized that their adoption in RP and near-RP varieties is, in many cases, nigh inconceivable in the immediate future (H-dropping, Cockney vowels, the glottal stop, etc.).

Among the consonants, Cockney is characterized by H-dropping, as just mentioned. While the spelling ⟨h⟩ at the beginning of words such as *hour* and *honour* is never pronounced in any standard variety and while its pronunciation in some items is variable (*hotel*, *herb*, *human*) depending on the region or the individual, there are no limits in Cockney on the words beginning with ⟨h-⟩ which may sometimes occur without /h/, for example, *'ouse* for *house* (see also 3.3.4).

The voiceless stops /p, t, k/ are frequently more strongly aspirated than in RP or GenAm. They are affricates in some cases: [tˢəɪ] (*tea*) or [kˣoʊ] (*call*). Furthermore, in final position the same stops may have glottal coarticulation, i.e. a glottal stop just before the oral one, e.g.

[εʔt] (*hat*). It is also possible for the glottal stop to replace /p, t, k/ completely. This could lead to a loss of the distinctions between *whip*, *wit* and *wick*, all as [wɪʔ] (Wells 1982: 323). In addition, intervocalic /t/ may be realized as tapped [ɾ] or as the glottal stop. The former is making inroads into RP; the latter is found in numerous urban dialects in Great Britain (but seldom in Ireland).

The fricatives /θ/ and /ð/ are very frequently, but not exclusively, pronounced as /f/ and /v/ respectively, i.e. *three free* and *mother* rhymes with *lover*. One exception is that initial /ð/ is not realized as /v/; instead /d/ may be used (*these* = *D's*) (ibid.: 328–30).

Following /t, d, n/, Cockney may have /uː/ instead of /juː/ (*tune* = *toon*, *dune* = *doon*, *news* = *noos*). In the case of /t/ and /d/ there seems to be a switch in progress towards /j/ and then a palatalized form, for example, /t/ + /j/ → /tʃ/ (*Tuesday* = *Chewsday*) (ibid.: 330f).

One last point about the consonants is the vocalization of /l/ (see 3.2). Here words such as *milk* may be pronounced with new diphthongs, as in [mɪʊk]. The same sort of thing is happening in Australia and New Zealand (cf. 13.1.1 and 13.2.1) and in the American South.

The traditional complex vowels (long vowels and diphthongs) of Cockney are noticeably different from their RP and GenAm equivalents. Those which are front or have a front second element in RP start at a progressively lower or more greatly backed position, (see figure 10.1). Those which are back or have a back second element in RP start at a progressively lower or more fronted position, (see figure 10.2). One of the consequences of these shifts in articulation is that RP *light* sounds virtually the same as Cockney *late* (figures adapted from Wells 1982: 308, 310).

Figure 10.1 Cockney diphthongs with a front second element in comparison with RP

Figure 10.2 Cockney diphthongs with a back second element in comparison with RP

10.4.2 British Black English

Since the early 1960s the ethnic make-up of most British cities has changed enormously. High levels of immigration from Commonwealth countries which are not primarily ethnically European has produced a 'multicultural Britain'. As positive as *multicultural* sounds on paper, the reality has been different. Prejudice and discrimination, subtle and open, have prevented the full assimilation of many of these 'New Commonwealth citizens'. While it is presumptuous to assume that these immigrants and their children want to become replicas of the English people around them, economic integration requires a command of General English. This means that there are two forces pulling on them. The one is towards General English, be it StE or the local vernacular; the other is towards an ethnic variety – Jamaican Creole, Bajan or some other **'patois'**).

For the most part, a koineized form of West Indian Creole is used by second generation British blacks. It resembles Jamaican Creole more closely than it does the Eastern Caribbean varieties. Although it differs from Jamaican Creole in avoiding many of the 'deeper' creole forms (cf. Sutcliffe 1984: 220–9), it has an overall resemblance to the Caribbean creoles treated in 12.7 and 16.3.1. For a more detailed linguistic characterization see Sutcliffe 1982: chapter 4; Sutcliffe 1984: 220–9; Wells 1973 is an early study of the pronunciation of Jamaicans living in London.

Sebba reports that there is 'considerable peer-group pressure' on young black males to learn the creole (Sebba 1986: 156). However, just what the nature of London Jamaican (Sebba) or British Jamaican Creole (Sutcliffe) is does not meet with agreement. Sebba thinks London Jamaican is nothing more than 'a set of rules applied to a London English "base" to "convert" London English to London Jamaican' (Sebba 1986: 160). Sutcliffe, in contrast, speaks of British Jamaican Creole as having 'its own grammatical stability and separate integrity' (Sutcliffe 1984: 231).

In any case, Britons of West Indian origin experience the same sort of phenomenon as many working-class whites: overt norm or covert norm? There are, however, some essential differences. One is the greater number of choices the black Briton faces.

To what extent the children of West Indian immigrants are Creole or General English speakers has not been clearly established (see discussion in Sutcliffe 1984: 231). What does seem fairly clear, however, is that most of these people speak the English vernacular of their region regularly and the patois only on certain occasions, but that the majority can speak patois if they wish. In regard to young London blacks, Sebba writes:

> . . . most of them are, first and foremost, speakers of London English. Among women nearly all conversation seems to be carried on in London English except in certain, reasonably well defined, circumstances, when Creole is used. Among males the situation is different. . . . In formal situations, such as at school and when white people are present, London English is likely to be used.

> (Sebba 1986: 151)

Furthermore, various investigators have suggested that the vernacular as spoken by black Britons is hardly different from that of their white peers. Yet the few differences which do crop up may be particularly significant as markers of identity (cf. Edwards 1986: 131). Sutcliffe calls this variety, located between the creole and the English vernacular, British Black English; Sebba uses the term Afro-Caribbean London English. Both seem to agree that the differences are small. One of these possibly lies in something in the tone of voice which has not been further defined (Sebba 1986: 152). A particularly indicative syntactic item is the use of *se* after verbs of speech and cognition in the manner of English *that* (*A all white jury found out se 'e was guilty*).

Young blacks may indulge in code-switching involving the vernacular and the patois. Since their interlocutors often understand both codes, the question is why they do this. Sebba suggests that 'code-switching is used as a strategic and narrative device, as well as an additional resource for conveying affective meaning, i.e. for giving information about the attitude or state of mind of the speaker' (Sebba 1986: 164). A switch may serve to show solidarity or distance, to mark off speech acts, to report speech, to frame a narrative (vernacular) or to create a black narrative persona (patois) (ibid.: 163–7; for a different view, see Sutcliffe 1982: 147–58).

REFERENCES

Abercrombie, D. (1979) 'The accents of standard English in Scotland', in A. J. Aitken and T. McArthur (eds) *Languages of Scotland*, Edinburgh: Chambers, pp. 68–84.

Aitken, A. J. (1980) 'New Scots: the problems', in J. D. McClure, A. J. Aitken and J. T. Low, *The Scots Language: Planning for Modern Usage*, Edinburgh: Ramsay Head, pp. 45–63.

—— (1984) 'Scottish accents and dialects', in P. Trudgill (ed.) *Language in the British Isles*, Cambridge: Cambridge University Press, pp. 94–114.

—— (1985) 'Is Scots a language?', *English Today* 3 (July): 41–5.

Barltrop, R. and Wolveridge, J. (1980) *The Muvver Tongue*, London: Journeyman.

Barry, M. V. (1984) 'The English language in Ireland', in R. W. Bailey and M. Görlach (eds) *English as a World Language*, Cambridge: Cambridge University Press, pp. 84–133.

Bertz, S. (1975) *Der Dubliner Stadtdialekt*, Dissertation, University of Freiburg.

Bliss, A. (1977) 'The emergence of modern English dialects in Ireland', in D. ÓMuirithe (ed.) *The English Language in Ireland*, Dublin: Mercier, pp. 7–19.

—— (1984) 'English in the South of Ireland', in P. Trudgill (ed.) *Language in the British Isles*, Cambridge: Cambridge University Press, pp. 135–51.

Catford, J. C. (1957) 'The linguistic survey of Scotland', *Orbis* 6: 105–21.

Cheshire, J. (1991) 'The UK and the USA', in J. Cheshire (ed.) *English around the World: Sociolinguistic Perspectives*, Cambridge: Cambridge University Press, pp. 13–34.

Coupland, C. H. (1990) *English in Wales*, Clevedon: Multilingual Matters.

Edwards, V. (1986) *Language in a Black Community*, Clevedon: Multilingual Matters.

English World-Wide (1983) 'In Memoriam John Thomas Low' (4): 85–91.

Filppula, M. (1991) 'Urban and rural varieties of Hiberno-English', in J. Cheshire (ed.) *English around the World: Sociolinguistic Perspectives*, Cambridge: Cambridge University Press, pp. 51–60.

Franklyn, J. (1960) *A Dictionary of Rhyming Slang*, London: Routledge & Kegan Paul.

Giles, H. (1990) 'Social meanings of Welsh English', in N. Coupland (ed.) *English in Wales*, Clevedon: Multilingual Matters, pp. 258–82.

Giles, H. and Powesland, P. F. (1975) *Speech Style and Social Evaluation*, London: Academic.

Giles, H., Coupland, N., Henwood, K., Harriman, J. and Coupland, J. (1990) 'The social meaning of RP: an intergenerational perspective', in S. Ramsaran (ed.) *Studies in the Pronunciation of English*, London: Routledge, pp. 191–211.

Gimson, A. C. (1980) *An Introduction to the Pronunciation of English*, 3rd edn., London: Edward Arnold.

Glauser, B. (1991) 'Transition areas versus focal areas in English dialectology', *English World-Wide* 12: 1–24.

Gregg, R. J. (1972) 'The Scotch-Irish dialect boundaries in Ulster', in M. F. Wakelin (ed.) *Patterns in the Folk Speech of the British Isles*, London: Athlone, pp. 109–39.

Grieg, J. Y. T. (1928) *Breaking Priscian's Head: English as She Will be Spoke and Wrote*, London: Kegan Paul, Trench, Trubner.

Harris, J. (1984) 'English in the North of Ireland', in P. Trudgill (ed.) *Language in the British Isles*, Cambridge: Cambridge University Press, pp. 115–34.

—— (1985) *Phonological Variation and Change: Studies in Hiberno-English*, Cambridge: Cambridge University Press.

—— (1991) 'Ireland', in J. Cheshire (ed.) *English around the World: Sociolinguistic Perspectives*, Cambridge: Cambridge University Press, pp. 37–50.

Henry, P. L. (1957) *An Anglo-Irish Dialect of North Roscommon*, Dublin: University College.

Honey, J. (1989) *Does Accent Matter?*, London: Faber & Faber (2nd edn 1991).

Hughes, A. and Trudgill, P. (1979) *English Accents and Dialects*, London: Edward Arnold.

Jones, B. M. (1990) 'Welsh influence on children's English', in N. Coupland (ed.) *English in Wales*, Clevedon: Multilingual Matters, pp. 195–231.

Jones, D. (1967) *Everyman's English Pronouncing Dictionary*, ed. A. C. Gimson, London: Dent.

Kallen, J. L. (1991) 'Sociolinguistic variation and methodology: *after* as a Dublin variable', in J. Cheshire (ed.) *English around the World: Sociolinguistic Perspectives*, Cambridge: Cambridge University Press, pp. 61–74.

Kolb, E., Glauser, B., Elmer, W. and Stamm, R. (1979) *Atlas of English Sounds*, Berne: Francke.

Lewis, J. W. (1990) '*HappY* land reconnoitred: the unstressed word-final -y vowel in General British pronunciation', in S. Ramsaran (ed.) *Studies in the Pronunciation of English*, London: Routledge, pp. 159–67.

Low, J. T. (1975) 'The Scots language: the contemporary situation', in J. D. McClure (ed.) *Scots Language in Education*, Aberdeen: Association for Scottish Literary Studies, Occasional Papers 3: 17–27.

Lunny, A. (1981) 'Linguistic interaction: English and Irish in Ballyvourney, West Cork', in M. V. Barry (ed.) *Aspects of English Dialects in Ireland*, Belfast: Institute of Irish Studies, pp. 118–41.

Macafee, C. (1981) 'Nationalism and the Scots renaissance now', *English World-Wide* 2: 29–38.

—— (1983) *Glasgow*, Amsterdam: Benjamins.

Macaulay, R. K. S. (1977) *Language, Social Class and Education: a Glasgow Study*, Edinburgh: Edinburgh University Press.

—— (1978) 'Variation and consistency in Glaswegian English', in P. Trudgill (ed.) *Sociolinguistic Patterns in British English*, London: Edward Arnold, pp. 132–43.

McClure, J. D. (1980) 'Developing Scots as a national language', in J. D. McClure, A. J. Aitken and J. T. Low, *The Scots Language: Planning for Modern Usage*, Edinburgh: Ramsay Head, pp. 11–14.

Mather, J. Y. and Speitel, H. H. (eds) (1975–7) *The Linguistic Atlas of Scotland*, London: Croom Helm.

Melchers, G. (1985) '"Knappin", "proper English", "modified Scottish": some language attitudes in the Shetland Islands', in M. Görlach (ed.) *Focus on: Scotland*, Amsterdam: Benjamins, pp. 87–100.

Miller, J. and Brown, K. (1982) 'Aspects of Scottish English syntax', *English World-Wide* 3: 3–17.

Milroy, J. (1981) *Regional Accents of English: Belfast*, Belfast: Blackstaff.

—— (1991) 'The interpretation of social constraints on variation in Belfast English', in J. Cheshire (ed.) *English around the World: Sociolinguistic Perspectives*, Cambridge: Cambridge University Press, pp. 75–85.

Milroy, L. (1984) 'Urban dialects in the British Isles', in P. Trudgill (ed.) *Language in the British Isles*, Cambridge: Cambridge University Press, pp. 199–218.

Murison, C. (1977) *The Guid Scots Tongue*, Edinburgh: William Blackwood.

Orton, H., Halliday, W. J., Barry, M. V., Tilling, P. M. and Wakelin, M. F. (eds) (1962–71) *Survey of English Dialects*, Leeds: E. J. Arnold.

Orton, H. and Wright, N. (1974) *A Word Geography of England*, London: Seminar.

Orton, H., Sanderson, S. and Widdowson, J. (1978) *The Linguistic Atlas of England*, London: Croom Helm.

Parry, D. (1972) 'Anglo-Welsh Dialects in South-West Wales', in M. Wakelin (ed.) *Patterns in the Folk Speech of the British Isles*, London: Athlone, pp. 140–63.

Parry, D. (1977, 1979) *The Survey of Anglo-Welsh Dialects*, Vol. 1, *The South-east*. Vol. 2, *The South-west*, Swansea: David Perry.

Philp, A. M. (1970) *Attitudes to Correctness in English*, London: Longman.

Ramsaran, S. (1990) 'RP: fact *and* fiction', in S. Ramsaran (ed.) *Studies in the Pronunciation of English*, London: Routledge, pp. 178–90.

Romaine, S. (1978) 'Postvocalic /r/ in Scottish English: sound change in progress?', in P. Trudgill (ed.) *Sociolinguistic Patterns in British English*, London: Edward Arnold, pp. 144–57.

Russ, C. V. J. (1984) 'The geographical and social variation of English in England and Wales', in R. W. Bailey and M. Görlach (eds) *English as a World Language*, Cambridge: Cambridge University Press, pp. 11–55.

The Scots Style Sheet (1974) *Lallans* 2: 4–5.

Sebba, M. (1986) 'London Jamaican and black London English', in D. Sutcliffe and A. Wong (eds) *The Language of Black Experience*, Oxford: Blackwell, pp. 149–67.

Sivertsen, E. (1960) *Cockney Phonology*, Oslo: Olso University Press.

Stewart, W. A. (1962) 'An outline of linguistic typology for describing multilingualism', in F. A. Rice (ed.) *A Study of the Role of Second Languages in Asia, Africa, and Latin America*, Washington: Center for Applied Linguistics, pp. 15–25.

Sutcliffe, D. (1982) *British Black English*, Oxford: Blackwell.
—— (1984) British Black English and West Indian Creoles', in P. Trudgill (ed.) *Language in the British Isles*, Cambridge: Cambridge University Press, pp. 219–37.
Thomas, A. R. (1984) 'Welsh English', in P. Trudgill (ed.) *Language in the British Isles*, Cambridge: Cambridge University Press, pp. 178–94.
—— (1985) 'Welsh English: a grammatical conspectus', in W. Viereck (ed.) *Focus on: England and Wales*, Amsterdam: Benjamins, pp. 213–21.
Todd, L. (1984) 'By their tongue divided: towards an analysis of speech communities in Northern Ireland', *English World-Wide* 5: 159–80.
Trudgill, P. (1972) 'Sex, covert prestige and linguistic change in the urban British English of Norwich', *Language in Society* 1: 179–95.
—— (1974) *The Social Differentiation of English in Norwich*, Cambridge: Cambridge University Press.
—— (1975) *Accent, Dialect and the School*, London: Edward Arnold.
—— (1990) *The Dialects of England*, Oxford: Blackwell.
Trudgill, P. and Chambers, J. K. (eds) (1991) *Dialects of English*, London: Longman.
Trudgill, P. and Hannah, J. (1982) *International English*, London: Edward Arnold.
Viereck, W. (ed.) (1985) *Focus on: England and Wales*, Amsterdam: Benjamins.
Wakelin, M. (ed.) (1972) *Patterns in the Folk Speech of the British Isles*, London: Athlone.
—— (1977) *English Dialects*, 2nd edn, London: Athlone.
—— (1983) 'The stability of English dialect boundaries', *English World-Wide* 4, 1–15.
—— (1984) 'Rural dialects in England', in P. Trudgill (ed.) *Language in the British Isles*, Cambridge: Cambridge University Press, pp. 70–93.
Wells, J. C. (1973) *Jamaican Pronunciation in London*, Oxford: Blackwell.
—— (1982) *Accents of English*, Cambridge: Cambridge University Press.
Williams, C. H. (1990) 'The Anglicisation of Wales', in N. Coupland (ed.) *English in Wales*, Clevedon: Multilingual Matters, pp. 19–47.
Wright, P. (1981) *Cockney Dialect and Slang*, London: Batsford.
Wyld, H. C. (1934) *The Best English: a Claim for the Superiority of Received Standard English*, Oxford: Society for Pure English, No. 39.

Chapter 11

Standard British and American English in comparison

Although by far the majority of linguistic forms in the English language are common to both BrE and AmE, there are a considerable number of points at which the two varieties diverge. Chapters 1 to 5 concentrated on a systematic presentation of the lexical, phonetic, orthographic, syntactic and pragmatic phenomena of StE largely ignoring possible variety differences. While some dissimilarities were mentioned, this was done only incidentally. The purpose of this chapter, in contrast, is to look at the differences between the two major varieties, BrE and AmE, in their *standard* forms area by area.

11.1 Pronunciation

It is in the area of pronunciation that BrE–AmE differences are most obvious. While divergent patterns of grammatical usage, vocabulary choice and spelling preference crop up only sporadically, pronunciation pervades and colours every aspect of oral communication. Much of this is due to the differences in what is called *articulatory set* (Honikman 1964), a predisposition to pronounce sounds and words in a particular fashion. This includes much that is difficult to describe, yet contributes to the typical voice quality of an accent. Many American speakers, especially from the Middle West, for example, have a 'nasal twang'. This is caused by the articulatory habit of leaving the velum open so that the nasal cavity forms a further resonance chamber. Coupled with this is a narrowing of the pharynx which occurs because the root of the tongue is pushed backwards more strongly (Higgs 1980); this gives the voice a tenser, darker quality. Southern American speakers, in contrast, are stereotyped by other Americans for their drawl. This drawing out of sounds is due perhaps to an overall lack of tension in articulation (Wells 1982: 93). British accents are often thought of as 'clipped' by Americans, possibly because of the greater tension and lesser degree of lengthening in stressed vowels (cf. Strevens 1972: 78).

In addition to these overall contrasting features there are a number of more specific differences. In making this comparison it seems best to proceed systematically, according to the type of difference involved. In the following, therefore, differences in the phonemic inventories of sounds in BrE as represented by RP and in AmE as realized by the GenAm accent will be recounted first; then the major differences in phonetic (or articulatory) realization and the phonotactic (or distributional) differences will be reviewed; after that divergent patterns of phoneme use in whole sets of words as well as a small list of individual words which differ in their pronunciations only by chance will be mentioned. A few remarks on differences in stress and intonation will close this section.

11.1.1 Differences in phoneme inventory

The consonants of RP and GenAm are identical. Both varieties contain the same twenty-four phonemes (cf. 3.3.1). The only possible difference lies in the maintenance of the /hw/ − /w/ distinction (as in *where* vs. *wear*) in some of the regions where GenAm is spoken, though the use of /hw/ seems to be recessive (cf. Wells 1982: 229f). Some RP speakers also retain this distinction through a conscious effort to do so, feeling perhaps that this is somehow 'more correct'.

With the vowels there is a clear difference in the number of phonemes available: RP has twenty; GenAm, sixteen. This may be credited to the fact that GenAm, which is a rhotic accent (cf. 3.4.3 and below), has no centring diphthongs. While RP has the phonemes /ɪə, ɛə, ʊə/, GenAm has the combinations /ɪr, ɛr, ʊr/, as in *lear*, *lair* and *lure*.

In addition, GenAm does not have the phoneme /ɒ/. Wherever RP has this sound, GenAm has either /ɑː/ or /ɔː/. This, as well as RP non-rhoticity, lies behind the following story:

> American (to an Englishman): Say, what's your job?
> Englishman: I'm a clerk.
> American (astonished): You mean you go 'tick-tock, tick-tock'?
> (Strevens 1972: 68)
> [RP /klɑːk/ 'clerk' = GenAm /klɑːk/ 'clock']

Corresponding to RP /ɒ/, GenAm has only /ɑː/ in some regions (for example, in parts of the Middle West and neighbouring Canada); in other areas two distinctive phonemes are retained. The distribution of RP /ɒ/ between GenAm /ɑː/ and GenAm /ɔː/ varies regionally in America; the following is one possible example of this split. Before /l, m, n/ (*doll, bomb, don*) GenAm has /ɑː/; the same is true before the stops, as in *top, rob, dot, God, dock*; however, before a voiced velar, as in *dog* or *fog*, /ɔː/ is widespread. The same is true of the position before the velar nasal /ŋ/ (*song*), before /r/ (*orange*), and before the (unvoiced) fricatives

/f, θ, s/ (*off*, *moth*, *moss*). However, GenAm has /ɑɪ/ before /ʃ/, as in *posh*, *slosh* or *gosh*). This distribution and regional modifications of it apply only to words with /ɒ/ in RP. It does not mean that GenAm never has /ɔː/ when a stop follows (cf. *gawdy* or *taught*) nor /ɑː/ when /r/ (*far*) or a fricative (*father*) follow.

11.1.2 Differences in the phonetic quality of phonemes

The chief consonant which may be noticeably different in its realization in the two accents is /r/. In GenAm there is a strong tendency for /r/ to be retroflex [ɻ] (made with the tip of the tongue turned backwards), while it is often the constricted continuant [ɹ] in RP (made with the tongue raised and tensed in the area just behind the alveolar ridge with relatively little retroflexion). In addition, an /r/ between two vowels (as in *very*) is sometimes articulated with a single flap of the tongue against the alveolar ridge [ɾ] in RP. It is also not particularly unusual to hear RP speakers who colour their /r/ with a /w/-like sound, so that *rap* sounds a bit like *wap*.

The /l/-sound differs inasmuch as GenAm tends to use a dark [ɫ] in most positions, where RP has clear [l] before vowels (*loop*) and dark [ɫ] before consonants (*help*), at word end (*sale*) or where /l/ is syllabic (*bottle*) (cf. 3.3.1 **The lateral**).

Among the vowels there are far more examples of different articulations. Most are slight, yet some are relatively readily perceptible. The first element of /əʊ/ is a central vowel (schwa) in RP, but a back vowel in GenAm, hence [oʊ]. In fact, the degree of diphthongization of GenAm [oʊ] may be almost non-existent, viz. [oː], just as /eɪ/ may be [eː]. In RP /ɔɪ/ may be so close as to sound almost identical with GenAm [oː]; in GenAm, on the other hand, /ɔɪ/ is relatively open (see 3.4.2).

/ʌ/ (as in *cut*) is more or less mid-central in GenAm, but open front in RP. Both GenAm and RP have a long, mid-central vowel realization of /ɜː/ (as in *bird*); however, in RP this vowel is almost never followed by an /r/ (exception: *furry* /fɜːrɪ/), while in GenAm it always is (and in this sense might be considered to be a variant or allophone of the central vowel /ʌ/ before /r/).

In GenAm /æ/ is usually longer than in RP. One of the consequences of this is that it is frequently at least somewhat diphthongized in stressed syllables in GenAm. Where the first element of the resulting diphthong is a high front vowel, as in New York City, the girl's name *Ann* and the (British) name *Ian* may become synonymous /ɪən/. In addition, GenAm /æ/ is often subject to nasalization if a nasal consonant follows. For some speakers the following nasal disappears completely leaving only the nasalized vowel, for example, *bank* /bæŋk/ first becomes /bæ̃ŋk/ and then possibly /bæ̃k/, which itself is distinguished from back /bæk/ only by means of nasalization.

11.1.3 Phonotactic differences

There are quite of number of contrasts between RP and GenAm that involve patterns of distribution and combinations of sounds.

Rhoticity   RP has an /r/ only where there is a following vowel (*red, every*). When this includes a vowel in the following word (*tear + up*), what is known as a 'linking *r*' may link or connect the two words into a single phonetic unit. Such linking may also occur where no *r* is present in the spelling (*law officer* /lɔːrɒfɪsə/); this is called an 'intrusive *r*' and may be found after final /ɔː, ə, ɑː/ before a vowel in the following word. GenAm regularly pronounces /r/ where the spelling indicates; it does not know an intrusive *r* (see also 3.4.3).

Intervocalic /t/   GenAm realizes what is written as a ⟨t⟩ with a flap of the tongue tip against the alveolar ridge when it comes between two vowels. Phonetically this is very much like the tapped [ɾ] of RP *very*, but it is usually perceived as a /d/. Indeed, intervocalic /d/ is also flapped in GenAm, which means that *latter* and *ladder* sound identical, both with flapped intervocalic [t̬]. This is also the case, for example, when the semivowel /r/ or the sonorant /l/ precedes (*hurting = herding*; *helter = held'er*) or a vocalized, syllabic /m/ or /l/ follows (*totem = towed'em*; *futile = feudal*). This voicing of intervocalic ⟨t⟩ does not apply if the syllable following the ⟨t⟩ is stressed, hence *'a-tom = 'A-dam*, both with a flapped [t̬], but *a-'tom-ic*, with /t/. In RP, in contrast, ⟨t⟩ is realized as /t/ wherever it is written, including the case in the next paragraph. (Note, however, that many urban accents of England and Scotland replace intervocalic /t/ with a glottal stop [ʔ]; see 3.3.2 and 3.3.4.)

Post-nasal /t/   In words such as *winter* or *enter*, where an unstressed vowel follows, the ⟨t⟩ is not pronounced at all in GenAm. As a result *winter = winner* and *intercity = innercity*. When the following syllable is stressed /t/ is pronounced as in *in-'ter*; /t/ is also pronounced if a consonant follows, as in *intracity*.

Dental and alveolar consonants + /j/   The combinations /nj, tj, dj, sj, zj, lj, θj/ do not occur in most varieties of GenAm, while they may in RP. Hence all those words spelled with ⟨u⟩, ⟨ew⟩, ⟨eu⟩, ⟨ui⟩, ⟨ue⟩, and a few other combinations with ⟨u⟩ (words such as *tune, thews, deuce, suit, sue, lieutenant*, etc.) usually have simple /uː/ in GenAm, but /juː/ in RP (on *lieutenant*, see 11.1.5). Sometimes, especially after /s, z, l/ (as in *suet, presume, lute*), there is free variation in RP between /juː/ and /uː/. Both RP and GenAm agree in having /uː/ where the spelling has ⟨oo⟩ (*noose, loose, doom*, etc.). Note that the combinations /nj/ and /lj/ are possible in

GenAm if there is an intervening syllable boundary, as in *Jan-u-ary*, *mon-u-ment*, *val-ue*, all with /juː/.

Palatalization   The lack of /j/ before /uː/ described in the preceding section represents a relatively late development in GenAm. Evidence that an earlier /j/ must have been present can be seen in the palatalization which took place in words such as *feature, education, fissure* or *azure*, in which original /t, d, s, z/, as reflected in the spelling, have moved slightly backwards in the mouth to a more palatal place of articulation. Furthermore, the stops /t/ and /d/ also changed to the affricates /tʃ/ and /dʒ/ while /s/ and /z/ merely became the palatal fricatives /ʃ/ and /ʒ/. In GenAm palatalization is regular when the following syllable is unstressed. There are a few well-known cases of palatalization before a stressed syllable, such as *sure, sugar, assure*. RP agrees in most cases with GenAm, but it has the additional possibility of unpalatalized /dj, tj, sj, zj/ in those cases where a ⟨u⟩ follows. This is phonotactically impossible in GenAm. Hence RP *education* may be /edjuːkeɪʃən/ or /edʒəkeɪʃən/ and *issue* may be /ɪʃuː/ or /ɪsjuː/.

When a ⟨u⟩ is not involved, but rather /iː/ or /ɪ/ + unstressed vowel, the situation is less predictable. RP has, for example, both unpalatalized *Indian* /ɪndɪən/ and (old-fashioned) palatalized /ɪndʒən/, unpalatalized *immediately* /ɪmiːdɪətlɪ/ and palatalized /ɪmiːdʒətlɪ/. GenAm has only the unpalatalized versions of each. A number of place names are unpalatalized in RP and palatalized in GenAm: *Tunisia*, RP /tjʊnɪzɪə/ and GenAm /tuːniːʒə/, or *Indonesia*, RP /ɪndəniːzɪə/ and GenAm /ɪndouniːʒə/ (see 11.1.4 for voicing differences, i.e. RP /ʃ/ vs. GenAm /ʒ/). Both agree in having palatalized *soldier, auspicious, financial*, etc; and both have unpalatalized *easier, Finlandia* or *rodeo* (see also 3.3.5 **Palatalization**).

Vowels   In the area of the vowels only two frequent and very noticeable points will be mentioned. GenAm does not allow any short vowels except for unstressed schwa to occur in unchecked syllables (ones that do not end with a consonant). This means that the only vowels which can come at the very end of a word are long vowels, diphthongs and schwa. RP makes an exception to this rule by allowing final unstressed /ɪ/. As a result, all those words ending in unstressed ⟨-y⟩ and ⟨-ie⟩, such as *cloudy* and *birdie*, have /ɪ/ in RP, but /iː/ in GenAm. /ɪ/ is retained even when an ending follows, hence in RP *candied = candid* /kændɪd/.

The other point with vowels also involves unstressed syllables. GenAm has a much greater tendency to reduce unstressed vowels to schwa, while RP retains /ɪ/, especially where the endings ⟨-ed⟩ and ⟨-es⟩ are involved. This distinguishes *boxes* /bɒksɪz/ from *boxers* /bɒksəz/. GenAm has schwa in both cases, but this causes no confusion because *boxers* is pronounced with an /r/.

11.1.4 Divergent patterns of phoneme use in whole sets of words

Among the consonants of English there is a noticeable difference in the way intervocalic ⟨-si-⟩ is realized before an unstressed syllable (see the remarks on palatalization in the preceding section). While in GenAm all the following have /ʒ/, in RP only those under (a) have this consonant; the ones under (b) have either /ʒ/ or /ʃ/ and the items in (c) have only /ʃ/.

(a) *vision, confusion, decision, measure, treasure, pleasure, usual, seizure*
(b) *Asia, aspersion* (GenAm: /ʒ/ or /ʃ/), *immersion, magnesia* (GenAm: /ʒ/ or /ʃ/), *Persia, perversion*
(c) *version, aversion, Indonesian* (RP: also /-zɪ-/ GenAm: /ʒ/ or /ʃ/)

In addition, *Malaysia, Melanesia, Micronesia* have /-zɪ-/ in RP and either /ʒ/ or /ʃ/ in GenAm; *euthanasia, Polynesia* and *Tunisia* have RP /-zɪ-/ and GenAm /ʒ/.

At least some areas of America, especially the South, have an /l/ in words with ⟨-alm⟩ (*alms, balm, calm, palm, psalm, qualms*). Furthermore, in those varieties in which there is an /l/, the vowel is not /ɑː/ but /ɔː/. In varieties of GenAm without an /l/ either vowel may occur. RP never has an /l/ and always has /ɑː/ (cf. also 3.6.2).

There are four important sets of words in which RP and GenAm generally differ in the vowel chosen. The largest and better known is the set of so-called *bath*-words, which have /æ/ in GenAm and /ɑː/ in RP. This set of words is defined by the occurrence of a spelling ⟨a⟩ followed by an ⟨s⟩, an ⟨f⟩ or a ⟨th⟩, as in *pass, after, path* or *rather*; in addition, the ⟨a⟩ may be followed by an ⟨m⟩ or an ⟨n⟩ plus another consonant, as in *example* or *dance*. Approximately 300 words fulfil these conditions, but only about one-third have /ɑː/ in RP; the remainder have /æ/ in both varieties (*ass, traffic, maths, gather, trample, Atlantic*). One word has /ɑː/ in both varieties (*father*), and some vary in RP between /æ/ and /ɑː/ (*lather, mass*) (cf. Lewis 1968–9: 65; see also 3.6.2).

The second set of words which vary between the two varieties comprises those in which an intervocalic /r/ follows a mid-central vowel, as in *borough, burrow, courage, concurrent, curry, flurry, furrow, hurricane, hurry, nourish, scurry, thorough, turret, worry*. Here GenAm has /ɜː/ while RP has /ʌ/. RP can have the combination /ɜːr/ only when a word otherwise ending in /ɜː/ has been given an ending beginning with a vowel, as in *furry, deterring* or *referral*.

The third set includes those words derived from Latin which end in ⟨-ile⟩. In RP the usual pronunciation is /aɪl/ while in GenAm it is /ɪl/ or /əl/, (*febrile, fragile, futile, missile, puerile, tactile, virile*). Note, however, that individual words in GenAm may vary, so that, for example, *textile*, *reptile* and *servile* commonly have either /aɪl/ or /ɪl/.

The final set of words includes names of countries, such as *Czecho-slovakia*, *Nicaragua*, *Rwanda*, *Surinam* or *Vietnam*. Here GenAm usually has /ɑː/ for the ⟨a⟩ in the stressed syllables while RP has /æ/, cf. /nɪkərægjʊə/ vs. /nɪkərɑːgwə/.

11.1.5 Individual words which differ

A few words have differing pronunciations in the two varieties without this divergence being systematic or belonging to a larger set which patterns in the same way. In the following list first the RP and then, following the slanted line, the GenAm pronunciation is indicated for each item or group of items: *schedule* (ʃ/sk), *lieutenant* (army: left-; navy: luɪt-/luːt-), *erase* (z/s), *gooseberry*, (z or s/s), *herb* (h/no consonant), *geyser* (iː/aɪ), *quinine* (iiː/aɪaɪ), stressed *been* (iː/ɪ), *aesthetic*, *evolution* (iː/e), *squirrel* (ɪ/ɜː), *(n)either* (aɪ/iː), *tryst* (aɪ/ɪ), *dynasty*, *midwifery*, *privacy*, *viola* (musical instrument) (ɪ/aɪ), *progress*, *process* (əʊ/ɑː), *date*, *apparatus*, *status* (eɪ/eɪ or æ), *leisure*, *zebra*, *zenith* (e/iː), *wrath* (ɒ/æ), *quagmire* (ɒ or æ/æ), *produce* (noun), *shone*, *scone*, *yoghurt* (ɒ/oʊ), *tomato*, *strafe* (ɑː/eɪ), *what*, *was*, *of* (ɒ/ʌ), *vase* (vɑːz/veɪz or veɪs), *plaque* (ɑː or æ/æ), *clerk*, *Berkeley*, *Derby* (ɑː/ɜːr), *route* (uː/uɪ or aʊ).

Stress and intonation The stress patterns of RP and GenAm are generally the same. One well-known difference is in the pronunciation of words ending in *-ary*, *-ery* or *-ory*. In RP they contain a single stressed syllable, which is the first or the second one in the word, and the second to last syllable is frequently elided. In GenAm the stress is on the first syllable; in addition, secondary stress falls on the next to last syllable:

secretary:	'sec-re-t(a)ry	/	'sec-re-ˌtar-y
library:	'li-br(ar)y	/	'li-ˌbrar-y
stationery:	'sta-tion-(e)ry	/	'sta-tio-ˌner-y
laboratory:	la-'bor-a-t(o)ry	/	'lab-(o)-ra-ˌtor-y
corollary:	co-'rol-la-ry	/	'cor-o-ˌlar-y

A number of individual words also carry their stress on different syllables in the two varieties. Here is a short list, always with the RP form first:

ad'vertisement/		*adver'tisement* (the ⟨i⟩ is ɪ/aɪ)
arti'san	/	*'artisan* (the second a is æ/ə)
'ballet	/	*bal'let* (the ⟨e⟩ is eɪ or ɪ/eɪ)
'baton	/	*ba'ton* (the ⟨a⟩ is æ/ə)
'chagrin (n.)	/	*cha'grin* (the ⟨a⟩ is æ/ə)

'detail	/*de'tail* (the ⟨e⟩ is iː/ɪ)
doc'trinal	/*'doctrinal* (the ⟨i⟩ is aɪ/ɪ)
'frontier	/*fron'tier* (the latter also in RP)
'garage	/*ga'rage* (the first ⟨a⟩ is /æ/ or aɪ/ə; the second ⟨a⟩ is /ɪ/ or aɪ/aɪ)
'lamentable	/*la'mentable* (læmənt-/ləment-)
'résumé (noun)	/*resu'me* (⟨re-⟩ is re or reɪ/re)
re'veille	/*'reveille* (rɪvæliː/revəliː)
'valet	/*va'let* (væ-lɪt or -leɪ/vəleɪ (and as in RP)

The intonation of both accents functions according to the same basic principles. Yet the intonation of RP is often characterized as more varied, that of GenAm as flatter. Some of the individual points of difference include the following. RP more frequently uses sharp jumps downwards, but has more gradual rises than does GenAm. In lengthy sentences GenAm will repeat the overall contour, leaving the final rise or fall until the very end; RP, in contrast, draws out the rise or fall in small increments from stressed syllable to stressed syllable. GenAm generally has falling intonation in *Wh*-questions while RP frequently uses an alternative pattern with a low rise at the end, something which is perceived as friendlier. *Yes–no* questions have a rapid rise in GenAm, remain high, and finish with a further small rise. In RP the final rise may be preceded by a falling contour. The same is true of echo-questions (cf. Engler and Hilyer 1971).

Useful literature on pronunciation includes (for RP) Gimson 1989, Roach 1983; (for GenAm) Bronstein 1960, Kenyon 1969; (for both) Lewis 1970–1, Wells 1982. Standard pronouncing dictionaries for RP are Jones 1988; for GenAm, Kenyon and Knott 1944; Wells 1990 gives both.

11.2 Spelling and punctuation

Spelling and punctuation differences are, much like the majority of differences in pronunciation, not merely haphazard and unsystematic. Instead, certain principles are involved, including simplification, regularization, derivational uniformity and reflection of pronunciation. Of course, there are also a number of individual, unsystematic differences. Although it is not always easy to attribute British-American divergencies unambiguously to a single principle, the following presentation will proceed as if this were no problem.

11.2.1 Spelling

Simplification This principle is common to both the British and the American traditions, but it is sometimes realized differently in each. AmE has a greater reputation for simplification, as often attested by such standard examples as *program* instead of *programme* (but note that BrE has *program* for computer software). Compare also measurement words ending in ⟨-gram(me)⟩ such as *kilogram(me)*, etc., where the form with the final ⟨-me⟩ is the preferred, but not the exclusive BrE form. Likewise, BrE *waggon* is still found next to AmE (and, increasingly, BrE) *wagon*. On the other hand, AmE has *counselor*, *woolen*, *fagot* as well as shared *counsellor*, *woollen* and *faggot*.

Simplification of *ae* and *oe* to *e* in words taken from Latin and Greek (*heresy*, *federal*, etc.) are the rule for all of English, but this rule is carried out less completely in BrE, where we find *mediaeval* next to *medieval*, *foetus* next to *fetus*, and *paediatrician* next to *pediatrician*. This is especially noticeable in view of the existence of AmE forms with simple *e* compared with the non-simplified forms of BrE, for example, AmE *esophagus* and BrE *oesophagus*, AmE *esthetics* and BrE *aesthetics* (also AmE), *maneuver*/*manoeuvre*, *anapest*/*anapaest*, *estrogen*/*oestrogen*, *anemia*/*anaemia*, *egis*/*aegis* (also AmE), *ameba*/*amoeba*. Note, however, that many words have only *ae* and *oe* in AmE, for example, *aerial* and *Oedipus*.

A further simplification in AmE is one which has not been adopted at all in BrE: the dropping of the ⟨-ue⟩ of ⟨-logue⟩ in words such as *catolog*, *dialog*, *monolog*. (Etymologically unrelated *back-log* or *ship's log* are identical in AmE and BrE.) This simplification, which does not extend to words such as *Prague*, *vague*, *vogue* or *rogue*, is not fully accepted for use in formal AmE writing. Note the simplification of words such as (BrE) *judgement* to (AmE) *judgment* (though both spellings occur in both varieties).

BrE employs some simplified spellings which have not been adopted in AmE, such as BrE *skilful* and *wilful* for AmE *skillful* and *willful*. BrE *fulfil*, *instil*, *appal* may be interpreted as simplification, but AmE double ⟨-ll-⟩ in *fulfill*, *instill*, *appall* may have to do with where the stress lies (see below **Reflection of pronunciation**). Nevertheless, AmE uses common *fulness* alongside (AmE) *fullness*; other words which have both forms in AmE are *instal(l)*, *instal(l)ment*, and *enthral(l)*.

BrE may simplify ⟨-ection⟩ to ⟨-exion⟩ in *connexion*, *inflexion*, *retroflexion*, etc. Here AmE uses *connection*, etc., thus following the principle of derivational unity: *connect* > *connection*, *connective*; *reflect* > *reflection*, *reflective*. For more on **Derivational uniformity** see below.

Regularization   This principle is again one which has been employed more completely in AmE than in BrE. It shows up most obviously in the regularization of the endings ⟨-or⟩ and ⟨-our⟩ to the single form ⟨-or⟩. This seems justified since there are no systematic criteria for distinguishing between the two sets in BrE: *neighbour* and *saviour*, but *donor* and *professor*; *honour* and *valour*, but *metaphor*, *anterior* and *posterior*; *savour* and *flavour*, but *languor* and *manor*; *behaviour* and *colour*, but *anchor* and *calor (gas)*.

Within BrE there are special rules to note: the ending ⟨-ation⟩ and ⟨-ious⟩ usually lead to a form with ⟨-or-⟩ as in *coloration* and *laborious*, but the endings ⟨-al⟩ and ⟨-ful⟩, as in *behavioural* and *colourful*, have no such effect. However, even AmE may keep ⟨-our⟩ in such words as *glamour* (next to *glamor*) and *Saviour* (next to *Savior*), perhaps because there is something 'better' about these spellings for many people. Words such as *contour*, *tour*, *four* or *amour*, where the vowel of the ⟨-our⟩ is never fully unstressed, are never simplified.

Note that, although unrelated to the preceding, AmE also has *mold*, *molt*, *smolder* and *mustache* where BrE has *mould*, *moult*, *smoulder* and *moustache*. Similar is AmE *gage* where BrE has *gauge*.

The second well-known case concerns ⟨-er⟩ and ⟨-re⟩. Here BrE words in ⟨-re⟩ are regularized to ⟨-er⟩ in AmE. For example, BrE *goitre*, *centre* and *metre* become AmE *goiter*, *center* (but the adjective form is *central*) and *meter* (hence levelling the distinction between *metre* '39.37 inches' and *meter* 'instrument for measuring'). This rule applies everywhere in AmE except where the letter preceding the ending is a ⟨c⟩ or a ⟨g⟩. In these cases ⟨-re⟩ is retained, as in *acre*, *mediocre* and *ogre*, in order to prevent misinterpretation as a 'soft' ⟨c⟩ /s/ or ⟨g⟩ /dʒ/. The spellings *fire* (but note: *fiery*), *wire*, *tire*, etc., are used to ensure interpretation of these sequences as monosyllabic. The fairly widespread use of the form *theatre* in AmE runs parallel to *glamour* and *Saviour*, as mentioned above: it probably suggests superior quality or a more distinguished tradition for many people.

Derivational uniformity BrE writes *defence*, *offence*, *pretence*, but *practise* (verb) (all are also possible alternatives in AmE), while AmE alone has *defense*, *offense*, *pretense*, but *practice* (verb). What appears to be arbitrary (now ⟨c⟩, now ⟨s⟩) is really the application in AmE of the principle of derivational uniformity: *defense > defensive*, *offense > offensive*, *pretense > pretension*, *practice > practical*. (cf. *connexion* vs. *connection* above under **Simplification**.)

In another case BrE observes this principle and AmE violates it, viz. *analyze* and *paralyze*. Here BrE *analyse* and *paralyse* (also possible in AmE) share the ⟨s⟩ with their derivational cognates *analysis* and *paralysis*.

Reflection of pronunciation The forms *analyze* and *paralyze*, which end in ⟨-ze⟩, may violate derivational uniformity, but they do reflect the pronunciation of the final fricative, which is clearly a lenis/voiced /z/. This principle has been widely adopted in spelling on both sides of the Atlantic for verbs ending in ⟨-ize⟩ and the corresponding nouns ending in ⟨-ization⟩. The older spellings with ⟨-ise⟩ and ⟨-isation⟩ are, however, also found in both AmE and BrE. The decisive factor here seems to be publishers' style sheets, with increasing preference for ⟨z⟩. However, some words such as *advertise*, *advise*, *compromise*, *revise*, *televise* appears only with ⟨-ise⟩.

In AmE, when an ending beginning with a vowel (⟨-ing⟩, ⟨-ed⟩, ⟨-er⟩) is added to a multisyllabic word ending in ⟨l⟩, the ⟨l⟩ is doubled if the final syllable of the root carries the stress and is spelled with a single letter vowel (⟨e, o⟩). If the stress does not lie on the final syllable, the ⟨l⟩ is not doubled.

re'bel → re'belling	'revel → 'reveling
re'pel → re'pelled	'travel → 'traveler
com'pel → com'pelling	'marvel → 'marveling
con'trol → con'trolling	'trammel → 'trammeled
pa'trol → pa'troller	'yodel → 'yodeled

Hence AmE spelling closely reflects pronunciation. (The AmE spellings *fulfill*, *distill*, etc., may be favoured over simplified BrE *fulfil*, *distil*, etc., because they indicate end stress.) A similar principle may apply to AmE *installment*, *skillful* and *willful*, where the ⟨ll⟩ occurs in the stressed syllable. BrE, in contrast, follows the principle of regularization, since all final ⟨l⟩'s, regardless of stress, are doubled (*revelling*, *traveller*, *marvelling*, *trammelled*, *yodelled*, etc.). These latter spellings are also accepted in AmE. In a few cases BrE doubles the final ⟨p⟩ where AmE does not, for example, *worship(p)er*, *kidnap(p)er*.

Perhaps the best-known cases of spellings adapted to reflect pronunciation are those involving ⟨-gh-⟩. Here AmE tends to use a 'phonetic' spelling so that BrE *plough* appears as AmE *plow*, BrE *draught* ('flow of air, swallow or movement of liquid, depth of a vessel in water'), as AmE *draft* (BrE has *draft* in the sense of a bank draft or a first draft of a piece of writing). The spellings *thru* for *through* and *tho'* for *though* are not uncommon in AmE, but are generally restricted to more informal writing; however, they sometimes show up in official use, as in the designation of some limited access expressways as *thruways*. Spellings such as *lite* for *light*, *hi* for *high*, or *nite* for *night* are employed in very informal writing and in advertising language. But from there they can enter more formal use, as is the case with *hi-fi*.

Individual words which differ in spelling   For a number of words there are alternatives between ⟨in-⟩ and ⟨en-⟩ without there being any clear principle involved, except for a slight preference in AmE for ⟨in-⟩ and in BrE for ⟨en-⟩, as in BrE *ensure*, *enclose*, *endorse* and AmE *insure*, *inclose*, *indorse*, but common *envelop* and *inquire* (beside BrE *enquire*).

The practice of writing compounds as two words, as a hyphenated word or as a single unhyphenated word varies; however, there is a marked avoidance of hyphenations in AmE. Hence while BrE writes *make-up* ('cosmetics'), AmE uses *make up*; BrE *neo-colonialism*, but AmE *neocolonialism*. Usage varies considerably from dictionary to dictionary, and no more can be said than that this is a preference; but there does seem to be an increasing tendency towards uniformity in the form of single unhyphenated words (cf. Benson *et al.* 1986a: 19). Many Americans (and Australians) write compound numbers without a hyphen (*twenty five*), but most retain one (*twenty-five*), as do most British writers.

In a similar vein, AmE drops French accent marks in some words (*cafe*, *entree*) while BrE may be more likely to retain them (*café*, *entrée*). However, the tendency towards anglicization (no accent marks) is great in both varieties. For more on internal variation within BrE, see Greenbaum 1986; for AmE, see Emery 1975.

The following list includes the most common differences in spelling, always with the BrE form listed first: *aluminium/aluminum*, (bank) *cheque/check*, *gaol* (also *jail*)/*jail*, *jewellery/jewelry*, (street) *kerb/curb*, *pyjamas/pajamas*, *storey* (of a building)/*story*, *sulphur/sulfur*, *syphon/siphon*, *tyre/tire*, *whisky/whiskey*.

In addition, nonce spellings, especially in advertising, can probably be found more frequently in AmE than in BrE, for example, *kwik* (*quick*), *donut* (now almost standard for *doughnut*), *e-z* (*easy*), *rite* (*right*, *write*), *blu* (*blue*), *tuff* (*tough*) and many more (cf. Gläser 1972).

11.2.2 Punctuation

Aside from the lexical differences in the designations for some of the marks of punctuation, there are only a few differences in practice worth mentioning here. First, the sometimes different names: a BrE *full stop* is an AmE *period*; BrE *brackets* are AmE *parentheses*, while BrE *square brackets* are AmE *brackets*. AmE and BrE *quotation marks* are sometimes *inverted commas* in BrE. Note also that BrE uses single quotation marks ('. . .') in the normal case and resorts to double ones (". . .") for a quotation within a quotation ('. . .". . .". . .'). AmE starts with double quotation marks and alternates to single ones for a quote within a quote. Common British-American *exclamation mark* is also called an *exclamation point* in AmE. And the *slash*, /, may be termed an *oblique (stroke)* in BrE and a *virgule*, a *solidus* or a *diagonal* in AmE.

Simplification vs. regularization AmE opts for simplification whenever closing quotation marks occur together with a period or a comma: the period or comma always comes inside the quotation marks whether it 'belongs' to the material quoted or not. BrE places its full stops and commas inside if they belong to what is quoted and outside if they do not.

Compare (a) where the punctuation belongs to the quotation vs. (b) where it does not:

(a) BrE: *'He belongs to the club,' he told her.* Or: *He answered, 'She left an hour ago.'*

AmE: Usage is identical here except that AmE sets double quotation marks instead of single ones.

(b) BrE: *These may be called 'corruptions', 'degradations' and 'perversions'.*

AmE: *These may be called "corruptions," "degradations," and "perversions."*

The principle of regularization is observed in AmE usage for all other marks of punctuation, i.e. question marks and exclamation points come inside the quotation marks if they belong, but are placed outside if they do not belong to the quotation itself.

Note also that in lists AmE usage is more likely than BrE usage to use a comma before the conjunction joining the final item in a list (*x, y, and z* vs. *x, y and z*). On the other hand, (conservative) BrE usage sets a comma between the house number and the street name in addresses (*331, High Street*), something which is not practised in AmE.

The use or not of a dot (period, full stop) after abbreviations, especially titles, also differs. While AmE opts for simplicity, always using a dot, BrE distinguishes abbreviations which end with the same letter as their unabbreviated form and which therefore have no dot, e.g. *Mister > Mr, Missus > Mrs, Sergeant > Sgt, Lieutenant > Lt*, etc. In contrast, abbreviations which end with a letter different from the final letter of the full form have a dot, e.g. *General > Gen., Captain > Capt., (the) Reverend > Rev.*, etc. Note that in the bibliographical information in this book *editor* is abbreviated as *ed.*, but *editors* as *eds* (without a dot).

Miscellaneous differences in punctuation   In business letters, the salutation (*Dear Sir, Dear Madam, Dear General Jones*) is followed by a colon in AmE, but by a comma in BrE. Salutations containing a name may have a comma in AmE. The colon, when used as punctuation between two main clauses, is followed by a small (lower case) letter in the second clause in BrE. In AmE, there may be capitalization, for example, *One solution is quite evident: check* (BrE)/*Check* (AmE) *the credit-worthiness of the client carefully*. When a colon is used to introduce lists it may sometimes be followed by a hyphen in BrE; this is never the case in AmE; e.g. *Several commodities have fallen in price significantly:- coffee, cocoa, tea and tobacco*.

The symbol ⟨%⟩ is written out as two words in BrE (*per cent*), but is a single one in AmE (*percent*). In addition, BrE uses the abbreviation *p.c.* or *pc*, as in *16 pc drop in unemployment*.

Dates can be the source of serious misunderstanding between the two varieties, since BrE goes with European usage in placing the date before the month between oblique strokes or separated by (sometimes raised) dots: *2 April 1992* is 2/4/92 or 2.4.92. In AmE 2/4/92 (oblique strokes only) is *February 4, 1992*. In cases of possible confusion it is recommendable to write out the name of the month or its abbreviation. The raised dots just mentioned are unknown in AmE, but are also used for decimals and times in BrE, for example, *3·1416* or *10·43 a.m.* A normal period/full stop may also be used in BrE.

Clock times use a dot in BrE (*3.45 p.m.*), but a colon in AmE (*3:45 p.m.*). Both varieties abbreviate *number(s)* as *No.* or *Nos* (capitalized or not, the latter with a dot or not according to AmE and BrE rules, e.g. *No. 8* or *nos(.) 5 and 8*); however, only AmE uses, for *number*, the symbol # (*#8*) and the possible plural # *#5 and 8*.

Information on punctuation is found in a very concise form at the front or back of most modern dictionaries. Most good dictionaries, whether AmE or BrE in their orientation, provide alternative spellings, but they cannot always be counted on to include the standard spellings of the other side of the Atlantic if they are not current at home. See also the references to chapter 3 for more titles on punctuation and spelling.

11.3 Grammar and morphology

The differences in grammar and morphology are not deeply significant; however, it is of interest to recount some briefly, but by no means all of them. The procedure will be area by area according to the parts of speech. In doing this, most space is reserved for the verb. A short note on word order differences closes this section.

11.3.1 The verb

Morphology The one relatively systematic difference between BrE and AmE as far as the verb is concerned is at the same time one of the more trivial ones. A number of verbs ending in a nasal (*dream*, *lean*) or an /l/ (*spill*) have two forms for their past tense and past participle; one is regular, adding ⟨-ed⟩; the other adds ⟨-t⟩ (sometimes with and sometimes without a change in the vowel). These include the following: *burn*, *dream*, *dwell*, *kneel*, *lean*, *learn*, *spell*, *spill* and *spoil*. In each case, AmE is more likely to have the regular form and BrE to have the form in ⟨-t⟩. For example, *leant* /lent/ is rare in AmE in contrast to *leaned* /liːnd/. Note, however, that there are verbs ending in /m, n, l/ which do not have two forms; for example, there is only irregular *meant* /ment/ in both varieties, just as there is only regular *quelled* and *teamed*.

A further widespread phenomenon is the greater tendency in AmE for non-standard past tense forms to be used higher up in the scale of stylistic formality. This is especially the case with the pattern *sprung* for *sprang* (cf. also non-standard simple past tense *rung*, *shrunk*, *sung*, *sunk*, *stunk* and *swung*).

Most other differences in the past tense and past participle forms are singular, incidental ones, including the differing pronunciation of the past tense forms *ate* (BrE /et/; AmE /eɪt/) and *shone* (BrE /ʃɒn/; AmE /ʃoʊn/) or AmE past tense *dove* and *snuck* (beside common *dived* and *sneaked*) or BrE *quitted*, *betted* and *fitted* (beside common *quit* and *bet* and AmE *fit*). AmE also sometimes uses *proven* and *shaven* as past participles next to common *proved* and *shaved*. Furthermore, AmE has the past participles *beat*, *shook* and *swelled* (beside normal *beaten*, *shaken* and *swollen*) in the expressions *to be beat* 'completely exhausted', *all shook up* 'upset' *and to have a swelled head* 'be conceited'. *Slay* (itself more common in AmE) has two past tenses: literal, though archaic, *slew* 'killed' and figurative *slayed*, as in *That slayed me* 'caused me to laugh vigorously'.

Get* and *have More significantly, *get* has two past participle forms in AmE, *got* and *gotten*, each used with a different meaning. *Have got* is used for possession, obligation or logical necessity in both varieties, as in possession: *I've got a book on that subject*; obligation: *you've got to read it*; logical necessity: *it's got to be interesting*. *Have got* for logical necessity, familiar in AmE, is apparently a more recent and less widespread phenomenon in BrE. *Have gotten*, which does not occur in BrE at all, means 'receive', as in *I've just gotten a letter from her*. In its modal sense *have gotten* means 'be able, have the opportunity', as in *I've gotten to do more reading lately*. These distinctions can be made by lexical means but not morphologically in BrE. In addition, the past form *had got* is not a real option for expressing possession in either variety, but it is just barely possible in the modal meaning of obligation in BrE (*They had got to reply by yesterday*) (Quirk *et al.* 1985: §3.45).

Do* and *have Further differences in ways of expressing possession and obligation (but also events) involve *have*. AmE treats *have* in these uses as a lexical verb and therefore uses periphastic *do* for negation and inversion; only the perfect auxiliary is an operator in AmE, which means that only it inverts and negates directly (cf. 4.1.3). In BrE this seems to be increasingly the case as well; however, lexical *have*, especially in the broad sense of possession, may also be treated as an operator, for example, *I haven't any idea*; *Have you a book on this subject?*; or *Hadn't she any news?* This use, which is as good as unknown in AmE, is becoming rarer in BrE, especially in questions and even more so in past tense use (cf. Quirk *et al.* 1985: §3.34).

Note that *do*-periphrasis is obligatory in both varieties for events such as having lunch, having a good time, having trouble, etc. One misunderstanding which is still just barely possible is based on the fact that possession may be expressed without *do* in BrE and *do* may be reserved for events; hence the following (possible, but unlikely) exchange:

American: Do you have children? ['possess']
Briton: Yes, one a year. [event, 'give birth to']

(Strevens 1972: 48)

Propredicate *do*   A further difference involves *do* as a propredicate. This is the use of one of its forms (*do, does, did, done, doing*) to replace a lexical verb instead of repeating it, for example, A: *Did you write to the hotel?* B: *Yes, I have done*. This type of construction is exclusively BrE; in AmE B's reply would be: *Yes, I have* or *Yes, I have done so*, both of which are also possible in BrE (see also 4.8.5).

Modal auxiliaries   Other differences between AmE and BrE in the area of the verb concern the frequencies of the modal verbs. *Should, shall, ought to, dare, need* and *must*, all of which are relatively infrequent in BrE, are even more so in AmE. *Dare* and *need*, furthermore, are more likely to be used as blends between operators and lexical verbs in AmE. This means that they will use *do*-periphrasis, but an unmarked infinitive, for example, *I don't dare think about it*. The use of *ought* without *to* in questions and negations (i.e. in non-assertive contexts; *he ought not do that*) is an increasingly frequent pattern not only in AmE and BrE, but also in AusE (cf. Quirk *et al*. 1985: 139; Collins 1989: 141f).

The modal *used to* still has direct negation relatively frequently in BrE (*used not to, usen't to*); in AmE (as well as in BrE) the preferred form of negation is with *do*-periphrasis (*didn't use(d) to*) (Quirk *et al*. 1985: §3.44).

The modal *would* is normally used in the *if*-clause of a conditional sentence when it indicates willingness (*If you would agree, everything would be fine*). Here the two varieties agree. However, AmE extends the use of *would* to *if*-clauses where no volition is involved (*If it would rain, everything would be okay*). A further point involving the *would* is that the expression *'d rather*, which is a contraction of *would rather*, is sometimes re-expanded to *had rather*, chiefly in AmE (Quirk *et al*. 1985: §3.45).

The growing use of the modal *will* with first person pronouns (*I/we will*) instead of traditional *shall* is an instance where British and American usage are converging: 'Increasingly even in Southern Standard BrE the forms formerly associated with AmE are becoming the norm' (Quirk *et al*. 1985: §4.50). *Shall* is heard in AmE almost only in questions inquiring about the desirability of the speaker's doing something, for example, *Shall I get you an ashtray?* More common, however, would be the phrasing, *Would you like me to . . .?*; *Should I . . .?*; or *Can I . . .?* (cf. Quirk *et al.* 1985: §4.58).

Modal *must*, mentioned as infrequent above, is losing ground to *have (got) to* in its obligation meaning, especially in AmE; in its epistemic use for logical necessity '*must* is very much alive and is now met with also in clauses negated by *not*, a usage that appears to be fairly recent in origin' (Jacobson 1979: 311); Quirk *et al.* consider negated *must*, as in *His absence must not have been noticed*, to be particularly American (1985: §4.54). For more on the modal verbs, see 4.4.5.

The subjunctive   In AmE the subjunctive is far more common than in BrE. This is less the case with the so-called formulaic subjunctive (*I wish I/he/she/it were . . .*; *If I were you, . . .*), which is becoming less and less current in both varieties. Rather, what is typically American usage is the so-called **mandative subjunctive**, used after predicates of command or recommendation and other predicates which mark something as desirable future action, for example, *we suggest/recommend that you be on time tomorrow*; *it is important/mandatory that you not misunderstand me*. While this is somewhat formal usage in AmE, it is by no means unusual in the everyday language. In BrE, on the contrary, it is largely restricted to formal written usage, though it seems to be making a come-back due to American influence (Quirk *et al.* 1985: §3.59). What BrE uses in its place is either what is called **putative** *should* (*it is mandatory that you should not misunderstand me*), which is also available in AmE, or the indicative (*it is mandatory that you don't misunderstand me*). This latter option is utterly impossible in AmE. See also 4.7.5, *Suggest*.

The perfect   The use of the perfect is interpreted somewhat differently in the two varieties. While there is basic agreement, AmE speakers may choose to use the past in sentences with the adverbs *yet*, *just* or *already*, all of which would almost automatically trigger the use of the present perfect in BrE, as in AmE *He just/already came* for BrE *He has just/already come* (the latter is clearly possible though somewhat less likely in AmE) (Vanneck 1958; Marshall 1979; cf. also 4.4.3).

Complementation   There are four relatively important differences in the patterns of complementation used in AmE and BrE. One of these has already been discussed, namely the use of a *that*-clause with the subjunctive after verbs of command, recommendation and desirable future action.

A second pattern is the use of an infinitive complement whose subject is introduced by *for* after verbs of emotion such as *love*, *like*, *hate* and *prefer*, as in *They would like for you to come*. While adjectives take such *for . . . to* complements in both varieties (*They would be happy for you to come*), the occurrence of the *for . . . to* construction after verbs is more typical of AmE. Note, however, that this pattern is not employed all the time in AmE, nor is it completely unknown in some varieties of BrE. When something separates the main verb from the infinitive complement, *for* will occur in both varieties, for example, *They would like very much for you to come*.

The third case involves copular verbs. These may be classified as ascriptive (*be, become*: *he is silly*), as cognitive (*seem, appear*: *he seems silly*) or sensorial (*look, sound, feel, smell, taste*: *he looks silly*). So long as what follows is an adjective, the two varieties pattern in the same way (as in the examples). When, however, a noun follows, there are divergencies. Both allow nouns following ascriptive *be* and *become*: *he is a fool*. The case is quite different with *appear* and *seem*, however, which may take noun predicative complements directly in BrE, but require *to be* in AmE (also possible in BrE): *he seemed (to be) a fool*. With sensorial copulas, finally, BrE once again allows a noun to follow directly while AmE requires intervening *like* (also possible in BrE): *he looked (like) a fool*. Note that even in BrE not every noun may follow directly (i.e. without *to be* or *like*); this seems to be possible only when the noun is more or less adjectival in nature (*to seem/look a fool* = *to seem/look foolish*). This practically dictates that the indefinite article be used, for then reference is general and serves the purposes of characterization just as an adjective does. In addition, the noun concerned must be gradable in the sense of more or less. For instance, someone can be *very much a fool*, but not the specific **very much my fool*. For more on complementation, see 4.7.

Concord   This is the final point concerning the verb. As elsewhere in the grammar the two varieties agree here almost completely. The one important divergency has to do with the greater degree to which **notional concord** is applied in BrE. While both types of English construe words such as *people* and *police* as plurals, in BrE a large number of collective nouns for groups of people are often seen as plural while they virtually never are in AmE, for example, *government, team, committee, council, board*, etc. Hence BrE frequently has *The council have decided to make further enquiries*, where AmE (but BrE as well) has *The council has decided . . ..*

A minor point in this context is the fact that BrE freely uses interrogative *aren't I* for the non-existent contracted form of *am*. This is not acceptable in AmE.

Tag questions   Tag questions, at least those which show changing grammatical correspondences according to the subject and auxiliary of the preceding main clause (*He's coming early, isn't he?*) are probably more common in BrE than in AmE. AmE seems to prefer the non-grammatical type (*I'll return it tomorrow, okay?*); certainly ones without reversed polarity are rare in AmE, for example *They are leaving tomorrow, are they?* (Benson *et al.* 1986a: 25; Algeo 1988: 11f).

11.3.2 The noun, the pronoun and the article

This area contains considerably less to report on.

The noun   Besides the difference in interpretation of some collective nouns as notional plurals, as discussed immediately above, there is nothing of great significance to add here. Perhaps it is of interest, however, to note that some words appear regularly in the singular in the one, but in the plural in the other variety: For example, BrE has the plural *overheads* and *maths* where AmE has singular *overhead* and *math*; on the other hand, AmE has plural *accommodations* and *sports* where BrE has abstract and non-count *accommodation* and *sport*. In AmE *inning* (as in baseball) is a count noun with a singular and a plural; in BrE there is only the unchanging singular and plural form *innings* (as in cricket). BrE can (but need not) give words such as *fish* or *shrimp* a plural ending (*fishes, shrimps*), while this is impossible in AmE. Furthermore, numbers are also sometimes treated differently: when a noun follows a number ending in *thousand, million*, etc., no plural {S} is added to the number in either (*five thousand books*); when the noun is elided BrE may add a plural (possible BrE: *five thousands*); AmE may not.

The pronoun   Two further observations can be added to what has already been said about collective nouns and notional concord. For one, both varieties agree in frequently, but not necessarily, using plural pronoun reference for such 'group' nouns (*their* in the following), irrespective of the verb form chosen: *The council is/are considering this at their next meeting*. The second point reveals greater divergency: a singular interpretation of a collective noun such as *committee* or *council* will lead to the use of the relative pronoun *which*, while the BrE plural interpretation will be more likely to take *who* (*The Committee, which is considering the move, . . .* vs. *The Committee, who are considering the move, . . .*).

An additional pronoun difference is the widespread use of a distinct second person plural pronoun in Southern AmE, *you all*, sometimes shortened to *y'all* (possessive *you all's* or *y'all's*). Although a few other second person plural forms exist in both BrE and AmE, such as *youse*, none of them has the relative acceptance of *you all*.

Traditionally, AmE used the indefinite pronoun *one* on first reference, but used *he, his* or *him* as appropriate to continue the reference, for example, *One tends to find himself in agreement in order to maintain his self-respect*. Here BrE would use *One . . . oneself . . . one's . . .* . Aside from the fact that indefinite *one* has always been overly formal and stiff and therefore hardly a part of lively colloquial English, AmE users are increasingly finding the use of the masculine form needlessly sexist and opting for either the BrE repetition of a form of *one* or the combination *he or she* or singular *they*, as in *One tends to find him- or herself/themself (*also *them-selves) in agreement in order to maintain his or her/their self-respect*. See discussion in 8.1, **Generic Reference**.

Two final points on pronouns are, first, that there is greater AmE use of the form *he* or *she* after the copula in the phrases *This is he/she* (used chiefly to identify oneself on the telephone; for example, BrE *Speaking*). Second, BrE may omit the pronoun in prepositional expressions of location, as in *We have a cellar with water in (it)*.

The article   A few differences in article choice include the following point: BrE *to/in hospital* vs. AmE *to/in the hospital*. While all the seasons (*spring*, *summer*, *autumn*, *winter*) can be used with or without the article in both varieties, the usual AmE word for *autumn*, viz. *fall*, cannot occur without it (*in the fall*, not **in fall*). Although there are other differences in usage, none of them is of great significance.

11.3.3 The preposition, the conjunction, and the adverb

Differing items   While BrE and AmE both prefer *while*, *among* and *amid*, BrE also uses the forms *whilst*, *amongst* and *amidst*, which are rare in AmE. BrE sometimes also employs *in respect of* where both normally have *in respect to*. Common to both is *behind*, *apart from* and *on top of*, but AmE also has *in back of*, *aside from* and *atop* respectively, which are unfamiliar in BrE. AmE uses *in behalf of* in addition to shared *on behalf of*. Next to common *off*, *opposite* and *alongside*, AmE also has *off of*, *opposite of* and *alongside of* without any difference in meaning. AmE prefers *different than* next to BrE *different from* and *different to*. Further-more, AmE usage is much more prone to leave the preposition out altogether in time expressions such as *Tuesdays*, where BrE has *on Tuesdays*. AmE also omits prepositions more freely in time expressions, as in *She starts work (on) Monday*.

Differing meanings   The preposition *out* (AmE, informal BrE) is not used in the same way as common *out of*. The former may only be employed with two-dimensional objects which designate paths of exit, as in *out the window*, *door*, etc. *Out of* may be used here as well, of course, in both varieties and, indeed, usually is in BrE.

The pair *round* and *around* also overlap in much the same way except that here it is AmE which has no choice, since the form *round* is scarcely found there. In BrE, on the other hand, *round* may be distinguished from *around* as in *to go round the earth* 'in a circular movement, as, for example, a satellite' vs. *to go all around the world* 'to travel to various places anywhere in the world'. This distinction is missing in AmE.

The preposition *through*, as in AmE *Volume one of the dictionary goes from A through G*, is not current in BrE, where the ambiguous *A to G* or the cumbersome *A to G inclusive* might be found.

The present perfect of verbs expressing continuous activity regularly has *for* to introduce periods of time in both varieties, for example, *I've been working for an hour*. For individual events within a period both varieties use *in*, for example, *I have gone twice in (the past) two weeks*. Usage differs when a verb expressing individual events is negated: here BrE uses *for*: *I haven't gone for (the past) two weeks*, while AmE prefers *in*: *I haven't gone in (the past) two weeks*. In other words, BrE usage is generalized from the continuity of non-action while AmE usage is generalized from the non-occurrence of individual acts.

An additional difference in application of generalities is the preference for *at* (BrE and common) vs. *over* (AmE) for longer holidays and week-ends (*at/over Easter*). Here *at* usage stresses the relatively punctual nature of the time unit, while AmE usage underscores its longer absolute length. The use of *at the week-end* (BrE; impossible in AmE) fits this pattern and treats *week-end* punctually (as *at the end*). AmE *on* (beside *over*) *the week-end* treats *week-end* in the same way as a week day (*on Monday*).

To indicate a fixed time in the future, the time of reference will always follow *from* in AmE while BrE may omit the preposition and even invert the elements (common *We'll meet two weeks from Saturday* and BrE *We'll meet Saturday fortnight*).

For clock time informal AmE uses *of* or *till* for common *to*, as in *It's quarter of/till ten*. The usage with *of* is unknown in BrE; *till* is rare there. Informal BrE, on the other hand, has the preposition *gone* 'past' as in *It's gone eight; we'd better get a move on*, which would puzzle an AmE speaker. Equally ununderstandable for this speaker is the time expression *It's half eight* for 'eight-thirty'. AmE frequently uses *after* (*It's twenty after nine*), while BrE uses only the shared form *past*; however, AmE favours *past* in combination with *quarter* and *half* (*a quarter/half past ten*).

A few usages show preferences in the one or the other direction, for example, *lest* is more common in AmE (*Be quiet lest he call the police*). In BrE this counts as somewhat archaic. Instead the informal *in case* might be used in much the same sense (*Be quiet in case he should call the police*), a usage which, however, is not possible in AmE. Note that both could have *. . . so that he won't call the police*. A final preference worth mentioning is the use of time expressions without a preposition, which is more common in AmE than in BrE, as in *The meeting started seven-thirty*.

Differing word class membership   In AmE the prepositions *plus*, *like* and *on account of* are sometimes used as conjunctions, as in *I don't feel like we should go out on account of it's late, plus I'm tired*. In BrE, on the other hand, the adverbs *directly* and *immediately* can also be conjunctions, as in

Immediately/Directly you came, he left. Furthermore, in BrE *nor* may be an adverbial conjunct and co-occur with the conjunctions *and* or *but*, for example *I don't like French cheese, but nor do I like cheddar*.

Adverbs   Perhaps the most noticeable difference in the use of adverbs is the greater tendency in AmE, especially in speech and in informal writing and sports journalism, to use adjectives rather than adverbs, as in *You did that real good*. While the use of an adjective in the function of a manner adverb (*good* in the example) is rejected in more careful usage, adjectives as intensifiers (*real* in the example) are used much further up the stylistic scale.

The use of adverbs formed from nouns plus the ending *-wise* (*time-wise* 'from the point of view of time' or *word-wise* 'as far as words are concerned') is considered more typically American. A further morphological difference is the partiality of AmE to the ending *-ward* (without a final *-s*) as in *toward* or *backward*.

To round off this section, here are a few examples of different preferences in the choice of adverbs: the expressions in AmE: *sure(ly)*; *why then*; *okay now*; *anyways*; *still and all*. More firmly BrE are the intensifiers *quite*, *fairly* and *rather*.

11.3.4 Word order

BrE has *Will you give it me?* for common *Will you give me it?* or *Will you give it to me?* In the complimentary close to business letters American usage has *Sincerely yours* while BrE uses *Yours sincerely*. In BrE, inversion such as *Monday last* can be found, but hardly in AmE. Compare also the *River Thames* (*Humber*, *Avon*, etc.), but *the Mississippi* (*Missouri*, *Hudson*, etc.) *River*. In contrast, AmE will more freely use post-modifiers of the type *Eggs Benedict* or *Pea Soup Louise* in the names of dishes. Premodifiers in journalistic style are more frequent in AmE than in BrE, for example, *British novelist Graham Greene*, where more formal styles would have *Graham Greene, the British novelist*.

11.4 Lexis

The lexical relations between BrE and AmE have been analysed in many different ways, of which only the most important can be mentioned in this section.

11.4.1 The developmental approach

What might be called the developmental approach takes the criteria of use, intelligibility and regional status to set up four groups which can be seen as the stages through which regional words have to pass before they are fully accepted into common StE. The first category consists of words that are neither understood nor used in the other variety, for example, AmE *meld* 'merge' or BrE *hive off* 'separate from the main group'. Group two contains items that are understood but not used elsewhere (AmE *checkers*, *cookie*, *howdy* or BrE *draughts*, *scone*, *cheerio*). In the third there are items that are both understood and used in both, but which still have a distinctly American or British flavour to them (AmE *figure out*, *movie*; BrE *car park*, *telly*). The last group, finally, includes lexical material that is not only completely intelligible and widely used in the other variety, but has also lost whatever American or British flavour it once had (originally AmE *boost*, *debunk*, *hi*; originally BrE *brass tacks*, *semi-detached*, *pissed off*). There can be no doubt that many items start in group one and end up in the last group. It has to be added, however, that there is often no agreement on which group an item is in. *Student*, for example, in the broader-than-university sense of 'young person at school', used to be common only in AmE, but is making its way into BrE as well; *The Advanced Learner's Dictionary* (1989) still labels it 'esp US', while *Collins English Dictionary* (1987) and *The Concise Oxford Dictionary* (1990) have no regional labels at all. The BrE word *trendy* may have overtaken AmE *chic* in America (Safire 1989). *Webster's New Collegiate Dictionary* (1975) labels it as chiefly British, but *Longman's Dictionary of Contemporary English* (1987), *Collins COBUILD* (1987) and the *Oxford Advanced Learners Dictionary* (1989) do not. Finally, though almost all dictionaries say that *bag lady* 'a homeless woman who carries everything she owns around with her' is an AmE word, it is frequently found in newspapers in Britain, where the phenomenon is also widespread. This lack of consensus does not, however, mean that the criteria and the four groups have no value or cannot be justified.

The national flavour of a word can be important in determining whether it is accepted or not. Some people in Britain seem to resent the great number of Americanisms in BrE. The controversy around the word *hopefully*, as in *hopefully, he will be back soon*, has frequently served as a call-to-arms for purists who condemned it by pointing out that it came from across the Atlantic. Other speakers in Britain, on the other hand, especially younger people, might perhaps welcome transatlantic items simply because they are AmE. Overall, Americans show a more tolerant attitude towards British loans than vice versa; however, there are far fewer of them in AmE than the other way around (for examples, see Mencken 1963: chapter 6.4; Trudgill and Hannah 1985: 76; Safire 1989).

11.4.2 The causal approach

Scholars have also enquired into the less subjective and more linguistic reasons why items are or are not borrowed from the one variety into the other (cf. Leisi 1985: 227f). In this causal approach, the vivid and expressive nature of a number of words and phrases is held to have helped them expand, for example, many of the informal or slang items from AmE such as *fiend* (as in *dope fiend* or *fitness fiend*), *joint* ('cheap or dirty place of meeting for drinking, eating etc.') and *sucker* ('gullible person'). Secondly, many borrowings are short and snappy and often reinforce the trend in common StE towards the monosyllabic word, such as AmE *contact* (beside *get in touch with*), *cut* (next to *reduction*) and *fix* (in addition to *prepare*, *repair*) or BrE *chips* (beside AmE *french fries*) and *dicey* (beside AmE *chancy*). The third reason has to do with the fact that some loans provide a term for an idea or concept where there was none before. Borrowings of this latter sort are particularly valuable because they fill a conceptual gap. Examples are originally AmE *boost*, *debunk*, *know-how* and *high/low brow* or originally BrE *brunch*, *smog*, *cop*, *tabloid* or *gadget* (cf. Mencken 1963: chapter 6.4).

Finally, part of the attraction of many loans may lie in their morphological make-up. When they conform to productive word formation patterns of English, they are more likely to be borrowed. This may include phrasal verbs or zero-derived items (see chapter 1). Examples of phrasal verbs: AmE *be into something* ('be passionately interested in'), *bone up (on)* ('study intensively'), *cave in* ('collapse; give up') or BrE *butter up* 'sweet talk' or *be cheesed off* 'annoyed' (both listed as BrE in Moss 1973, but now clearly shared). Among zero derivations of American origin, *brush-off*, *hairdo* and *showdown* can be mentioned.

Conversely, words current in the language of ethnic minorities in the United States, such as African-Americans, Jews, and people of Hispanic origin, may provide other examples. The same is probably true of words borrowed into BrE from many of Britain's former colonial holdings, for example, Anglo-Indian *pukka*, 'genuine, sound' or Arabic *shufti* 'a look at something'. Originally Yiddish words, for instance, which are known and used especially on the East Coast of the United States, such as *schlemiel* ('an awkward and unlucky person'), *schlep(p)* ('carry'; 'move slowly or with great effort') or *schlock* ('trash, cheap goods'), are said to be unattractive to British ears and tongues perhaps because of the initial consonant cluster /ʃl/. But it would be rash to maintain that this type of word will 'remain firmly unborrowed in British English' (Burchfield 1985: 163); all the same, the 1990 edition of the *Concise Oxford Dictionary* does still mark *schlemiel* and *schlock* as colloquial American; but the regional label is not attached to *schlep(p)* any longer.

Once the words and phrases from the one variety are admitted to the other, the question is where they manage to establish themselves. Ilson (1990), for example, thinks that there are few Americanisms in expository writing, while many loans have been imported into such spheres as poetry, fiction, conversation, some areas of technology, social organization, transport and communication. This is an interesting observation, but clearly in need of more substantiation.

11.4.3 The semantic approach

Perhaps the most common way to deal with the lexis of the two varieties is what may be called the semantic approach. This method compares words and phrases with their referents or meanings in terms of sameness and difference. Despite varying approaches with sometimes far more groupings (cf. Trudgill and Hannah: 1985: 4.3; Benson *et al*. 1986a: 28–41; Algeo 1986), five different groups may conveniently be recognized.

First of all, most words and their meanings are the same, which explains the fact that British and American speakers rarely experience any difficulty in understanding each other. As a result this first group is seldom mentioned.

The second group comprises words which are present in only one variety because they refer to something unknown in the other culture. This can be words for things in the natural environment such as BrE *moor* or *heath* and AmE *prairie* and *canyon*. It also may include social and political institutions (BrE *Yorkshire pudding* or *back bench* and AmE *succotash* or *favorite son*). Although cases in the second category make linguistic help necessary, they do not cause misunderstandings.

A variant on this type of distinction is what has been called a **lexical gap**. Here the referent or concept is known in the other variety but not lexicalized, that is only paraphrases are available, for example, BrE *chapel* 'a local (branch) of a printers' union' or BrE (slang) *to tart up* 'to dress up in a garish manner' (cf. Benson *et al*. 1986a: 29).

The third group covers those cases where different words and phrases are used to express the same meaning. BrE *petrol* is AmE *gas(oline)* and AmE *truck* is BrE *lorry*.

In the fourth category the two varieties share a word/phrase, but with a fully different meaning, as with *vest*, which in AmE is what is called a *waistcoat* in BrE, but which in BrE is what is called an *undershirt* in AmE.

A variation on this is the case in which the two varieties agree in the meanings, but one variety has an additional meaning not known or used in the other. For example, both agree in the meaning of *leader* 'someone who leads', but BrE also uses it in the sense of AmE (and shared) *editorial*. Conversely, both understand the noun *fall* as 'downward movement', but AmE also uses this word in the sense of BrE (and shared) *autumn*. In many cases special words and meanings arise only in certain contexts. Examples in BrE are *sit* or *enter for* when they collocate with *exam*, while *freshen* has the extra meaning 'add more liquid etc. to a drink' in AmE only in collocation with *drink*. BrE *set an exercise* is *assign an exercise* in AmE (Benson *et al*. 1986a: 89). For collocations see Benson *et al*. 1986b.

The final grouping is the very common instance in which both varieties share an expression and its meaning(s), but where one or both have a further expression for the same thing not shared by the other. Both AmE and BrE have *taxi*, while *cab* is AmE. Likewise, both share *raincoat*, but only BrE has *mac(intosh)* for the same thing. In one final example of this, *pharmacy* is common, while *chemist's* is BrE only and *drug store* is typically AmE.

11.4.4 Relative frequencies and cultural associations

Many writers make absolute statements and do not take into account the evidence for relative frequencies. Too little use has been made so far of the two large-scale corpora assembled at Brown University for AmE (Francis and Kučera 1982) and at Lancaster, Oslo and Bergen (LOB) for BrE (Hofland and Johansson 1982). It is not the case, for example, that *railroad* is found exclusively in AmE or *railway* only in BrE: 'in the Brown corpus *railroad* appears forty-seven times and *railway* ten; in LOB *railway* appears fifty-two times and *railroad* once' (Ilson 1990: 37).

Differences in cultural associations are almost wholly neglected. It is often pointed out, for example, that *robin* refers to two different birds, but it is hardly ever mentioned that the English bird is considered a symbol of winter while the American robin is a harbinger of spring (Ilson 1990: 40).

Scholars have also been prone to take meaning in a narrow sense which excludes such use aspects as field, regional and social distribution and differences in personal tenor (see chapter 1). AmE *vacation* is *holiday(s)* in BrE, as in *They are on holiday/vacation now*. But lawyers and universities in Britain use *vacation* to refer to the intervals between terms. AmE *pinkie*, an informal word for *little finger*, is an import from Scotland, where it is still the accepted word, as is borne out by the regional labels 'esp. US & Sc.' in the COD.

Difficult and controversial, though of great importance in both the United States and Great Britain, are the social class associations that items can have in the respective variety. It is therefore not unimportant for Americans to know that in BrE *lounge* 'is definitely non-U; *drawing room* definitely U' [*U* = 'upper class'] (Benson *et al.* 1986a: 36). Conversely, British people might be interested to hear about America that 'Proles say *tux*, middles *tuxedo*, but both are considered low by uppers, who say *dinner jacket* or (higher) *black tie*' (Fussell 1984: 152). Few writers and fewer word lists or dictionaries give help with class aspects, but the books by Buckle (mainly BrE; 1978); Cooper (BrE; 1981), Fussell (AmE; 1984; especially chapter 7) and Benson *et al.* (AmE and BrE; 1986a) provide some orientation.

11.4.5 The fields of university and of sports

While most comparisons of BrE and AmE lexis are arranged in alphabetical order (Schur, 1987), this makes them useful only for analytic purposes, but not for language production. Instead of listing further unconnected items we will now undertake a brief systematic comparison of two fields, universities and the two 'national' sports of cricket and baseball.

University lexis   For the sake of convenience our discussion of university lexis will come under the headings of people and activities.

People   In higher education (AmE) or tertiary education (BrE) a division may be made into two groups: the first are those who teach (the faculty, AmE; the (academic) staff, BrE) and commonly include:

AmE	*(full) professors*	BrE	*professors*
	associate professors		*readers*
	assistant professors		*senior lecturers*
	instructors		*lecturers*

And there are those who study:

	freshmen	*first year students or freshers*
	sophomores	*second year students*
	juniors	*third year students*
	seniors	*final year students*

The teaching and research is organized in *departments* (AmE) or *faculties* (BrE), and these are under the administrative supervision of *heads of department* (AmE) or *deans* (BrE). American colleges and universities also have *deans*, but they are placed higher administratively, at the head of a major division in a college (AmE, undergraduate education) or professional school (AmE, postgraduate, for example in a school of medicine, law, forestry, nursing, business administration, etc.). At the top in the American system is a *president*. This is not unknown in the UK: however, a *chancellor* (honorary) or *vice-chancellor* (actual on-the-spot chief officer) is more likely to be found there. On the other hand, a *chancellor* in America is often the head of a state university system.

Activities   Students in the United States *go to* a college and *study* a *major* and a *minor subject*; in the UK they *come up* and then *study*, or *read*, a *main* and a *subsidiary subject*. While at college or university they may choose to live in a *dorm(itory)* (AmE) or a *student hostel* (BrE) or one of the *halls (of residence)* (BrE). If they misbehave, they may be *suspended* (AmE) or *rusticated* (BrE); in the worst of cases they may even be *expelled* (common) or *sent down* (BrE). In their *classes* (common) they may be assigned (AmE) a *term paper* (AmE) or given a *long essay* (BrE) to write, and at the end of a *semester*, *trimester*, *quarter* (all AmE) or *term* (common) they *sit* (BrE) or *take* (common) exams which are *supervised* (AmE) or *invigilated* (BrE) by a *proctor* (AmE) or *invigilator* (BrE). These exams are then *corrected* and *graded* (AmE) or *marked* (BrE). The grades (marks) themselves differ in their scale: American colleges and universities mark from (high) *A*, via *B*, *C* and *D*, to (low = fail) *F*, which are marks known and used in the UK as well. Overall results for a term as well as for the whole of one's studies in the USA will be expressed as a grade point average, with a high of 4.0 (all *A*'s). In the UK a person's studies may conclude with a brilliant *starred first*, an excellent *first*, an *upper second*, a *lower second* or a *third* (a simple pass).

Particularly good students may wish to continue beyond the *BA* (common) or *BS* (AmE) or *BSc* (BrE) as a *graduate* (especially AmE) or *postgraduate* (especially BrE) student. In that case they may take further courses and write an *MA thesis* (AmE) or *MA dissertation* (BrE). Indeed, they may even write a *doctoral dissertation* (AmE) or *doctoral thesis* (BrE).

Sports expressions   Idioms, idiomatic expressions and figurative language are used especially frequently in colloquial speech, perhaps because they tend to be colourful. Although they are drawn from all sorts of areas, it seems that a very high proportion come from sports. Many different types of sports are involved (track and field: *the university's track record*, boxing: *saved by the bell*, or horse-racing: *on the home stretch*); yet, it seems that it is the two 'national sports', cricket and baseball, which have contributed especially many of these vivid idiomatic and figurative expressions to the language of everyday communication.

Since the two sports resemble each other (if ever so vaguely), they actually share some expressions: *batting order* 'the order in which people act or take their turn'; *to field* 'enter a competition' as in *to field candidates for an election*; *to take the field* 'to begin a campaign'. The user should, however, beware of the seemingly similar, but in reality very different, expressions (BrE) *to do something off one's own bat* 'independently, without consulting others' vs. (AmE) *to do something off the bat* 'immediately, without waiting'.

Most of the expressions are, however, part of only cricket or only baseball. Of these a couple from cricket are well integrated into both BrE and AmE without any longer being necessarily closely identified with the sport: *to stump* 'to baffle, put at a loss for an answer' ($<$ put out a batsman by touching the stumps); *to stonewall* 'to draw out discussion intentionally and avoid giving an answer' ($<$ slow, careful overly protective play by a batsman).

Further expressions from cricket which are known, but not commonly used in AmE, are *a sticky wicket* 'a difficult situation' and *(something is) not cricket* 'unfair or unsportsmanlike'. Less familiar or totally unknown in AmE are *to hit something for six* 'to score a resounding success', *to queer someone's pitch* 'to spoil someone's plans', *to be caught out* 'to be trapped, found out, exposed', *a hat trick* (also soccer) 'something phenomenally well done', *She has had a good innings* 'a long life'.

Baseball has provided the following collection of idiomatic expressions, most of which have a very distinctly American flavour about them: *to play* (*political, economic*, etc.) *hard ball* 'to be serious about something', *to touch base* 'to keep in contact', *not to get to first base with someone* 'to be unsuccessful with someone', *to pinch hit for someone* 'to stand in for someone', *to ground out/fly out/foul out/strike out* 'to fail', *to have a/one strike/two strikes against you* 'to be at a disadvantage', *to play in/to make the big leagues* 'to work/be with important, powerful people', *a double play* 'two successes in one move', *a rain check* 'postponement', *a grand slam* (also tennis and bridge) 'a smashing success or victory', *a blooper* 'a mistake or failure', *a doubleheader* 'a combined event with lots to offer', *batting average* 'a person's performance', *over the fence* or *out of the ball park* 'a successful move or phenomenal feat', *out in left field* 'remote, out of touch, unrealistic', *off base* 'wrong'.

What has been illustrated here is only exemplary of the many lexical and idiomatic differences between the two varieties. This also seems to be the case in government and politics, in cooking and baking, in clothing, and in connection with many technological developments up to World War II (*railroads/railways*, *trucks/lorries*, etc.). Nevertheless, as a matter of perspective, it is important to bear in mind that the vocabulary and idioms associated with national institutions such as the educational system and national sports will diverge more strongly than that of other areas. The vast majority of vocabulary used in everyday, colloquial speech as well as that of international communication in science and technology is common not only to AmE and BrE, but also to all other national and regional varieties of English.

REFERENCES

Algeo, J. (1986) 'The two streams: British and American English', *Journal of English Linguistics*, 19: 269–84.
—— (1988) 'British and American grammatical differences', *International Journal of Lexicography* 1: 1–31.
Benson, M., Benson, E. and Ilson, R. (1986a) *Lexicographic Description of English*, Amsterdam: Benjamins.
—— (1986b) *The BBI Combinatory Dictionary of English: a Guide to Word Combinations*, Amsterdam: Benjamins.
Bronstein, A. J. (1960) *The Pronunciation of American English: an Introduction to Phonetics*, New York: Appleton Century Crofts.
Buckle, R. (1978) *U and non-U Revisited*, New York: Viking.

Burchfield, R. (1985) *The English Language*, Oxford: Oxford University Press.

Collins, P. E. (1989) 'Divided and debatable usage in Australian English', in P. E. Collins and D. Blair (eds) *Australian English: the Language of a New Society*, St Lucia: University of Queensland Press, pp. 138–49.

Cooper, J. (1981) *Class*, London: Corgi.

Emery, D. W. (1975) *Variant Spellings in Modern American Dictionaries*, 2nd edn, Urbana: National Council of Teachers of English.

Engler, L. F. and Hilyer, R. G. (1971) 'Once again: American and British intonation systems', *Acta Linguistica Hafnensia* 13: 99–108.

Francis, W. N. and Kučera, H. (1982) *Frequency Analysis of English Usage: Lexicon and Grammar*, Boston: Houghton Mifflin.

Fussell, P. (1984) *Class*, London: Arrow.

Gimson, A. C. (1989) *Introduction to the Pronunciation of English*, 4th edn, rev. S. Ramsaran. London: Edward Arnold.

Gläser, R. (1972) 'Graphemabweichungen in der amerikanischen Werbesprache', *Zeitschrift für Anglistik und Amerikanistik* 20: 184–96.

Greenbaum, S. (1986) 'Spelling variants in British English', *Journal of English Linguistics* 19: 258–68.

Higgs, J. (1980) 'The American /r/ is advanced velar not postalveolar', *Work in Progress* 13, Edinburgh: Department of Linguistics, University of Edinburgh, pp. 112–16.

Hofland, K. and Johansson, S. (1982) *Word Frequencies in British and American English*, Bergen: Norwegian Computing Centre for the Humanities.

Honikman, B. (1964) 'Articulatory Settings', in D. Abercrombie, D. B. Fry, P. A. D. MacCarthy, N. C. Scott and J. L. M. Trim (eds) *In Honour of Daniel Jones*, London: Longman, pp. 73–84.

Ilson, R. (1990) 'British and American English: ex uno plura?', in C. Ricks and L. Michaels (eds) *The State of the Language*, 2nd edn, Berkeley: University of California Press, pp. 33–41.

Jacobson, B. (1979) 'Modality and the modals of necessity *must* and *have to*', *English Studies* 60: 296–312.

Jones, D. (comp.) (1988) *Everyman's Pronouncing Dictionary*, 14th edn, (rev. A. S. Gimson; revisions and supplement by S. Ramsaran) London: J. M. Dent.

Kenyon, J. S. (1969) *American Pronunciation*, Ann Arbor: Wahr.

Kenyon, J. S. and Knott, T. A. (1944) *A Pronouncing Dictionary of American English*, Springfield, Mass.: Merriam.

Leisi, E. (1985) *Das heutige Englisch*, 7th edn, Heidelberg: Winter.

Lewis, J. W. (1968–9) 'The so-called "broad a"', *English Language Teaching* 23: 65.

—— (1970–1) 'The American and British accents of English', *English Language Teaching* 25: 239–48.

Marshall, H. W. (1979) *The Colloquial Preterite vs. the Present Perfect: a Socio-linguistic Analysis*, Dissertation, Columbia University.

Mencken, H. L. (1963) *The American Language*, 4th edn, ed. R. I. McDavid, Jr., New York: Alfred Knopf.

Moss, N. (1973) *What's the Difference?*, London: Hutchinson.

Quirk, R., Greenbaum, S., Leech, G. and Svartvik, J. (1985) *A Comprehensive Grammar of the English Language*, London: Longman.

Roach, P. (1983) *English Phonetics and Phonology: a Practical Course*, Cambridge: Cambridge University Press.

Safire, W. (1989) 'Britishisms, taking some decisions', *International Herald Tribune*, April 17.

Schur, N. (1987) *British English*, New York: Facts on File.

Strevens, P. (1972) *British and American English*, London: Collier-Macmillan.

Trudgill, P. and Hannah, J. (1985) *International English*, 2nd edn, London: Edward Arnold.

Vanneck, G. (1958) 'The colloquial preterite in modern American English', *Word* 14: 236–42.

Wells, J. C. (1982) *Accents of English*, Cambridge: Cambridge University Press.

—— (1990) *Longman Pronouncing Dictionary*, London: Longman.

Chapter 12

English in America

English is spoken as a native language in two major spheres in America. The larger covers the United States and English-speaking Canada; the other, lesser sphere is the Caribbean area, centring on Jamaica, the Lesser Antilles and Guyana. A few peripheral areas, the creole-speaking sections along the Atlantic coast of Central America and the Gullah area of South Carolina and Georgia, will be considered in chapter 16 on pidgins and creoles; Puerto Rico is mentioned only in connection with Puerto Ricans living in the mainland United States (12.4.2).

These two areas are distinguished according to two linguistic criteria. The first is that educated Caribbean usage is relatively clearly oriented towards BrE while United States and Canadian English together make up AmE (despite numerous BrE features to be found in CanE). The second criterion is rooted in the Creole–English linguistic continuum which exists in CaribE, but not in AmE. A **continuum** is a spectrum of language forms between two extremes, but with only small, incremental differences as one moves from one point on the continuum to the next. At the one extreme, correlating with the lowest socio-economic and educational level of society, lie creole forms of English; at the other extreme there is StE in its West Indian form.

Both spheres, AmE and CaribE, encompass a fair amount of internal variation, and the overview in this chapter will attempt to distinguish the most important regional, social and ethnic varieties in both.

12.1 The languages of the United States and Canada

The largest single English-speaking area in the world is that formed by the United States and Canada. Approximately 85 per cent of the American and almost two-thirds of the Canadian populations have English as their native language. This is a sum total nearing a quarter of a billion speakers. Many (but by no means all) of the inhabitants of Canada and the United States who do not have English as their first language, nevertheless, use it in a multitude of different situations.

The next most widely used languages are Spanish and French. Significant numbers of Spanish-speaking residents, many of whom are recent immigrants (legal or illegal), live in Miami (especially from Cuba) and New York (especially from Puerto Rico), as well as in neighbourhood pockets in many large American cities (generally from Mexico and Central America). Others live in areas whose Spanish language traditions go back hundreds of years (chiefly Chicano communities of the Southwest).

French is the majority language of Quebec (over five million native speakers with an English-speaking minority of approximately 600,000). Ontario and New Brunswick also have sizable francophone minorities; relatively few French speakers live in the remaining provinces and territories. In the United States the only large concentrations of French are in New England, close to French Canada, and in Louisiana, where speakers are divided into those of the standard metropolitan variety (descendants of the original French settlers), of Cajun French (descendants of the Acadians, expelled in the eighteenth century from what was then renamed Nova Scotia) and speakers of Creole French (mostly descendants of slaves).

Needless to say, countries of immigration such as Canada and the United States have tremendous numbers of speakers of other mother tongues. Few of them, however, have settled in such a way that their languages have also been able to serve as community languages. Nevertheless, there are rural communities in both countries in which immigrant languages have been maintained over several generations (e.g. the German-speaking Amish of Pennsylvania and the Russian-speaking Doukhobors of Saskatchewan), and there are urban communities such as the numerous Chinatowns and Little Italy's, where languages besides English, French and Spanish are maintained.

Non-immigrant and non-colonial languages are still in daily use in some native American environments. About half a million of the more than one million American Indians and Alaskan natives can speak their traditional languages (Waggoner 1988: 82). In Canada approximately 62 per cent now have English as their native tongue (and 5 per cent have French); just over 150,000 (42 per cent) can speak their native languages, of which there are some fifty-three distinct ones in Canada alone (Labrie 1988: 1309).

Despite the large number of non-English native speakers (over half in New Mexico, over one-third in Hawaii, California, Arizona and Texas, and over a quarter in New York), there are few places in the United States and Canada where it is not possible to communicate in English. (Note that, despite highly developed French–English bilingualism, there are some four and a quarter million monolingual French speakers in Canada (Chambers 1991: 90). Language retention for English in Canada is given as 111.4 per cent, which means that English is spreading at the cost of other languages; for Canadian French the rate is 95.9 per cent; for all other languages, just over half (54.9 per cent) (Labrie 1988: 1311). In the United States several non-English speaking groups are expanding noticeably, above all Spanish and Chinese; but the retention rate for native-born children is generally not much higher than 50 per cent (Waggoner 1988: 91).

12.2 Regional varieties of AmE

12.2.1 Canada

CanE is solidly part of the American branch of the language (see Pringle 1986: 231). As such it shares most of the linguistic characteristics of AmE sketched out in the preceding chapter. Yet there are important features of CanE which distinguish it as an independent subvariety of AmE. 'What is distinctly Canadian about Canadian English is not its unique features (of which there are a handful) but its combination of tendencies that are uniquely distributed' (Bailey 1984: 161). Not the least of the factors contributing to the independence of CanE are the attitudes of anglophone Canadians, which strongly support a separate linguistic identity (cf. Avis 1983: 4, 11).

The effect of attitudes on language behaviour is revealed in a study in which Canadians with relatively more positive views of the United States and of Americans are also more likely to have syllable reduction in words such as the following: *mirror* (= *mere*), *warren* (= *warn*) or *lion* (= *line*). They also have fewer high diphthongs in words such as *about* or *like* (see below) and are more likely to voice the /t/ in words such as *party*, *butter* or *sister*. Finally, they use more American morphological and lexical forms. Pro-British attitudes correlate well with a preservation of vowel distinctions before an /r/, such as *spear it* vs. *spirit*, *Mary* vs. *merry* vs. *marry*, *furry* vs. *hurry* and *oral* vs. *aural* as well as distinct vowels in *cot* vs. *caught*. Pro-Canadian attitudes mean relatively more levelling of the vowel distinctions just mentioned, more loss of /j/ in words such as *tune*, *dew* or *new* (also true of speakers with positive attitudes towards the United States). Canadianisms are heard more among such speakers as well (Warkentyne 1983: 75f). A number of surveys have been conducted to register preferences in regard to the pronunciation of various individual words (*tomato* with /eɪ/ or /ɑː/, *either* with /iː/ or /aɪ/, *lever* with /e/ or /iː/, etc.) as well as spellings; 75 per cent say *zed* (BrE) instead of *zee* (AmE) as the name of the letter and just as many use *chesterfield* (specifically CanE) for *sofa* (AmE and BrE). Two-thirds have an /l/ in *almond* (GenAm), but two-thirds also say *bath* (BrE) the baby rather than *bathe* (AmE) it (Bailey 1984: 160). BrE spellings are strongly favoured in Ontario, AmE ones in Alberta (Chambers 1986: 8). Indeed:

Spelling can be a fairly emotional issue, even for those who care little for language. For in it are woven the problems of our British connection, the

American control over our cultural life, and to a very small extent, the struggle for a national identity, independent of both British and American influences.

(Fong 1967–8: 270)

As the preceding examples indicate, differences between CanE and the AmE of the United States are, aside from the rather superficial spelling distinctions, largely in the area of pronunciation and vocabulary. Grammar differences are virtually non-existent, at least on the level of StE (but cf. Chambers 1986: 9f).

Vocabulary provides for a considerable number of Canadianisms. As with many varieties of English outside the British Isles, designations for aspects of the topography, for flora and for fauna make up many of these items. Examples are *sault* 'waterfall', *muskeg* 'a northern bog', *canals* 'fjords' (topography); *cat spruce* 'a kind of tree', *tamarack* 'a kind of larch', *kinnikinnick* 'plants used in a mixture of dried leaves, bark and tobacco for smoking in earlier times' (flora); and *kokanee* 'a kind of salmon', *siwash duck* 'a kind of duck' (fauna) (Avis 1983: 11). Many words peculiar to Canada are, of course, no different in status from the regional vocabulary peculiar to the one or the other region of the United States, and much of the vocabulary that is not part of BrE is shared with AmE in general.

The pronunciation of CanE (sometimes called General Canadian, Avis 1973: 62) applies to Canada from the Ottawa Valley (just west of the Quebec–Ontario border) to British Columbia and is similar to what has been described as GenAm (see chapters 3 and 11). It shares the same consonant system, including the instable contrast between the /hw/ of *which* and the /w/ of *witch*. Its vowel system is similar to that of the northern variety of GenAm, which means that the opposition between /ɑː/ and /ɔː/, as in *cot* and *caught*, has been lost. The actual quality of the neutralized vowel is said to vary according to the phonetic environment; however, Chambers and Hardwick suggest [ɔ] (exclusively) as a possible regional realization in Edmonton (Chambers and Hardwick 1986: 43). The distinctions between /iː/ and /ɪ/ (the stressed vowel of *beery* vs. that of *mirror*), between /eɪ/, /e/ and /æ/ (*Mary* vs. *merry* vs. *marry*), and between /ɒ/ and /ɔː/ (*oral* vs. *aural*) are rapidly dying out in CanE as they are in most varieties of AmE (cf. Kinloch 1983).

What shows up as the most typical Canadian feature of pronunciation is what is generally called 'Canadian raising'. This refers to the realization of /aʊ/ and /aɪ/ with a higher and non-fronted first element [ʌu] and [ʌi] when followed by a voiceless consonant. Elsewhere the realization is [au] and [aɪ]. Hence each of the pairs *bout* [bʌut] – *bowed* [baud] and *bite* [bʌit] – *bide* [baɪd] have noticeably different allophones. While other varieties of English also have such realizations (e.g. Scotland, Northern Ireland,

Tidewater Virginia), the phonetic environment described here is specifically Canadian.

One of the most interesting aspects of Canadian raising is its increasing loss (realization as [au] and [ai] in all phonetic environments) among young Canadians. This movement may be understood as part of a standardization process in which the tacit standard is GenAm and not General CanE. This movement has been documented most strongly among young females in Vancouver and Toronto and is indicative of a generally positive attitude towards things American (as partially substantiated by lexical preferences as well). However, an independent development among young Vancouver males, namely rounding of the first element of /aʊ/ before voiceless consonants as [ou], is working against this standardization and may be part of a process promoting a covert, non-standard local norm (Chambers and Hardwick 1986).

Regional variation in CanE   The emphasis in the preceding section was on the English westwards of the Ottawa Valley (sometimes called Central/ Prairie CanE even though it reaches to the Pacific). It is an unusually uniform variety, at least as long as the focus is on urban, middle-class usage (ibid.: 24). Canada is, of course, overwhelmingly middle-class and urban (Chambers 1991: 90), and the bulk of the English-speaking population lives in the area referred to.

Working-class usage is said to differ not only from middle-class CanE, but also in itself as one moves from urban centre to urban centre (ibid.). Unfortunately, relatively little concrete data about it is available (but cf. Esling 1991). Woods, however, shows working-class preferences in Ottawa to be more strongly in the direction of GenAm than middle- and upper-class preferences are, at least in regard to the voicing of intervocalic /t/ and the loss of /j/ in *tune*, *new* and *due* words. Working-class speech patterns also favour /ɪn/ over /ɪŋ/ for the ending *-ing* and tend to level the /hw/ − /w/ opposition more completely (Woods 1991: 137–43).

Eastwards from the Ottawa Valley and including the Maritime provinces of New Brunswick, Nova Scotia and Prince Edward Island is the second major region of CanE. Here the norms of pronunciation (for this is what differs most noticeably) are varied. For the Ottawa Valley alone Pringle and Padolsky distinguish ten distinct English language areas. Much of the variation they recognize may be accounted for by the settlement history of the valley: Scots, Northern and Southern Irish, Kashubian Poles, Germans and Americans (especially loyalists who left the United States during and after the War of Independence) (Pringle and Padolsky 1983: 326–9). Although there is also much variation in the Maritimes as well, the Eastern Canadian region is perhaps best characterized overall as resembling the English of New England (Avis 1973: 45), which is where many of the earliest settlers came from; there is, for example, less /aː/ − /ɔː/ levelling, yet the

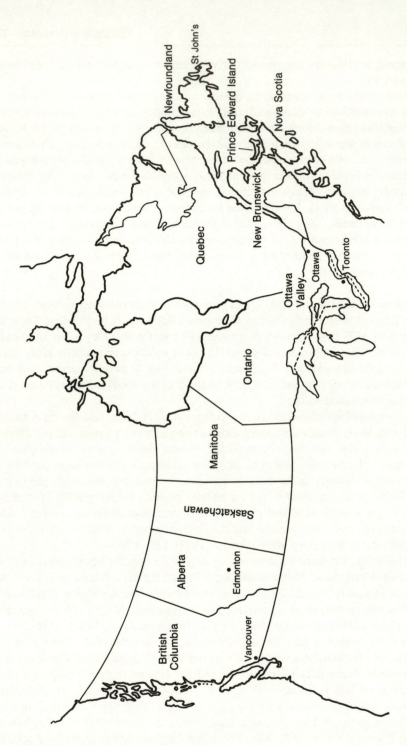

Map 12.1 Canada

English of this area is, like all of Canada, rhotic (i.e. /r/ is pronounced where spelled), while Eastern New England is non-rhotic.

The final distinct region of CanE is Newfoundland (population 568,000). Wells even speaks of the existence of traditional dialects in Newfoundland, something which exists in the English-speaking world only in Great Britain and Ireland and perhaps in the Appalachian region of the United States (Wells 1982: 4). The linguistic identity of Newfoundland is the result of early (from 1583 onwards) and diverse (especially Irish and Southwest English) settlement, stability of population (93 per cent native born) and isolation. Since it joined Canada in 1949 its isolation has been somewhat less. The influence of mainland pronunciation patterns has become stronger, and there is 'widespread diffusion within the province of the mainland North American standard' (Clarke 1991: 110). Yet the English of Newfoundland and specifically of St John's, its largest city, 'will retain its distinct phonological identity for some time to come' (ibid.: 119). Southwestern English influences have been observed in the voicing of initial /f/ and /s/ (cf. Kinloch 1985: 101f; however this is not mentioned in Wells 1982: 498–501). IrE influences include clear [l] in all environments, also monophthongal /e/ (for /eɪ/) and /o/ (for /əu/ or /ou/); /ʌ/ is rounded and retracted. Some speakers neutralize /aɪ/ vs. /ɔɪ/, realizing both as /aɪ/. The dental fricatives /θ/ and /ð/ are most often /t/ and /d/ (but also dental [t̪] and [d̪]) (cf. Clarke 1991: 109f). Furthermore, *pate* /pɛɪt/ and *bait* /bɛɪt/ do not traditionally rhyme; /h/ is generally missing except in standard speech; and consonant clusters are regularly simplified, for example, *Newfoun'lan'* or *pos'* ('post') (cf. Wells 1982: 498–501). 'Canadian raising' is universal in all phonetic environments for some speakers (Chambers 1986: 13).

Many of these features are typical only of older Newfoundlanders, 'while the speech patterns of certain teenage groups would be, to the untrained observer at least, virtually indistinguishable from those of teenagers in such major Canadian centres as Toronto or Vancouver' (Clarke 1991: 111). In other words, considerable change is taking place in Newfoundland English, and 'age is by far the most important' (ibid.: 113) of the sociolinguistic factors involved, with women generally taking the lead. In contrast, 'loyalty to the vernacular norm is most evident among older speakers, males, and lower social strata' (ibid.: 116).

The vocabulary of Newfoundland is well catered for in Story *et al*. *Dictionary of Newfoundland English* (1990). For mainland CanE see the general (rather than dialect) dictionary by Avis *et al*., *The Gage Canadian Dictionary* (1973).

12.2.2 The United States

The regional varieties of English in the United States consist of three general areas (see map 12.2): Northern, of which CanE is a part, Midland and Southern. Each of these may be further differentiated into sub-regions. Grammar is of relatively little importance for these three areas; most of the dividing and subdividing is based on vocabulary and pronunciation, though the two may not lead to identical areas (cf. Frazer 1986). However, the lexical distinctions are themselves most evident in the more old-fashioned, rural vocabulary which is investigated in the various dialect geographical projects in or related to the *Linguistic Atlas of the United States and Canada*: those covering New England (Kurath *et al.* 1939–43), the Middle and South Atlantic States (McDavid *et al.* 1980f), the North Central States (Marckwardt *et al.* 1976–8), the Upper Midwest (Allen 1973–6), the Pacific Coast (Bright 1971; Reed and Metcalf 1979), Colorado (Hankey 1960), Oklahoma (Van Riper), Texas (Atwood 1962), and of the Gulf States (Pederson 1981). See also Cassidy 1985, 1991. Increasingly, general North American terms are replacing such regional distinctions as Northern *(devil's) darning needle* or Midland *snake doctor/snake feeder* or Southern *mosquito hawk* 'dragon fly'. However, some urban terms continue to reinforce the older regional terms. For example, *hero* (New York), *sub/submarine* (Pittsburgh), *hoagie* (Philadelphia), *grinder* (Boston), *po' boy* (New Orleans) and a number of others all designate a roughly similar, overlarge sandwich made of a split loaf or bun of bread and filled with varying (regional) goodies. Each of the cities just mentioned is, more or less coincidentally, also the centre of a sub-region. Vocabulary on the whole, however, offers distinctions which often do not occur very frequently and which can usually easily be replaced by more widely accepted terms.

Pronunciation differences, in contrast to lexis, are evident in everything a person says and less subject to conscious control. The Southern accents realize /aɪ/ as [aˑ] or [a], that is, with a weakened off-glide or with no off-glide at all. Lack of rhoticity is typical of Eastern New England and New York City, but not the Inland North. It is also characteristic of Coastal Southern and the Gulf Southern, but not Mid-Southern (also known as South Midland). Northern does not have /j/ in words such as *due*, nor does North Midland, but /j/ may occur throughout the South. The /ɑː/ − /ɔː/ opposition is maintained in the South, but has been lost in the North Midland, and is weakening in the North. 'Canadian raising' is a Northern form which, despite its name, is common in many American cities of the Inland North (Vance 1987).

The pronunciation of the North Midland area, more or less from Ohio westwards, has often been referred to as General American (GenAm). This label is a convenient fiction used to designate a huge area in which there are surely numerous local differences in pronunciation, but in which there are none of the more noticeable sub-regional divisions such as those along the eastern seaboard. Furthermore, the differences between North Midland and Inland North are relatively insignificant. Both areas are rhotic, are not likely to vocalize /l/, have /aɪ/ as [æɪ] or [aɪ], do not distinguish /ɑː/ and /ɔː/ (or increasingly do not; note, however, that this opposition is still recognized in this book), and no longer maintain the /j/ on-glide in the *due*-words. Most significant of all for the selection of North Midland for the label GenAm is the fact that it is this type of accent more than any other which is used on the national broadcasting networks. For a summary of the varied history of the term, see Van Riper 1986.

The most noticeable and probably the major regional contrast is that between North and South. This division is, in addition to vocabulary and pronunciation differences, underscored to some extent at least by grammatical features. It seems that it is only in Southern varieties, including Black English (see below), that such, admittedly non-standard, features occur as perfective *done* (*I done seen it*), future *gon* (*I'm gon* [not *goin'*] *tell you something*), and several more far-reaching types of multiple negation, such as a carry-over of negation across clauses (*He's not comin', I don't believe* 'I believe he's not coming') (cf. Feagin 1979: 258).

It is also in the South that an area is to be found with speech forms approaching the character of a traditional dialect (such as otherwise found only in Great Britain and Ireland and possibly also in Newfoundland; cf. Wells 1982: 4). The dialect which is meant is Appalachian English and the related Ozark English, which are found in the Southern Highlands (Mid-Southern on map 12.2). The English of these regions is characterized by a relatively high incidence of older forms which have generally passed out of other types of AmE. Examples include syntactic phenomena such as *a*-prefixing on verbs (*I'm a-fixin' to carry her to town*), morphological-phonological ones such as initial /h/ in *hit* 'it' and *hain't* 'ain't', and lexical ones such as *afore* 'before' or *nary* 'not any' (cf. especially Wolfram and Christian 1976).

12.3 Social variation in AmE

Within any one region there is more than one form of English. Besides differences according to the gender of the speaker (cf. chapter 8) and race or ethnicity (see below, 12.4), there are significant differences according to the socially and economically relevant factors of education and social class.

In North America socio-economic status shows up in pronunciation inasmuch as middle-class speakers are on the whole more likely than those of the working class to adopt forms which are in agreement with the overt norms of the society. The now classic investigations of Labov in New York City in the 1960s provided a first insight into these relations (Labov 1966). This may be illustrated by the finding that initial voiceless ⟨th-⟩ (as in *thing*) is realized progressively more often as a stop [t] or an affricate [tθ] than as a fricative [θ] as the classification of the speaker changes from upper middle to lower middle, to working, to lower class (Labov 1972: 188–90).

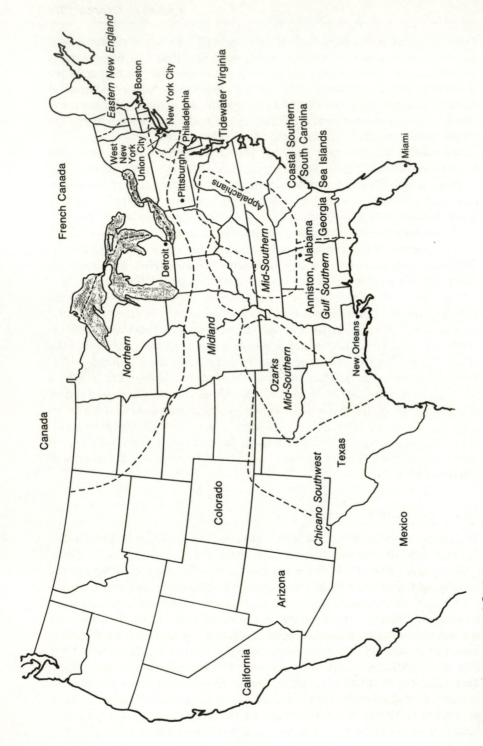

Map 12.2 The United States

Although variation is usually within a range of regional or local variants, it may in some cases be a non-regional standard which is aimed at. For example, New Yorkers increasingly (with middle-class women as leaders) pronounce non-prevocalic *r* even though rhoticity was not traditionally a feature of New York City pronunciation. Since younger speakers also favour pronunciation of this *r*, this is not only an excellent example of the differing speech habits of differing social classes and the greater norm-orientation of women, but also the gradual adoption of rhoticity by a new generation. This latter fact indicates a probable long-term change in the regional standard. Other cities in which sociolinguistic studies have been carried out include, for example, Detroit (Shuy *et al*. 1967), Philadelphia (Labov *et al*. 1972) and Anniston, Alabama (Feagin 1979).

Social distinctions are especially perceptible in the area of grammar, where a remarkable number of stigmatized features (often referred to as *shibboleths*) apply supra-regionally. Accordingly, a person who uses the following is regarded as uneducated, unsophisticated and uncouth.

1 *ain't* (*I ain't done it yet*);
2 a double modal (*I might could help you*);
3 multiple negation (*We don't need none*);
4 *them* as a demonstrative adjective (*Hand me them cups*);
5 no subject relative pronoun in a defining relative clause (*The fellow wrote that letter is here*);
6 *don't* in the third person singular (*She don't like it*);
7 *was* with a plural subject (*We was there too early*);
8 *come, done, seen, knowed, drownded* (<*drown*), for the simple past tense;
9 *took, went, tore, fell, wrote*, etc., as a past participle.

Investigations of usage have revealed that these and other non-standard forms are used most by the less well educated of the rural and urban working class (cf. Feagin 1979: passim). Users are also frequently the oldest and most poorly educated rural speakers such as were often sought out for studies in the framework of the *Linguistic Atlas*, the so-called Type I speakers (for an example, see Allen 1986: 253).

It would be a mistake, however, for the impression to arise that such non-standard forms are somehow strange or unusual merely because StE, and therefore the written language, does not include them. The contrary is the case. All of them are very common. Indeed, many of them may be majority forms. In Anniston, Alabama, for example, third person singular *don't* was found to be used more than 90 per cent of the time by all the working-class groups investigated except for urban adult males, whose rate was 69 per cent. The use of singular *don't* by the Anniston upper class, in contrast, ranged from 0 to 10 per cent (Feagin 1979: 208). This type of situation seems to be the case wherever English is spoken.

12.4 Ethnic varieties of AmE

As might be expected in countries of immigration, there are millions of inhabitants in the United States and Canada whose native language is not English and there are many more millions whose ethnic background is not English. In the immigrant generation and sometimes in the second generation many of these people spoke/speak English which was/is characterized by first language interference. Experience has shown, however, that by the fourth generation most of the descendants of immigrants have become monolingual English-speakers (Valdés 1988: 115f), and virtually all signs of interference have vanished. There are then no grounds for the speaking of an ethnic variety, for recognizing such a variety would be justified only if it could be viewed as distinct from mainstream AmE and as self-perpetuating.

Yet there are some groups of native English speakers in North America who have an ethnic identity and speak a type of English which is distinct in various ways from the speech of their neighbours of comparable age, class, sex and region. For two of these groups it is uncertain whether it is really suitable to speak of ethnic varieties of English: Native American Indians and Chicanos. The third group, American blacks, include a large number who speak the ethnic dialect Black English.

12.4.1 Native American English

Today the majority of Indians are monolingual speakers of English. For most of them there is probably no divergence between their English and that of their non-Indian fellows of equivalent age, sex, education and social status. However, among Native Americans who live in concentrated groups (on reservations) there are also 'as many different kinds of American Indian English as there are American Indian language traditions' (Leap 1986: 597). This is seen as the result of the on-going influence of the substratum (the traditional languages) on English, even if the speakers are monolingual. Many of the special features of this English are such familiar phenomena as word-final consonant cluster simplification (*west* > *wes'*), multiple negation, uninflected *be* (see below, 12.4.3), and lack of subject–verb concord. Although mainstream non-standard English has the same sort of 'surface phenomena', they are the products of 'different grammatical systems' (Toon 1984: 218). It is suggested, for example, that because some traditional Indian languages require identical marking of subject and verb, Indian English has such forms as *some peoples comes in* (ibid.).

12.4.2 Spanish-influenced English

Hispanic Americans are one of the two largest ethnic minorities in the

United States (blacks are the other). They consist of at least three major groups, Puerto Ricans, Cubans and Chicanos (or Mexican Americans).

Cubans Approximately 600,000 of the roughly one million Cuban Americans live in Dade County (or Miami) in Florida; another 20 per cent are in West New York and Union City, New Jersey. Because of this areal concentration they have been able to create unified communities with ethnic boundaries, i.e. Little Havana's. Nonetheless, integration with the surrounding Anglo community is relatively great (a high number of inter-ethnic marriages), perhaps because Cuban Americans, owing to the nature of emigration from Cuba, encompass all levels of education and class membership and are not relegated to a marginal position *vis-à-vis* the greater outside society. Only 6 per cent of the second generation of Cuban Americans were monolingual Spanish in 1976 (García and Otheguy 1988). 'Second-generation Cubans, as is usually the case with all second-generation Hispanics, speak English fluently and with a native North American accent' (ibid.: 183). Indeed, perhaps only the presence of loan words (and calques/loan translations) such as *bad grass* < Spanish *yerba mala* 'weeds'; ibid.: 184) may indicate the original provenance of the speakers.

Puerto Ricans As American citizens, Puerto Ricans have long moved freely between their native island and the mainland United States. Most originally went to New York City, and although a number have since moved to other cities, approximately 60 per cent of mainland Puerto Ricans are still to be found there, where they often live in closely integrated ethnic communities. Many members of these communities are bilingual (only 1 per cent of second-generation mainland Puerto Ricans are monolingual Spanish speakers; García and Otheguy 1988: 175), and there are a number of differing Spanish–English constellations of language usage within families. One investigation showed that those 'reared in Puerto Rico speak English marked by Spanish interference phenomena, while the second generation speaks two kinds of non-standard English: Puerto Rican English (PRE) and/or black English vernacular (BEV)' (Zentella 1988: 148). Some typical instances of interference will be provided in the next section; Black English will be discussed in 12.4.3. On English in Puerto Rico, see Werner 1988.

Chicanos Chicanos numbered an estimated 10.8 million people in early 1985 and are a rapidly growing group (Valdés 1988: 112). They include recent immigrants as well as native-born Americans who continue to live in their traditional home in the American Southwest (Texas, New Mexico, Arizona, Colorado and California), which was conquered from Mexico and annexed in the middle of the nineteenth century. Chicanos are most numerous in California, where they are an urban population, and in Texas, especially southwest Texas, where they are often relatively rural. Spanish is more commonly maintained in the Texas than in the California environment.

The type of English spoken by many of these people, some Spanish–English bilinguals, others monolingual English speakers (5 per cent of second-generation Mexican-Americans remain monolingual Spanish speakers; García and Otheguy 1988: 175), consists of several internal varieties. Among bilinguals it is characterized by frequent code-switching (sometimes referred to as Tex-Mex). For many speakers English is a second language and contains numerous signs of interference from Spanish. However, whether an 'interference variety' or a first language, the linguistic habits of a large portion of the Chicano community are continually reinforced by direct or indirect contact with Spanish, whose influence is increased by the 'isolation of Chicano from some Anglo groups' (Penfield and Ornstein-Galicia 1985: 1). Most important for regarding Chicano English as an ethnic variety of AmE is that it 'is passed on to children and . . . serves an important function in the speech community along with having its own norms of appropriateness' (ibid.).

The maintenance of Chicano English as a separate variety 'serves the functions of social solidarity and supports cohesiveness in the community' (Toon 1984: 223). It can be a symbol of ethnic loyalty, as when militant Chicanos use it as one means of identity *vis-à-vis* both Mexican and Anglo norms (Penfield and Ornstein-Galicia 1985: 17).

The linguistic features of Chicano English are most prominently visible in its pronunciation, including stress and intonation. There seems to be little syntactic and lexical deviation from English, though the norm adopted may be either StE or a non-standard form. As with Puerto Ricans, contact with blacks may result in the use of various features of Black English among working-class Chicanos (ibid.: 28).

Pronunciation shows obvious signs of Spanish influence. Among the twenty-three individual points enumerated in Penfield and Ornstein-Galicia (1985: 36f) are the following:

1 stress shift in compounds (*'miniskirt → mini'skirt*);
2 rising pitch contours (independent of the final fall) to stress lexical items;
3 rising pitch in declarative sentences;
4 devoicing and hardening of final voiced consonants (*please → police*);
5 realization of labio-dental fricative /v/ as bilabial stop [b] or bilabial fricative [ß];
6 realization of /θ/ and /ð/ as [t] and [d]
7 realization of central /ʌ/ as low [a];
8 simplification of final consonant clusters;
9 merger of /tʃ/ and /ʃ/ to /ʃ/ (*check → sheck*);

10 merger of /iː/ and /ɪ/ to /ɪ/ and of /eɪ/ and /e/ to /e/, and occasionally of /uː/ and /ʊ/ as /ʊ/.

The final two points distinguish Chicano English from the second language 'interference' variety. The predictable interference pattern would be a realization of /ʃ/ as /tʃ/, of /ɪ/ as /iː/, of /e/ as /eɪ/, and of /ʊ/ as /uː/ since Spanish has only the latter member of each pair. Actually, Chicano speakers often realize the member of each pair which is not predicted, and this is what distinguishes such Chicano speakers from both Mexicans and Anglos (ibid.: 21, 34).

Various studies have shown that there are considerable obstacles in the way of general acceptance of Chicano English as equivalent to other accents of StE (ibid.: 16). A matched guise test, for example, in which the participants were told that all the voices they heard were those of Mexican-Americans, showed a clearer association of pejorative evaluations (stupid, unreliable, dishonest, lazy, etc.) with a Chicano voice than with a near-Anglo accent (Arthur *et al.* 1974: 261; Hernández-Chavez *et al.* 1975).

12.4.3 Black English (BlE)

The most widely recognized and widely researched ethnic dialect of English is American Black English. Before looking at it more closely, it should be pointed out that many middle-class blacks do not speak BlE, but are linguistically indistinguishable from their white neighbours. Rather, it is the poorer, working- and lower-class blacks, both in the rural South and the urban North, who speak the most distinctive forms of this dialect. It is often distinctly associated with the values of the vernacular culture including performance styles especially associated with black males in such genres as the dozens, toasting, ritual insults, etc. (cf. Abrahams 1970; Kochman 1970) but also preaching (cf. Rosenberg 1970).

One of the main debates that has raged in connection with BlE concerns its origins. Some maintain that it derives from an earlier Plantation creole, which itself ultimately derives from West African Pidgin English (especially Dillard 1972; see chapter 16 for more details). This would mean that BlE contains grammatical categories (especially of the verb phrase) which are basically different from English. The converse view is that BlE derives from the English of the white slave owners and slave drivers, which ultimately derives from the English of Great Britain and Ireland (McDavid and McDavid 1971). BlE, so conceived, is divergent from StE only in its surface forms. Wolfram and Clarke (1971) contains a readable collection of articles on both sides of this issue. There are, in addition, a great number of researchers who take a position in between these two, maintaining that both have had influence on BlE (cf. Burling 1973: chapter 7; Fasold 1972: 218f; Feagin 1979: 8; Wolfram 1990).

In evaluating the question of origins it has generally been conceded that BlE has a phonological system which often differs greatly from that of GenAm, though it is often remarkably similar to white Southern Vernacular English. Since BlE has its more immediate origins in the American South, pronunciation similarities between the two are hardly astonishing. This explains the followed shared features:

1 realization of /aɪ/ as [a] before voiced consonants;
2 convergence of /ɪ/ and /e/ + nasal (*pin*<*pen*);
3 merger of /ɔɪ/ and /ɔː/, especially before /l/ (*boil*>*ball*);
4 merger of /i/ and /æ/ before /ŋk/ (*think*>*thank*);
5 merger of /i(r)/ and /e(r)/ (*cheering*>*chairing*) and of /ʊ(r)/ and /ɔ(r)/ (*sure*>*shore*).

Furthermore, both are non-rhotic, both vocalize /l/, and both simplify final consonant clusters.

It is this final point which, in the end, also distinguishes the two accents, for BlE carries the deletion of final consonants much farther than Southern White Vernacular does. While both might simplify *desk* to *des'* (and then form the plural as *desses*), only BlE regularly deletes the inflectional endings {S} and {D} so that *looked* becomes *look*, and *eats*, *tops* and *Fred's* become *eat*, *top* and *Fred*. The deletion of final consonants may take place even with a single consonant between two vowels, as when *applied afterward* appears as *apply afterward*. However, this is less frequent than when the following word begins with a consonant. On the conditions for, and frequency of, deletion, see Fasold 1972.

Some people have called the existence of the category of tense in BlE into question because the past tense marker {D} is so frequently missing. However, the past tense forms of the irregular verbs, where the past does not depend only on {D}, for example, *catch – caught* or *am/is/are – was/were* are consistently present. Hence any conclusion about the lack of tense would be mistaken (cf. Fasold 1972: chapter 2).

Nevertheless, there are some remarkable grammatical differences between BlE and comparable forms of Southern Vernacular White English. The lack of third person singular present tense {S} seems to be so far-reaching that it is not unreasonable to conclude that it is not well anchored in BlE. One study shows 87 per cent deletion in one study of BlE versus 11 per cent deletion for Southern White Vernacular (Wolfram 1971: 145; cf. also Fasold 1986: 453f). This, of course, is not a terribly serious loss since there is no potential confusion of meaning as there can be when {D} is lost. With plural {S}, which carries important meaning, there is much less frequent deletion than with the verb ending {S} (Fasold 1986: 454).

A number of other grammatical features specific to BlE have also been pointed out. They include:

1 *been* as a marker of the remote present perfect (*I been know him* 'I have known him for a long time'); this is rare in BlE;
2 *be done* as future resultative marker (*I'll be done killed that motherfucker if he tries to lay a hand on my kid again* 'I'll kill him if he should try to hurt my kid' (Labov 1987: 7f);
3 third person singular present tense {-S} used as a marker of narrative in contrast to unmarked non-narrative usage; this is viewed as a recent development (ibid.: 8f, but see 10.2.2 for a similiar feature in Scots).

The most discussion, however, has centred around what is called **invariant** or **distributive** *be*. In order to understand what this is, it is first necessary to note that there are two distinct uses of the copula *be* in BlE. The one involves zero use of the copula, for example, *She smart* 'She is smart', which describes a permanent state or *She tired* 'She is tired', which names a momentary state. Here colloquial white English might use a contraction (*She's smart*); BlE deletes instead of contracting. Where contraction is not possible in StE, neither is deletion in BlE, as in *Yes, she really is*. Invariant *be*, in contrast, is used to describe an intermittent state, often accompanied by an appropriate adverb such as *usually* or *sometimes*, as in *Sometimes she be sad*.

The major question is where this form comes from (origins again). It seems that invariant *be* does not occur in the most extreme creoles, though it does in some decreolized forms (Feagin 1979: 255, 262). Therefore they are an unlikely source. Some studies of White Southern Vernacular show it to be rare, and do not indicate clearly whether it carries the same meaning as in BlE or whether it is not merely an instance of *will/would be* in which *'ll* or *'d* have been deleted (Feagin 1979: 251–5; Sommer 1986: 184–90). The white vernacular is, therefore, not a very likely source of this construction either. One investigation of Southern BlE even reveals it to be something of a rarity there, too (Schrock 1986: 211–14). However, the *Linguistic Atlas of the Gulf States* (Pederson 1981) turns up instances of it in both black and (a very few instances of) white vernacular speech. In this data invariant *be* sometimes represents deletion of *will* and *would*, but more often it is used for an intermittent state (including negation with *don't*: *Sometime it be and sometime it don't*) and, with a following present participle, intermittent action (*How you be doing?*) (Bailey and Bassett 1986). If invariant *be* is an innovation of BlE, then this would speak for an at least partially increasing divergence of BlE from white vernacular forms. This question has been hotly, but inconclusively, debated (Fasold *et al.* 1987). Whatever its source, invariant *be* is a construction that speaks strongly for the status of BlE as an independent ethnic dialect of English.

12.5 The languages of the Caribbean

The Caribbean stretches over a wide geographical area and includes, for our purposes, at least nineteen political units which have English as an official language (see map 12.3): The Bahamas, the Turks and Caicos Islands, the Cayman Islands; in the Greater Antilles, Jamaica and Puerto Rico (with Spanish); in the Lesser Antilles the American and the British Virgin Islands, Anguilla, St Kitts-Nevis, Antigua-Barbuda, Montserrat, Dominica, St Lucia, St Vincent, Barbados, Grenada, Trinidad-Tobago; in South America Guyana; in Central America Belize. In addition to these countries and territories there are numerous others with Spanish as the official language (Cuba, the Dominican Republic, Puerto Rico (with English), Mexico, Guatemala, Honduras, Nicaragua, Costa Rica, Panama, Colombia and Venezuela), as well as a few with French (Guadeloupe, Haiti, Martinique) and Dutch (Aruba–Bonaire–Curaçao and Surinam). Although the majority of the islands are anglophone, the largest are not (Cuba and Hispaniola [the Dominican Republic and Haiti]); and Puerto Rico is chiefly Spanish speaking. The mainland all the way from Guyana to the United States is hispanophone with the exception of Belize. In the sub-United States Caribbean the five to six million inhabitants of the anglophone countries are greatly outnumbered by their Spanish-speaking neighbours (for demographic data, cf. Lawton 1984: 252f; Winford 1991: 567).

Below the level of official language policy lies the linguistic reality of these countries. Here English is truly a minority language, for the vast majority of people in the anglophone countries are speakers not of StE, but of English creoles. In addition, Guyana and Trinidad–Tobago have a number of Hindi speakers. Guyana also has Amerindian language speakers. Belize has Amerindian as well as Spanish speakers. Spanish is used by small groups in the American Virgin Islands and Jamaica. French Creole is widely spoken as a vernacular in Dominica and St Lucia as well as by smaller groups in the American Virgin Islands and Trinidad–Tobago. English creoles are, however, the major languages on most of the anglophone islands; furthermore, they are in use in several Central American countries (besides Belize) in some Atlantic coast areas, on the Bay Islands of Honduras (Roatan, Guanaja, Utila) and parts of the Honduran coast, in the Bluefields area of Nicaragua, among some citizens of Limón in Costa Rica, as well as by tiny populations in Livingston, Guatemala and Columbia's Corn Islands off the Nicaraguan coast (cf. Holm 1983; Lipski 1985).

The term **English creole** refers to a vernacular form which is strongly related to English in the area of lexis, since the English creoles share a major portion of their vocabulary with StE. Syntactically, however, they diverge so strongly that it is not unjustified to regard them as separate languages rather than dialects of English (for discussion of this relationship, see below 12.6; for some linguistic characteristics, see 12.7).

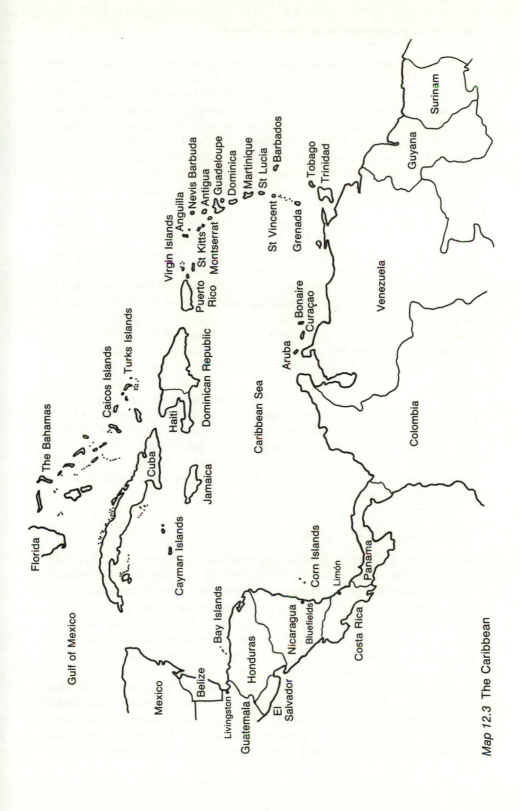

Map 12.3 The Caribbean

The various English creoles share a similar historical development (see chapter 16); in addition, migration patterns (Holm 1985) between the various Caribbean countries as well as with West Africa may have further heightened their mutual resemblance. More recently migration to and from the United States, Canada and Great Britain have been an added unifying factor for many West Indians. Furthermore, tourism has increased exposure to AmE speech. Despite all of this the various English creoles are, in actual fact, often so different that mutual comprehension between, for example, the inhabitants of Guyana and Barbados cannot be taken for granted (Haynes 1983: 211f), sometimes not even between StE speakers and Creole speakers within a single country such as Jamaica (Roberts 1988: 9).

The explanation lies in the fact that each of the territories has its own history. In the case of Barbados, for example, the vernacular has decreolized more strongly than the relatively conservative varieties of Guyana and Jamaica (Hancock 1980 even suggests that there was no real creolization in Barbados). Special factors influencing Barbados are the higher rate of British and Irish settlers in the early colonial period, the greater development of the infrastructure and relatively small size of the island, and the high degree of literacy (97 per cent) (cf. Roy 1985: 143f). Jamaica, in contrast, received slave imports much longer than Barbados; this led to a lengthening of the pidgin phase and a subsequent strengthening of the creole. Guyana is linguistically similar to Barbados because there was a great deal of immigration there from Barbados. However, besides its black population Guyana also has an approximately equal number of East Indians (most of whom have, in the meantime, adopted the creole for daily use); their arrival (between 1838 and 1924) slowed down the decreolization process by acting as a buffer between the StE top of society and the creole bottom (Roberts 1988: 6–9).

12.6 The linguistic continuum

Regardless of whether the various English creoles are more or less mutually comprehensible, more or less creolized, they all have one thing in common: all are diglossically Low languages in relation to the High language, which is StE in the anglophone countries, Dutch in Surinam, and Spanish in Honduras, Nicaragua, Costa Rica and Columbia. This means that StE (and Dutch and Spanish) are used in government administration and state schools (but changes are in progress in the direction of more use of the creoles, especially in Belize, Jamaica and Trinidad; Winford 1991: 578f). StE dominates in most of the printed media and all but a little of the electronic media. The creoles are the language of everyday life, the home, family and neighbourhood. Church sometimes uses the vernacular, sometimes the High language. Literature makes a few forays into creole (cf. Rickford and Closs-Traugott 1985). Only Sranan, a creole relatively distantly related to English, is used widely for literary (and religious) purposes.

If it is not unjustified to regard the English creoles as separate languages, as remarked above, it is also not fully justified to do so. Many people see StE and the creoles as two extremes related through a spectrum or **continuum** of language varieties, each of which is only minimally different from the nearest variety upwards or downwards from it in the scale. The lowest or broadest form is called the **basilect**; the highest, StE, the **acrolect**. In between lies the **mesolect**, which is any of numerous intermediate varieties. Evidence of a linguistic nature indicates, however, that there is a fairly strong, perhaps substantial break between the basilect and the mesolect. The underlying grammatical categories shared by the mesolect and the acrolect (though realized in distinct forms) are essentially different from those of the basilect (see below for exemplification).

The basilect lacks overt prestige while the acrolect commands respect. The lower a person's socio-economic status and the poorer his or her education, the more likely that person is to speak the basilect.

> A general pattern of correlation between creole and lower status on the one hand, and acrolect (English) and higher status on the other, is a fairly common feature of all the communities reported on in the literature.
>
> (Winford 1991: 572)

Rural dwellers will also be located closer to the basilect than will the urban part of the population. Age is an additional factor, since younger speakers generally seem more likely than older ones to adopt the more standard forms, which, however, need not be all the way up to the level of StE.

Despite the overt prestige of the acrolect, individual and group loyalties may lead to more use of the basilect for some speakers (ibid.: 574, 576f). There are covert local norms which favour creole language and culture. Indeed, certain speech genres, especially those associated with performance styles, can hardly be imagined apart from the vernacular: teasing, riddles, traditional folktales such as the Anansi stories with their spider hero, ritual insults and the like (ibid.: 577; Roberts 1988: chapter 6; cf. similar uses of American BIE as well). Furthermore, the forms people use with one another may be a good indication both of where they feel they belong on the social scale and how they feel towards their conversational partners:

> The speaker of Jamaican creole who controls a substantial segment of the linguistic spectrum on the island knows when he meets an acquaintance with the same control speaking with another speaker who controls a lesser range, that if his friend uses *nyam* and *tick* he is defining the situation on the axis of solidarity and shared identity whereas if he is using

eat and *thick* he is interested in the maintenance of social distance and formality.

(Grimshaw 1971: 437)

The continuum (however conceived) is not the same in all the territories mentioned. The English of Barbados, Trinidad and the Bahamas is so decreolized that it is possible to say there is, relatively speaking, no basilect (cf. Alleyne 1980: chapter 7). In countries where English is not the official language, the opposite might be said to be the case: there is no acrolect. This is actually the case only for Surinam, where Sranan has gone its own way, no longer oriented towards English. For in Honduras, Costa Rica or Nicaragua StE is always present in the wings, so to speak, as speakers there maintain connections with anglophone countries such as Jamaica.

12.7 Linguistic characteristics of CaribE

StE in the Caribbean area is syntactically the same as other standard varieties. Where there are BrE–AmE differences CaribE is oriented towards BrE; only in the American Virgin Islands and Puerto Rico – to the extent that English is spoken in the latter – is AmE the model.

The creole forms, on the other hand, offer an enormous contrast in grammar. A small selection of these will serve as an illustration. There is a partially different set of personal pronouns (Jamaican Creole *yu* 'you (sing.)' and *unu* 'you (plur.)'), often without case distinctions (Jamaican Creole *wi* 'we, us, our'). Plurals of nouns need not be marked but, if they are, the plural is marked by adding -*dem* < English *them* (*boddem* 'birds'). Possession is marked by juxtaposition: *Mieri gyardan* 'Mary's yard'.

The verb does not have to be marked for tense, although the particle *been* (or *did* or *had*) + verb is available for marking the past and *go* or *gain* + verb (sometimes + -*in*) are used for the future. However, aspect is always expressed, whether *process* (e.g. *da* or *duz* + verb, sometimes with the ending -*in*), *completive* or *perfective* (e.g. *dun* + verb), or *active* of a dynamic verb or *stative* of a state verb (zero marking). These particles can also be combined in various more complex structures. These examples of verb usage are taken from Bajan, the Barbados basilect (Roy 1985). For more treatment, see chapter 16. In addition, the creoles make use of serial verbs, such as *come* or *go*, indicating movement towards or away from the speaker (*carry it come* 'bring it') or instrumental *tek* (*tek whip beat di children dem* 'beat them with a whip') (Roberts 1988: 65). The passive is widely expressed by the intransitive use of a transitive verb (*The sugar use already* '. . . was used . . .'), but there is also a syntactic passive with the auxiliary *get* (*The child get bite up*) as well as the possibility of impersonal expressions (*Dem kill she* 'She was killed') (ibid.: 74f).

The vocabulary of CaribE contains a considerable number of terms not widely known outside the area. Inasmuch as its speakers move easily between the acrolect and the mesolect, it is only natural that standard CaribE draws on these lexical resources. The special regional (or subregional) vocabulary of the Caribbean draws ultimately on two major sources: the African languages of the slaves and non-standard regional English of the early settlers from Britain and Ireland. Craig provides a long exemplary list of creole words of originally Scottish origin which have become part of standard CaribE, for example, *lick* 'to hit, strike', *dock* 'to cut the hair', *heap* 'a great deal' (Craig 1983). Examples of Africanisms tend to be calques (loan translations) rather than direct borrowings, for example, *cry water* 'tears', *sweet mout'* 'flatter' and *hard ears* 'persistently disobedient, stubborn'. Reduplication (*little-little* 'very small') is also probably an African carry-over. An example of a direct borrowing from an African language is *John Canoe*, the term for the mumming parade at Christmas time. Its source is the Ewe language. Cassidy explains it as follows:

> The chief dancer in the underlying African celebration seems to have been a medicine man, and in Ewe we find *dʒɔnɔ* 'a sorcerer', and *kúnu* 'a cause of death', or alternatively *dʒonkɔ* 'a sorcerer's name for himself', and *-nu*, a common suffix meaning 'man'. Some African form or forms of this kind meaning 'sorcerer-man' has been rationalized into *John Canoe*.

> (Cassidy 1985: 137)

The pronunciation of CaribE marks it regionally more than anything else. Here the carry-over from basilect to acrolect is especially prominent. One of the most noticeable features is the stressing, which gives each syllable more or less equal stress (syllable-timing; cf. chapter 3). In addition, in a few cases pitch may play a decisive role in interpreting a lexeme; *kyan* with a high level tone is positive 'can', while the same word with a high falling tone means 'can't' (Lawton 1984: 257; cf. Wells 1982: 573).

The consonants in comparison with those of RP and GenAm include the following particularly noticeable differences (cf. Wells 1982: 7.2; Roberts 1988: 50–7):

1 /θ/ and /ð/ are freely, but not exclusively realized as [t] and [d] (*tick* for *thick*; *dem* for *them*);
2 /v/ may be a [b] or a bilabial fricative [ß] (*gib* for *give*, *bittles* for *vittles*);
3 the ending {-ING} is regularly /-ɪn/ (*talkin'*);
4 simplification of consonant clusters, especially if homorganic and voiced after /n/ and /l/ (*blind* → *blin'*); in the basilect even initial clusters are sometimes simplified (*string* → *tring*);

5 palatalization of /k/ and /g/ + /aɪ/: *car* /kjaɪr/;
6 clear /l/ in all phonetic environments.

Some territories are rhotic (Barbados); some are non-rhotic (Trinidad, the Bahamas); and some are semi-rhotic, i.e. stressed final *r* as in *near* is retained (Jamaica, Guyana) (Wells 1982: 570). In the basilect sometimes /r/ is realized as [l] (*flitters* for *fritters*), but this is growing less common (Roberts 1988: 54).

The vowels differ most *vis-à-vis* RP and GenAm. In Jamaica, for instance, /eɪ/ and /əʊ/ are the monophthongs [eː] and [oː]. /æ/ is realized as [a], which is also the realization of /ɒ/, so that *tap* and *top* are potential homophones. Both are distinguished by length from the vowel of *bath* [aː]. Central vowels are less a fixed part of the system; hence schwa is often [a] as well as [e]; /ʌ/ may be back and rounded, and /ɜː/ may be [o] (cf. Jamaican Creole *boddem* 'birds'). In the basilect /ɔɪ/ sometimes merges with /aɪ/, making *boy* and *buy* homophones. For more details including differentiation by territory, see Wells 1982: 7.2; Roberts (1988: chapter 4) contrasts the features of the major territories grammatically, lexically and phonetically.

REFERENCES

Abrahams, R. D. (1970) *Deep Down in the Jungle: Negro Narrative Folklore from the Streets of Philadelphia*, Chicago: Aldine.
Allen, H. B. (ed.) (1973–6) *The Linguistic Atlas of the Upper Midwest*, 3 vols, Minneapolis: University of Minnesota Press.
—— (1986) 'The linguistic atlas of the Upper Midwest', in H. B. Allen and M. D. Linn (eds) *Dialect and Language Variation*, Orlando: Academic, pp. 247–58.
Alleyne, M. C. (1980) *Comparative Afro-American*, Ann Arbor: Karoma.
Arthur, B., Farrar, D. and Bradford, G. (1974) 'Evaluation reactions of college students to dialect differences in the English of Mexican-Americans', *Language and Speech* 17: 255–70.
Atwood, E. B. (1962) *The Regional Vocabulary of Texas*, Austin: University of Texas Press.
Avis, W. S. (1973) 'The English Language in Canada', in T. Sebeok (ed.) *Current Trends in Linguistics*, Vol. 10, *Linguistics in North America*, The Hague: Mouton, pp. 40–74.
—— (1983) 'Canadian English in its North American Context', *Canadian Journal of Linguistics* 28: 3–15.
Avis, W. S., Crate, C., Drysdale, P., Leechman, D. and Scargill, M. H. (1967) *A Dictionary of Canadianisms on Historical Principles*, Toronto: Gage.
Avis, W. S., Drysdale, P. D., Gregg, R. J. and Scargill, M. H. (eds) (1973) *The Gage Canadian Dictionary*, Toronto: Gage.
Bailey, G. and Bassett, M. (1986) 'Invariant *be* in the Lower South', in M. B. Montgomery and G. Bailey (eds) *Language Variety in the South*, Alabama: University of Alabama Press, pp. 158–79.
Bailey, R. W. (1984) 'The English language in Canada', in R. W. Bailey and M. Görlach (eds) *English as a World Language*, Cambridge: Cambridge University Press, pp. 134–76.

Bright, E. S. (1971) *A Word Geography of California and Nevada*, Berkeley: University of California Press.

Burling, R. (1973) *English in Black and White*, New York: Holt, Rinehart & Winston.

Cassidy, F. G. (ed.) (1985, 1991) *Dictionary of American Regional English*, Cambridge, Mass.: Belknap.

Cassidy, F. G. and LePage, R. B. (1980) Dictionary of Jamaican English, 2nd edn, Cambridge: Cambridge University Press.

—— (1985) 'Etymology in Caribbean creoles', in M. Görlach and J. A. Holm (eds) *Focus on the Caribbean*, Amsterdam: Benjamins, pp. 133–9.

Chambers, J. K. (1986) 'Three kinds of standard in Canadian English', in W. C. Lougheed (ed.) *In Search of a Standard in Canadian English*, Kingston, Ont.: Queen's University Press, pp. 1–15.

—— (1991) 'Canada', in J. Cheshire (ed.) *English around the World: Sociolinguistic Perspectives*, Cambridge: Cambridge University Press, pp. 89–107.

Chambers, J. K. and Hardwick, M. F. (1986) 'Comparative sociolinguistics of a sound change in Canadian English', *English World-Wide* 7: 23–44.

Clarke, S. (1991) 'Phonological variation and recent language change in St John's English', in J. Cheshire (ed.) *English around the World. Sociolinguistic Perspectives*, Cambridge: Cambridge University Press, pp. 108–22.

Craig, D. R. (1983) 'Toward a description of Caribbean English', in B. B. Kachru (ed.) *The Other Tongue: English Across Cultures*, Oxford: Pergamon, pp. 198–209.

Dillard, J. L. (1972) *Black English: its History and Usage in the United States*, New York: Random House.

—— (1985) *Towards a Social History of American English*, Berlin: Mouton.

Esling, J. H. (1991) 'Sociophonetic variation in Vancouver', in J. Cheshire (ed.) *English around the World: Sociolinguistic Perspectives*, Cambridge: Cambridge University Press, pp. 123–33.

Fasold, R. W. (1972) *Tense Marking in Black English*, Washington: Center for Applied Linguistics.

—— (1986) 'The relation between black and white speech in the South', in H. B. Allen and M. D. Linn (eds) *Dialect and Language Variation*, Orlando: Academic, pp. 446–73.

Fasold, R. W., Labov, W., Vaughn-Cooke, F. B., Bailey, G., Wolfram, W., Spears, A. K. and Rickford, J. (1987) 'Are black and white vernaculars diverging?', *American Speech* 62: 3–80.

Feagin, D. (1979) *Variation and Change in Alabama English*, Washington: Georgetown University Press.

Fong, W. (1967–8) 'Canadian English spelling', *English Language Teaching* 22: 266–71.

Frazer, T. C. (1986) 'South Midland pronunciation in the North Central states', in H. B. Allen and M. D. Linn (eds) *Dialect and Language Variation*, Orlando: Academic, pp. 142–50.

García, O. and Otheguy, R. (1988) 'The language situation of Cuban Americans', in S. L. McKay and S. C. Wong (eds) *Language Diversity: Problem or Resource?*, Cambridge, Mass.: Newbury House, pp. 166–92.

Grimshaw, A. D. (1971) 'Some social forces and some social functions of pidgin and creole languages', in D. Hymes (ed.) *Pidginization and Creolization of Languages*, Cambridge: Cambridge University Press, pp. 427–45.

Hancock, I. (1980) 'Gullah and Barbadian: origins and relationships', *American Speech* 55: 17–35.

Hankey, C. T. (1960) 'A Colorado word geography', *Publications of the American Dialect Society* 34: 1–76.

Haynes, L. M. (1983) 'Caribbean English: form and function', in B. B. Kachru (ed.) *The Other Tongue: English across Cultures*, Oxford: Pergamon, pp. 210–26.

Hernández-Chavez, E., Cohen, A. D. and Beltramo, A. F. (eds) *El Lenguaje de los Chicanos*, Arlington, Va.: Centre for Applied Linguistics.

Holm, J. (1983) *Central American English*, Heidelberg: Groos.

—— (1985) 'The spread of English in the Caribbean area', in M. Görlach and J. A. Holm (eds) *Focus on the Caribbean*, Amsterdam: Benjamins, pp. 1–22.

Kinloch, A. M. (1983) 'The phonology of central/prairie Canadian English', *American Speech* 58: 31–5.

—— (1985) Review of R. W. Bailey and M. Görlach (eds) *English as a World Language*, in *Canadian Journal of Linguistics* 30: 97–105.

Kochman, T. (1970) 'Toward an ethnography of black American speech behavior', in N. E. Whitten and J. F. Szwed (eds) *Afro-American Anthropology*, New York: Free Press, pp. 145–62.

Kurath, H. *et al.* (eds) (1939–43) *Linguistic Atlas of New England*, 3 vols, Providence: American Council of Learned Societies.

Labov, W. (1966) *The Social Stratification of English in New York City*, Washington: Center for Applied Linguistics.

—— (1972) 'The study of language in its social context', in J. B. Pride and J. Holmes (eds) *Sociolinguistics*, Harmondsworth: Penguin, pp. 180–202.

—— (1987) 'Are black and white vernaculars diverging?', *American Speech* 62: 5–12.

Labov, W., Yaeger, M. and Steiner, R. (1972) *A Quantitative Study of Sound Change in Progress*, Philadelphia: US Regional Survey.

Labrie, N. (1988) 'Canada', in U. Ammon, N. Dittmar and K. J. Mattheier (eds) *Sociolinguistics Soziolinguistik*, Berlin: de Gruyter, pp. 1307–13.

Lawton, D. L. (1984) 'English in the Caribbean', in R. W. Bailey and M. Görlach (eds) *English as a World Language*, Cambridge: Cambridge University Press, pp. 251–80.

Leap, W. L. (1986) 'American Indian English and its implications for bilingual education', in H. B. Allen and M. D. Linn (eds) *Dialect and Language Variation*, Orlando: Academic, pp. 591–603.

Lipski, J. M. (1985) 'English–Spanish contact in the United States and Central America: sociolinguistic mirror images?', in M. Görlach and J. A. Holm (eds) *Focus on the Caribbean*, Amsterdam: Benjamins, pp. 191–208.

McDavid, R. I. Jr and McDavid, V. (1971) 'The relationship of the speech of American negroes to the speech of whites', in W. A. Wolfram and N. H. Clarke (eds) *Black–White Speech Relationships*, Washington: Centre for Applied Linguistics, pp. 16–40.

McDavid, R. I. Jr *et al.* (1980f) *Linguistic Atlas of the Middle and South Atlantic States*, Chicago: University of Chicago Press.

Marckwardt, A. H. *et al.* (ed) (1976–8) *Linguistic Atlas of the North Central States: Basic Materials*, Chicago: University of Chicago Press.

Pederson, L. (ed.) (1981) *Linguistic Atlas of the Gulf States: the Basic Materials* [microfilm], Ann Arbor: University of Michigan Press.

Penfield, J. and Ornstein-Galicia, J. L. (1985) *Chicano English*, Amsterdam: Benjamins.

Pringle, I. (1986) 'The concept of dialect and the study of Canadian English', in H. B. Allen and M. D. Linn (eds) *Dialect and Language Variation*, Orlando: Academic, pp. 217–36.

Pringle, I. and Padolsky, E. (1983) 'The linguistic survey of the Ottowa valley', *American Speech* 58: 325–44.

Reed, D. and Metcalf, A. (1979) *Linguistic Atlas of the Pacific Coast: Field Records and Guide* [microfilm], Berkeley: University of California Press.

Rickford, J. R. and Closs-Traugott. E. (1985) 'Symbol of powerlessness and degeneracy, or symbol of solidarity and truth? Paradoxical attitudes toward pidgins and creoles', in S. Greenbaum (ed.) *The English Language Today*, Oxford: Pergamon, pp. 252–61.

Roberts, P. A. (1988) *West Indians and Their Language*, Cambridge: Cambridge University Press.

Rosenberg, B. A. (1970) *The Art of the American Folk Preacher*, New York: Oxford University Press.

Roy, J. D. (1985) 'The structure of tense and aspect in Barbadian English Creole', in M. Görlach and J. A. Holm (eds) *Focus on the Caribbean*, Amsterdam: Benjamins, pp. 141–56.

Schrock, E. F., Jr, (1986) 'Some features of the *be* verb in the speech of blacks of Pope County, Arkansas', in M. B. Montgomery and G. Bailey (eds) *Language Variety in the South*, Alabama: University of Alabama Press, pp. 202–15.

Shuy, R. W., Wolfram, W. A., and Riley, W. K. (1967) *Linguistic Correlates of Social Stratification in Detroit Speech*, Washington: US Office of Education.

Sommer, E. (1986) 'Variation in Southern urban English', in M. B. Montgomery and G. Bailey (eds) *Language Variety in the South*, Alabama: University of Alabama Press, pp. 180–201.

Story, G. M., Kirwin, W. J. and Widdowson, J. D. A. (eds) (1990) *Dictionary of Newfoundland English*, 2nd edn, Toronto: Toronto University Press.

Toon, T. E. (1984) 'Variation in contemporary American English', in R. W. Bailey and M. Görlach (eds) *English as a World Language*, Cambridge: Cambridge University Press, pp. 210–50.

Valdés, G. (1988) 'The language situation of Mexican Americans', in S. L. McKay and S. C. Wong (eds) *Language Diversity: Problem or Resource?*, Cambridge, Mass.: Newbury House, pp. 111–39.

Vance, T. J. (1987) '"Canadian raising" in some dialects of the Northern United States', *American Speech* 62: 195–210.

Van Riper, W. R. (1986) 'General American: an ambiguity', in H. B. Allen and M. D. Linn (eds) *Dialect and Language Variation*, Orlando: Academic, pp. 123–35.

Waggoner, D. (1988) 'Language minorities in the United States in the 1980s: the evidence from the 1980 census', in S. L. McKay and S. C. Wong (eds) *Language Diversity: Problem or Resource?*, Cambridge, Mass.: Newbury House, pp. 69–108.

Warkentyne, H. J. (1983) 'Attitudes and language behaviour', *Canadian Journal of Linguistics* 28: 71–6.

Wells, J. C. (1982) *Accents of English*, Cambridge: Cambridge University Press.

Werner, A. B. (1988) *Language Mixture in the Spontaneous Speech of Puerto Ricans in San Juan*, University of Michigan dissertation.

Winford, D. (1991) 'The Caribbean', in J. Cheshire (ed.) *English around the World: Sociolinguistic Perspectives*, Cambridge: Cambridge University Press, pp. 565–84.

Wolfram, W. A. (1971) 'Black–white speech differences revisited', in W. A. Wolfram and N. H. Clarke (eds) *Black–White Speech Relationships*, Washington: Center for Applied Linguistics, pp. 139–61.

—— (1990) 'Re-examining Vernacular Black English', *Language* 66: 121–33.

Wolfram, W. A. and N. H. Clarke (eds) (1971) *Black–White Speech Relationships*, Washington: Center for Applied Linguistics.

Wolfram, W. A. and Christian, D. (1976) *Appalachian Speech*, Arlington: Center for Applied Linguistics.

Woods, G. R. (1971) *Vocabulary Change: a Study of Variation in Regional Words in Eight of the Southern States*, Carbondale: Southern Illinois University Press.

Woods, H. B. (1991) 'Social differentiation in Ottawa English', in J. Cheshire (ed.) *English around the World: Sociolinguistic Perspectives*, Cambridge: Cambridge University Press, pp. 134–49.

Zentella, A. C. (1988) 'The language situation of Puerto Ricans', in S. L. McKay and S. C. Wong (eds) *Language Diversity: Problem or Resource?*, Cambridge, Mass.: Newbury House, pp. 140–65.

Chapter 13

English in Australia, New Zealand and South Africa

These three countries have been grouped together for a number of reasons. First of all, they are the only large areas in the southern hemisphere in which English is spoken as a native language. This itself is related to the relatively large-scale settlement of all three by English-speaking Europeans at roughly the same time (Australia from 1788 on, South Africa essentially from 1820 on, New Zealand officially from 1840 on). All three were, for a considerable period of time, British colonies and hence open to British institutions (government, administration, courts, military, education and religion) as well as the use of English as an official language. Finally, the type of English spoken in all three is closely related to the StE of Britain and Ireland, the United States and Canada. That is, despite the fact that all three countries contain significant numbers of ethnically non-European inhabitants, often speaking languages other than English, there is relatively little use of pidgin or creole varieties of English (but see below on Australia).

Other places in the southern hemisphere such as the Falkland Islands, South Georgia, Fiji or Samoa will not be considered. Zambia and Tanzania are included in chapter 14 in the section on East Africa. Vanuatu and Papua New Guinea are treated in chapter 16.

In each section of this chapter there will be a short sketch of settlement history, which will provide the background to the establishment of English as a local language. Mention will also be made of the number of speakers of English and other important languages as well as official language policies. This is followed by an estimate of the status of English. The chief object, however, is to provide a characterization of English in these countries, taking into consideration pronunciation, grammar and vocabulary as well as social, regional and ethnic varieties.

13.1 Australian English (AusE)

When the first European settlers reached Port Jackson (present-day Sydney) in New South Wales in 1788 the only people inhabiting the continent were the native or Aboriginal peoples. Since these peoples were linguistically divided and technologically far less advanced than the European newcomers, they had little impact on further developments, including language. Today the Aborigines number about 230,000 in a total population of approximately sixteen million.

Initially Australia served as a penal colony and was populated chiefly by transported convicts. With the economic development of the country (wool, minerals) the number of voluntary immigrants increased, and there was a boom after the discovery of gold in 1851. The convict settlers were chiefly Irish (30 per cent) and southern English. The latter had the strongest influence on the nature of AusE. Because of their largely urban origins, the English they used contained relatively few rural, farming terms and perhaps a greater preponderance of words considered to be less refined in polished English society. The pronunciation which has developed, while distinctly Australian, has a clearly urban southern English bias; and although it is often compared with Cockney, the similarities are only partial (see especially Cochrane 1989 and below).

Today the vast majority of the population speaks English, according to Clyne (drawing from the 1976 census), 98.6 per cent of the population – over 80 per cent of them as their native language. Aboriginal languages are in wide use only in Western Australia and the Northern Territory, where the figure was 27.4 per cent (Clyne 1982: 6). Non-British immigration has been significant since World War II. The long practised 'white Australia' policy, which discouraged non-European, even non-British immigration (except for New Zealanders) has yielded to more liberal policies: by the 1970s a third of the immigrants were Asians and only a half were Europeans. In 1976 one in eight of the population over five years of age indicated that they regularly used a language other than English (ibid.); yet the languages of the immigrants have neither called the primacy of English into question nor influenced its character beyond providing loan words.

13.1.1 AusE pronunciation

AusE is most easily recognized by its pronunciation. The intonation seems to operate within a narrower range of pitch, and the tempo often strikes non-Australians as noticeably slow. Overall, rural pronunciations are slower than urban ones. Besides this there is no systematic regional variation, but there are significant social differences. Frequently AusE pronunciation is classed in three categories. The first is referred to as **Cultivated** and resembles RP relatively closely; it may, in fact, include speakers whose pronunciation is 'near-RP'. It is spoken by proportionately few people (in one investigation of adolescent speakers – Delbridge 1970: 19 – approximately 11 per cent), but it is, by the way, the type of pronunciation given in *The Macquarie Dictionary*. The second type is called **General**, spoken by the majority (Delbridge: 55 per cent); its sound patterns are clearly

Map 13.1 Australia

Australian, but not so extreme as what is known as **Broad** (Delbridge: 34 per cent), which realizes its vowels more slowly than General.

In the light of Australia's early history, in which two groups stood in crass opposition to each other, namely the convicts and the officer class which supervised them, the following remark seems fitting:

> In sum, Australian English developed in the context of two dialects — each of them bearing a certain amount of prestige. Cultivated Australian is, and continues to be, the variety which carries overt prestige. It is the one associated with females, private elite schools, gentility, and an English heritage. Broad Australian carries covert prestige and is associated with males, the uneducated, commonness, and republicanism. The new dialect is 'General' which retains the national identity associated with Broad but which avoids the nonstandardisms in pronunciation, morphology, and syntax associated with uneducated speech wherever English is spoken.
>
> (Horvath 1985: 40)

Today teenage speakers are tending to cluster in the area of General, perhaps being pushed there to distinguish themselves from the large number of immigrants who have adopted Broad (ibid.: 175f).

AusE intonation   In addition to the remark made above on the narrower range of pitch in AusE, one further comment is appropriate. This is the use of what is called the high rising tone (sometimes also called the Australian question intonation), which involves the use of rising contours (tone 2, cf. 3.5.3) for statements. It is part of the turn-taking mechanism, and it is used chiefly in narrative and descriptive texts. 'And finally, at the heart of it all is a basic interactive meaning of soliciting feedback from the audience, particularly regarding comprehension of what the speaker is saying' (Guy and Vonwiller 1989: 28). Like adding, 'You know' to a statement, it requests the participation of the listener; see appealer, 6.3.4. It is apparently a low prestige usage, favoured more by young people; it is also more common among females than among males (ibid.: 29; Horvath 1985: 122, 132).

AusE consonants   There are a few significant differences in the realization of AusE consonants as compared sometimes with RP and sometimes with GenAm. Among these few is the tendency to flap and voice intervocalic /t/ before an unstressed syllable in Broad and General, though hardly in Cultivated (ibid.: 99). T-flapping is very similar to the same phenomenon in GenAm and in some varieties of Belfast English. This necessarily means that there is an absence of the glottal stop [ʔ], which many urban varieties of BrE have in the same environment (*butter* is [bʌdə] '*budder*' rather than [bʌʔ] '*buh'er*'.

Unlike GenAm, but like RP, AusE is non-rhotic. As in Cockney there is also a certain amount of H-dropping ('*ouse* for *house*). However, Horvath's Sydney investigation turned up relatively little of this (ibid). In addition, the sound quality of /l/ is even darker than a normal velarized [ɫ]; it is, rather, pharyngealized [lˤ] in all positions (Wells 1982: 603). Furthermore, there seems to be widespread vocalization of /l/ (Taylor 1973–4, pace Wells 1982: 594), which leads to a new set of diphthongs (see examples under NZE, which is similar).

AusE vowels   In the following the vowel system of General/Broad AusE will be presented schematically in comparison with that of RP. One of the main differences, noted by various observers, is a general raising of the simple vowels (see figures 13.1 and 13.2), a lowering and retraction of the first element in the diphthongs which move towards a high front second element (figure 13.3), and a lowering and fronting of the first element of the diphthongs which move towards a high back second element (figure 13.4). To some extent AusE represents a continuation of the Great Vowel Shift, which began in the Middle English period and which is continuing in the

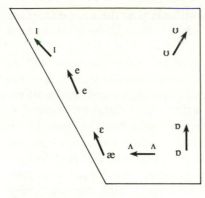

Figure 13.1 The short vowels
(RP → AusE)

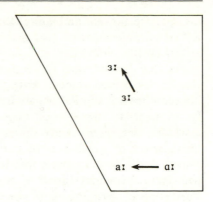

Figure 13.2 The vowels of 'start'
and 'nurse' (RP → AusE)

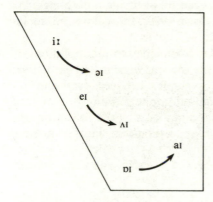

Figure 13.3 The vowels of 'fleece',
'face' and 'price' (RP → AusE)

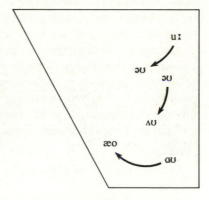

Figure 13.4 The vowels of 'goose',
'goat' and 'mouth' (RP → AusE)

same sense in London English (Cockney). For details, see Cochrane 1959; Turner 1972; Wells 1982.

Beyond such differences in the phonetic realization of the vowels, it is notable that far fewer unstressed vowels are realized as /ɪ/ in AusE than in RP (Bernard and Lloyd 1989: 288). This means that the distinction maintained in RP between ⟨-es⟩ and ⟨-ers⟩ (as in *boxes* /ɪz/ and *boxers* /əz/ or *humid* /ɪd/ and *humoured* /əd/) is usually not made. Indeed, it may be possible to say that there is a certain centralization of /ɪ/ which brings it closer to /ə/, but also sometimes to fronted [ʉː] as well. An Australian newsreader working for the BBC is supposed to have caused some consternation by reporting that the Queen had *chattered* /əd/ rather than *chatted* /ɪd/ with workers (Wells 1982: 601f; cf. Taylor 1973–4). However, most AusE speakers probably could make the distinction if necessary to prevent ambiguity. In addition, note that the final unstressed RP /ɪ/ pronunciation of ⟨-y⟩ and ⟨-i(e)⟩ (*hurry, Toni, hurries*) is realized as /iː/ (Wells 1982: 602).

The /æ/–/aː/ contrast in words of the type *ask, after, example, dance*, etc., shows divided usage in AusE, reminiscent of the same type of contrast between GenAm and RP. Apart from the fact that vowel realization differs from word to word (i.e. does not affect this class of words as a whole), one recent study shows significant regional distinctions. In an identical set of words (*castle, chance, contrast, demand, dance, graph, grasp*) Adelaide lies closest to RP with a proponderance of /aː/ (only 9 per cent /æ/) while Hobart is closest to GenAm with 72 per cent /æ/. Furthermore, working-class speech favours /æ/, with the difference between working and middle class largest in Melbourne (33 percentage points) and least in Brisbane (3 percentage points) (Bradley 1991: 228–31). For further regional differences in pronunciation (centring diphthongs, lax front vowels), see Bradley 1989; also Oasa 1989; for details on socio-linguistic distinctions, see Horvath 1985.

Among the vowels there is, finally, also a tendency to monophthongize the centring diphthongs through loss of the second element (Bernard 1967: 52f). This levels the distinction, for example, between /eə/ and /e/ (*bared > bed*). Together with the fronting and monophthongizing of /aʊ/ this can occasionally lead to misunderstandings such as the following one quoted in Taylor between himself and a postal agent in the outback (1973–4: 59):

Author: Do you sell stamps?
Agent: Yes.
Author: I'd like airmail [= *our mail* for Australian ears], please.
Agent: Sorry, but your mail hasn't come in yet.

Years of prescriptive schooling have not failed to have their effect on Australians, who have only recently begun to gain a more positive attitude towards their own variety of English (mostly pronunciation). One researcher reports that Broad speakers often become General ones by the time they arrive at the recording laboratory (Delbridge 1970: 19; cf. Bernard 1969: 70). Interesting in this context is the discovery that Cultivated forms correlate 'strongly with sex (nine girls for every one boy), with superior education (especially in independent, fee-paying schools), and comfortable urban living' (Delbridge 1990: 72). Finally, another linguist (Poynton) is quoted as remarking that Cultivated was 'good speech used by phony people whereas Broad was bad speech used by real people' (quoted in Horvath 1985: 24).

13.1.2 Grammar and morphology in AusE

It can be said with a great deal of certainty that there are no really significant differences in grammar between standard AusE and standard BrE or
AmE, although formal usage in all areas seems to tend more towards BrE
(Leitner 1984, passim; Turner 1972: 95). An investigation of the use of *dare*
and *need* as modal or lexical verbs has shown, for example, that there are
some differences in preferred usage, but no absolute ones (Collins 1978).

Non-standard AusE usage is also very much like that of other countries
in which English is a widely spoken native language. If there are any
differences in non-standard AusE, they are in relative frequencies. For
many AusE speakers, however, the use of the plural verb in existential
there-constructions, even with singular subjects, is virtually categorical
(Eisikovits 1991: 243f). Gender differentiation seems, for example, to be
stronger in Australia than in the United States or Great Britain (especially
in pronunciation, cf. Guy 1991: 222). A study of Inner Sydney usage reveals
greater use of third person singular *don't* by males, probably 'as a marker
of group identity, "maleness" and working-class values' (Eisikovits 1991:
238f).

In morphology AusE reveals a preference for several processes of word
formation which are considerably less frequent in English at large. One of
those is the relatively greater use of reduplication, especially in designations
for Australian flora and fauna borrowed from Aboriginal languages (*ban-
dy-bandy*, a snake, *gang-gang*, a kind of cockatoo) proper names (*Banka
Banka*, *Ki Ki*, *Kurri Kurri*), and terms from Aboriginal life including
pidgin/creole ones (*mia-mia* 'hut', *kai kai* 'food') (Dabke 1976: 24). In
addition the endings ⟨-ee/-y/-ie⟩ /iː/ (*broomy*, *Aussie*, *Tassie*, *Brizzie*,
surfy) and *-o* [ʌʊ] (*bottlo*, *smoko*) occur more often in AusE than in other
varieties (ibid. 33ff; Turner 1972: 101f; Gunn 1970: 55ff).

13.1.3 AusE vocabulary

Next to pronunciation it is the distinctively Australian words which give this
variety its special character. Slang, including rhyming slang, is often
regarded as especially typical of AusE. Baker's pioneering book, *The Australian Language*, devotes most of its space to Australian words. This
includes both slang and more formal usage. See also *A Dictionary of Australian Colloquialisms*. (For examples of AusE vocabulary, see also Delbridge 1990; Eagleson 1967; Ramson 1966; Sharwood and Gerson 1963;
Turner 1972.) *The Macquarie Dictionary*, the *Heinemann New Zealand
Dictionary* and *The Australian National Dictionary* all cater to both
Australia and New Zealand; *The Australian Concise Oxford Dictionary*

of Current English includes only AusE and not NZE. For a report on regional variation in AusE vocabulary, see Bryant 1985.

There are quite a few Australian words which originate in English dialects and therefore are not a part of StE elsewhere, for example, *bonzer* 'terrific', *chook(ie)* 'chicken', *cobber* 'mate', *crook* 'ill', *dinkum* 'genuine', *larrikin* 'rowdy', *swag* 'bundle', *tucker* 'food'.

Other words are general StE, but may be applied somewhat differently in AusE. For example, you may *shout* someone (order, treat to) a drink. A *station* is a farm (from earlier *prison station*). *Paddocks* are fields. A *mob* of sheep is a flock or herd. *Store* has the AmE meaning. Other AmE borrowings include older *block* 'area of land for settlement, etc.', *township*, *bush* 'the countryside as opposed to town', and more recently *french fries*, *cookies*, *movies*, *truck* 'lorry' and *service station*. Taylor (1989) provides a number of further items borrowed from AmE to which he adds comments on spelling, morphology and syntax; for GenAm as a pronunciation model, see Sussex 1989.

In more formal domains there are, of course, words that are Australian by origin but accepted throughout the English-speaking world because what they designate is some distinctively Australian aspect of reality. Chief among these are words for the flora, fauna and topography of Australia as well as aspects of Aboriginal life. These can be borrowings from Aboriginal languages, of which some forty words are still current in AusE, such as *barramundi* (a fish), *kookaburra* (a bird), *koala* (an animal), *mallee* (a tree, scrub), *billabong* ('dried out river'), *woomera* ('throwing stick, boomerang'). They can also be new words, or compound words, using English elements: *trumpeter* (fish), *lyrebird* (bird), *ironbark* (tree), *outback* ('remote bush') or *throwing stick* ('woomera, boomerang').

Place names, of course, are often specifically Australian (*Wallaroo*, *Kwinana*, *Wollongong*, *Wagga Wagga*), and sometimes there is uncertainty even among Australians about how to pronounce them. So the anecdote about the train approaching Eurelia, where one porter goes through the cars announcing /juːrəlaɪə/ ('You're a liar') and is followed by a second yelling /juːriːliːaː/ ('You really are') (Turner 1972: 198).

AusE shares all but a small portion of its vocabulary with StE; however this small Australian portion is important for giving AusE its own distinctive flavour.

13.1.4 Ethnic groups and language in Australia

With the loosening of immigration policies Australia has ceased to be the almost totally English-speaking country it once was. Immigrants from Asia, America and Europe use some 140 languages as their mother tongues, many regarded as 'community languages' (Delbridge 1990: 66), i.e. 'languages used within the Australian community to emphasize the justification of their continuing existence' (Clyne 1982: 2). The two largest communities are the Italian (48,333 in 1976) and the Greek (30,081) (ibid.: 8). In her study of Sydney English pronunciation Horvath found it useful to add to the Cultivated—General—Broad division the further one which she terms Ethnic Broad (1985: 69). However, as is also the case in the United States, the children of immigrants switch rapidly not only to English, but to English virtually indistinguishable from that of their peers with native-born parents (ibid.: 94).

Particularly interesting is the existence of what are called 'industrial pidgins', which are simplified versions of English used for communication by non-native speakers who do not share another language. What is fascinating about these pidgins is that they do not so much reflect interference from the users' first language, but rather universal processes of simplification (ibid.: 114; cf. 16.2.3).

It has already been mentioned that a number of Aboriginal languages are still spoken. Although about 1 per cent of the Australian population is Aboriginal, only those in the remoter parts of the interior still speak these languages. Furthermore, in parts of Queensland and Western Australia and in the Northern Territory the mixing of Aboriginals with varying, mutually unintelligible mother tongues has led to their adoption of (Roper) Kriol, Torres Strait Broken (Cape York Creole) and Aboriginal English (see also 16.3.3).

Kriol is spoken by at least 15,000 people in the north of Australia. Like Torres Broken, which is spoken on many of the islands between Australia and New Guinea and on Cape York, it is a pidgin for many speakers, but the first language, i.e. a creole, for numerous others. Aboriginal English, spoken especially in remote areas, is 'a term used generally to denote speech varieties between so-called St AusE and creoles' (Sandefur 1983: 55). In the cases of Kriol and Aboriginal English, both languages are recognized as mother tongues in bilingual educational programmes. As far as their status is concerned,

> These Creoles are distinct languages. . . . They show an ingenious blend of English and Australian structural features, producing a language that seems quite appropriate to the bicultural milieu in which many Aboriginal Australians find themselves. Indeed, in some areas an increasing number of young Aborigines are speaking Kriol – instead of or as well as an Australian language – and it is coming to be thought of by them as 'the Aboriginal language'.
>
> (Dixon 1980: 73f)

In most Aboriginal communities there is a continuum which runs from standard AusE to Aboriginal English. However, those Aborigines who live in urban areas such as Sydney speak like their non-Aboriginal neighbours, though the variety of AusE they use tends to be on the non-standard side (cf. Eagleson 1978).

13.2 New Zealand English (NZE)

The language situation in New Zealand resembles that in Australia in many ways. For one, virtually everyone can speak English, and most have it as their native language. The large minority of Maoris, the native Polynesian people of New Zealand, are rapidly losing their native tongue. At the end of the 1970s only about 20 per cent of them, which is approximately 3 per cent of the population of the country, were still fluent in it, and few of these speakers were younger people (Benton 1991: 187). The decision in 1987 to give Maori the status of official language (ibid.: 188–90) is unlikely to change anything.

The historical development of New Zealand is closely related to that of Australia. Before British sovereignty over the territory was officially proclaimed in 1840 there were already some 2,000 English-speaking people there. They had come, mostly via Australia, to establish whaling stations or to work as Christian missionaries to the Maoris. After 1840 European settlement was more closely regulated (but with no transported convicts and no penal stations) and grew gradually in the next decades, drawing on immigration chiefly from Great Britain and Australia. Of the immigrants who arrived between 1854 and 1870, 7,239 came from Britain and 4,523 from Australia (Gordon and Deverson 1985: 18). It was these people, Australians and many English immigrants with a London bias to their speech, who determined the linguistic character of New Zealand.

The English spoken by the present New Zealand population of just over three million (including approximately 12 per cent Maoris) is very much like AusE: 'Even now the similarities in pronunciation and older vocabulary suggest a single dialect area with two major subdivisions' (Turner 1970: 85). Indeed, it has sometimes been said that, linguistically speaking, New Zealand is to Australia as Canada is to the United States. The differences within each of the pairs are small, but for the smaller partner psychologically vital.

The grammar of NZE is fully standard, differing from other standard varieties only in preference of use of some forms:

> Those changes which do affect New Zealand English are confined to pronunciations (accent) and vocabulary (word and meanings); grammar shows no significant change here from the parent variety.
>
> (Gordon and Deverson 1985: 12)

The differences between NZE and other varieties are to be found in matters of degree rather than in categorical distinctions, but NZE is not

Wellington

Otago

Southland

Map 13.2 New Zealand

just the same as BrE or AmE: it is a distinct variety, in grammar as well as in lexis and pronunciation

(Bauer 1989: 82).

What is most noticeably particular to NZE is, as with AusE, its pronunciation and some of its vocabulary.

13.2.1 The pronunciation of NZE

For all practical purposes New Zealanders sound like Australians, at least to outsiders; of course, 'to New Zealanders the Australian accent seems quite different' (Gordon and Deverson 1985: 13). There seems to be little or no regional difference in pronunciation despite the fact that New Zealanders feel there is (but see remarks below on Otago and Southland). Social or class differences do, however, show up, though 'not as clearly marked as in the U.K.' (Bayard 1991: 183). It may also be the case that RP is still more a model in New Zealand than in Australia; certainly it is favoured in 'serious' broadcasting and the news. Investigations of attitudes show associations of RP with ambition, education, reliability, intelligence, and higher income and occupational prestige, but association of NZE accents with friendliness and a sense of humour (Gordon and Abell 1990: 40). While RP has high overt prestige, North American accents show the overall highest covert prestige (Bayard 1990a: 92). In contrast to AusE: 'A true New Zealand standard is still evolving' (ibid.: 57; cf. Bell and Holmes 1991: 160–2). Note, too, that correction in the direction of the prestige sometimes results in such hypercorrect forms as /eɪ/ for /aɪ/ in such words as *I* or *like* (Gordon and Deverson 1985: 64).

The explication and figures presented above for AusE apply to NZE as well. The shifts shown there include such items as the growing merger of /e/ and /eə/, which compounded with the raising of /æ/ to /e/ led to the following misunderstanding. A visiting American phoning a colleague at his house got one of the man's children on the line. The American heard, much to his astonishment, 'He's dead' rather than the intended 'Here's Dad' (Gordon and Deverson 1985: 82).

While much of NZE pronunciation is the same as in AusE, including the even more frequent use of the high rising tone (Allan 1990: 127; Bell and Holmes 1991: 162), a few points are arguably different and merit pointing out. One of these is the greater retraction and centralization of /ɪ/ in NZE, a point which non-New Zealanders have often commented on. Hence the vowel of *kit* becomes [ɨ] or even a stressed schwa [ə]. This explains the surprise of an American hearing Flight 846 at Wellington Airport announced as follows: 'Flight ite four sucks' (Gordon and Deverson 1985: 82).

There is also a very noticeable tendency to vocalize /l/ in NZE (see Bauer 1986: 243ff), something which Wells does not consider to be the case in AusE (Wells 1982: 594). The result has had a far-reaching effect on the vowel system because it has created a number of new diphthongs. This occurs more commonly after front than after back vowels and often involves **neutralization** (i.e. otherwise different vowels are no longer distinguished when followed by /l/), for example, *bill = bull*, *fool = full* and *kill = cull*, or, even more extremely, *pool = pull = pill = pall*, all of which might be rendered as *pooh* (cf. ibid; Gordon and Deverson 1985: 20). An /l/-related phenomenon is also the lowering of /e/ (or the neutralization of the /e/–/æ/ opposition) in words such as *helicopter*, *help*, *Wellington*, which then sound like *hallicopter*, *halp* and *Wallington*.

The centring diphthongs /ɪə/ and /ɛə/ (*beer = bear*) are merging for more and more young people, as in AusE and SAE as well. This is 'the only point at which the New Zealand vowel system actually differs phonemically from that of RP' (Gordon and Maclagan 1990: 132). Especially clear is the loss of the distinction between /w/ and /hw/ (cf. Bell and Holmes 1991: 158f; Bayard 1991: 181). On the other hand, young people show signs of increasing use of the glottal stop in words with final /t/ (Bayard 1991: 184).

Two final, somewhat minor points are, for one, that some speakers in Southland and Otago, where Scottish settlement was strong, are reported to have a rhotic accent (Gordon and Deverson 1985: 59) and, for another, that sometimes a distinction is made between monosyllabic *groan* and bisyllabic (and bimorphemic) *grown* = *grow-n* (likewise: *throne—thrown*, *moan —mown*) (ibid.: 25; cf. 10.2.3). Bayard finds that rhoticism in the general population is sporadic only and that bisyllabic *grown* is a widespread conservative NZE feature; its loss tends to occur among 'Yank-influenced' speakers and to correlate with other pronunciation innovations such as distinguishing singular *woman* from plural *women* or adopting American pronuncations of *garage*, *dynasty*, *missile* and *Z* (Bayard 1990b: 158f).

13.2.2 NZE vocabulary

The vocabulary of NZE has been influenced by new flora, fauna, topography and institutions, and the presence of a non-English-speaking people. In addition, it shares many items with AusE that differ from other national varieties of English. What distinguishes NZE most from AusE is the existence in NZE of a sizable number of borrowings from Maori. Examples include the following: *hoot* 'money', *kiwi* 'a kind of (flightless) bird, the NZ symbol', *mana* 'prestige, status', *marae* 'courtyard, forum', *ngaio* 'a kind of tree', *pakeha* 'white New Zealander', *wahine* 'woman', *whare* 'small house, hut', *yacker* 'work'.

The fact that /aɪ/ as in *whare* /waɪriː/ (see above) can become /ɒ/ in NZE led one schoolboy to make the following spelling mistake: 'Dad thought Mum looked tired so he hired a whore for the holidays' (Turner 1972: 129).

The following excerpt is taken from a newspaper review of the supplement on Australian and New Zealand vocabulary in *The New Zealand Pocket Oxford Dictionary*. The passage makes highly intensive and unauthentically exaggerated use of NZE and AusE colloquial vocabulary; however, it also offers a little of the flavour of the language:

> Stone the crows, sports, but with no more bobsy-die than a dag-picking bushy claiming compo from out in the boo-ay, the sticky-beaks of the Oxford University Press have been taking a squiz at Aussie and Enzed slang. They've now published a beaut new supplement to the Pocket Oxford Dictionary – 1200 dinkydi words and expressions which are certainly giving the chooms something to chiach at.
>
> (quoted in Gordon and Deverson 1985: 51)

To help out, here is a short glossary:

stone the crows – expression of surprise
sports – 'guys'

bobsy-die — 'fuss, panic'
dag-picking — 'sorting the wool from the dags'
dag — 'wool around a sheep's hindquarters, often dirty with mud and excreta'
bushy — 'someone from the countryside, from the bush'
compo — 'worker's compensation'
boo-ay — 'backblocks, remote country district'
sticky-beaks — 'priers, meddlers'
squiz — 'a look'
beaut — 'fine, good'
dinkydi — 'true, honest, genuine'
choom — 'English person' (variant of chum)
chiach — 'jeer, taunt, deride, tease'

13.2.3 Maori English

Although the Maoris (as opposed to the Aborigines of Australia) have a single language, it has not provided significantly more loan words to NZE than Aboriginal languages have to AusE, and it has been constantly giving way to English. There are over a quarter of a million Maoris, but fewer than 10 per cent of young Maoris speak the Maori language fluently (Huygens and Vaughan 1983: 208).

> The relationship between English and Maori in New Zealand is rather like that between Germanic and Celtic languages in fifth-century Britain. Loans from the conquered to the conquering language are few and are especially in place-names and otherwise mainly in words for the natural environment and for unpretentious things.
>
> (Turner 1972: 126)

Most Maoris have adopted English, and they speak it indistinguishably from Pakehas (New Zealand whites) (cf. Benton 1985: 111) of the same socio-economic stratum. There is, for example, no Pidgin English in New Zealand. For proportionately more Maoris this means a broad, working-class type of NZE.

In an experiment, recorded samples of Maori speech were rated lower in social prestige than samples from High and Middle Status Pakehas, but the Maori recordings were given high ratings on the 'warm' scale (as opposed to the 'hard-working' and 'intelligent' scales). Overall, the conclusion was drawn that 'even if there are characteristics of spoken English which are distinctly Maori, New Zealand listeners are generally not distinguishing them' (Huygens and Vaughan 1983: 222). Maoris seem to be evaluated 'as if Low Status Pakehas' (ibid.).

13.3 South African English (SAE)

In this section only South African English (SAE) will be treated. A similarly oriented variety is said to be spoken in Lesotho, Swaziland, Botswana, Namibia, Zambia, Malawi, Zimbabwe and Kenya (Trudgill and Hannah 1982: 24; for sociolinguistic views see Chishimba 1991; cf. also chapter 14). When the first group of English-speaking settlers arrived at Cape Town in 1820 there were not only black Africans living in the colony (principally the Khoikhoi or Hottentots, the San or Bushmen and the Xhosa), but also the descendents of Dutch settlers, called Afrikaners, who had begun arriving in 1652 and over whom the British had established permanent control in 1806. Both the Afrikaners and the British treated the native Africans much as the Europeans had treated the Aborigines in Australia and the Maoris in New Zealand, for the latter were unable to offer resistance to the Europeans or to influence the technologically more advanced culture they represented. The British and Afrikaners, however, became rivals, and their subsequent history has been characterized by political, economic, cultural and linguistic competition.

Between 11 and 12 per cent of the population, namely two-fifths of the white, somewhat more than one-tenth of the coloured (of mixed black and white ancestry) and virtually all of the Indian population, altogether somewhat more than 2.8 million people, speak English as their home language. This makes it the fifth largest language of the country. Around seventeen million speak a black African language, four of which are major languages (North, South and West Sotho; Zulu; Xhosa; Tswana). Just under five million are speakers of Afrikaans, the language of the Afrikaners, but also of the vast majority (between 80 and 90 per cent) of the coloureds as well as a few others (Aldridge 1988: 1400).

After the Afrikaner National Party victory in the 1948 election English was no longer automatically the favoured language in South Africa. Despite its relatively small number of native speakers it has, however, retained considerable influence and prestige. It and Afrikaans have numerous advantages over the black African languages:

1 they are not divided into dialects;
2 they are the official languages of the country;
3 they are spoken by a culturally, politically, and economically dominant white population;
4 they offer access to technological and scientific knowledge (and here English has the advantage over Afrikaans).

English is a world-wide language of wider communication, and for this reason many black Africans are eager to learn it, despite their resentment of white hegemony in economic and political life (cf. Schuring 1979).

Map 13.3 South Africa

The official policy of the government in South Africa has been protective of Afrikaans and cool towards English. As a result most schools within the white community have become monolingual as far as the language of instruction is concerned (39.2 per cent English medium; 59.2 per cent Afrikaans medium; 1.6 per cent dual medium; Kloss 1978: 34). This has helped to prevent further flight from Afrikaans into English, which generally has high prestige and is the language of international commerce, science and technology. Overall, however, English has remained predominant in public life (Chishimba 1991: 438).

For black Africans English was the primary language of instruction until the Bantu Education Act of 1953. After that the black population was to be taught in their native languages until junior high school. Although the advantages of native language learning are undisputed for establishing literacy in primary education, it can be a disadvantage to postpone education in an important library language or language of wider communication too long, as this may cement deficits which can be made up for only at great cost. It has been said that this was intended, as it would not only weaken the position of English, but also cement ethnic–linguistic differences within the black community (Dunjwa-Blajberg 1980: 33ff).

Since 1969 both English and Afrikaans have been the media of teaching at (senior) high school level; however, the black population prefers English both because of its utilitarian value and because it is more closely identified with liberal ideas than is Afrikaans. One study of blacks' attitudes towards English and Afrikaans shows that English is associated with better-looking, more sociable and kinder people with higher-status jobs (Vorster and Proctor 1976: 108). Indeed, English, in contrast to Afrikaans, is seen less as a group language and more as an 'out-group' language, one shared by various ethnic groups. This function is the result of the fact that English-speaking white South Africans have relatively little group feeling, and it is strengthened by the fact that English is a widely used second language for all groups in South Africa including the Afrikaners (cf. Dunjwa-Blajberg 1980: 111, passim).

13.3.1 White SAE

The white English-speaking community in South Africa of approximately 1.8 million (not counting numerous Afrikaans–English bilinguals) uses a variety of English which is close to StE in both grammar and vocabulary. Variation within this community is largely in the dimension of pronunciation: SAE is phonologically virtually identical with the English of southern England. However, phonetically there are numerous differences, most noticeably in the variety referred to as Extreme SAE, less so in what is called Respectable SAE, and least so in Conservative SAE. These three distinctions correlate to some extent with class and, as comments will show, to region and to the gender of the speaker.

Conservative SAE is very similar to RP, and, indeed, it is said that most white SAE-speakers cannot distinguish the two. Among the few differences between the two is vowel retraction before /l/ ([tʃɵldrən] for *children*), centralization of [uː], especially after /j/, and raising of /ɔː/ to back, half close [oː] (Lanham 1984: 338). All of these features turn up in AusE and NZE as well.

In contrast to AusE and NZE, however, Conservative SAE, which has 'a clear correlation with the highest socio-economic status' (Lanham 1985: 243), remains the widely accepted standard of pronunciation in South Africa as seen in its use in radio and television.

Respectable SAE is 'accepted as an informal, local standard expressing high social status if not correctness in English speech' (Lanham 1984: 331). This type of SAE has developed from Natal English, is recognized as local in Natal, and is therefore not so highly regarded there (Lanham 1985: 246); however, it is representative of 'upwardly mobile groups elsewhere' (ibid.: 243). Natal SAE differs from RP because of its tendency to monophthongize /aɪ/ to [a], especially before /l, m, n, v, z, s/.

SAE pronunciation is generally non-rhotic; however, because of the influence of rhotic Afrikaans, it is not consistently so. It may be characterized by the following eight features (cf. Lanham and Macdonald 1979: 46f; Lanham 1984: 339):

1 /eɪ/ starts lower: [əɪ] (*may*);
2 /əʊ/ starts lower as well: [ʌʊ] (*go*);
3 /e/ raised to near Cardinal 2: [eː] (*yes = yace*);
4 /æ/ likewise raised: [e] (*man* = RP *men*);
5 /ɔː/ raised to near Cardinal 7: [oː] (*four = foe*);
6 /ɪ/ realized as [i] (*kiss*) in stressed syllables next to velars, after /h/, and initially; otherwise as [ə] (*pin* = GenAm *pun*) (cf. Wells 1982: 612);
7 final /ɪ/ is longer and closer: /iː/ (*city = citee*);
8 /eə/ is monophthongized: /eː/ (*shared = shed*, except the latter is longer; ibid.: 613).

All of these characteristics, as well as the occasional occurrence of a flapped and voiced /t/ (*latter = ladder*), are reminiscent of AusE and/or NZE. In addition, /dj/ and /tj/ are palatalized /dʒ/ (*due = Jew*) and /tʃ/ (*tune = choon*) (cf. Trudgill and Hannah 1982: 25f).

Extreme SAE has low social prestige, but is connected with the covert values of toughness and manliness, independence, and lack of regard for what is considered refined. Its speakers are marked by gregariousness and unselective social relations, un-Englishness, strong local loyalties and Afrikaner patriotism (Lanham and Macdonald 1979: 25ff). It shares some features with Afrikaans English and is associated with the Eastern Cape. These phonetic characteristics include the use of an obstruent, often trilled /r/, a retracted /aɪ/ (so that *park* is like RP *pork*), and fronted and glide-weakened /aʊ/ = [æʊ] as well as [ɒɪ] for /aɪ/ (much as in AusE and NZE) (ibid.: 38ff and Wells 1982: 614). Yet even this 'broadest' of SAE varieties does not share such working-class variables as /ɪn/ for ⟨-ing⟩ or *h*-dropping, which are typical of Cockney, perhaps because there is virtually no white working class in South Africa (Wells 1982: 622).

Although the influence of Afrikaans on SAE may justifiably be called into question, especially in regard to pronunciation, some evidence of grammatical influence remains. One such item is the construction *I'm busy verbing*, which is a kind of progressive form. In StE only an action verb may occur in the blank (*I'm busy working*). In SAE non-activity verbs are possible as well (*I'm busy waiting*). This construction seems to be modelled on the Afrikaans progressive with *besig* 'busy' (Lass and Wright 1986: 219f).

Other syntactic features include *no* as a sentence initiator (*No, that'll be fine; we can do that easily for you*), third person address (*Will Doctor* [said to this person] *lend me two rand?*), incomplete predications (A: *I was looking for some shoes in town.* B: *And did you find?*), third person single present tense without an {S} (*I'm no musician but the wife play*), prepositions (*to be scared for* [= of] *something; explain me* instead of *explain to me*) (examples from Branford 1978: xv).

There are, of course, some lexical items specific to SAE. These are largely loans from Afrikaans (*brak* 'salty, alkali water or soil', *lekker* 'pleasant, excellent, delicious', *trek* 'arduous trip', *veld* 'open country'); from Nguni/Zulu or Xhosa (*donga* 'river bank, gully', *kaross* 'skin blanket', *mamba* 'a type of snake') or from other languages (Portuguese Pidgin *brinjal* 'egg plant', Hindi *dhobi* 'washerman', Portuguese *kraal* 'native village').

Beyond these, however, there are further words which have entered other forms of StE, usually items reflecting South African life or politics, for example, *apartheid, commando, exit permit* 'permit to leave the country without the right to return', *homeland* 'black ethnic area', *Immorality Act* (former anti-miscegenation law). Branford 1987 is the best source for SAE lexical items; see also Beeton and Dorner 1975.

13.3.2 Afrikaans SAE

Since English is recognized as extremely useful in business life and since English culture is attractive for numerous young Afrikaners, many of them use it widely. More than one in eight claims to be fully bilingual, while fewer than 10 per cent of white SAE-native speakers know Afrikaans well enough to make a similar assertion (Lanham 1984: 335f). Together with less fluent Afrikaans users of English, then, a large number of these South Africans speak Afrikaans English. Generally, this variety carries little prestige and is associated closely with Extreme SAE, which it also resembles to a large extent. Additional linguistic features include deaspiration of stops and /j/ for /h/, as in *hill* /jil/ or *here* /jəˑ/ (ibid.: 340).

13.3.3 Black SAE

Black South Africans speak a kind of English which is clearly identifiable as a second language variety. Despite the large number of English native speakers in South Africa, few teachers in black schools have a sufficiently good command of the language to offer a native-speaker-like model. Nevertheless, somewhat more than a third of the black population read, speak or understand English (Schuring 1979: 11–13). This means that an additional six million South Africans use English, even though this English reflects 'Bantu-language phonology, idioms and fixed expressions, redefined semantic content, and peculiar grammatical structures' (Lanham 1985: 244). These are largely urban dwellers who read English-language newspapers, listen to the English media, and need English in education and in their work lives (Lanham 1984: 333, 347). The higher a person is on the social-educational scale, the more likely her/his English is to resemble white SAE.

Phonetically black SAE is shaped by the pronunciation patterns of the African mother tongues of its users. Among other things this means that the long–short contrasts of English are not maintained (*tick = teak*; *head = haired*; *pull = pool*). Furthermore, there are no central vowels. This means that *bird* may be confused with *bed* and that there is no schwa (Lanham 1984: 342).

13.3.4 Coloured SAE

The coloured population has traditionally spoken Afrikaans; however, a certain shift in loyalties to English may be observed, perhaps because of the negative associations caused by the apartheid policy of the Afrikaners. The characteristics of this variety are similar to (low-prestige) Extreme SAE or Cape English. Yet its speakers seem to cultivate it as a symbol of group identity and solidarity (Lanham 1984: 348).

13.3.5 Indian SAE

This variety of SAE is spoken by approximately three-quarters of a million South Africans of Indian extraction; most of them live in largely English-speaking Natal. It is predicted that English will eventually replace those Indian languages which are still spoken not only in education and economic life, but also as the home language (Lanham 1984: 338, 348).

Linguistically Indian SAE, especially that of older speakers, has a number of characteristics of IndE (cf. 15.2.1), such as the merger of /w/ and /v/, the use of retroflex alveolar consonants, and [eː] and [oː] for /eɪ/ and /əʊ/ (ibid.: 343). Yet Conservative SAE appears to be the overt standard of pronunciation and younger speakers seem to be shifting towards it (ibid.: 334).

Some observations on the grammar of South African Indian English point out that many basilect speakers employ non-standard constructions to form relative clauses, using, for example, personal pronouns instead of relative ones (*You get carpenters, they talk to you so sweet*) or allowing the relative to precede the clause containing the noun to which it refers (*Which one haven' got lid, I threw them away* 'I threw the bottles that don't have caps away') (Mesthrie 1991: 464–7). Furthermore, in basilect speech *that faller*, pronounced *daffale* in rapid delivery, is used as a personal pronoun (ibid.: 472).

It is also reported that the area of topicalization (for example, the fronting of elements in a sentence to make them thematic) and the use and non-use of the third person present tense singular and the noun plural ending {S} vary according to various sociolinguistic criteria (ibid.: 464, 472).

Despite the constructions and usages just mentioned, younger and better educated South Africans of Indian ancestry, who are usually native speakers of English, share most features of their English with other mother-tongue speakers of SAE (ibid.: 462).

REFERENCES

Aldridge, M. V. (1988) 'South Africa', in U. Ammon, N. Dittmar, and K. J. Mattheier (eds.) *Sociolinguistics Soziolinguistik*, Berlin: Walter de Gruyter, pp. 1400–5.

Allan, S. (1990) 'The rise of New Zealand intonation', in A. Bell and J. Holmes (eds) *New Zealand Ways of Speaking English*, Clevedon: Multilingual Matters, pp. 115–28.

The Australian Concise Oxford Dictionary of Current English (1987) 7th edn, ed. G. W. Turner, Melbourne: Oxford University Press.

The Australian National Dictionary (1988) ed. W. S. Ramson. Melbourne: Oxford University Press.

Baker, S. J. (1945, 1966, 1978) *The Australian Language*, 1st–3rd edns, Sydney: Currawong.

Bauer, L. (1986) 'Notes on New Zealand English phonetics and phonology', *English World-Wide* 7: 225–58.

—— (1989) 'The *have* in New Zealand English', *English World-Wide* 10: 69–83.

Bayard, D. (1990a) '"God help us if we all sound like this": attitudes in New Zealand and other English accents', in A. Bell and J. Holmes (eds) *New Zealand Ways of Speaking English*, Clevedon: Multilingual Matters, pp. 67–96.

—— (1990b) 'Minder, mork and mindy? (-t) glottalisation and post-vocalic (-r) in younger New Zealand speakers', in A. Bell and J. Holmes (eds) *New Zealand Ways of Speaking English*, Clevedon: Multilingual Matters, pp. 149–64.

—— (1991) 'Social constraints on the phonology of New Zealand English', in J. Cheshire (ed.) *English around the World: Sociolinguistic Perspectives*, Cambridge: Cambridge University Press, pp. 169–86.

Beeton, D. R. and Dorner, H. (1975) *A Dictionary of English Usage in Southern Africa*, Cape Town: Oxford University Press.

Bell, A. and Holmes, J. (eds) (1990) *New Zealand Ways of Speaking English*, Clevedon: Multilingual Matters.

—— (1991) 'New Zealand', in J. Cheshire (ed.) *English Around the World: Sociolinguistic Perspectives*, Cambridge: Cambridge University Press, pp. 1531–68.

Benton, R. A. (1985) 'Maori, English, and Maori English', in J. B. Pride (ed.) *Cross Cultural Encounters*, Melbourne: River Seine, pp. 110–20.

—— (1991) 'Maori English: a New Zealand myth?', in J. Cheshire (ed.) *English Around the World: Sociolinguistic Perspectives*, Cambridge: Cambridge University Press, pp. 187–99.

Bernard, J. R. L. (1967) 'Length and the identification of Australian English vowels', *Australian Modern Language Association* 27: 37–58.

—— (1969) 'On the uniformity of spoken Australian English', *Orbis*, 18: 62–73.

Bernard, J. R. and Lloyd, A. L. (1989) 'The indeterminate vowel in Sydney and Rockhampton English', in P. Collins and D. Blair (eds) *Australian English: the Language of a New Society*, St. Lucia: University of Queensland Press, pp. 288–300.

Bradley, D. (1989) 'Regional dialects in Australian English phonology', in P. Collins and D. Blair (eds) *Australian English: the Language of a New Society*, St. Lucia: University of Queensland Press, pp. 260–70.

—— (1991) '/æ/ and /aː/ in Australian English', in J. Cheshire (ed.) *English Around the World: Sociolinguistic Perspectives*, Cambridge: Cambridge University Press, pp. 227–34.

Branford, J. (1978, 1987) *A Dictionary of South African English*, 1st and 3rd edns, Cape Town: Oxford University Press.

Bryant, P. (1985) 'Regional variation in the Australian English lexicon', *Australian Journal of Linguistics* 5: 55–66

Chishimba, M. M. (1991) 'Southern Africa', in J. Cheshire (ed.) *English Around the World: Sociolinguistic Perspectives*, Cambridge: Cambridge University Press, pp. 435–45.

Clyne, M. G. (1982) *Multilingual Australia: Resources – Needs – Policies*, Melbourne: River Seine.

Cochrane, G. R. (1959) 'The Australian English vowels as a diasystem', *Word* 15: 69–88.

—— (1989) 'Origins and development of the Australian accent', in P. Collins and D. Blair (eds) *Australian English: the Language of a New Society*, St. Lucia: University of Queensland Press, pp. 176–86.

Collins, P. (1978) '"Dare" and "need" in Australian English: a study of divided usage', *English Studies* 59: 434–41.

Dabke, R. (1976) *Morphology of Australian English*, Munich: Fink.

Delbridge, A. (1970) 'The recent study of spoken Australian English', in W. S. Ramson (ed.) *English Transported*, Canberra: Australian National University Press, pp. 15–31.

—— (1990) 'Australian English now', in L. Michaels and C. Ricks (eds.) *The State of the Language*, 2nd edn, Berkeley: University of California Press, pp. 66–76.

A Dictionary of Australian Colloquialisms (1990) ed. G. A. Wilkes, South Melbourne: Sydney University Press.

Dixon, R. M. W. (1980) 'The role of language in Aboriginal Australian society today', in *The Languages of Australia*, Cambridge: Cambridge University Press, pp. 69–96.

Dunjwa-Blajberg, J. (1980) *Sprache und Politik in Südafrika*, Bonn: Informationsstelle Südliches Afrika.

Eagleson, R. D. (1967) 'The nature and study of Australian English', *Journal of English Linguistics* 1: 11–24.

—— (1978) 'Urban Aboriginal English', *Australian Modern Language Association* 49: 52–64.

Eisikovits, E. (1991) 'Variation in subject–verb agreement in Inner Sydney English', in J. Cheshire (ed.) *English Around the World: Sociolinguistic Perspectives*, Cambridge: Cambridge University Press, pp. 435–55.

Gordon, E. and Abell, M. (1990) '"This objectionable colonial dialect": historical and contemporary attitudes to New Zealand speech', in A. Bell and J. Holmes (eds) *New Zealand Ways of Speaking English*, Clevedon: Multilingual Matters, pp. 21–48.

Gordon, E. and Deverson, T. (1985) *New Zealand English*, Auckland: Heinemann.

Gordon, E. and Maclagan, M. A. (1990) 'A longitudinal study of the "ear/air" contrast in New Zealand speech', in A. Bell and J. Holmes (eds) *New Zealand Ways of Speaking English*, Clevedon: Multilingual Matters, pp. 129–48.

Gunn, J. S. (1970) 'Twentieth-century Australian idiom', in W. S. Ramson (ed.) *English Transported*, Canberra: Australian National University Press, pp. 49–67.

Guy, G. (1991) 'Australia', in J. Cheshire (ed.) *English Around the World: Sociolinguistic Perspectives*, Cambridge: Cambridge University Press, pp. 213–26.

Guy, G. and Vonwiller, J. (1989) 'The high rising tone in Australian English', in P. Collins and D. Blair (eds) *Australian English: the Language of a New Society*, St. Lucia: University of Queensland Press, pp. 21–34.

Heinemann New Zealand Dictionary (1979) ed. H. W. Orsman, Auckland: Heinemann.

Horvath, B. M. (1985) *Variation in Australian English*, Cambridge: Cambridge University Press.

Huygens, I. and Vaughan, G. M. (1983) 'Language attitude, ethnicity and social class in New Zealand', *Journal of Multilingual and Multicultural Development* 4: 207–23.

Kloss, H. (1978) *Problems of Language Policy in South Africa*, Vienna: Braumüller.

Lanham, L. W. (1984) 'English in South Africa', in R. W. Bailey and M. Görlach (eds.) *English as a World Language*, Cambridge: Cambridge University Press, pp. 324–52.

—— (1985) 'The perception and evaluation of varieties of English in South African society', in S. Greenbaum (ed.) *The English Language Today*, Oxford: Pergamon, pp. 242–51.

Lanham, L. W. and Macdonald, C. A. (1979) *The Standard in South African English and its Social History*, Heidelberg: Groos.

Lanham, L. W. and Traill, A. (1962) 'South African English Pronunciation', *English Studies in Africa* 5: 171–208.

Lass, R. and Wright, S. (1986) 'Endogeny vs. contact: "Afrikaans influence" on South African English', *English World-Wide* 7: 201–23.

Leitner, G. (1984) 'Australian English or English in Australia: linguistic identity or dependence in broadcast language', *English World-Wide* 5: 55–85.

The Macquarie Dictionary (1981) ed. A. Delbridge, Dee Why, NSW: Macquarie Library.

Mesthrie, R. (1991) 'Syntactic variation in South African Indian English: the relative clause', in J. Cheshire (ed.) *English Around the World: Sociolinguistic Perspectives*, Cambridge: Cambridge University Press, pp. 462–73.

The New Zealand Pocket Oxford Dictionary (1986) ed. R. Burchfield, Auckland: Oxford University Press.

Oasa, H. (1989) 'Phonology of current Adelaide English', in P. Collins and D. Blair (eds) *Australian English: the Language of a New Society*, St. Lucia: University of Queensland Press, pp. 271–87.

Ramson, W. S. (1966) *Australian English: an Historical Study of the Vocabulary 1788–1898*, Canberra: Australian National University Press.

Sandefur, J. R. (1983) 'Modern Australian Aboriginal languages: the present state of knowledge', *English World-Wide* 4: 43–68.

Schuring, G. K. (1979) *A Multilingual Society: English and Afrikaans amongst Blacks in the RSA*, Pretoria: Human Sciences Research Council.

Sharwood, J. and Gerson, S. (1963) 'The vocabulary of Australian English', *Moderna Språk* 57: 1–10.

Sussex, R. (1989) 'The Americanisation of Australian English: prestige models in the media', in P. Collins and D. Blair (eds) *Australian English: the Language of a New Society*, St Lucia: University of Queensland Press, pp. 158–68.

Taylor, B. (1989) 'American, British and other foreign influences on Australian English since World War II', in P. Collins and D. Blair (eds) *Australian English: the Language of a New Society*, St Lucia: University of Queensland Press, pp. 225–54.

Taylor, C. V. (1973–4) 'Ambiguities in spoken Australian English', *English Language Teaching* 28: 59–64.

Trudgill, P. and Hannah, J. (1982, 1985) *International English: a Guide to Varieties of Standard English*, 1st and 2nd edns, London: Edward Arnold.

Turner, G. W. (1970) 'New Zealand English today', in W. S. Ramson (ed.) *English Transported*, Canberra: Australian National University Press, pp. 84–101.

—— (1972) *The English Language in Australia and New Zealand*, London: Longman.

Vorster, J. and Proctor, L. (1976) 'Black attitudes to "white" languages in South Africa: a pilot study', *Journal of Psychology* 92: 103–8.

Wells, J. C. (1982) *Accents of English*, Cambridge: Cambridge University Press.

Preface to chapters 14 and 15
English as a second language

The previous, geographically oriented chapters in this part have provided a look at those countries in which English is spoken as a native language, if not by the total population, at least by a significantly large group. The following two chapters continue the geographic survey of English by observing its use as a second language. Chapter 14 deals with English in Africa; chapter 15, with English in Asia.

The idea of **second language** is only gradually different from that of **foreign language**, for it is less the quality of a speaker's command than the status of the language within a given community that determines whether it is a second or a foreign language. In an unambiguous case a foreign language is a language learned in school and employed for communicating with people from another country. A second language, in contrast, may well be one learned in school, too, but one used within the learner's country for offical purposes, i.e. 'by the government for its own internal operating and promoted through the power of the state' (Conrad and Fishman 1977: 8).

As far as English is concerned, second-language status is quite common. Not only are bilingual French–English Canada (chapter 12), Irish–English Ireland (chapter 10), and Afrikaans–English South Africa (chapter 13) cases where, for some people, it is a second language; it is also a second language in numerous countries in Asia and Africa. In the latter it is the official or semi-official language, a status sometimes shared with one or more other languages, and is typically not the native language of more than a handful of people. There are some thirty-five such countries, twenty-six in which English is an official language and nine further ones in which it is de facto so. The first group includes Botswana, Cameroon (with French), Fiji, Gambia, Ghana, Hong Kong, India (with Hindi), Lesotho (with Sesotho), Liberia, Malawi (with Chichewa), Malta (with Maltese), Mauritius, Namibia (with Afrikaans and German), Nauru (with Nauru), Nigeria (with Igbo, Hausa and Yoruba), the Philippines (with Filipino/Pilipino/Tagalog), Sierra Leone, Singapore (with Chinese, Malay and Tamil), Swaziland (with Siswatsi), Tanzania (with Swahili), Tonga (with Tongan),

Uganda, Vanuatu (with Bislama and French), West Samoa (with Samoan), Zambia and Zimbabwe. The second group consists of Bangladesh, Burma, Ethiopia, Israel, Kenya, Malaysia, Pakistan, Sri Lanka and Sudan.

The number of second-language users of English is estimated (pace Crystal 1985, who opts for 600 million and even quotes one billion) at about 300 million, i.e. roughly the same number as that of English native speakers. Whatever the exact figure may be, 'English is the major language of wider communication and the primary natural language candidate for an international language in the world today' (Conrad and Fishman 1977: 7).

The circumstances that have led to the establishment of English, an outside or 'exoglossic' language, as a second language in so many countries of Africa and Asia are not education and commerce alone, however important English is for these activities everywhere in the modern world and however strong the economic hegemony of the English-speaking world. Quite clearly it is the legacy of colonial rule that has made English so indispensable in these countries, of which only Ethiopia was never a British or American colony or protectorate. (Where the colonial master was France, Belgium or Portugal, French and Portugese are the second languages.) The retention of the colonial language is a conscious decision and may be assumed to be the result of deliberate language policy and language planning. Among the factors which support the use of English as an official language are the following:

1 the lack of a single indigenous language that is widely accepted by the respective populations; here English is neutral *vis-à-vis* mutually competing native languages and hence helps to promote national unity;
2 the usefulness of English in science and technology as opposed to the underdeveloped vocabularies of the vernaculars;
3 the availability of suitable school books in English;
4 the status of English as an international language of wider communication, useful in trade and diplomacy.

In these countries English plays an important role in government and administration, in the courts, in education (especially secondary and higher education), in the media, and for both domestic and foreign economic activity. English is, in other words, an extremely utilitarian, public language. It is also used, in a few cases, as a means of expressing national unity and identity versus ethnic parochiality (especially in Singapore). As a result second-language English users are in the dilemma of **diglossia**: they recognize the usefulness of English, yet feel strong emotional ties to the local languages. English is the diglossically High language *vis-à-vis* the indigenous languages, which are more likely to be diglossically Low, and therefore to be preferred in private dealings and for intimacy and emotion. Family life is typically conducted in the ethnic or ancestral vernaculars.

English, in other words, is far from displacing the vernaculars. Historically, the conditions for language replacement have been, as the cases of Latin and Arabic show, (1) military conquest, (2) a long period of language imposition, (3) a polyglot subject group and (4) material benefits in the adoption of the language of the conquerors (cf. Brosnahan 1963: 15–17). In modern Africa and Asia additional factors such as (5) urbanization, (6) industrialization/economic development, (7) educational development, (8) religious orientation and (9) political affiliation (Fishman *et al.* 1977: 77–82) are also of importance. Yet the period of true language imposition has generally been relatively short and economic development at the local level has been less directly connected with the colonial language, so that English has tended to remain an urban and an elite High language.

All the same, where English is widely used as a second language there is often as much local pride in it on the part of the educated elite as there is resentment at its intrusion. As a result there has been widespread talk of the recognition of a 'local' standard, especially in pronunciation, either a regional one such as standard West African English or a national one such as standard Nigerian English. Some have emphasized the negative aspects of such 'nativization' or 'indigenization', which is said to tend towards a fall in (international) intelligibility (Prator 1968: 466, 473) and, in Africa for example, to 'preclude the development of African languages' (Bokamba 1983: 95). A neglect of the vernaculars includes the danger of producing 'thousands of linguistically, and hence culturally "displaced persons"' (Spencer 1963: 3). On the other hand, English may be spreading 'apparently accompanied by relatively little affect [*sic*] – whether positive or negative' (Fishman 1977: 126). Indeed, some would go so far as to maintain: 'The use of a standard or informal variety of Singaporean, Nigerian, or Filipino English is . . . a part of what it means to *be* a Singaporean, a Nigerian, or a Filipino' (Richards 1982: 235). As the following chapters show, there is, indeed, room for a wide diversity of opinions on this subject, and the developments in one country may be completely different in tendency from those in another.

REFERENCES

Bokamba, E. G. (1983) 'The Africanization of English', in B. B. Kachru (ed.) *The Other Tongue*, Oxford: Pergamon, pp. 77–98.
Brosnahan, L. F. (1963) 'Some historical cases of language imposition', in J. Spencer (ed.) *Language in Africa*, Cambridge: Cambridge University Press, pp. 7–24.
Conrad, A. W. and Fishman, J. A. (1977) 'English as a world language: the evidence', in J. A. Fishman, R. L. Cooper and A. W. Conrad (eds) *The Spread of English*, Rowley, Mass.: Newbury House, pp. 3–76.
Crystal, D. (1985) 'How many millions? The statistics of English today', *English Today* 1: 7–9

Fishman, J. A. (1977) 'The spread of English as a new perspective for the study of "language maintenance and language shift"', in J. A. Fishman, R. L. Cooper and A. W. Conrad (eds) *The Spread of English*, Rowley, Mass.: Newbury House, pp. 108–33.

Fishman, R. A., Cooper, R. L. and Rosenbaum, Y. (1977) 'English around the world', in J. A. Fishman, R. L. Cooper and A. W. Conrad (eds) *The Spread of English*, Rowley, Mass.: Newbury House, pp. 77–107.

Prator, C. H. (1968) 'The British heresy in TESL', in J. A. Fishman, C. A. Ferguson and J. Das Gupta (eds) *Language Problems of Developing Nations*, New York: Wiley, pp. 459–76.

Richards, J. C. (1982) 'Rhetorical and communicative styles in the new varieties of English', in J. Pride (ed.) *New Englishes*, Rowley, Mass.: Newbury House, pp. 227–48.

Spencer, J. (ed.) (1963) 'Introduction', in *Language in Africa*, Cambridge: Cambridge University Press, pp. 1–5.

Chapter 14

English in Africa

Second-language English in Africa may be divided into three general geographic areas: the six anglophone countries of West Africa (Cameroon, Gambia, Ghana, Liberia, Nigeria and Sierra Leone, plus Fernando Poo, where Creole English is spoken), those of East Africa (Ethiopia, Somalia, Uganda, Kenya, Tanzania, Malawi and Zambia), and those of Southern Africa (Namibia, Botswana, Zimbabwe, Swaziland, Lesotho and South Africa; cf. 13.3 on South Africa). 'English is . . . an official language for over 160 million Africans, though its native-speaking population amounts to little more than 1% of this.' (Angogo and Hancock 1980: 88).

The first group includes two countries which have native speakers of English (Liberia, 5 per cent) or an English creole (Sierra Leone, also 5 per cent) (percentages according to Brann 1988: 1421). All six are characterized by the presence and vitality of Pidgin English, used by large numbers of people. Neither Eastern nor Southern Africa have pidgin or creole forms of English. However, South Africa, Zimbabwe and Namibia all have a fair number of non-black native speakers of English (South Africa: approximately 40 per cent; Namibia, 8 per cent; Zimbabwe, virtually all the white population). There are, however, statistically speaking, no native speakers of English among the black African population and, except for the possibly more direct influence of native-speaker English in Southern Africa, there is no reason for distinguishing these countries from those of East Africa. Indeed, in the following only the basic division into West and East Africa has been maintained.

English in Africa, though chiefly a second language and rarely a native language of African blacks, is, nevertheless, sometimes a first language in the sense of familiarity and daily use. Certainly, there are enough fluent, educated speakers of what has been called African Vernacular English who 'have grown up hearing and using English daily, and who speak it as well as, or maybe even better than, their ancestral language' for it to serve as a model (Angogo and Hancock 1980: 72). Furthermore, the number of English users is also likely to increase considering the number of Africans who are learning it − '47.1 percent of primary school students and 96.9

percent of those in secondary schools throughout the continent' (Conrad and Fishman 1977: 16).

Despite numerous variations, due especially to the multitudinous mother tongues of its speakers, this African Vernacular English is audibly recognizable as a type and is distinct from, for instance, Asian English.

It tends to have a simplified vowel system *vis-à-vis* native-speaker English. Furthermore, it shares certain grammatical, lexical, semantic and pragmatic features throughout the continent. These include different prepositional, article and pronoun usage, comparatives without *more*, pluralization of non-count nouns, use of verbal aspect different from StE, generalized question tags, a functionally different application of *yes* and *no*, semantic extension, shift and transfer, as well as the coinage of new lexical items. Various expressions, such as the interjection *Sorry!*, are employed in a pragmatic sense unfamiliar to StE.

14.1 West Africa

The six anglophone West African countries of Cameroon, Gambia, Ghana, Liberia, Nigeria and Sierra Leone (see map 14.1) are themselves polyglot. Nigeria has up to 415 languages; Cameroon, 234; Ghana, 60; and even Liberia, Sierra Leone, and Gambia have 31, 20 and 13 respectively (Brann 1988: 1418f). In this situation it is obvious that any government has to be concerned about having an adequate language for education and as a means of general internal communication. Where there is no widely recognized indigenous language to do this, the choice has usually fallen on the colonial language. When the two Cameroons were united, both colonial languages, French (80 per cent of the country) and English (the remainder), were adopted. A bilingual French–English educational policy is pursued. Of the six states just mentioned, only Nigeria has viable native languages which are readily available for written use, most clearly Hausa in the north, but also Yoruba in the west and Igbo in the east; all three are being developed as official languages. However, in Nigeria as a whole, as well as the other five countries, it is English which fulfils many or most of the developmental and educational functions of language. It is possible to speak here of **triglossia**: at the bottom, the autochthonous languages; at an intermediate level, the regional languages of wider communication; and superimposed on the whole, the outside or exogenous language, English (ibid.: 1416). For the most part the vernaculars and English are not in conflict, but are complementary (Adekunle 1972: 100), with English reserved for the functions of a High language in the sense of diglossia, viz. use on formal and public occasions and as the written language, while the local languages are the Low languages of informal, private, vernacular, oral communication. Note that speakers who do not share a native language prefer to communicate in a regional one. If that is not feasible, they will choose pidgin English.

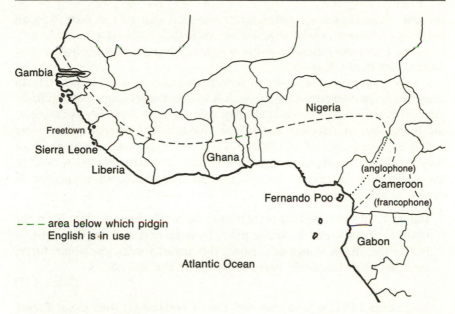

Map 14.1 West Africa

'English is generally utilised in horizontal communication as the "default" code: when there is no other alternative' (Bokamba 1991: 499).

14.2 English in West Africa

The English language is a complicated phenomenon in West Africa. It is present in a continuum of sorts which runs from British StE with a (near) RP accent (in Liberia the orientation is towards AmE), via a local educated second-language variety, to a local vernacular and to West African Pidgin or one of its creolized varieties. This diversity of levels is one of the results of the history of European–African contact on the West Coast of Africa.

14.2.1 Pidgins and creoles

Europeans went to the Atlantic coast of Africa in the first phase of European imperialism from 1450 on, during what was known as the Age of Discovery. Initial trade contacts gradually expanded as a part of the West Indian–American plantation and slave system, in which West Africa's role was chiefly that of a supplier of slaves. Throughout the era of the slave trade (Britain and the United States outlawed it in 1808; other European countries slowly followed) Europeans and Africans conducted business by means of contact languages called **pidgins**. Although simplified linguistic systems, their grammatical structure resembled that of the West African languages (themselves relatively similar) while their vocabulary came largely from the European language involved – first Portuguese, later French and Dutch, and finally English.

Pidgin English continues to be used today all along the West African coast from Gambia to Gabon, though it is not always immediately intelligible from variety to variety. It is a diglossically Low language like most of the indigenous vernaculars and is, for example in Cameroon, 'the most widely used language' (Todd 1982: 132). It is perhaps so easily learned not only because it is simplified, but also because it is structurally so close to the indigenous languages. Its spread and importance in Cameroon is described as follows:

> Pidgin English is used on plantations, on work-sites, in church, in the market, in playgrounds, and in pubs, by preachers and by politicians. It is also the lingua franca of prisons, the armed forces, the police force, and the most commonly heard language in the law courts.
>
> (ibid.: 137)

> As a contact Pidgin in various varieties of Weskos [< *West Coast* Pidgin English], it may be spoken occasionally by as many as 30 millions in the 5 'anglophone' states of West Africa and Cameroon, either as an inter-ethnic lingua franca, or as a relaxed or joking language.
>
> (Brann 1988: 1421)

Furthermore, creolized (mother tongue) forms of pidgin are in wide use in Sierra Leone, where it is becoming more important than English (Fyle 1976: 47), and in Liberia, both of which are countries to which slaves were returned – either from America, Canada and the West Indies or from slave ships seized by the British navy – from the late eighteenth century on. Their first language was or became a form of (creole) English. This accounts for the approximately 5 per cent of Liberians who are native speakers of English and the 2 to 5 per cent of Sierra Leoneans who speak Krio, the English-based creole of that country. Today, creolized forms of pidgin English are continuing to emerge among the children of linguistically mixed marriages in many urban centres, especially in Cameroon and Nigeria (cf., for example, Shnukal and Marchese 1983; Agheyisi 1988). For more on pidgins and creoles, see chapter 16.

14.2.2 Standard English

Standard English was introduced in the second major phase of colonialism in the nineteenth century, when the European powers divided up as much of Africa and Asia as they could. As a part of this movement there was a wave of Christian missionary effort in Africa: 'English was to become the language of salvation, civilisation and worldly success' (Spencer 1971: 13). Although the Church made wide use of the native languages and alphabetized various of them for the first time, it had little use for Pidgin English. The result was the suppression of Pidgin and Creole English by school, church and colonial administration in favour of '"correct" bourgeois English' (ibid.: 23). StE was and is used in education, in government, in international trade, for access to scientific and technical knowledge and in the media. It is a status symbol, a mark of education and Westernization. While StE thus functions as the badge of the local elite, Pidgin English has little prestige, but does signal a good deal of group solidarity. A passage from Chinua Achebe's novel *No Longer at Ease* (p. 77) provides an example of the complex linguistic situation in Nigeria:

'Good! See you later.' Joseph always put on an impressive manner when speaking on the telephone. He never spoke Ibo or pidgin English at such moments. When he hung up he told his colleagues: 'That *na*[1] my brother. Just return from overseas. B.A. (Honours) Classics.' . . .

'What department he *de*[2] work?'

'Secretary to the Scholarship Board.'

''E *go*[3] make plenty money there. Every student who wan' go England *go*[3] *de*[2] see *am*[4] *for*[5] house.'

''E no *be*[6] like dat,' said Joseph. 'Him *na*[1] gentleman. No *fit*[7] take bribe.'

Notes:

[1] *na* 'be' (marker for a following predicative complement)
[2] *de* + infinitive (progressive, cf. StE *be* + *Ving*)
[3] *go* 'will' (future, cf. *going to*)
[4] *am* 'him, her, it, etc.' (transitive verb object marker)
[5] *for* 'to, at, etc.' (generalized preposition of place)
[6] *be* 'be' (copular verb, uninflected)
[7] *fit* 'be able to' (modal verb)

To return to the continuum of Englishes in West Africa today, it might be remarked that StE at the upper end, with no syntactic or semantic differences to native-speaker StE and few if any *phonological* differences to RP, is spoken by no more than a few *been-to*'s, i.e. those who have returned from Great Britain or the United States. Although it is internationally intelligible, it is not socially acceptable for native Africans in local West African society. At the other extreme are the pidgins and creoles, which, linguistically speaking, are often regarded as independent languages, and hence outside the continuum of English (Bamgbose 1983: 101f); for 'throughout West Africa, speakers are usually able to say at any time whether they are speaking the one or the other' (Angogo and Hancock 1980: 72). Nevertheless, the situation is not quite so straightforward inasmuch as many people as well as the governments generally view pidgin and creole as English, albeit of an 'uneducated' variety. Furthermore, for speakers who have a limited command of the stylistic variations of native-speaker English, Pidgin English can make possible the needed change to an informal register (Egbe 1979: 103; Adetugbo 1979: 156). However, whatever perspective is taken, it is a fact that only a local, educated variety may be regarded as a serious contender for the label West African StE. Such a form of English, which implies completed primary or secondary education, is available to perhaps 10 per cent of the population of anglophone West Africa. A study of prepositional use in Nigerian English provides support for the view that an independent norm is growing up which contains not only evidence of mother tongue interference, but also of what are termed 'stable Nigerianisms'. In addition, this study shows that a meaningful sociolinguistic division of Nigerian English is one which, reflecting the educational structure of the country, provides for 'two or three broad categories (corresponding to the masses/sub-élite/élite classification)'(Jibril 1991: 536). Some of the characteristics of this variety will be enumerated in the following section.

14.3 Linguistic features of educated West African English (WAE)

Within WAE there is a great deal of variation; indeed, the higher the education of a user, the closer his or her usage is likely to be to StE. In this sense WAE is perhaps less a fixed standard than a more or less well-learned second language. This is substantiated to some extent by the fact that a good deal of the difference between the StE of native speakers and that of educated West Africans can be explained by interference from the first language of the latter. All of this notwithstanding, there are, nevertheless, features of educated WAE which form a standard in the sense that (a) they are widely used and no longer amenable to change via further learning (cf. the non-acceptance of *been-to* StE mentioned above) and (b) they are community norms, not recognized as 'errors' even by the relatively most highly trained anglophone West Africans.

14.3.1 The pronunciation of WAE

Most noticeable to a non-African is, as with all the types of StE reviewed in this book, the pronunciation. Generally speaking, West Africans have the three diphthongs /aɪ, aʊ, ɔɪ/ and a reduced vowel system which can be represented as in table 14.1. What is noticeable about the list is the lack of central vowels. This means that schwa /ə/ is also relatively rare, which fits in with the tendency of WAE to give each syllable relatively equal stress (syllable-timed rhythm). Furthermore, stress is realized differently and the intonation is less varied. Important grammatical distinctions made by

Table 14.1 The vowels of WAE in comparison with those of RP

WAE	RP	as in	WAE	RP	as in
i — iː		bead	ɔ — ɜː		bird
ı		bid	ʌ		bud
			ɒ		bod(y)
e — eɪ		bayed	ɔː		bawdy
ɛ — e		bed	o — əʊ		bode
a — æ		bad	u — ʊ		Buddha
ɑː		bard	uː		booed

(adapted from Angogo and Hancock 1980: 75)

intonation, such as the difference between rising and falling tag questions, may be lost. Emphasis may be achieved lexically, by switching from a short to a long word, for instance, from *ask* to *command* to show impatience (Egbe 1979: 98–101). In the same way cleft sentences are likely to be more frequent in the spoken language of Nigerian speakers than of non-African native speakers (Adetugbo 1979: 142). The consonant system is the same as in RP, but there is a strong tendency towards spelling pronunciations of combinations such as *-mb* and *-ng*; this also means that although WAE is non-rhotic, less educated speakers may pronounce /r/ where it is indicated in the spelling. There are, of course, numerous regional variations such as that of Hausa speakers, who tend to avoid consonant clusters, so that *small* becomes /sᵘmɔl/ (Todd 1984: 288). Among other things, for some speakers /θ/ becomes /t/. For further details, see Bamgbose 1983; Jibril 1982; Todd 1984; Willmott 1978–9.

14.3.2 The grammar of WAE

The syntactic features of standard WAE are much more difficult to define. A study of deviation from StE in Ghanaian newspapers reveals numerous syntactic problems, but very few general patterns (Tingley 1981). Among the points that are frequently mentioned and which therefore presumably have a fair degree of currency are the following:

1 the use of non-count nouns as count nouns (*luggages, vocabularies, a furniture, an applause*);
2 pleonastic subjects (*The politicians they don't listen*);
3 an overextension of aspect (*I am having a cold*);
4 the present perfect with a past adverbial (*It has been established hundreds of years ago . . .*);

5 comparatives without *more* (*He values his car than his wife*);
6 a generalized question tag (*It doesn't matter, isn't it?*);
7 a functionally different use of *yes* and *no* (*Isn't he home? Yes* [*he isn't*]).

See Angogo and Hancock 1980; Bamgbose 1983; Tingley 1981; Todd 1984 for these and further examples. Most of these points (except 5) show up in Asian English as well, which suggests that their source may well lie in the intrinsic difficulty of such phenomena in English.

14.3.3 The vocabulary of WAE

The English vocabulary of West Africa, like that of any area, has special words for local flora, fauna and topography. In addition, the special elements of West African culture and institutions have ensured the adoption of numerous further items. This, more than grammar, is said to give WAE 'its distinctive "flavour", because it reflects the sociolinguistic milieux in which English is spoken' (Bokamba 1991: 502). The words themselves may be:

1 English words with an extension of meaning, e.g. *chap* 'any person, man or woman';
2 semantic shifts, e.g. *smallboy* 'low servant'; *cane* 'bamboo';
3 new coinages using processes of affixation, compounding, or reduplication, e.g. *co-wives* 'wives of the same husband'; *rentage* '(house)rent'; *bush-meat* 'game'; *slow slow* 'slowly';
4 new combinations, e.g. *check rice* 'rice prepared with krain-krain'; *head tie* 'woman's headdress';
5 words now outdated in Britain/America, e.g. *deliver* 'have a baby'; *station* 'town or city in which a person works';
6 calques/loan translations, e.g. *next tomorrow* 'day after tomorrow' from Yoruba *otunla* 'new tomorrow';
7 borrowings from a native language, e.g. *awujor* 'ceremony giving the ancestors food'; *krain-krain* 'a leaf vegetable';
8 borrowings from pidgin/creole, e.g. *tai fes* 'frown'; *chop* 'food';
9 borrowings from other languages, e.g. *palaver* (Portuguese) 'argument, trouble'; *piccin* (Portuguese) 'child'.

Most of these are restricted in use to West Africa, but some may be known and used more widely, for example, *calabash*, *kola* or *palm wine*. For the examples above and further ones, see especially Pemagbi 1989; Bokamba 1991; but also Jibril 1982; Bamgbose 1983; Willmott 1978–9.

14.3.4 Some pragmatic characteristics of WAE

The cultural background of West African society often leads to ways of expression which are unfamiliar if not misleading for outsiders. This is surely one of the most evident ways in which second-language English becomes 'nativized' or 'indigenized'. A frequently quoted example is the use of *Sorry!* as an all-purpose expression of sympathy, that is, not only to apologize for, say, stepping on someone's toes, but also to someone who has sneezed or stumbled. Likewise, *Wonderful!* is used to reply to any surprise (even if not pleasant), and *Well done!* may be heard as a greeting to a person at work (cf. Bamgbose 1971: 44; 1983: 107).

The difference in family structure between the Western world and West Africa means that kinship terms (*father*, *mother*, *brother*, *sister*, *uncle*, *aunt*, etc.) may be used as in the West, viz. in regard to the kernel family. Because polygyny is practised in West African society the terms may be extended to the father and all his wives and all their children. An even more extended concept may be adopted to include a father and all his sons and their wives, sons and unmarried daughters. The terms *father* and *mother* are sometimes also applied to distant relatives or even unrelated people who are of the appropriate age and to whom respect is due. When far away from home, kinship terms may be applied to someone from the same town or ethnic group, or, if abroad, even to compatriots (Akere 1982: 91; cf. also 9.2.2). One further example of such culturally constrained language behaviour concerns greetings. The indigenous (Yoruba) culture provides for far more variants than StE English does, such as special greetings for various activities and emotions. It also prescribes different norms of linguistic politeness:

> The terms *Hi*, *Hello*, and *How are you* can be used by older or senior persons to younger or junior ones, but not vice-versa. Such verbal behavior coming from a younger person would be regarded as off-hand.
>
> (ibid.: 92)

14.4 East Africa

The main countries of East Africa as far as this review is concerned are Tanzania, Kenya and Uganda (see map 14.2). All three of them share one important feature: the presence of Swahili as a widely used lingua franca. Structurally within East African society this language is therefore somewhat parallel to Pidgin English in West Africa. However, while Pidgin English is almost totally without prestige, the same cannot be said of Swahili, which, together with English, is the official language in Kenya and Tanzania. In each of these countries English is used widely in education, especially at the secondary and post-secondary levels. However, in Tanzania, despite the continued prominence of English in learning and much professional activity, Swahili is the preferred national language; it is also probably slowly displacing the autochthonous mother tongues.

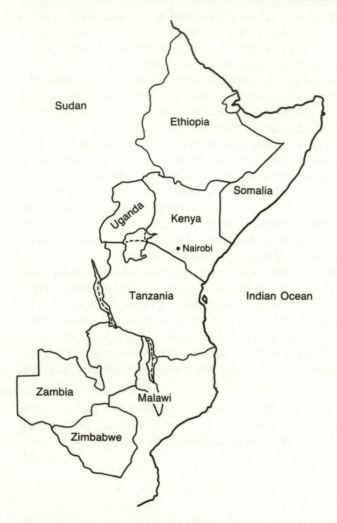

Map 14.2 East Africa

The situation in Uganda is more ambiguous because of the ethnic rivalries between the large anti-Swahili Baganda population (approximately one-sixth are Luganda native speakers and an additional almost one quarter speak Luganda as a second language) and the anti-Baganda sections of the population, who favour Swahili. In the meantime, while Swahili is used in the army and by the police, English remains the medium of education from upper primary school (year four) on, if not earlier (cf. Abdulaziz 1988: 1348–51; Ladefoged *et al.* 1972: 25). In all three countries English is a diglossically High language in comparison with Swahili; but Swahili itself is High in regard to the various local mother tongues. In Tanzania and in Kenya the (local) mother tongues provide ethnic identity and solidarity; Swahili contributes to national identity; and English serves to signal modernity and good education (Abdulaziz 1991: 392, 400).

Ethiopia and Somalia to the north (see map 14.2) are countries in which English plays a much more restricted role. While Amharic is the official language of Ethiopia (spoken by approximately 25 per cent of the population) English is used in secondary and higher education and in various areas of public life (for example, radio and newspapers; laws are published in Amharic and English). Somalia is virtually monolingual in Somali, but English, Italian and Arabic are the chief written languages because Somali has little tradition of writing. Furthermore, English is used in the civil service, secondary school, radio, newspapers, local novels and correspondence (cf. Whiteley 1971: 550–2; Bender *et al.* 1976: 12–19; Schmied 1985b: 241).

To the South lie Zambia and Malawi (see map 14.2), in both of which English is the official language. Little information is available on Malawi, but it is reported that 'English permeates all these official activities [i.e. school, radio, government] as a separate, nationwide code which in most respects carries a superior status' (Serpell 1982: 104).

14.5 English in East Africa

A survey of the domains of English in all these East African countries (plus Zimbabwe and the Seychelles) reveals that it is used in a full range of activities in Uganda, Zambia, Malawi, Kenya and Zimbabwe: high (but not local) court, parliament, civil service; primary and secondary school; radio, newspapers, films, local novels, plays, records; traffic signs, advertisements; business and private correspondence; and also at home (Schmied 1985b: 241). For instance,

> most literature in Kenya is indeed in English, and the publications are increasing, from dime-store novels to more sophisticated examples which form part of the African literature syllabus in schools and the university.
> (Zuengler 1983: 114)

In Tanzania, where Swahili is well established, English is used in the high courts, secondary schools, radio, newspapers, local novels and films, correspondence, and, sometimes, advertisements (Schmied 1985b: 241). The image which English has is relatively more positive than Swahili over a range of criteria, including beautiful, colourful, rich; precise, logical; refined, superior, sophisticated – at least among educated Tanzanians (ibid.: 244–8).

Kenya and Tanzania are, despite many parallels, not linguistic twins. After independence the position of English weakened in Tanzania as the country adopted a language policy which supported Swahili. In Kenya, where Swahili was also officially adopted, English continued to maintain a firm role as second language. There attitudes towards the language are generally positive, being associated with high status jobs; English has even become the primary home language in some exclusive Nairobi suburbs; and many middle- and upper-class children seem to be switching gradually to English. In Tanzania, in contrast, attitudes vary considerably from a great deal of acceptance to indifference (Abdulaziz 1991: 393, 397f).

In Kenya, in particular, the sometimes unstable situation of multi-lingualism and the overlap in the functional roles of the various languages has led both to a great deal of code-switching in conversation among urban dwellers and to mother tongue–Swahili–English code-mixing. The latter has even given rise to a mixed language jargon called Sheng (ibid.: 397f). In Tanzania school students use an interlanguage called Tanzingereza (< Swahili *Tanzania + Kiingereza* 'English language') (Schmied 1985a: 260).

14.6 Linguistic features of East African English

The heading of this section is somewhat doubtful, for it has not been ascertained whether 'the three East African countries (Kenya, Uganda, and Tanzania – each having different historical, political, and linguistic characteristics) share an English that could be called "East African English"' (Zuengler 1983: 112). Nonetheless, a number of factors have contributed to a levelling process which has led to the existence of a distinguishable variety of East African English. For one thing, these three countries share a colonial past which included numerous common British East Africa institutions (the mass media, university education, the post office and governmental enterprises) and free movement of people and goods. In addition, many of the ethnic languages are closely related: over 90 per cent in Tanzania and over 75 per cent in Kenya speak the one or the other Bantu language. Furthermore, the linguistic target has generally been a bookish variety with a pronunciation norm free of local interference (Abdulaziz 1991: 391f).

All this notwithstanding, many of the same types of interference and nativization processes described for WAE apply in East Africa as well. This includes a simplified five-vowel system as outlined in table 14.2.

All the consonants of English except /ʒ/ have counterparts in Swahili, and some speakers do not differentiate /r/ and /l/. Nevertheless, there are considerable differences in realization. /r/ may be flapped or trilled; /l/ is usually clear; /dʒ/ may be realized as /dj/; /θ, ð/ may be [t, d], [s, z] or even [f, v]; /p, t, k/ are likely to be unaspirated (Schmied 1985a: 230, 243f; for interference from local languages, cf. Schmied 1991).

As in WAE, rhythm is syllable-timed, and there is a tendency to favour a consonant-vowel-consonant-vowel syllable structure (ibid.: 248–51). Yet

Table 14.2 The vowels of EAE in comparison with those of RP

EAE	RP	as in	EAE	RP	as in
i ⟨	iː	bead	oˡ ⟨	ɒ	body
	ɪ	bid		ɔː	bawdy
				əʊ	bode
ɛˡ ⟨	eɪ	bayed			
	e	bed	u —	ʊ	Buddha
				uː	booed
a ⟨	æ	bad			
	ɑː	bard			
	ɜː	bird			
	ʌ	bud			

(adapted from Angogo and Hancock 1980: 75)

East African English is said to differ not only from RP, but also from WAE in its patterns of intonation (Abdulaziz 1991: 395).

Beyond syntactic and lexical differences which are similar in type to those in West Africa, there are culturally determined ways of expression that reflect the nativization of English as a second language. For example, a mother may address her son as *my young husband*; and a husband, his wife as *daughter*. A brother-in-law is a *second husband* (Zuengler 1983: 116). How differences work in the social reality which are implied by a language can be seen not only in the differing prestige and domains of, say, English and Swahili, but also in the behavioural roles associated with each (pidgin English in West Africa, for instance, is stereotyped as a joking, funny language):

> Certain social-psychological situations seem to influence language maintenance among the bilinguals. One of the respondents [among a group of fifteen informants] said that whenever he argued with his bilingual wife he would maintain Swahili as much as possible while she would maintain English. A possible explanation is that Swahili norms and values assign different roles to husband and wife (socially more clear cut?) from the English norms and values (socially less clear cut, or more converging?). Maintaining one language or the other could then be a device for asserting one's desired role.
>
> (Abdulaziz 1972: 209)

REFERENCES

Abdulaziz, M. H. (1972) 'Triglossia and Swahili–English bilingualism in Tanzania', *Language in Society* 1: 197–213.

—— (1988) '150: A sociolinguistic profile of East Africa', in U. Ammon, N. Dittmar, and K. J. Mattheier (eds) *Sociolinguistics Soziolinguistik*, Berlin: Walter de Gruyter, pp. 1347–53.

—— (1991) 'East Africa (Tanzania and Kenya)', in J. Cheshire (ed.) *English Around the World: Sociolinguistic Perspectives*, Cambridge: Cambridge University Press, pp. 391–401.

Achebe, C. (1960) *No Longer at Ease*, London: Heinemann.

Adekunle, M. A. (1972) 'Sociolinguistic problems in English language instruction in Nigeria', in D. M. Smith and R. Shuy (eds) *Sociolinguistics in Cross-Cultural Analysis*, Washington: Georgetown University Press, pp. 83–101.

Adetugbo, A. (1979) 'Appropriateness and Nigerian English', in E. Ubahakwe (ed.) *Varieties and Functions of English in Nigeria*, Ibadan: African Universities Press, pp. 137–66.

Agheyisi, R. N. (1988) 'The standardization of Nigerian Pidgin English', *English World-Wide* 9: 227–41.

Akere, F. (1982) 'Sociocultural constraints and the emergence of a Standard Nigerian English', in J. Pride (ed.) *New Englishes*, Rowley, Mass.: Newbury House, pp. 85–99.

Angogo, R. and Hancock, I. (1980) 'English in Africa: emerging standards or diverging regionalisms', *English World-Wide* 1: 67–96.

Bamgbose, A. (1971) 'The English language in Nigeria', in J. Spencer (ed.) *The English Language in West Africa*, London: Longman, pp. 35–48.

—— (1983) 'Standard Nigerian English: issues of identification', in B. B. Kachru (ed.) *The Other Tongue: English across Cultures*, Oxford: Pergamon, pp. 99–111.

Bender, M. L., Bowen, J. D., Cooper, R. L. and Ferguson, C. A. (eds.) (1976) *Language in Ethiopia*, London: Oxford University Press.

Bokamba, E. G. (1991) 'West Africa', in J. Cheshire (ed.) *English around the World: Sociolinguistic Perspectives*, Cambridge: Cambridge University Press, pp. 493–508.

Brann, C. M. B. (1988) '159: West Africa', in U. Ammon, N. Dittmar, and K. J. Mattheier (eds) *Sociolinguistics Soziolinguistik*, Berlin: Walter de Gruyter, pp. 1414–29.

Conrad, A. W. and Fishman, J. A. (1977) 'English as a world language: the evidence', in J. A. Fishman, R. L. Cooper and A. W. Conrad (eds) *The Spread of English*, Rowley, Mass.: Newbury House, pp. 3–76.

Egbe, D. I. (1979) 'Spoken and written English in Nigeria', in E. Ubahakwe (ed.) *Varieties and Functions of English in Nigeria*, Ibadan: African Universities Press, pp. 86–106.

Fyle, C. (1976) 'The use of the mother tongue in education in Sierra Leone', in A. Bamgbose (ed.) *Mother Tongue Education: the West African Experience*, London: Hodder & Stoughton; Paris: UNESCO, pp. 43–62.

Jibril, M. (1982) 'Nigerian English: an introduction', in J. Pride (ed.) *New Englishes*, Rowley Mass.: Newbury House, pp. 73–84.

—— (1991) 'The sociolinguistics of prepositional usage in Nigerian English', in J. Cheshire (ed.) *English around the World: Sociolinguistic Perspectives*, Cambridge: Cambridge University Press, pp. 519–44.

Ladefoged, P., Glick, R. and Criper, C. (1972) *Language in Uganda*, London: Oxford University Press.

Pemagbi, J. (1989) 'Still a deficient language?', *English Today* 17: 20–4.

Schmied, J. J. (1985a) *Englisch in Tansania*, Heidelberg: Groos.

—— (1985b) 'Attitudes towards English in Tanzania', *English World-Wide* 6: 237–69.

—— (1991) 'National and subnational features in Kenyan English', in J. Cheshire (ed.) *English around the World: Sociolinguistic Perspectives*, Cambridge: Cambridge University Press, pp. 420–32.

Serpell, R. (1982) 'Learning to say it better: a challenge for Zambian education', in J. Pride (ed.) *New Englishes*, Rowley, Mass.: Newbury House, pp. 100–18.

Shnukal, A. and Marchese, L. (1983) 'Creolization of Nigerian Pidgin English: a progress report', *English World-Wide* 4: 17–26.

Spencer, J. (ed.) (1971) 'West Africa and the English Language', in *The English Language in West Africa*, London: Longman, pp. 1–34.

Tingley, C. (1981) 'Deviance in the English of Ghanaian newspapers', *English World-Wide* 2: 39–62.

Todd, L. (1982) 'English in Cameroon: education in a multilingual society', in J. Pride (ed.) *New Englishes*, Rowley, Mass.: Newbury House, pp. 119–37.

—— (1984) 'The English language in West Africa', in R. W. Bailey and M. Görlach (eds) *English as a World Language*, Cambridge: Cambridge University Press, pp. 281–305.

Whiteley, W. H. (1971) 'Language policies of independent African states', in T. A. Sebeok (ed.) *Current Trends in Linguistics*, Vol. 7, *Linguistics in Sub-Saharan Africa*, The Hague: Mouton, pp. 548–58.

Willmott, M. B. (1978–9) 'Variety signifiers in Nigerian English', *English Language Teaching* 33: 227–33.

Zuengler, J. E. (1983) 'Kenyan English', in B. B. Kachru (ed.) *The Other Tongue: English across Cultures*, Oxford: Pergamon, pp. 112–24.

Chapter 15

English in Asia

In this chapter three Asian countries in which English plays an important role will be reviewed: India, Singapore and the Philippines. In none of these countries is English a native language; in all of them it is part of the colonial legacy. In other former colonial possessions in Asia in which English once had a similar status, such as Sri Lanka or Malaysia, its role has gradually been reduced to that of an important foreign language.

The remarks on each of these countries will be centred first on the status of English (numbers of speakers, its use in government, education, economic life, the media, etc.) and people's attitudes towards it; in a second section the linguistic characteristics of each local variety will be sketched out.

15.1 India

In India, the largest of the South Asian countries, English plays a special role. The remaining countries which were once, like India, British colonial possessions are Pakistan and Bangladesh, Sri Lanka and Nepal. Each of them has a certain amount of linguistic diversity and each continues to use English in some functions. The most data, however, are available on India, which dwarfs its neighbours with its ethnic diversity, its large geographic size, and its enormous population of around 800 million.

English has been used in India for hundreds of years, but it was an outsider's language for most of this time. The British colonial administration employed it, and colonial educational policy encouraged its wider use for the creation of a local elite which was to be 'Indian in blood and colour; but English in taste, in opinion, in morals and in intellect', according to a proposal on Indian education by T. B. Macaulay, which was accepted in 1835 (Macaulay 1967). To a limited extent, these goals have been reached, for English is well established as one of the most important diglossically High languages of India. The National Academy of Letters (Sahilya Academi), for example, recognizes literature by Indians in English as a part of Indian literature (Kachru 1986b: 32). It is a 'link language' for the Indian

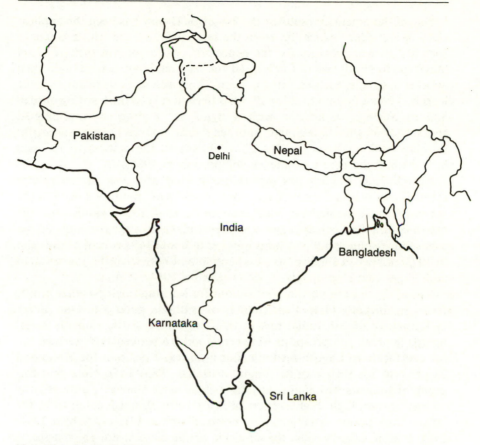

Map 15.1 South Asia

Adminstrative Service (the former Indian Civil Service), a medium in the modernization and Westernization of the country, and an important language of higher education, science, and technology.

The role of English is owing, in part, to the general spread and use of English throughout the world, especially in science and technology, trade and commerce. However, English also has an official status. Fifteen 'national languages' are provided for in the Indian constitution; one of them, Hindi, the language of over one-third of the population, is the official language. In addition, English is designated the 'associate official language'. Its status is supported by continuing resistance in the non-Hindi parts of India, especially the south, to the spread of Hindi, which automatically puts non-Hindi speakers at a disadvantage. Where everyone must learn English, everybody is on a par linguistically.

One of the practical results of this linguistic rivalry has been the application, in secondary education since the late 1950s, of the 'three language formula', which provides for the education of everyone in their regional language, in Hindi and in English. (If the regional language is Hindi, then another language, such as Telugu, Tamil, Kannada or Malayalam, is to be learned.) The intention of this policy has been to spread the learning burden and to create a population with a significant number of multilingual speakers, but this 'integrative approach' has not been very successful (Kachru 1984: 355). As for English, estimates set the number of its users in India at 3 per cent (= some 23 million plus in 1985).

Nevertheless, English has maintained a kind of hegemony in several areas: English-language newspapers or magazines are published in all of the states of India (something which cannot be said about Hindi) and the readers of the English-language newspapers make up approximately 23 per cent of the reading public. A large number of books (45 per cent of the titles in 1973) appear in English, as do scientific and non-scientific journals (74 and 83 per cent respectively in 1971) (Kachru 1984: 356).

One of the most important motivations for learning English is that people feel it significantly raises their chances of getting a good job. One survey in Karnataka (South India) reveals that two-thirds of the students investigated felt their job prospects were very good (16 per cent) or excellent (52 per cent) with an English-medium education (vs. 7 per cent for Hindi and 28 per cent for their mother tongue) (Sridhar 1983: 145). Note that this group of students was aiming at jobs such as bank manager, university or college teacher, high level civil servant, or lawyer. 'English is felt to be the language of power, a language of prestige' (ibid.: 149, cf. Sahgal 1991: 299). It is, in other words, the language of the classes, not the masses.

Even so English is 'the language of our intellectual make-up – like Sanskrit and Persian were before – but not of our emotional make-up' according to the Indian author Raja Rao (in the foreword to *Kanthapura*). One study which substantiates this reveals that English intrudes less on intimate areas such as communication with family or neighbours than on domains of business, politics, technology, communication with strangers or pan-Indian communication (Sridhar 1983: 148f; cf. also Sahgal 1991: 305). Where English is used it not only signals a certain level of education; it also serves to cover over differences of region and caste. Through a judicious use of **code-switching** (the change from one to another language) and **code-mixing** (the use of elements of one language within communication which is basically in another) various speaker identities can be revealed. English, for example, is used not only for certain domains and to fill in lexical gaps in the vernacular, but also to signal education, authority and a cosmopolitan, Western attitude (Kachru 1978: 110–14).

Overall, it might be said that, despite the relatively small numbers of English-users in India, it is precisely these people who have the most status and power; English is not only 'an "access" language among ethnically and linguistically diverse Indians', but also a language which brings 'monetary gains, professional mobility, and social prestige' (Kachru 1986b: 31). 'In its Indianized variety, it has become a pan-Indian elite language' (Kachru 1988: 1283). The following section describes some of the characteristics of this form of English.

15.2 Indian English (IndE)

IndE is not a native but a second language (note that a small group of Anglo-Indians, perhaps about 100,000 [estimated, 1966], have English, derogatively termed *Chee Chee*, as their mother tongue; Spencer 1966). Yet this second language is far too entrenched in Indian intellectual life and traditions to be regarded as a foreign language. 'So long as English continues to have the status of a second language (and not a foreign language) in India, it will create its own local standard' (Verma: 1982: 176). This statement is plausible; yet the acceptability of a local standard is not universally acknowledged. Kachru quotes a study in which two-thirds reported a preference for BrE and only just over a quarter accepted Indian English as their preferred model (1986a: 22). Some, while realizing that IndE is not and cannot be identical with its one-time model, BrE, have fears of a chaotic future in which 'English in India . . . will be found disintegrating into quite incomprehensible dialects' (Das 1982: 148). There seems to be little doubt that IndE has established itself as an independent language tradition. While most of the English which educated Indians produce is close to StE, there are obvious differences in pronunciation, some in grammar, and a noticeable number in vocabulary and usage. In looking briefly at each of these areas, it is not the English of the highly trained (often '*England-returned*') nor the very imperfectly learned English of the 'unlicensed and self-appointed tourist guides, small shopkeepers, hotel-bearers, street vendors, narcotics dealers, porters, beggars, boatmen, rickshaw pullers, taxi-drivers, and commercial agents' (Mehrotra 1982: 156) which will be considered, but that of the majority of educated Indians. (For an extended example of the lower variety, see ibid.: 156–9.)

15.2.1 The pronunciation of IndE

Pronunciation offers the greatest number of difficulties for native speakers unfamiliar with this variety. To begin with there is a great deal of local variation which depends especially on the native language of any given IndE user and is further influenced by spelling pronunciations; even within India mutual comprehension cannot always be expected. However, despite this diversity there do seem to be a number of relatively widespread features in the pronunciation of IndE.

What is perhaps most noticeable is the way words are stressed in IndE. Often (but not universally) stress falls on the next to last syllable regardless of where it falls in RP or GenAm. This produces, for example, Pro'testant rather than 'Protestant and 'refer rather than re'fer (Vermeer 1969: 60; cf. also Wells 1982: 630).

The effect of education is often evident. Among the segmental sounds one of the most common features is the pronunciation of non-prevocalic ⟨r⟩ (a non-standard feature), at least among 'average' as opposed to 'prestigious' speakers, who include especially the young and women (Sahgal and Agnihotri 1988: 57–62). Note also that Khan found more instances of final consonant cluster simplification (*fast* → *fas'*) among women and the young in northern India; Khan's subjects were from a notably less affluent, less well educated traditional Muslim community and therefore presumably less susceptible to Western influence (Khan 1991: 293f).

A further (though again not universal) difference is the use of retroflex [ṭ] and [ḍ] (produced with the tongue tip curled backwards) for RP/GenAm alveolar /t/ and /d/. Note, however, that in one study IndE retroflex [ṭ] was used in fewer than half the possible cases (Sahgal and Agnihotri 1988: 55). The dental fricatives /θ/ and /ð/ of RP/GenAm are often realized as the dental stops [ṭ] and [ḍ], and the labio-dental fricatives /f/ and /v/ as [pʰ] and [bʰ]. The latter sound and [ʋʰ] is also frequently used for /w/, which does not seem to occur in the phonology of IndE (ibid.: 63).

For Hindi and Urdu speakers initial consonant clusters are difficult and may be pronounced with a preposed vowel, so that *school* becomes /ɪskul/, *station*, /ɪsteʃan/, and *speech* /ɪspitʃ/. As the example of *station* reveals, unstressed syllables often have a full vowel (/-an/).

Many of these points as well as numerous differences (always as compared with RP/GenAm) in the vowel system (phonemics) or in vowel realization (phonetics) are not the result of a local IndE norm, but are owing, in the end, to the phonetic and phonological nature of the varying mother tongues of the speakers of IndE. Even within the IndE community there can be difficulties in communication. Hence the panic among the guests at a Gujarati wedding when the following was announced over the public address system: 'The snakes are in the hole.' The subsequent run for the exit could be stopped only when someone explained that, actually, the refreshments (snacks) were in the hall (Mehrotra 1982: 168).

15.2.2 The grammar of IndE

This is hardly deviant *vis-à-vis* StE; yet, here, too, there are differences. Some of the points commonly mentioned include

1 invariant tag questions: *isn't it?* or *no?*, e.g. *You went there yesterday, isn't it?*;

2 the use of the present perfect in sentences with past adverbials, e.g. *I have worked there in 1960*;

3 the use of *since* + a time unit with the present progressive, e.g. *I am writing this essay since two hours*;

4 a *that*-complement clause after *want*, e.g. *Mohan wants that you should go there*;

5 Wh-questions without subject–auxiliary inversion, e.g. *Where you are going?* (all examples from Verma 1982: 181–3).

It has been questioned whether, at least for well educated speakers in South Delhi, patterns such as these are not perhaps independent ones which are passed on from generation to generation rather than learning and inter-ference errors (Sahgal and Agnihotri 1985); however that may be, such forms (as well as further deviant structures) seem to be relatively common, even if IndE-speaking experts such as university and college English teachers reject them (Parasher 1983).

15.2.3 The vocabulary of IndE

IndE vocabulary is universally recognized as containing numerous charac-teristic items. For convenience they can be classified as follows:

1 English words used differently, e.g. *four-twenty* 'a cheat, swindler';

2 new coinages, e.g. *black money* 'illegal gains'; *change-room* 'dressing room';

3 hybrid formations, e.g. *lathi charge* 'police attack with sticks'; *coolidom*;

4 adoption of Indian words, which often 'come more naturally and appear more forceful in a given context than their English equivalents. *Sister-in-law* is no match for *sali*, and *idle talk* is a poor substitute for *buk-buk*' (Mehrotra 1982: 160–2).

The use of Indian words in English discourse is said to be more common in situations that are 'more informal, more personal, more relaxed, and sometimes more culture-sensitive' (ibid.); nevertheless, there may be oppor-tunity or need enough to use Indian terms in formal texts as well, as in the following:

> Urad and moong fell sharply in the grain market here today on stockists offerings. Rice, jowar and arhar also followed suit, but barley forged ahead.
>
> (Kachru 1984: 362)

For a collection of IndE vocabulary items, see *The Little Oxford Dictionary* with a 29-page supplement by R. A. Hawkins, containing approximately 1500 IndE words.

15.2.4 Style and appropriacy

These are the final areas to be reviewed. It has often been pointed out that IndE diction has a bookish and old-fashioned flavour to it because the reading models in Indian schools are so often older English authors (e.g. Mehrotra 1982: 163; for numerous examples cf. Das 1982). Certainly, the standards of style and appropriacy are different in IndE as compared with most native-speaker varieties. There is a 'tendency towards verbosity, preciosity, and the use of learned literary words', a 'preference for exaggerated and hyperbolic forms' (Mehrotra 1982: 164); 'stylistic embellishment is highly valued' (Kachru 1984: 364). While, for example, profuse expressions of thanks such as the following are 'culturally appropriate and contextually proper in Indian situations' (Kachru 1986b: 33), they would seem overdone to most native speakers:

> I consider it to be my primordial obligation to humbly offer my deepest sense of gratitude to my most revered Guruji and untiring and illustrious guide Professor [. . .] for the magnitude of his benevolence and eternal guidance.
>
> (Mehrotra 1982: 165)

In an effort to use the idioms and expressions learned, an IndE user may, of course, as a non-native speaker, mix his/her levels of style, as did a clerk who, in asking for several days leave, explained that 'the hand that rocked the cradle has kicked the bucket' (ibid.: 162). Likewise the following wish: 'I am in very good health and hope you are in the same boat' (Das 1982: 144).

Less easy for a native speaker to penetrate are differing communicative strategies, for example *yes–no* answers, where the IndE speaker may agree or disagree with the form of a statement while the native speaker will agree or disagree with its content. IndE can, therefore, have the following types of exchanges:

> A: Didn't I see you yesterday in college?
> B: Yes, you didn't see me yesterday in college.
>
> (Kachru 1984: 374)

Equally difficult for the outsider to comprehend is the way a subtle change in perspective via an active–passive switch may be perceived:

> A subordinate addressing his boss in an office in India writes, 'I request you to look into the case,' while the boss writing to a subordinate will normally use the passive, 'you are requested to look into the case.' If the latter form is used by a subordinate, it may mean a downright insult.
>
> (Mehrotra 1982: 166)

15.3 Singapore

The English language plays a special role in Southeast Asia in both Singapore and Malaysia, a role, however, which is developing in two very different fashions. The demographic situation in each state is comparable inasmuch as both have major ethnic elements in the population, consisting of Malays, Chinese and Indians. In peninsular Malaysia this is 53 per cent Malays to 35 per cent Chinese to 10 per cent Indians. In Singapore, which lies at the tip of the Malay Peninsula, the relationship is 15 to 76 to 7 per cent. In addition, both states were formerly under British colonial administration, and in both English was an important administrative and educational language. For a short period in the 1960s the two were federated and shared the same 'national language', viz. Malay (or Bahasa Malaysia). After Singapore left the federation, it retained Malay as its national language alongside its further 'official languages', English, Mandarin Chinese and Tamil. Malaysia, on the other hand, abandoned English as a second language (National Language Policy of 1967) and became officially monolingual in Bahasa Malaysia. In the intervening years the level of English in Malaysia has declined, although it remains an important foreign language (cf. Augustin 1982).

In Singapore much the opposite has happened. While this city-state continues to uphold its policy of maintaining four official languages, the de facto status of each has been changing. The Chinese ethnic part of the total population of over 2.3 million (1980), which is divided into speakers of several mutually unintelligible dialects (above all, Hokkien, Teochew and Cantonese), has been encouraged to learn and use Mandarin, and indeed, younger Singaporeans of Chinese descent are increasingly using Mandarin, especially in more formal situations, though it is far from displacing the vernacular dialects in everyday situations.

Malay remains the 'national language' and it is widely used as a lingua franca; yet it is English which is on the increase, so much so, in fact, that it has been referred to as 'a language for the expression of national identity' (Tay 1982a: 52). For Malay is associated with the ethnic Malays, just as Mandarin and the Chinese vernaculars are associated with the ethnic Chinese, and Tamil with the ethnic Indians. In contrast, English, the native language only of (most of) the small (approximately 0.5 per cent) Eurasian community, is viewed as an inter-ethnic lingua franca (Platt 1988: 1385); it is 'a unifying working language at the national level' (Kuo 1980a: 59). For 'English is seen as having a key role in increasing levels of modernization and development in Singapore' (Gopinathan 1980: 184).

The pre-eminent position of English in Singapore is most evident in the area of education. Since the all-party report of 1956, which instituted bilingual education, the teaching medium was to be one of four official languages; if this was not English, English was to be the second school

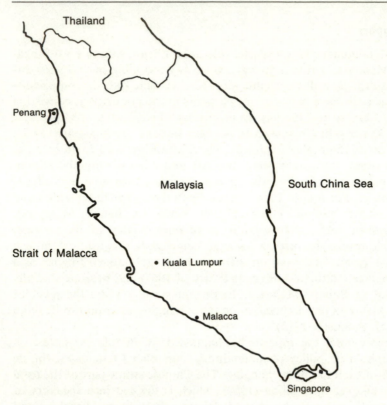

Map 15.2 Malaysia and Singapore

language. Since that time virtually 100 per cent of the students in Singapore have been in English-medium schools (Platt 1988: 1384; 1991: 377). What this means is that about 60 per cent of teaching time is in English. Yet with 40 per cent for Mandarin or Malay or Tamil, literacy in these languages is assured. This is important in the case of Malay because the neighbouring states of Malaysia and Indonesia both use forms of Malay as their national languages. Mandarin is obviously useful because of the size and importance of China. Tamil – never the language of more than about two-thirds of the ethnic Indians – is apparently losing ground, largely to English.

Beyond the areas of education, all four languages are prominent in the media, both print and electronic. In both cases English is gaining proportionately and it alone draws on a readership and audience from all three major ethnic groups (Kuo 1980b: 121, passim). Most parliamentary work is conducted in English, which is also the sole language of the courts. Naturally, it is predominant in international trade.

The fact that English is so widely used does not mean that it is a universal language. It is generally a High (H) language, reserved for more formal use, though a local Low (L) vernacular variety of SingE, sometimes called Singlish (not to be confused with Sinhalese English, which is also sometimes referred to as Singlish), is used in a wider range of more informal situations including both inter-ethnic and intra-ethnic communication. English is, however, despite its increasing spread, seldom a home language (Platt 1988: 1385f). Nevertheless, Platt does see English in Singapore as 'probably the classic case of the indigenisation' because its range of domains is constantly expanding, and this includes its use among friends and even in families (Platt 1991: 376). It is 'fast becoming a semi-native variety' (Platt and Weber 1980: 48).

15.4 Singaporean (and Malaysian) English (SingE)

Within SingE there is a variety of levels. At the upper level (the acrolect) there is little difference in grammar and vocabulary between SingE and international StE. As in any regional variety there are, of course, local items of vocabulary, more of them as the level broadens to the mesalect and basilect.

15.4.1 The vocabulary of SingE

Borrowings from Chinese and Malay are especially prominent, for example, Malay *jaga* 'guard, sentinel', *padang* 'field', *kampong* 'village', *makan* 'food' and Hokkien *towday* 'employer, business person'. But other languages have also contributed to SingE, for example, *dhobi* 'washerman' is from Hindi; *peon* 'orderly, office assistant' from Portuguese; *syce* 'driver' from Arabic via Hindi; and *tamby* 'office boy, errand boy' from Tamil (cf. Tongue 1974: 69; Platt and Weber 1980: 83–7).

Differences in SingE vocabulary *vis-à-vis* international StE also include colloquialisms. *To sleep late* means, on the Chinese pattern, to go to bed late and hence possibly to be tired. This, of course, stands in contrast to StE *to sleep late*, which indicates longer sleep in the morning and probably being refreshed (Tongue 1974: 78). The loan translation of Malay *goyang kaki* as *shake legs*, rather in contrast to StE *shake a leg* 'hurry', means, in SingE, 'take it easy', as in '*stop shaking legs and get back to work la*' (Tay 1982a: 68).

The element *la*, just quoted, probably comes from Hokkien. It is almost ubiquitous in informal (or diglossically Low) SingE: 'Perhaps the most striking and distinctive feature of L English' (Richards and Tay 1977: 143). Its function is to signal the type of relationship between the people talking: 'there is a positive rapport between speakers and an element of solidarity' (ibid.: 145).

15.4.2 The grammar of SingE

SingE grammar is virtually identical with that of StE in the formal written medium. In speech and more informal writing (including journalism) and, increasingly, at a lower level of education, more and more non-standard forms may be found, many of them reflecting forms in the non-English vernaculars of Singapore (and Malaysia).

The verb   Verbs are perhaps most central. Since the substratum languages do not mark either concord or tense (Platt 1984: 398f), it is no wonder that the third person singular present tense {-S} is often missing (*this radio sound good*, ibid.: 399) and that present forms are frequently used where StE would have the past (*I start here last year*, ibid.: 398; cf. especially Platt and Ho 1988). This tendency is reinforced by the substratum lack of final consonant clusters, but it also includes the use of past participles for simple past (*We gone last night*, Tay 1982a: 64). On the other hand, while Malay and Chinese mark aspect, the transfer to English often leads to misuse. Thus the StE progressive is overused (*Are you having a cold?*; Tongue 1974: 46) and *used to* is employed not only for the habitual distant past as in StE, but also for the present habitual as in

> SingE speaker: The tans [military unit] use to stay in Serangoon.
> Non-SingE speaker: Where are they staying now?
> SingE speaker (somewhat sharply): I've just told you. In Serangoon.
> (from Tongue 1974: 44)

Numerous other points, including modal use, the auxiliary *do*, the infinitive marker *to* and the deletion of the copula, might be added (cf. Tongue 1974, chapter 2; Tay 1982a: 64f; Wong 1982; Platt 1984: 398ff; 1991).

The noun   Nouns are perhaps less noticeably deviant *vis-à-vis* StE usage. The differences to be observed in local basilect forms include the lack of plural {-S}, probably attributable to the different nature of plural marking in Chinese (a plural classifier) and Malay (reduplication), hence *how many bottle?* (Platt 1984: 400); however, deeper semantic influences may also be involved (cf. Platt 1991). There is also a tendency to have fewer indefinite articles (*You got to have proper system here*; Tay 1982a: 64) and to use non-count nouns like count nouns (*chalks, luggages, fruits, mails, informations*, etc.; Tongue 1974: 49f).

Sentence patterns   These may also differ from those of StE. Indirect questions often retain the word order of direct questions (as they do increasingly often in StE as well), as in *I'd like to know what are the procedures?* (Tay 1982a: 63). Both subjects (especially first person pronoun subjects) and objects may be deleted where StE would have them:

A: Can or cannot?
B: Cannot
A: Why cannot?

(Tay 1982a: 65)

One last point is the widespread use of the invariant tag question *is it?/isn't it?*, as in *the Director is busy now, is it?* (Tay 1982a: 64) or *you like Carlsberg [beer], isn't it?* (Platt 1984: 401). For more details, see Tongue 1974; Richards 1977; Tay 1982a; Wong 1982; Platt 1977 and 1984; Platt and Weber 1980: chapter 4).

15.4.3 The pronunciation of SingE

Pronunciation is the most distinctive aspect of SingE. Once again this is the result of interference from the non-English vernaculars. The vernacular influence may be direct — because of the speaker's own language — or indirect — because of the effect of other speakers whose pronunciation reflects first language interference.

Rhythm   The rhythm of SingE, which is staccato-like and syllable-timed, is one of its most noticeable features. This means each syllable gets approximately equal stress, where RP, GenAm and most other native-speaker varieties have a rhythmical pattern which places the stressed syllables at approximately equal intervals, often separated by one or more unstressed syllables. This has the effect of levelling the distinction made in RP and GenAm between the noun *'in-crease* and the verb *in-'crease*. In SingE both sound more like the latter (Tay 1982a: 61). Furthermore, SingE has less range in pitch and fewer distinctive intonational patterns (ibid.: 65), owing perhaps to the fact that Chinese, as a tone language, does not use word stress as English does: stress is signalled by greater length and loudness in SingE, while native-speaker type stressing also includes pitch change (Tay 1982b: 139).

Vowels   The vowels of SingE are generally shorter or less tense than in RP/GenAm, and diphthongs are often monophthongized, for example /əʊ/ → [oː], /eɪ/ → [eː], /ɛə/ → [ɛː].

Consonants   The consonants of the acrolect are distinguished by a lack of voicing of obstruents in word final position; furthermore, there is less frequent release of all final stops and affricates. In the mesolect final consonant clusters are simplified to a realization of the first consonant only (see above, *sound* for *sounds* as a third person present tense form), and often the final stops are replaced by a glottal stop. /θ/ and /ð/ are commonly realized as

[t] and [d]. In the basilect, finally, Chinese speakers realize /r/ as /l/ (*rice = lice*); Malay speakers may replace /f/ with /p/ (*face = pace*); and Indian speakers may fail to distinguish between /v/ and /w/ (*vary = wary*). For more details on SingE pronunciation, cf. Tay 1982b; Platt and Weber 1980: chapter 4.

15.5 The future of SingE

While it is evident that the role of English will continue to decline in Malaysia as Bahasa Malaysia extends its domains, it is clear that Singapore is, and will remain, a multilingual state in which English is taking a position of increasing pre-eminence before Mandarin, Malay and Tamil. In Singapore, speech patterns are **polyglossic**. This means, concretely, that there is more than one High language (usually English and Mandarin) and several Low ones (usually Bazaar Malay, Hokkien and, increasingly, Singlish). (Compare the situation in Hong Kong, where about 90 per cent of the students (1979) attended English-medium schools. Since, however, 98 per cent of the population is Chinese, mostly Cantonese speaking, Hong Kong is an example of 'diglossia without bilingualism' (Kang-kwong and Richards 1982: 51f). For more on Hong Kong, see also Tay 1991: 327f.)

English is seldom the first language in the sense of the first learned; it is, however, the first school language of practically everybody who has entered Singapore schools since the early 1980s. It has also grown to be the language of national identity, of work and of inter-ethnic (and even some intra-ethnic) communication.

> Unless there is a radical change in policy it can be assumed that the use of English will continue to increase. . . . the use of Colloquial Singapore English can be expected to continue. Paradoxically, the higher the proportion of Singaporeans with English-medium education, the more a colloquial subvariety will develop.
>
> (Platt 1988: 1387)

15.6 The Philippines

Aside from the very size (a population well over fifty million) and the regional significance of the Philippines, they constitute the only example to be treated in which the tradition of AmE is of importance. The islands had formed a Spanish colony for well over 300 years when the American government took them over as one of the results of the Spanish-American War (1898). Despite considerable Filipino resistance (1898–1901) to the new colonial master, the United States was soon firmly in control and established English as an offical language alongside and fully equal to Spanish in 1901. English was given favourable treatment (government jobs were

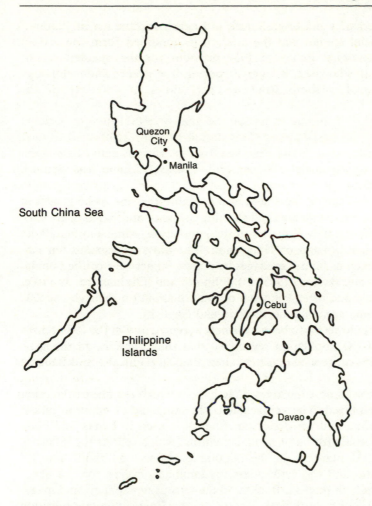

Map 15.3 The Philippines

more readily available to those who could use English) and soon began to displace Spanish. By the time the Philippines entered the status of Commonwealth with the United States in 1936, English was pre-eminent. It is true that the Constitution of 1936 provided for a national language (Filipino, a modified form of Tagalog), but in fact English had just been established as *the* language of education in the preceding year.

After independence in 1946 little changed at first, but in the early 1950s a policy of vernacular education in years one and two of school with a later shift to English was implemented. In 1974 the new Bilingual Education Policy was initiated, in which Pilipino/Filipino and English were to be the shared languages of education. This policy provided for the teaching of

science, mathematics and English itself in English and the use of Pilipino/
Filipino in social studies and the arts. In its modified form the revised
Bilingual Educational Policy of 1987 provides for the maintenance of
English, since this language is highly important for science and technology
and international relations (trade, worker flows in and out of the
Philippines).

The Philippines continue to pursue the goal of establishing a national
language, and the post-Marcos Constitution of 1987 reaffirmed as that
language Filipino, which is to be evolved from the various native languages,
but which is approximately 80 per cent Tagalog/Pilipino and Spanish
(Gonzales 1988: 47).

In addition to Tagalog there are seven to eight other major languages in
the Philippines and over a hundred all told. Cebuano and Tagalog are each
spoken by approximately a quarter of the population, while another 20 per
cent speak either Ilokano or Hiligaynon. The most widespread ten languages are spoken as home languages by almost 90 per cent of the population (Gonzales and Bautista 1985: 54). Filipinos and Filipinas are, as a rule,
at least bilingual and often trilingual or quadrilingual (in their vernacular,
the regional language, Filipino/Pilipino and English).

Pilipino/Filipino seems to be increasingly accepted and in the 1980 census
77 per cent of the population responded that they knew it. In the same
census 64.5 per cent replied that they knew English (Gonzalez and Bautista
1985: 59).

It is of interest to note the areas of activity in which the one or the other
language is employed. The vernacular is the language of emotion and is
used for swearing and for dreaming. English is used in banks and book
stores and especially for numbers and counting, which reflects the influence
of schooling. At markets, in the popular press and on radio and TV
Pilipino/Filipino and the vernaculars predominate, except for the news,
which is generally in English. Books and the serious newspapers and magazines are in English; technical reports are in English; communication
upwards – with a department head or boss – will tend to be in English.
'English now has a life of its own in the Philippines, albeit confined to the
elites and the educated. It is among these elites and educated that communication in a veriety [sic] called Philippine English is carried on' (Gonzalez
1982: 218). In other words, the more formal the occasion is and the higher
the level of education, the more likely it is that English will be used
(Gonzalez and Bautista 1985: chapter 2). It is even possible to say that
Filipinos and Filipinas have an integrative motivation for learning English
(in addition to the obvious instrumental motivations), namely to identify
with the native English-speaking elites (ibid.: 46).

Despite the spread of Pilipino/Filipino, English remains predominant in
what are referred to as the 'controlling domains of language': government
administration, legislation, the law and the judiciary, higher education and

the professions, business and commerce, science and industry (Sibayan 1988: 92). The bar exams, Certified Public Accountant exams, engineering and medical board exams, and the National College Entrance Examination are all in English; the Senate and the House of Representatives are conducted mostly in English; laws are passed in English with a Filipino translation (Pascasio 1988: 117). Indeed, it has been pointed out that the bilingual education policy has served, on the one hand, to spread Pilipino/ Filipino (*vis-à-vis* other Philippine languages) and, on the other, to have furthered the elite, who have access to English, for with the lessening of access to English on a broad scale there will be 'a loss of access by the talented of the masses to social mobility, a worsening social stratification based on language' (Gonzalez and Bautista 1985: 119).

The Philippine population is obviously quite aware of the advantages of English, and parents want their children to learn it because of the advantages it offers, namely social mobility, higher paying jobs, power and prestige (Pascasio 1988: 117).

15.7 Philippine English

After the immediately preceding remarks it is not surprising to read:

> The better educated, the better the approximation (in lexis and in morphology and syntax though not in pronunciation) to Standard American English; the less educated, the more the discrepancies in word usage and especially in morphology and syntax (with likewise a more varied pronunciation) as compared to Standard American English.
>
> (Gonzalez and Bautista 1985: 25)

Pronunciation   The pronunciation of Filipino English is strongly characterized by the native language of the speaker. For this reason it is no surprise should a speaker say *as a matter of pact* (Llamzon 1969: 14), since this reflects the fact that Pilipino has no /f/. Among the differences in pronunciation there is

1 the absence of aspiration of /p, t, k/;
2 fuller value of schwa and a tendency towards syllable-timing;
3 spelling pronunciations;
4 dental [t̪] and [d̪];
5 lack of release of all final stops.

(Bautista 1988: 72; Llamzon 1969: 39)

Grammar   Filipino grammatical features include 'local rules for agreement, tense, tense sequence, article usage and prepositional usage as well as localized usage of the progressive, present perfect, and past perfect tenses' (ibid.: 48).

Lexis Lexical items which are specific to the Philippines are often patterned on Tagalog expressions. Examples are *I will go ahead of you* as a leave-taking formula; *my head/tooth is painful* 'I have a headache/toothache'; *close/open the light* 'turn the light off/on'; or *I slept late yesterday* 'I went to bed late yesterday' (examples from Llamzon 1969: 47).

Code-switching In a society in which two languages, English and Tagalog/Pilipino/Filipino, play such a prominent role it is not surprising that a great deal of code-switching occurs. The use of English may be functional and prestigious, but the intermixture of Tagalog/Filipino establishes sender—receiver solidarity and may mark the speaker as a (Westernized) nationalist (Gonzales 1982: 214, 217). This mixing is pejoratively referred to as Mix-Mix (or Halo-Halo). If there is more Tagalog it is sometimes called Taglish; if more English, Engalog (ibid.: 214). The following illustration of it comes from the beginning of a short story:

> Maniwala ka kaya, pare, kung sabihin ko sa iyo that a mere whisper can cause death. It may even create chaos.
> Tipong heavy and intro ko, pero it happened one night dito sa destitute place namin. Ganito iyon, listen carefully. . .
> [Can you believe it, friend, if I were to tell you that a mere whisper can cause death. It may even create chaos.
> It looks like my introduction is heavy [too serious], but it happened one night here at our destitute place. It was like this, listen carefully. . .]
>
> (quoted from Gonzalez 1982: 213)

15.8 Outlook

Although there is a steady move to Filipino in all domains, English will remain important for economic reasons – both because widespread knowledge of English may induce foreign employers to move to the Philippines (especially Manila) and because it facilitates the ability of Filipinos and Filipinas to find jobs abroad (a half a million go yearly, cf. Gonzalez 1988: 10). However, despite claims 'that there is a standard variety of English which has arisen in the Philippines' (Llamzon 1969: 84), this applies only to the better educated parts of society. In general the level of Philippine English is and will remain relatively low and may even fall to the status of a foreign, rather than a second, language, albeit an important one.

REFERENCES

Augustin, J. (1982) 'Regional standards of English in peninsular Malaysia', in J. B. Pride (ed.) *New Englishes*, Rowley, Mass.: Newbury House, pp. 249–58.

Bautista, M. L. S. (1988) 'Domains of English in the 21st century', in A. Gonzales (ed.) *The Role of English and Its Maintenance in the Philippines*, Manila: Solidaridad, pp. 71–7.

Das, S. K. (1982) 'Indian English', in J. B. Pride (ed.) *New Englishes*, Rowley, Mass.: Newbury House, pp. 141–9.

Gonzalez, A. (1982) 'English in the Philippines', in J. B. Pride (ed.) *New Englishes*, Rowley, Mass.: Newbury House, pp. 211–26.

—— (ed.) (1988) *The Role of English and its Maintenance in the Philippines*, Manila: Solidaridad.

Gonzalez, A. and Bautista, M. L. S. (1985) *Language Surveys in the Philippines (1966–1984)*, Manila: De La Salle.

Gopinathan, S. (1980) 'Language policy in education: a Singapore perspective', in E. A. Afendras and E. C. Y. Kuo (eds) *Language and Society in Singapore*, Singapore: Singapore University Press, pp. 175–202.

Hawkins, P. A. (1986) Supplement of Indian Words in J. Swannell (ed.) *The Little Oxford Dictionary*, 6th edn, Oxford: Clarendon Press.

Kachru, B. B. (1978) 'Code-mixing as a communicative strategy in India', in J. E. Alatis (ed.) *International Dimensions of Bilingual Education*, Washington: Georgetown University Press, pp. 107–25.

—— (1984) 'South Asian English', in R. Bailey and M. Görlach (eds) *English as a World Language*, Cambridge: Cambridge University Press, pp. 353–83.

—— (1986a) *The Alchemy of English*, Oxford: Pergamon.

—— (1986b) 'The Indianization of English', *English Today* 6: 31–3.

—— (1988) 'India', in U. Ammon, N. Dittmar, and K. J. Mattheier (eds) *Sociolinguistics Soziolinguistik*, Berlin; de Gruyter, pp. 1282–7.

Kang-kwong, L. and Richards, J. C. (1982) 'English in Hong Kong: functions and status', *English World-Wide* 3: 47–64.

Khan, F. (1991) 'Final consonant cluster simplification in a variety of Indian English', in J. Cheshire (ed.) *English around the World: Sociolinguistic Perspectives*, Cambridge: Cambridge University Press, pp. 288–98.

Kuo, E. C. Y. (1980a) 'The sociolinguistic situation in Singapore: unity in diversity', in E. A. Afendras and E. C. Y. Kuo (eds) *Language and Society in Singapore*, Singapore: Singapore University Press, pp. 39–62.

—— (1980b) 'Multilingualism and mass media communications in Singapore', in E. A. Afendras and E. C. Y. Kuo (eds) *Language and Society in Singapore*, Singapore: Singapore University Press, pp. 116–36.

Llamzon, T. A. (1969) *Standard Filipino English*, Manila: Ateneo University Press.

Macaulay, T. B. (1967) 'Indian education: minute of the 2nd of February, 1835', in G. M. Young (ed.) *Prose and Poetry*, London: Hart-Davis, pp. 719–30.

Mehrotra, R. R. (1982) 'Indian English: a sociolinguistic profile', in J. B. Pride (ed.) *New Englishes*, Rowley, Mass.: Newbury House, pp. 150–73.

Parasher, S. V. (1983) 'Indian English: certain grammatical, lexical and stylistic features', *English World-Wide* 4: 27–42.

Pascasio, E. M. (1988) 'The present role and domains of English in the Philippines', in A. Gonzales (ed.) *The Role of English and its Maintenance in the Philippines*, Manila: Solidaridad, pp. 114–24.

Platt, J. T. (1977) 'The sub-varieties of Singapore English: their sociolectal and functional status', in W. Crewe (ed.) *The English Language in Singapore*, Singapore: Eastern Universities Press, pp. 83–95.

—— (1984) 'English in Singapore, Malaysia, and Hong Kong', in R. Bailey and M. Görlach (eds) *English as a World Language*, Cambridge: Cambridge University Press, pp. 384–414.

—— (1988) 'Singapore', in U. Ammon, N. Dittmar and K. J. Mattheier (eds) *Sociolinguistics Soziolinguistik*, Berlin: de Gruyter, pp. 1384–8.

—— (1991) 'Social and linguistic constraints on variation in the use of two grammatical variables in Singapore English', in J. Cheshire (ed.) *English Around the World: Sociolinguistic Perspectives*, Cambridge: Cambridge University Press, pp. 376–87.

Platt, J. T. and Ho, M. L. (1988) 'Language universals or substratum influences? Past tense marking in Singapore English', *English World-Wide* 9: 65–75.

Platt, J. T. and Weber, H. (1980) *English in Singapore and Malaysia*, Kuala Lumpur: Oxford University Press.

Richards, J. C. (1977) 'Variation in Singapore English', in W. Crewe (ed.) *The English Language in Singapore*, Singapore: Eastern Universities Press, pp. 68–82.

Richards, J. C. and Tay, M. W. J. (1977) 'The *la* particle in Singapore English', in W. Crewe (ed.) *The English Language in Singapore*, Singapore: Eastern Universities Press, pp. 141–56.

—— (1991) 'Patterns of language use in a bilingual setting in India', in J. Cheshire (ed.) *English Around the World: Sociolinguistic Perspectives*, Cambridge: Cambridge University Press, pp. 299–306.

Sahgal, A. (1991) 'Patterns of language use in a bilingual setting in India', in J. Cheshire (ed.) *English around the World: Sociolingistic Perspectives*, Cambridge: Cambridge University Press, pp. 299–307.

Sahgal, A. and Agnihotri, R. L. (1985) 'Syntax: the common bond: acceptability of syntactic deviances in Indian English', *English World-Wide* 6: 117–29.

—— (1988) 'Indian English phonology: a sociolinguistic perspective', *English World-Wide* 9: 51–64.

Sibayan, B. P. (1988) 'Social engineering strategies for the maintenance of English', in A. Gonzalez (ed.) *The Role of English and its Maintenance in the Philippines*, Manila: Solidaridad, pp. 91–6.

Spencer, J. (1966) 'The Anglo-Indians and their speech: a socio-linguistic essay', *Lingua* 16: 57–70.

Sridhar, K. K. (1983) 'English in a South Indian urban context', in B. B. Kachru (ed.) *The Other Tongue: English across Cultures*, Oxford: Pergamon, pp. 141–53.

Tay, M. W. J. (1982a) 'The uses, users, and features of English in Singapore', in J. Pride (ed.) *New Englishes*, Rowley, Mass.: Newbury House, pp. 51–70.

—— (1982b) 'The phonology of educated Singapore English', *English World-Wide* 1: 135–45.

—— (1991) 'Southeast Asia and Hong Kong', in J. Cheshire (ed.) *English around the World: Sociolinguistic Perspectives*, Cambridge: Cambridge University Press, pp. 319–32.

Tongue, R. (1974) *The English of Singapore and Malaysia*, Singapore: Eastern Universities Press.

Verma, S. K. (1982) 'Swadeshi English: form and function', in J. B. Pride (ed.) *New Englishes*, Rowley, Mass.: Newbury House, pp. 174–87.

Vermeer, H. J. (1969) *Das Indo-Englische: Situation und linguistische Bedeutung*, Heidelberg: Groos.

Wells, J. C. (1982) *Accents of English*, Cambridge: Cambridge University Press.

Wong, I. (1982) 'Native-speaker English for the third world today?', in J. Pride (ed.) *New Englishes*, Rowley, Mass.: Newbury House, pp. 261–86.

Chapter 16

Pidgin and Creole English

No consideration of modern English is complete without taking into account the varieties of English which emerged, above all, through the activity of Europeans in the Third World in the period of classical imperialism and colonization. Over a period of some 350 years (from the beginning of the seventeenth century) Great Britain was a major power which through trade and colonization exerted an enormous influence on the economy and the societies of many parts of the world. This influence may be seen not least in the international spread of the English language today. English, however − as extensively illustrated in this book − has numerous different varieties. Among these are the so-called **mixed languages**. This frequently used term comes from the assumption that such languages derive their lexicon from a prestigious language, their **lexifer** (usually a European language such as English), and their syntax from the substratum languages (say West African languages as a group). (This conception has been called into question; see below, 16.2, for discussion.) However this may be, contacts between English-speaking seamen, merchants, plantation owners and overseers, missionaries, colonial magistrates and officers, and many others, on the one hand, and native colonial populations, on the other, did lead to new languages whose

> very existence is largely due to the processes − discovery, exploration, trade, conquest, slavery, migration, colonialism, nationalism − that have brought the peoples of Europe and the peoples of the rest of the world to share a common destiny.
>
> (Hymes 1971b: 5)

In this chapter the two basic types of such languages, pidgins and creoles, will first be defined. In a second step some of the ideas about the possible origins and historical development of those pidgins and creoles which have an English base element in their lexis will be outlined. They will then be reviewed according to major geographic areas and illustrated with an enumeration and examples of some of their linguistic features. Furthermore, the differing political−cultural context of these languages will be dealt with, and the social functions briefly characterized. Useful introductions are Hall 1966; Hymes 1971a; Todd 1974 and 1984a; Mühlhäusler 1986a; Wardhaugh 1986: chapter 3; Romaine 1988; Holm 1988, 1989; Fasold 1990: chapter 7.

16.1 Definition of pidgins and creoles

The attempt to explain what pidgin and creole languages are leads in three different directions: the linguistic, the social and the historical. The nature of a pidgin or creole language can only be understood as a combination of all three.

16.1.1 Pidgins

From the linguistic point of view pidgins are second languages; no one has a pidgin as their mother tongue. This is so because pidgins grow out of contact situations in which none of the people who need to communicate with each other have an established language in common. (If an already existing language is chosen, possibly in a simplified form, this will be known as a **lingua franca**; this did not happen in the cases reviewed here.) Motivated by the necessity of communicating, pidgin speakers have made do, by taking the majority of the vocabulary from the most prestigious of the languages involved, the so-called **lexifer** language, and resorting to grammatical patterns whose sources are uncertain, but may be either a common denominator of sorts or the result of universal processes of language acquisition innate in every human (for discussion, see below 16.2.3).

In comparison with the native languages of their speakers, pidgins are less elaborated. This means that they have a smaller vocabulary, a reduced grammar, and a less differentiated phonology. Furthermore, pidgins are used in a much more limited set of circumstances and are stylistically less varied than first languages. In Melanesian Pidgin English (which is now often called Tok Pisin) or in Hawaiian Pidgin English (Hawaiian PE), for example, this looks as follows.

1 Reduced vocabulary leads to extensive use of paraphrase and metaphor to supply lexical units, for example in Tok Pisin: /skru bɪlɔŋ arm/ 'screw of the arm' is the word for elbow, just as /gras bɪlɔŋ hɛd/ 'grass of the head' means hair (Hall 1966: 90f).
2 As compared with StE there is a simplified and changed phoneme inventory: often missing are, for example, /ð/ and /θ/, cf. Hawaiian PE /t^{h}ri ijá/ 'three years' (Carr 1972: 20). Often mentioned also is the lack of consonant clusters and the resultant sequences of consonant–vowel–consonant–vowel.
3 Inflections are rare as compared with StE; for example, there is no plural {-S} in Hawaiian PE /t^{h}ri ijá/ 'three years'.

4 Syntactic reduction as compared with StE frequently leads to the lack of the copula, of prepositions, of determiners and of conjunctions, for example Hawaiian PE *I think one year me school teacher* 'I think that I was a school teacher for one year'; *Baby name me no like* 'I did not like the baby's name'; *All auntie, uncle, all small* 'All of your aunts and uncles were small' (Carr 1972: 30f).

The historical situations which led to the development of pidgins were ones involving trade and plantation work. From the fifteenth century on Europeans ventured out into the (for them) newly discovered lands of Africa and Asia in order to engage in trade. There they met with peoples all the way down the coast of West Africa around the Cape of Good Hope and across the Indian Ocean to India and the Spice Islands and China. To communicate they relied largely on pidgins. Note that the more reduced pidgins are sometimes called **trade jargons**.

The second characteristic situation was closely tied to the European procurement of labour for plantations. Those established in the Caribbean area as well as Brazil and what is now the southern United States relied on the massive importation of slaves from West Africa. Later plantation systems employed contract labour and also moved workers from their homelands, sometimes for a set period of time, sometimes as permanent immigrants. The sugar growing area of Queensland represents the first type; the sugar and pineapple growing areas of Hawaii, the second. In all of these places pidgins which drew on English for their lexicon came into existence.

The social situation in which these pidgins were spoken was characterized by the very limited needs and circumstances in the trading posts in West Africa. Consequently, it is no wonder that the registers which developed were equally limited.

With reference to the various uses to which language is put, this characterization means a language is used to talk about less topics, or in fewer contexts, to indicate fewer social relations, etc.

(Samarin 1971: 126)

Pidgins have sometimes been referred to as **marginal languages** because they are indeed marginal 'in the circumstances of their origin, and in the attitudes towards them on the part of those who speak one of the languages from which they derive' (Reineke 1937 in Hymes 1971b: 3). Nevertheless, quite a number of pidgins have been able to survive long enough to develop beyond the stage of a trade jargon. This was especially the case in the plantation situation, where pidgins were used not only to facilitate communication between master and servant, which was surely very limited, but also among the various labourers, who seldom shared a common mother tongue. These pidgins gained in stability and entered into a process of linguistic and functional elaboration.

16.1.2 Creoles

At the 'end' of this process of elaboration lies the creole, which is a pidgin that has become the first language of its speakers. This means that it may be a mother tongue or a primary language, i.e. the speakers' dominant language (cf. Mühlhäusler 1986a: 12; Todd 1984a: 16). A creole is enriched, expanded and regularized; it has the full complexity characteristic of any natural language.

This seems to have happened quite rapidly on the plantations of the New World. African slaves who were able to communicate with each other only in a pidgin had children for whom this language was, practically speaking, the only medium available. They must have added to the vocabulary and gradually arrived at a relative stability of grammatical forms and phonological norms. Yet it would be mistaken to think that all creoles are necessarily substantially different from the pidgins which the first generation of creole speakers have as their language-learning model. If the parents speak an elaborated pidgin, the creole may be only minimally different. However, in the course of time regional and stylistic differentiation are likely to become increasingly evident.

Many present-day pidgins and creoles are nearly identical. In West Africa, for example, Pidgin English is the home language of some people in urban areas (and the mother tongue of children in these homes; cf. Shnukal and Marchese 1983). One might expect Pidgin English used so constantly in the routines of daily life to be relatively more greatly expanded. However, pidgin is also widely employed as a market language. Here it may be considerably simpler. Pidgin and creole, in other words, can stand at the two ends of a linguistic continuum which stretches 'all the way from true creole . . . to what one might call minimal Pidgin' (Mafeni 1971: 96; for more on the idea of continuum, see 12.6). The same is true of Tok Pisin, the pidgin-creole of New Guinea, which is a native language in the towns and is becoming progressively more elaborated. It exists, however, in ever more simplified and pidgin-like forms as one moves into the rural and mountainous areas.

It is this continuum and the historical relationship between a pidgin and its creolized form which distinguish a creole from any other natural language. Viewed on its own, as an independent linguistic system, there is nothing about a creole which is essentially different from any other natural language (cf. Washabaugh 1981; Woolford 1981).

16.2 The origins of English pidgins and creoles

A great deal of discussion by linguists has centred around the question of how pidgins and creoles come into existence. One of the intriguing points of departure for the various considerations involved is the high degree of structural similarity between many of the English pidgins and creoles (for examples, see 16.3). These are too different from StE to be related to it as the regional dialects of Britain are. The latter are (among other things) the result of hundreds of years of relatively great social, political, cultural and regional isolation working on a set of more or less closely related Germanic dialects in England and Scotland. The pidgins and creoles, in contrast, were presumably the result of necessarily rapid change in a contact situation involving numerous obviously different languages. Furthermore, not only are the English pidgins and creoles similar as a group, but there is also an astonishingly high degree of structural correspondence between them and the pidgins and creoles which have lexicons based chiefly on French, Spanish, Portuguese and Dutch. The similarities are too great to be the product of pure coincidence. Three different views are offered to explain the similarities (see Muysken 1988 for an annotated list of nine different theories of the origins).

1 These languages all share a common source (the **monogenetic hypothesis**).
2 The historical conditions for the genesis of each were similar and hence they developed in the same way (the **parallel development hypothesis**).
3 All pidgins are subject to the same principles of reduction and simplification, and all creoles expand according to the same principles of elaboration and extension of grammatical categories (the **hypothesis of universals of language acquisition**).

16.2.1 The monogenetic hypothesis

This approach assumes that the first Europeans who came into contact with West Africans in the fifteenth century, the Portuguese, used a simplified language. This may have been a form of the original Lingua Franca (Latin: 'French language'), which had been in use for trade throughout the Mediterranean for centuries (cf. Whinnom 1965; Todd 1974: 33–42; Wardhaugh 1986: 73). However that may be, this language, also known as Sabir, was, according to this theory, employed by the Portuguese in West Africa and in the course of time along the trade routes in the Indian Ocean to China. Its grammatical structure remained basically unchanged, but its vocabulary drew heavily on Portuguese. This language would then have been firmly entrenched in the ports of West Africa, so that when, from 1630 on, the Dutch began to make incursions on the Portuguese slave trade, they would have made use of the same language; however, Portuguese words would begin to be replaced by Dutch ones, and instead of Portuguese Pidgin there would develop *Negerhollands*. Where the French established themselves, the same process would result in *petit nègre*.

In the seventeenth century English, too, became a party to this process. The English began participating in the slave trade, which they dominated by the eighteenth century. In addition, they were intent on acquiring colonial territories in the Caribbean. The first settlements were in the Lesser Antilles (St Kitts, 1624; Barbados, 1627; Nevis and Barbuda, 1628; Antigua, 1632; Montserrat, 1633; Anguilla 1650). In 1651 they began a colony on the mainland of South America in Surinam, which they ceded to the Dutch in 1667 (the last English plantation owners did not leave until about 1680). At about the same time (from 1655) the English captured the Greater Antilles island of Jamaica from the Spanish (for extensive details on the language history of the Caribbean area, see Holm 1986). In all of these territories and in the slave trade, Pidgin English would have been used.

The actual mechanism by which the originally Portuguese proto-pidgin vocabulary became Dutch or French or English (should this indeed be what transpired) is referred to as **relexification** (Stewart 1962: 46f), a process in which words originating in one language are replaced by those of another without there being any comparable change in the grammatical structure. This can be illustrated in the following manner (cf. Dillard 1970: 122; Alleyne 1971: 174). The perfective aspect (i.e. the designation of an action as completed) drew on the Portuguese marker *acabar de*; it was adopted as proto-pidgin *kabe*, which was relexified as French pidgin/creole *fèk* (from *faire*) in Haiti and as English pidgin/creole *done*, as in . . . *ain't I done tell you 'bout dat* (J. C. Harris, *Nights with Uncle Remus*, p. 211). The word changed, but what remained was the perfective aspect, referring to something completed in the past. Not all the Portuguese words were replaced; this would explain the presence in English pidgins and creoles of such words as *pickaninny* 'small child' (from Portuguese *pequenino*) or *savvy* 'know' (from *saber*) (for these and other examples, cf. Dillard 1973: 122).

16.2.2 The parallel development hypothesis

According to this explanation the pidgins came into existence under a set of conditions so similar that languages with comparable structures were bound to be the result. The most important of those conditions include the similar grammatical structure of many West African languages, the influence of pidgin Portuguese, and possibly similar processes of simplification (for example, something like baby-talk for communication with slaves, cf. Koefoed 1979) on the part of the European native speakers who provided the language model.

There is evidence for this in the fact that many non-linguistic features of shared West African culture survived under New World slavery, including elements of folklore, religion, family structure, music and performance styles (cf., for example, Herskovits 1941; Whitten and Szwed 1970; Dalby 1971). Some linguistic features can also be traced fairly directly back to

African languages (cf. Turner 1949; Alleyne 1971: 170, 175f; Baudet 1981; Traugott 1981; Holm 1988, 1989). Dalby makes clear that he sees African influence when he defines Black English as

> all those forms of speech in which an English or English-derived vocabulary is used with a grammatical structure divergent at a number of points from so-called 'standard' English, but reminiscent at those same points of certain widespread features in West African languages.
>
> (Dalby 1971: 116)

Sometimes this theory is restricted to the Atlantic pidgins and creoles with English as their lexifer language. In such cases a separate development of the Pacific pidgins and creoles based on the common features of local Pacific languages is also advanced.

16.2.3 The hypothesis of universal processes of language acquisition

The basis of this approach is the assumption that people everywhere simplify language in the same way, for example, by

1 using a simplified phonology such as the sequential structure Vowel–Consonant–Vowel–Consonant (cf. Nigerian PE /filag/ 'flag' with an intrusive vowel, or /tori/ 'story' with one consonant deleted from the initial cluster, examples from Barbag-Stoll 1983: 65, 62);
2 placing markers directly in front of the propositions to which they apply; this involves the markers for negation, past, aspect and irrealis (conditional); as an example, note the pre-posed negative particle *no* in Neo-Solomonic *no kæčɪm ɛni ples i-kwajtfɛla* (literally: no catch-him any place he-quiet-fellow) '[we] did not come to any place which was quiet' (example from Hall 1966:151);
3 leaving off inflectional endings, for example, Australian PE *aj* 'eye' or 'eyes' (ibid.: 152).

In a converse procedure people are then said, under certain circumstances, to enrich and expand pidgins to creoles in accord with universal principles (cf. Bickerton 1977: 65). One of the pieces of evidence adduced is the presence of similar categories of tense, modality and aspect expressed as particles (e.g. Sranan *ben* for past tense, *sa* for modality-future, and *e* for progressive aspect). All three appear in pre-verbal position, and all three always appear in the same relative order, as listed above, when they occur simultaneously. This approach, relying as it does on universal, innate processes, is sometimes referred to as **bioprogram hypothesis** (Bickerton 1988; Fasold 1990: 202–7).

All three hypotheses have something to recommend them, and currently there is little chance that conclusive evidence can be produced for any one of them. Perhaps factors involved in all three have had at least partial effects on the English pidgins and creoles presently spoken in the world. In the next section we will leave speculation and take a concrete look at some of them.

16.3 English pidgins and creoles

At present pidgins and creoles with English as their lexifer are spoken in three general areas: the Caribbean, West Africa and the Pacific. Each of these areas will be briefly reviewed below. Comments will also be made on the social situation of some of the more prominent pidgins and creoles, and some of their linguistic features will be exemplified.

Although the social situation of each is in some way different from that of every other, there are three basic paradigms in regard to the political–cultural framework, one of which affects them all.

1 The pidgin/creole is spoken in a country in which English is the official language and no other (non-English related) languages are in general use. This is the case throughout most of the Caribbean, in Australia and in Hawaii.
2 The pidgin/creole is spoken in an officially English-speaking country, but one in which there are few native speakers of English. This is the case in most of West Africa and in Papua New Guinea and Vanuatu.
3 The pidgin/creole is in use in a country in which English is neither the official language nor the diglossically available High language. Surinam is an example of this, and the same may apply on a smaller scale in parts of West Africa, such as the francophone part of Cameroon.

These differences in language orientation have an important effect on the status and the stability of the pidgins/creoles of each of the regions to be reviewed.

16.3.1 The Caribbean

No pidgins are present in the Caribbean, but English creoles are spoken throughout the Caribbean basin as well as on the mainland of South America (Surinam and Guyana), in Central America (above all in Belize, but see Holm 1983) and, though not part of the Caribbean, along the Georgia–South Carolina coast in the United States. For details on the Caribbean territories including demographic information, see 12.5 and map 12.3.

In most of the Caribbean countries there is a continuum between the creole and StE. This is a series of more or less closely related forms ranging from the broadest creole (the basilect) at one extreme to StE (the acrolect) at the other. Although deep creole is structurally very different from English, its speakers usually consider themselves to be speakers of English, however 'bad' or 'broken' they may regard their 'patois' as being. Furthermore, English is the public language of government, school and most of the media, and StE is regarded as a means of social advancement. As a result of all this there has been a continuous pull towards the standard, and this has a decreolizing effect on the creole. Chapter 12 (see 12.6) contains more discussion of the continuum.

Some people believe that American Black English is precisely this, a decreolized form of an earlier plantation creole, which was allegedly spoken throughout the American South (cf. 12.4.3). Gullah, the creole still spoken along the coast and on several of the islands off the coast of South Carolina and Georgia, is possibly related to this putative plantation creole. Today it is spoken by fewer and fewer people as it gives way to local forms of English. Among the more extensively treated creoles of the Caribbean are Jamaican Creole (cf. LePage and DeCamp 1960; Cassidy 1961; Bailey 1966), Guyanese Creole (Bickerton 1975) and Belizean Creole (Dayley 1979), all of which are decreolizing in varying degrees. Some of the anglophone territories in the Caribbean have local basilect forms which have so few creole elements as to be considered more dialects of English than creoles; this is the case with Bajan, as the vernacular of Barbados is called.

Only in Surinam is English completely missing as the diglossically High language. As a result there is no continuum and no process of decreolization there. The major creole of the country, Sranan (earlier known as Taki Taki), is, consequently, only historically related to English and not in the least mutually intelligible with it. As an independent language it is meanwhile developing its own literary tradition. For its linguistic details, see Voorhoeve 1962.

Even where mutual intelligibility is not given, the English creoles of the Caribbean share numerous linguistic features. For example, all of them have lost the inflections of English, i.e. they do not use the noun plural morpheme {-S}, as in Sranan *wiki* 'week' or 'weeks'. In mesolect varieties the plurals may be restored and marked as in English; however, this can lead to a double plural with the basilect morpheme *dem* (from English *them*) added to the English plural, as in Guyanese Creole *di aafisiz-dem*, *di skuulz-dem* 'the offices, the schools' (Devonish 1991: 593f).

Likewise, the past tense marker {-D} is typically missing from the basilect, as in Sranan *bribi* 'believe' or 'believed'. Yet past may optionally be marked with the pre-verbal particle *ben/bin*, as in Sranan *ben de* 'was somewhere, existed' (ibid.) or Guyanese *bin gat* 'had' (Bickerton 1975: 35) or Bajan *been walk* (in standard spelling) 'walked' (Roy 1986: 151). The particle *ben/bin* is found throughout the Caribbean and, indeed, elsewhere as well (cf. Nigerian PE *been meet* (standard spelling) 'met', Barbag-Stoll 1983: 106; Australian PE *bin si* 'saw', Hall 1966: 151). In mesolect varieties creole *bin* may be replaced by forms closer to StE, such as *had* or *did* in Bajan (Roy 1986: 148) or *did* or *woz* in Guyanese (Devonish 1991: 591).

The Caribbean creoles also share the durative aspectual marker *a* or *de/da* + verb, for example, Belizean creole *de slip* 'is/was sleeping' (Escure 1991: 608). In Belizean this is decreolized either to absence of the marker in the mesolect or to an inflected form of *be* in the upper mesolect/acrolect (ibid.: 597). Much the same sort of thing takes place in the other Caribbean creoles as well.

The future and irrealis (conditional) marker *sa* from English *shall* (Sranan, Guyanese Creole, but rare in the latter) or its more general West Indian equivalent *go* or decreolized *gain* (cf. Roberts 1988: 69) or *gwain*, for example, *ju gwain fáin óut* 'you will/are going to find out' (Hall 1966: 154) is a further form common to the Caribbean creoles. Likewise, past perfective or completive *done* (as mentioned in 16.2.1) is found.

Further characteristics of Caribbean creoles, such as personal pronouns, serial verbs, passive and possessive constructions, as well as some remarks on pronunciation and vocabulary are illustrated in 12.7. All of these points make the close relationship within this 'family' of creoles clear. These correspondences have sometimes been strengthened and sometimes weakened by one factor or another, such as population movement in the historical–cultural development of these territories (see discussion in 12.5). The single most important factor, however, is the degree to which speakers of the English creoles of the Caribbean do or do not stand in a continuum with standard Caribbean English.

16.3.2 West Africa

The linguistic situation in West Africa is significantly different inasmuch as there is no large native English-speaking population in this region. English is, it is true, the official language of Cameroon (with French), Gambia, Ghana, Liberia, Nigeria and Sierra Leone, but it is almost exclusively a second language (see Preface to chapters 14 and 15 as well as chapter 14 itself). One of the chief results of this is that there is no continuum like that found in the Caribbean. Instead, English is the diglossically High language (as are such regional languages as Yoruba, Igbo and Hausa in Nigeria), and West African Pidgin English (WAPE) is diglossically Low (as are the numerous local indigenous languages). There are intermediate varieties of English and, therefore, a continuum of sorts. However, these forms are not like the mesolects of the Caribbean, but are forms of second-language English noticeably influenced by the native languages of their various speakers. Note that in West Africa there are relatively few creole speakers and relatively many pidgin users. West African Standard English is in wide use by the more highly educated in the appropriate situations (administration, education, some of the media); WAPE is employed as a lingua franca in inter-ethnic communication in multilingual communities and as a market language. However, because the pidgin has such a great amount of internal variation, some people feel that there is a need for some type of standardization (cf. Agheyisi 1988: 240). The latter can also be found in the non-anglophone countries of West Africa (cf. Todd 1982: 132; 1984b: 284). However, even the pidgin exists in more than one type. Sometimes it involves a **marginal pidgin** or **jargon**, 'limited as to use, lexis and structural flexibility', and sometimes an **extended pidgin**, which has all the linguistic markers of a creole without actually being a mother tongue (Todd 1979: 282).

It is only in the area of Freetown, Sierra Leone, that a sizable community of creole speakers exists. Their language, Krio, was established there by Africans freed from the illegal slave trade by the British Navy in the nineteenth century and by former slaves who were transported from North America and resettled in Freetown in the eighteenth and nineteenth centuries. For further discussion of the social and historical relationship between WAPE and StE, see 14.1.1 and map 14.1.

Linguistically, WAPE has many parallels with the Caribbean creoles, and, indeed, the historical connections between the two areas are well known. Here, too, for example, the past marker is *bin* (cf. Bickerton 1979); the aspect marker is *a* or *da/de/di*. (For more details, see Taylor 1971; Alleyne 1980.) The pronoun system is remarkably like that of the Caribbean creoles as well (cf. Barbag-Stoll 1983: 72; Faraclas 1991). Nouns may be followed by *den* to mark the plural in Liberia, but they may also be followed by {-S}. Here, interestingly, the basilect–acrolect dimension is of less importance than semantic considerations, since *den* is used most often to mark the plural of nouns designating humans (Singler 1991: 552–6). The pronunciation of WAPE is, however, distinctly African, reflecting the phonology of the first languages of its speakers. Furthermore, there are numerous lexical borrowings from the local vernaculars in it.

Linguistic and social details on individual varieties of WAPE are recounted in Barbag-Stoll 1983 for Nigerian PE; in Todd 1982 for Cameroon PE; in Jones 1971 as well as in Fyle and Jones 1980 for Krio; and in Todd 1979, which compares Cameroon PE and Krio.

16.3.3 The Pacific

The major focus of interest in the Pacific has been on the pidgins and creoles of Melanesia, especially Tok Pisin in Papua New Guinea (cf. Dutton 1985; Wurm and Mühlhäusler 1985); Neo-Solomonic or Solomon Islands Pijin; Bislama of Vanuatu (the New Hebrides) (cf. Crowley 1981); and Australian PE (cf. Sharpe and Sandefur 1976; Sandefur and Sandefur 1980; Steffensen 1991). There is also increasingly more information available about Fiji (cf. Siegel 1987). On the Pacific mainland coast Chinese PE is often mentioned, but is no longer attested. In Polynesia there is the minor case of Pitcairn Island, where there is a creole spoken that grew up as a

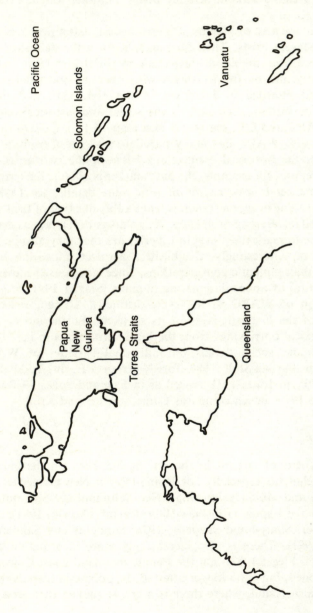

Fiji

Pacific Ocean

Solomon Islands

Vanuatu

Papua
New
Guinea

Torres Straits

Queensland

Map 16.1 The Pacific Region

result of the mutineers from the *Bounty* (1790) and their Polynesian companions; this creole was later spread to Norfolk Island (cf. Ross and Moverley 1964). Polynesia also includes the major case of Hawaii, where Hawaiian PE, Hawaiian Creole English, and a spectrum of decreolized varieties are in use (cf. Carr 1972). A general survey is presented by Romaine (1991).

Fiji and Hawaii are cases in which there is a continuum similar to that of the Caribbean, which means that there is a great deal of decreolization. This is also the case in Australia wherever contact with speakers of AusE is strong. Solomons Pijin, Bislama and Tok Pisin, on the other hand, are relatively independent pidgins/creoles despite the fact that they co-exist with English as official language. In the following Tok Pisin will be discussed in somewhat more detail.

In Papua New Guinea, Tok Pisin is the most widely used language even though English is the official one. It is 'the linguistically most developed and the socially most established variety' of the Pacific pidgins, with between three quarters of a million and a million users among the two million inhabitants of the country; some 20,000 households have it as their first language (Mühlhäusler 1986b: 549). It is 'a complex configuration of lects [varieties] ranging from unstable pidgin to fully fledged creole varieties' (Mühlhäusler 1984: 441f). Creolization is relatively rapid both in the towns and in non-traditional rural work settlements (ibid.: 452). Even in the parliament, the House of Assembly, the vast majority of business is conducted in this language, and university level teaching is conducted in it as well (Romaine 1991: 628). It is, in other words, in the process of establishing itself independently of English.

However, owing to the fact that more and more people are learning English, there is some evidence of an incipient continuum. This is most noticeable in urban Tok Pisin, or Tok Pisin bilong taun 'Tok Pisin of the town', or in anglicized Tok Skul, where mixing and switching between English and Tok Pisin is more frequent, and, especially, where borrowing from English is stronger. One of the results of this is that the mutual comprehensibility of urban Tok Pisin and Tok Pisin bilong ples, or rural Tok Pisin, is becoming less complete, to say nothing of the more distant Tok Pisin bilong bus or bush pidgin used as a contact language and lingua franca in remoter areas.

Tok Pisin ultimately derives much of its vocabulary from English, but there is also evidence of borrowing from other sources, both Melanesian (Tolai *tultul* 'messenger, assistant village chief') and European (*sutman* from German *Schutzmann* 'policeman'); however, the major source of new vocabulary lies within the productive capacity of the language itself. In this way, *vot*, which is both a noun 'election' and a verb 'vote' is semantically transparent (cf. also *hevi* (adj.) 'heavy' and *hevi* (n.) 'weight'). In urban varieties numerous loan words from StE are replacing Tok Pisin vocabulary and dispensing with native Tok Pisin means of word formation. Under the influence of English the nouns *ileksen* and *wait* have been introduced (Mühlhäusler 1984: 445). Much the same thing applies when *smokbalus* 'jet' (from *smok* 'smoke' and *balus* 'bird, airplane') gives way to *setplen* (Mühlhäusler 1986b: 559–61). This process of approximation to English is sometimes referred to as **metropolitanization**.

As the forms that English words borrowed into Tok Pisin reveal, the phonologies of the two languages differ considerably. This is most dramatically illustrated by the convergence of English /s, ʃ, tʃ, dʒ/ as Tok Pisin /s/, which together with the lack of a Tok Pisin /iː/–/ɪ/ distinction and the devoicing of final obstruents renders *ship*, *jib*, *jeep*, *sieve* and *chief* homophonous as Tok Pisin *sip*. Likewise, since /b/, /p/ and /f/ are not distinguished, Tok Pisin *pis* may be equivalent to English *beach*, *beads*, *fish*, *peach*, *piss*, *feast* or *peace*. Here, of course, borrowing might profitably be employed to reduce the number of words which are pronounced identically. Too much homophony can lead to misunderstandings, as when a member of the House of Assembly said: *les long toktok long sit nating*, meaning 'tired of talking to empty seats (sit nating)', but was mistranslated as saying 'tired of talking to a bunch of shits' (Mühlhäusler 1986b: 561).

The grammar of Tok Pisin has re-expanded, as is typical of elaborated and, especially, creolized pidgins.

1　Past tense marked by *bin*: *Na praim minista i bin tok olsem* 'The prime minister spoke thus' (Romaine 1991: 629).
2　Continuative aspect expressed with verb + *i stap* (literally 'he/she/it stops', i.e. 'remains unchanged'), as in *em i slip i stap* 'he/she is sleeping' (ibid.: 631).
3　Completive or perfective aspect has the particle *pinis* (from English *finish*), as in *em i lusim bot pinis* 'he had got out of the boat' (Mühlhäusler 1984: 462).
4　Transitive verbs end in *-im* (from English *him*); hence the verb *pinisim* 'finish' differs from the completive or perfective marker: *yu pinisim stori nau* 'finish your story now' (ibid.: 640).
5　Future uses the particle *bai* (pace Bickerton 1988: 278), shortened from English *by and by*; Solomons Pijin uses unshortened *bambae* as well as shortened *babae* or *bae*: *Em bai ol i go long rum* 'They will go to their rooms now' (Mühlhäusler 1991: 642).
6　The ending *-pela* (from English *fellow*) is used with monosyllabic adjectives or determiners, as in *dispela boi* 'this bloke' (ibid.: 640); furthermore, it is used as a plural marker for pronouns, as in *mipela* 'we' and *yupela* 'you all'.
7　The prepositions *long* (generalized locative 'at, in, on, with, to, until, etc.'), as in *Mipela i go long blekmaket . . .* 'We went to the black market . . .' and *bilong* (generalized genitive–ablative–dative 'of, from, for') *ki*

bilong yu 'your key' or *ol bilong Godons* 'they are from Gordon's' (ibid. 640f).

In Papua New Guinea, as in other countries in which there is widespread use of a pidgin/creole, speakers seem to be in a permanent dilemma as to its status. The local pidgin/creole is often not regarded as good enough for many communicative functions and is rejected in education in favour of a highly prestigious international language such as English. On the other hand, some people argue that such pidgins/creoles should be espoused and developed because of their contributions to the internal integration of the country and possible favourable effects on literacy if used in the schools. Pidgins and creoles are certainly emotionally closer to local culture than StE, which is often extremely distant. In most of the countries reviewed in this chapter, there will probably be continued decreolization. A few creoles may stay on an independent course, most likely Sranan, possibly Tok Pisin, Solomons Pijin and Bislama. Some will eventually disappear entirely: Gullah seems to be on that course. And in many cases the status quo will surely be maintained for an indefinite period.

REFERENCES

Agheyisi, R. N. (1988) 'The standardization of Nigerian Pidgin English', *English World-Wide* 9: 227–41.

Alleyne, M. C. (1971) 'Acculturation and the cultural matrix of creolization', in D. Hymes (ed.) *Pidginization and Creolization of Languages*, Cambridge: Cambridge University Press, pp. 169–86.

—— (1980) *Comparative Afro-American: an Historical-Comparative Study of Some Afro-American Dialects in the New World*, Ann Arbor: Karoma.

Bailey, B. (1966) *Jamaican Creole Syntax*, Cambridge: Cambridge University Press.

Barbag-Stoll, A. (1983) *Social and Linguistic History of Nigerian Pidgin English*, Tübingen: Stauffenberg.

Baudet, M. M. (1981) 'Identifying the African grammatical base of the Caribbean creoles: a typological approach', in A. Highfield and A. Valdman (eds) *Historicity and Variation in Creole Studies*, Ann Arbor: Karoma, pp. 104–17.

Bickerton, D. (1975) *Dynamics of a Creole System*, London: Cambridge University Press.

—— (1977) 'Pidginization and creolization: language acquisition and language universals', in A. Valdman (ed.) *Pidgin and Creole Linguistics*, Bloomington: Indiana University Press, pp. 49–69.

—— (1979) 'The status of *bin* in the Atlantic creoles', in I. F. Hancock (ed.) *Readings in Creole Studies*, Ghent: Story-Scientia, pp. 309–14.

—— (1988) 'Creole languages and the bioprogram', in F. J. Newmeyer (ed.) *Linguistics: the Cambridge Survey*. Vol. 2, *Linguistic Theory: Extensions and Implications*, Cambridge: Cambridge University Press, pp. 268–84.

Carr, E. B. (1972) *Da Kine Talk: From Pidgin to Standard in Hawaii*, Honolulu: University of Hawaii Press.

Cassidy, F. G. (1961) *Jamaica Talk: Three Hundred Years of the English Language in Jamaica*, London: Macmillan.

Crowley, T. (1981) *Grama Blong Bislama*, Port Vila, Vanuatu: University of the South Pacific Press.

Dalby, D. (1971) 'Black through white: patterns of communication in Africa and the new world', in W. A. Wolfram and N. H. Clarke (eds) *Black–White Speech Relationships*, Washington: Center for Applied Linguistics, pp. 99–138.

Dayley, J. P. (1979) *Belizean Creole*, Brattleboro, Vt: Action/Peace Corps.

Devonish, H. (1991) 'Standardisation in a creole continuum situation: the Guyana case', in J. Cheshire (ed.) *English around the World: Sociolinguistic Perspectives*, Cambridge: Cambridge University Press, pp. 585–94.

Dillard, J. L. (1970) 'Non-standard Negro dialects: convergence or divergence?', in N. E. Whitten and J. F. Szwed (eds) *Afro-American Anthropology*, New York: Free Press, pp. 119–27.

—— (1973) *Black English: its History and Usage in the United States*, New York: Vintage.

Dutton, T. E. (1985) *A New Course in Tok Pisin (New Guinea Pidgin)*, Canberra: Pacific Linguistics, D-67.

Escure, G. (1991) 'Gender roles and linguistic variation in the Belizean Creole community', in J. Cheshire (ed.) *English around the World: Sociolinguistic Perspectives*, Cambridge: Cambridge University Press, pp. 595–608.

Faraclas, N. (1991) 'The pronoun system in Nigerian Pidgin: a preliminary study', in J. Cheshire (ed.) *English around the World: Sociolinguistic Perspectives*, Cambridge: Cambridge University Press, pp. 509–18.

Fasold, R. (1990) *The Sociolinguistics of Language*, Cambridge, Mass.: Blackwell.

Fyle, C. N. and Jones, E. D. (1980) *A Krio–English Dictionary*, New York: Oxford Univesity Press.

Hall, R. A. (1966) *Pidgin and Creole Languages*, Ithaca: Cornell University Press.

Harris, J. C. (1881) *Nights with Uncle Remus*, Boston: Houghton Mifflin.

Herskovits, M. (1941) *The Myth of the Negro Past*, Boston: Beacon.

Holm, J. A. (ed.) (1983) *Central American English*, Heidelberg: Groos.

—— (1986) 'The spread of English in the Caribbean area', in M. Görlach and J. A. Holm (eds) *Focus on the Caribbean*, Amsterdam: Benjamins, pp. 1–22.

—— (1988, 1989) *Pidgins and Creoles*, Vol. 1, *Theory and Structure*, Vol. 2, *Reference Survey*, Cambridge: Cambridge University Press.

Hymes, D. (ed.) (1971a) *Pidginization and Creolization of Languages*, Cambridge: Cambridge University Press.

—— (1971b) 'Preface', in D. Hymes (ed.) *Pidginization and Creolization of Languages*, Cambridge: Cambridge University Press, pp. 3–11.

Jones, E. (1971) 'Krio: an English-based language of Sierra Leone', in J. Spencer (ed.) *The English Language in West Africa*, London: Longman, pp. 66–94.

Koefoed, G. (1979) 'Some remarks on the baby talk theory and the relexification theory', in I. F. Hancock (ed.) *Readings in Creole Studies*, Ghent: Story-Scientia, pp. 37–54.

LePage, R. and DeCamp, D. (1960) *Jamaican Creole*, London: Macmillan.

Mafeni, B. (1971) 'Nigerian Pidgin', in J. Spencer (ed.) *The English Language in West Africa*, London: Longman, pp. 95–112.

Mühlhäusler, P. (1984) 'Tok Pisin in Papua New Guinea', in R. W. Bailey and M. Görlach (eds) *English as a World Language*, Cambridge: Cambridge University Press, pp. 439–66.

—— (1986a) *Pidgin and Creole Linguistics*, Oxford: Blackwell.

—— (1986b) 'English in contact with Tok Pisin (Papua New Guinea)', in W. Viereck and W.-D. Bald (eds) *English in Contact with Other Languages*, Budapest: Akadémiai, pp. 549–70.

—— (1991) 'Watching girls pass by in Tok Pisin', in J. Cheshire (ed.) *English around the World: Sociolinguistic Perspectives*, Cambridge: Cambridge University Press, pp. 637–46.

Muysken, P. (1988) 'Are creoles a special type of language?', in F. J. Newmeyer (ed.) *Linguistics: the Cambridge Survey*, Vol. 2, *Linguistic Theory: Extensions and Implications*, Cambridge: Cambridge University Press, pp. 285–301.

Roberts, P. A. (1988) *West Indians and Their Language*, Cambridge: Cambridge University Press.

Romaine, S. (1988) *Pidgin and Creole Languages*, London: Longman.

—— (1991) 'The Pacific', in J. Cheshire (ed.) *English around the World: Sociolinguistic Perspectives*, Cambridge: Cambridge Univesity Press, pp. 619–36.

Ross, A. S. C. and Moverley, A. W. (1964) *The Pitcairnese Language*, London: Deutsch.

Roy, J. (1986) 'The structure of tense and aspect in Barbadian English Creole', in M. Görlach and J. A. Holm (eds) *Focus on the Caribbean*, Amsterdam: Benjamins, pp. 141–56.

Samarin, W. J. (1971) 'Salient and substantive pidginization', in D. Hymes (ed.) *Pidginization and Creolization of Languages*, Cambridge: Cambridge University Press, pp. 117–40.

Sandefur, J. R. and Sandefur, J. (1980) *Language Survey: Pidgin and Creole in the Kimberleys, Western Australia*, Darwin: Summer Institute of Linguistics.

Sharpe, M. C. and Sandefur, J. (1976) 'The creole language of the Katherine and Roper River areas, Northern Territory', in M. G. Clyne (ed.) *Australia Talks*, Canberra: *Pacific Linguistics* 23: 63–77.

Shnukal, A. and Marchese, L. (1983) 'Creolization of Nigerian Pidgin English: a progress report', *English World-Wide* 4: 17–26.

Siegel, J. (1987) *Language Contact in a Plantation Environment: a Sociolinguistic History of Fiji*, Cambridge: Cambridge University Press.

Singler, J. V. (1991) 'Plural marking in Liberian English', in J. Cheshire (ed.) *English Around the World: Sociolinguistic Perspectives*, Cambridge: Cambridge University Press, pp. 545–61.

Steffensen, M. S. (1991) 'Australian Creole English: the effect of cultural knowledge on language and memory', in J. Cheshire (ed.) *English around the World: Sociolinguistic Perspectives*, Cambridge: Cambridge University Press, pp. 256–67.

Stewart, W. A. (1962) 'Creole languages in the Caribbean', in F. Rice (ed.) *Study of the Role of Second Languages in Asia, Africa and Latin America*, Washington: Center for Applied Linguistics, pp. 34–53.

Taylor, D. (1971) 'Grammatical and lexical affinities of creoles', in D. Hymes (ed.) *Piginization and Creolization of Languages*, Cambridge: Cambridge University Press.

Todd, L. (1974) *Pidgins and Creoles*, London: Routledge & Kegan Paul.

—— (1979) 'Cameroonian: a consideration of "what's in a name?"', in I. F. Hancock (ed.) *Readings in Creole Studies*, Ghent: Story-Scientia, pp. 281–94.

—— (1982) *Cameroon*, Heidelberg: Groos.

—— (1984a) *Modern Englishes: Pidgins and Creoles*, Oxford: Blackwell.

—— (1984b) 'The English language in West Africa', in R. W. Bailey and M. Görlach (eds) *English as a World Language*, Cambridge: Cambridge University Press, pp. 281–305.

Traugott, E. C. (1981) 'Introduction', in A. Highfield and A. Valdman (eds) *Historicity and Variation in Creole Studies*, Ann Arbor: Karoma, pp. 1–6.

Turner, L. D. (1949) *Africanisms in the Gullah Dialect*, Chicago: University of Chicago.

Voorhoeve, J. (1962) *Sranan Syntax*, Amsterdam: North Holland.

Wardhaugh, R. (1986) *An Introduction to Sociolinguistics*, Oxford: Blackwell.

Washabaugh, W. (1981) 'Pursuing creole roots', in P. Muysken (ed.) *Generative Studies on Creole Languages*, Dordrecht: Foris, pp. 85–102.

Whinnom, K. (1965) 'The origins of the European-based creoles and pidgins', *Orbis* 14: 509–27.

Whitten, N. E. and Szwed, J. F. (eds) (1970) *Afro-American Anthropology*, New York: Free Press.

Woolford, E. (1981) 'The developing complementizer system of Tok Pisin', in P. Muysken (ed.) *Generative Studies on Creole Languages*, Dordrecht: Foris, pp. 85–102.

Wurm, S. A. and Mühlhäusler, P. (eds) (1985) *Handbook of Tok Pisin*, Canberra: Australian National University.

Index